THE INSTITUTE FOR POLISH–JEWISH STUDIES

The Institute for Polish–Jewish Studies in Oxford and its sister organization, the American Association for Polish–Jewish Studies, which publish *Polin*, are learned societies that were established in 1984, following the International Conference on Polish–Jewish Studies, held in Oxford. The Institute is an associate institute of the Oxford Centre for Hebrew and Jewish Studies, and the American Association is linked with the Department of Near Eastern and Judaic Studies at Brandeis University.

Both the Institute and the American Association aim to promote understanding of the Polish Jewish past. They have no building or library of their own and no paid staff; they achieve their aims by encouraging scholarly research and facilitating its publication, and by creating forums for people with a scholarly interest in Polish Jewish topics, both past and present.

To this end the Institute and the American Association help organize lectures and international conferences. Venues for these activities have included Brandeis University in Waltham, Massachusetts, the Hebrew University in Jerusalem, the Institute for the Study of Human Sciences in Vienna, King's College in London, the Jagiellonian University in Kraków, the Oxford Centre for Hebrew and Jewish Studies, the University of Łódz, Kraków, th University College London, and the Polish Cultural Institute and the Polish embassy in London. They have encouraged academic exchanges between Israel, Poland, the United States, and western Europe. In particular they seek to help train a new generation of scholars, in Poland and elsewhere, to study the culture and history of the Jews in Poland.

Each year since 1986 the Institute has published a volume of scholarly papers in the series *Polin: Studies in Polish Jewry* under the general editorship of Professor Antony Polonsky of Brandeis University. Since 1994 the series has been published on its behalf by the Littman Library of Jewish Civilization, and since 1998 the publication has been linked with the American Association as well. In March 2000 the entire series was honoured with a National Jewish Book Award from the Jewish Book Council in the United States. More than twenty other works on Polish Jewish topics have also been published with the Institute's assistance.

Further information on the Institute for Polish–Jewish Studies can be found on its website, <www.polishjewishstudies.co.uk>. For the website of the American Association for Polish–Jewish Studies, see <www.aapjstudies.org>.

This publication has been supported by
a donation in memory of

DR GEORGE WEBBER
(1899–1982)

scholar, Hebraist, jurist

THE LITTMAN LIBRARY OF
JEWISH CIVILIZATION

Dedicated to the memory of

Louis Thomas Sidney Littman

who founded the Littman Library for the love of God
and as an act of charity in memory of his father

Joseph Aaron Littman

and to the memory of

Robert Joseph Littman

who continued what his father Louis had begun

יהא זכרם ברוך

'Get wisdom, get understanding:
Forsake her not and she shall preserve thee'

PROV. 4: 5

The Littman Library of Jewish Civilization is a registered UK charity
Registered charity no. 1000784

From *Shtetl* to Socialism

Studies from Polin

Edited by
ANTONY POLONSKY

Published for
The Institute for Polish–Jewish Studies

The Littman Library of Jewish Civilization
in association with Liverpool University Press

The Littman Library of Jewish Civilization
in association with Liverpool University Press
4 Cambridge Street, Liverpool L69 7ZU, UK

www.liverpooluniversitypress.co.uk/littman

Managing Editor: Connie Webber

Distributed in North America by
Oxford University Press Inc., 198 Madison Avenue,
New York, NY 10016, USA

First published in paperback 1993

Catalogue records for this book are available from the
British Library and the Library of Congress

ISSN 0268 1056
ISBN 978–1–874774–14–3

Publishing co-ordinator: Janet Moth
Design: Pete Russell, Faringdon, Oxon.
Typesetting: Footnote Graphics, Warminster, Wilts.

Printed and bound by CPI Group (UK) Ltd, Croydon, CR0 4YY

For my wife Arlene
and my children Leah and Jake
in fondest love

Editors and Advisers

POLIN

We did not know, but our fathers told us how the exiles of Israel came to the land of Polin (Poland).

When Israel saw how its sufferings were constantly renewed, oppressions increased, persecutions multiplied, and how the evil authorities piled decree on decree and followed expulsion with expulsion, so that there was no way to escape the enemies of Israel, they went out on the road and sought an answer from the paths of the wide world: which is the correct road to traverse to find rest for their soul? Then a piece of paper fell from heaven, and on it the words:

Go to Polaniya (Poland)!

So they came to the land of Polin and they gave a mountain of gold to the king, and he received them with great honour. And God had mercy on them, so that they found favour from the king and the nobles. And the king gave them permission to reside in all the lands of his kingdom, to trade over its length and breadth, and to serve God according to the precepts of their religion. And the king protected them against every foe and enemy.

And Israel lived in Polin in tranquillity for a long time. They devoted themselves to trade and handicrafts. And God sent a blessing on them so that they were blessed in the land, and their name was exalted among the peoples. And they traded with the surrounding countries and they also struck coins with inscriptions in the holy language and the language of the country. These are the coins which have on them a lion rampant from the right facing left. And on the coins are the words 'Mieszko, King of Poland' or 'Mieszko, Król of Poland'. The Poles call their king 'Król'.

And those who delve into the Scriptures say: 'This is why it is called Polin. For thus spoke Israel when they came to the land, "Here rest for the night [*Po lin*]." And this means that we shall rest here until we are all gathered into the Land of Israel.' Since this is the tradition, we accept it as such.

S. Y. AGNON, 1916

POLIN
Studies in Polish Jewry

VOLUME 1 *Poles and Jews: Renewing the Dialogue* (1986)

VOLUME 2 *Jews and the Emerging Polish State* (1987)

VOLUME 3 *The Jews of Warsaw* (1988)

VOLUME 4 *Poles and Jews: Perceptions and Misperceptions* (1989)

VOLUME 5 *New Research, New Views* (1990)

VOLUME 6 *Jews in Łódź, 1820–1939* (1991)

VOLUME 7 *Jewish Life in Nazi-Occupied Warsaw* (1992)

From Shtetl to Socialism (1993): selected articles from volumes 1–7

VOLUME 8 *Jews in Independent Poland, 1918–1939* (1994)

VOLUME 9 *Jews, Poles, Socialists: The Failure of an Ideal* (1996)

VOLUME 10 *Jews in Early Modern Poland* (1997)

VOLUME 11 *Aspects and Experiences of Religion* (1998)

VOLUME 12 *Galicia: Jews, Poles, and Ukrainians*, 1772–1918 (1999)

Index to Volumes 1–12 (2000)

VOLUME 13 *The Holocaust and its Aftermath* (2000)

VOLUME 14 *Jews in the Polish Borderlands* (2001)

VOLUME 15 *Jewish Religious Life, 1500–1900* (2002)

VOLUME 16 *Jewish Popular Culture and its Afterlife* (2003)

VOLUME 17 *The Shtetl: Myth and Reality* (2004)

VOLUME 18 *Jewish Women in Eastern Europe* (2005)

VOLUME 19 *Polish–Jewish Relations in North America* (2006)

VOLUME 20 *Making Holocaust Memory* (2008)

VOLUME 21 *1968: Forty Years After* (2009)

VOLUME 22 *Social and Cultural Boundaries in Pre-Modern Poland* (2010)

VOLUME 23 *Jews in Kraków* (2011)

VOLUME 24 *Jews and their Neighbours in Eastern Europe since 1750* (2012)

VOLUME 25 *Jews in the Former Grand Duchy of Lithuania since 1772* (2013)

Acknowledgements

THE essays in this volume have all appeared previously in *Polin: a Journal of Polish–Jewish Studies*. Chapters 1, 2, 5, 12, 16, 23, and 26 appeared in Volume 1, Chapters 6, 14, 17, 20, and 21 in Volume 2, Chapters 7, 9, and 24 in Volume 3, Chapters 3, 4, 10, 11, 15, 19, 22, and 25 in Volume 4, Chapters 27 and 28 in Volume 5, Chapters 8 and 18 in Volume 6, and Chapter 13 in Volume 7. For permission to reproduce the maps I should like to thank the following: John Murray (Publishers) Ltd. for 'The Kingdom of Bolesław the Brave in 1025' and 'Poland under Kazimierz the Great, 1370', taken from A. Zamoyski's *The Polish Way*; Columbia University Press and Herbert Kaplan for 'Poland in 1771', taken from H. H. Kaplan, *The First Partition of Poland*; PWN–Polish Scientific Publishers for 'The Partitions of Poland' and 'The Congress Kingdom of Poland', taken from S. Kieniewicz (ed.), *History of Poland*; Wilfred Laurier University Press for 'The Territorial Settlement of 1815 in Eastern Europe', taken from R. A. Prete and A. Hamish Ion (eds.), *Armies of Occupation*; Basil Blackwell for 'The Territories making up the Polish State in 1921', from C. Abramsky, M. Jachimczyk, and A. Polonsky (eds.), *The Jews in Poland*; Oxford University Press for 'The German Occupation, 1939–1945' and 'Post-war Poland' both from N. Davies, *God's Playground: A History of Poland*. The glossary is partly based on that in my edition of Artur Eisenbach, *The Emanicipation of the Jews in Poland 1780–1870*, published by Basil Blackwell, and the chronology has been adapted with permission from S. Kieniewicz (ed.), *History of Poland*.

This volume is the first product of the collaboration between the Institute for Polish–Jewish Studies, the American Association for Polish–Jewish Studies, and the Littman Library of Jewish Civilization, which will henceforth also be publishing *Polin*. It has been a pleasure to work with the Littman Library and we are convinced that we shall have a long and fruitful relationship. I should like, in particular, to thank Connie Wilsack, managing editor of the Library, for her constant encouragement and counsel. The book is also the first to appear under the joint imprint of the Oxford Centre for Postgraduate Hebrew Studies and the Institute for Polish–Jewish Studies, and it marks the increasing closeness of their relationship. We are grateful to the former President of the Centre, Dr David Patterson, the current President, Professor Philip Alexander, and particularly the Chairman of the Publications Committee, Dr Jonathan Webber, who is also the Treasurer of the Institute, for their aid in developing this relationship. *From* Shtetl *to Socialism* would never have appeared without the support of Professor Jehuda Reinharz, Provost and Senior Vice-President for Academic Affairs, and of the Near Eastern and Judaic Studies Department at Brandeis University. I also owe a special debt to Professor Richard and Mrs Irene Pipes.

Waltham, Mass. A.P.
May 1993

Contents

Maps

Introduction

Gentle Poland, ancient land of Torah and learning
From the day Ephraim first departed from Judah

From a *selihah* by Rabbi Moshe Katz Geral

What then is the meaning of the era of the Jews in Poland in the context of the history of the Jewish people? ... If the concept of Jewish history can be said to have had a plastic *gestalt*, then Polish Jewry, individually and collectively, was the mould which formed it. Such was perhaps the dialectic of its fate and the meaning of its demise. Jewish history had reached in Polish Jewry one of the peaks of its arduous uphill climb.

Yeshaia Trunk, *Poyln*

In recent years there has been a great revival of interest in the history of Polish Jewry. By the early seventeenth century this community had become the largest in the Jewish world, and in the years of its flourishing it gave rise to a unique religious and secular culture in Hebrew and Yiddish and enjoyed an unprecedented degree of self-government. In a penitential prayer composed in the aftermath of the massacres which occurred during the Cossack uprising of the mid-seventeenth century, Rabbi Yom-Tov Lipman Heller looked back to a golden age, recalling 'Poland, a country of royalty where we have dwelled from of old in tranquil serenity'.[1] Yet even after the devastating effect of these upheavals, which also marked the beginning of the downfall of the Polish–Lithuanian Commonwealth, the Jewish community continued to increase in size and was able to recover some of its vitality. The partition of Poland at the end of the eighteenth century divided Polish Jewry between the Tsarist, Habsburg, and Prussian states. Throughout the nineteenth century, the lands of the former Polish–Lithuanian Commonwealth remained the home of the largest concentration of Jews in the world. It was here that the new religious movement of Hasidism emerged and gained a mass following and that later those movements developed—Zionism, Socialism, Neo-Orthodoxy—which were to transform the Jews' perception of themselves. From the 1860s the swelling tide of emigration from these lands took the cultural patterns of Polish Jewry to western Europe, the New World, and the Antipodes. In the words of the great Jewish historian, Salo Baron, himself of Polish origin, American Jewry

[1] Quoted by Rosman in Ch. 4.

is 'a bridge built by Polish Jews'. After 1921 Poland was still the second-largest Jewish community in the world after that in the United States, while the next in numbers which also derived from the Polish–Lithuanian Commonwealth were those in the Soviet republics of Ukraine and Belarus.

This East European Jewish world was almost entirely wiped out by the Nazis. The traumatic effect of this catastrophe, in which the majority of Jewish historians of the area also perished, has meant that it is only in recent years that scholarly investigation into this now lost world has revived. It has become increasingly clear that an understanding of the nature of the Jewish experience, good and bad, in the thousand years that Jews lived on Polish soil is an essential element in Jewish self-knowledge. In Poland, too, it has also become increasingly evident that a proper understanding of the Polish past will have to take into account the presence of substantial national minorities on Polish soil. The implications of the fact that the Jews made up nearly a third of the urban population and not only developed their own rich cultural life but also interacted constantly with their neighbours are now much more widely recognized.

One product of the revived interest in Polish–Jewish history was the conviction that it could only be studied in a framework that transcended national and disciplinary barriers: hence the establishment of the yearbook *Polin*. This title, which means 'Poland' in Yiddish and Hebrew, was chosen because of its long associations with the Jewish vision of that country; it is a term that echoes back from the long and complex history of Polish Jewry and somehow embodies the mixture of affection and suspicion with which Jews regarded the country in which they lived for so many centuries. The great Hebrew writer S. Y. Agnon, who created an earlier journal with the same name, expressed this in a passage which attempted to reproduce the flavour of Aggadic commentary:

> Said the exegetes: The land was called Poland (Polin) because when Israel arrived there they exclaimed: *po lin*! That is, *po nalin*, here we shall spend the night until we are privileged to go up to the Land of Israel.
> If she receives us, we shall receive her![2]

In the first issue of *Polin*, the editors wrote:

> The founder of Hasidism, Israel Baal Shem Tov, observed that 'forgetting leads to exile, remembering is the path to salvation.' Our aim is to preserve and enlarge our collective memory, to investigate all aspects of our common past. We believe that there should be no topics that are too sensitive to be discussed. Our columns are open to all those of good will. We ask only that they write honestly and with respect for historical facts. We do not believe in

[2] S. Agnon, *Hatekufah*, 5 (1920), 23–4.

a definitive historical truth, still less a Jewish or a Polish historical truth. In these pages, we meet, as in life, not as representatives of groups or ideological camps, but as individuals. The dialogue we favour is many-sided and through it we hope we will gain a greater understanding of ourselves, of each other and of those developments in the past which have sometimes united and sometimes divided us, on occasion cruelly and brutally.[3]

How far these ambitious goals have been achieved the reader will be able in part to judge from the essays in this volume, all of which previously appeared in *Polin*. While they do not provide a fully comprehensive account of the history of the Jews in Poland, they do furnish illumination of the most critical aspects of that history and illustrations of the way these issues are being treated by the leading and most innovative scholars in the field. The essays are divided into five sections, reflecting the chronological division of Polish and Polish Jewish history. The first of these deals with the period from the establishment of the first Polish state at the end of the tenth century to the partition of the Polish–Lithuanian Commonwealth at the end of the eighteenth. No aspect of Polish Jewish history is more obscure than the process by which the community itself became established. We do know that by the end of the fifteenth century it numbered between 10,000 and 30,000 out of a total population of around four million (population estimates in the period before the development of modern census-taking techniques are notoriously unreliable). By this stage, its institutions, in particular the charters by which it sought to guarantee its security and its right to practise its religion and carry on its economic pursuits, were derived from the German-speaking lands of central Europe. The language which the community used in every-day life was also medieval Judaeo-German, which was to evolve into Yiddish. The theory that the Jewish community traced its origin to the Khazar kingdom north of the Black Sea, whose Turkic nobility had converted to Judaism in the early middle ages, is now largely discredited. Yet it is still unclear whether there was some form of organized Jewish life in Poland before the arrival of Jews from the German lands. This occurred between the twelfth and fourteenth centuries, partly as a result of the worsening conditions for Jews in these territories in the aftermath of the first three Crusades and the Black Death, accompanied as it was by accusations of Jewish well-poisoning, and partly as a result of the new opportunities that were developing in Poland with the emergence of a consolidated kingdom under Kazimierz the Great, who ruled from 1333 to 1370.[4] The

[3] *Polin: A Journal of Polish–Jewish Studies*, 1: 1–2.

[4] On early Jewish settlement in Poland, see Bernard D. Weinryb, *The Jews of Poland: A Social and Economic History of the Jewish Community in Poland from 1100 to 1800* (Philadelphia, 1973), 17–103; id., *The Beginnings of East European Jewry in*

presence of a small Slavic- and possibly Greek- and Tartar-speaking community before the major Ashkenazi emigration is strongly maintained by the philologist Paul Wexler in an article which is a demonstration of how the techniques of his discipline can be used to illustrate thorny and otherwise insoluble historical problems (Chapter 1).

The consolidation and flourishing of the Jewish community on the Polish lands was a feature of the next 150 years. It was in this period that it grew in size to between 150,000 and 300,000 (out of a total population of perhaps ten million) and that it became a major centre of Jewish life, with *yeshivot* (rabbinical academies) renowned throughout the Jewish world and scholars like Rabbi Moshe Isserles of Kraków, whose critical glosses to the *Shulkhan arukh*, the rabbinic code of Joseph Caro, enabled this work, written by a Sephardi scholar in Safed, to become the basic regulator of the mores of Ashkenazi Jewry. The expansion of the Jewish community in these years was the result of the prosperity which Poland enjoyed as a consequence of the development of the international grain trade down the Vistula, in which Jews played an important part. It was also the result of the social and economic dominance established in these years by the Polish nobility (*szlachta*). In the sixteenth and early seventeenth centuries, the *szlachta* was able to reduce the king to an elected cipher, and ruled the country through the Sejm, the parliament, which it dominated. Serfdom was imposed on the overwhelming bulk of the rural population, while the towns, with the exception of the great grain port of Danzig, were also subjected to noble hegemony, and the rights of their burghers, mostly of German origin, were severely restricted. In these circumstances, a 'marriage of convenience' developed between the nobility and the Jews, which led to the commonly expressed contemporary view that Poland was 'hell for the serfs, purgatory for the burghers, heaven for the *szlachta*, and paradise for the Jews'. The Jews were a convenient partner for the nobility, because they did not in any way seek to challenge their political and social hegemony, while at the same time performing important services for them, particularly in the noble-owned towns which increased significantly in number in this period and in which the Jews were mostly settled. Different aspects of the noble–Jewish partnership and the way it was understood by its respective partners are analysed in the articles by Gershon Hundert (Chapter 2), Janusz Tazbir (Chapter 3),

---

Legend and Historiography (Dropsie College, 1962); S. Ettinger, 'Kievan Russia', in C. Roth (ed.), *World History of the Jewish People: The Dark Ages* (Tel Aviv, 1966), 329–34; A. Gieysztor, 'The Beginnings of Jewish Settlement in Polish Lands', in C. Abramsky, M. Jachimczyk, and A. Polonsky (eds.), *The Jews in Poland* (Oxford, 1986), 15–21.

Moshe Rosman (Chapter 4), and Anna Żuk (Chapter 6). This was not, of course, a relationship of equals. The attitude of the nobles to the Jews was one of paternalistic contempt. The Jews for their part, while accepting their inferior position and greatly valuing the protection they enjoyed because of *szlachta* patronage, saw the Christian world of the nobility as characterized by violence, idolatry, and lack of trustworthiness.

Yet the danger to the Jews in the alliance did not lie in the distance between the two groups. It was, rather, the consequence of the hostility which the Jewish–noble links aroused in the subject population and, in particular, among the Greek Orthodox population of south-east Poland. The early seventeenth century saw an intensification of efforts by the nobility to profit from the fertile lands of the Ukraine, which had been a part of the Grand Duchy of Lithuania, and which had become a part of Poland as a result of the union of the Kingdom of Poland and the Grand Duchy achieved at Lublin in 1569. This had been followed by a tightening of the bonds of serfdom and also, with the triumph of the Counter-Reformation in Poland, by attempts to force a union with Rome on the Orthodox Church in these lands. At the same time, the Poles found themselves increasingly in conflict with the Cossacks, Greek Orthodox free settlers established on the Polish eastern frontier to protect it from Tartar and Turkish invasion. These developments led to the fusion of social, religious, and proto-national grievances, which culminated in the revolt of the polonized Cossack, Bohdan Khmelnytsky, in 1648. The results of this upheaval were disastrous for the Polish–Lithuanian Commonwealth. It led to twenty years of war, described in Polish tradition as the 'Flood', with foreign invasion by Swedes and Muscovites, the devastation of the territory of the Republic, and the loss of its territories on the east bank of the Dniester. The Republic never really recovered from these events. Religious intolerance and pressure on non-Catholic (dissident) Christians, witch burning, and ritual murder accusations against Jews became features of Polish life. The Great Northern War saw a further stage in Poland's decline, and at its conclusion in 1721 the country was in effect reduced to the status of a Russian satellite. It was only the first partition of the Republic in 1772 which sparked off attempts at reform. These succeeded in introducing significant changes in Polish life, based on the philosophy of the Enlightenment. The Constitution adopted by the reformers on 3 May 1791 was the first written constitution in Europe and, while it did still maintain noble political hegemony, it was an important stage on the path to the creation of modern political and social conditions. The experiment aroused the hostility of Poland's neighbours, who made use of conservative opposition in Poland to the changes to effect the final partition of the country between 1793 and 1795.

Jewish life seemed to recover relatively rapidly from the catastrophic events of 1648–67, which saw the worst massacres of Jews since the Crusades, and in which between 40,000 and 50,000 people perished, often after appalling tortures (although Jewish chroniclers may have exaggerated the number of dead). The Jewish population continued to increase rapidly and by 1764 probably numbered around 750,000 out of a total of fourteen million. But the Jews never again enjoyed the security which they had earlier felt and the prosperity of the community was undermined by the general economic decline of Poland. The intolerance which followed the twenty years of foreign invasion during which the Catholic Poles had been adjured to drive out the dissident Swedes and schismatic Muscovites and the increasing sway within the country of the values of the Counter-Reformation also adversely affected Jewish life. Yet with the impact of the ideas of the Enlightenment, which called for the transformation of the Jews into citizens with the rights and obligations of their fellow-countrymen, attitudes began to change. These problems are set out clearly and authoritatively by Jacob Goldberg (Chapter 5).

Some topics are not extensively discussed. There is little detailed discussion of the emergence and functioning of the institutions of Jewish autonomy, which were so crucial to the sense of security of the Jewish community.[5] There is also little on Jewish religious life in the sixteenth and early seventeenth centuries,[6] on the vexed question of whether the mid-seventeenth-century Messianic pretender Shabbetai

[5] On this see I. Lewin, 'The Protection of Jewish Religious Rights by Royal Edicts in Pre-Partition Poland', in M. Giergieliewicz (ed.), *Polish Civilization: Essays and Studies* (New York, 1979), 115–34; B. Brilling, 'The Struggle of the Va'ad Arba Aratzot for the Jewish Right of Religious Worship in Breslau', *YIVO Annual*, 2: 162–87; M. Wischnitzer, 'The Lithuanian Va'ad', *Menorah Journal*, 19 (Mar. 1931), 261–70; Jacob Goldberg, 'The Privileges Granted to Jewish Communities of the Polish Commonwealth as a Stabilizing Factor in Jewish Support', in Abramsky *et al.* (eds.), *The Jews in Poland*, 31–54; Shmul Ettinger, 'The Council of the Four Lands', in A. Polonsky, J. Basista, and A. Link-Lenczowski, *The Jews in Old Poland* (London, 1993), 89–105; Israel Bartal, 'The *Pinkas* of the Council of the Four Lands', ibid. 105–13; Jacob Goldberg, 'The Jewish Sejm: Its Origins and Functions', ibid. 142–60; Gershon Hundert, 'The *Kehilla* and the Municipality in Private Towns at the End of the Early Modern Period', ibid. 169–81; Shmuel Shilo, 'The Individual versus the Community in Jewish Law in Pre-Eighteenth Century Poland', ibid. 212–27.

[6] On this see H. H. Ben-Sasson, *Hagut vehanhagah* (Jerusalem, 1959); J. Elbaum, 'Aspects of Hebrew Ethical Literature in Sixteenth-Century Poland', in B. D. Cooperman (ed.), *Jewish Thought in the Sixteenth Century* (Cambridge, Mass., 1983), 146–66; id., *Petichut vehistagerut* (Jerusalem, 1990); L. Kaplan, 'Rabbi Mordekhai Jaffe and the Evolution of Jewish Culture in Poland', in Cooperman, *Jewish Thought*, 266–82; E. J. Schochet, *Rabbi Joel Sirkes* (New York, 1971).

Zevi had significant support in Poland,[7] and on the character and importance of the movement inspired by the enigmatic figure of Jacob Frank.[8] Above all, there is little on the character of Hasidism, on the reasons for the emergence of this innovative antinomian religious movement in Poland, and on the factors which fostered its rapid, if not universal, spread.[9]

The nineteenth century saw a fundamental transformation of the situation of the Jews in Europe. The Enlightenment and the politicians of the French Revolution had proclaimed the ideal of Jewish emancipation. Its basis was clearly articulated by Stanislaus de Clermont-Tonnerre in the revolutionary French National Assembly in December 1789: 'The Jews should be refused everything as a Nation, and granted everything as individuals. The Jews should give up their autonomy and as citizens should be incorporated into the political organism of the French nation.'[10] In return for abandoning their separate status as a European (indeed, worldwide) community with a shared set of religious, moral, and social values, the Jews would acquire the status of citizens. Jews would purge their religion of its 'medieval' and 'obscurantist' features, so that it would be in harmony with the progressive temper of the age. They would abandon those occupations to which Christian prejudice and persecution had relegated them—money-lending, peddling, petty trading—and become 'productive' members of the wider community. They would reform the education they provided for their children. The exclusive study of the Bible and Talmud would be replaced by more 'modern' concepts of religious education, together with instruction in secular subjects and in European languages. These ideas quickly found a response in significant sections of the Jewish world. Here the idea of Enlightenment, *haskalah* in Hebrew, was first proclaimed by Moses Mendelsohn and his followers in Berlin. In an attempt to wean his readers from Yiddish and outmoded ideas of biblical exegesis he published a German translation of the Bible printed in Hebrew characters with a commentary

[7] See G. Scholem, 'Shabbetai Zevi', in *Encyclopedia Judaica*, xiv (Jerusalem, 1971), cols. 1219–54; id., *Sabbatai Sevi: The Mystical Messiah*, trans. R. J. Z. Werblowsky (Princeton, 1973).

[8] See G. Scholem, 'Jacob Frank', in *Encyclopedia Judaica*, vii. 55–72; Jan Doktor, *Jakub Frank i jego nauka* (Warsaw, 1991).

[9] G. Hundert (ed.), *Essential Papers on Hasidism: Origins to Present* (New York, 1991); J. Weiss, *Studies in East European Jewish Mysticism* (Oxford, 1985); Ada Rapoport-Albert (ed.), *Hasidism Reappraised*, to be published by the Littman Library of Jewish Civilization.

[10] Quoted in A. Eisenbach, *The Emancipation of the Jews in Poland, 1780–1870* (Oxford, 1991), 60.

reflecting modern 'rational' concepts of how the divine revelation should be understood. In this way he sought to propagate his views throughout the entire Ashkenazi world.

The results of these attempts to reform Jewish life from within and without were different in western and eastern Europe. In the west, where liberal values were able to find a significant buttress in the rising middle class and where national states consolidated themselves, Jews received their civil rights with the gradual establishment of constitutional government. The progress of the Industrial Revolution enabled them to find new sources of livelihood and they embarked on a transformation, the final outcome of which was to make them Englishmen or Frenchmen of the Jewish faith.

The process was much slower in German-speaking central Europe, and it was even less successful on the lands of the former Polish–Lithuanian Commonwealth. The reasons for this divergent development and its outcome are explored in the essays on the nineteenth century. As is convincingly demonstrated in Chapter 7 by Stefan Kieniewicz, the doyen of Polish nineteenth-century historians, who died last year, the problem in the first half of the nineteenth century was complicated both by the continued social domination of Polish society by the nobility and by the pre-eminent importance of the national question: how to regain the independence of the country, whose partition had been confirmed, though with somewhat different boundaries, at the Congress of Vienna in 1815? As Kieniewicz shows, the Polish aristocracy and the civil servants derived from it who ruled the autonomous Polish kingdom linked with the Tsarist Empire which had been established at the Congress of Vienna held that the Jews would have to demonstrate their 'civilized' character by a substantial degree of acculturation and polonization before they could be emancipated. This viewpoint explains the somewhat ambivalent reaction of the Polish insurrectionaries in 1830 to Jewish attempts to participate in their revolt against Russia. The failure of this revolt led to the emigration of about 7,000 Poles, who established a powerful emigré centre in France and who hoped to become the nucleus from which the independence of Poland would be achieved. From the late 1830s, some members of this emigration began to proclaim the need to enlist the Jews in the struggle for national liberation. Their call had some resonance in Austrian Poland and the Republic of Kraków in 1846 and 1848. In Prussian Poland, they were not responded to by the Jewish community, which by and large identified with the German element and with the Prussian government which had granted them at least partial emancipation. Their most significant, if somewhat delayed, impact was in Russian Poland, and above all in Warsaw, where calls for Polish–Jewish brotherhood were increasingly widely heeded in the run-up to the insurrection which began in January 1863. Following the demonstrations of 25 and 27 February 1861, which led to the deaths of five protesters, two of them Jews, a city delegation of twelve leading citizens of Warsaw was elected. It included the chief rabbi, Dov Ber Meisels, who had also participated in the 1848 revolution in Kraków. The next day Meisels went to the palace of the leading Polish reformer, Count Andrzej Zamoyski, to sign a petition to the tsar calling for the restoration of the 'rights of the Polish nation'. Kieniewicz relates how Zamoyski spoke of the 'Old Testament Believers' (a Polish nineteenth-century term for Jews) as 'our countrymen and brothers, the children of one land', while Meisels replied, 'And we too feel that we are Poles and we love the Polish land as you do.'

The uprising failed disastrously and was followed by two generations of severe repression and russification. The last vestiges of the autonomy granted to the Kingdom of Poland were now done away with and a substantial Russian army was quartered in the territory, now called the 'Vistula land', in order to prevent the outbreak of any further insurrections. In the run-up to the revolt, in order to diminish Jewish support for Polish independence, the tsarist authorities had allowed their Polish viceroy, Count Alexander Wielopolski, to abolish all the main restrictions on Jewish activity on 4 June 1862, in effect establishing the Jews as equal citizens. Similarly, in its aftermath, unfree cultivation was done away with, and, in the hope of winning the peasants' support, the tsarist authorities granted them the freehold of the land they were given on much more favourable terms than their counterparts in the rest of the Empire.

The 1863 uprising was a decisive turning-point in Polish history. The bankruptcy of the Polish insurrectionary tradition had been clearly demonstrated; new political strategies would have to be adopted in order to preserve the Polish national identity. Two groups were now dominant. The first was the Galician conservatives, who advocated close co-operation with the Austrian authorities who had given self-government to Austrian Poland in the 1860s. In the Kingdom of Poland, the Warsaw Positivists saw themselves as the upholders of the liberal political tradition that was now dominant in western Europe. Like their namesakes in France and Britain, they stressed the importance of scientific knowledge and of the progressive character of industrial development. Certainly, the abolition of unfree cultivation, the emancipation of the Jews, and the ending of the tariff barrier between the Kingdom of Poland and the rest of the Russian Empire led to a substantial industrial upsurge in the years after 1863. By 1914, the Kingdom of Poland, with industrial centres in Łódź, Warsaw, and the Dąbrowa basin was the most highly industrialized part of the Tsarist Empire and one of the more industrialized parts of Europe. By the outbreak of the First World War, nearly two-thirds of the population of its two most industrialized provinces, Warsaw and Piotrków, derived their livelihood from sources other than agriculture. The Positivists believed that the Polish struggle to regain national sovereignty had been too narrowly based. What was necessary was work 'at the foundations' to win over those groups—peasants, Jews, women—who lay outside the bounds of Polish noble society. The Jews, with their commercial expertise, could contribute to the industrialization of the Polish lands, which would make possible the creation of the secular and tolerant society sought by the Positivists. The way this issue is reflected in Positivist writing is described by Magdalena Opalski (Chapter 11).

The Jewish Enlightenment had been relatively slow to develop in the Polish lands, where traditional values were strong within the Jewish community and where the authorities had, for the most part, not been willing to intervene actively to 'civilize' the Jews. The implications of early marriage, which was common in Jewish life in Poland, and the associated pattern of a young man leaving his home to board with his in-laws, for the development of views sympathetic to the Haskalah (Enlightenment) is described in a path-breaking article by David Biale (Chapter 12). Only by the reform of traditional Jewish society, the *maskilim* claimed, could a form of marriage be established in which love and partnership would be the essential elements. They also held that traditional society denied women their appropriate place, and in particular was unwilling to grant them any sort of education. The *maskilim* often cited as proof of this the talmudic text that 'anyone who teaches his daughter Torah teaches her *tiflut*' (indecency or frivolity). This view is challenged by Shaul Stampfer, who argues that women in nineteenth-century Jewish eastern Europe received much more of both religious and secular education than has sometimes been realized (Chapter 13). The separateness of the Jewish community and the gulf which divided it from the rest of society emerges clearly in the way traditional Jewish stereotypes of the non-Jewish world are reflected in nineteenth-century Yiddish and Hebrew literature; this is examined in Israel Bartal's article (Chapter 10). He demonstrates that these views are shared by the principal writers of the Haskalah like Mapu, Judah Leib Gordon, Isaac Meir Dik, and Abraham Ber Gottlober, and their successors Sholem Abramovich (Mendele Mokher Seforim), Sholem Aleichem and Yitshak Leibush Peretz, who were the creators of modern Yiddish literature. Yet a significant segment of Jewish society did respond to the Positivist calls to transform themselves into 'Poles of the Mosaic faith'. This movement had most support in towns like Warsaw and Łódź, which grew enormously in size in the second half of the nineteenth century. Warsaw's population grew from 223,000 in 1864 to 885,000 in 1914, while that of Łódź rose in the same period from 42,500 to 513,000. At this time Jews numbered just over a third of the population of both towns. Within the burgeoning Jewish urban society acculturation and assimilation made significant strides. One reflection of this, described in the article by Maria and Kazimierz Piechotka, was the synagogues they built (Chapter 14). These were not 'reformed' synagogues on the German pattern, but they did involve a new understanding of the nature of Jewish worship. They introduced a more orderly pattern of worship, with a trained choir, employed an organ at weddings and at minor Jewish festivals like Purim and Chanukah, and instituted an upstairs gallery for women, who had previously been segregated behind a curtain. In these new synagogues, whether in Warsaw, Łódź, Lwów, or Kraków, great stress was placed on preaching, which also occasioned a change in the position of the *bimah*. Initially, the sermon was delivered in German, the language of the Haskalah, but increasingly, as the Jewish élite became polonized, Polish was used.

By the 1880s, the assimilationist dream of transforming the Jews into 'Poles of the Mosaic faith' was clearly failing. The Poles, outside Galicia, did not control the educational system, which was the only real means through which a substantial degree of acculturation could be achieved. The Jewish community was also too large and too conservative to respond rapidly to demands that it totally transform itself. The benefits of such a transformation in the political conditions which prevailed in Russian Poland after 1863 were also not that obvious. Within Polish society, as Opalski demonstrates, there was growing disillusionment with the results of industrialization. According to the turn-of-the-century critic Ignacy Matuszewski, cited in Chapter 11 below:

> Alas! The golden age remained a dream, the heroic engineers, praised by contemporary writers, were transformed into legal bandits. [Organic] work, which was to raise the spirits of the individual and of the collective, changed into a nightmare which preyed on the sweat of the poor and the brains, nerves and hearts of the rich and those determined to become rich.

This change in attitude inevitably had an adverse effect on attitudes to the Jews, who were widely blamed for the defects of capitalism. As Opalski shows there is a whole series of *fin-de-siècle* Polish novels which describe the unsuccessful attempts of Polish characters to free themselves from the capitalist cobwebs that entangle them. 'In all cases, the "flies" are ultimately strangled and become the prey of a swarm of Jewish "spiders".' Around the same time, the European-wide revival of nationalism led to the emergence in Poland of the

National Democratic Movement. Its chief ideologist, Roman Dmowski, was a Social Darwinist who believed that if Poland was to survive as a nation it would have to abandon the naïve belief in international brotherhood which had characterized the gentry revolutionaries of 1830, 1848, and 1863. 'Struggle and ... oppression are a reality and universal peace and universal freedom are a fiction',[11] he asserted. In these conditions, the Poles should create an organic national movement which would defend their national interests. In this movement, there could be no place for the Jews, who were a disruptive force and who could never be integrated into the national substance.

These developments both caused and were stimulated by the transformation of the Jewish consciousness which occurred in the Pale of Settlement, the area in the Tsarist Empire to which Jews were confined in the 1880s. Increasingly, the assimilationist solution was rejected as unrealistic and involving a series of compromises which had proved both humiliating and fruitless. Autonomist Jewish political movements now emerged, of which the most important were Zionism, Folkism (which sought Jewish cultural autonomy in the Diaspora), and Jewish Socialism, which believed that Jewish national autonomy should be sought within the framework of the Socialist millennium. These movements were underpinned by the development of a modern Hebrew and Yiddish literature which is described by Chone Shmeruk (Chapter 9). The new politics, characterized as it was by a more strident and antisemitic form of Polish nationalism, by a Socialist challenge to the Tsarist Empire, and by Jewish autonomist claims, was both more populist and more demagogic. Its impact on Łódź, the second-largest town in the Polish lands, is described by Paweł Samuś (Chapter 8). Boycotts and anti-Jewish violence followed the elections to the Fourth Russian Duma in Warsaw and Łódź. The old Jewish–noble alliance was now clearly dead. So, too, was the assimilationist idea that the Jews would become 'Poles of the Mosaic faith'. Whether the autonomist solutions of the 'Jewish problem' were realistic and whether the Jews could find for themselves a place in Polish society, on the eve of the greatest war mankind had thus far experienced, remained open to question. There is certainly something plaintive in Peretz's observations in 1911 in his significantly titled article 'I Give Up':

> It was not I who allowed Poland to be partitioned, because of family intrigue and hope of material gain. It was not I who put foreign rulers on the Polish throne.... It was not I who brought modern civil law from Paris. It was not I who brought religion and the Jesuits from Rome. It was not I who delayed

[11] *Myśli nowoczesnego Polaka* (first pub. Lwów, 1903, repr. London, 1953), 87.

the emancipation of the peasants, so that it had to come from Petersburg. Dear nobleman, this culture, with all its virtues and mistakes is *yours* . . . my only sorrow is that in this Poland which is *yours*, besides me, who works and trades in the town, so also, the peasant, who ploughs and sows has no share. There is also no place in *that* culture which you have created with foreign ideologies and laws for those who feel and act in a human (*menshlekh*) and not in an aristocratic (*pritsish*) way. I know, too, that in the Poland that is coming, there will be a place for the humanist, for the peasant and for me.

The First World War radically transformed the situation of the Jews in the Polish lands. It saw the collapse of the three empires which had partitioned Poland and the emergence of an independent Polish state. The establishment of this state was the central element in the Wilsonian plan for the reconstitution of east central Europe. The national and democratic principles, which had shown their superiority in the conflict with autocracy, would make it possible rapidly to overcome the economic backwardness which had long plagued the area. The rights of the national minorities in the new state—which included, along with the three million Jews (just over 10 per cent of the total population), Ukrainians, Byelorussians, and Germans—would be safeguarded by the provisions of the Polish constitution guaranteeing their rights and by the treaty between Poland and the Allied and Associated Powers, which gave an international aspect to that guarantee. It was always unlikely that the high hopes with which the new Poland was born would be fulfilled. As Eugene Black shows (Chapter 17), the international guarantee of Jewish rights which had been achieved by the veteran Anglo-Jewish diplomat Lucien Wolf at Versailles was a response to the serious deterioration of the position of the Jews on the Polish lands which had occurred as a result of the First World War. Wartime devastation had been on an immense scale in the east, the result both of the many shifts of the front here and the German exactions of goods and raw materials in response to the Allied blockade. The Jews had also suffered from the paranoiac suspicion of Russian commanders, who had executed many Jewish 'spies' and expelled nearly half a million Jews from the western areas of the Empire on the grounds of their potential disloyalty. The end of the war was marked by large-scale anti-Jewish violence in Russian Poland, Galicia, and above all Ukraine. In Poland, the violence resulted partly from the breakdown of law and order at the end of the German occupation, from wartime privations and the belief that Jews were responsible for hoarding the shortages, and from fears that the Jews were the avant-garde of the Bolshevik revolution. Anger at the Jewish failure to support the Polish claims to towns like Lwów and Vilna also played a role.

The conditions in which the new Poland emerged were thus not conducive to the establishment of harmonious relations between Poles and Jews. In an article published in 1986 and provocatively titled 'Interwar Poland: Good for the Jews or Bad for the Jews?',[12] Ezra Mendelsohn observed that in the historiography of inter-war Polish Jewry two basic camps, one 'optimistic' the other 'pessimistic', can be observed. He continued:

> The attitude of most Jewish scholars has been, and continues to be, that interwar Poland was an extremely anti-semitic country, perhaps even uniquely anti-semitic. They claim that Polish Jewry during the 1920s and 1930s was in a state of constant and alarming decline, and that by the 1930s both the Polish regime and Polish society were waging a bitter and increasingly successful war against the Jewish population.[13]

This point of view is most clearly expressed by Celia Heller in her book *On the Edge of Destruction* (New York, 1977). Her thesis is clearly encapsulated in the title. In her view, the period between the two world wars was a rehearsal for the Holocaust. Polish actions had by 1939 pushed the Jews to 'the edge of destruction' and it only remained for the Nazis to complete what they had begun.

This 'pessimistic' view of the situation of Jews in inter-war Poland has not gone unchallenged, by both Jewish and non-Jewish (mostly Polish) historians. The most eloquent of the Jewish 'optimists' is Joseph Marcus. Marcus, who is a supporter of the Orthodox party, Agudas Yisroel, reserves his greatest condemnation for what he refers to as the 'reformers' of Jewish life in Poland. Blinded by their Zionist and Socialist obsessions, they had a great deal to do with the economic decline of Polish Jewry. According to Marcus, Jews in Poland were able to hold their own economically and were, in fact, better off than the majority of the population. They were more than capable of

[12] *The Jews in Poland*, 130–9.

[13] Among those who hold this view, he cites R. Mahler, *Yehudei polin bein shtei milkhamot olam* (Tel Aviv, 1968); J. Lestchinsky, 'The Anti-Jewish Program: Tsarist Russia, the Third Reich, and Independent Poland', *Jewish Social Studies*, 3/2 (Apr. 1941), 141–58; Y. Trunk, 'Der ekonomisher antisemitizm in Poyln', in Joshua A. Fishman (ed.), *Studies on Polish Jewry 1919–1939* (New York, 1974), 3–98; Pawel Korzec, *Juifs en Pologne: La question juive pendant l'entre-deux-guerres* (Paris, 1980); id., 'Antisemitism in Poland as an Intellectual, Social and Political Movement', *Studies on Polish Jewry*, 12–104; Moshe Landau, *Miut le'umi lochem: Ma'avak Yehudei polin 1918–1928*, (Jerusalem, 1986); Shlomo Netzer, *Ma'avak Yehudei polin al zekhuyoteihem ha'ezrachiot vehaleumuiot (1918–1922)*, Publications of the Diaspora Research Institute, Tel Aviv University (Tel Aviv, 1982); Emanuel Meltzer, *Ma'avak medini bemalkodet: Yehudei polin 1935–1939*, Publications of the Diaspora Research Institute, Tel Aviv (Tel Aviv, 1982).

withstanding the assaults to which they were subjected in the 1930s. The real problem in Marcus's view was Polish poverty and Jewish over-population: 'The Jews in Poland were poor because they lived in a poor, undeveloped country. Discrimination added only marginally to their poverty.'[14]

These views have been echoed by many Polish scholars. Their position has been best articulated by the British historian of Poland, Norman Davies. In his challenging and stimulating history of Poland, he claims that 'the condition of Polish Jewry in the interwar period is often described out of context'. This, he claims, is the responsibility of the Zionists, who needed to paint the situation in Poland in the blackest colours in order to justify their own political position. Like Marcus, he argues that the intractable nature of the Jewish question was the result of the poverty of the reborn Polish state and 'an unprecedented demographic explosion' which 'countermanded all attempts to alleviate social conditions'. The Jews were only one of many ethnic groups in conflict in Poland; they were not singled out for special treatment by Polish chauvinists—the latter were no less hostile to Germans and Ukrainians. Moreover, they had important allies on the Polish political scene. Davies also argues that the scale of anti-Jewish violence in Poland has been exaggerated, referring to the 'so-called pogroms' of 1918 and 1919. He cites the cultural creativity of the Polish Jewish community as evidence that its situation was not as desperate as has sometimes been claimed: 'Anyone who has seen the remarkable records which these people left behind them, and which have been collected in YIVO's post-war headquarters in New York, cannot fail to note the essential dynamism of Polish Jewry at this juncture. All was not well: but neither was it unrelieved gloom.' He explicitly rejects Heller's claim that the oppression which the Jews experienced in the last years before the outbreak of the war paved the way for the successful implementation by the Nazis of their policies of mass murder.[15]

It is easy to understand why the history of the Jews in Poland in these years should have aroused such passion. In the inter-war years, Poland's Jewish community was second only in size to that of the United States and its fate was seen as a touchstone for how the Jews would fare in the newly independent states of east central Europe. The country was also seen as a laboratory in which the various autonomist Jewish ideologies—Zionism, Bundism, Folkism—could

[14] Joseph Marcus, *Social and Political History of the Jews in Poland, 1919–1939* (Berlin, New York, Amsterdam, 1983).

[15] Norman Davies, *God's Playground: A History of Poland in Two Volumes* (2 vols.; Oxford, 1981), ii. 240–66.

be tested. Summing up his view of the controversy, Ezra Mendelsohn wrote:

> Interwar Poland was therefore bad for the Jews, in the sense that it excluded them from first-class citizenship in the state. This led, by the late 1930s, to a widespread feeling among Polish Jews, and especially among the youth, that they had no future in Poland and that they were trapped. Interwar Poland was good for the Jews because, among other things, it provided an environment in which forces were unleashed in the Jewish world which many Jews regarded then, and today, as extremely positive.[16]

These issues are explored in the articles on the inter-war period. Versions of the 'optimistic' view of the situation of the Jews are set out by Norman Davies (Chapter 15) and Jerzy Tomaszewski (Chapter 16), while Szymon Rudnicki highlights one aspect of the 'pessimistic' thesis, showing the success of the nationalist campaign in reducing and ultimately excluding the Jews from Polish universities (Chapter 21). In inter-war Poland, the legal status of the *kehillot*, which governed Jewish communal life, had been regulated by the statute in October 1927 and March 1930. In terms of this legislation, the *kehillot* were defined as autonomous organizations which had both religious and social functions. They were to provide rabbinical services and maintain religious institutions, cemeteries, and Jewish religious schools. They were also responsible for supplying Jews with kosher meat and with providing welfare for needy Jews. They were governed by boards elected by universal male suffrage, which were authorized to levy taxes. All adherents of the 'Mosaic faith' were required to belong to a *kehillah* and one could not withdraw except through baptism. The 'autonomists' had wanted the *kehillot* to have wider powers and to form the basis for a system of Jewish self-government, headed by a Jewish Council elected by the *kehillot*. For a brief period, such a system functioned in Lithuania. In Poland, the narrower religious character of the *kehillot* was the result of the close relationship which developed between the regime of Józef Piłsudski, which took power after a coup in May 1926, and the main Orthodox party, Agudas Yisroel. How this alliance and the *kehilla* itself functioned in Łódź is the theme of Robert Shapiro's article (Chapter 18). Both Mendelsohn and Davies allude to the cultural efflorescence of Polish Jewry in this period. Different aspects of this flourishing cultural scene are described by Michael Steinlauf and Eugenia Prokopówna. Steinlauf examines a specific feature of Jewish life in Poland, the existence of daily newspapers in Polish intended for a Jewish readership (Chapter 20). Prokopówna's article (Chapter 19) has a wider scope: it describes the way the *shtetl*, the typical Jewish small town, has been

[16] 'Interwar Poland: Good for the Jews or Bad for the Jews?', 139.

described in both Polish and Polish Jewish literature. The *shtetl* was, until the early twentieth century, the characteristic institution of Polish Jewry, and one index of the changing social geography of the community is the novels written in Polish by Maurycy Szymel, Stefan Pomer, and Czeslawa Rosenblattowa which all recount the experience of having to leave the town in which one was born. Their work is suffused by nostalgia, melancholy, and a sense that the traditional Jewish world is disappearing. In his prose and poetry, Szymel evokes the world of the *shtetl* and, in particular, the *shtetl* on the Sabbath. He draws it in bright colours:

> The polished candlesticks absorbed the liquid gold
> of the evening glow that flowed down the wet window panes.
>
> In the small *bes-medresh* the sky opened for me,
> The old Sabbath sky of mother, warm and womanly.

But he is aware that he can no longer fit into this world:

> All too often we are late on Friday evenings,
> And keep old woman-Sabbath waiting in the glimmer of candles.[17]

The sense of foreboding was even more clearly articulated by the Polish Jewish poet, Hersz Avrohom Fenster. In his poem 'Elegy on a Sabbath Evening', he asks his mother to relate to him Sabbath legends, but his nostalgic mood is dispelled by his inability to believe. Referring to the Jewish legend of the wild river Sambation which only rests on the Sabbath, he is brought back to his own alienation from the world in which this legend was a reality:

> ... tell me why the old and tired Sambation does not rest even on the Sabbath?
> I know that we are the Sambation, but why is our path so slippery and steep
> That our bones never know peace ...[18]

These forebodings were in fact justified, for, as we know, the Nazi conquest of Poland enabled Hitler to carry out a genocide from which very few Polish Jews escaped. It is in the discussion of the Holocaust that the views of Polish and Jewish historians have been furthest apart. Many Jewish historians have argued that by its attempt to undermine the economic viability of the Jewish community after the death of Piłsudski in 1935, the Polish government made Hitler's task easier. The great increase in antisemitism in the late thirties, which resulted from the persistence of the economic crisis, the example of

[17] Quoted in E. Prokopówna, 'The Sabbath Motif in Interwar Polish–Jewish Literature', in Yisrael Gutman, Ezra Mendelsohn, Jehuda Reinharz, and Chone Shmeruk (eds.), *The Jews of Poland Between Two World Wars* (Hanover and London, 1989), 429–30.

[18] Ibid. 432.

Nazi Germany, and the attempt of some members of the government to widen its support by gaining the adherence of the young antisemitic zealots of the nationalist opposition, is also held to have created a climate of opinion which was not willing during the Nazi occupation to see the Jews as fellow citizens. This connection between the pre-war and the wartime situations is denied by many Polish historians. Their position has been accurately stated by Norman Davies, who has asserted that: 'the destruction of Polish Jewry during the Second World War was . . . in no way connected to their earlier tribulations'.[19] Rejecting this view, many Jewish historians have claimed that during the Nazi occupation Poles, far from aiding Jews in their hour of need, at best displayed indifference and, at worst, were willing accomplices of the Nazis. On the Polish side, the harshness of the Nazi occupation has been stressed, together with the difficulty of providing aid to the Jews, sealed off as they were by the Germans in ghettos, and the fact that the penalty for providing assistance to Jews was death. In recent years, the heat has, to an extent, gone out of this controversy and there has been a significant narrowing of the gulf between the two sides. Most scholars now accept that there was a significant increase in antisemitism in Poland in the last years before the outbreak of the war, and that this had something to do with the general indifference with which most Poles observed the mass murder of the Jews. It is also accepted that under the conditions of Nazi terror there was little that Poles could do to assist their Jewish fellow citizens and that those who offered assistance, whether as individuals or as members of the Council for Aid to the Jews (Żegota) set up by the Home Army (Armia Krajowa), the main resistance movement in Poland, should be honoured as heroes. There is less agreement on the scale of and motives for assistance to the Nazis and on the attitude of the Home Army and the Polish Government in London which controlled it to the Jewish tragedy. These thorny issues are only tangentially discussed in the section on the Second World War in this volume. The best introductions to them are provided by the essays by Władysław Bartoszewski, Teresa Prekerowa and Yisrael Gutman, which were first delivered as papers at the Conference on Polish–Jewish Studies held in Oxford in September 1984, and by the record of the discussion which followed, by the account of this problem by Yisrael Gutman and Shmuel Krakowski, and by the collection of essays edited by Antony Polonsky dealing with the recent controversy in Poland on the degree of Polish responsibility for the fate of the Jews during the Second World War.[20]

[19] *God's Playground*, ii. 263.

[20] Władysław Bartoszewski, 'Polish–Jewish Relations in Occupied Poland 1939–1945', in Abramsky *et al.*, *The Jews in Poland*, 147–60; Teresa Prekerowa, 'The Relief Council for Jews in Poland, 1942–1945', ibid. 161–76; Yisrael Gutman, 'Polish

Each of the three essays printed here in the section on the Second World War discusses a particular problem relating to the *shoah* on the Polish lands. In recent years, a great deal has been written on the reaction of the Jews to the Soviet annexation of eastern Poland (western Ukraine and western Byelorussia) at the beginning of the war and to the vexed question of how far alleged Jewish 'collaboration' with the Soviets affected subsequent Polish attitudes towards the Jews.[21] This issue is investigated in the article by Paweł Korzec and Jean-Charles Szurek (Chapter 22). The equally controversial issue of whether the Western governments could have done more to assist the Jews under Nazi rule is examined by David Engel (Chapter 23), while Ewa Kurek-Lesik analyses the hiding of Jewish children in Catholic religious houses, as a result of which at least 1,500 lives were saved (Chapter 24).

At the end of the war barely 300,000 members of the community that had numbered 3.3 million in 1939 had survived, most of them as refugees in the Soviet Union. The survivors of this ordeal found themselves caught up in the civil war conditions which prevailed in post-war Poland and which were caused by the attempt to impose an unpopular and unrepresentative Communist government on the country. In the attendant violence, at least 1,500 Jews lost their lives. In the worst incident, the pogrom in Kielce in July 1946, forty Jews lost their lives following the disappearance of a Christian boy whom, it was rumoured, the Jews had killed while trying to extract blood from him to cure the anaemia from which they were suffering as a result of their wartime deprivations. The panic which followed this appalling event led to the emigration of the bulk of the Jews remaining in Poland. The boy himself later reappeared.[22] A small community has, however, remained in spite of subsequent vicissitudes and further large-scale emigration in 1956 and in the aftermath of the 'anti-Zionist' campaign of 1968. This community now numbers at least

and Jewish Historiography on the Question of Polish–Jewish Relations during World War II', ibid. 177–89; id., 'Polish–Jewish Relations During the Second World War: A Discussion', *Polin*, 2: 337–58; Yisrael Gutman and Shmuel Krakowski, *Unequal Victims: Poles and Jews During World War II* (New York, 1986); A. Polonsky (ed.), My Brother's Keeper? *Recent Polish Debates on the Holocaust* (London, 1990).

[21] Jan T. Gross, *Revolution from Abroad: The Soviet Conquest of Poland's Western Ukraine and Western Belorussia* (Princeton, N.J., 1988); Ben-Cion Pinchuk, *Shtetl Jews under Soviet Rule: Eastern Poland on the Eve of the Holocaust* (Oxford, 1990); Norman Davies and Antony Polonsky (eds.), *Jews in Eastern Poland and the USSR, 1939–1946* (London, 1991).

[22] On these events, see Michal Borwicz, 'Polish–Jewish relations, 1944–1947', in Abramsky *et al.* (eds.), *Jews in Poland*, 190–8; Lucjan Dobroszycki, 'Restoring Jewish Life in Post-war Poland', *Soviet Jewish Affairs*, 2 (1973) 58–72.

10,000, and in recent years strenuous efforts have been made to strengthen it and renew its links with Western Jewry. Although the Jewish community was very small from 1947 onwards, the Jewish issue played a disproportionate role in the politics of Communist Poland. Why this was the case is examined by Krystyna Kersten and Paweł Szapiro (Chapter 25). Hegel observed that 'the owl of Minerva takes flight in the dusk'. It is paradoxical that after the almost total destruction of the Jewish community of Poland, a number of Polish Jewish writers have emerged. Among the most notable figures of this group have been Roman Brandstetter, Adolf Rudnicki, Kazimierz Brandys, Julian Stryjkowski, and the much younger Henryk Grynberg. The character of this school is examined by Jan Błoński (Chapter 26) and the work of Julian Stryjkowski is discussed in more detail by Laura Quercioli-Mincer (Chapter 27). The greatest Yiddish prose writer of the twentieth century is probably Isaac Bashevis Singer. He moved to the United States from Poland in 1936, but his fiction has been preoccupied with bringing to life the lost world of Polish Jewry. His treatment of Poles and Poland is examined by the Polish literary critic, Monika Adamczyk-Garbowska (Chapter 28).

The Polish Jewish community is today tiny in comparison with the past and it is not clear how long organized Jewish life can survive in a land which was for long one of the main centres of the Jewish world. The small number of Polish Jews who survive often feel that we, the Jews of the West, most of whom derive our cultural roots from Polin in the broadest sense, do not understand them and are not interested in hearing what they have to say. At the beginning of the 1960s, Stryjkowski went to California, where a number of his friends had settled. He found this encounter with American Jewish life, which he described in his essay 'On the willows ... our fiddles', disconcerting (the willow is the tree most characteristic of the Polish countryside). It lacked any authenticity. There was a rabbi, his head covered with a very small *yarmulkah*, a 'ritual relic ... as shameful as a figleaf', married to a (converted) Hawaiian woman, people sang Hasidic songs, but 'the young did not know the psalm, had no idea what it had sounded like in their fathers' and grandfathers' time'. A Sephardic rabbi had never heard of the Marranos. Instead of history, 'I teach boys not to be afraid of anybody'. Stryjkowski felt unable to communicate his own Jewish experience:

> What can I say?—I reflected, as if I really wanted to make the declaration that from the first moment they had been expecting from me. ... The seconds passed in silence. I dried the sweat with my handkerchief.
> —My dear friends—I began—I have nothing to say to you.
> The guests looked at each other and returned to their dinner.

In spite of the reproaches of his friends, he returns to Poland:

A whole people has perished. How can you walk on that earth? Under every stone is a brother who has been killed....—But I belong in the cemetery.[23]

A similar sense of isolation and of being the last of many generations is articulated by Henryk Grynberg. In his novel *Kaddish*, he describes sitting with his mother and her friends of the Nowy Dwór *landsmanshaft* after the doctor has revealed that she has a fatal cancer. The members of the *landsmanshaft* are his last links with the world 'of authentic Jewry which consists of people declaring and nurturing the human virtues of solidarity, compassion and sincerity, brought from their little Mazovian town'. He continues:

Red Indians from the Nowy Dwór tribe, from the past, of whom apart from ourselves nothing is left, moved and gesticulated in a natural and unpretentious way, using warm, unpretentious words. They were old and I knew that before long, I would be left alone: they understood this and so sat close to me silently in a warm, family silence.[24]

It is our task as Jews to demonstrate that we do hear these voices from this world which has been destroyed, but which is still very much a part of our own world. For those Poles concerned to remember and honour the Polish Jewish past, the task is different. It is to integrate posthumously the Jewish community of Poland into the historic consciousness of the Polish people. This also will not be easy. As the Polish poet Jerzy Ficowski wrote in his poem 'The Way to Yerushalaim':

... through woodland rivers
through an autumn of bowed candlesticks
through gas chambers
graveyards of air
they went to Yerushalaim
both the dead and the living
into their returning olden time

and that far they smuggled
a handful of willow pears
and for a keepsake
a herring bone
that sticks to this day[25]

[23] J. Stryjkowski, *Na wierzbach ... nasze skrzypce* (Warsaw, 1974), 189, 231, 177.

[24] Quoted in Jozef Wrobel, 'Henryk Grynberg Calls Poland to Account', *Polin*, vol. 7.

[25] Jerzy Ficowski, *A Reading of Ashes*, trans. Keith Bosley and Krystyna Wandycz (London, 1981), 4.

PART I

Pre-partition Poland (to 1795)

1

THE RECONSTRUCTION OF PRE-ASHKENAZIC JEWISH SETTLEMENTS IN THE SLAVIC LANDS IN THE LIGHT OF LINGUISTIC SOURCES

Paul Wexler

The historian naturally favours written documentation over all other sources in reconstructing the history of both literary and pre-literary periods; when written documentation is sparse or unavailable, he has traditionally sought out the assistance of the archaeologist. Rarely does the historian turn to the linguist – though the latter often has much to contribute to the historian. The task of reconstructing the history of pre-Ashkenazic Jewish settlement patterns in the Slavic lands forcefully illustrates the usefulness of collaboration between historian and linguist. In this paper, the present writer, a linguist, will first survey briefly the insights of historians on early Jewish settlement history in the Slavic lands, and then explore some linguistic data which raise some tantalizing questions for the historian.

The student wishing to reconstruct the early history of Jewish settlement in Europe during the first millenium AD can turn to a small number of historical documents, but rarely from the lands occupied by the Slavs.[1] The written sources can be supplemented by a fair number of archaeological remains; for example, epigraphical materials from synagogue ruins and occasionally from gravestones attest to a Jewish presence in territories adjoining the northern Mediterranean and Black Sea littorals.[2] However, the further north one proceeds, away from the Greco–Roman cultural orbit, the more difficult it becomes to reconstruct Jewish settlement history – for both textual and archaeological remains are lacking. The penetration of the Jews into the Slavic lands prior to the year 1200 has long been written off by historians as a topic barely accessible to description.[3] The documentation for this early period consists of scraps of textual evidence – most of which is preserved in documents recorded many centuries after the events transpired, and often by scribes ignorant of the language of the original documents. The main sources are as follows: a late 8th–early 9th-century Latin mention of a Slavic-speaking Jewish physician in Salzburg;[4] a reference to peripatetic Jewish merchants (also residents?) in the Slavic lands in the Arabic writings of the 9th-century Persian geographer ibn Xordāδbeh;[5] the first mention, in *c*.965, of a permanent Jewish settlement in the West Slavic lands given in the fragmentary Arabic accounts of Ibrāhīm ibn Jaʿqūb (al-Isrāʔīlī or aṭ-Ṭorṭōsī), a Catalan Jewish traveller (known only from the later Arab writers, none earlier than the 11th century);[6] a Khazar Hebrew document dated *c*.930 from Kiev containing what is possibly the first reference to that city;[7] a Hebrew letter composed in Saloniki, perhaps in the year 1000, mentioning a monolingual Slavic-speaking Jewish visitor from the East Slavic lands;[8] the mention of a purported visit of a Czech rabbi, Eliezer of Prague, to 'Russia' in the late 12th century,[9] and of the settlement of 'Western' Jews in Kiev;[10] references to Jews residing in the West Slavic lands in the remarks of Kalonimos bɛn Šabtaj (10th century – but preserved in an early 13th-century text),[11] in the *Sefɛr hadinim* of Jəhuda bɛn Meir Ha-Kohen (early 11th century, but the work survives in two 13th-century German Rabbinical texts);[12] the *Sefɛr hašoham* of Mošɛ bɛn Jicxak ha-Nəsia (second half of the 13th century) relates the visit of a Jew from Černihiv to England;[13] and finally, there is a reference to Slavic-speaking Jews in Lausitz, south-eastern Germany, from as late as the 14th century.[14] Even if these fragmentary sources all prove to be reliable, the historian still has little way of reconstructing the native languages of these Jewish communities, or their paths of migration into and across Slavic Europe.

It is the paucity of reliable evidence which led the historian B. D. Weinryb to dismiss most of the outlines of Slavic Jewish history sketched above as a myth.[15] I may add that even in the interpretation of the texts, historians have often failed to grasp all the implications. For example, the reader finds repeated mention of the Hebrew letter from Saloniki dated *c*.1000 as support for the hypothesis that there were monolingual Slavic-speaking Jews in the East Slavic lands prior to the arrival of the Yiddish-speaking Jews in the late 14th century; yet no onc appears to have stated explicitly that the letter also shows that Jews in Saloniki were themselves conversant in Slavic.[16] Appreciating the limitations of collaboration with archaeologists, a few historians have turned to linguistic data. The pioneer in this field was A. A. Harkavi, who offered the first systematic analysis of the Slavic glosses recorded in Hebrew characters from the West and East Slavic lands between the mid-10th and 17th centuries.[17] In our century, the number of Slavic historians who have examined linguistic materials has grown considerably and the percentage of Polish-born scholars in this group is striking.[18] For example, I. Sziper (Šiper) studied the naming patterns of Jews in Poland, Yiddish and Hebrew sources spanning the 14th–16th centuries (1924, 1926);[19] B. D. Weinryb has evaluated Slavic toponyms and anthroponyms used by Jews as indices of their settlement history (1957, 1962a, 1962b, 1973);[20] S. M. Dubnow and M. Bałaban have studied the status of a Slavic-speaking Jewry in Poland, Byelorussia and the Ukraine before the Ashkenazic migrations (1909, 1913; 1917, 1920, 1930–31 respectively);[21] B. Nadel has studied the epigraphic data from the Black Sea (Crimea) and the possibility of Khazar-Karaite contacts (1959, 1960, 1961); M. Gumowski has written about the Polish coins from the late 12th–13th centuries minted by Jews with Hebrew and Polish inscriptions (in Hebrew characters) (1962, 1975); T. Lewicki (both independently and in collaboration with F. Kupfer, 1956) has studied linguistic and non-linguistic evidence from Arab and Jewish sources relating to the Slavic Jewish settlements and the early history of the Slavs (1956a, 1956b, 1958, 1984); E. Ringelblum has examined fragments of Polish speech by Jews from the 15th century as well as Old Yiddish materials from the 15th century (1926, 1932); T. Kowalski has examined the Arabic-language text of Ibrāhīm ibn Jaʿqūb (1946).

However, it is rare to find a historian who cites Jewish languages by their proper name or who appreciates the significance of world-wide Jewish linguistic phenomena. For example, Leon (1960) concludes that deviations from standard Latin in the Jewish inscriptions in the Roman catacombs are proof that the Jews knew Latin poorly (and not that they may have developed a judaicized version of that language), while Xananel and Eškenazi (1960: 227–8) interpret Slavisms in an early-17th century Hebrew text from Vidin, Bulgaria as 'deviations' from standard Bulgarian. Even Kupfer and Lewicki (1956), who collected most of the West Slavic glosses in Hebrew characters from the mid-10th to mid-13th centuries, display an appalling ignorance of the nature of linguistic judaicization. Yet if historians have shown some interest in linguistic facts, it must be stated, with regret, that linguists are often oblivious to historical research (an exception is H. Birnbaum, 1981a) and have rarely studied the linguistic evidence which would be invaluable for historians.[22] Most linguists who dabble in Jewish history have contented themselves with impressionistic formulations devoid of factual authority. Thus, S. A. Birnbaum (1926: 1), M. Altbauer (1929: 106) and H. Teszler (1942: 6) all talk about an 'Eastern' origin of the Polish Jews, while F. J. Beranek writes of an 'Asian' origin for the first Jewish settlers in Polesia (1958: 5). M. Šapiro has suggested that the first Jews in Byelorussia and Lithuania were settlers from no fewer locales than Arabia, Asia, Egypt, Greece, and especially from the Caucasus and Volga regions; further, he claims to see an impact from these languages on the Jewish successor language – Yiddish – though no evidence is forthcoming (1939: 119). M. Šulman, finally, thinks that Yiddish in the Slavic lands contains Slavicisms introduced by 'Eastern' Jews – but he neglects to say if the latter were Slavic-speaking or not (1939: 109).

Barring the discovery of new documents,[23] historians have probably reached the limits of their ability to reconstruct pre-Ashkenazic Jewish settlement history in the Slavic lands. Hence, it is now up to linguists to sift through the Jewish languages spoken in the Slavic lands (e.g. Yiddish, Karaite, Judeo-Slavic and Judeo-Spanish), as well as the coterritorial Slavic languages, for evidence of a pre-Ashkenazic linguistic and cultural presence. These data will permit a better understanding as well as reconceptualization of early Jewish migration to the Slavic lands.

In the discussions below, I will present linguistic evidence in a variety of forms which can either clarify hypotheses already formulated by historians or suggest the need for new hypotheses. The main source of our data is Yiddish – the only surviving Jewish language in contact with Slavs since the 10th century. Yiddish, especially in its older forms, preserves elements from Judeo-Greek, Judeo-Iranian, Judeo-Slavic and possibly even Judeo-Turkic. Apart from Yiddish, we also have some fragmentary Judeo-Slavic materials (emanating from the Czech and Sorbian lands from between the mid-10th and mid-13th centuries, and from the East Slavic lands from the late-16th to early-17th centuries). The Judeo-Iranian and Judeo-Turkic component in Yiddish is far too small to allow us to posit an Iranian or Turkic settlement in the Slavic lands and eastern Germany; I therefore assume that these few elements came into Yiddish directly from a Judeo-Slavic community which itself had contact with Iranian and Turkic Jewries. The examples are discussed under five headings: (1) Judeo-Greek; (2) Judeo-Iranian; (3) Judeo-Turkic; (4) Judeo-Slavic; (5) non-Ashkenazic corpus and pronunciation of Hebrew.

(1) *Judeo-Greek*. A number of Grecisms are attested in languages spoken by the Jews in the Slavic lands (Yiddish, Polish in Hebrew characters) and by the coterritorial non-Jews; some of these Grecisms appear to be unique to Jewish languages.

(a) The Judeo-Greek expression *hē megalē hēmera* 'Yom Kippur',[24] literally 'the great day' (itself ultimately calqued perhaps on the synonymous JAr *jōmāʔ rabbāʔ*), is attested in a cluster of contiguous languages – Cz *dlouhý den*, Hg *hosszúnap*, G *der lange Tag* – which are used by both Jewish and non-Jewish speakers.[25] See also Balkan J Spanish *el dia grande* 'Tišʿāh bəʔāv (a fast day commemorating the destruction of the two Temples, 586 BC and 70 AD); a day for accomplishing an important event (e.g. marriage).'

(b) The etymology of Y *katoves* 'jest', first encountered in German Yiddish of the early 15th century, is in dispute.[26] I am inclined to regard the Yiddish term as a direct borrowing from Gk *katavasion* 'church hymn'; the Russian (or Ukrainian, Byelorussian) intermediary proposed by Joffe (e.g. R *katavasija* 'church hymn; disorder, confusion, jumble') is unappealing because of the presence of the term in 15th-century Bavarian

Yiddish. Of course, if an East Slavic etymon is to be preferred, then the problem would be to account for the diffusion of an East Slavic Grecism all the way to eastern Germany (Se *katavasija* has only the original Greek ecclesiastical meaning). The semantic and formal differences between Yiddish and East Slavic also mitigate against a direct Slavic source for Yiddish.

(c) Y *dukes* 'duke; powerful noble with a large estate' can only be derived from Byzantine Gk *doukas*, itself a Hellenized form of La *dux* 'leader'. Outside of Byzantine Greek, the term appears to be used in Europe only in Jewish languages: in Yiddish (the earliest attestation is in the famous German Yiddish epic poem, the *Dukus horant*, 1382),[27] on Polish coins minted by Jews which have Hebrew and Polish inscriptions in Hebrew characters (dated 1242–57),[28] in Hebrew-Aramaic, and in early 16th-century Balkan Judeo-Spanish (as a family name). The coterritorial non-Jewish languages use only the original Latin root, see e.g. Fr *duc*, It *duca* (the probable source of Se *duca*, late 14th century).[29]

(d) The presence of a number of Greek male names in Western Yiddish also points to a not insignificant Greek element in the early Ashkenazic Jewish population. See Y *kalmen* (first encountered in 13th-century documents),[30] coexisting with its etymon, JGk *kalonymos* (literally 'good name' – and unattested among non-Jewish Greeks); *sendir* (14th century), a hypocoristic form of Gk *aleksandros*.[31] The practice of truncating the first two unstressed syllables to form a familiar name is only typical of non-Jewish languages which were historically coterritorial with Greek or which were receptive to Hellenization (accompanying the spread of Christianity in its Byzantine form); this type of abbreviation is unknown in German and North Slavic languages. Consider examples of the type Hg *Sándor*, Rumanian *Şandu*, Bulgarian *San(d)o*, Ossete *Sandyr*, Georgian, It *Sandro* vs. Polish abbreviations of the type *Leksa*, *Olecha*, *Olechno*, OPo *Leksand(e)r*,[32] Austrian G *Xandl*.[33]

(2) *Judeo-Iranian*. The most certain Iranianism in the Ashkenazic culture and language area is Y *šabaš*, known across a broad area extending from the East Slavic lands to Lithuania and eastern Poland as an interjection or noun signifying an invitation to the guests at a wedding to contribute money to the musicians. The term is found in Eastern Yiddish beginning with the early 1500s (from Lida, now in the Hrodna oblast of Byelorussia).[34] In Western Yiddish, the spelling *cwbwš*/cubuš/ appears in an anonymous Rhineland study of Rashi's Bible commentary from the 13th–14th century.[35] In addition, all the Yiddish dialects seem to have a cognate of *cwbwš* in *šibeš* 'small coin; trifle'. The etymon of all three forms is Iranian, see Persian *šabaš* 'money, tip (to musicians and dancers at weddings, banquets; to newly-weds at the wedding); bravo!'. Attempts to derive the Yiddish terms from East Slavic are unconvincing; see e.g. R, Br,

Ukrainian *šabaš* 'time off from work; finish work; enough!', or R *šabaški* 'wood cuttings taken home by carpenters from work',[36] (Don dialect) *na šabašax* 'free, at someone else's expense'.[37] I suggest that the Slavic terms are also reflexes of the same Iranian root, but came into the Slavic languages from a Turkic intermediary – unlike Yiddish, which received the terms directly from a Judeo-Iranian speech community. The reasons for this conclusion are twofold: (a) the Slavic and Yiddish surface cognates are semantically disparate (Yiddish is closer to the original Iranian meaning); and (b) Yiddish uses the Iranianism much further to the west than Slavic. Karłowicz lists *szabasz* for Polish dialects but fails to indicate which dialects use the term (the eastern areas coterritorial with Ukrainian and Byelorussian?). However, Polish musicians' slang from Warsaw has a truncated form, e.g. *baś* 'money'[38] – possibly from PoY musicians' slang *baš* (also *šab*, *šap*, *čap*).[39] If Y *šabaš*, *šibeš* and *cwbwš* are all related, then I could suppose that (J)Ir *šabaš* reached Yiddish via a specifically Judeo-Slavic carrier in two separate waves. (a) Via Judeo-East and Judeo-West Slavic to the Slavicized Jews resident in what is now eastern Germany, the form *šabaš* became *šibeš* in Yiddish through stress retraction and vowel harmony: *šabaš* > **šábeš* > *šibeš* (on the pattern of He *pānīm* 'face' > Y *pónem*, but *pénemer* plural < **pónemer*). The Medieval Hebrew spelling *cwbwš* with *vav* may have been a typographical error for the similar looking *jod* letter.[40] (b) Via Judeo-West or Judeo-East Slavic, Ir *šabaš* was borrowed a second time without being altered in form.

(3) *Judeo-Turkic*. The fate of the Khazar-speaking Jews after the collapse of the Khazar Empire in the 9th century is shrouded in mystery. A number of hypotheses have been advanced but in the absence of serious linguistic or historical evidence. There is the view that the Khazars were absorbed by the Karaites,[41] by two groups presently inhabiting the Daghestan ASSR – the Judeo-Tats (also known as 'Mountain Jews')[42] and the Kumyks (a Muslim people),[43] by the Crimean Krymčaks,[44] the Bukharan Jews[45] and the Cossacks.[46] Theories about Khazar migrations to Hungary, Czechoslovakia, Poland and Lusatia, or to the Černihiv area of the Ukraine in the 11th–12th centuries cannot be proven.[47] The once popular allegation that Khazar toponyms could be found in Poland has absolutely no basis.[48] The only secure scrap of information is the presence of a Khazar Jewish presence in Kiev in the early 10th century related in a Hebrew document (see Golb and Pritsak, 1982). In addition, there may be some linguistic evidence for a Judeo-Turkic (Khazar?) impact on West European Jewish languages. The Ukrainian Khazar Hebrew document gives the earliest example known of the male name *pesah*, derived from the Hebrew holiday term 'Passover'. This name has a revealing geography; it is popular in Eastern Yiddish and in German Yiddish almost exclusively from the originally Slavicized German lands east of the Elbe River,[49] and among

Karaite and Iranian Jewries. The name is unknown in the Iberian Peninsula and rare in the Balkans (where it is often borne by Jews of Ashkenazic origin). The name is very common in Old Polish and East Slavic records – often adapted to Old South Polish pronunciation patterns – e.g. -*ḥ* (*x*) > -*k* (this Old South Polish sound law is first noted in 15th-century manuscripts),[50] e.g. Po *Pessac* (Wrocław 1351–6).[51] Reflexes with -*k* also appear in German documents, e.g. *Petsak* (Wiener-Neustadt 1455).[52] The change of -*x* > -*k*, the far greater popularity of the name in Slavic- rather than German-speaking Europe, and the use of the name among Asian Jews all suggest that an autochthonous Slavic Jewry may have acquired the habit of naming male children born on Passover by the holiday term from the Khazar Jews in the Ukraine and adjoining lands to the east. This assumption would explain how the Old South Polish habit of pronouncing final *x* as /k/ was found in German documents. While among Jews the name may have been diffused from east to west (from Khazaria to the East Slavic lands to Slavicized eastern Germany), the change of -*x* to -*k* itself, among non-Jews, may actually point to an eastward diffusion, since Middle Low German loans with -*x* can appear in Polish with -*k*.[53]

The idiosyncratic nature of the Turkic component in Balkan Judeo-Spanish also suggests independent channels of diffusion not shared by the coterritorial non-Jewish populations in the Balkans.

(4) *Judeo-Slavic*. The Slavic languages have a sizeable number of native terms associated with Jews and Jewish culture which do not appear to be loan translations of Hebrew or Yiddish expressions. I posit three possible sources for such terms: (a) borrowings from Judeo-Slavic;[54] (b) independent innovations by non-Jewish speakers of Slavic; and theoretically (c) innovations of Judaizers (see M. Mieses 1933–4, Sh. Ettinger 1960). The last source cannot at present be illustrated, but the possibility of such a source is not in doubt. A clear borrowing from Judeo-Slavic is Po *szkoła* 'synagogue' (in addition to the native meaning 'school'; see also JIt *scuola*, New Testament JGk *sxolē*).[55] An example of a possibly Christian (though not necessarily Slavic) lexical innovation is the use of 'trumpet' to designate the Jewish New Year, as e.g. Po *święto trąbek*, *trąbki*. Ukrainian and Byelorussian have cognates. The customary Jewish term is He *roš hašānnāh* (literally 'head of the year'). While the ram's horn is sounded in the synagogue service on this holiday, Jewish languages do not use an expression containing 'trumpet'. The Slavic expression has a basis in Byzantine Gk *tē aorta tōn salpiggōn* (the earliest example known to me is from Anatolia, 13th century).[56] There are quite a number of native expressions in Slavic languages associated with Jews whose communal origins are unclear. Some Old Polish examples are *chłodnica*, (PoLa) *chlodnicza* (1424) 'Tabernacles, Succot';[57] *kozubalec*, -*s*, *kožubalec* 'tax paid by Jews for the purpose of purchasing writing materials for poor Christian

students' (late 16th–18th centuries);[58] *bożnica* (17th-century or modern *bóż-*) 'synagogue';[59] *kuczka* 'Succot' (16th-century).[60] For additional native Slavic terms in Polish and other Slavic languages, see Wexler ms.

A probable Judeo-Slavicism in Yiddish (and through Western Yiddish in German, Czech and Croatian slang) is *nebex* 'poor, unfortunate (person)'. The extreme westward diffusion of the term suggests that this is an early loan from a West Slavic language, from Upper Sorbian *njeboh* 'deceased' or OCz *nebohý* 'deceased'; modern Cz 'unfortunate, poor'.

(5) *Non-Ashkenazic corpus and pronunciation of Hebrew*. All the European languages in contact with Ashkenazic Jews have a small Hebrew-Aramaic component which in the main reflects the pronunciation norms of the coterritorial Yiddish-speaking Jews (see Wexler 1983). An example is Po *szabas* 'Sabbath' borrowed from Y *šabes*. While most Hebrew-Aramaic components in non-Jewish languages share the lexical and phonetic norms for Hebraisms and Aramaisms in Yiddish, there are a few Hebrew-Aramaic loans in European languages which cannot be attributed to the Ashkenazic Jews or to direct learned Christian borrowing from Hebrew-Aramaic texts. Such terms point to contact with a pre- (non-)Ashkenazic Jewish community in the Slavic lands. Presumably, this community was Slavic-speaking, since the examples appear primarily in Slavic lands and in the formerly Slavicized areas of Germany. Examples of Hebraisms which lack a plausible Ashkenazic (Yiddish) origin follow below.

(a) G *Pinke(pinke)* 'money', Cz, Hg *pinka* 'box for money paid by card-players to the innkeeper'. The source is JAr *pinxāh*, *-ā?* 'plate', ultimately from Gk *pinaks*, etc. 'board; dish'. The Judeo-Aramaic term is also marginally used in literary Hebrew, but not in colloquial Jewish languages (but see Y *pinkes* 'protocol' < He *pinqās* < Gk *pinaks*). The German, Czech and Hungarian terms (with the same geographical distribution as for the Grecism 'the great day' = 'Yom Kippur' discussed above) are clearly from Hebrew-Aramaic – but not via a Yiddish intermediary.

(b) Po *kahał* 'Jewish community' < He *qāhāl* '(Jewish) community; gathering' has surface cognates in East Slavic languages – see Br *kahal* 'Jewish community; crowd, (noisy) gathering; relatives' (in different dialects), *kahalam* 'all together'. In Eastern Yiddish, the Hebraism is pronounced as *kōl* or *kūl*. While early Western Yiddish has k^h*āl* (still attested in some dialects), there is no bisyllabic pronunciation in Yiddish; the Eastern Yiddish dialects in contact with Polish and East Slavic give no evidence of k^h*āl* (the oldest Byelorussian example of *kahal* is from 1663; Polish *kahał* from the 17th century).[61] Hence, it is not unreasonable to derive this Slavic Hebraism from a Jewish language other than Yiddish, possibly even from a Caucasian Jewish language, since Kumyk, a Turkic language spoken in the Caucasus, has the Hebraism in the form *qaġal* in the multiple meanings 'matzah; Passover; noise'.

(c) Two Polish Latin documents from near Sandomierz (1387) and from Kraków (late 14th century) contain the intriguing term *kawyary* and *kawyory* respectively for 'Jewish cemetery'.[62] The village name *Kawiory* is cited in a Latin document dated 1318 in the form *Kauor* – without the plural suffix.[63] Surface cognates are found in German sources (pre-16th century)[64] and in Polish and East Slavic slang lexicons (beginning with the late 17th century).[65] M. Altbauer interpreted the Old Polish form as a reflection of the Yiddish pronunciation of He *qɛvɛr* 'grave', but there is no motivation for this (1977: 48: originally 1961). The fact is that Eastern Yiddish rarely uses this term in the plural (see He *qvārīm*, *qvārōt*), except in the compounds *kejver-oves* 'parental graves' (< He *qɛvɛr ʔāvōt*), *bejsakvures* 'cemetery' (< *bēt haqvārōt*). The importance of Y *bejs* 'house of' in the construction is shown by the Yiddish–Polish blend used dialectally in Yiddish – *bejs-smentaž* (M. Weinreich 4: 1973: 328) < Po *cmentarz*. In view of the wide territorial expanse from once slavicized Germany (Magdeburg, Erfurt, Regensburg) to Russia in which reflexes of He *qɛvɛr* occur, and the antiquity of the citations – it may be possible to regard the Slavic and German Hebraism as a common loan from a Jewish language other than Yiddish. Moreover, the Old Polish Latin variant *kawyary* (1387) points to a very old borrowing – prior to the settlement of Ashkenazic Jews in Western Poland. For example, in Old Polish, the changes of original *ē* > *ā* > *a* and *e* > *a* > *o* are believed to have been completed by the 11th century.[66] If we suppose that He *qɛvɛr* > **q(')ɛ̄v'ɛr* > **qāv'ar* > **qav'or*, then the Polish Latin variant with *-ya-* could be the earliest of the two variants. This implies that the Hebraism was already in the Polish lexicon perhaps 200–300 years earlier than the oldest Polish attestation. The *-y* is the Polish plural marker.

The sharp differences in Hebrew pronunciation norms between Sephardic Jews in Spain and the Balkans (also, the first Jews in Zamość were Spanish Jews who came in the late 16th century)[67] suggest that Sephardic Jews must have been heavily influenced by autochthonous Jewish communities (Turkic-, Greek-, Slavic-[?]speaking) prior to submerging the latter in Judeo-Spanish language and culture.

The examples discussed above constitute a small fraction of the extant materials that could attest to non-Ashkenazic Jewish settlement on the Slavic territories eventually occupied by the Ashkenazic Jews. If these examples do not prove beyond doubt the existence of Turkic or Iranian Jewries in the German- and West Slavic-speaking lands, they certainly do suggest a certain amount of cultural and linguistic impact – probably through an intermediary Judeo-Slavic community in the West and possibly East Slavic lands. The impact of Slavic Jewries on Ashkenazic Jewry has so far been speculative. The existence of Slavic glosses in Hebrew characters and native terms in the Slavic languages with (often unique) Jewish associations, also attest to the existence of monolingual

(Judeo-)Slavic-speaking Jews. Finally, I should add that the findings of Jewish linguistic research are useful for corroborating developments postulated for European civilization at large. For example, the role of Saints Cyril and Methodius, the Slavic apostles, in propagating Greek-Byzantine culture in the Great Moravian Empire in the 9th–10th centuries finds a parallel in the diffusion of colloquial Grecisms to early German Yiddish. Also, the existence of a colloquial Greek, Iranian and Turkic impact on Central European or 'Danubian' languages (e.g. Bavarian German, Hungarian, Polish) has been appreciated for some time – but the Jewish data show that these influences may have penetrated (at least among the Jews) as far west as Western Germany.

NOTES*

1 See materials in Aronius 1902.
2 See Frey 1936–52; Nadel 1960, 1961; Roth 1966. Jewish tombstone inscriptions, mainly in Judeo-Greek, are attested from the northern shore of the Black Sea and from Roman Pannonia, from the first millenium AD, but not from the period of Slavic settlement in those areas.
3 See Baron 1957; Friedman 1959; Halpern 1960; Ettinger 1966; Roth 1966.
4 See Aronius 1902: 80.
5 See Lewicki 1956b: 74–5, 118ff.
6 See Kowalski 1946.
7 See Golb and Pritsak 1982 and discussion below.
8 The first to discuss the letter was Marmorstein 1921.
9 See Zunz 1876: 83.
10 See Rawita-Gawroński 1924.
11 See Kupfer and Lewicki 1956: 61ff. This passage describes Jewish settlements in Hungary and Jewish trade between Regensburg and the East Slavic lands.
12 The text contains a mention of Greek Jews in the town called *prjmwṭ*, interpreted by Schall 1932, Kupfer and Lewicki 1956: 32ff, 41–4, Baron 1957: 219 and others as **prjmwš/Przemyśl*. For serious objections to this interpretation, see Weinryb 1962b: 494–5, who suggests the possibility of linking the toponym to the Czech lands; Wexler explores other possible locales in the German lands (ms, chapter 1, fn. 13).
13 See Kupfer and Lewicki 1956: 173–5.
14 See the remarks by Johannes of Saxony in Boncompagni 1862–3.
15 See Weinryb 1957, 1962a, 1962b, 1973.
16 Nor do Jewish historians appear to appreciate the fact that at this time Greek Macedonia was largely bilingual – in Greek and Slavic (Macedonian) – including the hinterland of Saloniki. Suffice to note that Sts. Cyril and Methodius, the two Slavic apostles who developed an alphabetic writing system for the Slavs and who translated the liturgy into Old Macedonian (Old Church Slavic) in the late 9th century, hailed from Saloniki.
17 See Harkavi 1865, 1867. Most recently, see Kupfer and Lewicki 1956, Jakobson 1957, 1984, Jakobson and Halle 1964. For a comprehensive discussion of Judeo-Slavic speech and an extensive bibliography, see Wexler ms.
18 It is worth noting, in passing, that among Slavs, Polish-born scholars also predominate in the study of Jewish languages in the Slavic lands and of Jewish-Slavic

* In this article, Prof. Wexler adheres to the standard transliteration scheme used by linguists.

linguistic contacts. For example, Yiddish linguistics owes much to the scholarship of Rubštejn (1913, 1922); Mieses (1924), who has also written on historical topics as well, e.g. 1933–4; U. Weinreich (1952, 1958, 1962) and M. Weinreich (1973); Polish-Yiddish linguistic contacts have been explored by Ohr (1905), Altbauer (1928, 1932, 1934), Brzezina (1979); Polish slang-Jewish contacts by Kurka (1896 ff), Estreicher (1903), Prilucki (1918, 1924), Ludwikowski and Walczak (1922). Slavic Jewish and Yiddish onomastics have been discussed by Bystroń (1936) and Taszycki (1965 ff). For studies of Karaite spoken in the Lithuanian, Byelorussian and Ukrainian lands long occupied by Poland, see Zajączkowski (1947, 1961a, 1961b) and Altbauer (1979–80); for Khazar studies, see Gumplowicz (1903), Modelski (1910), Brutzkus (1929, 1930, 1939), Nadel (1959) and Altbauer (1968). Finally, for Judeo-Slavic studies, see Altbauer (1972, 1977) and M. Weinreich (1973). It is too much of a digression to discuss here the importance of Polish periodicals in the interbellum period (mainly in Yiddish) for the above topics.

19 The bibliography for Šiper and others discussed here makes no pretence at being complete.

20 See the discussion of *prjmwţ* in note 12 above.

21 See also Centnerszwerowa 1907 and Rubštejn 1913.

22 It is also to be regretted that linguists have been slow to avail themselves of the priceless onomastic materials gathered by historians such as Beršadskij (1882–1903), Bersohn (1911) and Huberband (1951).

23 The most dramatic development in recent years is the identification by Golb and Pritsak (1982) of a Ukrainian Khazar document in Hebrew from Kiev, containing a brief runic inscription and thought to date from *c.* 930.

24 Language abbreviations used here with examples are: Ar – Aramaic, Br – Byelorussian, Cz – Czech, Fr – French, G – German, Gk – Greek, He – Hebrew, Hg – Hungarian, Ir – Iranian, It – Italian, J – Judeo-, La – Latin, O – Old, Po – Polish, R – Russian, Se – Serbian, Y – Yiddish.

25 The earliest example of the term outside of Greek is the German variant, cited by a Bavarian Jewish convert to Christianity, Anthonius Margaritha (1530).

26 See *ktvwt* in the Hebrew writings of Iserlin, a Bavarian rabbi (1440, published in 1519). Joffe 1959: 78–9 argues for a Russian etymology, Prilucki 1926–33: 293–7 for a Hebrew etymology.

27 See discussion in M. Weinreich 1960.

28 See Gumowski 1975.

29 See Vasmer 1944: 55. Outside of Europe, the Hellenized form with *-s* appears in Syriac.

30 See attestation in Šiper 1926: 287. In a Greek form, the name is spelled in Hebrew as *qlwnjmws* on a Mainz tombstone from 1096 (M. Weinreich 1: 1973: 350–1; 3: 374–7). The original Greek form of the name may have been imported into Germany from Italy (after 1000) by Greek-speaking Jews.

31 See Kracauer 1911: 462.

32 See Taszycki 3, 2: 1972.

33 See Jakob 1929.

34 See Harkavi 1865: 39 ff; Levin 1984.

35 See Bar-El 1984.

36 See Dal' 1863–6.

37 See Ovčinnikova *et al.* 3: 1976: 198.

38 See Wieczorkiewicz 1974: 410.

39 See Prilucki 1918: 276, 279, 290.

40 The existence of variant forms of the same root are important clues to multiple borrowings, i.e. migrations. For example, the Yiddish variants *čolnt* (now common in Eastern Yiddish) ~ *šālet* (Western Yiddish) 'Sabbath dish prepared on Friday'

reflect two stages in Old French phonological development – pre-14th century *ch* /č/ and post-14th century *ch*/š/. A cognate is OFr *chauld* 'warm'.
41 See Zajączkowski 1947.
42 See Brutzkus 1939: 30.
43 See Brutzkus 1930: 347. Kumyk is related to Karaite.
44 See Brutzkus 1930: 347; 1939: 30.
45 See Brutzkus 1939: 30.
46 See Friedman 1959: 1511.
47 See Hunfalvy 1877: 218ff; Brutzkus 1930: 347–8; 1939: 22; Shevelov 1979: 211.
48 See Altbauer 1977: 48 (originally written in 1961).
49 The oldest Western Yiddish examples known to me come from Fulda (early 13th century: Salfeld 1898, index) and a tombstone inscription from Budapest dated 1278 (Kaufmann 1895: 307). See also Baron 1957: 202.
50 See Stieber 1973: 69–70, 144.
51 See Bondy and Dvorský 1906: 128.
52 See Schweinburg-Eibenschütz 1895: 113 and index of names.
53 See Borchling 1911: 86.
54 See Wexler ms for the claim that the Jews developed judaicized dialects of Slavic.
55 The term first appears in a Latin privilege granted the Jews by Kazimierz the Great in 1334 (see Bałaban 1: 1931: 324). See also Bersohn 1911, 21a and Wexler 1981.
56 See Davreux 1935: 101.
57 See Winkler 1960: 100. Nitsch and Urbańczyk give 1431 as the first attestation (1953ff).
58 See Bałaban 1: 1931: 177, 392, 553–60; 2: 1936: 199, facing 368.
59 See Nitsch and Urbańczyk 1953ff and surface cognates in other West and East Slavic languages.
60 Ibid. See also surface cognates in Ukrainian, Byelorussian, Russian and Church Slavic.
61 See Bulyka 1980: 42.
62 See Bałaban 1930–31: 11; Nitsch 1954: 206.
63 See Sulimierski *et al.* 15,2: 1902.
64 See M. Weinreich 1: 1973: 211; 3: 214–15.
65 See Wexler ms for details.
66 See Stieber 1973: 24–5, 36–7, 60.
67 See Morgensztern 1961.

REFERENCES

Abbreviations used:
AŠ – *Afn špraxfront* 2nd–3rd series. Kiev 1934–9.
BG – *Bleter far gešixte* 1–13. Warsaw 1948–60.
BŻIH – *Biuletyn Żydowskiego Instytutu Historycznego*. Warsaw 1951ff.
JP – *Język polski*. Kraków 1913ff.
MGWJ – *Monatsschrift für die Geschichte und Wissenschaft des Judentums* 1–83. Wrocław 1851–1939.
MŻ – *Miesięcznik żydowski* 1–5. Warsaw 1931–6.
REJ – *Revue des études juives*. Paris 1880ff.
YF – *Yidiše filologye*. Warsaw 1924.

Altbauer, M. (1928). Jeszcze o *mizińcu//mizynku*. *JP* 13(2), 49–50.
—— (1929). O błędach ortograficznych i gramatycznych w zadaniach polskich Żydów przemyskich. *JP* 14(4), 105–110, 139–46.

—— (1932). *Bałaguła, belfer, cymes, kapcan, łapserdak, ślamazarny*. *JP* 17(2), 47–9, 76–8.
—— (1934). *Di kegnzajtike pojliš-jidiše hašpoes ojfn šprax-gebit*. Warsaw.
—— (1961). Mεxkaro šεl Jicxak Šiper al hajəsod hakuzari-jəhudi bəmizrax eropa. *Hε'avar*. Reprinted in *Sefεr Jicxak Šiper*, ed. S. Eidelberg, New York 1966, 47–58 and in Altbauer 1977: 44–50.
—— (1968). Jeszcze o rzekomych 'chazarskich' nazwach miejscowych na ziemiach polskich. *Onomastica* 13, 120–8.
—— (1972). Achievements and tasks in the field of Jewish-Slavic language contact studies. Unpublished paper delivered to the Russian and East European Center, UCLA.
—— (1977). *Mεxkarim bəlašon*. Jerusalem.
—— (1979–80). O tendencjach dehebraizacji leksyki karaimskiej i ich wynikach w *Słowniku Karaimsko-rosyjsko-polskim*. *Harvard Ukrainian Studies* 3–4, 51–60.
Aronius, J. (1902). *Regesten zur Geschichte der Juden im fränkischen und deutschen Reiche bis zum Jahre 1273*. Berlin.
Bałaban, M. (1917). Początki Żydów na ziemiach ruskich i polskich. *Almanach żydowski*. Vienna.
—— (1920). Jakim językiem mówili Żydzi w Polsce? In his *Z historji Żydów w Polsce. Szkice i studja*, 22–31. Warsaw. Originally appeared in *Kurjer lwowski* 1907, numbers 26, 28, 30.
—— (1930–1). Kiedy i skąd przybyli Żydzi do Polski? *MŻ* 1 (1930), 1–12; 2 (1931), 112–21. Reprinted as Ven un fun vanen zenen di jidn gekumen kejn pojln. *BG* 12 (1960), 3–24.
—— (1931–6). *Historya Żydów w Krakowie i na Kazimierzu 1304–1868* 1–2. Kraków.
Bar-El, J. (1984). A toes un a šibes. *Baj zix* 25, 200–2.
Baron, S. W. (1957). Eastern Europe. In his *A Social and Religious History of the Jews* 3, 173–222; 313–40. New York-London-Philadelphia. 1964[3].
Bεn Šabtaj. See Kupfer and Lewicki 1956.
Beranek, F. J. (1958). *Das Pinsker Jiddisch*. Berlin.
Beršadskij, S. A. (1882–1903). *Russko-evrejskij arxiv* 1–3. St. Petersburg.
Bersohn, M. (1911). *Dyplomataryusz dotyczący Żydów dawnej Polsce na źródłach archiwalnych osnuty (1388–1782)*. Warsaw.
Birnbaum, H. (1981a). On Jewish life and anti-Jewish sentiments in Medieval Russia. In his *Essays in Early Slavic Civilization*, 215–45. Munich.
—— (1981b). On the Slavic word for Jew: origin and meaning. Ibid., 26–35.
Birnbaum, S. A. (1926). Die jüdische Literatur Osteuropas. *Jahresbücher für Kultur und Geschichte der Slaven* n.F. 2, 1–8.
Boncompagni, B. (1862–3). Intorno ad un trattato d'aritmetica stampato nel 1478. *Atti dell'Accademia Pontificia de nuovi lincei* 16, 692.
Bondy, G. and F. Dvorský (1906). *K historii židů v Čechách, na Moravě a v Slezku, 906 až 1620*, Prague. Also in German, Prague 1906.
Borchling, C. (1911). Der Anteil des Niederdeutschen am Lehnwörterschatze der westslawischen Sprachen. *Jahresbuch des Vereins für niederdeutsche Sprachforschung* 37, 75–95.
Brutzkus, J. (1929). Di eršte jedijes vegn jidn in pojln. *Historiše šriftn* 1, 55–72.
—— [J.B.] (1930). Chasaren. *Encyclopaedia Judaica* 5, col. 337–50. Berlin.
—— (1939). Istoki russkogo evrejstva. *Evrejskij mir* 1, 17–32.
Brzezina, M. (1979). *Języki mniejszości narodowych w tekstach literackich i folklorystycznych* 1. *Południowo-kresowa polszczyzna Żydów*. Warsaw-Kraków.
Bulyka, A. M. (1980). *Leksičnyja zapazyčanni w belaruskaj move XIV–XVIII stst*. Minsk.
Bystroń, J. St. (1936). *Nazwiska polskie*. Lvov-Warsaw.
Centnerszwerowa, R. (1907). *O języku Żydów w Polsce, na Litwie i Rusi*. Warsaw.
Dal', V. I. (1863–66). *Tolkovyj slovar' živogo velikorusskogo jazyka* 1–4. Moscow; 1955[6].

Davreux, J. (1935). Le codex bruxellensis (graecus) II4836 (de Haeresibus). *Byzantion* 10, 91–106.
Dubnow, S. M. (1909). Razgovornyj jazyk i narodnaja literatura pol'sko-litovskix evreev v XVI i pervoj polovine XVII veka. *Evrejskaja starina* 1, 7–40.
—— (1913). Etlixe verter cum forigen artikel. *Der pinkes* 1, col. 36–8.
Estreicher, K. (1903). *Szwargot więzienny*. Kraków. Reprinted in Horbač 1979, 1.
Ettinger, Sh. (1960). Hahašpa'a hajəhudit šɛl hatsisa hadatit bəmizraxa šɛl eropa bəsof hame'a ha-15. *Sefɛr hajovɛl J.Bɛr*, ed. Sh. Ettinger *et al.*, 228–47. Jerusalem.
—— (1966). Kievan Russia. In Roth and Levine 319–24; 442–5.
Frey, P. J. B. (1936–52). *Corpus inscriptionum iudaicarum*, 1–2. Rome; 1, New York 1975 (second ed.).
Friedman, P. (1959). The first millenium of Jewish settlement in the Ukraine and in the adjacent areas. *Annals of the Ukrainian Academy of Arts and Sciences in the U.S.* 7(1–2), 1483–1516.
Golb, N. and O. Pritsak (1982). *Khazarian Hebrew Documents of the Tenth Century*. Ithaca-London.
Gumowski, M. (1962). Monety hebrajskie za Piastów. *BŻIH* 41, 3–19; 42, 3–44.
—— (1975). *Hebräische Münzen im mittelalterlichen Polen*. Graz.
Gumplowicz, M. (1903). *Początki religji żydowskiej w Polsce*. Warsaw.
Ha-Kohen. See Kupfer and Lewicki 1956.
Halpern, I. (1960). The Jews in Eastern Europe. In L. Finkelstein, ed., *The Jews. Their History, Culture and Religion* 1, 287–320. New York.
Ha-Nəsia. See Kupfer and Lewicki 1956.
Harkavi, A. A. [Garkavi, A. Ja.] (1865). *Ob jazyke evreev živšix v drevnee vremja na Rusi i o slavjanskix slovax vstrečaemyx u evrejskix pisatelej*. St. Petersburg. Also in *Trudy Vostočnogo Otdelenija Imperatorskogo Arxeologičeskogo Obščestva* 14, 1865.
—— (1867). *Hajəhudim usfat haslaviim*. Vilna.
Horbač, O., ed. (1979). *Polnische Gaunersprache* 1–2. Frankfurt.
Huberband, S. (1951). Mekojrim cu der jidišer gešixte in di slaviše lender, bifrat in pojln, rusland un lite. *BG* 4(4), 93–130.
Hundert, G. and G. C. Bacon (1984). *The Jews in Poland and Russia. Bibliographical Essays*. Bloomington.
Hunfalvy, P. (1877). *Ethnographie von Ungarn*. Budapest.
Ibn Ja'qūb. See Kowalski 1946.
Ibn Xordāđbeh. See Lewicki 1956b.
Iserlin, J. b. P. (1519). *Trumat hadɛšɛn*. Venice.
Jakob, J. (1929). *Wörterbuch des Wiener Dialektes mit einer kurzgefassten Grammatik*. Vienna.
Jakobson, R. (1957). Řeč a písemnictví českých židů v době přemyslovské. *Kulturní sborník ROK*, ed. L. Matějka, 35–46. New York.
—— (1984). Iz razyskanij nad staročešskimi glossami v srednevekovyx evrejskix pamjatnikov. In his *Selected Writings* 6, ed. S. Rudy, 855–857. Berlin – New York – Amsterdam.
—— and M. Halle (1964). The term *Canaan* in Medieval Hebrew. In L. Dawidowicz *et al.*, eds, *For Max Weinreich on his Seventieth Birthday. Studies in Jewish Languages, Literature and Society*, 147–72. The Hague.
Joffe, J. A. (1959). The etymology of *davenen* and *katoves*. *American Academy of Jewish Research. Proceedings* 28, 77–92.
Johannes of Saxony. See Boncompagni 1862–3; Jakobson and Halle 161, fn. 71.
Karłowicz, J. A. (1885). Mémoire sur l'influence des langues orientales sur la langue polonaise. *Actes du sixième Congrès international des orientalistes (1883)*, part 2, section 1, 411–41. Leiden.
Kaufmann, D. (1895). Der älteste jüdische Friedhof Ungarns. *MGWJ* 39, 305–9.

Kowalski, T. (1946). *Relacja Ibrāhīma ibn Ja'kūba z podroży do krajów słowiańskich w przekazie al-Bekrīego*. Kraków.

Kracauer, I. (1911). Die Namen der Frankfurter Juden bis zum Jahre 1400. *MGWJ* n.F. 19, 447–63; 600–13.

Kupfer, F. and T. Lewicki (1956). *Źródła hebrajskie do dziejów Słowian i niektórych innych ludów środkowej i wschodniej Europy*. Wrocław-Warsaw.

Kurka, A. (1896). *Słownik mowy złodziejskiej*. Lvov; 1899², 1907³; in Horbač 1979, 2.

Kurzowa, Z. (1983). *Polszczyzna Lwowa i kresów południowowschodnich do 1939 roku*. Warsaw-Kraków.

Leon, H. J. (1960). *The Jews of Ancient Rome*. Philadelphia.

Lewicki, T. [Levicki] (1956a). Hebreiše mekojrim cu der gešixte fun di slaviše felkeršaftn. *BG* 1–2, 16–35.

—— (1956b). *Źródła arabskie do dziejów słowiańszczyzny* 1. Wrocław-Warsaw-Kraków-Gdańsk.

—— (1958). Źródła arabskie i hebrajskie do dziejów Słowian w okresie wczesnego średniowiecza. *Studia źródłaznawcze* 3, 61–99.

—— (1984). Początki osadnictwa żydowskiego w Europie środkowej i wschodniej. *Kalendarz żydowski 1984–1985*, ed. E. Świderska, 36–9. Warsaw.

Levin, J. F. (1984). Two exclamations: Russ. *šabaš!*, Eng. *bushwa! Wiener slawistischer Almanach* 13, 161–9.

Ludwikowski, W. and H. Walczak (1922). *Żargon mowy przestępców*. Warsaw. Reprinted in Horbač 1979, 2.

Margaritha, A. (1530). *Der gantz Jüdisch glaub*. Augsburg.

Marmorstein, A. (1921). Nouveaux renseignements sur Tobiya ben Eliézer. *RÉJ* 73, 92–7.

Mieses, M. (1924). *Die jiddische Sprache*. Berlin-Vienna.

—— (1933–4). Judaizanci w Wschodniej Europie. *MŻ* 3(1933), 41–62; 169–85; 4 (1934), 147–59; 241–60; 342–58; 566–76.

Modelski, T. E. (1910). *Król 'Gebalim' w liście Chasdaja*. Lvov.

Morgensztern, J. (1961). Uwagi o Zydach sefardyjskich w Zamościu w latach 1588–1650. *BŻIH* 38, 69–82.

Nadel, B. (1959). Karaimer un kuzaren in frien mitlalter. *Folks-štime* (Warsaw) 136–41, 143–4.

—— (1960). *Jidn in mizrex-ejrope fun di eltste cajtn biz der mongoliše invazie*. Warsaw.

—— (1961). *Di eltste jidiše jišuvim in mizrex-ejrope*. Warsaw.

Nitsch, K. (1954). W sprawie *kirkutu*. *JP* 34, 204–6.

—— and S. Urbańczyk *et al*. (1953 ff). *Słownik staropolski*. Warsaw.

Ohr, J. (1905). *Polszczyzna w żargonie żydowskim*. Warsaw.

Ovčinnikova, V. S. *et al*. (1975–6). *Slovar russkix donskix govorov* 1–3. Rostov.

Prilucki, N. (1918). Ləšon ha"klezmarim" bəpolonia. *Rəšumot* 1, 272–91.

—— (1924). Špet-lošn. *YF* 1, part 3, 338–82.

—— (1926–33). Katoves. *Arxiv far jidišer špraxvisnšaft, literaturforšung un etnologje*, ed. N. Prilucki and Š. Leman 1, 292–97; 437–8. Warsaw.

Rawita-Gawroński, F. [1924]. *Żydzi w historji i literaturze ludowej na Rusi*. Warsaw.

Ringlblum, E. (1926). Adnotacjes un bamerkungen in lošn-kojdiš in altjidiš fun 15tn j.h. *Filologiše šriftn* 1, 333–8.

—— [Ringelblum] (1932). *Żydzi w Warszawie* 1. Warsaw.

Roth, C. (1966). The early Jewish settlements in Central and Eastern Europe 1. General setting. In Roth and Levine, 302–4.

—— and I. H. Levine, eds. (1966). *The World History of the Jewish People* 11. *The Dark Ages. Jews in Christian Europe 711–1096*. New Brunswick, NJ.

Rubštejn, B.-C. (1913). Di amolige šprax fun juden in di rusiše gegenden. *Der pinkes* 1, col. 21–35.

—— (1922). *Di antšteung un antviklung fun der jidišer šprax*. Warsaw.

Salfeld, S. (1898). *Das Martyrologium des Nürnberger Memorbuches*. Berlin.
Šapiro, M. (1939). Der gramatišer min in jidiš. *AŠ* 3, 111–63.
Schall, J. (1932). Najdawniejsze osadnictwo żydowskie w Przemyślu. *MŻ* 2(7–12), 159–61.
Schweinburg-Eibenschütz, S. (1894–5). Documents sur les Juifs de Wiener-Neustadt. *RÉJ* 28, 247–64; 29, 272–81; 30, 101–14.
Shevelov, G. Y. (1979). *A Historical Phonology of the Ukrainian Language*. Heidelberg.
Šiper, I. (1924). Der onhejb fun 'lošn aškenaz' in der balajxtung fun onomatiše kveln. *YF* 2–3, 101–12; 4–6, 272–87.
—— (1926). Jidiše nemen in pojln un rajsn bejs dem 15tn j"h. In his *Kultur-gešixte fun di jidn in pojln bejsn mitlalter*, 283–7. Warsaw.
Stieber, Z. (1973). *A Historical Phonology of the Polish Language*. Heidelberg.
Sulimierski, F., *et al.* (1880–1904). *Słownik geograficzny Królestwa Polskiego i innych krajów słowiańskich* 1–15. Warsaw.
Šulman, M. (1939). Slavizmen in der leksik fun jidiš. *AŠ* 3, 71–109.
Taszycki, W. (1965 ff). *Słownik staropolskich nazw osobowych*. Wrocław-Warsaw-Kraków-Gdańsk.
Teszler, H. (1942). *A héber elem a jiddis (zsidó-német) nyelvben*. Budapest.
Vasmer, M. (1944). *Die griechischen Lehnwörter im Serbo-Kroatischen*. Berlin.
Weinreich, M. (1960). Old Yiddish poetry in linguistic-literary research. *Word* 16, 100–18.
—— (1973). *Gešixte fun der jidišer šprax* 1–4. New York.
Weinreich, U. (1952). *Sábesdiker losn* in Yiddish: a problem of linguistic affinity. *Slavic Word* 1, 360–77.
—— (1958). Yiddish and Colonial German: the differential impact of Slavic. *American Contributions to the Fourth International Congress of Slavists*, 369–421. The Hague.
—— (1962). Multilingual dialectology and the new Yiddish atlas. *Anthropological Linguistics* 4(1), 6–22.
Weinryb, B. D. (1957). Origins of East European Jewry. *Commentary* 24, 509–18.
—— (1962a). Reappraisals in Jewish history. In his *Beginnings of East European Jewry*, 939–74. Leiden.
—— (1962b). The beginnings of East European Jewry in legend and historiography. In M. Ben-Horin *et al.*, eds., *Studies and Essays in Honor of Abraham A. Neuman*, 445–502. Leiden-Philadelphia.
—— (1963–76). The Khazars, an annotated bibliography. *Studies in Bibliography and Booklore* 6, 111–29; 11, 57–74.
—— (1973). *The Jews of Poland. A Social and Economic History of the Jewish Community in Poland from 1110 to 1800*. Philadelphia.
Wexler, P. (1981). Terms for 'synagogue' in Hebrew and Jewish languages. Explorations in historical Jewish interlinguistics. *RÉJ* 140(1–2), 101–38.
—— (1983). Hebräische und aramäische Elementen in den slavischen Sprachen: Wege, Chronologien und Diffusionsgebiete. *Zeitschrift für slavische Philologie* 93, 229–79.
—— (ms). *Explorations in Judeo-Slavic Linguistics*. Leiden. In press.
Wieczorkiewicz, B. (1974). *Gwara warszawska dawniej i dziś*. Warsaw.
Winkler, E. (1960). Il piu antico dizionario latino-polaco (del 1424). *Ricerche slavistiche* 8, 96–111.
Xananel, A. and E. Eškenazi (1960). *Evrejski izvori na obštestvenno-ikonomičeskoto razvitie na balkanskite zemi* 2. *Prez XVII vek*. Sofia.
Zajączkowski, A. (1947). *Ze studiów nad zagadnieniem chazarskim*. Kraków.
—— (1961a). *Karaims in Poland: History, Language, Folklore, Science*. Warsaw.
—— (1961b). Khazarian culture and its inheritors. *Acta Orientalia* (Budapest) 12(1–3), 299–307.
Zunz, L. (1876). Aelteste Nachrichten über Juden und jüdische Gelehrte in Polen, Slavonien, Russland. In his *Gesammelte Schriften* 3, 82–7. Originally in *MGWJ* 1846, 382–6.

2

SOME BASIC CHARACTERISTICS OF THE JEWISH EXPERIENCE IN POLAND*

Gershon David Hundert

To speak of basic characteristics is to generalize and to generalize is to endanger the truth. None of the six constructs or schemata which will be suggested here is absolutely true in the sense that one could not prepare lists of exceptions to each, as well as dozens of quibbles and qualifications. This understood, it is proposed that these six constructs are essential filaments in the web of the historical experience of the Jews in the Polish Commonwealth. In other, paradoxical words, it is being asserted here that these are the fictions by which the truth can be discovered.[1]

The first item on the list will be also the most objective. As Professor Salo Baron has taught us, one properly opens the description of a Jewish community with a discussion of numbers. For much of its history the Polish-Jewish community was the largest in the world. Indeed, even today, their descendants include most of the Jews in the Soviet Union and North America and about half of the Jewish population of the State of Israel. Furthermore Polish Jews comprised a very substantial proportion indeed of the population of the Polish Commonwealth as a whole. It may be that during the 18th century nearly a majority of the town-dwellers in Poland-Lithuania were Jews. Recent work on the demographic history of Poland, however, has called into question virtually every estimate of the population of historical Poland. Church records of births, baptisms, weddings and deaths, which are the most objective and reliable sources of information, are least useful in computing the Jewish population. Estimates of Jewish numbers have been based mainly on fiscal records, especially the hearth taxes, which are notoriously unreliable. Further, there is no agreement whatsoever as to how many Jews lived in each dwelling. As a result, estimates of the mid-17th century Jewish population, for example, range between 170,000 and 450,000. Virtually all Jewish historians have accepted Raphael Mahler's carefully calculated figure of 750,000 Jews in Poland-Lithuania in 1764–5. Recently, however, even Mahler's methods have been called into question. Furthermore, there is a large number of equally important subsidiary questions about demographic history which remain

* Paper based on lecture delivered at conference on Polish-Jewish Relations held at Columbia University, March 1983.

unresolved, most notably the rate of expansion of the Jewish population during different periods. It is generally asserted that there was dramatic growth in Jewish numbers during the 16th century, but it is also known that the proportion of Jews in the towns of Poland-Lithuania increased dramatically during a 150-year period beginning in the late-17th century and continuing through the 18th century. It was only during that era that the 'Jewish town' came into being. Could this latter development be attributed to the agrarianization of the Catholic population; to the likely difference in the rates of infant mortality among Jews and among Catholics or in the birth rates of the two groups, or both; or to the fact-hypothesis that Jewish losses during the wars and epidemics of the middle of the 17th century were substantially less severe than those of the Catholic population? These are issues of considerable significance which have not yet been thoroughly investigated. If, for example, the Jewish population was growing very quickly during the 18th century because of a relatively low death rate, meaning, in those days, a relatively low rate of infant mortality, this would mean that every year there were more and more young people proportionally. And this could mean, in turn, that accounts of the early Hasidic movement ought to be revised to include the possibility that Hasidism was, in its early, radical stages, an expression of generational conflict. Be that as it may, the sheer size of the Jewish community of Poland-Lithuania must be the first item on this list of general characteristics.[2]

Though of course the cliché does not always hold true, in this case there *was* relative security in numbers. More than security, there was a sense of rootedness and permanence about this community. These qualities were attributed to the Jewish community by Poles as well. As early as the 15th century, Jan Długosz recorded the famous and oft-repeated legend of Casimir the Great's Jewish mistress, Esterka. She purportedly used her feminine wiles to persuade the 14th-century monarch to invite the Jews to come to Poland and to grant them their extensive privileges. The story also includes the detail that by Esterka the King had four children, two boys and two girls. The former were raised as Christians and the latter as Jews. Aside from what is evidently a desire to cast aspersion on the legitimacy of the Jews' privileges, there is the clear sense in the tale that:

(1) the Jews had resided in Poland for a long time;
(2) their residence in Poland was permanent – Jews were a fixed and continuing part of the social landscape;
(3) the Jews had extensive rights and privileges;
(4) the Jews were protected by the crown.

During the period in which this legend was first recorded, the leading German rabbi of the time, Moshe ben Yitshak – MaHaRaM – Mintz, recorded his own view that the lands of Poland had, 'from of old been considered a refuge for the exiled sons [of Israel]'. He himself spent his last years in Poznań. Other evidence could be adduced easily to show that at least through the 16th and the first part of the 17th centuries there was a relatively low level of what might be termed 'exilic consciousness' among Polish Jews. Preachers and rabbis quoted the following passage to describe their contemporaries: *sevurim hem deyabashta hava ve-leka galuta* (they think they have found dry land and that their exile is ended). Even subsequent to *gzeyres takh ve-tat* (the mid-17th century disasters), no messiah or messianic movement was produced on Polish soil. During the 18th century the dominant note was struck by the revivalist Hasidic movement, which was much more concerned with personal, individual redemption than with the final collective redemption of the Jewish people. It can be argued that in this general absence of political activism Polish Jews were merely the continuators of broader Ashkenazic traditions.[4]

This is indeed the third filament in the web of the interrelated basic characteristics of the historical experience of Polish Jewry, namely, the Ashkenazic character of that community. Not only was the overwhelming majority of the Jews of Poland-Lithuania descended from migrants from central and western Europe, but also their language, their communal institutions, and their religious-cultural traditions all came from the West. Solomon Luria (the MaHaRShaL, a great 16th-century Polish rabbi) in proudly tracing his lineage back to *Hasidei Ashkenaz* (medieval German-Jewish pietists), claimed more than biological descent. Those *hasidim* of the twelfth and thirteenth centuries were considered the models of the most lofty spiritual values by Polish Jews. *Sefer Hasidim* ('Book of the Pious' – the most important collection of their teachings) held almost canonical status in the eyes of the folk. The critical ingredients here were a stress on personal humility, a negative valuation of *hana'ah* (physical, this-worldly pleasure), the quest for the 'will of the creator' beyond the simple requirements of Jewish law and which sometimes involved difficult and painful penances, and finally a kind of interior focus of spirituality which if it was not precisely mystical was at least psychological and individual.[5]

Beginning with medieval Ashkenazic forms, the Jews of the Polish Commonwealth developed the most ramified and durable of the autonomous institutions of Ashkenazic Jewry. The *kahals* (communities) came to be, partly as a consequence of demographic developments, the administrators of Jewish towns, taking decisions regarding aqueducts and road repair, rent control and consumer protection. The so-called Council of Four Lands, the national institution of Polish Jews, sometimes made representations to foreign governments, negotiated a global sum to be collected in taxes from Polish Jews with the Royal Treasury, and enacted laws concerning copyright. These are but well-known samples of the extent of the autonomy of the Jewish community in the Polish Commonwealth.[6] The degree of elaboration and ramification reached by the Jewish communal and inter-communal institutions can be attributed in part to the size of the community, and in part to its occupational diversity – a characteristic which distinguished Polish Jews from their Ashkenazic ancestors. In part, the extensive development of those institutions can be attributed also to a certain notable characteristic of society in general in the Polish Commonwealth, that is, its heterogeneity. Polish society was heterogeneous not only in that there was more than one autochthonous nationality but also because various other groups were to be found, mainly in the towns, such as Italians, Scots, Armenians, Tatars, Greeks, Hungarians, etc. During the 17th century less than one-fifth of the Commonwealth's population was urban, and less than two-fifths of the Commonwealth's population was Polish. Some of these non-Polish, non-autochthonous groups, including the Armenians, the Italians and the Scots, developed communal and even inter-communal institutions parallel to those of the Jews. Thus, not only did the relative autonomy of the towns themselves, based mainly on the Magdeburg law brought to Poland by German migrants, provide a formal precedent for the development of these institutions, but also the ethnic heterogeneity of the Polish town, as long as it lasted, itself contributed, along with other incentives, to the tendencies of various groups to preserve and institutionalize their distinctiveness. In this connection one should recall also what Professor Baron has termed 'something approaching an historical law', namely, that the status of the Jew was most favourable in states of multiple nationality in which they were less conspicuous.[7] Another factor contributing to the relative security in which the Jews of the Polish Commonwealth lived was their success in forging an alliance with the upper stratum of the *szlachta*.

The lynchpin of Jewish 'foreign policy' in pre-modern times was the forging of alliances with the crown or with the highest authority in the state. This general rule, however, was not appropriate during the period of the Polish Commonwealth because of the strength of the centrifugal forces in that polity. The central issue in the history of Jewish political strategy in Poland was the response of the Jews to the gradual decentralization of political power and its concentration in the hands of the *szlachta* and particularly the great magnate-aristocrats. The ability of the Jews to forge alliances with the Polish nobility was essential to their security. The Jews' success accounts in significant measure for the relative peace in which Polish Jews lived. During the 16th and 17th centuries Jews preferred to settle in private towns. Even before 1539 when the crown surrendered jurisdiction over Jews in private towns to the town-owners, a step which accelerated the movement of Jews into those towns, Justus Deciusz made the following observation: 'There is hardly a magnate . . . who does not hand over the management of his estates to a Jew . . . and more zealously protects them against any wrong, real or imaginary, than he protects

Christians.' Deciusz made these remarks in 1521, the very year in which the only known attempt of the burghers of the leading cities to combat Jewish competition *collectively* was made. This attempt failed and subsequently the struggles were conducted on the local level, where with the exception of some crown cities, mainly during the 16th century, the burghers failed to limit their Jewish competitors.[8] The Jews, then, successfully allied themselves with the magnate-aristocrats and also benefited from the virtual political impotence of the citizens of the Polish cities.

One important factor which made the alliance between the Jews and the landowners possible and which was the sign of the success of this convergence of interests was the rise of the Jewish arendator and the association of the Jews particularly with the trade in alcoholic beverages in Eastern Europe. The Jews' successful political strategy of the early modern period became a liability as political and economic conditions changed and they were left dependent for their livelihoods and security on the crumbling old order. A further dimension of this dynamic is connected with the disintegration of Jewish communal institutions during the 18th and 19th centuries. One of many factors which contributed to that development is germane here because it arose from the relationship between the magnate-aristocrats and the Jews. By the 18th century, it should be noted, one-half to three-quarters of the Jews in Poland-Lithuania lived on private holdings. The following incident will illustrate the point. In Opatów, a private town in Little Poland, the arendator missed a payment in 1771, claiming that the money had been stolen from him. The townowner's administrator did not believe this claim and 'suggested' that the *kahal* take action, and he detailed those actions. They were to assemble one hundred householders and kindle in their presence twenty-four black candles and pronounce a severe ban against this man. During the holy ceremony, the administrator continued, the defendant and his wife should be carefully interrogated as they stood barefoot holding a copy of the Torah. Time after time during the 18th century in this same town Jews brought their disputes not before their own court but before that of the townowner. The poor and the disenfranchised, when they had complaints about the *kahal* elders brought them before the townowner and not before any Jewish authority.[9] Magnate authority, then, contributed significantly to the disintegration of the Jewish corporation and therefore to the freeing of the Jewish individual in a way that is somewhat analogous to what happened to the Jews in the Absolutist states of Central Europe.

We arrive finally at the last and most elusive of the items on this list of basic characteristics. That is, the self-sustaining quality of Polish-Jewish creativity and something more than this. Professor Benzion Dinur wrote of the creation by Polish Jews of almost a national entity with the *Torah* as its constitution. Even when that constitution's hold began to weaken there remained something more visceral. Two anecdotes will illustrate this. The first is from a rabbinic responsum which dates from the period between 1640 and 1647. It speaks of a Jew who went out with 'soldiers' to plunder and rob villages. The text of the responsum makes clear 'that there was no war at all, rather the armed men went to plunder the village'. In the text also it is stated explicitly that the Jew was part of some sort of regular unit with a commanding officer and so on. Unfortunately for Hendl (this was the Jew's name) 'one villager pursued the Jew who had stolen his horse and killed him with . . . a musket'. Now this responsum exists because his widow wanted to remarry and the rabbi, Joshua Hoeschel ben Yosef, was examining the evidence of his death. In the text of the responsum there is no sense that the man was a renegade or an apostate. He remained a Jew even though in his behaviour he was indistinguishable from his fellow brigands.[10]

The second anecdote touches on a characteristic of Polish Jewry which has not been mentioned – their mobility. They moved across the Commonwealth from west to east, participating in the great colonization of the Ukraine in the 16th and 17th centuries. They moved to Western Europe in the 17th century in small numbers and in ever-increasing waves in subsequent years. These remarks will conclude with a brief description of a Polish Jew who came to America, to Newport, Rhode Island, in November, 1772. There is a description of him in Ezra Stiles' Literary Diary, the manuscript of which is preserved in the Yale Library. His name was Moshe bar David and he had a letter of introduction from the head of the Portuguese synagogue in London. He told Stiles that he had left Poland in 1741 at the age of twenty and had returned there in 1755. 'He went to Jerusalem, Cairo, Tiberias, Saphat, Aleppo, Ur of the Chaldees, the R. Chebar, Mosul, Bagdat, Mt. Ararat, Bassora, Ispahan, Cassan, Hamadan, and Surat in India where he lived 2½ years.' This is of course striking and reminiscent of Raphael Hayyim Isaac Carigal who visited Stiles some months later. Moshe bar David, 'had with him the itinerary of R. Benjamin Tudelensis in A.D. 1170 but says he could not find many places mentioned by him . . . he could find none of the ten tribes.' It turns out that in addition to Benjamin's itinerary, he had with him *Sefer Sha'arei Orah* and *Sefer Sha'arei Zion* which contains *Sefer Yetsira*, these being Kabbalistic works. For all of his world travels this Polish Jew inhabited a Jewish universe. When Ezra Stiles took out his newly arrived copy of the *Zohar* to show his visitor, Moshe bar David told him that if he – Stiles – could comprehend that book he would be a master of Jewish learning and of the greatest philosophy in the world.[11]

Wherever they went Polish Jews carried with them something which characterized them at home too: a very particular attachment to their people and a uniquely positive view of their identity as Jews.

NOTES

1 For a survey of the literature on the historical experience of the Jews in the Polish Commonwealth see Gershon David Hundert, Gershon Bacon, *The Jews in Poland and Russia: Bibliographical Essays* (Bloomington, Indiana, 1984).

2 Irena Gieysztorowa, *Wstęp do demografii staropolskiej* (Warsaw, 1976); Raphael Mahler, *Yidn in amolikn Poyln in likht fun tsifern*, 2 vols (Warsaw, 1958); Tomasz Opas, 'Sytuacja ludności żydowskiej w miastach szlacheckich województwa lubelskiego w XVIII wieku', *Biuletyn Żydowskiego Instytutu Historycznego* 67 (1968), pp. 3–37; the following article, to my mind, does little more than express puzzlement in a tone which one rather wishes had been banished from Polish literature: Zygmunt Sułowski, 'Mechanizmy ekspansji demograficznej Żydów w miastach polskich XVI–XIX wieku', *Zeszyty Naukowe Katolickiego Uniwersytetu Lubelskiego* 17, no. 3 (1974), pp. 93–110.

3 See Chone Shmeruk's magisterial study, 'Ha-maga''im bein ha-sifrut ha-polanit le-vein sifrut yidish al pi sippur esterkah ve-kazimir ha-gadol melekh Polin', in Shmeruk's *Sifrut Yidish be-Polin* (Jerusalem, 1981), pp. 206–80. Cf. Bernard Dov Weinryb, 'Poland through the eyes of Polish Jews', in his *The Jews of Poland: A Social and Economic History of the Jewish Community in Poland from 1100 to 1800* (Philadelphia, 1973), pp. 156–76; Haim Hillel Ben-Sasson, 'Poland', *Encyclopaedia Judaica* (Jerusalem, 1972); Benzion Dinur, 'Darkah ha-Historit shel Yahadut Polin', *Moznaim* 11 (1940–1941), pp. 163–71 and in his *Dorot ve-Reshumot* (Jerusalem, 1978), pp. 193–201.

4 Gerson D. Cohen, 'Messianic Postures of Ashkenazim and Sephardim', *Leo Baeck Memorial Lecture* 9 (New York, 1967) and reprinted in *Studies of the Leo Baeck Institute* edited by Max Kreutzberger (New York, 1967), pp. 115–56. And see my 'No Messiahs in Paradise', *Viewpoints: The Canadian Jewish Quarterly* II, no. 2 (Fall, 1980), pp. 28–33 for an unannotated but expanded version of this point.

5 Haim Hillel Ben-Sasson, 'Shorshei ha-Mahshavah shel Hokhmei Polin', in his *Hagut ve-Hanhagah* (Jerusalem, 1959), pp. 11–17. On 'Hasidei Ashkenaz', see Yosef Dan, *Torat ha-Sod shel Hasidut Ashkenaz* (Jerusalem, 1968); Yosef Dan (ed.), *Iyyunim be-Sifrut Hasidei Ashkenaz* (Ramat Gan, 1975); Ivan G. Marcus, *Piety and Society: The Jewish Pietists of Medieval Germany*, Etudes sur le Judaïsme médiéval (Leiden, 1981).

6 See the various studies by Israel Halpern on the Council of Four Lands which are collected in his, *Yehudim ve-Yahadut be-Mizrah Eiropa* (Jerusalem, 1968), pp. 37–107.

7 See my article, 'On the Jewish Community in Poland during the seventeenth century: Some comparative perspectives', *Revue des études juives* 142 (1983), 349–72.

8 See Salo W. Baron, 'Poland-Lithuania 1500–1650', volume XVI of his *Social and Religious History of the Jews* (New York and Philadelphia, 1976), pp. 164–312; Maurycy Horn, *Żydzi na Rusi Czerwonej w XVI i pierwszej połowie XVII w.: Działalność gospodarcza na tle rozwoju demograficznego* (Warsaw, 1975), pp. 218–85; Gershon David Hundert, 'Jews, money and society in the seventeenth-century Polish Commonwealth: The case of Krakow', *Jewish Social Studies*, 43 (1981), pp. 261–74.

9 Warsaw, Archiwum Główne Akt Dawnych, Archiwum Gospodarcze Wilanowskie: Administracja Dóbr Opatowskich I/38.

10 *She'elot u-teshuvot ge'onei ba-tra'ei* (Czernowitz [Chernovtsy]: 1860), qu. 2, pp. 2b–3a.

11 New Haven, Conn., Yale University Library, Ezra Stiles Papers: The Literary Diary, vol. III, pp. 277–8. The published version of these passages in *The Literary Diary of Ezra Stiles*, edited by F. B. Dexter, vol. I (New York, 1901), pp. 299–303, and reproduced in George Alexander Kohut, *Ezra Stiles and the Jews* (New York, 1902), pp. 79–83, elides some important material.

3

IMAGES OF THE JEW IN THE POLISH COMMONWEALTH

Janusz Tazbir

The sources and literature for the theme of this study[1] present particular difficulties. The former consist largely of pamphlets, texts which have to be approached with great care. The same can be said of the literature on the subject, which is often far from objective. With a few commendable exceptions,[2] there is a dearth of studies on attitudes to Jews in the context of attitudes to outsiders in general, although it is clear from many pre-partition Polish sources that the commercial activities of Armenians, Scots, Italians and Germans were often criticized in much the same way. Accusations were not only levelled against Judaism, but also against Islam (practised by Tatars settled in the noble Republic) or supporters of the Reformation who, it was claimed, secretly wanted to destroy both human souls and the Republic itself. The writers who made these accusations were often the same people who were offended by every 'outsider', that is by anyone different from them in language, traditions or religion. The Jews, although settled in Poland since the Middle Ages, represented a classical and principal example of such an outsider.

It was claimed that Jews, by not eating pork and practising circumsion, 'in many of their rites resemble the Turks'. They were also said to follow the wishes of the Turks by abducting Christian children and then taking them to the sultan after circumcising them. Although in the first half of the 18th century fear of Turkish invasion had subsided, the accusation that 'they pass all state secrets to other countries and make pacts with enemies of the Republic . . .'[3] continued to be levelled at Jewish society.

The heretic, the Jew, the witch, all of them, since they had lost contact with God, were considered to be servants of the devil. It is not surprising that there was a proverb that a Jew feared holy water as much as Satan did. It was claimed that all of them used charms, in case of need, to cause personal misfortunes, natural disasters (particularly epidemics), cattle plagues and even Tatar invasions. Gypsies and Tatars who had settled in the Grand Duchy of Lithuania were also accused of practising witchcraft.

It was widely believed, although the clergy denied it, that Jewish practices included drawing blood from the host and from Christian children, because Jews were born blind and could only see after rubbing their eyes with this blood. (In many regions of the noble Republic it was claimed that the inhabitants of Mazowsze were also born blind and could only see nine days later.) Jews were also accused of having an unpleasant smell. This was caused by Jewish people eating large amounts of onions or garlic ('the smell of garlic spreads over a quarter of a mile'). Italian culinary tastes were also criticized, but with the crucial difference that the Italians failed to convert the Poles to their salads, whereas certain elements of Jewish cooking acquired citizen's rights within Polish national cuisine. Despite this, the general image of the Jew was of someone who loved garlic, in much the same way as the present-day image of the Frenchman is someone who eats snails or of the Italian as someone who eats pasta.

The Jews stood out from the rest of the population above all by their dress. The difference in their clothes and features could prompt certain associations, since many paintings showed the devil with a hooked nose and curly hair. Furthermore, Jewish dress was mainly black and this colour also evoked comparison with the forces of hell. In the popular imagination, a heretic was a strange foreigner in German dress. The impression of strangeness was accentuated by the Jews' distinctive hairstyle and particularly their side-locks. These were the principal distinguishing features, as beards were also worn by the Christian population. The Jews also stood out by their specific mannerisms: their nervous gestures, continually emphasizing the spoken word, and their characteristic feverish haste, an inevitable product of the way they lived. The excitable temperament of these voluble southerners always contrasted with the more languid disposition of the Christian population, as did their exaggerated oriental way of speaking.

Their incomprehensible language was dismissed as gibberish, which was found as irritating as the German from which Yiddish had, after all, largely developed. This was linked with a phenomenon which can be described as 'linguistic xenophobia', since almost all languages apart from one's own would be considered inferior, peculiar, ugly to hear or even odious. Latin, of course, was an exception, as this was the language used to communicate with God, as were written Greek and Hebrew, which were known from the Scriptures. However, the spoken Hebrew used during Jewish services was found irritating.

The Jew as a blasphemer, who denied the divinity of Christ, an economic rival, an onerous creditor, accused of arrogance and impudence, also appeared as a buffoon character, clumsy, mangling the Polish language, and willing to suffer any humiliation for even a small gain. He provided the comic element in many plays: in nativity plays 'a Jew and Jewess, and a Jewish dance, were always a source of general and perpetual amusement'.[4] This picture of the Jew was used to show the difference between the value-system recognised (though not always realised in practice) by aristocratic society, and those features considered dominant in the Jewish racial character. High in the scale of values, not only among the *szlachta*, were chivalrous ones: skill in battle, courage, physical strength, and not showing fear even in moments of mortal danger. On the other hand every Jew was generally held to be a weak and cowardly person who fled not only from an armed enemy but even from a dog. A Jew setting off for war was also the subject of jokes, situation comedies and proverbs, just as a servant of the church was.

Even if the *szlachta* sometimes engaged in trade, they never considered this their main activity; in *szlachta* circles it was often repeated emphatically that 'It is a sin and shame to trade'.[5] In the opinion of this estate, every merchant whether Italian, German or Jewish, whether dealing on a large scale or merely from house to house (the latter were mainly Scots) was by nature a swindler, deceiver and criminal. Although it had long been held that religious minorities provided necessary service industries, which the native population either could not or did not wish to undertake, nevertheless, these alien religious (or racial) groups did not enjoy social approval.

The Jews were widely considered harmful or parasitic, partly because of the belief that their occupations did not deserve to be called 'work'. Only agriculture was worthy of this description, unlike trade, credit deals or 'rocking' over the Talmud. Talmudic studies were doubly discredited: on the one hand Jews were thought to blaspheme against the true God in pursuing these studies, and on the other hand there could be no respect for occupations which involved working with books (the analysis and commentary of texts). The fame which the noble Republic's rabbinical schools enjoyed all over Europe until the mid-17th century was of little interest to anyone. One exception was Szymon Starowolski, who reported in 1632 that the Jews in Brześć, Lithuania, ran 'their own school. It was famous throughout Europe and people come from Italy, Germany, Moravia, and Silesia to study and to advance themselves by becoming rabbis and on returning to their own lands being able to direct synagogues'.[6]

Hostile views of Jews appeared as soon as printing began to develop. But they were found even earlier, as in the 15th century, in Jan Długosz who wrote with approval of bloody pogroms in Prague (1389) and Kraków (1407). The forge where these anti-Jewish pamphlets were fashioned was the 16th-century Polish capital of Kraków. These works not only repeated individual opinions about the Jews, but also created a kind of picture of them as a group, a register of accusations. This served at the same time as a tool for the further development of opinions decidedly hostile towards followers of Judaism. These pamphlets came mainly from burgher circles but were also written by minor clergy or poor *szlachta*. The authors did not include members of the wealthier landowning class, nor better-known writers: Jews do not seem to have interested Jan Kochanowski at all; Mikołaj Rej criticized them, but only in passing. Scholars point out that at a time when there was an incredibly large and varied anti-Jewish literature in Western Europe (particularly Germany), there were strikingly few Polish works containing occasional attacks on Jews or dedicated specifically to them, while the content of those that do exist is also comparatively restrained. Hardly thirty appeared in the years 1588–1668, 90 per cent of which were produced during the reigns of the first two Vasa monarchs (1587–1648). Their contents were unspeakably monotonous, repeating the same arguments.[7]

The principal image was that of the Jew as a dangerous economic rival, increasing his wealth quickly, *per fas et nefas*, at the expense of the Christian. It was no accident that the wave of pamphlets which reached its apogee at the close of the 16th century and in the first half of the 17th century, coincided with the beginning of the decline of Polish towns. In a situation where market outlets for goods were contracting and the chances for trade decreasing, and with restrictions on credit, burgher writers became very sensitive to every sign of competition.

There was general anxiety at the rapid growth of the Jewish population, caused in part by the influx of immigrants from Germany, Italy and even Spain. 'All these exiles have one goal before them, and that is Poland', wrote Majer Bałaban, adding that 'the destruction of any larger commune in the West' meant a growth of the Jewish population in Poznań, Kraków, Lublin, Lwów, or 'even distant Wilno'.[8] Another reason was the way Jews reproduced. As Sebastian Miczyński wrote: none of them dies in war or of the plague; furthermore they marry when they are twelve and so ... multiply rampantly'.[9] At the close of the Middle Ages the Jews made up 0.6 per cent of the population of Poland and Lithuania; in the mid-17th century there were half a million of them and therefore 5 per cent of all inhabitants of the Republic. This figure amounted to 30 per cent of the whole Jewish diaspora. Their economic activity also developed rapidly and was all the more noticeable compared with the general decline in prosperity.

Both in the works dedicated specifically to Jews and in tracts concerning the principal grievances of the noble Republic, we find, almost without exception and repeated with a certain monotony, a list of profitable leases and positions which ought to be removed from Jewish hands. Some of these even included inns and mills. Appropriate proposals were made at the *szlachta sejm* and the regional diets by representatives of the middling, and particularly the poorer *szlachta*, who felt threatened by Jewish financial competition and by the leasing of toll-posts and custom-houses as well as land and salt-mines. Jews were also accused of counterfeiting and exporting money, of practising usury at the expense of the Christian population, of systematically evading civic taxes and military service.

It should be mentioned that while the regional diets often simply reported the complaints of the towns about economic competition from the Jewish tradesmen and craftsmen, they also protected Jews, condemning the sporadic pogroms, and granted Jews privileges such as trade with the East.

The *szlachta* moreover cannot have been very concerned about the Jews taking over commerce and crafts or their activities in the area of free trade of which the burgher writers complained so often and with such passion. The latter described the particular ways in which Jews brought about the ruin of Christian master-craftsmen and so on. However, the Hungarian Martin Csombor, who travelled round Poland at the beginning of the 17th century, wrote: 'The Jews are very active in trade which, though sometimes causing losses for the burghers, is also convenient for the latter, as one can buy any commodity from a Jew, so that it has become common to say: "If you can not find something at a Jew's, you will search for it in vain elsewhere".'[10] Christian competitors obviously had a different opinion of this 'convenience'.

The *szlachta* viewed foreigners in a similar way to that in which Polish burghers regarded the Jews. Foreigners, thanks to the protection of the king, seemed to wrest profitable leases and well-paid posts from deserving citizens and, furthermore, ruined them by dishonestly trading in luxury goods (at which the Italians supposedly excelled). The only difference was that the king supported foreigners to the detriment of the *szlachta* whereas the noble gentlemen – it was claimed – protected Jews at the expense of the lower sections of society, the poor and oppressed Christians. The latter 'must revere them (the Jews), respect and even bow down to the ground before them when requesting something from them', claimed the Jesuit Mateusz Bembus.[11]

Just as the *szlachta* showed their xenophobia in criticizing the foreigners coming to court, and thus indirectly the monarch who protected them, anti-magnate or even anti-*szlachta* feelings were also expressed by writing about Jewish competitors 'lording it' on magnates' estates. The basic contradiction within these various positions came from the fact that for the burgher estate (the Germans, Ruthenians and Armenians as well as Poles) the Jews were a harmful element in economic life, while the magnates or wealthy *szlachta* saw Jewish activities fitting into the model of the state envisaged by its noble owners. For in their eyes they alone made up the nation: the role of the other sections of society was purely one of service. The *szlachta* was, on the whole, indifferent to the descent, language or faith of the people who sold them goods or worked the land, especially since neither the peasants nor the burghers were entirely of Polish descent. The magnates willingly employed those who were dependent only on them.

And the Catholic clergy could rage in vain that Jews 'are a nation dear to many lords'. 'Who has easiest access to the lord? The Jew. Who is most trusted at the manor house? The Jew', wrote Szymon Starowolski.[12]

The Jews were necessary to the magnates and to the *szlachta* as tenants, innkeepers, moneylenders and merchants. The Jew represented an indispensable intermediary in the economic system of the time: he provided large and small amounts of credit and he helped the landowner in many trading activities. He also frequently kept him informed of what was happening in the wider world, shaved and nursed him, and played at his receptions and weddings (Jewish barbers, surgeons and musicians appear in many memoirs, and have also been immortalised in paintings and engravings). In a variety of ways the Jew helped overcome the isolation of thousands of *szlachta* farms, scattered throughout the huge noble Republic. In the eyes of the magnate or wealthy member of the *szlachta*, the Jew was sometimes an irritating creature – more often simply funny –, but indispensable none the less. The Jews acted as intermediaries in the feudal exploitation of the peasant. Above all they could be blamed for the various levies imposed by the magnates and *szlachta* on their subjects.

It is not strange, then, that Jews were found intolerable by the Orthodox and Ruthenian peasantry in the Ukrainian lands belonging to the Republic. Conditions prevailing there 'allowed Jews to conduct forms of exploitation impossible elsewhere'.[13] In some areas they apparently even leased sources of church income, namely payments for christenings, weddings and funerals. Economic conflicts overlapped with racial and religious differences; thus the image of the Jew in Ukrainian popular writing of the 17th to 18th centuries is a far more hostile one than in Polish literature of the same period. Equally the great Cossack Uprising under Bohdan Chmielnicki (1648) and the rebellions of the so-called *hajdamaki* (Kolivshczyzna) in the following century, were conducted under the slogans of slaughtering the *Lachy* (masters), Jews, and Catholic priests, that is those groups held responsible for political, economic and religious oppression. The Jewish settlements in the east of the noble Republic paid for their close economic cooperation with the *szlachta* and magnates with thousands of victims (in the mid-17th century 100,000 Jews were to die, victims of the Cossack knife and lance). Mass pogroms erupted in those lands vacated by the Polish armies and authorities.

The image of the Jew held by the magnates and *szlachta* was opposed by the most radical writers, who had a vision of the Republic without Jews whose activities harmed the whole state materially (for example by counterfeiting and ruining money and taking it out of the country). In the credit sphere – they wrote – Christians could easily take the place of the Jews or special institutions could be established to do so (*montes pietatis*). The most radical views came primarily from burgher circles; very few members of the *szlachta* demanded the expulsion of the Jews from Poland.

Some writers, however, demanded that they should be made to work on the land. Clerical writers hoped that in this way the Jewish population could be gradually persuaded to be christened. These arguments were welcomed in burgher circles, where Jews were called 'cruel beasts', 'locusts', 'venomous reptiles and foul vermin'.

Both Polish publicists and foreigners travelling in the noble Republic believed the Jews made up a kind of separate estate because of the privileges they enjoyed. The Jewish settlements did indeed enjoy considerable legal autonomy, guaranteed and observed by the state authorities and local feudal lords.

Most accusations levelled against Jewish merchants, artisans or moneylenders, tended to owe more to class criticism than to anti-semitism. This trend emerged constantly in feudal society, and a much larger volume could be compiled from the criticisms of peasants, burghers and *szlachta* than that produced seventy years ago by Kazimierz Bartoszewicz on anti-semitism in pre-partition Polish literature.[14]

From the 16th century the image of the Jew in Polish literature was linked with a particular social issue, although it was not possible at the time to identify it. Although it was known that the population was steadily increasing (which caused some anxiety), this did not seem then to be the most important issue in the multi-racial Republic. The most crucial cause for concern was the obvious decline in the overall economic situation. The signs could be read by everyone and easily enumerated, but the causes were far less clear. Burgher writers in particular explained the decline partly by the growing role of Jews in the economy. The more this economic decline increased, the more it was written about and explained by the activities of a specific group rather than through particular economic mechanisms. The Jew became a 'scapegoat', a guilty party (if not the principal culprit), for the economic decline of the noble Republic. With every subsequent financial crisis the ones chiefly to blame were identified as foreigners, more frequently Jews than, for example, Italians, who also managed the mint.

Public opinion did not consider Jewish innkeepers, tenants, moneylenders or merchants the descendants of David, Solomon, Jeremiah, let alone of the apostles, the Holy Family and Christ. They had crucified him and were still blind to the light of true faith. They were ungrateful sinners, and, for this, God, 'in whose eyes nothing is more ugly than ingratitude', had turned away from them.[15] What is worse, the Jews continued to repeat the deicide they had committed centuries ago. They profaned the host of the living God and murdered innocent children who were the image of the Saviour (hence the frequent motif of crucifixion of the victim in trials over alleged ritual murders).

The memory of their role as murderers of Christ was revived in presentations of the Passion during Holy Week, or in works on the

Suffering of Christ. In the second half of the 17th century there was an increase in the number of paintings representing the judgement of Christ and his suffering. The members of the Sanhedrin and those responsible were usually portrayed dressed as wealthy Jewish merchants. In one of these paintings (in the cloisters of the Dominican Fathers at Janów Podlaski) the Jewish wise men are shown plotting against the Christian faith. Anti-Jewish features were also present in paintings depicting Christ's casting out of the merchants from the temple. The message was clearly aimed 'first at merchants, but also at Jews engaged in trade and usury'.[16]

The regional diet in Łęczyca in 1669 even demanded that the Jews should be held collectively responsible for desecrating the host and for ritual murders: all Jews from one province should be punished by expulsion and the confiscation of their property. Severe punishments were also demanded by other regional diets. Belief in these accusations led to trials described in many publications. They served to develop an image of the Jew as a dangerous enemy of all Christians, whose blood was supposedly used for the practice of his religion. These beliefs encouraged hanging paintings in churches and monasteries (e.g. in Sandomierz cathedral, the Bernardine Fathers in Kalwaria Zebrzydowska), showing scenes of ritual murder, woodcuts of similar design and coffins depicting the remains of murdered children. There were, however, no written works on this theme.

Similar propaganda was received best in the towns; there above all (and not on the estates of the *szlachta* or on royal property) anti-Jewish trials took place. The crucial role played by economic antagonism is shown, because in some instances these cases preceded the expulsion of the Jewish population from a town. The *Sejm* and other authoritative bodies tried to prevent these accusations: only royal and *sejm* courts, not municipal courts, could examine them. However, this was not adhered to in practice. Sigismund III in 1618 banned the publication and distribution of Sebastian Miczyński's pamphlet *Zwierciadło Korony Polskiej* (Mirror of the Polish Crown), as a work which could, by discussing ritual murder, provoke religious outrage and anti-Jewish rioting.

For three hundred years (from the 16th to 18th century) very few authors attempted to present the image of the Jews in a better light, or even to show any understanding for their situation. However, in 1517 Maciej Miechowita had written that in Lithuania or Russia one meets many Jews, 'not the exploitative types found in Christian countries, however, but working farmers and great merchants, often running customs and tax offices'. He had also praised them for taking up 'the humanistic sciences, astronomy and medicine'.[17] At the beginning of the following century Jan of Kijan (in the poem *Lichwa polska* [Polish usury]) had argued that Jews practising usury were less insensitive than their Christian colleagues. Similarly,

Daniel Bratkowski (1697) had written that in collecting their percentage the Christian pupils outdid their Jewish teachers.

In popular literature one can also find some traces of compassion towards Jews persecuted by students. These may be rare but they do appear in dramas such as P. Baryka's *Z chłopa król* (From Peasant to King) (1637) or Fr D. Neserowicz's *Świat na opak wywrócony* (The World Turned Upside Down) (1663), where Jews demand compensation from the students, while berating them for stealing and participating in pogroms. Similarly, Pęski, a Jesuit and member of the *szlachta*, in his quarrel with those who called the Republic a paradise for Jews, wrote that he himself would flee such a paradise if he had to go about in tattered clothes, to buy protection from persecution or to be victimized by schoolboys.

These voices begin to increase under the gradual influence of the Enlightenment. Bishop Józef Andrzej Załuski, for example, appealed for a whole nation not to be blamed for a crime (the crucifixion of Christ) committed by individuals centuries ago. Józef Pawlikowski, one of the most vociferous and influential polemicists of the time, warned against imitating the treatment meted out to Jews earlier by the fanatical Spaniards. The Jews were also defended by such journals appearing in the second half of the 18th century as *Monitor* or P. Świtkowski's *Pamiętnik Polityczny i Historyczny*.

In the noble Republic Jews had become, as it were, a part of the human landscape, one of the most permanent colours in the palate of a multiracial community. In the second half of the 18th century the painter's brush incorporated them into the portrayal of the general ruin of Polish towns (B. Vogel did this with great panache, cf. the view of the market square in Olkusz and other works by this artist), who depicted these wretched abodes, worthy of 'the peasant and the Jew', to quote the words of the poet, Ignacy Krasicki. Immortalised in paintings and engravings also were the Jewish inn and its owners, the synagogue with the faithful returning home, Jewesses dressed for holy days and Jewish children outside the *heder* and, finally, Kazimierz near Kraków, which was inhabited mainly by Jews. We owe most of these works to the talent of Piotr Norblin who frequently, with obvious pleasure and the eye of a true reporter, portrayed Jews trading, haggling fiercely with noble or peasant.

Foreigners visiting Poland were surprised at the size of the Jewish population (some even wrote exaggeratedly that it reached 2 million), their privileges, which gave them greater freedom than 'anywhere else in the world except Holland and England', and their dress and traditions which differed completely from those in Western Europe. Some above all noted the wealth of Jewish merchants or the flourishing state of their affairs, while others only saw poor Jews, dressed in black tattered robes. Some recognised their indispensability in the economic system of the noble Republic, while others blamed them for the economic ruin of the state, the decline of the towns and the universal drunkenness (particularly among the peasants), and accused them of benefiting from commercial fraud, usury and swindling. In sum, their opinions largely matched the image of the Jew in Polish sources. It should be remembered, however, that foreign travellers used the works of Polish writers (the marginalia of foreign accounts refer to them), and they must also surely have discussed the theme with native Poles. Paradoxically, the travellers in Poland stressed that on Saturday evenings only Jews remained sober (indeed Jews were the only group in the Polish Commonwealth whom nobody accused of drunkenness).

Jewish omnipresence, their monopoly of most areas of economic life (crafts as well as trade) and their close links with the *szlachta* were noted by almost all foreigners. This, in their view, reflected badly on the Jews as well as on the Poles themselves, or rather on the 'fecklessness and apathy of the *szlachta*', 'the oppressed peasant', and the inertia of the native burgher class. All these indulged in drink and allowed themselves to be exploited, but could not conduct trade themselves, run inns or engage in credit activities, areas where English, French and German merchants had not allowed themselves to be ousted by foreign immigrants.[18]

Returning to the image of the Jew held by the Poles themselves, it should be mentioned that it was formed through economic contacts and religious conflicts, those areas where they appeared rivals. The stereotype was developed therefore in very unfavourable circumstances, in the area of contact between a merchant (or moneylender) and his client (or debtor). Jews were not encountered, however, in political life, in their traditional or family life, as might be the case, for example, with the *szlachta*, who belonged to various Christian denominations. Furthermore, only a tiny percentage of Jews was Polonized and assimilated into the nationalities then living in the noble Republic. Whereas in the 16th and 17th centuries Germans, Ruthenians, Armenians and Lithuanians, and even the Tatar *szlachta* living in the Grand Duchy began to be assimilated, the Jews – apart from a few individuals – remained completely resistant to this process. It was not until the second half of the 18th century that the so-called Frankists began the assimilation of Polish Jewry; their descendants played a significant role in the cultural history of the 19th century. The promoters of the Polish Enlightenment were also moving in the same direction. On the one hand they demanded the Polonization of the Jewish population by gradually limiting publications in Hebrew, abandoning distinctions in dress, and introducing compulsory education and even military service. On the other, they demanded that Jews should be productive (which involved removing them from usury and trade and directing them towards work in agriculture and manufacturing). This was to be accompanied by lifting all legal barriers dividing the Jews from the rest of society. No follower of the Enlightenment favoured expelling the Jews from Poland. There was also anger at their persecution at the hands of town mobs. 'How can we suffer this barbaric vestige of older practices and allow this banditry which brings shame on a great nation and age', wrote Piotr Świtkowski in *Monitor* (1783).[19] Accusations of ritual murder or desecration of the host also became less and less frequent at this time.

In conclusion, let us try to discover the image of the Poles and the noble Republic which appeared in the consciousness and literature of its Jewish inhabitants. It is difficult to give a complete answer without studying Hebrew writings. We know, from much later translations, that Polish tolerance was praised, a tolerance which allowed Jews expelled from beyond the Warta, Vistula and Dniepr to find food and freedom of worship. It was for this reason that David Gans, a Jewish chronicler from Prague, mourned the 'righteous' King Sigismund Augustus. The Hebrew poets often took up the same theme, and the famous religious polemicist, Izaak ben Abraham of Troki, contrasted the religious tolerance at the end of the 16th century in the 'state without stakes' with the religious persecution in Western Europe. He wrote that in England the 'papists' were treated with such cruelty that it 'made one's hair stand on end', and that in France and Spain Protestants were dealt with in the same way. This was God's punishment, for all three states had once persecuted Jews, and then expelled them completely. In Poland, however, the followers of Judaism were protected. 'And that is why God has granted this land great power and such peace that those of different faiths are not enemies and do not fight each other'.[20] In the mid-16th century Moses Isserles, an outstanding Jewish scholar who found refuge in Kraków, wrote to one of his pupils that it was better to be satisfied with a piece of dry bread and live peacefully in Poland than to live in Germany where Jews were surrounded by universal hatred.

A hostile image of the Jew is also found in French, German and English writing of the 16th to 18th centuries; Polish literature was not therefore an exception. Furthermore, as far as the *szlachta* was concerned, and they were the ones with whom Jews had most contact, it was more a question of anti-Judaism than anti-semitism, if the question arose. As soon as the disciples of Moses were christened they were regarded as citizens with full rights; for as soon as they did so they ceased to be Jews. Converts were not reminded of their non-Christian descent, as was the case in Spain, for example. Moreover, in the Grand Duchy of Lithuania between 1588–1764, Jewish converts were made members of the *szlachta*, although no statute provided for this for burghers or peasants. Polish members of the *szlachta* knew that there were many assimilated newcomers in their midst, ranging from Christians whose mother tongue was German, Lithuanian or Ruthenian, to former adherents of Islam (the Tatars) or Judaism (the Jews). The *szlachta* was unconcerned about this; at the most it was occasionally mentioned in anecdotes about new Christians. The burghers looked on these matters rather differently, writing with hostility about the Frankists.

To conclude, the image of the Jew throughout the three centuries covered in this study is a very stable one, a feature of all stereotypes. This was because of the influence of the Church, which did not revise its approach to the Jewish question until the 20th century, and because of the inertia and size of Jewish centres. In the 16th and 17th centuries the noble Republic held the largest concentration of Jews outside the Ottoman Empire, and on a scale unprecedented in Western Europe: 44 per cent of the Jewish diaspora lived in the lands of the former Polish state in 1800. This must have had definite repercussions on attitudes to Jews; the popular view was that of someone who was an outsider, and such a person is never represented very positively in any country. Neither the Reformation nor the Enlightenment brought about any radical changes: the only difference lay in the fact that the future of the Jews was perceived in a different way from the traditional view. In the 16th and 17th centuries Catholics and Protestants hoped that at least some Jews would be gradually absorbed into society through conversion, whereas in the following century it was not hoped there would be racial assimilation. However, no one approached the problem from a wider social perspective: arguments for granting the Jewish population equal rights were not broached until the 19th century.

NOTES

1 This article is a shortened version of a longer study in German ('Das Judenbild der Polen im 16–18 Jahrhundert', *Acta Poloniae Historica*, vol. 50 (1984), pp. 29–56) and French ('Les Juifs vus par l'opinion polonais des XVIe, XVIIe et XVIIIe siècle', *Literary Etudes in Poland*, vol. 19 (1988), pp. 41–77).

2 These include the excellent collection of studies by A. Hertz, *Żydzi w kulturze polskiej* (Paris, 1961) (particularly pp. 224 ff.: 'Obraz Żyda'). Cf. also J. Goldberg, 'Poles and Jews in the 17th and 18th Centuries. Rejection or Acceptance', *Jahrbücher für Geschichte Osteuropas*, vol. 22 (1974), no.2, and M. Fuks, Z. Hoffman and J. Tomaszewski, *Die Juden in Polen. Geschichte und Kultur* (Warsaw, 1982).

3 W. Konopczyński, *Polscy pisarze polityczni XVIII w.* (Warsaw, 1966), p. 30.

4 J. St. Bystroń, *Dzieje obyczajów w dawnej Polsce, wiek XVI- XVIII*, vol. 1 (Kraków, 1932), pp. 65–5.

5 J. Tazbir, *Świat panów Pasków. Eseje i studia* (Łódź, 1986), p. 217. Ibid. 'Żydzi w opinii staropolskiej', pp. 213 ff.

6 Sz. Starowolski, *Polska albo opisanie położenia Królestwa Polskiego* (Warsaw, 1976), p. 88.

7 Cf. D. Tollet, 'La litérature antisémite polonaise de 1588 à 1668', *Revue française d'histoire du livre*, no. 14 (1977) and in a separate edition (Bordeaux, 1977).

8 M. Bałaban, 'Umysłowość i moralność żydowstwa polskiego XVI w.', *Kultura staropolska* (Kraków, 1932), p. 607.

9 S. Miczyński, *Zwierciadło Korony Polskiej* . . . (Kraków, 1618), p. 3.

10 M. Csombor, *Podróż po Polsce* (Warsaw, 1961), p. 101.
11 M. Bembus, *Kometa, to jest pogrożka z nieba* (Kraków, 1619), p. 36.
12 Sz. Starowolski, *Wady staropolskie*. A shortened version of the work: *Robak sumienia złego*. . . (Kraków, 1853), pp. 86–7.
13 J. St. Bystroń, op. cit., vol. 1, p. 68.
14 K. Bartoszewicz, *Antysemityzm w literaturze polskiej XV-XVII w.* (Warsaw, 1914).
15 J. Tazbir, op. cit., p. 229.
16 M. Gutowski, *Komizm w polskiej sztuce gotyckiej* (Warsaw, 1973), pp. 169 and 203.
17 M. Miechowita, *Opis Sarmacji azjatyckiej i europejskiej*, (Wrocław, 1972), pp. 62–3 and 71.
18 Cf. J. Tazbir, op. cit., pp. 235–7.
19 W. Smoleński, *Przewrót umysłowy w Polsce wieku XVIII* (Warsaw, 1979), p. 386.
20 M. Bersohn, *Tobiasz Kohn, lekarz polski w XVII wieku* (Kraków, 1872), pp. 32–33.

4

A MINORITY VIEWS THE MAJORITY: JEWISH ATTITUDES TOWARDS THE POLISH LITHUANIAN COMMONWEALTH AND INTERACTION WITH POLES*

M. J. Rosman

The behaviour of the various subordinate minorities of the Polish Lithuanian Commonwealth towards Polish hegemony covers the entire theoretical spectrum: from rebellious through resigned, to accepting, to assimilationist.[1] At one extreme are the Germans, Scots, and others who reached an accommodation with Polish domination that resulted in their eventual assimilation and integration. At the other extreme are the Arians, whose failure to submit to the demands of subordinate status led in 1667 to their expulsion. Somewhat different was the response of the Cossacks and, at times, the Ruthenian peasants. The posture they maintained was frequently one of antagonism and conflict, and even led to militant secessionist tendencies as expressed in various uprisings.

The Jews' position was between the extremes. Polish society supported the Jews' communal institutions, tolerated their cultural differences, and offered opportunities for successful articulation with the general economic order. In exchange, the Jews resigned themselves to domination and, by and large, remained within the bounds of the economic, social, and political roles that the majority defined for them. Significantly, the first act of the umbrella institution of Jewish autonomy, the Council of Four Lands, was intended to guarantee that Jewish economic activity would not infringe on the prerogatives of Poles. This decree, issued in 1580, forbade Jews to lease royal concessions in the western parts of Poland. The probable reason for the Council taking such action was the fear that competition with Polish noblemen for these leases might elicit a reaction that would endanger all Jews.[2]

* This article, based on a lecture I delivered at the Conference on Polish-Jewish History held in Jerusalem in February 1988, was completed during my tenure as a visitor in the Department of History at the University of Michigan. I would like to express my gratitude to the Department and the University for their hospitality.

The Jews were generally supporters of the political *status quo*. As I have pointed out elsewhere, Jewish leaders were convinced that the graciousness of kings and nobility was what guaranteed their security and prosperity.[3] They regarded the Polish kings as the guarantors of the Jews' safety and freedom and generally perceived their interests as being linked with those of the king or local magnate.[4] The clearest expressions of Jewish support for the Polish political order come from the period of the Chmielnicki uprising (1648–57). The Jews were not passive observers waiting for the accursed houses of the protagonists to be put in order so that Jewish suffering would cease; rather, they were active allies of the Commonwealth. In Tulczyń, for example, according to the Jewish chronicler, Meir of Szczebrzeszyn,[5] writing no later than 1650:

> About 600 courageous men, the nobles, barricaded themselves in the fortress. Approximately 2,000 of the scattered sheep [the Jews], accurate marksmen, joined them. The noblemen received them and they joined together, making an honest covenant between them; each would help the other. The noblemen were deployed inside the fortress; the Jews stood around on the battlements, on guard with bow and arrow. When the smouldering butts [Cossacks and Tartars] attacked, they shot at them with arrows and flames. The Greeks recoiled in fear and trembling and the noblemen and Jews chased them, smiting a mighty blow against the rebels.

The Polish anti-rebel forces, according to Frank Sysyn, 'depicted the revolt as a bloody *jacquerie* against society and civilization. They condemned the Cossacks as the driving force of the revolt and portrayed the uprising as a rebellion of subjects against their lawful masters.'[6] The Jews certainly shared this view. Obviously, it was in the interests of the Jews to support the *Rzeczpospolita* against those who had targeted them, along with the Polish side, as objects of their resentment. What is interesting, however, is how the Jews explained their own support of the Poles to themselves. For the most part, they did not see the alliance in pragmatic terms, but supported the Poles because right was on the Polish side. While some of them expressed awareness of the heavy price the feudal yoke exacted from the Ruthenian peasantry,[7] they still regarded the existing structure of the Commonwealth as right and proper. In the Jews' opinion, the rebels who intended to create a new order were clearly in the wrong. As the chronicler Shabbetai HaKohen asserted, the Ruthenian villains (whom he also styles 'Greeks' and 'Cossacks'), were 'a contemptible nation . . . vile, base, unreliable and vacuous . . . Peasants and farmers gathered from near and far and raised their hand against the king, his noblemen and retainers, a great and powerful nation, like the giants'.[8] R. Meir of Szczebrzeszyn was no less hostile in his assessment. 'Cruel men, the sons of cruel men, as they have been for generations ... their words appear sincere, but their intentions (are) to spill blood in stealth and to destroy cities ... They all revolted; betraying their Catholic masters ... Slaves ruled over masters'.[9] Gabriel Shusberg's reaction to Jan Kazimierz's predicament at Zbaraż and subsequent compromise settlement with the Cossacks at Zborów would have been appropriate from an anti-rebel nobleman:

> But the King, the royal officials and the noblemen were forced to fulfil all of [the rebels'] desires, handing over a large ransom. Then, after an agreement was reached, the Greek [i.e. Cossack] hetman and Tartar king returned in great honour to their land; they had almost attained sovereignty. What humiliation and disgrace.[10]

Jews not only supported the Polish political constellation. Some also displayed an interest in Polish history. David Ganz, a German Jew who had studied in Poland as a young man, wrote a chronicle of world and Jewish history that was published in Prague in 1592, which treats Poland as a major power and its political history as an important part of world history.[11] Nathan Hannover, a Jewish chronicler writing in the early 1650s about the roots of Cossack Polish antagonism, displayed a fairly sophisticated understanding of the far-reaching changes in Polish society wrought by Zygmunt III, champion of the Counter-Reformation. Hannover related how Zygmunt III abandoned the tradition of treating noblemen equally, regardless of their religious faith, and favoured the Catholics; he also attempted to induce the Ruthenian nobility to abandon their faith and embrace Catholicism. Subsequently, the Ruthenians were impoverished and relegated to a wretched and lowly status. The exceptions to this were the registered Cossacks charged with protecting the south-eastern border against the Tatars, in return for which they were granted special privileges.[12]

The Jewish chronicler most familiar with Polish history, government, and society at this time was the eighteenth-century wine merchant, Dov Ber of Bolechów. Despite certain *lacunae*, he was acquainted with such events as the post-Altranstadt machinations involving the supporters of King Augustus II and their rivals supporting Leszczyński; Count Poniatowski's rise to power; Moscow's intervention in favour of the election of Augustus II; Frederick William of Prussia's role in aggravating Polish inflation; and the Confederation of Bar. In the light of such knowledge, it is hardly surprising that he also understood the workings of such Polish institutions as the *Sejm* and High Tribunal at Lublin.[13] He held the High Tribunal in great esteem:

> This Tribunal was the supreme court over all the courts which existed in each *starostwo*. Each province and district used to elect a

> number of wealthy noblemen, learned in the law, who assembled at Warsaw, the capital of Poland, and there the Diet chose from among them men known for their high character, fear of God, love of truth and incorruptibility.[14]

While the Jews may have generally supported the Polish political configuration, and individuals among them may have taken an interest in Polish history and institutions, for the most part Jewish political involvement was marginal. There were, it is true, some instances of successful Jewish lobbying at the *Sejm* and regional *Sejmiki* (dietines), but this was in an attempt to defeat specifically anti-Jewish legislation or to prevent an increase in the taxes on Jews.[15] The Jews may have shown political astuteness in securing their own interests,[16] but they held no formal political positions and played no defined role.[17]

The Jews were resigned to their relative exclusion from the formal political process before partition and never attempted to do more than lobby behind the scenes. By the eighteenth century, however, in the classic fashion of subordinate minority groups, discontent began to be apparent in their literature and folklore. The Jews, like most minority groups, tended to interpret the political history of their country ethnocentrically.[18] Thus, typically, the Jews who called the Polish kings 'hasid' were motivated to do so by their favourable assessment of the royal policy on Jews. Shabbetai Hakohen, for example, said that Władysław IV was worthy of being numbered among the righteous because of his graciousness and fidelity to the Jews.[19] But not all Jews held favourable views of the Commonwealth. Dov Ber of Bolechów, for example, claimed that the partitions of Poland came as a punishment for the dissolution of the Council of Four Lands:

> Then the Polish people and their kingdom were deprived of all honour, and the verse was fulfilled: 'And I will lay vengeance upon Edom . . . by the hand of my people Israel'; that is to say that as they had dealt with Israel so were they dealt with. All the honour of their country was taken away from them, and they were enslaved forever. And so perish our foes who denounce us![20]

Jewish fantasies also embroidered their own role in the political process: the Polish government held the power – legitimately, one might add – and Jews wanted to share in it. The most famous example of this type of thinking is the legend of a Jew called Saul Wahl, which was first written down in 1733 but is probably much older. According to the various versions of this legend, Wahl, who won the admiration of the *Sejm*, became Polish regent for a day; while ruling justly over the Poles, he instituted legislation favourable to the Jews, and finally crowned Zygmunt III king of Poland.[21] Similarly, later Hasidic legend asserted that the founder of

Hasidism, the Baal Shem Tov, had intervened to assure victory for a cossack ('Greek') ruler over a Tatar ('Ishmaelite') in order to prevent suffering for the Jews.[22] Another Hasidic legend reported that the election of Stanisław August Poniatowski was merely a confirmation of a choice made by the Maggid of Międzyrzecz in consultation with R. Pinhas of Korzec.[23]

Pinhas of Korzec (d. 1790) claimed that the Jews had a stake in preserving Poland because 'the exile (in Poland) is less bitter than anywhere else'. Thus, as long as R. Nahman Horodenker prayed to keep the Russians out of Poland, the power of his prayer was sufficient to assure it. But when in 1764 R. Nahman left for the Land of Israel, the Russians succeeded in crossing the Dniepr in order to act against the Confederation of Bar. After that, R. Pinhas himself worked to limit the effects of partition; only following his death was Poland completely dismembered.[24]

A clear instance of Polish Jews' insistence on their central importance in the country, despite the apparent reality, is to be found in a statement made by Rabbi Levi Yitshak of Berdichev to his followers in the late eighteenth century:

> Know that all of the nations that were created were created for the sake of Israel, for the good of Israel; for sometimes, for some reason, good comes to Israel from the nations. Thus their sustenance is from a holy source; were it not that there is some good [that comes from them] they would not have been created at all . . . And know that each ruler of the nations must serve our God who is the God of gods and the Lord of lords . . .[25]

The fact that Dov Ber of Bolechów and Pinhas of Korzec held different attitudes towards the partition of Poland raises another subject for examination: Jewish attitudes towards Poland and their opinions on how Jews should interact with Poles were not monolithic. It has long been accepted that Polish attitudes towards Jews in the pre-partition period varied with social groups. Thus, although certain religiously-based and other Jewish stereotypes were widespread, Jacob Goldberg, for one, has demonstrated that the stances of magnates, *szlachta*, townsmen, peasants, and high and low clergy each bore characteristically distinguishing features.[26] By contrast, Jewish historians portraying the Jewish attitude towards Poles under the Commonwealth have tended to postulate a general position. Bernard Weinryb, for example, although recognising negative reactions among Polish Jews holds that the prevailing attitude among at least the élite of the Jewish community, was one of sympathy with the Poles and trust, confidence, and even pride in Poland.[27] Jacob Katz subsumes Polish Jewry under the general rubric of Ashkenazic Jewry, thereby implying that there was no attitude towards the Gentiles around them particular to Polish Jews. He posits, rather, that the attitude of Ashkenazi Jewry towards all non-Jews was directly linked to the norms of Jewish religious law, and it was this that resulted in the Jewish stance of isolation and estrangement throughout Central and Eastern Europe.[28]

In my opinion, the distance between these apparently opposed viewpoints can be bridged if one concedes that in the Jewish community, there was not a single 'Jewish attitude' towards Poles, but rather a spectrum of attitudes, which depended on their holders' vantage points within society no less than they derived from traditional norms. While on the face of it this proposition seems logical, the scarcity of Jewish sources that document attitudes makes it difficult to substantiate. Only in the eighteenth century does one find sufficient sources to permit the identification of different approaches to Poles on the part of Jews from different sectors of the Jewish community.

The first is the best known and represents the view of what sociologists might term the 'accommodation-leadership', those charged with liaising with the majority.[29] In the case of the Polish-Jewish interaction, these were the *kahal* leaders. Their attitude towards the Polish environment can be seen in the legislation that they passed and which appears in the communal record books that have survived. One of the important features of their legislation was prohibitions on individuals from entering into politically or economically significant relationships with Poles.[30] These prohibitions demonstrate that their authors were convinced that powerful Poles and Polish institutions represented a potential threat to the stability of the Jewish community and the prerogatives of the autonomous Jewish institutions. They never challenged the legitimacy of Polish authority; their approach was to accept Polish authority as a given, to negotiate with it when possible, but to minimize its impact (and preserve their own status) by restricting contact between Jews and Poles or Polish institutions.[31] Loans, tax payments, business partnerships, adjudication before non-Jewish authorities, *arenda* leases and political lobbying efforts were all to be mediated, or at least approved by the *kahal*. By limiting contact to routine bureaucratic channels, Polish influence on the Jewish community could be anticipated, controlled, and reduced to the minimum extent possible.

A different approach was advocated, in the eighteenth century at least, by some who were not part of the *kahal* establishment and managed to establish close relationships with powerful Poles (and after partition with Germans, Austrians, and Russians). People like Dov Ber of Bolechów, or later Moshe Wasserzug, saw close relationships with powerful non-Jews as potentially advantageous, rather than potentially dangerous. All that was necessary, they said, was to keep one's wits about one and know how to deal properly with such people. Both men took obvious pride in their relationships with powerful Gentiles – relationships which, while based on utilitarian considerations, clearly acquired other significance. Dov Ber goes to great lengths to impress upon his readers – his family – how he had genuinely friendly relations with certain noblemen, while several Jews cheated him and caused him trouble. Far from avoiding relations with Poles, then, such men were eager to develop economic, social, and even cultural ties with them.[32]

More complex than either the attitudes of the official leadership or the individuals with special relations with Poles was the attitude expressed in early Hasidic sources. *Shivhei Ha-Besht* (first published in 1814) is the earliest collection of oral traditions concerning the activities of the founder of Hasidism, Israel ben Eliezer Baal Shem Tov (died 1760) and some of his disciples.[33] It is imbued with a sense of the demonic character of non-Jews and the dangers inherent in encounters with them. One of the most common motifs is how in situations where contacts between Jew and non-Jew – Cossack, robber, nobleman, peasant, priest, or sorcerer – could result in the victimization of the Jew, the Baal Shem Tov's intervention could assure a happy ending.[34]

Alongside the belief in the non-Jews' demonic nature and the fear and mistrust of Gentile society, some of these tales hint at a very different evaluation of the theological-moral standing of the non-Jew. According to Jacob Katz, given the religious rivalry between Judaism and Christianity, the members of each group adopted a double standard of morality towards each other. There was no religious rationale for treating outsiders according to ethical norms. Jews frowned on mistreating or cheating non-Jews not on moral grounds but from enlightened self-interest: such behaviour would bring Jews into disrepute and result in sanctions or even violence being brought to bear against them.[35]

In *Shivhei Ha-Besht* other considerations seem to come into play. In one story, the Baal Shem Tov's disciple Jacob Joseph of Polnoye has a dream in which he enters a palace in paradise. There Satan accused an *arendator* of defrauding the villagers in his area. This sin was deemed to outweigh the fact that the man 'studied constantly' and gave money to charity. A punishment was decreed, and on earth the lord of the estate confiscated the *arendator*'s possessions and put him and his family in jail. The moral of the story is actually spelled out: 'From this it can be seen that one should refrain from robbing the Gentiles, since, as it is written in the books, Satan deducts this sin from one's holy merits, God forbid'.[36] The point here, then, is not that one should deal honestly with Gentiles out of consideration of expedience in this world, but that cheating non-Jews is a sin that will be punished by the heavenly court. Thus, in another story, the Baal Shem Tov tells his disciples how 'he saw that in heaven Jews who live in the villages were accused of cheating the Gentiles in their accounts'.[37] The warning is clear.

When the question of interaction with Poles was considered at greater remove, as in the case of eighteenth-century Polish Jews who had emigrated and had been influenced by Western European culture, attitudes could be more extreme. Such men seem to have absorbed the deprecatory attitudes towards Poland common in the West and mince no words in their description of Poles (and Polish Jews as well). The physician Tobias Kohn, born in Poland, but educated in universities in Italy and Germany, wrote in 1707 concerning causes of *plica polonica* (trichosis or elflock), a disease of the hair and scalp for which there was no known cure in Poland.[38] He noted that, as a young man in Poland, he had seen at first hand:

> . . . this country is more fertile than all the other lands of the nations,[39] but it is full of filth and offal . . . people's homes stink and their clothes are dirty. They do not comb their hair or beards even once a year . . . Their diet is bizarre, mainly beans, pickles and, on an empty stomach, radishes, onions and garlic. They drink liquor that burns the heart and the soul as well and mead and beer and other unhealthy drinks that unquestionably cause serious diseases . . . so there is no wonder that they suffer such illnesses due to their bad habits . . . [Furthermore] even if demons had never been created they would have had to have been created for the people of this country; for there is no land where they are more occupied with demons, talismans, oath formulas, mystical names and dreams . . .

If Tobias criticized Polish hygiene and superstition, Solomon Maimon, who had attached himself to the intellectual circles of Berlin, recorded his negative opinion of Polish political, economic, and social organization. According to Maimon, Poland's political policies were informed by ignorance, and its non-Jewish and non-serf population were distinguished by laziness.[40] I have not found such negative statements as these made by Jews who were living in Poland, even in texts intended for a Jewish readership.

The Jews' accommodation to their political status in Poland combined moderation on the practical level with an imaginative interpretation of reality that gave expression to their desire for power and their belief in their ultimate superiority. By contrast, attitudes towards interaction with Poles and other non-Jews were rooted more in the actual experiences and position of the members of the various Jewish sub-groups within society. Thus, Jewish emigrés, who no longer had any ongoing relationship with Poles, criticized them. The representatives of the institutional establishment, who wanted to consolidate their power within the Jewish community, saw Poles as a threat to their position. This threat could best be managed by maintaining correct relations between Polish and Jewish institutions and maximum distance between Polish and Jewish societies. Jews who benefited from close relationships with non-Jews tended to admire their interlocutors and take pride in such relationships. One of the characteristics of early Hasidism may have been an attempt by a leadership sensitive to the unpredictability and possible violence of everyday encounters with Gentiles to explore new bases for the relationship between Jew and non-Jew. From this variety of attitudes, it is evident that, although Jews' reactions to minority status were typical and predictable, their stance towards interaction with the non-Jewish environment cannot be characterized by one paradigm only, and was connected closely enough to reality as to be susceptible of change.

NOTES

1 For a description of the typology of responses see Floyd James David, *Minority-Dominant Relations: A Sociological Analysis* (Arlington Heights, III: 1978); Minako Kurokawa, ed., *Minority Responses* (New York, 1970); cf. P.R. Brass, ed., *Ethnic Groups and the State* (Totowa, N.J., 1985), pp. 34–47, 171–173, 184–186; W.F. Mackey and W. Verdoodt, eds., *The Multinational Society* (Rowley, Mass., 1975), pp. 329–353.

2 Israel Halpern (ed.), *Pinkas Va'ad Arba Aratsot* (Jerusalem, 1945), p. 1. For an analysis of the background to this declaration see S.A. Cygielman, 'Leasing and contracting interests (public incomes) of Polish Jewry and the foundation of *Vaad Arba Aratsot*', *Tsion*, vol 47, (1982) pp. 112–144. For other examples of the Jews' conviction that they must keep a low profile and conform to the requirements of the majority, see M.J. Rosman, 'Jewish Perceptions of Insecurity and Powerlessness in 16th-18th century Poland', *Polin*, vol I, pp. 19–27.

3 Rosman, 'Perceptions', p. 23. For a discussion of how Jewish political consciousness in Poland developed in post-Partition times see: Jack Kugelmass, 'Native Aliens', unpublished Ph.D. dissertation (New School for Social Research, New York, 1980), esp. pp. 52–54, 253–54.

4 B.D. Weinryb, *The Jews of Poland* (Philadelphia, 1973), pp. 165–167; Rosman, 'Perceptions', pp. 20–22.

5 *Tsok Ha-Itim* (Kraków, 1650, new edition, Jerusalem, 1981), p. 6. Other Hebrew chronicles contain several mentions of Jews' fighting alongside Poles against the rebels; e.g. Shabbatai Ha-Kohen, *Megilat Eifa* (Amsterdam, 1651, reprinted in *Beit Yisrael Be-Polin*, I. Halpern, ed. vol. 2, Jerusalem, 1953), p. 253; Nathan Hannover, *Yeven Metsula* (Venice, 1953, translated *Abyss of Despair* by A.J. Mesch, New York, 1950, reprinted New Brunswick, N.J., 1983), pp. 54, 63, 80..

6 F.E. Sysyn, 'Seventeenth-Century Views on the Causes of Khmel'nysts'kyi Uprising: An Examination of the "Discourse on the Present Cossack or Peasant War"', *Harvard Ukrainian Studies* 5 (1981), p. 446.

7 See Hannover, pp. 27–28, 38.

8 Ha-Kohen, p. 252. See also Weinryb, *The Jews of Poland*, p. 200. The terms used by Shabbetai and other Jewish chroniclers to describe the Ukrainians are parallel to those used by Poles; compare the Hebrew *nivzim* (contemptible), *shefalim* (base), *pohazim* (fickle), *raikim* (vacuous) with the Polish *swawolny* (dissolute), *zdrajca* (traitor), *niecnota* (scoundrel), *hultaj* (good-for-nothing). See: A.Z. Baraboy, et al., eds., *Dokumenty osvoboditelnoi voine Ukrainskovo naroda* (Kiev, 1965), passim.

9 Meir ben Samuel, p. 3.

10 Gabriel ben Joshua Shusberg, *Petah Teshuvah* (Amsterdam, 1651), p. 12b.

11 David Ganz, *Zemah David*, M. Breuer, ed. (Jerusalem, 1983), pp. 314. See the index under Poland for other events of Polish history reported in the book.
12 N.N. Hannover, pp. 27–28.
13 Ber Birkenthal, *The Memoirs of Ber of Bolechow*, M. Vishnitzer, ed. (London, 1922, reprinted New York, 1973) pp. 52–53, 73–74, 125, 127, 131–2, 150, 172.
14 Ber Birkenthal, p. 124. Note that the Hebrew terms used here to characterise the members of the High Tribunal (see Hebrew edition of the memoirs, p. 75) are the same ones employed in the Bible to describe the type of people Jethro told Moses to pick to serve as judges in the courts of Biblical Israel (*Exodus* 18, 21).
15 Isaac Lewin, *The Jewish Community in Poland* (New York, 1985), pp. 67–96; Birkenthal, p. 143.
16 Rosman, 'Perceptions', pp. 19–20.
17 Dov Ber of Bolechów did several times house the officer who brought money from Paris for the support of the Confederation of Bar (Birkenthal, p. 92 [Hebrew Edition]; Vishnitzer's translation, p. 150, is not accurate on this point). Sometimes non-Polish Jews did play a role in high level Jewish politics; see Cecil Roth's articles: 'Dr. Solomon Ashkenazi and the Election to the Throne of Poland', *Oxford Slavonic Studies* 9 (1960), pp. 8–20; 'A Mantuan Jewish Consortium and the Election to the Throne of Poland in 1587' [Hebrew], *Yitzhak F. Baer Jubilee Volume*, S.W. Baron, et al., eds. (Jerusalem, 1960), pp. 291–296. On the role of the German Court Jew, Berend Lehmann, in the election of August II, see Selma Stern, *The Court Jew* (Philadelphia, 1950), pp. 80–82.
18 On covert aggression of minority groups against the dominant group see Davis, pp. 50, 131–132, 138, 145. Particularly relevant for our discussion is the notion of expressive hostility (p. 138).
19 *Ha-Kohen*, p. 252.
20 Birkenthal, p. 149–151.
21 P. Bloch, 'Die Sage von Saul Wahl, dem Eintags König von Polen', *Zeitschrift den Historischen Gessellschaft für die Provinz Posen* 4 (1889) p. 234ff; Majer Balaban, *Yidn in Poyln* (Wilno, 1930), pp. 17–38; there is also the legend of Prochownik which while it may date from an earlier period does not appear until the nineteenth century: see B. Weinryb, *The Beginnings of East European Jewry in Legend and Historiography* (Leiden, 1962), pp. 1–11.
22 Dov Ber ben Samuel, *Shivhei ha-Besht: In Praise of the Ba'al Shem Tov*, D. Amos and J. Mintz, trans. and eds., (Bloomington, Indiana, 1972) (henceforth SB) No.174; the Baal Shem Tov also supposedly brought about the wartime destruction of the town of Balta. (SB No.45).
23 A.J. Heschel, *The Circle of the Baal Shem Tov*, (Chicago, 1985), p.22.
24 Heschel, p. 40–43.
25 Levi Yitshak of Berdichev, *Kedushat Levi* (Slavita, 1798), p. 106. On Levi Yitshak's political activism under both Polish and Russian rule see I. Halpern, *Yehudim Ve-Jahadut be-Mizrah Europa*, (Jerusalem, 1968), p. 340–47.
26 J. Goldberg, 'Poles and Jews: in the 17th and 18th centuries. Rejection or Acceptance' in *Jahrbücher für Geschichte Osteuropas*, vol. 22 (1974) No.2, pp. 248–82. See also R. Mahler, *History of the Jews in Poland* (Hebrew), (Merhavia, 1946) pp. 164–188. For discussion of some of the stereotypical ideas about Jews, see A. Kamiński, 'Poland as a Host Country of the Jews' *Proceedings of the Conferences on Poles and Jews: Myth and Reality in Historical Context*, J. Micgiel et al, eds. (New York, 1986), p. 16–31 and M.J. Rosman, *The Lords' Jews* (Cambridge, Mass., 1989), Conclusion.
27 The Jews of Poland, pp. 165–176.
28 J. Katz, *Exclusiveness and Tolerance* (New York, 1952), pp. 56–7; idem., *Tradition and Crisis* (New York, 1971), pp. 18–42. Cf. Kugelmass, p. 254.

29 Davis, pp. 133–5.
30 For examples see: ***The Lords' Jews***, Chapter 7, 'The Magnates and the Jewish Community', notes 1, 8, 9.
31 For modern examples of minority accommodation leadership acceding to the essential legitimacy of the majority-dominated political system see: ***Brass***, pp. 34–35, 39; M.S. Dhami, ***Minority Leaders' Image of the Indian Political System*** (New Delhi, 1975), pp. 27–28, 35, 57. For a discussion of the threat that the power of the state represents to ethnic élites in modern developing countries, see: ***Brass***, pp. 27–36.
32 Birkenthal, pp. 55–57, 65–67, 75, 89, 94, 102, 107, 120, 135, 148–149, 152, 156–158, 162, 167–168, 176–177 (Dov also has some uncomplimentary things to say about particular noblemen of his acquaintance, see pp. 74, 85, 106–107, 170); ***Korot Moshe Wasserzug*** (The Life of Moshe Wasserzug), H. Loewe, ed. (Berlin, 1911) pp. 6, 15–17, 19, 23–27.
33 Despite its relatively late date, there are good grounds for believing that many of the traditions recounted in Shivhei Ha-Besht are authentic; see M.J. Rosman, 'Międzybóż and Rabbi Israel Ba'al Shem Tov' (Hebrew), ***Tsion*** 52 (1987), pp. 177–189; idem, 'The Quest for the Historical Ba'al Shem Tov,' ***Tradition and Crisis Revisited*** (Harvard Center for Jewish Studies: in preparation).
34 SB Nos.4, 23, 30, 41, 69, 77, 82, 103, 123, 150, 167, 171, 180, 198, 218, 224, 229, 232, 235.
35 ***Exclusiveness and Tolerance***, pp. 56–63; ***Tradition and Crisis***, pp. 35–42.
36 SB, No.90.
37 SB, No.236.
38 ***Ma'ase Tuviah*** (The Exploits of Tobias), (Venice, 1707), p. 110d.
39 Earlier in the text Tobias had remarked that Poland had a large population and was richly endowed with water resources.
40 ***The Autobiography of Solomon Maimon***, J. Clark Murray, trans. (London, 1888, reprinted 1954), pp. 11–13.

5

THE CHANGES IN THE ATTITUDE OF POLISH SOCIETY TOWARD THE JEWS IN THE EIGHTEENTH CENTURY

Jacob Goldberg

The transformations in the social structure, politics and culture of 18th-century Poland had their impact upon the evolution of the predominant attitudes of Polish society towards the Jews. The large numbers of the latter constituted in the second half of the century the largest concentration of Jews in the world. They amounted to about 1,000,000 or 10 per cent of the country's population,[1] which means that their numbers roughly equalled those of the *szlachta*. This is why in the last century of the Commonwealth's existence, the demographic factor determined Polish attitudes towards the Jews far more than ever before. However, the growth in the demographic potential of the Jewish population coincided with the impact of the ideas of the Enlightenment, with the result that the two factors compounded one another in rendering all problems concerning the Jews highly visible and in considerably influencing the designs for social and political reforms at the time of the Four-Year Diet. I wish to call attention here to those aspects of the process which have been overlooked or neglected in the rather scanty and mostly obsolete literature on the subject. Furthermore, in my own study, *Poles and Jews in the 17th and 18th Centuries: Rejection or Acceptance*,[2] I failed to address some pertinent issues, which are dealt with here.

The fact that Polish attitudes towards the Jews were subject to an evolution over time can best be assessed through a comparison between the realities of the first and second halves of the century. The comparison would have to be carried out in terms of (1) the growth or decline of extreme forms of anti-Jewish repression; (2) fiscal burdens; (3) the degree to which the enlightened part of the *szlachta* and the magnates sympathized with the economic hardships of the Jews; (4) the attitude of the Catholic clergy; (5) the differences in the respective standpoints of the advocates of the early and advanced forms of the Enlightenment; (6)

hostility between the Jews and the burghers; (7) factors conditioning the peasant attitudes towards the Jews; and (8) the remedial measures for improvement of mutual relationships advocated by various figures within Polish society.

As is known, hatred of the Jews reached its highest intensity during the period of the cultural decline which marked the first half of the century. During that period, xenophobia and obscurantism gained momentum.[3] Never in the history of Poland were the repressive measures against the Jews so brutal, nor the anti-Jewish attitudes of the Poles so widespread and extreme.[4] Repression against the Jews was harsher than against any other ethnic or religious minority. True, the Armenians were pressured to join the Uniate Church, and the events accompanying the so-called Toruń tumult of 1724 point to the growing tendency to persecute the Protestants.[5] A commission was set up by the assessorial court in Toruń to investigate the affair of the desecration of a Catholic procession and Catholic relics by German students of a Protestant high school. The commission issued 16 death verdicts (four of which were against town mayors), some with additional rigours attached, such as quartering of the body or amputation of the hand prior to the execution. Yet the case was isolated, in that neither before nor afterwards did anti-Protestant reprisals reach comparable extremes of severity. On the other hand the case does bear resemblance to the numerous blood libel cases which took place in the Commonwealth at that period. (Their exact number is not known.) Unlike the Toruń verdict, these cases were by no means isolated. They are to be regarded as the most extreme and repressive measures used against the Jews. Throughout the 18th century, the blood libel trials almost always ended in collective death verdicts for something in the area of a dozen Jews each time, and the forms of execution tended to be similar to those applied against the German Protestants in the 1724 Toruń case.[6] It should also be pointed out that, rather significantly, the growth in the incidence of blood libel cases was concurrent with the proliferation of indictments for witchcraft. Forty-six per cent of all the witchcraft trials which took place in Poland between the 16th and 18th centuries occurred in the years 1701–50.[7] Simultaneously some 17 trials against Jews took place; the Jews were accused primarily of using the blood of Christian children.[8] In nearly all instances, the trials of witches ended with the condemnation of innocent Polish burghers or peasant women to the stake.[9] Originally, both the blood libel and the witchcraft trials had been imports from Western Europe.[10] But for nearly 300 years, both institutions found hospitable ground in Poland, and the first half of the 18th century marks the apogee of their popularity. The witchcraft trials – which, after all, took a much heavier toll of victims than the blood libel trials of Jews, for the number of those innocently indicted peasant women and townswomen runs in the thousands[11] – begin to disappear only under the influence of the culture of the Enlightenment, which spread to the Polish Commonwealth in the second half of the 18th century. Four per cent of the total number of witchcraft trials still took place in that period, the last of which in 1775.[12] All of those trials ended in death by torture. During the same period, six trials were held against Jews accused of using blood for ritual purposes. The last took place in 1786.[13]

Proceeding to fiscal matters, we need to point out that from about 1600 until 1764 these constituted virtually the sole area of Jewish-related concern on the part of state authorities, the Diets and the Dietines.[14] *Inter alia*, this concern manifested itself in attempts to turn the collection of Jewish taxes into a repressive measure. It began in the second half of the 17th century when revenues from the Jewish Pogłówne (poll tax) were allocated as 'Gifts to the Tatars', or ransom paid to the Tatars to make them desist from forays into the Commonwealth's territory. When in 1662 the State Treasury did not receive the Jewish Pogłówne by the deadline, the Crown Treasurer Jan Kazimierz Krasiński ordered that Jews be rounded up on the roads and at the fairs, with the professed aim of delivering them to the Tatars in lieu of the ransom. Naturally, the Jews took the threat seriously and paid the overdue amount, as a result of which the delivery of the captured Jews to the Tatars as a 'gift' did not take place.[15] Several proposals for fiscal repression against the Jews were motivated by fear of the growth of the Jewish population. An example is the speech of Deputy Horain of the Wilno voivodship at the Diet of 1744. Horain proposed 'reducing the Jewish numbers by making them abstain from matrimony until they reached the age of 30; and then imposing payments in talers, in proportion to the missing years on all youths, male and female alike, who nevertheless insist on marrying'.[16] Such ideas are not to be looked upon as oddities, for they were typical manifestations of negative attitudes towards Jews characteristic of the Polish political culture at the time.[17] But whether due to the anarchic mode of the Diets' proceedings or to the countervailing efforts of Jewish lobbyists, such suggestions failed to materialize as laws. To be sure, the Diet of 1775 did enact a law proscribing the marriages of Jews who had insufficient resources to pay taxes: but indolence and the ineffectuality of the state machinery foiled its enforcement.[18]

In the years which followed, however, the issue of Jewish marriages ceased to be discussed by publicists and by deputies to the Diet eager to use reprisals against Jews or impose fiscal burdens. Now the subject was broached from an entirely new angle. The new suggestion was to alter the age structure of Jewish brides and bridegrooms in such a way as to provide young Jewish couples with basic economic security. Their purposes coincided with *maskilic* ideas for Jewish reform, and their appearance shows that an 'enlightened' segment of Polish society was changing its attitudes towards the Jews. But as a group they lacked understanding of the opposition to their views among traditional Jews.

Let us now proceed to the attitude of enlightened Poles towards the economic hardships to which the Commonwealth Jews were subjected in the 18th century. The crucial problem here was the enormous indebtedness of Jewish communities to the Church and to the *szlachta*. Towards the end of the century the problem of this indebtedness increasingly absorbed the attention of the Diet deputies and of the newly established organs of state administration. The problem was aggravated by the abolition of the Jesuit order in 1773 and the subsequent takeover of the Jesuit property and financial stock by the Commission for National Education. It turned out that some former Jesuit capital was frozen in the form of the so-called Jewish debts which could not be exacted. Obviously this matter, documented by an exceptionally abundant supply of historical sources, has attracted considerable attention from Polish historians.[19] A study by Sobczak which appeared several years ago attributes Jewish indebtedness to the devastation of the towns and to the economic decline during the first half of the 18th century.[20] But Sobczak gives no indication that attitudes towards Jews contributed. Although overlooked by Sobczak, this factor actually was of crucial significance. It must be borne in mind that in order to fend off persecutions and the imposition of legal and administrative restrictions, as well as to secure the right to live and work in the cities and freedom of worship, the Jews had to bribe virtually all existing institutions.[21] The expenditure thus incurred included not only overt payments, for example to Church institutions and parish priests, but also a variety of ordinary bribes. In the year 1788 representatives of Warsaw burghers claimed that 'Jews borrowed money from clergy, and people of secular professions, ostensibly for the sake of securing the debts, and made the Jewish communites responsible for them', and that 'having borrowed all this money, the Jews got themselves protectors'[22] [who were paid by the Jews in due course]. Jan Stanisław Jabłonowski, author of a pamphlet published in 1730, compares the Jews with the treasurers, who were known for their corruption. As he put it: 'It can be truly said about [the treasurers] what is said about the Jews: whoever speaks about them favourably, receives their reward, and whoever is against them, merely desires to receive one.'[23] It is noteworthy that over half a century later an enlightened magnate, Andrzej Ogiński, dealt with the same subject, but from a perspective strikingly different from that of Jabłonowski: Ogiński saw the economic hardships of the Jews as stemming from the need to bribe multifarious officials. In his *Economic Instruction Sheet for Persons Performing Economic Services* (1786), Ogiński wrote that a Jew 'must keep a teacher for his children, must save for the dowry for his sons and daughters, must pay the rabbi, must pay dues to the community he belongs to so that the latter can receive supplies and pay its debts, must support the communities' elders, must contribute to its legal expenses, must help maintain the synagogue and prayer services, must finance his own lawsuits and disputes . . . and still cannot receive even half his due justice . . . without gifts and payments.'[24] If Jabłonowski had not gone beyond the observation that the Jews used to pay bribes, Ogiński showed an understanding of the conditions of life in Jewish society and of the causes of the inordinate expenditures borne by Jewish communities in the Polish Commonwealth.

In the second half of the 18th century certain circles began to reveal concern creating the conditions which would enable the Jewish communities to repay the debts contracted from clerical institutions and the *szlachta*.[25] This proved to be a factor which restrained the anti-Jewish repression initiated by the burghers and also brought about a more moderate attitude of a part of Polish society towards the Jews. The stand in the matter of Andrzej Młodziejowski, the Crown Grand Chancellor and the Bishop of Poznań is more representative. In a letter written on 17 August 1744 he demanded from the Lublin *starosta*, 'Find a way to make the Lublin merchants stop persecuting Jews and commiting those acts of outrage. The Jewish community in Lublin and the provinces took out a considerable mortgage from the clergy; nearly every one of them owes money either to the *szlachta* or to persons of other status. If they continue to be persecuted by the merchants and wronged in their property rights, their creditors will be those to be most harmed.' In a *post scriptum* to the same letter, the Crown Grand Chancellor expressed his basic attitude to the Jews, which was so characteristic of the changes taking place in Poland during the age of Enlightenment. He wrote, 'The Lublin Merchant Guild knows well that I do not favour the Jews and will not allow it that they should breed in the town, but I cannot persecute them with impunity.'[26]

The Catholic Church always exercised an overpowering influence upon the attitudes of Poles towards the Jews. The role of the Church was particularly prominent in the first half of the 18th century: i.e. in the period of intensified religious intolerance and at the same time of advanced disintegration of the Polish state. As an outcome of this latter process, the Church became the only powerful and effectual institution in the Polish Commonwealth.[27] Rulings enjoining the Christians to segregate themselves from Jews and to distrust them were passed in resolutions of provincial synods, included in the pastoral letters of Polish bishops and disseminated through sermons, which then were the most efficient medium of communication. It was the pamphlet 'Sekret żydowskiej przewrotności wyjawiony i światu polskiemu w przestrodze pożytecznej pokazany' [The secret of Jewish perfidy revealed and presented to the Polish public as a useful warning], written by Wilno Jesuits and several times re-published after 1700, which served as a major source for general opinions about the Jews as pronounced from the pulpits. The contents of the pamphlet lacked originality: for the most part it reiterated the familiar story of the alleged talmudically-prescribed hatred of Jews for the Christians.

Already in the first half of the 18th century some Polish bishops took a positive stand towards the Jews, but their dissent lacked firmness or consistency. The most prominent among them was the Bishop of Volhynia, Franciszek Kobielski, who after having protected the Jews, protested in the Diet of 1748 against new tax burdens to be imposed upon them. He was the first Polish clergyman to preach in synagogues. He also published appeals, in Polish, calling upon the Jews to convert to Catholicism. But his pro-Jewish sympathies, motivated as they merely were by the hope of inducing the Jews to convert, turned out to be short-lived. Once his missionary endeavours ended in resounding failure, he shifted to hatred and harrassment of the Jews, to the point of sponsoring blood libel suits. He cooled down only after the Jewish representatives complained to the Pope, who referred the matter to the nuncio in Warsaw for investigation.[28]

However, the learned Bishop of Kujawy, Józef Andrzej Załuski, who is considered a representative of the early Enlightenment in Poland, wrote an essay under the heading 'La Pologne, dite Paradis de Juifs', in which he refuted the then widespread claim that the Talmud enjoins the Jews to kill Christian children. Probably as a result of the intervention of Frankists, he was compelled to withdraw from this position. He excused his withdrawal by the impossibility of analysing more precisely this complex matter. Yet he wrote at the same time that though admittedly a Jew who hates Christians is capable of killing a Christian child, the whole nation should not be indicted for crimes committed by individuals.[29] This dualism characterized the attitude of the Catholic Church in the Polish Commonwealth in the age of the early Enlightenment not only in matters regarding Jews but in several other issues.[30]

On the other hand, the most outstanding advocate of early Enlightenment in Poland, Father Stanisław Konarski, portrayed the Jews in his writings in a very unfavourable light, to the point of positing the need for imposing restrictions upon their entrepreneurial activities.[31]

Among the secular personalities the most typical representatives of the attitudes of the early Enlightenment towards the Jews were Stefan Garczyński, Voivoda (Palatine) of Poznań, and Stanisław Poniatowski, father of King Stanisław August. Derogatory opinions about the Jews were expressed in their writings, but they did not affect the practical steps taken by their authors. As a Voivoda of Poznań, Garczyński was known for his favourable adjudications of those administrative cases concerning the Jews that were brought to his attention. It cannot be precluded that, as was then the custom, he received money or gifts for such adjudication, but this would still mean that his hostility towards the Jews was neither consistent nor ruthless. As for Poniatowski, he donated a quite considerable amount of money for relief of the Jewish poor living in the town of Jazłowiec, which he owned.[32]

None of the representatives of the early Enlightenment in the Commonwealth formulated any programme for solving the Jewish question. All that they (in particular Konarski) did formulate, were proposals for proscriptive legislation. This limitation of the early Enlightenment was transcended between 1770 and 1780, that is, in the era of the advanced Enlightenment. These two decades marked the crystallization of the view point that the situation of the Jews was in need of reform. But at the same time the evaluation of some Jewish customs and of traits attributed to the Jews changed. Even though offensive and condescending references to the Jews continued to appear in contemporary writings, their form and style was already different. The espousal of the reform approach implied the abandonment of the idea previously held not only by the clergy but also by the considerable segment of *szlachta*, namely, the idea of conversion to Christianity as the only solution of the Commonwealth's Jewish problem. Even some clergymen now opposed this idea openly, the best case in point being the Bishop of Wilno and one of the founders of the Commission for National Education, Ignacy Massalski. Not a figure of singular personal integrity but nonetheless a fervent advocate of the ideas of Enlightenment, Massalski condemned the practice of kidnapping Jewish children for the sake of baptizing them, and opposed the intensification of proselytizing efforts aiming at the Jews.[33] Likewise Father Jan Bohomolec, while discussing in his sermons the custom of referring to the Jews as 'faithless' people, agreed that they were indeed faithless, but at the same time insisted that 'their faithlessness is more innocent than our faith, for they abide by what we also recognise as God's commandments, while we do not so abide.'[34]

The economic situation inclined a segment of the *szlachta* and some magnates to a favourable attitude to the Jews as early as the first half of the 18th century. At that time the Jews constituted a demographic reserve which could populate the villages and small towns, ravaged by war and disease. For the above reasons a delegation of deputies to the *Sejm* complained to the Primate and bishops in 1720, saying that '. . . landed property and the *szlachta* hereditary towns are bound to decline, when some of the "honourable" clergy find any pretext to be against the Jews or other non-Catholic persons, such as tradesmen, merchants, stallkeepers . . . as a result of which towns become deserted.'[35] They also had in mind the disastrous state of the depopulated towns which belonged to the clergy. One of the reasons for this state of affairs was undoubtedly the fact that the Jewish population was forbidden to enter the towns owned by the clergy.[36]

A certain polarization of attitudes toward the Jews was bound to occur. On the one hand, *Gazeta Warszawska* under Father Łuskina's editorship continued to attack the Jews in the old style, resorting to obscurantist arguments which included the blood libel theme.[37] On the other hand, Łuskina was attacked by *Pamiętnik Historyczno-Polityczny* under the editorship of an ex-Jesuit Piotr Świtkowski, who, along with Piotr Butrymowicz and the leading advocate of Polish Enlightenment Vice Chancellor Hugo Kołłątaj, stood for a programme of reforms aiming at a rapprochement between the Jews and the Poles.[38] Such a rapprochement was partly conceived in terms of Jewish assimilation, and partly in terms of the abolition of a number of traditional Jewish institutions, such as *Kehillah* (demanded by Kołłątaj).[39] The latter programme had its opponent in the person of Józef Pawlikowski, a *szlachcic* and subsequently a Jacobin. Of all advocates of Enlightenment in Poland, Pawlikowski was most pro-Jewish. He was probably alone among contemporary Poles in his full identification with the need to preserve Jewish traditions.[40] When Kołłątaj proposed to prohibit the Jews from wearing a distinct garb, Pawlikowski opposed the idea forcefully: 'We have agreed to be tolerant of their religion. By what logic, then, shall we now interfere with it, with its holidays, with its fasts? Why should we be towards them like the Spaniards of old? Let us not force them to change their garb! Let us instead act towards them so as to make them feel not aggrieved but happy with being Poles.'[41]

A different position in regard to Jewish traditions was expounded by another prominent advocate of Polish Enlightenment, Stanisław Staszic. Staszic granted that 'Jews are superior to us [i.e. the Poles] in the ways in which they establish the authority of fathers and husbands and in their marital regulations.' But in contrast to Pawlikowski, Staszic, who was a fervent enemy of the Jews, considered it necessary to suppress Jewish distinctness.[42]

Staszic represented the interests of the renascent Polish burgher class, which perceived the Jews as economic competitors and fought them vigorously.[43] In Warsaw, the burghers demanded the deportation of the city's Jewish population on the basis of the privilege *De Non Tolerandis Iudaeis* which had been granted to the Polish capital in the 16th century.[44] This was the background of the pogrom of 1790 in Warsaw, which also had reverberations in the provinces. The growing hostility between the burghers and the Jews was also responsible for the 1791 anti-Jewish violence in Łęczyca, sparked by a burgher dispute with Jewish leaseholders of town inns.[45] But the burghers were not united against the Jews, for already in 1792 a group of Łęczyca burghers jointly with the town's *szlachta* filed with the police a complaint on behalf of Jews harassed by the municipality.[46] Acting in his capacity of Vice Chancellor, Kołłątaj called upon the Łęczyca municipality to desist from further persecutions of the Jews, and shortly afterwards protested against harassment of the Jews in Cracow.[47] Moreover, in May 1792 Kołłątaj wrote a letter to the Speaker of the Four-Year Diet, Stanisław Małachowski, urging him to investigate

Jewish matters, 'lest the persecution of Jews be launched not just in Warsaw, but in the whole of Poland . . .'.[48]

The burgher attitudes towards the Jews found expression in demands voiced in the era of the Four-Year Diet by the newly-arisen burgher political movement. At the rallies electing the delegates to the burgher convocation in Warsaw, resolutions were passed against granting municipal citizenship to the Jews; and at some of these rallies demands were even made to prohibit Jewish settlement in the towns.[49] There were only a few exceptions: several towns in Lithuania, Piotrków in central Poland, and the towns in the vicinity of Sieradz, where the passage of such resolutions was blocked by the area's native son, the Jacobin Józef Pawlikowski whom we have already mentioned.[50] There was still another exception: the mutual economic cooperation agreements concluded by burghers of several towns with the local Jewish communities. Such agreements involved the burgher's consent to granting the Jews municipal citizenship.[51]

Yet the overwhelming majority of Polish society was composed of a peasantry which throughout remained totally unaffected by the ideas and the programmes of the Enlightenment. The attitudes of the peasants towards the Jews were determined by two facts. First, by the time-honoured and petrified notions about the Jews retained in peasant consciousness throughout generations. And second, by the ever-intensifying conflicts with Jews leasing inns from the landowners. Since within their estates, the *szlachta* had a monopoly on the production and sale of vodka and beer, the peasant in search of a drink had no choice but to go the inn leased by the Jew. In the process, the former was often stripped of his last penny and sometimes also of a cow, a horse, or other belongings. As if this were not enough, the peasants owed serf labour to Jewish innkeepers, a fact which further contributed to inflaming mutual hostility. The conflict was particularly intense in royal villages where the peasants had the right to bring lawsuits against the Jews.[52] Interestingly, however, there exists no documentary evidence that would warrant linking the Polish peasant attitudes towards the Jews either with the Cossack rebellions of the beginning of the century in the eastern parts of the Commonwealth, or with the Hadjamak riots, which subsequently lasted for decades and which were also directed against the Jews. In this respect the situation changed markedly from the 17th century when the slogans of Chmielnicki and the Cossack pogroms of Jews found resonance in the Polish rural population.[53] Jacek Jezierski, the Castellan of Łuków and other Polish reformers of the Age of Enlightenment, headed by Kołłątaj, were still incapable of preventing the growing conflict of interests between peasants and Jews.[54] Yet they attempted to pursue this goal by introducing a new restriction, namely by forbidding the Jews to take on the leases of inns, distilleries or breweries in villages and towns. But at the same time Kołłątaj in his *Political Right of the Polish Nation* wrote that 'the human rights of Jews are to be respected no less than the rights of any other human beings.'[55] This sentence epitomizes the direction of the change which the advocates of Enlightenment in the Commonwealth intended to bring about for the sake of reshaping the whole configuration of mutual relationships between the Jews and the Poles.

NOTES

1 Z. Sułowski, 'Mechanizmy ekspansji demograficznej Żydów w miastach polskich XVI–XIX wieku', in: *Zeszyty Naukowe Katolickiego Uniwersytetu Lubelskiego*, vol. 17 (1974), no. 3, p. 95.

2 J. Goldberg, 'Poles and Jews in the 17th and 18th centuries. Rejection or acceptance', in: *Jahrbücher für Geschichte Osteuropas*, vol. 22 (1974), no. 2, pp. 248–82.

3 *Rzeczpospolita w dobie upadku 1700–1740. Wybór źródeł*. Ed. J. Gierowski (Wrocław, 1955), pp. 89–116; H. Olszewski, *Doktryny prawno – ustrojowe czasów saskich (1697–1740)* (Warsaw, 1961); J. Michalski, 'Sarmatyzm a europeizacja Polski w XVIII wieku', in: *Swojskość i cudzoziemczyzna w dziejach kultury polskiej* (Warsaw, 1973), pp. 114–28.

4 N. M. Gelber, 'Die Taufbewegung unter den polnischen Juden im XVIII. Jahrhundert', in: *Monatsschrift für Geschichte und Wissenschaft des Judentums*, vol. 32 (1924), pp. 226–7.

5 S. Salmonowicz, 'O problematyce politycznej i prawnej tzw. tumultu toruńskiego z 1724 roku', in: *Czasopismo Prawno – Historyczne*, vol. 24 (1972), no. 1, pp. 223–37; J. Feldman, 'Sprawa dysydencka za Augusta II', in: *Reformacja w Polsce*, vol. 3 (1924), p. 89; S. Salmonowicz, 'O sytuacji prawnej protestantów w Polsce (XVI–XVIII w.)', in: *Czasopismo Prawno – Historyczne*, vol. 26 (1974), no. 1, pp. 172–3; J. Dworzaczkowa, 'Reformacja a problemy narodowościowe w przedrozbiorowej Wielkopolsce', in: *Odrodzenie i Reformacja w Polsce*, vol. 23 (1978), pp. 91–2.

6 S. Żuchowski, 'Proces kryminalny o niewinne dziecię Jana Krasnowskiego. w.p. 1713'; 'Dekret o zamęczeniu przez Żydów dziecięcia katolickiego ferowany w grodzie żytomirskim, w.p. 1753'; S. Załęski, *Jezuici w Polsce*, vol. 3 (Kraków, 1902), p. 673.

7 Calculated according to the date by B. Baranowski, *Procesy czarownic w Polsce w XVII i XVIII wieku* (Łódź, 1952), p 29.

8 Calculated according to the date by Gelber, 'Die Taufbewegung unter den polnischen Juden im XVIII. Jahrhundert', pp. 227–8.

9 Baranowski, *Procesy czarownic w Polsce w XVII i XVIII wieku*, pp. 76–81; see: B. Groicki, 'Postępek sądów około karania na gardle', in: B. Groicki, *Artykuły prawa majdeburskiego. Postępek sądów około karania na gardle. Ustawa płacej u sądów*, Ed. K. Koranyi (Warsaw, 1954), pp. 117, 123. First Edition 1559.

10 'This case is taken from the Rights of Emperors which Emperor Carl V had given in all his countries which are given those teachings in which cases the verdict of death should be pronounced', Groicki, 'Postępek sądów około karania na gardle', p. 101; J. Tazbir, 'Procesy o czary', in: *Odrodzenie i Reformacja w Polsce*, vol. 23 (1978), pp. 152–5.

11 Baranowski, *Procesy o czary w Polsce w XVII i XVIII wieku*, pp. 30–1, 175; Tazbir, 'Procesy o czary', p. 152.

12 Baranowski, *Procesy czarownic w Polsce w XVII i XVIII wieku*, pp. 66–72, 29. To be

sure, sporadic cases of blood libel and witchcraft accusations were to persist throughout the nineteenth century into the twentieth, but without outcomes as ghastly as in earlier times.

13 Gelber, 'Die Taufbewegung unter den polnischen Juden im XVIII. Jahrhundert', pp. 227–8.

14 A. Pawiński, *Dzieje ziemi kujawskiej oraz akta historyczne do nich służące* (Warsaw, 1888), p. 99.

15 Roman Rybarski, the leading scholar of the Polish Treasury and the leader of the anti-semitic Stronnictwo Narodowe wrote in this connection, 'Jan Kazimierz Krasiński, the Crown Treasurer applied *the most interesting measures to the execution of the taxes* . . .' (emph. J. G); R. Rybarski, *Skarb i pieniądz za Jana Kazimierza, Michała Korybuta i Jana III* (Warsaw, 1939), p. 223.

16 'Dyaryusz sejmu ordynaryjnego, sześcioniedzielnego grodzieńskiego in anno 1744', in: M. Skibiński, *Europa a Polska w dobie wojny o sukcesyę austryjacką w latach 1740–1745*, vol. 2 (Cracow, 1912), p. 312; see: I. Halpern, 'Nisuei behalah be-Mizrah Eiropa', *Zion*, vol. 27 (1962), no. 1–2, pp. 36–58.

17 Olszewski, *Doktryny prawno – ustrojowe czasów saskich (1697–1740)*, pp. 136, 181, 187, 197–8, 294.

18 J. Goldberg, 'Die Ehe bei den Juden Polens im 18.Jahrhundert', in: *Jahrbücher für Geschichte Osteuropas*, vol. 31 (1983), p. 495.

19 S. Muznerowski, *Krzepice w przeszłości* (Włocławek, 1914), pp. 97–9. *Wojewódzkie Archiwum Państwowe*, Lublin, Lubelskie Grodzkie RMO No. 385/21544, folio 830–860; No. 383/21542, folio 74,722–723; Krasnystaw Grodzkie RMO 80/19799, folio 748–748v; Chełm Grodzkie RMO 20270/186, folio 201–203; *Wojewódzkie Archiwum Państwowe*, Kraków, Archiwum Sanguszków, Teki tzw. arabskie, Teka 50; *Archiwum Państwowe*, Poznań, Kaliskie Ins. No. 130 Hub. 133, pp. 572–6; *Archiwum Główne Akt Dawnych*, Warszawa/AGAD/, Zbiór Czołowskiego No. 3101.

20 J. Sobczak, 'Zadłużenie kahałów żydowskich w końcu XVIII wieku w świetle obliczeń sądu ziemiańskiego w Kaliszu', in; *Rocznik Kaliski*, vol. 11 (1978), pp. 108–9.

21 *Acta Electorum Communitatis Judaeorum Posnaniensum* (1621–1835). Ed. A. Avron (Jerusalem, 1966), p. 41; I. Lewin, 'Udział Żydów w wyborach sejmowych w dawnej Polsce', in: *Miesięcznik Żydowski*, vol. 2 (1932), no. 1–6, pp. 46–65; T. Zielińska, 'Mechanizm sejmikowy i klientela radziwiłłowska za Sasów', in: *Przegląd Historyczny*, vol. 62 (1971), no. 4.

22 'Ekspozycyja praw miasta Warszawy względem Żydów oraz odpowiedź na żadana przez nich w tymże mieście lokacyja', in: *Materiały do dziejów Sejmu Czteroletniego*, vol. 2 (Warsaw, 1959), p. 27. In this matter the Jews quoted the arguments of their opponents in 'Wyłuszczenie praw wolnego mieszkania i handlu Żydów w Warszawie pozwalających, z odpowiedzią na pisma magistratu warszawskiego przeciw Zydom r. 1789 wydanej', in: *Materiały do dziejów Sejmu Czteroletniego*, vol. 6 (Wrocław, Warsaw, Cracow, 1969), p. 35.

23 [J. S. Jabłonowski], *Skrupuł bez skrupułu w Polszcze albo oświecenie grzechów narodowi polskiemu zwyczajniejszych*, w.p. 1730.

24 'Instruktarz ekonomiczny dla ludzi będących w służbie gospodarskiej do druku podany w Warszawie w drukarni Nadwornej J. K. Mości i Prześwietnej Komisyi Edukacyi Narodowej w roku 1786', in: *Polskie Instruktarze ekonomiczne z końca XVII i z XVIII wieku*, Ed. S. Pawlik, vol. 1 (Cracow, 1915), p. 252.

25 See: A. Zahorski, *Ignacy Wyssogota Zakrzewski prezydent Warszawy* (Warsaw, 1963), pp. 50–1.

26 The copy of the letter of Chancellor Andrzej Młodziejowski, Łopaciński Library in Lublin Ms. 109.

27 E. Rostworowski, 'Spór Stefana Garczyńskiego z braćmi Załuskimi o rolę

duchowieństwa w "Anatomii Rzeczypospolitej"', in: *O naprawę Rzeczypospolitej XVII–XVIII. Prace ofiarowane Władysławowi Czaplińskiemu w 60 rocznicę* urodzin (Warsaw, 1965), p. 230.

28 J. Goldberg, 'Die getauften Juden in Polen – Litauen im 16.–18.Jahrhundert. Taufe, soziale Umschichtung und Integration', in: *Jahrbücher für Geschichte Osteuropas*, vol. 30 (1982), no. 1, pp. 63–4.

29 S. Turowski, 'Polska rajem dla Żydów, ('la Pologne, ditte des Juifs' przez Józefa Andrzeja Załuskiego. 1760 r. Rękopis'), in: *Kwartalnik Poświęcony Badaniu Przeszłości Żydów w Polsce*, vol. 1 (1912), no. 3, pp. 72–100; see: S. Kot, *Polska rajem dla Żydów, piekłem dla chłopów, niebem dla szlachty* (Warsaw, 1937), p. 27.

30 J.Gierowski, 'U źródeł polskiego Oświecenia', in: *Wiek XVIII. Polska i świat. Księga poświęcona Bogusławowi Leśnodorskiemu* (Warsaw, 1974), p. 47. J. Gierowski, 'Kościół katolicki wobec wczesnego Oświecenia w Polsce', in: *Roczniki Humanistyczne*, vol. 25 (1977), No. 2, p. 28. S. Kot in his discussion of these matters regarded the essay of Załuski as unequivocally anti-Jewish, since research on the early Enlightenment in Poland had not been developed yet, see: *Polska rajem dla Żydów, piekłem dla chłopów, niebem dla szlachty*, p. 27.

31 S. Konarski, *O skutecznym rad sposobie albo o utrzymywaniu ordynaryjnych seymów*, vol. 2 (Warsaw, 1761), p. 6; S. Konarski, 'O uszczęśliwieniu własnej ojczyzny', in: *Pisma wybrane*. Ed. J. Nowak-Dłużewski, vol. 2 (Warsaw, 1955), p. 347.

32 For their views, see S. Garczyński, *Anatomia Rzeczypospolitej Polskiej* (Wrocław, 1751), pp. 8, 133–4, 141 and S. Poniatowski, 'List ziemianina do pewnego przyjaciela z innego województwa', in: K. Kantecki, *Stanisław Poniatowski kasztelan krakowski, ojciec Stanisława Augusta*, vol. 2 (Poznań, 1880), p. XCIII. For Garczyński's actions L. Wegner, 'Stefan Garczyński wojewoda poznański i dzieło jego Anatomi Rzeczypospolitej Polskiej (1706–1755)', in: *Roczniki Towarzystwa Przyjaciół Nauk Poznańskiego*, vol. 6 (1871), p. 18. When Stanisław Poniatowski granted the privilege to the Jewish community of Jazłowiec in Podolia in 1753, he donated the substantial sum of 10,000 złotys to the community, part of which was devoted to the relief of poor Jews to assist them in the development of Trade, *Jewish Privileges in the Polish Commonwealth. Charters of Rights Granted to Jewish Communities in Poland-Lithuania in the Sixteenth to Eighteenth Centuries*. Ed. J. Goldberg (Jerusalem, 1985), p. 104.

33 J. Kurczewski, *Biskupstwo wileńskie* (Wilno, 1912), p. 506. Goldberg, 'Die getauften Juden in Polen-Litauen im 16.–18. Jahrhundert', p. 67.

34 J. Ch. Bohomolec, 'Nauka dla włościan o zacności stanu małżeńskiego przez Jana Chryzostoma Bohomolca proboszcza Pragi i Karyszewa własnoręcznie w testamencie jego napisana r. 1793', in: *Starożytności Warszawy*. Ed. A. Wejnert, vol. 4 (Warsaw, 1856), p. 132; E. Ringelblum, 'The Underside of the Inner Life of the Jews at Warsaw in the 18th Century', in: *Fun Noentn Ever*, (Yiddish) vol. 1 (1937), p. 181; Goldberg, 'Poles and Jews in the 17th and 18th Centuries', p. 256.

35 J. Podoski, *Teka*, vol. 2. Ed. K. Jarochowski (Poznań, 1855), p. 42; see also p. 47.

36 W. Rusiński, 'O rynku wewnętrznym w Polsce w drugiej połowie XVIII w.', in: *Roczniki Dziejów Społecznych i Gospodarczych*, vol. 16 (1954), p. 121.

37 E. Ringelblum, 'Żydzi w świetle prasy warszawskiej wieku XVIII-go', in: *Miesięcznik Żydowski*, vol. 2 (1932), pp. 459–518; see: J. Łojek, *'Gazeta Warszawska' księdza Łuskiny* (1774–1793) (Warsaw, 1959).

38 The book, *De la Reforme des Juifs par Mr C. G. Dohm Conseller de guerre etc. Traduit de p. Allemand*, 1782 was given a good press by Świtkowski, *Pamiętnik Historyczno – Polityczny*, vol. 7 (1783), pp. 58–62; 'Myśli względem założenia osad żydowskich po wsiach', *ibidem*, vol. 8 (1785), pp. 414–23; 'Uwagi względem reformy Żydów uprojektowanej przez jw Butrymowicza', in: *Pamiętnik Historyczno – Polityczno – Ekonomiczny*, vol. 13 (1789), pp. 1153–4, 1160–7; I. Homola-

Dzikowska, *Pamiętnik Historyczno-Polityczny Piotra Świtkowskiego 1782–1792* (Cracow, 1960), pp. 209–12; see also: E. Ringelblum, 'Zydzi w świetle prasy warszawskiej wieku XVIII – go'. W. Smoleński, *Stan i sprawa Żydów polskich w XVIII wieku* (Warsaw, 1876); E. Deiches, *Sprawa żydowska w czasie Sejmu Wielkiego* (Lwów, 1891); N. M. Gelber, 'Żydzi i zagadnienie reformy Żydów na Sejmie Czteroletnim', in: *Miesięcznik Żydowski*, vol. 2 (1931), no. 10, pp. 326–44; no. 11, pp. 429–40; K. Zienkowska, *Jacek Jezierski kasztelan łukowski (1722–1805). Z dziejów szlachty polskiej XVIII w. Warszawa* (1963), pp. 188–92; H. Kołłątaj, *Listy Anonima i Prawo Polityczne Narodu Polskiego*, vol. 2. Ed. B. Leśnodorski, H. Wereszycka (Cracow, 1954), pp. 323–3; see also *Materiały do dziejów Sejmu Czteroletniego*, vol. 6.

39 Kołłątaj, *Prawo Polityczne Narodu Polskiego*, p. 332: 'Kahały i przykahałki znoszą się.'

40 [J. Pawlikowski], *Myśli polityczne dla Polski* (Warsaw, 1789), pp. 101–115. E. Rostworowski, 'Jakobin Józef Pawlikowski anonimowym autorem słynnych pism politycznych', in: *Kwartalnik Historyczny*, vol. 63 (1956), no. 1, pp. 74–94; T. Pawlikowski, S. Jaros, 'Kiedy i gdzie urodził się jakobin Józef Pawlikowski', in; *Kwartalnik Historyczny*, vol. 77 (1970), pp. 95–6; W. Olszewicz, 'Jeszcze o Józefie Pawlikowskim', in: *Kwartalnik Historyczny*, vol. 80 (1973), pp. 914–17; T. Pawlikowski, S. Jaros, 'Jeszcze raz o miejscu i dacie urodzenia jakobina Józefa Pawlikowskiego', in: *Kwartalnik Historyczny*, vol. 82 (1975), pp. 110–16; E. Rostworowski, 'Myśli polityczne Józefa Pawlikowskiego', in his *Legendy i fakty XVIII w.* especially p. 243. W. Kalinka, *Sejm Czteroletni*, vol. 2 (Cracow, 1896), pp. 536–7. I do not agree with Rostworowski that Józef Pawlikowski aimed at the assimilation of the Polish Jewry, see: ibidem, p. 244.

41 Kołłątaj, *Prawo Polityczne Narodu Polskiego*, vol. 2, p. 239; Pawlikowski, *Myśli polityczne dla Polski*, p. 113.

42 S. Staszic, 'O przyczynach szkodliwości Żydów i o środkach usposobienia ich, aby się społeczeństwu użytecznemi stali', in: *Gazeta Wieyska* (1818), no. 26, pp. 201–8; no. 27, pp. 209–16; no. 28, pp. 217–24; see: Goldberg, *Poles and Jews*, p. 257.

43 Kalinka, *Sejm Czteroletni*, vol. 2, p. 369; W. Smoleński, *Jan Dekert prezydent Starej Warszawy i sprawa miejska podczas Sejmu Wielkiego* (Warsaw, 1912), p. 12; W. Smoleński, 'Mieszczaństwo warszawskie w końcu wieki XVIII'. Ed. M. H. Serejski, A. Wierzbicki (Warsaw, 1976), pp. 102–3; J. Goldberg, 'Wystąpienie Hugona Kołłątaja w r.1791 w obronie Żydów w Łęczycy', in: *Biuletyn Żydowskiego Instytutu Historycznego*, vol. 21 (1957), pp. 14–18; J. Michalski, 'Rola polityczna mieszczaństwa warszawskiego w okresie Sejmu Czteroletniego', in: *Rocznik Warszawski*, Vol. 7 (1966), pp. 174–6; Zienkowska, *Jacek Jezierski kasztelan łukowski* (1722–1805), pp. 189–90; K. Zienkowska, *Sławetni i urodzeni. Ruch polityczny mieszczaństwa w dobie Sejmu Czteroletniego* (Warsaw, 1976), pp. 269–73; see: *Materiały do dziejów Sejmu Czteroletniego*, vol. 5 (Wrocław, Warsaw, Cracow, 1964); *Materiały do dziejów Sejmu Czteroletniego*, vol. 6.

44 AGAD Parchment Documents no. 1618, 1627, 6185; 'Przywileje królewskiego miasta stołecznego Starej Warszawy, 1376–1772'. Ed. T. Wierzbowski (Warsaw, 1913), no. 85; Y. Shatskii, *Geshikhte fun Yidn in Varshe* of vol. 1 (New York, 1947), p. 49.

45 Shatzkii, pp. 88–9; Kalinka, *Sejm Czteroletni*, vol. 2, p. 369; Smoleński, *Jan Dekert prezydent Starej Warszawy*, p. 12; Smoleński, 'Mieszczaństwo warszawskie w końcu wieku XVIII', pp. 158–61. Deiches, *Sprawa żydowska w czasie Sejmu Wielkiego*, pp. 52–3; F. Friedman, 'Odgłos warszawskiego "tumultu żydowskiego" w maju 1790 roku na prowincji.Tumult żydowski w Łęczycy w sierpniu 1790 r.', in: *Lodzer Wisenshaftleche Shryftn*, (Yiddish) vol. 1 (1938), pp. 247–51; Goldberg 'Wystąpienie Hugona Kołłątaja w r. 1791 w obronie Zydów w Łęczycy', pp. 15–17.

46 'Memoriał od obywatelów miasta Łęczycy do J. O. Komisyi Policji Obojga Narodów podany, zwłoki niecierpiący': 'Żydów także w mieście tym podług swoich przywilejów mieszkających i znacznym handlem bawiących się, już przez oddawanych podatków publicznych na swój użytek obrócenie, już przez wzbranianie budowania się na ich i własnych placach pokrzywdzają. Przez którą bezrządność i absolutności, nie tylko potrzebnych temu miastu rzemieślników odstręczają, ale też życzących municypalności związku szlachtę ... odsunęli', *AGAD* Archiwum Królestwa Polskiego no. 86/1, folio 99–99v.

47 Goldberg, 'Wystąpienie Hugona Kołłątaja w r. 1791 w obronie Żydów Łęczycy', p. 18; Deiches, *Sprawa żydowska w czasie Sejmu Wielkiego*, pp. 52–3.

48 B. Dembiński, 'Z listów Kołłątaja do marszałka Małachowskiego', in: *Kwartalnik Historyczny*, vol. 14 (1900), p. 632.

49 Materiały do dziejów Sejmu Czteroletniego, vol. 6, pp. 146–68; Michalski, *Rola polityczna mieszczaństwa warszawskiego w okresie Sejmu Czteroletniego*, pp. 174–5; Zienkowska, *Sławetni i urodzeni*, pp. 269–70.

50 Materiały do dziejów Sejmu Czteroletniego, vol. 6, pp. 148–66. See also Zienkowska, *Sławetni i urodzeni*, p. 349.

51 Goldberg, 'Poles and Jews in the 17th and 18th Centuries', pp. 278–9.

52 *Księgi Referendarii Koronnej z czasów saskich*. Sumariusz. Ed. M. Woźniakowa, vol. 1 (Warsaw, 1969), pp. 39, 43, 44, 47, 53, 101, 148, 152, 153, 172, 187, 189, 210, 213, 222, 248; vol. 2 (Warsaw, 1970), pp. 44, 45, 56, 75, 84, 86, 87, 89, 98, 309, 315, 317; *Księgi Referendarii Koronnej z drugiej połovy XVIII* w., vol. 1 (1768–1780). Ed. A. Keckowa, W. Pałucki (Warsaw, 1955), pp. 108, 117, 140–1, 231, 232, 320, 506, 602–3, 683; vol. 2 (1781–1794) (Warsaw, 1957), pp. 180, 181, 183, 191, 194, 489, 508, 514.

53 Goldberg, 'Poles and Jews in the 17th and 18th Centuries', pp. 262–8.

54 Zieńkowska, *Jacek Jezierski kasztelan łukowski*, p. 188; J. Jezierski, 'Miasta bez prawa', in: *Materiały do dziejów Sejmu Czteroletniego*, vol. 4 (Wrocław, Warsaw, Cracow, 1961), pp. 50–1; Kołłątaj, *Prawo polityczne narodu polskiego*, vol. 2, p. 331; 'Szynkowa Żydom zabrania się', 'Dyspozycja H. Kołłątaja dla dóbr Krzyżanowice, 1786', in: *Instrukcje gospodarcze dla dóbr magnackich i szlacheckich z XVII–XIX wieku*, vol. 1. Ed. B. Baranowski, J. Bartyś, A. Keckowa, J. Leskiewicz (Wrocław, 1958), p. 178.

55 '... w Żydzie, jak i we wszystkich ludziach praw człowieka przestrzegać należy', Kołłątaj, *Prawo polityczne narodu polskiego*, vol. 2, p. 329.

6

A MOBILE CLASS. THE SUBJECTIVE ELEMENT IN THE SOCIAL PERCEPTION OF JEWS: THE EXAMPLE OF EIGHTEENTH-CENTURY POLAND

Anna Żuk

I apply the term 'mobile class' to a social grouping, which becomes the object of emotions usually directed towards several different classes. A characteristic feature of a mobile class is that its place in the subjectively-perceived social structure changes, depending upon who is making the assessment and the degree of his familiarity with the group. The aim of this paper is to show how Jews can be considered a 'mobile class', since they are the subject of emotions usually directed by more highly-placed social groups to the lower classes, and, conversely, by the lower social strata to groups of higher social ranking. To illustrate my argument I shall use examples from eighteenth century Poland.

For a mobile class to come into being, a pre-requisite is, in most cases, the decay and disappearance of those characteristics which indicate social ranking. What then occurs is identification of the group on the basis of attributes belonging to various social strata. However the kind of perception which results is brought about by subjective factors. It consists essentially of a number of generalizations that do not have a real basis in reality; or which are based on some specific features of the group, rather than all its characteristics.

The Jews in eighteenth century Poland belonged, together with the burghers and the peasants, to the lower classes. Some of them were engaged directly in servicing the magnate and gentry classes. The subjective categories in which Jews were included were two-fold: the upper classes regarded the Jews as belonging to the lower orders and bestowed upon them emotions reserved for these classes. To them this seemed justified by the position of Jews in the social order. In turn the lower classes tended – especially during periods of social conflict – to identify all Jews on the basis of functions which some of them performed for the upper classes.

Thus they looked on the Jews as a group with emotions normally reserved for these classes.

In both cases, subjective categorization becomes at the same time generalization; feelings which might have been justified if directed towards a section of the Jewish community were extended to the group as a whole. Before discussing this problem, I should like to point out that the phenomenon of the mobile class is not the only area of the sociology of affect, in which Jews were in the past, or are currently, the subject. It should also be stressed that this study contains a series of hypotheses, the validity of which should be tested in research which goes beyond the history of Polish Jews and the framework of a single historical era. Furthermore, while it is not only the Jews who can be characterized as a mobile class, they are a prime example – almost the embodiment – of this phenomenon.

JEWS AS SEEN BY THE UPPER CLASSES

The question of the functions performed by a section of the Jewish community in the service of the upper classes in old Poland requires further research. At this stage I would merely like to emphasize the political aspect of these functions. They were usually services of an economic nature, and explanations for this have been sought either in the cultural sphere (for example, the fact that the nobility [*szlachta*] were prevented from engaging in commerce), or else in the personal traits of the upper classes. Thus Graetz writes that Jews 'brought benefits to the frivolous and masterful Polish lords'.[1] In accordance with this view it is argued that the nobility and gentry entrusted their interests to Jews in order to devote themselves wholeheartedly to frivolity. Some individuals were certainly motivated by considerations of this nature. Yet on the whole, the practice has a certain logic and can be seen as contributing to the continuing domination of the noble class. If one wishes to maintain a monopoly of power and privilege, it is a considerable advantage if a serving group does not aspire to the prizes which social advancement offers, but is satisfied with merely financial rewards. To use a simple comparison, the Jews serving the nobility were in the position of a foreign work-force accepting half-pay. The full payment accorded to a serving group which provides services directly and possesses qualifications (particularly in the field of management) consists, as a rule, apart from financial remuneration, of rewards of a social and political character – in the shape of rights and privileges. This is one of the mechanisms by which members of the lower class advance to middle class status. The serving class becomes a pressure group, directing its aspirations towards areas of privilege and decision-making which are within the domain of the class being served.

Since the latter attach considerable importance to those they consider indispensable, the aspirations of the servicing group sometimes meet with a favourable response. As a rule, however, the situation as it unfolds is one of conflict. How, and by what means, this conflict is resolved may depend upon the particular circumstances. It lies in the interests of the upper classes, who wish to retain their dominance, to avoid not only the conflict itself, but also the possibility of its arising. One way of achieving such security would be to recruit a serving group which does not harbour any aspirations towards those rights and privileges which are the preserve of the upper classes.

In the case of the Jews of old Poland, their social aims were limited. They were restricted to the confines of their own community, which was isolated both culturally, and, because of the self-government granted to them, also politically. The Jews were not the only group which can be seen to have been optimally functional in a service role and, at the same time, to have been 'protective', i.e. unlikely to seek conflict itself, while insulating the nobility and gentry from other groups which had the potential for conflict. Another such group was the lower clergy. In this case too, the reference system of values and rewards – in the sense, for example, of social and political advance – lay outside that monopolized, at least at the parish level, by the nobility. The conflicts which did arise in the political arena related rather to the Church hierarchy and the ruling élite, two circles which it is not always easy to separate. At the parish level the clergy were able to provide the nobility and gentry with support. This went beyond simply legitimizing power and assumed more direct forms. A foreigner who travelled in Poland at the time of King Stanisław August Poniatowski noted:

> A very small part of his [the vicar's] affairs concerns matters of religion; most of the time which his church and household leave him, he spends with the squire or is engaged in the latter's affairs. Hence one often meets, whether at home or abroad, a Polish nobleman in the company of a clergyman. The other of his inseparable companions is the Jew. They, like two guiding spirits, protect at each step every Pole of importance. All matters which are thought to be too important or too sensitive for a Jew are entrusted to the clergyman and, therefore, the priests are often, and for long periods, absent from their parishes.[2]

The clergy and the Jews, groups that were socially distant and culturally opposed to each other, in practice, in everyday life in old Poland were bound by frequent social contact centred on the squire and his interests. These contacts may have been reflected in some customary practices. Thus a foreigner found in a Polish inn that 'the postmaster, an old drunken Jew, drank vodka with a stalwart and corpulent village priest.'[3]

Summarizing these reflections, it is clear that the political role of those Jews directly involved with serving the nobility contributed towards the stabilization and preservation of the upper class monopoly of power. In this role, apart from Jews, there were also some members of the lower clergy and also foreigners, such as Germans. Their usefulness and efficiency as a group serving the economic – and indirectly the political – interests of the upper class, resulted from their membership of social spheres which were culturally or institutionally isolated, a fact which excluded them from the political game.

To underline the importance of the problem, let us imagine a situation in which the squire administered his domain with the help and co-operation of its inhabitants. This would imply a degree of peasant emancipation which can not be reconciled with serfdom. It therefore endangered the class domination of the nobility. The Cossacks, by contrast, were an example of a group which provided services of a specific kind, but at the same time possessed considerable potential for conflict. This conflict potential, the effects of which were decidedly harmful for Polish statehood, stemmed largely from the fact that the Cossacks demanded social and political rights as payment for their military services.

The link which bound the squirearchy together with the Jews who serviced it may be defined as comparative exploitation. Its relative character becomes evident when comparison is drawn with other groups which, if they had füllfilled the same functions as the Jews, would have been rewarded differently.

The stereotype of the Jew held by the upper classes, and its subjective colouring, may reflect this relative exploitation. As a consequence, features which should have been evident because of the Jews' functions and their contacts with the nobility disappear from their actual status. The question of rewards in the area of social and political rights or prestige also disappears, since the stereotype does not include those cultural and personal attributes which could form the basis for the grant of such rights.

And so, at the time of the Four Year *Sejm*, in upper class journalism, the Jews were presented stereotypically as an undifferentiated mass: 'greedy, cunning, fanatical, marked by a low cultural, mental and moral level'.[4] We should note that upper classes frequently formulate their feelings towards lower classes in this kind of language. A 'low cultural, mental and moral level' is usually attributed to lower classes, irrespective of who they are. We can see this process at work, for example, when a peasant or a worker is defined as 'uncultured, dirty, ignorant,'. Only the term 'fanatical', as applied to religious practices and customs, is linked specifically to the stereotype of the Jew. The adjective 'greedy' is applied to the under-privileged classes to such a degree, since it serves to deny or restrict their rights to acquisition and ownership. In the minds of those who regard the privilege of ownership as belonging exclusively to themselves, an acquisitive drive on the part of the underprivileged classes is judged in terms that are morally negative; the man is 'greedy' if he wishes to acquire goods or services, and 'cunning' if he is able to realise that wish. In the culture of Polish stereotypes, such attributes are also ascribed to peasants.

This stereotype of the Jew contains an element of mystification originating from the principle of taking the part for the whole. It leaves out a large number of Jews who did not fit the stereotype of the lower classes, for the simple reason that they did not belong to them. The proximity referred to, which included contact on the social plane, excluded individuals of a 'low cultural and mental level'. Its frequency is hard to ascertain, but in eighteenth century memoirs, for example, the Jewish agent or manager is described as a member of the household,[5] and a foreigner visiting Poland wrote; 'It is certain that in any other country an infected Jew would not be admitted to a nobleman's house.'[6] Hence the conclusion that even a reasonable excuse, such as disease, was not used as a barrier to continued contacts with Jews in Poland.

And yet the day to day presence in upper class houses of Jews, fulfilling both functional and social roles, does not seem to have had any significant effect on the stereotype of the Jew, in which he is denied cultural and moral virtues. The general attitude of the nobility and the gentry towards the Jews is best described in the words of Adolf Pawiński:

> In relation to the lower strata, discriminated against politically and socially, there prevails in the main an indifference to their fate or even a tendency to oppress them. And so, for example, Jews who have long lived either in the villages or in towns, or even in the cities, are an object of aversion or contempt as well as being exploited in financial and fiscal terms. In the eyes of the ruling estate they do not deserve any kindness. On the contrary, in the instructions of the *sejmiki* (regional assemblies of the gentry) attention is repeatedly drawn to the Jews as a convenient and necessary source of financial pillage for the benefit of the Republic. Whenever the need arises in the Sejm to vote a tax for defence purposes, and the gentry and nobility are called upon to contribute, they point to the Jews as the first and most plentiful source (. . .) After each taxation measure or increase of the tax levels affecting Jews, there follows a new demand issued by the deputies of the *sejmiki*. It all reminds one of the digestive processes of an animal's body; satiation is followed by emptiness, and emptiness by renewed filling of the stomach.[7]

The nobility and gentry push the Jews aside, ascribe them without exception to the lower orders and, at the same time, establish them as an object of exploitation. This occurs despite the many benefits derived from Jews, either in the form of services of various kinds, or through direct material profit.

The political benefits which accrued to the upper classes were considerable, but they were disregarded or unappreciated by them. Nathan Hannover, for example, writes in his chronicle dating from the period of the Cossack wars in the seventeenth century: 'The Jews in Ruś were lords and rulers of Ruthenian towns; hence the misfortunes which befell the Jews.'[8] This sounds improbable, but Hannower is not guilty of misrepresentation; he merely uses language which is inadequate to describe the political system in the Ukraine, in which Jews did, to a certain extent, participate. Apart from the role of 'middleman' in economic life, Jews in Old Poland were very important in the circulation of information. In such a vast, underpopulated country they were often messengers, and because of their mobility and the nature of their occupations, which required meeting people regularly, they acquired a relatively large stock of information.

Adam Moszczeński, describing the period of the Humań massacre, recalls; 'As for the provincial governor (*wojewoda*) of Kiev, his door was always open to the Jews, and he believed their tales and complaints to such lengths that if any official or cashier had the Jews against him, he could not retain his post.'[9] This seems possible, as the Jews in the Ukraine were the only possible ally of the gentry classes. There was no other social group which could provide support for the ruling power; the burgher class was insignificant, while an immense social gulf, as well as economic and religious conflicts, separated the nobles and gentry from the peasantry. Relations with the Cossacks were similarly plagued with conflict. Nevertheless, irrespective of the benefits which the gentry classes received from the Jews, the latter were treated in the way an upper class treats a lower one, and were accorded the emotional response usually reserved for the lower classes.

This relationship is well captured by Marchlewski:

> Within the conservative, gentry camp . . . there was an active tradition of treating Jews with contemptuous patronage, a tradition maintained since the times of serfdom. This relationship is expressed in one word which hides an infinity of contempt: *żydek*. . . . Even among people of unquestionably high cultural level, who had, however, absorbed the ideas and assumptions appropriate to their class, there was the same tone and the same attitude towards Jews. So, for example, J.I. Kraszewski tries to be 'fair' to the Jews, but whenever he writes about them one senses the gulf which separates him from these pariahs. He treats them in almost the same way as a European ethnographer would describe an exotic African tribe. For him, a gentleman with his own coat of arms, it would be out of the question

> to consider a Mosiek or a Lejbuś as his peer. Until now, for politicians of this camp, the 'Jewish question' existed only in the sense that decisions regarding the Jews' future need to be taken; equality of rights for Jews is a notion which eludes their grasp completely . . . It is, however, this same gentry tradition which will not be reconciled to anti-semitism, to the struggle against the Jews. Between the nobles and their *żydki*, whatever we think about the policies of the gentry class, there was always that sense of lordliness which recoils from flattering the instincts of the masses and attempts to retain a semblance of culture . . . Journalists of this camp too did not degrade themselves by exploiting zoological anti-semitism for political purposes. They had no need to dirty their hands.[10]

The nobility and gentry bestowed on the Jews emotions reserved for the lower classes, treating them with disrespect, patronisingly, fully confident of their own superiority. But this was not anti-semitism, which, according to this gentry scheme of values, was plebeian and therefore unworthy.

JEWS AS SEEN BY THE LOWER CLASSES

Here the paradoxes which lead to the creation of a mobile class are fully revealed; the inclusion of Jews in a subjective category with groups with which, in objective terms, they have little in common, and this categorization process carried out on the basis of very scanty evidence. Emotions are clearly the motive force behind generalization.

Our hypothesis as to how the Jews appeared to the lower classes is as follows: these classes exhibited a tendency to include Jews in the same subjective category as the privileged classes on the evidence of the service function performed by certain Jews for these classes and the type of social dependence (patronage) involved. The extensive mystification process involved here consisted of all Jews being subjected to the emotions which may have been justified in relation to a small number of them, so that Jews who occupied an equally low and underprivileged position in society as those who attacked them became the object of aggression directed against the upper classes. This allows us to explain the different interpretations of certain events which are sometimes treated as anti-Jewish or anti-semitic, but are also interpreted in terms of class conflict.

So, for example, according to Kitowicz, the expulsion of Jewish artisans from Warsaw in 1794 frightened contemporaries, who saw in it the beginnings of a social upheaval along the lines of the French Revolution.[11] Kitowicz, in his description of the Warsaw riots, gives the following sequence of events: 'The first outbreak' – Warsaw artisans demand the expulsion of Jews. 'The second outbreak' – appeared to be modelled on the initial stages of the French Revolution. Three villains were seen at Krakowska Street with cockades fastened to their caps. They were immediately taken off to the guardhouse on Marszałkowska Street. Nothing else was heard of them and it was dangerous to ask lest the enquirer were counted as one of their companions.[12] 'The third outbreak' – anti-Jewish excesses break out in the wake of the attack by the tailor, Fox, on a Jewish tailor. The furrier, Mariański, who had said; 'Today the apprentices are rioting; tomorrow it will be their elders', was dragged from his bed by soldiers who forced their way into his house . . . and led him down to the guardhouse.[13]

In the light of these events 'the *Sejm* considered banning the indulgence festival at Bielany on Whit Monday, which had always attracted Varsovians in their thousands to the forest of the Cameduli monks, – and also the public processions during Corpus Christi. A request was also made that detachments of soldiers disperse all crowd gatherings in which twelve or more people took part.'[14]

However the Bielany festival and the Corpus Christi procession 'passed off peacefully as usual'. Kitowicz, in his description of the Warsaw riots concludes that 'the Warsaw mob is not as frightening as, for example, the French'. Examining this question in more detail, he anticipates Tocqueville's later argument that the social basis of revolutions are not those who are underprivileged absolutely, but those whose underprivileged status is relative and who aim to improve their position:

> The Polish mob is not supported by the gentry, and it has no access to the army because officers and members of the cavalry are recruited exclusively from the noble class. Its voice carries no weight in public debates. All legislative, defence and financial functions of the state are in the hands of the noble estate. Hence the Polish mob could never be as dangerous to this country as the French mob became. It might become so when the burgher class is admitted to the legislature and to other public offices.[15]

These conclusions, which may be recognized as a valuable contribution to the sociological theory of revolution, were reached by Kitowicz on the basis of events which could be defined as an anti-Jewish riot. In this latter interpretation the facts alone are taken into account, while in the version given by Kitowicz, the thoughts and motives of those involved are considered, and here, in fact, the Jews appear as an intermediate element in the conflict between the mob and the upper classes. In the thoughts, and even more, in the emotions, of the common people these riots are not solely anti-Jewish, but have a further object in the shape of the privileged classes. The privileged group grasps this true context, and hence the severe measures taken against the artisan who spoke of a further stage of rebellion; hence also the discussion of such radical measures as the prohibition of meetings or the ban on public Catholic rites. And yet the fear which provoked the above sentiments proved unfounded, since 'the Polish mob is not as dangerous as, for example, the French mob'.

In the seventeenth and eighteenth centuries during the conflicts between the nobility on the one hand and the peasants and Ukrainian Cossacks on the other, the full force of what we have termed 'subjective generalization' is revealed. In the heat of the dispute the Jews, together with the Catholic clergy and the gentry, are lumped together in a single category of adversaries. In this case, and it is a rare occurrence in Jewish history, these attitudes had grounds for justification; their logic is borne out by consideration of the system of power relations and the position of Jews within it.

Some contemporary Jews were conscious of this. Nathan Hannover writes in his Chronicle:

> Some Cossacks were freed from taxation and enjoyed the same freedom as the nobility and the gentry. But the remainder of the Ruthenian people worked as serfs on the estates of the magnates and gentry who oppressed them. They dug clay and made bricks and laboured hard in the house and in the fields. The gentry class placed a heavy burden on their shoulders and some of the gentry used dreadful measures to force them to accept the faith of their rulers. They were degraded to such an extent that all nations, even that poorest of all [i.e. Jews] ruled over them.[16]

However such a measure of rationality in according Jews the emotions reserved for the ruling classes is a very rare occurrence. As a rule, the image of the Jew in the emotions of the lower classes is a highly mystified one, and the generalization is constructed on the basis of features that are unrepresentative of Jewish society as a whole. The social consciousness of the common people, touched to only a small degree by intellectualism, seems to suffer from the mis-application of empiricism. What is experienced directly is thought to hold good as a general rule. Hence, a part is identified with the whole and appearance with essence. In the feudal order, this arises when the peasantry direct their hopes and aggressions not against those who really dispose of power, but against those who are intermediaries.[17] All kinds of requests are addressed to leaseholders, estate stewards, and similar officials who also become the first victims of a desperate peasant rebellion. Jews are victims of emotions which should properly be addressed to members of the groups in power: the nobility, or else the clergy. Jews become victims because of this misuse of empirical knowledge; it is they whom the Ruthenian peasant encountered most frequently in the market place or in the inn, and the repression which the peasant experienced flowed directly from them, although its true source lay beyond them.

The mechanism of this kind of subjective construct can be illustrated by one of Spinoza's reflections: affect leads to a vision in which a part is identified with the whole; if this part is bad, then the whole may be treated with antipathy and aggression. 'But one must observe that in ordering our thoughts and images, we should always take into account what is good in each thing, so that we are always moved to action by feelings of joy.' The perception of the whole through what is bad and partial is:

> . . . the common characteristic of all those whom luck does not favour and who are weak in spirit. Thus a miser, even a poor one, talks unceasingly of the financial abuses and failings of the wealthy, tormenting himself and showing others that he cannot tolerate with equanimity either his own poverty, or the riches of others. Those who are ill-received by their mistresses talk in the same vein, thinking only of the volatile nature of women, their deceitfulness and other commonplace faults of this kind; it is all forgotten when the mistress accepts them back again.[18]

Such emotions are seemingly a natural tendency of human kind and are present in force in popular thinking, which is little penetrated by reason and is, as a rule, associated with the lower and oppressed classes, those 'whom luck does not favour'. Yet where the treatment meted out to Jews by their Christian neighbours is concerned, the tendency to emotions of this kind is both more specific and intense. This may be explained by the general attitude of the Church towards the Jews, an attitude which does not, as is usually argued, originate in the assertion that the Jews 'killed Christ' or refused to recognise him (which would be a Freudian rationalisation), but in their failure to recognize the Church itself – a step which, of course, would be impossible without recognising Christ too. For centuries the Church had been an institution which tended towards totalitarianism, a system which in the very nature of things behaves with intolerance and aggression towards groups threatening its legitimacy.

A totalitarian institution – and this is proved in the twentieth century by the experience of peoples living under totalitarian systems – rejects groups which challenge its legitimacy. There is no threat or warning issued – 'We shall persecute you because you do not recognize us.' The non-conformist groups are simply branded as sick, evil and in conspiracy with a demonic force which is interpreted according to the particular social and historical context. The Christian-Jewish conflict, rooted in the question of legitimacy of Church power, provided an environment in which Christians were inclined to see in Jews all that is evil, and to equate the part that is evil with the whole. Where popular consciousness was concerned, this tendency is particularly strong and it increased in the case of those 'whom luck does not favour'.

The nature of the understanding appropriate to a Ruthenian peasant in the eighteenth century, has been characterized as a distorted empiricism. It had particularly unfortunate effects when it came into contact with popular Jewish consciousness, which in turn was marked by distorted *apriorism*. This *a priori* thought results from enclosure in a particular ethnic, cultural and religious environment, and it produces patterns of thought and behaviour determined in advance by what was regarded as compatible with Jewish tradition. *A posteriori* thought – the process of reconciling knowledge and assumptions with experience and reality – was comparatively weakly developed. If the values of individual and collective life are established by such *a priori* thinking, and are shaped to only a small degree in accordance with external reality, the result may be that grasp of that reality is lost and the group becomes unable to foresee the dangers that reality bears. The social consciousness of the Jews, largely determined by *a priori* thought, and the social consciousness of the lower classes within Christian society, interacted and produced a tangled knot of mutual incomprehension and antipathy.

For centuries the Jews depended upon a system of logic and reasoning which restricted their ability – already limited in the conditions of the Diaspora – to act or exercise influence in the political sphere. From the point of view of the sociology of knowledge it is interesting that this *a priori* style, in a purer intellectual form, was quite widely represented in Jewish historiography. Majer Bałaban writes:

> In science research is usually based on facts – most importantly derived from the observation of phenomena – and only subsequently followed by conclusions arrived at by deduction. The scholar does not look to left or right and his conclusions sometimes destroy what generations have sanctified and centuries accepted as dogma. And this is true science, free from the influences of the street, from the considerations of the moment and of factions or groups. In the historiography of Polish Jews it is usually the other way round. The author has a chosen thesis and looks for evidence with which to back it up – he has the conclusions and seeks merely the initial premise.[19]

It can even be argued that these characteristics can be observed to a significant degree in present-day Jewish historiography, perhaps because of the persistence even in scholarly work of sublimated traits of that common Jewish consciousness or, in other words, the misapplication of *a priori* thought.

In conclusion, we may advance the following hypotheses: First, the perception of Jews in the group consciousness of the lower classes was based on a false analogy, which seemed to have a logical base but was rooted in emotion. One part, usually the 'bad' part, would became the whole. An intermediary role in carrying out a decision would be conceived as the process of decision-making itself. A typical feature of the feudal order – peasants focussing their hopes and emotions towards those who mediate between them and the true wielders of power – can be seen as typical of a far more general phenomenon.

Second, the ability of Jews to influence or determine events remained severely limited while they maintained their separate national and cultural identity under the conditions of the Diaspora. Jewish group consciousness, which concentrated on preserving that separate identity, diminished this ability even further, testifying to the weakness of *a priori* thought. It meant that the perception of reality was formed to only a small degree by contact with it, so that the values of individual and collective life (religious, national or cultural) were determined by abstract principles.

The combination of these two factors: peasant cognitive thought directing aggression against what was immediately perceived, and Jewish group consciousness which shaped cognition by *a priori* thinking, and resulted in a weak perception of reality, seem to have created a situation which for the Jews was particularly unfortunate. It made possible the manipulation of the Jews, putting them in a mediating position as a highly visible link which became the focus for the aggression of the lower and oppressed classes. This state of affairs existed during the seventeenth and eighteenth centuries in the Ukraine, where the Polish nobility made the Jews the visible tool of their own exploitative policies.

LANGUAGE AND THE JEWS AS A MOBILE CLASS

In Polish memoirs of the eighteenth century the linguistic order in which basic social groups are described seems to reflect the order of their stratification. The sequence in which these groups are cited is as follows: nobility peasants, Jews. This order follows from the way in which the social order was perceived, yet it also has a subjective basis: a generalization of speaking habits – 'I and you' rather than 'you and I'. In other words the feeling towards oneself or one's own group is very warm and positive. When Poles say 'Poles and Jews', and Jews – 'Jews and Poles', Czechs – 'Czechs and Slovaks' and Slovaks – 'Slovaks and Czechs', that priority given to one's own group of origin is a linguistic habit rooted in well-defined emotions. This linguistic principle is particularly apparent when the utterance expresses emotion. Let us take, as an example, a sentence from an eighteenth century memoir: 'All the Starzeński family liked greyhounds extraordinarily, but they detested Germans.'[20] Greyhounds are mentioned first, since they were liked, whereas the Germans, since they are disliked, are relegated to second place.

If we have in the Polish language of the eighteenth century an established sequence 'nobility, peasants, Jews', which reflected the order of social stratification and also the order of emotions, we may ask whether this order is ever reversed. This does sometimes take place in particularly dramatic occurrences, such as when death disrupts the sequence of these terms. Because the expressions 'gentry, peasantry, Jews', and nowadays 'Poles and Jews', come to one's lips readily, as if they were single phrases whose sense in common speech is not reflected upon, we may assume that breaking the internal order of such expressions demands some mental effort. The first requirement is a degree of analytical sense, or the awareness that behind the formal structure of the expression lies content and meaning. The second requirement is motivation, the desire to express a new content on the level of syntax. These two prerequisites must be satisfied for a linguistic pattern of this kind to be broken up. So, a modern Pole, irrespective of his attitude towards Jews and of the subject being considered, would say 'Poles and Jews'. It is the pattern of language which determines the phrase, and the reversal of order, to the extent that it is consistent and goes beyond mere chance or accident, requires both analytical sense and motivation.

The Polish language of the eighteenth century was, in some respects, more precise than present-day Polish, seen in terms of the sociology of knowledge. This could be attributed to the influence exerted by the system of direct democracy, a system which produced an analytical sense as a matter of course, because a forum in which contradictory views are brought into agreement generates a definite linguistic culture in which concepts must be sharp and sentences clear. Similarly the fact that the Talmudic hermeneutics of Jews in old Poland were dominated by the analytical method of the *pilpul* can be explained by the influences exercised by their social organization, based also on the principle of the clash of opinions. Its functioning required skill in reconciling contradictory views, since the essence of *pilpul* lay in bringing opposed viewpoints into agreement. There is a close relationship between the type of social organization and the type of hermeneutics used.

The way in which language was used in eighteenth century memoirs seems to indicate a high degree of awareness, so that already at the level of syntax it produces meaningful pronouncements. When human groups or things are listed, the order as a rule is from the most to the least important and from the largest to the smallest. Apart from the analytical sense which is perhaps due to direct democracy, we also find reflected a vision of the social world in terms of an inflexible hierarchy, which is believed to be in harmony with the objective state of things. So Kitowicz writes that in 1794 'the Muscovites engaged in considerable pillage of noblemen's palaces, the gentry's mansions, churches and the Jews; and last, of the humble peasants.'[21] The order in which the listing is made reflects both the social hierarchy and the scale of the plunder.

Even in the sight of the executioner the gentry take precedence over Jews. Writing about criminal offenders threatened with death for the crimes they had committed, Kitowicz writes: 'when a member of an influential family committed a crime . . . or a Jew'.[22] In another passage, he observes that the rebellious Cossacks 'pillaged noblemen and gentry, Jews and peasants',[23] or: 'members of the Roman Catholic faith, Jews and various Ruthenians'.[24]

Although the ordering of social groups, expressed in the terms 'nobles and gentry, Jews, peasants' or, more rarely, 'nobles and gentry, peasants, Jews', is a linguistic convention well established in the social reality of eighteenth-century Poland, the convention could collapse when particularly dramatic events were being described. As stated earlier, death sometimes forces an interruption in the linguistic sequence. And so, we find in a memoir that: 'Cossacks . . . committed terrible abuses and cruelties against the Jews under the pretext of avenging the death of the Saviour; at the same time they did not spare village vicars and landowners.'[25] The Jews, as the group suffering most, are mentioned before the clergy and gentry class.

Interesting material, relevant to our theme, can be found in the accounts of the Humań massacre of 1768. According to some Polish accounts, the Jews were the main defenders of Humań. The daughter of the governor of Humań, who survived the massacre, wrote: 'I remember seeing . . . Jews with singed beards and sidelocks who were shooting and defending themselves with great spirit – only Jews, I might add.'[26]

In Tuczapski's manuscript of 1788 we read:

> Szafrański, having collected all the guns, armed Jews with them and was thus in active command of the armoury and the entire defence. When the rebels approached the gates, leading peasants armed with hatchets to cut down the palisade, they were struck by cannon fire from the soldiers, while the Jews, shooting through the palisades, forced them to retreat. The Jews contributed actively to the defence and executed all Szafrański's orders.[27]

Adam Moszczeński's account reveals that the Jews in Humań conducted themselves with greater dignity than the gentry. It is true that Moszczeński does not write about the role played by the Jews in defending the fortress, but from his description of events, it appears that the Jews were more far-sighted and less prone to panic than the gentry. He writes:

> The Jews, seeing how the noblemen Ciesielski, Mładanowicz and Rogaszewski treated the Cossacks and their commander unjustly, naturally realised that it would bring repercussions when Żeleźniak approached at the head of the rebellious peasantry and the Cossacks. They went to the nobleman Ciesielski and suggested to him that Gonta was sure to have some agreeement with Żeleźniak.[28]

The Jews' warnings were disregarded. On the whole the image conveyed of their behaviour is more positive than that of the gentry. Moszczeński does not praise the Jews in so many words but, significantly, he breaks with linguistic convention and in his account, as a rule, gives the Jews precedence over the gentry:

> Here Gonta joined forces with the hordes led by Żeleźniak, and they marched together on Humań; wherever, on their way, they found Jews, gentry and Poles, these were cut to pieces.[29] . . . And then they covered the whole town of Humań with corpses. The deep well in the market place was filled with the bodies of dead children. The peasants in the villages robbed and killed Jews and their children, while the gentry and landowners were bound up and taken by cart to Humań where drunken Cossacks were killing them.[30]

Although in her memoir cited earlier, Mrs Krebs, the daughter of the governor of Humań, refers to the Jews as the main defenders of the fortress, the linguistic convention does not change when she writes that in Humań 'there were many merchants, Turks, Greeks, Muscovites, and Jews.'[31] In Moszczeński's account, however, 'many Jews, Greeks, Armenians, Turks and Tartars had settled [in Humań].'[32]

Generally speaking, the sequence in which people and objects are listed can be regarded as an expression of emotion, or as a reflection of social hierarchy in social consciousness, or both; our interpretation would depend on the context. Let us consider, for example, the meaning contained in one sentence, written by the Prussian subject George Forster, during his travels in Poland: 'At seven I arrived at Kęty, a miserable little town, where, because of the fair, the place was packed with carts, horses, peasants, oxen and swine, and also Jews.'[33]

This kind of ordering is completely unknown in Polish literature, although its essence can be found in the sentence quoted earlier, written by a nobleman who, in accordance with family tradition, gave greyhounds precedence over the Germans.

In conclusion we can state that, generally speaking, language used at the level of common speech is subjected to strong schematization. Although in eighteenth century accounts the phrase 'nobles and gentry, Jews, peasants' is usually found – and more rarely, 'nobility and gentry, peasants, Jews' – when particularly dramatic events are being described, engaging deep emotions and moral judgments, this schema can break down. So, Jews could be mentioned first, before the gentry, when they are the victims suffering most or when, in a given situation, as in Adam Moszczeński's account of the Humań massacre, evaluation in moral and subjective categories places them ahead of the noble and gentry class. Thus in language too, although in a limited sense, the Jews appear to be a mobile class.

NOTES

1 H. Graetz, *Historia Żydów*, vol. 8, (Warsaw, 1929), p. 52.
2 *Polska Stanisławowska w oczach cudzoziemców*, vol. 2, (Warsaw, 1963), p. 321.
3 Ibid., p. 95.
4 See A. Eisenbach, *Z dziejów ludności żydowskiej w polsce w XVIII i XIX wieku. Studia i szkice*, (Warsaw, 1983), p. 34.
5 *Z dziejów Hajdamaczyzny*, vol. 2, (Warsaw, 1905), p. 48.
6 *Polska Stanisławowska w oczach cudzoziemców*, vol. 2, p. 299.
7 A. Pawiński, *Rządy Sejmikowe w Polsce 1572–1795*, (Warsaw, 1978), pp. 169–70.
8 Natan Hannower, 'Jawein Mecula, tj. Bagno głębokie. Kronika Zdarzeń z Lat 1648–1652', translated by M. Bałaban in: *Sprawy i Rzeczy Ukrainne*, (Lwów, 1914), p. 18.
9 Adam Moszczeński, *Pamiętniki do historii polskiej w ostatnich latach panowania Augusta III i pierwszych Stanisława Poniatowskiego*, (Poznań, 1858), p. 137.
10 J.B. Marchlewski, *Antysemitizm a Robotnicy*, (Kraków, 1913), p. 55.
11 See J. Kitowicz, *Pamiętniki czyli Historia Polska*, (Warsaw, 1971).
12 Ibid., p. 439.
13 Ibid., p. 441.
14 Ibid., p. 441.
15 Ibid., p. 443.
16 Ibid., p. 443.
17 See W. Kula, *Teoria ekonomiczna ustroju feudalnego*, (Warsaw, 1983).
18 B. Spinoza, *Etyka*, (Warsaw, 1954), pp. 348–9.
19 M. Bałaban, *Z historii Żydów w Polsce. Studia i szkice*, (Warsaw, 1920), p. 23.
20 M. Starzeński, *Na schyłku dni Rzeczypospolitej*, (Warsaw, 1914), p. 2.
21 J. Kitowicz, *Pamiętniki czyli Historia Polska*, (Warsaw, 1971), p. 595.
22 J. Kitowicz, *Opis obyczajów za panowania Augusta III*, (Wrocław, 1970), p. 263.
23 Ibid., p. 304.
24 Ibid., p. 329.
25 M. Starzeński, *Na schyłku dni Rzeczypospolitej*, p. 25.
26 *Opis autentyczny rzezi humańskiej przez córkę Gubernatora Humania z Mładanowiczów zameżną Krebsową*, (Poznań, 1840), p. 23.
27 *Z dziejów hajdamaczyzny*, p. 57.
28 A. Moszczeński, *Pamiętniki do historii polskiej* . . ., pp. 139–40.
29 Ibid., p. 142.
30 Ibid., p. 144.
31 *Opis autentyczny rzezi humańskiej* . . . , p. 10
32 A. Moszczeński, *Pamiętniki do historii polskiej* . . . p. 145.
33 *Polska stanisławowska w oczach cudzoziemców*, vol. 2, p. 48.

PART II

The Nineteenth Century

7

THE JEWS OF WARSAW, POLISH SOCIETY AND THE PARTITIONING POWERS 1795–1861

Stefan Kieniewicz

The history, spanning almost two centuries, of the Jews of Warsaw, who represented the greatest concentration of Jews in Poland and one of the largest Jewish communities in the world, has been broadly documented. The literature is concerned mostly with the internal life of the Jewish commune (*kehilla*) and the economic structures of Jewish life. An important part looks at the process of legal emancipation of the Jews which took place during the 19th century together with the gradual liquidation of the feudal system. This process, as is generally known, brought the Jews concrete advantages and freed them from age-old limitations imposed by Christian society. However, the process also involved certain negative side-effects: 'coming out of the ghetto' threatened the Jews with being engulfed by the indifferent environment of the capitalist world and thus with the loss of their religious and national identity.

I wish to consider this question within the narrow limits of my own field: considering mutual relations between Jewish and Christian society in Warsaw against the background of the process of emancipation and, broadly speaking, between the mid-18th century and the mid '60s of the following century.

Warsaw, both as a fast developing industrial and trading centre since the Enlightenment and as the seat of political power, had always attracted Jews. Here, in the centre of the Republic, they searched for advantageous conditions for economic activity, and also hoped that here they could most effectively work for improvements in their condition on a national scale: by approaching the King, *Sejm* or central authorities.

The Jews had further obstacles to overcome in realising these aims, beginning with overturning or evading the privilege *de non tolerandis Judaeis*, in operation in Warsaw from the 16th century. They wanted the right of access to the capital and the right to settle there in the unrestricted areas of the city without incurring any further penalties. These issues were related to the question of the 'Jewish district', or more specifically the ban on settling by Warsaw's thoroughfares and the levy enforced on Jews arriving in the city, the so-called *biletowy* (*Tagzettel*). The right to carrying out any profession came next on the agenda, followed by assurance of autonomy for the religious commune (*Kahal*) and, finally, the granting of full citizens' rights.

The restrictions listed above were gradually overcome by the Jews via legislative or administrative orders, but also *via facti* – entering the city despite prohibitions, supported in one form or another by some patron. A reliable indication of the successful incursion of Jews into the Polish capital is the steady growth in absolute figures and percentages: 6,750 Jews in Warsaw (8.3 per cent) according to the first census of 1792, that is immediately before the Partitions; 73,000 in 1862, just after formal emancipation (32.6 per cent); 337,000 at the outbreak of war in 1914 (38.1 per cent).[1] The first figure may not be quite accurate; all three are based on religious criteria and do not include baptised Jews.

Towards the end of the Tsar's reign, the Jews in Warsaw had limited access to certain educational institutions and some political positions. In the independent capital after 1918 only one administrative prohibition was maintained with regard to the Jews. Access to certain gardens, as notices on their gates declared (I saw these myself in my youth), was permitted only to 'members of the public in European dress'. The park-keepers did not therefore admit what were then referred to as *chałaciarzy* (Jews wearing gaberdines). Thus a traditionally-dressed Jew could not enjoy the beauties of the Łazienki gardens; or, what was more onerous, could not take a short cut while hurrying about his business, through the Saxon Gardens, which were in the very centre of the town, directly next to the Jewish district. This rather petty irritation essentially affected the Jewish poor, as most wealthy Jews had abandoned the gaberdine and skullcap at the turn of the twentieth century.

The Christian middle classes of Warsaw remained permanently and unremittingly antagonistic towards the Jews throughout the whole of this period. Economic competition obviously played a part in this; it found emotional nourishment in the prevailing religious dislike of the 'enemies of Christianity', a dislike which was greatest among the poor Catholic population. The *magistrat* (municipal authorities) which voiced the interests of the Christian tradesmen and artisans' guilds stood by the privilege *de non tolerandis Judaeis* within the walls of 'Old and New Warsaw'. The Jews, on the other hand, were until the end of the 18th century under the patronage of the magnates (including some clergy), who were linked with the Jews by a whole network of interests, including their position as property owners of the *jurydyki* or jurisdictions, that is, private enclaves encircling Warsaw which did not come under the civil jurisdiction. The Republic's authorities, beginning with King Stanisław August, were undecided in their attitude towards the Jews. The leading thinkers of the Polish Enlightenment spoke of the need to 'reform' the Jews, but hesitated before the postulate of granting full equal rights.[2]

After 1795 a new element enters the conflict in the shape of the partitioning powers, the Prussians in the first instance (till 1806) and from 1815 the Russians. It is not difficult to find instances of anti-Jewish elements in the politics of the partitioning monarchies, especially in the Tsarist policies of imposing petty restrictions on the Jews, or even persecuting them. There is, however, also evidence of the reverse, instances when Warsaw Jews, or certain groups among them, attacked by the Polish element, sought the protection of the alien patron, sometimes successfully.

One of the earliest examples of this arrangement of forces was noted by Krystyna Zienkowska in her perceptive study of the dispute surrounding the 'New Jerusalem', a town settlement set up at Warsaw's gates in 1775 by Prince August Sułkowski. The Warsaw *magistrat* protested against the formation of this new centre of artisan and trade competition, and gained the support of the Crown Marshal Stanisław Lubomirski. Sułkowski, the owner of the settlement, was supported by the majority of the Permanent Council, that is, the government, with Adam Poniński the Treasurer (and main supporter of Russia at that time) at their head. As usual, Stanisław August Poniatowski vacillated. And so Sułkowski ensured the protection of the Russian army for himself. Thus when the marshal's guard came to 'New Jerusalem' to confiscate Jewish goods, thrusting the Russian guards to one side, the Russian resident in Warsaw, Baron d'Asch, lodged a protest at the Permanent Council against the assailing of the Russian army's safety in Poland, appealing to the guarantee of the Empress Catherine.[3] This incident had no further consequences: the *magistrat* won the legal dispute with the Jews. Formally 'New Jerusalem' was liquidated . . . only to re-emerge in another guise.

The Constitution of 3 May 1791 sanctioned the social and political advance of the Christian middle classes. Among other things it also liquidated jurisdictional differences; by the same token it weakened the position of the Jews, whose fate it passed over in silence – apart from very general assurances about state protection for people of all religious faiths. During the 1794 insurrection, Kościuszko, who was well-disposed towards the Jews, called to them not only to make sacrifices for the cause of the insurrection, but to serve in the civil militia to protect the capital. The later famous Berek Joselewicz organized a regiment of soldiers in the district of Praga.[4] However, these efforts did not save Warsaw or the country.

Warsaw found itself under Prussian rule, as the capital of the 'Department of Southern Prussia'. The Prussian government regulated social relations in the annexed province, including Jewish ones, in a spirit of enlightened absolutism. The 'General-Juden-Reglement für Süd- und Neu-Ostpreussen' of 17 April 1797 imposed on the Jews numerous irksome limitations, especially in ways of earning a living; it also attempted to transfer poor Jews beyond the border.[6] Otherwise, the Prussian government did not feel bound by anti-Jewish laws dating from the time of the Republic; in 1802 it abolished the feudal civic privileges including the Warsaw privilege of *de non tolerandis Judaeis*. A decree allowed Jews, from 21st December 1799, to 'live and conduct economic activity on all the streets and squares of Warsaw' on payment of a 'ticket' [*bilet*] levy for new arrivals of 1 zlp daily.[7] This opened the gates of the town to wealthy Jews, though more poor Jews continued to flow in less legally. In 1805, 11,911 Jewish residents were counted in Warsaw (17.4 per cent). They were mainly petty traders, who settled in the so-called Pociejów in the very centre of the town (around today's Teatralny Square), much to the disgust of the old Varsovians.

On the eve of Corpus Christi, 16 June 1805, a church procession passed by that way. It appears that a few wooden shingles fell onto the canopy veiling the Holy Sacrament – possibly from the neighbouring, old roof. 'Some even claimed to have seen falling stones.' Someone must have shouted that it was Jews desecrating a Christian holiday. The excited crowd broke into the nearest building, and 'many Jews were beaten up and windows, doors and stoves in their houses damaged'. The riot lasted three days, and many shops were raided in Pociejów. The Prussian army intervened, arresting 95 people for looting. One was stabbed by a bayonet, and the majority were punished by flogging. The official communique given to the press claimed that those who joined in the unrest were 'masons' and carpenters, some without work, some blacksmiths and some chimney sweeps'; whereas the townspeople (*scilicet* – the wealthy) 'did not belong to this crowd'. This communique admitted that the 'bitterness was great on both the Jewish side and that of the common people', and, characteristically, 'Many Jews suspected of having prompted this unrest have already been arrested'. There was no mention in this report of the number of Jewish victims.[9]

The long history of Israel's diaspora is full of such incidents. A trivial circumstance allows moods in a Christian environment, fed by an exaggerated dislike, to be vented; there are also always people to be found on the spot who are willing to take advantage of the situation and indulge in looting. Press information on which historians have hereto relied does not appear completely trustworthy; we do have another source, however. Joachim Lelewel, who later became an eminent historian, was then a 19-year-old student at the University of Wilno. He received a letter from his younger brother with a description of the riot, and this news aroused him in a surprising way.

'Thank you, Brother' – he replied from Wilno on 18/30 June 1805 – 'for writing to me about the incidents involving the Jews in Warsaw. Various things have been said here. Hardly a week had gone by before it became much talked about . . . Please let me know how it ended, how many Jews died; for here the figure has grown from 50 to a thousand. They say priests were wounded by stones at the procession, and other strange things. There was great joy that the Varsovians did not fear the army . . . this was much admired here in Wilno and arouses hope for something more . . . they say that the instigators were German Lutherans who incited the Jews.'[10]

This letter seems to indicate indirectly that some Polish circles in Warsaw saw the anti-Jewish riots in a different light: as a test of strength of the Polish populace in Warsaw and that of the partitioning power. The Varsovians stood up to the Prussian soldiers who were defending the Jews; the Jewish arrivals were thus seen as the tools of the Prussians. This was obviously an irrational way of looking at the situation; it was in some way connected with the fact that quite influential Jewish entrepreneurs who shared good relations with the authorities were arriving in 'Southern Prussia' from Berlin. The similarity of Yiddish to the German language was immediately perceived. It was also at that time (from 1797) that the Jewish population received formal surnames at the instigation of the Prussian authorities – surnames which in the majority of cases sounded German.

On 17 July 1806 the Warsaw *magistrat* ordered the removal of Jews from a few of the city's main thoroughfares over a two-year period.[11] This step, taken by the Prussian authorities, probably as a result of the petitioning of Christian tradesmen, was not in keeping with their general policies, which tolerated, or even favoured, the influx of Jews into Warsaw. It is debatable whether the anti-Jewish occurrences of the previous year had encouraged the Prussian authorities to remove the cause of the conflict, which had also served to arouse the Warsaw populace against Prussian rule. However, the Prussians did not succeed in realising the above decree, for in November 1806 the Napoleonic army entered Warsaw. The Treaty of Tilsit in 1807 established the Duchy of Warsaw, affiliated to France.

The re-establishment of Polish authority and general patriotic euphoria accompanied a venting of anti-German feeling, and indirectly anti-Jewish feeling also – in so far as Warsaw's Jews were seen as German allies. This situation was taken advantage of by the persistent opponents of Jewish trade, who sent memoranda to the new Warsaw authorities. The Ruling Commission, established by Napoleon by a resolution of 26 January 1807, reintroduced the former civic privileges abolished by the Prussian government. The new president of Warsaw, Paweł Bieliński, declared that on this basis the status of Jews in Warsaw should return to its pre-partition norm. He refused recognition to the representatives of the Jewish commune, established in 1801, and appointed a Jewish adviser (*shtadlan*), according to the system of organization functioning in Warsaw between 1759–1794. The choice fell on Mosko Szmulowicz from Kutno. The Jewish representatives protested violently. The dispute was brought before the courts and ruling authorities who, after a few weeks of tension, gave up this idea, and, instead of imposing such an advisor on the Jews, returned (despite the protests of the *magistrat*) to the unofficial practice of coming to an agreement via 'the Jewish elders of Warsaw'.[12]

One of the circumstances that might have restrained the authorities of the new state from antagonising the Jews was the continuing war, which demanded great expenditure to maintain Napoleon's 'Grand Army' which, it seemed at the time, was returning Poland's independence to her. Thus the supply of meat, flour, cereal and forage for hundreds of thousands of soldiers and their horses, rested almost exclusively in the hands of Jewish suppliers.[13] It is often pointed out that it was during these war years that the careers of various Warsaw financiers began: the Fraenkels, Laskis, Epsteins and Kronenbergs, and that they earned their first millions supplying the army. This could be presented in another way. The Polish armed forces of the Duchy of Warsaw were born of patriotic fervour and social sacrifice, and proved themselves on the field of battle both by the fighting spirit of their soldiers and the performance of their leaders. But the army would have been unable to organize itself and to function without a constant vast supply of food, clothing, harness gear and transport. To provide a regular supply of biscuits and vodka, uniforms and footwear, arms and ammunition required particular energy and the full support of various *liweranci*: Neumark, Bergsohn, Fürstenberg and the most powerful of them: Judyta Jakubowiczowa, the widow of the famous Szmul Zbytkower. Samuel Antoni Fraenkel saw not only to the needs of the army, but also gave credits to the French resident in Warsaw during the winter crisis of 1812–1813. The Kingdom's Treasury undoubtedly overpaid these suppliers – but in Napoleon's catastrophe they suffered losses of millions. The organizational contribution of the Warsaw financiers to the Polish armed effort deserves to be remembered.

At this time, however, the authorities of the Duchy of Warsaw were far from recognising the Jewish population as a whole as equal citizens. The Duchy's Constitution as provided by Napoleon stated: 'All religious worship is to be free and public' (art.2) and: 'All citizens are equal before the law' (art.4). It would appear from this that the Jews, together with the Christians, gained, among other things, the right to participate in community gatherings, made up of 'property-owning citizens not of the *szlachta*', (art.21) and thus the right to elect deputies to the *Sejm* and participate in it. This seemed unthinkable, even for enlightened public opinion, during an epoch when the majority of Jewish communes, particularly in the provinces, were separated from the Polish populace by their traditions and beliefs. And just as the 'December decree' of 1807 had excluded the peasants from sharing in the benefits of the democratic constitution, which denied them rights to land, so did another decree of 17 October 1808 (that is directly before the first elections to the *Sejm*) postpone the Jews' right to citizens' rights for ten years. Though it was said that by favour of the monarch the right in question could be obtained by individual Jews, this promise remained on paper.[14] The suspension of political rights brought with it not only a ban on participation in the elections, but also on performing public functions, and a series of other restrictions on freedom of movement, conducting a profession, and tax obligations, of which more will be said below.

This decision had particular consequences for the Warsaw Jews. The Prussian decree of 18 July had ordered that they be removed from the town-centre over a two-year period. Before the limit was up 'the elders of the Warsaw Assembly of the Orthodox Faith' (*Starozakonne wyznanie*) turned to the government, now Polish, to have this eviction order lifted. On its part the *magistrat*, together with the representatives of the artisans' guilds, petitioned the King for the complete removal of Jews from the capital. The State council discussed this subject on a number of occasions; one of the ministers in favour of retaining the Jews was Prince Józef Poniatowski. Nevertheless in March 1809 the resolution to evict the Jews from the Old Town, and a few main thoroughfares (including the streets crossing them) was carried, to be realised by 4 October of that year. On these streets banned to the Jews (*egzymowane*), those Jews who had appropriate funds were allowed to stay, namely bankers and merchants able to 'read and write in Polish or French, or at least in German', who sent their children to public schools and who did not display 'any external signs which distinguished the Orthodox from other inhabitants'. However even this privilege for visibly assimilated Jews was limited to two Jewish families per street.[15]

A few weeks after this decree was announced, the Austrian army entered the Duchy of Warsaw. For 40 days, from the end of April to the beginning of June 1809, Warsaw found itself under hostile occupation. Meanwhile the Polish armies were enjoying some successes on the Galician front, and in July Napoleon's victory at Wagram ended this auspicious campaign. During this war, states a competent historian, 'The Warsaw Jews showed themselves on the whole to be loyal to Poland and did not incur charges of serving the aggressor in any way'.[16] In essence, the Polish Jews had no particular reason to sympathise with the Austrian regime which had been very hard on them during the reforms of Joseph II.

Despite this, hardly had the Austrians departed from Warsaw, when the *magistrat* began to expel the Jews from the town-centre, beginning with the Pociejów area, already mentioned. There was talk (avoiding the term 'ghetto') of establishing a Jewish 'district' in Warsaw. This was not legally very precise; there was no law forcing Jews to live in a given part of the city; it stipulated only where they could not live. *De facto*, however, such a district began to form in the northern part of the city, which retained its Jewish character right until the 2nd World War. In the first years the Jews erected rented houses hurriedly, which resulted in great overcrowding. There were tens of families to a house, in the annexes of some magnates' palaces which were beyond the town centre. One of the dignitaries who derived a substantial income from these compulsory tenants was Łubieński, the Minister of Justice.[17] After 1815, together with the stabilization of the economic situation, the Jews began to build up streets: Nalewki, Franciszkańska, Gęsia; some of the one-storeyed buildings then put up, built in the classical style, survived into the 20th century.

During the first years of the constitutional Congress Kingdom of Poland, between 1818 and 1822, over 40 articles appeared in Polish on Jewish questions.[18] They discussed which rights could and should be granted to the Jews. Apart from a few exceptions, they were mainly hostile towards their emancipation. The latter was seen as dependent on the assimilation of the Jews, but evaluated the chances of assimilation sceptically. Nor was this period of relative political freedom a happy one for the Jewish populace in general. The Polish establishment, made up of aristocrats (partly recent ones) and of higher officials of Enlightenment formation, such as Staszic, had a negative stance towards a social group which, they believed, held on stubbornly to anachronistic traditions. The more old-fashioned among them were shocked by the flaunted wealth of Warsaw financiers, the majority of whom were Jewish. J. U. Niemcewicz, in a biting pamphlet, (not currently in print) – 'The Year 3333', foretold that one need only look to the future and the Jews would be living in magnates' palaces, whereas the descendants of the *szlachta* would sink to the station of labourers. This prompted fear of the advance of those Jews who were assimilating, and repugnance for the way of life of those who did not wish to assimilate. Hence the unwillingness to promote reform. Therefore the exclusion of Jews from citizens' rights continued to be upheld after 1815, as were the streets from which Jews were barred in central Warsaw. In 1825 the *biletowy* levy was re-introduced – a daily fee for Jews coming to the capital (it had been abolished in 1811). Other taxes affecting the Jews were also introduced, the most severe being the kosher tax. The authorities began to bar Jews from running village inns, blaming them for the drunkenness of the peasants. This ban indirectly affected a few hundred Warsaw tavern-keepers of the Mosaic persuasion.

Legal discrimination against the Jews was based on religious criteria. Converts had access to all positions in theory, as the careers of many Frankists bear witness, with the Wołowski brothers at their head. Among the *Sejm* deputies of the city of Warsaw two outstanding representatives of the liberal opposition, the lawyers Dominik Krysiński and Antoni Łabecki were Frankists. However when the Chamber of Deputies, during the 1831 uprising, decided to promote a few of its members to the Senate and when one of those trying for such an advance turned out to be the Frankist Franiciszek Wołowski, 'his efforts did not achieve the desired results, for as a neophyte ('one of ours' according to the name given them) it was hesitated to present him for this aristocratic function'.[19]

Lack of understanding in conservative circles of Jewish emancipation was to have grave consequences. The Jewish financiers searched – and found – support for their interests above the heads of Polish society, among the Russians. One should remember that even though current adminstrative affairs at that time remained in the hands of Polish ministers and state advisers, the main political line, personnel issues, particularly government supplies, were decided by the Grand Duke Constantine and Senator Novosiltsov.

The Army of the Polish Kingdom absorbed almost a half of the income of the small state. For the Commander-in-Chief, the Tsar's brother, it was the apple of his eye and he equipped it richly, not allowing expenditure to be controlled in any way, so that it reached 30 million zlp annually. The supplies of cloth, linen, footwear, gold and silver braid, the equipment of the field hospitals, and food for the army, were all sources of great income. They were sought after by a process of acute competitive struggle, and not without taking advantage of illegal patronage. 'The greater part of this income', writes an expert on these questions 'was scooped up by the great Warsaw trade bourgeoisie: Jakubowicz, the Sonnenbergs, Löbensteins, Epsteins, Trzcińskis and Bansemerows; next came the capital's financiers, such as the Epsteins, Samuel Leizor Kronenberg, Samuel Antoni Fraenkel.'[20] These contracts for supply made possible access to the Grand Duke and his acolytes.

The leasing out of government monopolies and direct taxation (including Jewish taxes) were decided solely by Senator Novosiltsov, at least until the time that Minister Lubecki took over the Treasury and Taxation portfolios (1822). His right hand man was Leon Newachowicz, a baptised Jew from Petersburg who controlled, among other things, the consumer licence (for importing food into Warsaw), and was hated by the poorest people of the capital. Newachowicz's biography[21] places him among the wealthiest people of the Congress Kingdom. Novosiltsov himself arranged honorific loans which he never intended repaying, which included enormous sums from all the government suppliers.[22] The Senator also accepted bribes from the Warsaw *kahal* in return for lifting or reprieving the ban which deprived them of the licence to sell liquor. Novosiltsov squeezed contributions out of the Jews, failed to honour his promises to them, exacerbated relations between enlightened Jews and the Poles, and also used Jews unduly for purposes of political intelligence.[23] The Warsaw Jews, rich and poor, had no reason to respect Novosiltsov, who preyed on their persecution. This did not alter the fact that in the eyes of Polish patriotic opinion (which was at bottom well-disposed towards the Jews) many leading Jewish activists could be seen as creatures of the partitioning power.

The Jews had to face further trials during the November uprising (1830–

31). In Warsaw itself, they found themselves in the fire of the street battle of 29 November. Next they had to take a stance in the face of the opposing camps – between the National Government and the Patriotic Society, between the supporters of capitulation, or those of a battle to the end. The uprising brought crisis to all of Warsaw's poor: unemployment, high prices, a cholera epidemic, the threat of conflagration and destruction. The Jews were burdened with a double 'recruitment' tax, paid in return for exemption from military service.

On the Jewish question, as also in the case of the peasantry, the conservative authorities who led the uprising failed to decide on any reforms which might have won the support of previously indifferent sectors of the population for the national cause. It did not, therefore, occur to them to return citizens' rights to the Jews or to abolish discriminatory laws. Jews were not permitted to take part in the elections in the capital. The Supreme National Council promised the citizens' rights to those Jews who volunteered for the army, but only after ten years of service, (or sooner if they performed an 'exceptional act').[24]

In Warsaw, the National Guard provided an opportunity to engage in the battle in progress. This organization, based on the French model, was to be made up of wealthy citizens (the owners of property and enterprises) who were to equip themselves at their own cost, and whose role was to maintain order in the city. The Guard was to help the army with street patrols and to support them when necessary. Also (according to the understanding of its conservative leaders) it was to restrain the unruly populace. Jews also began to apply to join the Guard: not only because they wished to manifest their solidarity with the Poles, but also because they hoped that by engaging in an all-Polish movement they could gain equal rights for themselves.

As is known, the Warsaw bourgeoisie reacted negatively to the November uprising. On the first night of the insurrection the army fought, supported by volunteers from the intelligentsia and by Christian plebeians. The following two days saw riots breaking out in the city, the armed crowd attacking food shops and Russian military warehouses. It was to restrain this 'rabble' that a 'guard' was hurriedly improvised, made up of the affluent citizens, which was, later, named the National Guard. By December Jews also could be found in this patrolling guard.[25] On 10 December, Stanisław Hernisz, a student at the Rabbinical School, turned to General Chłopicki, offering to establish a separate Jewish regiment.[26] 10 days later a group of Jewish activists turned to Chłopicki with a concrete request: to allow at least assimilated Jews into the Warsaw National Guard. The dozen or so people who wished to enlist included financiers (Jakub Epstein, Samuel Kronenberg, two Teoplitz's), the bookseller Merzbach, a few doctors, and, above all, Antoni Eisenbaum, the spirtual leader of the Warsaw *Haskala*.[27] Chłopicki agreed, limiting entry into the guard to those Jews who were allowed to reside on the restricted streets, in accordance with the resolutions of 1809. Immediately the 'Orthodox . . . began to gather to enlist into the Guard. The most reliable managed to get uniforms and showed uncommon zeal in their service; the youth in particular who had attended Polish schools, crowded to this new profession.'[28]

In January 1831 Governor Antoni Ostrowski stood at the head of the capital's Guard, one of the few Polish aristocrats to have any understanding for the Jewish question. He was of the opinion that the surest way of assimilating the Jews into Polish society was by their complete emancipation. Ostrowski also categorically opposed any current antisemitic opinion, such as that: 'Jews are scoundrels, spies, allies of the Muscovite, damn this nation and so forth.'[29] He supported the recruitment of Jews into the Guard. The Christian Guard members from trade spheres were less well-disposed towards them: a deserving Jew distinguishing himself in armed service could become even more of a threat competitively! The following argument was therefore constructed by them: the decree of 1809 formulated to define the conditions of participation in the Guard allowed for no 'external features which have hereto distinguished the Orthodox from the rest of the people'. The beards of the Orthodox Jews were included among these 'external features'. The Christian youth did not wear beards at that time and beards in the army were regarded as particularly intolerable. The leader of the Guard, Ostrowski, agreed: Jews could enter the Guard if they shaved off their beards. Representatives of the Orthodox Jews argued that 'shaving off one's beard adds neither good will towards the country nor courage'. Rabbi Salomon Lipszyc, asked for his opinion, expressed himself carefully: he did not forbid Jews to don the uniform of the Guard, but he could not order them to shave their beards – although there were other methods, apart from the razor, to trim them.[30]

Antoni Ostrowski found a compromise. For those Jews who applied to the guard but who refused to shave off their beards, he created a separate 'Civil Guard'; he spoke of it as an institution which would be 'preparatory and transitory, less honorific than the National Guard itself, but close to it'.[31] But this formation also met with obstacles: members of the 'national' guard wanted to deny the 'civil' guard members the right to wear confederates' caps, Polish eagles, even arms. They were successful on only one point, the Civil Guard received with its navy blue uniform tobacco-brown, instead of amaranth, lapels. This petty persecution of Jewish volunteers weakened their desire to enlist. The Civil Guard was slow in acquiring new members and it was not until mid-August 1831 that its numbers reached around 1,000 people. The Polish leadership spoke of its service with full recognition. At the beginning of 1831 the National Guard had over 6,000 volunteers, over 5,000 by the summer, including 300–400 Jews who had shaved off their beards. Some were chosen to be officers.[32]

Service in both guards mobilized and encouraged the solidarity in its ranks of the rebelling townspeople – Christians as well as Jews – who had until then not been involved at all in politics. However the Guard did not affect the course of military events; the Polish leadership did not trust it and did not want to use it, even during the decisive September battles in Warsaw.

One should look separately at the involvement of Jewish converts in political life in 1831. A few outstanding men such as Krępowiecki or Czyński found themselves on the left wing of the Patriotic Society; their Jewish descent was maliciously pointed out by their opponents. Czyński was one of the few who spoke out in the Society in favour of granting Jews full rights.[33] Then and later there was much discussion about the role played during the uprising by the Frankists, but it was not unambiguous. It is sufficient here to mention three close relatives, the Krysińskis. Aleksander Krysiński was the general secretary of General Chłopicki, then an aide-de-camp and delegate of the Commander-in-Chief Skrzynecki. On the left he was spoken of as the 'evil spirit' of the insurrection, accused publicly of treachery and scheming with Petersburg.[34] Deputy Dominik Krysiński, mentioned above, attacked the dictatorship in the *Sejm* and opposed the capitulators.[35] Finally, General Jan Krysiński was the commander of the fortress of Zamość; he was the last to capitulate in the November Insurrection, honourably, and not until 21 October 1831, seven weeks after the fall of Warsaw.[36]

The November uprising opened before Jewish society a temporary prospect of entering the Polish struggle for independence. In Warsaw this idea was taken up by quite large groups of Jews, not only assimilated ones or those prompted by the thought of emancipation. This commitment of the Jews was not employed as fully as it deserved to be, among other reasons because of continuing mistrust and dislike on the Polish side. Meanwhile the defeat of the uprising nipped the possibility of cooperation in the bud.

The system of repression inaugurated after the uprising by Governor-General Paskievich affected both the Christian and Jewish populace of Warsaw. A citadel was erected on the outskirts of the city, and around 250 houses were destroyed on its site. A few thousand people were rehoused, a large percentage of whom were Jews, who had lived in this area. During the uprising, police rigour had slackened, and many Jews had moved to the restricted districts; now they were evicted again.[37] Military contributions were paid by all Varsovians, regardless of their religion.

The wealthiest social sectors adapted to the new regime most easily and willingly: that is, a fraction of the aristocracy and all the financiers. Business deals were conducted – on credits from the Bank of Poland, by leaseholding monopolies, and later by building railways in agreement with the higher authorities – by all kinds of speculators, not only Jews, although the latter were most successful – more particularly, Fraenkel, Epstein,

Kronenberg, Rosen – alongside these native Varsovians a man who had come from Russia, Maurycy Koniar. It was business people, above all, who crowded into the apartments of the Governor-General; but patriotic opinion was more upset by the servility of the bankers than that of the native *szlachta*.

> It is not until you get there [Warsaw] that you will hear and understand what Poland is today, how fawning everyone is, how corruptible, how it is ten times worse to have Poles in office than the Muscovite; how the last shreds of honour are collapsing around the nation's ears, how the Jews and Germans are profiting from poverty and disgrace, how the Jews settle on the ruins of our palaces, how everywhere it is Jews and Jews only who have influence, meaning, power, means.

These words were written five years after the uprising by Zygmunt Krasiński,[38] author of the 'Undivine Comedy' (*Nieboska Komedia*), in which drama he accuses the 'converts', among others, of cooperating with world revolution.

In the ranks of the 'Great Emigration' of Poles to Western Europe there were indeed a few democratic activists of Jewish descent. But in Warsaw in the 1830s and 40s there is no note of any Jews in the revolutionary underground. Of course the appeal 'To the Israelites' written by Ludwik Lubliner and supported by Lelewel did reach Warsaw from Brussels. Listing the wrongs done them by the partitioning power, the appeal turns to the Jews saying: 'There is no other way of suspending these wrongs than by achieving citizenship and uniting with the Polish nation! . . . then, when the Polish nation achieves its full rights, that is when a restored democratic Poland is established.'[39] Aleksander Wężyk, the leader of the Warsaw cell of the clandestine 'Association of the Polish People' (*Stowarzyszenie Ludu Polskiego*) reworked this appeal and made it more concrete. Demonstrating the similar fate of both nations, Polish and Jewish, equally persecuted by the Tsar, he states categorically: 'Divided, we shall both perish . . . only mutual assistance and aims can be effective. In an independent Poland there shall in future be no differences between the Christian Pole and the Pole of the Mosaic faith. In a future Poland, if through work God permits us to have it, all will be free, all will enjoy equal rights, we will all be joined by a bond of brotherly love.'[40]

This was a significant declaration. Polish democrats for the first time offered the Jews 'freedom, equality and brotherhood,' in exchange for their participation in the struggle and in the building in the future of a common nation. In Warsaw this appeal, for the moment, made no impact. One of the conspirators, without giving the matter any thought, took the appeal to the banker Loewenstein in an envelope. He, however, handed it to the police.

This was the start of the arrest and collapse of the conspiracy in Warsaw.[41] In Kraków, in this year, the Polish conspirators already had links with Jewish circles. In the Warsaw of Paskievich, it was still too early for such links.

In May 1846 Sir Moses Montefiore was passing through Warsaw. He was returning from Petersburg, where he had met Tsar Nicholas, interceding on behalf of the Jewish people persecuted within the empire. His arrival in Warsaw aroused the local Jews and was reported to London by the British consul Du Plat:

'Their hopes are raised to the highest pitch, and his presence here has caused a most extraordinary sensation amongst all classes. The hotel where he lives is literally besieged from morning to night; the small square in its front is filled with persons of all ages. Police agents are obliged to guard the door of the house, and even the doors of his apartments, and he cannot stir beyond their threshold, no matter whether on foot, or in a carriage, without being followed by a dense crowd that increases as it moves along, and fills whole streets . . . As for the poor Jews themselves, they look upon him, and actually call him, their Messiah'.[42]

The consul himself wondered if placing their hopes for help in the West might not bring disappointment to the Polish Jews.

The turning point in mutual relations between the Jews and Polish patriotic circles took place in Warsaw at the beginning of the second half of the century. A few elements come into play here: the unremitting anti-Jewish policies of Nicholas's regime, marked by new administrative and fiscal rigours and the delaying of further discussions concerning Jewish emancipation; the Jews could expect nothing from the Tsar.[43] I have already mentioned the inclusion of the Jewish question in the programme of the independent Polish struggle. However it was the Warsaw circle of the *Haskala*, above all, which began to work for closer cooperation with the Poles from the mid-19th century.

This was due in the first place to Antoni Eisenbaum, the director of the so-called Rabbinic School, in which lay subjects were taught in Polish alongside study of the Talmud and Hebrew tongue. Treated with some mistrust by Orthodox circles, Eisenbaum managed to gain the support of a few financiers, such as Matias Rosen and Teodor Toeplitz, and began to campaign for the introduction of the Polish language into the 'reformed' synagogues. The first Polish sermon in the synagogue on Nalewki Street was given by Rabbi Izaak Kramsztyk in 1852. Of greater significance was winning over the so-called German synagogue which was attended by the majority of assimilated Jews. Jakub Bossakowski, a Polish official in the Russian administration, includes the following description of the synagogue in 1860 in his report on the state of the Polish Kingdom:

> This synagogue, situated in one of the houses on Danilowiczowska Street is exceptionally well appointed; elegant and yet simple, it

> reminds one in many respects of a Christian house of prayer. A separate committee runs the synagogue . . . and the whole of Warsaw's enlightened Jewry belongs to it. In this remarkable synagogue I attended services with uplifting, harmonious singing of good voices, and also sermons in the German language, given with conviction by the well-known, educated and enlightened Rabbi Jastrow (Ph.D.). He is zealously studying the Polish language in order to be able to deliver sermons in this language, in accordance with the wishes of the synagogue committee.[44]

In January 1859 *Gazeta Warszawska*, in an incidental article on musical life, included offensive, anti-semitic remarks directed against local Jews. Over two hundred well-known Jews from assimilated circles turned to the editor Lesznowski with a demand for public compensation. The editor acted in bad faith, turning to the Russian director of the Commission for Internal Affairs, Mukhanov. This very unpopular and well-known anti-semite put Lesznowski under police protection. The polemic took fire in the whole of the Polish press, beyond the borders of the Tsarist Empire of course, as the Tsar's censorship silenced pro-Jewish voices in Warsaw. This storm in a teacup did indeed have favourable repercussions for Polish-Jewish understanding. Anti-semites were compromised in the eyes of the public: the Jews on the other hand found that they could expect support and understanding from certain circles. The writer and emancipationist Narcyza Żmichowska, connected with organic work circles, who was aware of this 'Jewish struggle', wrote to a friend in Poznań:

> You should know first of all that the Congress Jews are not at all like your Poznań masses; there they have joined with the Germans, here they stand as a crowd, but separately, strong in their unity and industry; I think that generally they do not love Poland as they should. I know for sure, however, that after a few dozen years of recruitment [into the army] they sincerely detest the Muscovites . . . The whole of the Jewish intelligentsia, that is the whole of the academic intake educated in various universities, with all their skills and energy, stand openly and sincerely on the side of the nation assigned them by God . . . And of course I admit that this alien element is harmful to us in that they grow wealthier as we grow poorer, they swindle, speculate and above all make gains. Still, I must admit that they constitute a force, and simple political reason indicates that it is better to have such a force with one than against one.[45]

The Warsaw banker Leopold Kronenberg also drew appropriate conclusions from the 'Jewish war'. He bought up the *Gazeta Codzienna*, rival to the *Gazeta Warszawska*, brought in J. I. Kraszewski as its editor –

one of the most widely-read writers of the time – and Kraszewski, till then considered an anti-semite, ran the *Gazeta Codzienna* in a liberal spirit, in a spirit of understanding with the Jews.

The death of Nicholas I and the reform policies begun by his successor awakened the Jews' hope of achieving emancipation. Beginning in 1856 the council of the Jewish *kahal* in Warsaw submitted memoranda to the local authorities concerning the need to lift discriminatory restrictions. However, all these attempts met with categorical refusals.[46] Given these circumstances, it comes as no surprise that, when there was an outbreak of Russo-Polish conflict, the representatives of the *kahal* came out on the Polish side.

On 25 and 27 Feburary 1861 there were clashes between the people and the army on the streets of Warsaw. Shots were fired, and there were some victims. On the night of the 27th, a City Delegation was elected at a crowded meeting made up of a dozen leading citizens. Rabbi Meisels was also requested to attend – it was remembered that in his previous post at Kraków during the revolutionary year of 1848 he had shown solidarity with the Polish movement. The next morning Meisels reported to the palace of Count Andrzej Zamoyski, and was one of the first to sign an address to the Tsar asking, in general terms, that the Polish nation should have its rights restored. The statement was made public. Zamoyski spoke of the 'Orthodox as our countrymen and brothers, the children on one land'. Meisels replied 'And we too feel that we are Poles, and we love the Polish land as you do'.[47] Two days later Rabbis Meisels and Jastrow took part in the funeral of five victims of the uprising. Meisels was co-opted into the City Delegation. In a solemn procession of the members of the Delegation to the Town Hall Meisels walked at the side of Fr. Stecki and the banker Rosen with Fr. Wyszyński.[48]

On 11 March the British consul Stanton expressed the opinion that reaching an agreement with the Jews constituted the Polish 'national party's' strongest trump-card at that moment.[49] An appeal written in Hebrew and composed by Meisels was launched throughout the country. It reminded the Jews of all the persecution they had suffered at the hands of Mukhanov, whom he compared to the biblical Haman. He announced the wilingness of the Poles to grant the Jews equal rights; the appeal also called on the Jews to support the Polish national movement. The Austrian consul, Lederer, called the appeal 'an open declaration of war' on the Tsarist government.[50] The Polish-Jewish fraternal demonstrations in Warsaw have been described many times. Władysław Mickiewicz, son of the poet, who was visiting in Poland at the time, wrote to his fiancée from Warsaw on 2 July 1861:

> The Jews here are the best in all of Poland. They sing national anthems in the synagogues. The sermons they give in the synagogues

about love of the fatherland unite Poles and Jews in a single emotion, and the thought that a Poland will arise wakens hope in the Jews that their dispersal is coming to an end. A certain rabbi when asked what he wished for his co-religionists answered: that they should be forbidden to buy land as they should hold themselves in readiness for the return to Jerusalem.[51]

Today we look at 1861 and the rather unusual fraternization between the two nations with some detachment: the Poles with a kind of emotional tolerance at most, the Jews with ironic scepticism.[52] In essence, the January uprising was a failure, and with this failure was shattered the hope for a mutually fought and won victory. The paths of the two societies began to part once more, as the nationalist feelings of both grew. Among the Poles anti-semitism increased again; among the Jews – a tendency appeared here and there to seek understanding with the victorious partitioning power. Leopold Kronenberg, banker to the National Government, was transformed a few years after the uprising into a delegate of the Tsarist Governor-General Berg.

But one can look at that long dead history from another point of view. The Polish-Jewish rapprochement, born in a revolutionary situation, brought both sides clear advantages. For the Jews of Warsaw themselves it opened up the possibility of public action in defence of their own interests; it is enough to look at *Jutrzenka, tygodnik dla Izraelitów polskich*, which Daniel Neufeld edited in Warsaw from July 1861, to see how these were expressed.[53] Above all, the emergence of the Polish movement and Jewish support of it precipitated Jewish legal and political emancipation by the Tsarist government. Senator Valerian Platonov, delegate of Alexander II, formulated the question thus in his memorandum of 6/18 April 1861:

Today we have against us (the fact cannot be hidden) in the first place all the women and all the clergy, land-owners, clerks, particularly in subordinate positions, the inhabitants of the towns, above all those of Warsaw. The Jews also have yielded to the pressure exerted against them. Since they are not motivated by patriotism their defection must be attributed, in the first place to fear, in some degree to vanity, since they are at this moment treated as equals by the Poles, finally to the promises that the Poles have not hesitated to make to them, but which they have no intention of fulfilling, should they prove successful.

If the inhabitants of the Kingdom persist in their illusions and refuse to cooperate loyally with the government, there will be no alternative but to establish a military government in this country. It will be necessary resolutely to base oneself on the support of the

> peasants and the Jews . . . granting to the Jews the civil and political rights enjoyed by the other inhabitants of the Kingdom of Poland.[54]

Alexander II's *ukase* of 23 May/4 June 1862 was the realisation of just such a policy.

At the same time, for the Polish patriots, Jewish access to the national movement strengthened their self-confidence and their position in relation to the partitioning power and also to the hereto passive peasantry. It also provided the uprising with many dedicated Jewish co-workers in the national organization and in armed battle.[55] The most well known exiles should be named here: Paweł Landowski, Władysław Rawicz, Henryk Wohl.

So much for the immediate evaluation. But taken from a longer perspective? I cannot make any statements about the gains or losses from the Jewish point of view. But, from the Polish side, active participation in the events of 1861–3 won many outstanding people for the Polish cause, who performed many services for both sectors of society in the post-uprising period. Suffice it to mention, among many others, the sociologist Ludwik Gumplowicz, Aleksander Kraushar the historian, Aleksander Lesser the painter, medalier Jan Minheimer, Jakub Natanson the chemist, Hilary Nussbaum the pedagogue, the bookseller Maurycy Orgelbrand and the journalist Chaim Slonimski. They were all more or less deeply committed to the national movement of the 60s, and each of them also owed something to it.

One last reflection: in our century of rampant national egoism, and intensified scorn for 'alien' elements, it is worth showing more understanding for such a distant, fleeting attempt at Polish-Jewish rapprochement, an attempt to overcome old antagonisms – an attempt which could indeed have proved more fruitful, but which did not disappear completely, not without leaving echoes.

NOTES

1 S. Szymkiewicz, *Warszawa na przełomie XVIII i XIX w.* (Warsaw, 1959), pp. 139–140; A. Eisenbach, *Kwestia równouprawnienia Żydów w Królestwie Polskim* (Warsaw, 1972), p. 65; *Rocznik statystyczny Królestwa Polskiego. Rok 1914* (Warsaw, 1915).

2 The history of the Jewish question during the Enlightenment does not fall within the limits of this article. Cf. A. Eisenbach 'Żydzi warszawscy i sprawa żydowska w XVIII w' in *Warszawa XVIII w.*, no. 3 (Warsaw, 1975). A collection of articles: *Materiały do dziejów sejmu czteroletniego*, vol. VI (Wrocław, 1969).

3 K. Zienkowska, 'Spór o Nową Jerozolimę', *Kwartalnik Historyczny*, 1987, p. 370. The Aleje Jerozolimskie, one of Warsaw's main thoroughfares, took its name indirectly from this 'new Jerusalem'.

4 A. Zahorski, *Warszawa w powstaniu kościuszkowskim* (Warsaw, 1967), pp. 167, 175.

5 J. Wasicki, *Ziemie polskie pod zaborem pruskim. Prusy Południowe 1793–1806.* (Wrocław, 1957), pp. 292–4.

6 A. Eisenbach, *Kwestia* . . . , p. 100.
7 Ibid., 'Mobilność terytorialna ludności żydowskiej w Królestwie Polskim' in: *Społeczeństwo ludności żydowskiej w Warszawie w świetle spisu 1810 r.*, *Biuletyn Żydowskiego Instytutu Historycznego* (Ż.I.H.), no. 13–14, 1955, p. 87.
8 Ibid., p. 82.
9 'Gazeta Warszawska', 23 VI, 2 VII 1805. Cf. F. M. Sobieszczański, *Rys historyczny wzrostu i stanu miasta Warszawy* (Warsaw, 1974), pp. 137–8. H. Nusbaum, *Szkice historyczne z życia Żydów w Warszawie* (Warsaw, 1981), pp. 26–7, with the incorrect date 1804 (possibly a misprint).
10 J. Lelewel, *Listy do rodzeństwa pisane*, vol. I (Poznań, 1878), pp. 32–33.
11 A. Eisenbach, *Mobilność* . . . p.187. W. Sobociński, *Historia ustroju i prawa Księstwa Warszawskiego* (Toruń, 1964), p. 89.
12 A. Eisenbach, 'Status prawny ludności żydowskiej w Warszawie w końcu XVIII i na początku XIX w.', *Biul.ŻIH*, no. 39, 1961, pp. 5–11.
13 Abundant material exists relating to these supplies: J. Kosim, *Losy pewnej fortuny* (Wrocław, 1972), a monograph on the firm of Ignacy Neumark & Co., section II, On Fraenkel: *Instrukcje i depesze rezydentów francuskich w Warszawie* (Kraków, 1914), vol. II (according to the index).
14 *Ustawodawstwo Księstwa Warszawskiego* vol. I (Warsaw, 1964), pp. 143, 148. A. Eisenbach, *Kwestie* . . . , pp. 26–7.
15 *Protokoły Rady Stanu Księstwa Warszawskiego* (Toruń, 1962), vol. I, section 2, p. 317; vol. II, section 1, pp. 112, 137. *Ustawodawstwo Księstwa Warszawskiego*, vol. II, pp. 26–30. A. Szczypiorski, *Ćwierć wieku Warszawy 1806–1830* (Wrocław, 1964), p. 11.
16 B. Pawłowski, *Warszawa w roku 1809* (Torun, 1948), p. 127.
17 A. Eisenbach, 'Rozprzestrzenienie i warunki mieszkaniowe ludności żydowskiej w Warszawie w świetle spisu w 1815 r.', *Biul. ŻIH*, 1953, pp. 63–4.
18 Cf. *Bibliografia historii Polski XIX w.*, vol. I (Wrocław, 1958), sections 3864–3903.
19 W. Wężyk, *Kronika rodzinna* (Warsaw, 1987), p. 299.
20 J. Kosim, op.cit., p. 52.
21 Biography of Newachowicz, *Polski Słownik Biograficzny*, XXII pp. 699–700.
22 J. Kosim, op.cit., pp. 90, 197–9, 224–5 and others.
23 D. Kandel, 'Nowosilcow a Żydzi', *Biblioteka Warszawska*, 1911, vol. III. S. Askenazy, *Łukasiński* (Warsaw, 1929), vol. I, p. 64. One should mention here also the well-known case of the spy Joel Birnbaum, who terrorized, almost exclusively, Jews in Warsaw. On Birnbaum: M. Karpińska, 'Policje tajne w Królestwie Kongresowym', *Przegląd Historyczny*, 1985, pp. 684–6. On p. 696 the author calculates that the number of Jews among secret agents between 1815–30 came to 23.2 per cent.
24 W. Lewandowski, 'Materiały do udziału Żydów w gwardii narodowej, gwardii miejskiej i straży bezpieczeństwa w powstaniu listopadowym 1830–31', *Biul.ŻIH*, no. 19/20, 1956, p. 117.
25 M. Meloch, 'Warszawa w pierwszych dniach powstania listopadowego' in: *Studia z dziejów Warszawy 1830–31* (Warsaw, 1937), p. 70.
26 W. Lewandowski, op.cit., p. 115.
27 S. Warszawski, 'Gwardia miejska miasta stołecznego Warszawy podczas powstania listopadowego 1830–31', *Miesięcznik Żydowski*, vol. I p. 56.
28 A. Ostrowski, *Pamiętnik z czasów postania listopadowego* (Wrocław, 1961), p. 129.
29 Ibid. p. 127. An overview of the polemics of 1831 on Jewish subjects: A. Eisenbach, *Wielka Emigracja wobec kwestii żydowskiej 1832–1848* (Warsaw, 1976), pp. 80–107.
30 S. Warszawski, op.cit., pp. 56–8.
31 A. Ostrowski, op.cit., p. 131.

32 Ibid., pp. 130, 185 passim. S. Warszawski, op.cit., pp. 58–60. W. Lewandowski, op.cit., pp. 120–7.

33 W. Zajewski, *Walki wewnętrzne ugrupowań politycznych w powstaniu listopadowym* (Gdańsk, 1967), p. 191.

34 J. Ziółek, 'Dziennik Aleksandra Krysińskiego z 1830/31 r.', *Przegląd Historyczny*, 1974.

35 W. Zajewski, op.cit., pp. 69, 162–4.

36 Cf. biography of J. Krysiński, *PSB* XV pp. 478–9.

37 A. Szczypiorski, *Warszawa, jej gospodarka i ludność w latach 1832–1862* (Warsaw, 1966), p. 203.

38 Z. Krasiński, *Listy do Adama Sołtana* (Warsaw, 1970), p. 98, letter from 1.8.1836.

39 J. Lelewel, *Polska, dzieje i rzeczy jej*, vol. XX (Poznań, 1864), p. 260. Cf. A. Eisenbach, *Wielka Emigracja* . . . p. 371.

40 *Odezwa do Żydów, maj 1838, Stowarzyszenie Ludu Polskiego i świetokrzyżcy* (Wrocław, 1978), pp. 207–8.

41 Ibid., p. 48, introduction by W. Djakow.

42 Du Plat to Aberdeen, 16.V.1846, PRO FO 65/285.

43 On the anti-Jewish Tsarist policies as one of the causes of Jewish interest in the independent Polish cause see Rabbi M. Jastrow who wrote very clearly on the subject in: *Die Vorläufer des polnischen Aufstandes* (Leipzig, 1864), p. 27.

44 J. Bossakowski, *Gospodarka i finanse Królestwa Polskiego przed powstaniem styczniowym* (Warsaw, 1969), p. 393. Cf. H. Nusbaum, op.cit., pp. 91–102 who notes that Jastrow had already given a sermon in Polish in 1859.

45 N. Żmichowska, *Listy*, vol. II (Wrocław, 1960), pp. 131–2, letter dated 6.II.1859. Cf. W. Przyborowski, *Historia dwóch lat*, vol. I (Kraków, 1892), pp. 243–58. A. Eisenbach, *Kwestia* . . . p. 272–81.

46 Ibid., pp. 257–8, 284–306.

47 S. Kieniewicz, *Powstanie styczniowe* (Warsaw, 1983), p. 117.

48 J. K. Janowski, *Pamiętniki o powstaniu styczniowym* vol. III (Warsaw, 1931), p. 208.

49 Stanton to Russell, 11.III.1861. PRO FO 65/583.

50 N. Gelber, *Die Juden und der polnische Aufstand 1863* (Vienna, 1923), p. 161 n. The most accurate Polish translation of the reply: D. Kandel, 'Z roku 1861', *Kwartalnik poświęcony przeszłości Żydów w Polsce*, vol. I, 1912, pp. 144–7. Cf. F. Kupfer, *Ber Meisels* (Warsaw, 1953), pp. 89–92.

51 W. Mickiewicz, *Pamiętniki* (Warsaw, 1927), vol. II, p. 114.

52 The following article, among others, by M. Opalska is written in this tone: 'Polish-Jewish Relations and the January Uprising. The Polish Perspective', *Polin*, vol. I, 1986.

53 Cf. M. Fuks, *Prasa żydowska w Warszawie 1823–1939* (Warsaw, 1979), pp. 128–9.

54 *Korespondencja namiestników Królestwa Polskiego z 1861 roku* (Wrocław, 1964), pp. 128–9.

55 Cf. a variety of sources: *Żydzi a powstanie styczniowe. Materiały i dokumenty* (Warsaw, 1963).

8

THE JEWISH COMMUNITY IN THE POLITICAL LIFE OF ŁÓDŹ IN THE YEARS 1865–1914

Paweł Samuś

Social and political life in Łódź after the January Uprising of 1863 was influenced by numerous factors. These include the dynamic economic development of the city, the rapid growth of its population and its multinational structure. The socio-national conglomeration stimulated the growth of nationalist feelings, but also, on the other hand, provided a favourable background, especially in workers' circles, for the spread of internationalist ideas. The city's political life certainly developed in unfavourable legal and constitutional conditions. Among them were the reactionary political system of the Russian state, the lack of democratic institutions and national freedom in the Kingdom of Poland, the ban on meetings, political parties and trade unions (until 1906), and the extensive police control.[1] Łódź had no self-government, but a bureaucratic municipal council nominated by the Russian authorities. In addition, other public institutions which were necessary to create bonds of community and improve the quality of life of the many immigrants of different nationalities and social status who were attracted by this Polish 'Promised Land'[2] and who were lacking in the elements of civilization were either created too late, or had a very little influence. The ban on legal, political and social activity forced people to conspiracy. Many Polish and Jewish workers came to the conclusion that only violent forms of struggle were effective and often adopted terrorist methods.

Political life in Łódź in the period between the January Uprising and the First World War was marked by a characteristic irregularity. Long periods of quiescence were followed by violent outbreaks – short periods of unnatural acceleration such as, for example, the Łódź Uprising of May 1892, or the 1905–1907 Revolution. This pattern was, of course, closely related to the general situation the Polish Kingdom, where the rhythm of political life was similar. Yet nowhere else on Polish territory did this acceleration demonstrate such an extraordinary pace, or reveal itself with such force.

The position of Jews was determined not only by these factors but also by additional elements, among them the legal conditions under which they lived. Aleksander Wielopolski's reforms of 1862 abolished almost all discriminatory regulations which affected the Jewish population in the Polish Kingdom. These had affected freedom of settlement, purchase of land and the granting of civic rights. As a consequence, equality before the law was established. Yet the period after the 1863 Uprising saw many of these rights restricted and equality before the law in fact abolished. The policy of Russification initiated by the Tsarist authorities in the Polish Kingdom also brought with it the limitation of the rights of the Jewish community.

The enfranchisement *ukase* had already restricted Jewish communal self-government. That of 3 May 1882 introduced a temporary prohibition on the sale, lease or mortgage to Jews of estates outside town limits. They were also forbidden to settle in the country. Four years later, stricter penalties were imposed on Jews refusing to serve in the army. The right of Jews to participate in the governing of primary schools was limited in the late 'eighties. They were not allowed to fulfil public services, except as medical doctors and engineers. Their access to the legal profession was limited, and they were only permitted to fulfil the function of a commissioner of oaths. At the beginning of the 'nineties, restrictions on the change of Jewish names were tightened and Jews were issued with special identity documents. The period of the 1905–1907 revolution saw some relaxation of anti-Jewish legal discrimination. Yet as early as 1908–1909, a *numerus clausus* was introduced in universities (10 per cent) and high schools (15 per cent). The discriminatory policy of the Tsarist authorities created an atmosphere favourable to anti-Jewish pogroms. Legal discrimination affected the poorer sections of the Jewish population most severely, since the bourgeoisie and the better-off Jews in general were able, in various ways, to ease their situation and evade discriminatory laws.

The religious community *(kehilla)* played an important role in the life of the Jewish community. Officially its functions were limited to religious matters, as the Tsarist authorities did not concede to it prerogatives of self-government. After 1862, the *kehilla* was placed under stricter government supervision. The regulations of the *Komitet Urządzający* (The Organizing Committee) in the Polish Kingdom of 1867–68, laid down that rabbis, deputy-rabbis and cantors be appointed and dismissed from their functions by provincial governors. In reality, these officials merely confirmed candidates elected by the community. The *kehilla* was also subject to the control of another organ of the state administration as well, the Municipal Office.[3]

The influence of the *kehilla* went far beyond the sphere of religion and the control of the community's property. It affected the cultural and socio-political life of the Jewish population, and backed, financially and morally, Jewish social and cultural institutions, such as schools and charity organizations.

Rabbi Eliasz Chaim Majzel (1821–1912) was the head of Łódź *kehilla* for several decades. Born in Grodek, in the Wilno gubernia, of a rich family, he distinguished himself by his exceptional abilities already as a boy. He received the title of rabbi very early and took an appropriate post in his home town when only nineteen. In 1853 he became a rabbi in Dereczyn and next in Pruzan (1861–1867), where he founded a hospital during a cholera epidemic. He himself took an active part in fighting the disease. Finally he became the rabbi of Łomża, where he also worked to help the Jewish population. A year after the death in 1872 of the Łódź rabbi, Mojżesz Lipszyc, Majzel was elected to this post. He held the office for almost forty years and throughout that time was the initiator of, and participant in, many Jewish social and philanthropic undertakings in Łódź. He founded *Talmudei-Tora* with a reformed study programme. With his own capital, he opened a factory to give work to the unemployed, although, lacking the backing of industrialists, the enterprise failed. He also attempted to establish a settlement society to purchase land from Jewish land-owners in Poland and to organize agricultural settlements. Young Jews were to acquire agricultural qualifications and knowledge and with the help of the society emigrate to Palestine to work on farms there. The concept had many supporters, but also aroused opposition and in the end was never realized. Rabbi Majzel was very popular among Jews in Łódź and in the whole Russian empire. In his last years he was probably the most senior rabbi in the Russian Empire.

The dominant role in the *kehilla* in Łódź was played by the bourgeoisie, and industrialists and merchants were also often elected to the synagogal supervising body (elected every three years). In the seventies and eighties such functions were held by such men as Jakub Dobraniecki, Abram Prussak, Izrael Poznański and Szaja Rosenblatt.

The social inequalities within the Jewish community and discrimination against the poor in the *kehilla* were manifested in various ways. For example, the poor were, in effect, unable to pray in the magnificent synagogue at the corner of the Spacerowa (today Kościuszko) and Zielona Streets, as they could not afford to buy, or lease, a seat. The beginning of the twentieth century, as was reported by the contemporary Łódź press,[4] saw a number of incidents, sometimes even brawls, at the entrance to the synagogue, when its officials prohibited poor, badly-dressed Jews who wanted to participate in the religious ceremonies, from entering. There were not enough synagogues in the city; only three existed down to 1900 and a fourth was constructed in the years before the outbreak of the First World War.[5] In this situation, the poor had to satisfy themselves with modest prayer houses organized in hired apartments or other premises.

The capitalist conditions of the second half of the nineteenth century were not the only cause of the increasing differentiation within the Jewish community. Although Jews preserved their religious and national isolation, they were affected by the process of Jewish emancipation and by the religious reforms within Judaism. Already in the early sixties, a journalist of the periodical *Jutrzeńka* (1862) described the growing divisions within the Łódź Jewish community. He characterized two groups as follows:

> One, grouping almost a third [there were then about 5,000 Jews in Łódź], does not differ either in appearance, in customs, or in language from true Poles . . . They eagerly send their children to state schools, and have even attempted to open an elementary and an evening school . . . they take their place in the new synagogue constructed in the Old Town, yet for themselves they are organizing a separate prayer house, where they want to introduce reforms like those in practice in the Warsaw synagogue. The second category forms, alas, a sad contrast. Outlandish dress, Babylonian speech, disorderly religious services, odd customs, superstitious visions – these are their main characteristics.[6]

Throughout this period, Orthodox groups, devoted followers of hasidism and defenders of tradition, held a strong position among the Łódź Jews. They opposed any reforms, kept apart from non-Jews, and their attitude towards the outside world retained the traditional dichotomies. Yet in the conditions of rapid social and political change, new ideas and attitudes became more attractive, especially among the young Jewish intelligentsia. This was made up of doctors, hospital attendants, bank and trade clerks and white-collar workers. Tradition and religion were regarded as outmoded within this progressive intelligentsia. Its members were inclined towards modernity and assimilation and favoured professional and social contacts with Christians and, in particular, with progressive Polish groups. The majority of the Jewish community, as is often the case, probably took an intermediate position, while advocates of radical solutions of both the secular and religious sort found themselves in sharp conflict, and the leader of the Łódź community, Rabbi Majzel attempted, with varying results, to reconcile their clashes.[7]

The Jewish bourgeoisie was also not homogenous. Two rival groups emerged. One, headed by a group of rich settled Łódź bourgeois, the other by the 'Litvaks'. The latter were Jews who had emigrated from the western territories of the Russian empire in the eighties after they were allowed to move out of the 'Pale of Settlement' into the Polish Kingdom. They had capital at their disposal, were very enterprising, and became serious economic rivals to the old Łódź bourgeoisie. The 'Litvaks' were not a cohesive group. Partly Russified and lacking links with Polish traditions as well as any sympathy for Polish aspirations for independence, they opposed assimilation. Some supported nationalist trends and the Zionist movement within the Jewish community. Others, especially the young, showed great interest in social matters and often engaged in revolutionary activity.

Part of the middle and upper Jewish bourgeoisie, attracted by German culture, the power of the German Reich and of the German element in the city, with its strong middle-class and active intelligentsia, became Germanized. Łódź was, at this time, the largest German centre in the Polish Kingdom. Here were found German organizations, cultural, social, and sporting societies, as well as newspaper offices. This minority placed a characteristic German stamp on many aspects of life in Łódź over a relatively long period of time.

At the same time, as a result of the assimilation processes within the Jewish community especially among the *petite bourgeoisie* and the intelligentsia, the number of Jews who regarded themselves as Poles of the Mosaic faith grew. They participated actively in the Polish cultural and social life and in Polish societies, social and political organizations.[8] The progress of Polonization was connected with the increasing vigour of the Polish community in the city. Poles, although the bulk of the city's population, for many years did not have their own press, publishing houses, theatres, societies and other social bodies. The establishment of the *Dziennik Łódzki* (1884–1892), whose editorial committee sought to create a centre of Polish public opinion, and to direct the local Polish intelligentsia into social and cultural work, led to significant changes. Henryk Elzenberg (1845–99), born in Warsaw of a Polonized Jewish family was one of the founders and an editor of this daily. Baptised a Catholic at birth, he graduated in law at the Law Faculty of the Warsaw *Szkoła Główna*. In his youth he was active as a writer and was a frequent contributor to the Positivist Press in Warsaw. In the mid-seventies he settled in Łódź, where he worked as a Commissioner of Oaths and legal advisor to the largest factory of Karol Scheibler. He became a strong proponent of the promotion of Polish culture in Łódź.[9]

The *Dziennik Łódzki* devoted much space to Jewish problems. The editors attacked Jewish 'separatism' and advocated the positivist idea of assimilation through Polonization. In religious matters, they argued that it was possible to be a Pole while retaining one's Mosaic faith. The paper encouraged the study of the Polish language, popularized Polish literature, called for a reform of the 'separatist' Jewish education in *hadarim*, criticized 'jargon' (Yiddish) literature and theatre and condemned what it regarded as signs of cultural backwardness and religious fanaticism among Łódź Jews. The campaign of the *Dziennik Łódzki* was criticized both in the Jewish and Polish communities, and did not achieve any significant results. After some time, it was abandoned.[10]

The situation changed in the nineties, when the Polish intelligentsia in Łódź grew in size and became more established. It then devoted more attention to the city's problems. With the appearance of Polish books and newspapers (at first, from 1897 the daily *Rozwój* and, later the *Goniec Polski*, as well as other papers, literary and scientific journals), the monopoly of the German press was broken. At the turn of the century, the city saw the founding of many Polish cultural, cooperative, sporting and philanthropic societies. The growth of interest in Polish culture among the inhabitants of Łódź was evident. Merchants and industrialists began to employ the Polish language in their correspondence; factory administrators as well as the Jewish and German intelligentsia also started to use it.[11]

It is hard to determine the extent of Jewish assimilation. Łódź was a city of dynamic demographic growth, and its population was made up of an extraordinary national mosaic. The 1897 general census in the Russian empire gives some idea of the scale of Jewish assimilation. 92,400 people or 29.4 per cent of the city's population gave Yiddish as their mother tongue.[12] Yet the same census revealed 98,700 inhabitants of the Mosaic faith or 32 per cent of the total population, whilst Catholics made up 48 per cent, Protestants 18 per cent and Orthodox 2 per cent.[13] 93.6 per cent of those of Mosaic faith gave Yiddish as their mother tongue, while the same ratio for the whole Russian Empire was 96.9 per cent. In Łódź, the remaining adherents of the Mosaic faith spoke either Polish (4.1 per cent) or German (1 per cent).[14] These figures show that Łódź was inhabited by over 4,000 Polonized and about 1,000 Germanized Jews. At the end of the nineteenth century the real number of 'Poles of Mosaic faith' in the city was larger, since, as historians have shown, in the census some Polonized Jews were included in the Yiddish-speaking category.

Assimilation was mostly restricted to the intelligentsia and the bourgeoisie. The impoverished Jewish masses were too poor to gain access to Polish and German culture and were less subject to Polonization or Germanization.[15] Assimilation continued in the following years. The evidence suggests that the number of 'Poles of Mosaic faith' in Łódź nearly doubled in the period between 1897 and the First World War. Yet people within this group using Yiddish grew by only several thousand, while those speaking Polish or German rose by some tens of thousands.[16]

A section of the Jewish bourgeoisie and middle class in Łódź remained indifferent to Polish issues and to politics in general. This was also true of a part of Łódź's German population. According to the contemporary observers, these people, the typical *Lodzhermenshen* were characterized by egoism and desperate quest for profit. At the beginning of the present century a Polish publicist wrote of them: 'These are usually people with no political principles – they have found their motherland in Łódź, here they acquire the means to live, and they are tied only to the city . . . '[17]

As time went by, these attitudes, characteristic of the first generation of immigrants, weakened. They disappeared with the growth of the general cultural level of the subsequent generations of the Łódź bourgeoisie, often educated in leading European universities. Their horizons broadened and their interest in the city's problems and the conditions of life of its inhabitants grew, and resulted, in the European fashion, in philanthropic activity. At the same time, the Jewish and German bourgeoisie was loyal to the Tsarist authorities. Its richest members were eager to finance Russian cultural and philanthropic societies, even contributing on a large scale to the construction of Orthodox churches. Some were honoured by the Russian government with Russian orders and titles of councillors of state. Others, like Izrael Poznański and his son Ignacy were nominated to the post of councillor in the Łódź Municipal Council.[18]

The Zionist movement developed among the Łódź Jews from the end of the nineteenth century, that is at a period when the ideology of Polish nationalism also started to gain followers. Soon after the first Zionist Congress (1897) its supporters started to form organizations in Łódź, hold meetings, distribute shares of the London Zionist Bank and collect money for the Jewish National Fund. They aimed to reach all levels of the Jewish community. The leader of Łódź Zionists was rabbi Izrael Jelski, who played an important role in the Zionist movement of the Tsarist Empire.

Zionists advocated the creation of a Jewish state in Palestine and sought to strengthen Jewish national feelings and oppose assimilation. They also called for the democratization of Russia's political system, with the establishment of full citizens' rights for Jews and a system of Jewish self-government in which the rights of the Hebrew and Yiddish languages would be recognized. The Zionist activists in Łódź attempted to stimulate Jewish culture, backing cultural societies such as the Jewish Musical and Literary Society *Hatsomir*.

From its inception, the Zionist movement in Łódź suffered ups and downs. Initially, the leaders of the Jewish religious community, fearing the loss of their influence, regarded it with hostility. Zionist ideas were most popular in some bourgeois circles, mainly among 'Litvaks', the intelligentsia and high-school students. Yet the Zionist activists also aimed at winning followers among Jewish workers, offering also employment and professional training. Zionism was also propagated in the Jewish press, which started to appear in Łódź, in such papers as *Lodzher Togblat* (established 1908) and *Lodzher Morgenblat* (established 1912), which were widely read in the Jewish community.[19]

At the end of the nineteenth century, socialist ideas, already popular among the Polish working class, started to reach the Jewish workers in Łódź. The socialist movement soon found many followers among the Jewish proletariat, with its social and political difficulties, as well as among some groups of the intelligentsia. At the end of the nineteenth century, Jews made up, according to some estimates, about 11–12 per cent, Poles about 57 per cent and Germans 25 per cent of Łódź industrial and artisan workers. A similar ratio prevailed in subsequent years. In 1901 67,000 and in 1913, 93,000 workers were employed in the Łódź industry, while Łódź crafts employed over 20,000 employees in 1913.[20] At the end of the nineteenth century, Jewish workers worked mainly as weavers in small workshops or as weaver cottage-workers. With the rapid growth of the mechanical weaving mills, and, as a result, the growing pauperisation and proletarianisation of independent weaver cottage-workers and owners of small workshops at the beginning of the twentieth century, Jewish workers started to move into textile factories. Even then, they were mostly to be found in small enterprises. One reason was the reluctance of the Jewish workers to work on Saturdays, which disinclined industrialists to employ them. As hired labour, Jews found employment in artisan workshops, but also in trade, where they made up most shop assistants, as well as taking up small-scale trade and agencies themselves. Unskilled workers were among the poorest Jews, prepared to take even the hardest physical work.

The conditions of life and work of Jewish workers, like their Polish and German counterparts, were determined by their legal status. In this respect, factory legislation in the Russian Empire lagged far behind that of the western countries. Only in 1897 was the working day limited to 11.5 hours. Yet in small factories and workshops, where the majority of Jewish workers were employed, the working day often lasted as many as 14 to 16 hours. As there were no collective agreements regulating wages, workers' pay differed widely, determined as it was by individual industrialists. It often fluctuated with the economic situation and was much lower than in western countries. At the beginning of the twentieth century, weavers in large factories received around 6–7 roubles a week, while employees in small factories and workshops earned only 4 roubles. The latter worked much longer hours, so that, in effect, they earned approximately 2.5 times less per hour. What is more, a much higher percentage of women and children, whose pay was half that of men, were employed in small enterprises. A lack of insurance, inadequate medical help, very bad safety and hygienic conditions, insufficient food and clothing, not to mention appalling living conditions, were the lot of this group.[21]

For many years Jewish workers lived in religious, cultural and linguistic isolation. Their poor knowledge of the Polish language made their contacts with the Polish community rather difficult. The Jewish proletariat was exposed to anti-semitism, probably on a larger scale than other social groups. They also experienced oppression from Jewish industrialists and factory masters, who, in economic conflicts, were supported by the Jewish religious leaders. As a result, the Jewish proletariat in Łódź provided a ready audience for socialist ideas.

At the turn of 1897 to 1898 a branch of the General Jewish Workers' Society in Lithuania, Poland and Russia *Ogólno-żydowski Związek Robotniczy na Litwie, w Polsce i w Rosji*, known as the *Bund* was organized in Łódź. It was founded by emissaries from the Central Committee of the party which had just been established in Wilno: Abraham Mutnik, Borys

Frumkin, Izaak Pejsachsohn, and Roza Grinblat. The Łódź Committee of the *Bund* was formed at the same time, but was soon broken up by arrests. Its reconstruction was undertaken by the local Jewish intelligentsia and workers, including Beresz Winograd, Pinkus Kalstein and Estera Lipszyc.[22]

The *Bund* party circles were formed by Jewish workers in small factories, but were also joined by teachers, office clerks and high school students. The Łódź *Bund* organization was considered to be one of the most numerous in the Tsarist Empire and it was dominated by young people. In 1898 an underground printing house, run by Cywia Hurwicz, a member of the *Bund's* Central Committee, was organized in the town. *Di Arbayter Shtyme*, the central organ of the party, was published here for some time, as well as the proclamations of the Central Committee; in 1901–1902 a local paper *Der Frayhayts Glok* as well as other publications were printed there.

Bund activists propagated the slogans of class struggle and proletarian internationalism. Socialism was the ultimate goal of their struggle, while their more immediate aims were the overthrow of Tsarism and the creation of a democratic Russian republic, in which the Jews would enjoy national and cultural autonomy. The members of the *Bund* claimed their party was the only representative of the Jewish proletariat, disputing the right of Polish socialist organizations to represent Jews. This standpoint caused a deterioration of relations with these parties, as both the Polish Socialist Party (*Polska Partia Socjalistyczna – PPS)* and the Social Democracy of the Polish Kingdom and Lithuania (*Socjaldemokracja Królestwa Polski i Litwy – SDKPiL*) were active among the Jewish workers and craftsmen in Łódź, where they had succeeded in gaining some influence. In 1901, Salomon Chomentowski had been sent by the leadership of the *PPS* to its Łódź organization and had pursued with some success political agitation among the Jewish proletariat. Local Jewish intellectuals, like Juda Hercman were also active in the *PPS*. It was mainly representatives of the Polonized Jewish intelligentsia, some of whom played an important role in the party, as well as assimilated Jewish workers, who joined this party. A Jewish organization of the *PPS* functioned in Łódź within the framework of the party on the eve of the 1905 revolution.

A group of young intellectuals of Jewish origin, including Józef Berencwajg and Teodor Breslauer, were active in the years 1901–1904 in the Łódź organization of the *SDKPiL*. Some of them had earlier been linked for short periods with the *Bund* or the *PPS*. They had grown up in bourgeois and intellectual families which often were polonized. Some of them had become polonized in the course of education in schools and universities at home or abroad, which had led them to break with the religion and traditions of their family and social environments. Under the influence of socialist lectures and activity in youth circles, they became linked with the revolutionary movement, eagerly propagating the idea of social revolution. The *SDKPiL* also gained some influence in Łódź among Jewish artisans.

Cooperation between the *Bund* and the *SDKPiL* began to develop in the years before the 1905 revolution. The two organizations jointly created the United Committee of the Red Cross (*Zjednoczony Komitet Czerwonego Krzyża*) whose aim was to aid political prisoners and their families. *Bund* activists helped the *SDKPiL* reconstruct its organization after it was broken up by mass arrests in 1903.[23]

The Łódź *Bund* organization also suffered from police repression. What is more, its activists were also bitterly attacked by the Jewish religious leaders and bourgeoisie. In Łódź, the Bundists often referred to themselves as *akhusnikes*, a name also used by their opponents. In the years before the revolution, the *Bund*, like the Polish socialist parties, was still a small organization. At the end of 1904, it numbered in Łódź about 200 persons, although the circle of its sympathizers was much larger. Its characteristic form of propaganda was 'exchanges' (*giełdy*) – meetings of party members and followers at which literature was handed out, speeches delivered and discussions organized. In 1904, these took place on Wschodnia Street, often with several hundred people present. In the atmosphere of growing political and social tension in the Tsarist Empire, *Bund* activists in Łódź managed to mobilize many followers for demonstrations. One of the first of these took place on 14 June 1903 on Wschodnia, Kamienna and Piotrkowska Streets. Several hundred Jewish and Polish workers protested under red and black flags against the recent Kishinev pogrom. When the police attacked the demonstration fighting followed, as a result of which people were injured, and many demonstrators arrested. In the following autumn, the streets of Łódź saw stormy anti-Tsarist demonstrations, organized by the *Bund* and *PPS* in protest against conscription into the Russian army.[24]

Jewish and Polish workers in Łódź were active from the very earliest days of the revolution. They participated in strikes, demonstrations and meetings, street fighting against the police and the army; they demanded better living conditions, the democratization of the state and the granting of citizens' rights. Together they shed blood during the fights on the Łódź barricades (22–24 June 1905). Jews were the most numerous victims of the unequal struggle against the Russian police and army. The official announcement gave the number of civilians killed as 151, with 234 injured. 79 of those killed were of 'Mosaic faith', 55 were Catholics and 17 Protestants. These figures are certainly too low, and the victims among the Łódź proletariat probably number as many as 1500–2000 killed and wounded.[25]

The first year of the revolution saw political life emerge from underground, activating many thousands of citizens in the Kingdom of Poland. The massive character of the revolutionary events led them to experience political ideas in public and obtain a basic political education. The political general strike of October-November 1905 was, in this respect, a turning point.

The first ten days of October, the 'decade of freedom', saw an explosion of open political life in the Congress Kingdom. In Łódź, in spite of the introduction of martial law after the unrest in the previous June, the masses controlled the streets. Their victory was hard won, achieved with bloodshed and many killed and wounded in clashes with the police and the army. Rallies, meetings and demonstrations took place, during which various programmes and political options clashed. Organizations, cultural and educational societies, trade unions, started to function openly. The revolutionary wave made conspiracy unnecessary and led to the open functioning of the socialist parties as well as of anti-revolutionary groups. This situation developed still further after martial law was lifted (1 December 1905). The Łódź intelligentsia of all nationalities also became active in organizing various societies and trade unions.

In the first days of the revolution, the police tried unsuccessfully to provoke anti-Jewish excesses in Łódź. Anti-Jewish agitation became more intensive in the city in November and December 1905. The tension and fear among the citizens of Łódź were exacerbated by news of anti-semitic excesses in Russia. Proclamations calling for the organization of pogroms were distributed in the streets and signs painted by anti-semitic agitators on Jewish houses. Socialist activists and representatives of the progressive intelligentsia were conscious of the real danger of disturbances in the city, with its complicated social, national and religious structure. The Socialists carried on an intensive campaign, calling on citizens to organize for self-defence. Self-defence committees and parties were organized in factories and private homes, and were armed with all means available. They maintained order, ready to repulse an attack of the Black Hundreds. The most critical moment was in second decade (10th-20th) of December 1905, yet at this time attempts to provoke pogroms failed. A similar danger was averted in July 1906, when news of the Białystok pogrom reached Łódź, and in September, after the pogrom in Siedlce.

Anti-semitic sentiments could certainly be perceived, which was probably inevitable in such tempestuous times, when masses of people of widely different background and national origin were involved in politics. Anti-semitism was a major element in the propaganda of the Polish Nationalist camp, (*Endecja)* and was widely disseminated in their pamphlets. The argument that it was a marginal phenomenon, which has been expressed in some Polish historical writing, is naive.[26]

The massive joining of political parties and trade unions was a sign of the rapid development of political life, and affected all national groups in Łódź including Jews. At this time, workers dominated political life in all national groups. The workers' parties became massive organizations, and their growth took on the character of an avalanche. By the end of 1906, the socialist parties in Łódź numbered 40,000 members and another 10,000 joined their auxiliary organizations.

The *Bund* numbered about 4,000 persons, ranking third in the socialist camp after the *PPS* and the *SDKPiL*. Its activists managed to form an efficient organization, which directed the political and economic struggle of the Jewish proletariat, spread propaganda and published pamphlets. Bundists gave their backing to the workers' struggle in the whole Russian state to overthrow Tsarism, and demanded national and cultural autonomy for the Jewish population. The growing autonomist trends within the *Bund* led to conflicts between its activists and the representatives of the *PPS* and the *SDKPiL*. These two parties also gained adherents among Jewish workers in their Jewish organizations, and grew in strength, and soon comprised several hundred members. The number of Jews in both of them was indeed greater than the membership of their Jewish branches, as many Jewish workers joined the principal organizations, not to speak of the numerous assimilated Jewish intellectuals who were found in their ranks.

Bundist activists formed trade unions; at first these were firmly linked with the party, but they became more independent after their legalisation. In mid-1907, 3,500 members were united in the nine *Bund* trade unions in Łódź and included 1200 weavers and 750 employed in trade. At that time 76 trade unions existed in Łódź with a membership of over 85,000 members, making up half of the working population and a quarter of that of the town as a whole.

Smaller organizations such as the Zionist-Socialist Workers' Party (*Syjonistyczno-Socjalistyczna Partia Robotnicza*) and the Jewish Socialist Workers' Party *Poalei Tsion* (*Żydowska Socjalistyczna Partia Robotnicza)* rivalled the *Bund* for influence among the Jewish proletariat. Their activists linked socialist and Zionist slogans, advocating the solution of the problems of the Jewish proletariat through the creation of a socialist Jewish state in Palestine.

Anarchist ideas and terrorist slogans also obtained backing in some Jewish workers' circles, as well as among the bourgeoisie, especially among the young. They were found in such groups as the Łódź Group of Anarchists-Communists – International (*Łódźka Grupa Anarchistów-Komunistów – Internacjonal*), the Łódź Federal Group of Anarchists-Communists (*Łódzka Federacyjna Grupa Anarchistów-Komunistów*) and the Anarchist Communists (*Anarchiści-Komunisci*).[27]

The middle class and intelligentsia, joined by a small group of merchants and smaller industrialists, were also active during the revolution. Their main political party was the Jewish Territorial-Zionist Society (*Żydowskie Towarzystwo Terytorialno-Syjonistyczne*) legalized in May 1907, and founded by Dr. L.H. Prybulski, I. Szlamowicz and Rabbi Jelski. The

Jewish Elective Committee (*Żydowski Komitet Wyborczy*) established before the elections to the State Duma constituted the political representation of the Jewish middle class. It was not homogenous as its several dozen members represented different factions within the community. At first the representatives of national and conservative groups were dominant. They included Zionists and 'Litvaks', headed by a lawyer I. Zalszupin, and the Orthodox Jews, led by Rabbi Majzel. Representatives of the liberal-democratic and assimilatory circles led by Dr. M. Likiernik were less influential.[28]

The great Łódź factory owners and much of the middle class were not, for the most part, personally involved in political activity. The short period of autumn 1905, after the proclamation of a constitution for the Tsarist Empire is an exception. It was then that some bourgeois circles displayed an interest in the possibility of creating an elected local government body in Łódź. There was still no unanimity on how to deal with working-class unrest. From the very start of the revolution, some industrialists upheld their traditional view that in case of a conflict with the workers the best solution was to seek the assistance of the Russian authorities. Others, in the face of strike activity, considered the possibility of making concessions. For example Maurycy Poznański, whose thinking was representative of those bourgeois circles which were interested in liberal political changes in the Russian empire, refused to allow the army to enter his factory during the strike of October-November. He publicly announced that he would pay his workers for the period of the strike's duration until the proclamation of the Tsar's manifesto of October 1905. His views were not, however, shared by the majority of the Łódź industrialists.

The representatives of the Łódź bourgeoisie sought in vain the right to a seat in the Duma established by the October manifesto. They also failed to place their candidate in the State Council. The great Łódź bourgeoisie did not form its own political body; nor did it cooperate with the political organizations of the bourgeoisie either in Warsaw or in the Tsarist Empire as a whole. It took a loyal stand towards the Tsarist government, cooperating closely with it. In social matters it remained interested in the reconstruction of the pre-revolutionary relations in factories. To obtain these goals, it made use of the existing employers' societies. The most powerful of them was the Society of the Łódź Industrialists of the Cotton Industry (*Związek Fabrykantów Łódzkich Przemysłu Bawełnianego*).

The campaign for the election of the State Duma, the lower chamber of the Russian parliament, established in 1905 also saw bitter political struggles in Łódź. These elections took place in two stages, with electors, selected from four groups of voters, divided on the basis of property, electing a representative to the Duma. The spring 1906 elections to the 1st Duma were boycotted by the socialist parties. The Jewish pre-electors of the Łódź electoral circle established, as we have seen, the Jewish Electoral

Committee. A conflict broke out over its tactics and the candidates who were to run in the election. In the end the committee proposed M. Kohn, I. Zalszupin and S. Silberstein. The Committee gained 35 electors, while the Polish-German bloc (in which the National Democrats – *ND* – was the strongest party) managed to have ten times as many. As a result Antoni Rząd, representative of the *Endecja* became the deputy from Łódź to the 1st Duma.

The *Bund* took part in the January-February 1907 elections to the 2nd Duma. It formed a Social-Democratic Electoral Committee together with the *SDKPiL*, and their list won in the workers' electoral group (the fourth group) in Łódź. The Tsarist authorities intervened to disallow this result in favour of the nationalist groups. The Jewish Electoral Committee now adopted a new strategy, a sign of the radicalization of the Jewish community. Liberal-democratic Jewish circles now sought cooperation with Polish democrats in the Progressive-Democratic Alliance (*Związek Postępowo-Demokratyczny*, which was very active during these elections. Many Warsaw activists, in addition to those from Łódź, took part in its campaign; among them were many polonized Jews. In the end, the Jewish Electoral Committee and the Progressive Democratic Society put forward a common candidate, A. Mogilnicki, in the municipal electoral group. The Polish community was, however, dominated by nationalist sentiments and once more the candidate backed by the *Endecja*, Aleksander Babicki, was elected.

The autumn 1907 elections to the 3rd Duma took place in an atmosphere of growing anti-revolutionary repression. The *Bund* formed an electoral coalition in the workers' electoral group with the Polish socialist parties, but this alliance was defeated by the more nationalistic groups. Only Polish parties stood on this occasion in the municipal electoral group. As in January-February, in spite of the backing of the Jewish pre-electors, the Progressive-Democratic Alliance lost, and once again the candidate of the *Endecja*, Antoni Rząd, was elected.[29]

The defeat of the revolution was followed by a period of reaction. N. Kazankov, the temporary general-governor, succeeded, with particular ruthlessness, in crushing the revolutionary movement in Łódź. Here, more death sentences were pronounced in the military court than anywhere else in the Kingdom of Poland, and thousands of persons were sentenced to prison and exile. Martial law remained in operation here longer than anywhere else in Russian Poland. At the same time, industrialists started to re-introduce the pre-revolutionary order in their factories.

The city's political life was suppressed. Police repression led to the breaking up of workers' parties and trade unions. Most activists found themselves in prison or in exile. Some tried to save themselves by escaping abroad. Terror and lockouts by industrialists against stubborn employees resulted in the atmosphere of panic and apathy among workers, who left their parties and trade unions *en masse*. The socialist parties had to change their forms and methods of functioning, returning to conspiracy to save themselves from total disaster. The political activity of practically all groups in Łódź ceased. The majority of the intelligentsia and middle class, terrified by the extent of the repression organized by the Tsarist authorities against the revolutionary movement, gave up all public activity.

The Łódź *Bund* organization was almost completely broken by massive arrests at the turn of 1907 to 1908. Arrests after that date effectively paralysed any attempts at the reconstruction of the party. Its activists did not take up any wider political actions, limiting themselves to work in the legal, cultural and educational institutions and the trade unions, which also suffered a severe crisis.

July 1912 saw a revival of political activity in the city as a result of the electoral campaign to the 4th Duma. In the workers' electoral group, the *Bund* ran in the elections together with Polish socialist parties. The election of the plenipotentiaries in this group saw a socialist victory, with the *Bund*'s candidate, J. Oberman winning one of the seven mandates.

In the municipal electoral group, the pre-electoral campaign was marked by another bitter conflict between Polish nationalist opinion, represented in the *Endecja*, and the Polish progressive groupings who were allied with the main Jewish middle-class organizations. The outcome was determined by the limited suffrage introduced under the new electoral law. In terms of these regulations, Jews now constituted the absolute majority on pre-electoral lists in four, and Germans in one, out of six electoral districts. In this situation the *Endecja* realized it could not elect its candidate and advanced instead demagogic slogans in defence of the Polish character of Łódź. The Progressive-Democratic Alliance (which included representatives of the Jewish intelligentsia), on the other hand, called for a Polish or Jewish deputy to be elected who would uphold the principle of the political and social equality of all nationalities, and, moreover, defend the interests of the workers. The Germans ran in the elections alone. They formed a committee, which represented the intelligentsia, craftsmen, merchants and some industrialists. In their electoral campaign they advanced liberal and democratic ideas, although the campaign also included some nationalist elements.

The Jewish Electoral Committee brought together various groups with contradictory programmes. After many discussions and inner clashes, a compromise was reached, and a Łódź doctor, Mejer Bomasz, known for his progressive attitude, was chosen to stand for the Duma. His candidature was acceptable to progressive Poles and Germans, as well as to the representatives of the less wealthy groups of the Jewish community. The Committee did not put forward any concrete programme. Aiming to win the votes of various groups it advanced general slogans of democratic reform, equality of all nationalities and defence of Jewish rights.

In the municipal electoral group, the first round of elections took place on 16 October 1912. The voting frequency was rather low – 54 per cent, the result of the boycott by some Poles and Germans. The Jewish list won in two districts, the German in two others. It was violently opposed, however, by the *Endecja*, as well as by German nationalist circles, which now began an anti-Jewish campaign similar to that which was being waged simultaneously in Warsaw. In the end, M. Bomasz was elected the Łódź representative in the 4th Duma on 7 November 1912. He later joined the parliamentary faction of Kadets, as the members of the Constitutional-Democratic Party were called.[30] His victory, along with that of the *PPS-Left* candidate in Warsaw, Eugeniusz Jagiełło, who was elected by Jewish votes, was followed by the initiation by the *Endecja* in the whole of the Congress Kingdom of a violent anti-Jewish campaign. At the same time, some attempts were made within workers' circles in Łódź and elsewhere in Russian Poland to revive socialist fortunes by undertaking a campaign on behalf of the unemployed and for a better system of unemployment and accident insurance. It was in this atmosphere of national and social tension that Łódź entered the First World War.

NOTES

1 K. Grzybowski, *Historia państwa i prawa Polski*, vol. IV, *Od uwłaszczenia do odrodzenia państwa* (Warsaw, 1981), pp. 82, 91, 113–14, 118–20, 122, 136.
2 *Yevreyskaja Entsiklopediya*, vol. X (St. Petersburg), pp. 540–505; *Encyclopaedia Judaica*, vol. 11 (Jerusalem, 1982), p. 792.
3 H. Banner, *Gmina żydowska w Łodzi. Krótki zarys dziejów ustrojowo-gospodarczych* (Łódź, 1938), pp. 4, 21–7.
4 *Rozwój* 16 July 1901, no. 162, p. 6; 25 April 1903, no. 94, p. 3.
5 Before the First World War, synagogues in Łódź were situated in 8 Wolbromska St., 2 Spacerowa St., 6 Wolczańska St., and 36 Zachodnia St. Cf. *Kosmopolita*, a 10 copeck map of Łódź (1911), reprinted in: *Łódź die Stadt der Volkerbegegnung im Wandel der Geschichte*, ed. P. Nasarski (Köln, 1978); Cf. also *Informator miasta Łodzi z kalendarzem na 1920 r.* (Łódź, 1920), p. 385.
6 Quoted in: E. Rosset, *Łódź w latach 1860–70. Zarys historyczno-statystyczny* (Łódź, 1928), p. 42.
7 *Pietrokovskaya guberniya 1890–1904 gody* (Piotrków, 1904), pp. 324–5.
8 Ibidem, pp. 454–6.
9 R. Kaczmarek, 'Henryk Elzenberg' in: *Polski Słownik Biograficzny*, vol. VI (Kraków, 1948), pp. 238–9.
10 Z. Gostkowski, *Dziennik Łódzki' w latach 1884–1892. Studium nad powstawaniem polskiej opinii publicznej w wielonarodowym mieście fabrycznym* (Łódź, 1963), pp. 14–20, 123–8.
11 *Łódź. Dzieje miasta*, vol. I, ed. R. Rosina (Warsaw, 1980), pp. 398–9, 537–49, 555–9.
12 In the light of the 1897 census, based on the criterion of mother tongue, the city's total population of 314,000 was made up of: Poles – 145,600 (46.4 per cent), Jews – 92,400 (29.4 per cent), Germans – 67,300 (21.4 per cent), Russians – 7,400 (2.4 per cent) and other nationalities – 1,300 (0.4 per cent): ibid., p. 219.

13 Ibid., p. 215; *Encyclopaedia Judaica*, vol. 11, p. 425.
14 *Yevreyskaya Entsiklopediya*, vol. X, p. 328.
15 A. Żarnowska, *Klasa robotnicza Królestwa Polskiego 1870–1914* (Warsaw, 1974), p. 70.
16 According to the data gathered in the 1911 census, 52 per cent of the total population of 513,000 (including Bałuty) consisted of Catholics, 14 per cent of Protestants, 1 per cent of Orthodox, and 33 per cent (i.e. 169,000) of people of Mosaic Faith (cf. *Łódź. Dzieje miasta*, vol. I, p 215). Another statistical report from 1912 gives the following figures: 201,679 persons used the Polish language (43.9 per cent), 151,407 German language (32.9 per cent), 97,339 Yiddish language (21.2 per cent), 4,807 Russian language and 4,121 other languages (1.0 per cent) (Cf. W.L. Karwacki, *Związki zawodowe i stowarzyszenia pracodawców w Łodzi* (do roku 1914), Łódź 1972, p. 8).
17 S. Górski, *Łódź wspolczesna, Obrazki i szkice publicystyczne* (Łódź, 1904), p. 22.
18 *Pietrokovskaya guberniya* . . . , pp. 288, 336.
19 Ibid., pp. 527–8, 562–95; *Encyclopaedia Judaica*, vol. XI, p. 431.
20 W.L. Karwacki, *Związki* . . . , pp. 1–10; A. Zarnowska, op. cit., pp. 90–1.
21 *Yevreyskaja Entsiklopediya*, Vol. X, p. 330; W. L. Karwacki, op. cit., pp. 19–20, *Łódź, Dzieje miasta*, vol. I., pp. 323–51.
22 *Źródła do dziejów klasy robotniczej na ziemiach polskich*, vol. III, part 1, ed. S. Kalabinski (Warsaw, 1968), pp. 322–8, 339–41, 345, 350, 357–61.
23 W. L. Karwacki, *Łódźka organizacja PPS (1893–1907)* (Wrocław, 1978), pp. 55–8, 114–15; P. Samuś, *Dzieje SDKPiL w Łodzi 1893–1918* (Łódź, 1984), pp. 42–52.
24 More information on the Łódź *Bund* organization is to be found in: *Historia Bundu*, vol. I, prepared for publication by I.Sz. Herc (New York, 1960), passim; *W dymach czarnych budzi się Łódź. Z dziejów łódzkiego ruchu robotniczego 1882–1948* (Łódź, 1985), pp. 100–3, Cf. also note 23 above.
25 On the June uprising see: L. Mroczek, W. Bortnowski, *Dwa powstania* (Łódź, 1974), pp. 61–122.
26 W. L. Karwacki, *Łódź w latach rewolucji 1905–1907* (Łódź, 1975), pp. 149–60, P. Korzec, *Walki rewolucyjne w Łodzi i okręgu łódzkim w latach 1905–1907* (Warsaw, 1956), pp. 244–69; P. Samuś, op. cit., pp. 145–8.
27 W. L. Karwacki, *Łódzka organizacja* . . . , pp. 63–9; Idem, *Związki* . . . , pp. 67–70, 107–17; H. Piasecki, op. cit., pp. 152–4, 217–19; P. Samuś, op. cit., pp. 82–103.
28 K. Badziak 'Burżuazja łódzka w rewolucji 1905–1907', in: *Rewolucja 1905–1907 w Łodzi i okręgu. Studia i materiały*, ed. B. Wachowska (Łódź, 1975), pp. 62, 68–77, 82; W. L. Karwacki, Łódź . . . , pp. 37–8.
29 K. Badziak, op. cit., pp. 77–84; *Łódź, Dzieje miasta*, vol. I. pp. 425–7, 439–40; E. Rosset, *Oblicze polityczne ludności miasta Łodzi w świetle statystyki wyborczej* (Łódź, 1927), pp. 7–27; T. Stegner, 'Liberałowie Królestwa Polskiego wobec kwestii żydowskiej na początku XX w', *Przegląd Historyczny* 1989, fasc. 1, pp. 70–87.
30 E. Rosset, *Oblicze* . . . , pp. 28–32; *Łódź, Dzieje miasta*, vol. I, pp. 449–50.

9

ASPECTS OF THE HISTORY OF WARSAW AS A YIDDISH LITERARY CENTRE

Chone Shmeruk

The leading role of Warsaw on the eve of the Holocaust in Yiddish literature is well-known and generally accepted. Yet, apart from a large number of memoirs, dating especially from the period between the two world wars,[1] we do not possess even a single attempt at a broad survey of this centre. What is envisaged here is not a history of Yiddish literature in Warsaw as such, or of the theme of Warsaw in Yiddish literature. What is required is a study which will make us aware of the many factors in the wider background of Jewish Warsaw, which made possible the emergence of such a large and bustling – alas now merely historical – literary centre. In this article I want only to indicate some significant moments in the history of Yiddish literature in Warsaw, mainly in the period down to the First World War, with no intention of exhausting an extensive and truly fascinating theme.

Let us start with some history: from 1795, when the total Jewish population of Warsaw was 6,000, and certainly most of them without full and legal right of abode, the Jewish population grew constantly. Although Jews were not allowed to live in all the parts of the city, their population in 1861 had already reached 43,000. In the course of twenty years, until 1882, their number tripled to 130,000. In 1914, just before the First World War, 337,000 Jews were living in Warsaw.[2]

This steady growth of the number of Jews was not, of course, merely a result of natural increase, but was principally caused by the rapid urbanization of the Jews in Poland, by internal migration from the *shtetlekh* and the provinces to the big city. Warsaw, from the middle of the nineteenth century, exercised an enormous pull, not only on Jews within the borders of Congress Poland, but also on all Jews living in the Russian Pale of Settlement. It should be emphasized here that in addition to the stream of Jewish emigration overseas after 1881, there was an equally large internal migration, so that in the course of 32 years, from 1882 to 1914, over 200,000 Jews came to Warsaw. As we shall see, this steady influx of Jews into Warsaw was to have a particular influence on its development as a Jewish literary centre.

It is of course well-known that the process of Jewish assimilation was more rapid in Warsaw than anywhere else in Congress Poland. Assimilated Polish Jews, already in the nineteenth century, had greater opportunities for publication than Yiddish-speaking Jews. It is sufficient to mention the Polish section of the *Beobachter an der Weichsel* (The Observer on the Vistula) – *Dostrzegacz Nadwiślański* of 1823–24, *Jutrzenka* of the years 1861–1863 and *Izraelita*, which appeared in Warsaw from 1866 to 1912.[3] The existence of these publications should not, however, mislead us, since the overwhelming majority of Warsaw's Jews were Yiddish speakers. Polish assimilation, at least in the nineteenth century, only attracted a very thin layer of the Jewish population in Warsaw, although the city was already famed for its plutocracy of assimilated and, in part, converted Jews.

Ideally one would have wished to provide a more precise basis for the assertion, but here it must suffice to say that from the second half of the nineteenth century until the Second World War, Warsaw had the greatest concentration of Yiddish speaking Jews in Europe. What is relevant is that, at least from the middle of the nineteenth century until the Holocaust, Warsaw had the greatest number of potential readers of Yiddish literature in one place. The fact that they were, during this time, only potential readers needs some emphasis, since *talking* Yiddish did not mean *reading* Yiddish, and even more so reading modern Yiddish literature. It is clear, however, that the gradual realisation of this enormous potential was a significant factor in the development of Warsaw as a Yiddish literary centre. In this context, by Yiddish literature we mean modern Yiddish literature, which in Eastern Europe can be traced back to the last decade of the eighteenth century. At that time, parallel with the widespread, older traditional religious books in Yiddish or in Hebrew with a Yiddish translation, one can identify the sporadic appearance of isolated Yiddish works, with an open or a concealed maskilic attitude. Hebrew printing had been developing in Warsaw from 1797, at first in the hands of a group of non-Jews, and later almost exclusively in Jewish hands. The ban on Hebrew (and Yiddish) printing houses in the Russian Empire, outside Zhitomir and Wilno from 1836 until the eighteen-sixties, certainly stimulated the development of Hebrew presses within the borders of Congress Poland, especially in Warsaw. By 1859 there were already eight Hebrew presses here.[4] This development was to proceed apace until the Second World War. According to one incomplete list, there were in Warsaw on the eve of the Holocaust, 25 Jewish printing houses, in addition to the presses of the Jewish newspapers.[5]

We lack a comprehensive history of the Warsaw Hebrew presses, and we do not have a bibliography of their Hebrew and Yiddish book production.[6]

We can therefore only assume that until the eighteen-fifties, with few exceptions, they published only traditional Yiddish books and *mayse*-booklets. It is true that there were sporadic signs of something new. In 1840, for example, the Yiddish translation of Campe's *Robinzon Krazue (!) der yungere* (Robinson Crusoe the Younger) was published and was later republished twice, in 1850 and in 1874. We possess another version of the book, dating from this period, in Yiddish, translated from German, published in Lwów and also in Wilno. This was not, however, known in Warsaw, where the book was translated instead from Polish. The language of the Warsaw edition does perhaps tell us something about the Yiddish in Warsaw until the eighteen-eighties – it is quite Germanized in style, although Hebraisms and, above all, Polonisms are very evident.[7] We can expect the discovery of other examples of books of this type from Warsaw up to the mid-nineteenth century. We should not, however, overestimate their worth and significance, since most of the Yiddish speaking population of Warsaw during this period and for many years thereafter was of a strictly traditional character.

From the eighteen-fifties onwards, one can see many clearer and more substantial indications of modern Yiddish literary activity here. First of all, one finds original and adapted Yiddish pieces by local authors, some even with an expressly Warsaw colouring and Warsaw themes. Research on this literature has already made familiar the names of Gedalia Bellou, Avigdor Ruf and Gustav Makman, whose work has been described in N. Oyslender's pioneering work on the beginnings of Yiddish literature in Warsaw[8] and in J. Shatsky's *Geshikhte fun yidn in varshe* [The History of Jews in Warsaw].[9] Further research will perhaps reveal no less important literary works, such as Yehoshua Gershon Munk's hitherto almost forgotten abbreviated translation of *Mistorey Pariz, Di geheymnise fun pariz* [The Mysteries of Paris] which, despite its Hebrew title, was indeed 'translated from the French', and was published in Warsaw in five volumes in 1865–1866.[10] It would seem, however, that until well into the eighteen-eighties despite all these books and booklets, there is nothing of permanent literary value. Nevertheless the growing number of Yiddish books produced in Warsaw in this period offer us very specific pointers for the theme we are discussing. It should be stressed that if we wish to discover signs of reading habits, we must take into account the substantial amount of traditional *mayse*-literature, hasidic and non-hasidic, including hagiography, and not only what was published in Warsaw. The fact is that readers in Warsaw often read material published elsewhere. Many of these people also became readers of modern Yiddish literature.

We have already mentioned that the Warsaw Hebrew presses also served outside authors and publishers. Even after the ban on Hebrew presses in Russia was lifted, Warsaw remained a publishing centre for Jewish books, not necessarily written in Warsaw and certainly not published for local use only. Let us give some examples: one can find in Roskies' Dik bibliography, that of Ayzik-Mayer Dik of Wilno's first 21 Yiddish booklets in the eighteen-fifties, only 5 were printed in Wilno, the remainder, three times as many, appeared in Warsaw.[11] This is a dramatic example from the period, when restrictions on Hebrew printing were still in force in Russia. We should, however, mention that Sholem-Yankev Abramovitsh (Mendele Moykher Sforim), then of Berditchev had the first edition of his *Vinshfingerl* [Wish ring] printed in 1865 in Warsaw, and that later, in 1875, when he was already living in Zhitomir, he had his poem *Yudl* published in Warsaw. This tendency was also evident in the eighteen-eighties. Thus, the first edition of Shatskes' *Der yidisher far-pesakh* [The Jewish Pre-pesach] came out in Warsaw in 1881 – Shatskes at that time was living in Kiev – while the first edition of Yehuda-Leyb Gordon's Yiddish *Sikhas khulin* [Small Talk] was issued in 1886 by the Warsaw bookseller and publisher Eliezer-Yitskhok Shapiro[12] of Nalewki – Gordon was then living in St. Petersburg. In all these towns, there were Hebrew presses, which also printed Yiddish books and booklets. Warsaw was used, however, because it was either cheaper or easier to publish and to distribute books from there.

In the 19th century, there were no special presses for Yiddish publications. It would seem, however, that there is no Warsaw Hebrew press known to us which was not also involved in printing Yiddish books and booklets, religious and non-religious. There was a dynasty of printers in Warsaw – the Lebensohns – who began their activities in the second decade of the 19th century. On a very large number of Yiddish books published in Warsaw we can find the names of three generations of Lebensohns, beginning with the grandfather, Avigdor, and up to the grandsons Gershon and Pesakh at the end of the century. The Yiddish publisher and bookseller was also linked with the printing network. The division of functions amongst them did not always remain the same. There were some printers who were also publishers and booksellers, and booksellers who issued various Yiddish publications on their own initiative. From the mid-19th century, the Morgenshtern family of Franciszkańska Street were very much involved in printing Yiddish books in Warsaw. They were also involved in the book trade and in publishing over several generations.[13]

Although we lack detailed research on the Yiddish production of the Warsaw Hebrew printing network in the 19th century and its system of distribution, there is no doubt that from the mid-19th century this network became strengthened and enlarged, so that it could satisfy not only local needs of all kinds, but could also produce for export and serve the needs of authors and publishers in far away places.

The rapid development of Hebrew printing, publishing and distribution in both languages, Hebrew and Yiddish, has to be considered in very close connection and even very strong ties with the parallel simultaneous growing of Polish presses and the trade in Polish books in Warsaw. One has to keep in mind that Warsaw Jews were very prominent in the printing, publishing and distributing of Polish books. Some of them were active in both the Jewish and Polish fields. It is sufficient to mention here Samuel Orgelbrand the founder of the famous printing firm in Warsaw which published important Jewish and Polish books in a handsome way. These ties and the development of Jewish printing and publishing in Warsaw have still to be investigated thoroughly.[14]

The very important, and perhaps decisive, role of Yiddish periodicals in the development of modern Yiddish literature is generally well known. I have dealt more broadly with this issue elsewhere,[15] and have pointed out that in the eighteen-sixties, A. B. Gottlober, A. Goldfaden, S. Y. Abramovitsh, Y. L. Gordon, Y. Y. Linetski and M. L. Lilienblum all made their Yiddish debuts in the Odessa *Kol mevaser* [The Voice of the Herald]. Similarly, in the eighteen-eighties, M. Spektor, Sholem Aleykhem, S. Frug and D. Frishman first appeared in print in the St. Petersburg *Yudishes folksblat* [Yiddish People's Paper]. Who can say how Yiddish literature would have looked without them and who can say whether they would have come to Yiddish at all, without these journals. Yet, in the list of Yiddish writers of this period, there is still not one from Warsaw. It would seem that Warsaw still stood aside from the significant development of modern Yiddish literature in the eighteen-sixties, a situation which continued even until the eighties.

In the course of the nineteenth century, Warsaw did not have much good fortune with its own Yiddish papers which might well have offered many more openings for the development of her writers. The first Jewish newspaper in Eastern Europe did indeed come out in Warsaw in 1823–1824. The section of the bi-lingual *Beobakhter an der Weichsel – Dostrzegacz Nadwiślański* – which was printed with Hebrew letters was, however, much nearer to German than to Yiddish. The paper was, indeed, certainly intended for readers whose mother tongue was Yiddish. It is doubtful, however, if the average Yiddish speaker of that time would have been able to read and understand the newspaper. It is certainly absurd to believe that, thanks to the German in the newspaper, a Jew would be able to improve his 'corrupted' language – that is his Yiddish – and begin to talk a pure and 'correct' German. This does seem to have been the attitude of the editor of the newspaper himself, Antoni Eisenbaum. Indeed the newspaper was unable to survive for very long, even though it certainly received considerable subsidies. Only 150 copies of each issue were printed, and it ceased after merely 44 issues. It would indeed be quite wrong to look for the real beginnings of the Yiddish press in such a newspaper, whose failure in the eighteen-twenties was inevitable from the outset. This is not, however, to decide which factor was most important in this failure: the unintelligible languages – German and Polish, its maskilic point of view, unacceptable to the overwhelming majority of Warsaw Jews, the small interest of the contents, or perhaps mainly the lack of a habit of reading modern materials among most traditional Yiddish readers, who made up the potential readers of the newspapers.[16]

When in 1867–1868 there was another attempt to publish a weekly newspaper – the *Varshoyer yudishe tsaytung* [The Warsaw Jewish Newspaper] – it, too, did not succeed. It collapsed after only 50 issues, and had no more than 180 subscribers, 150 of them in Warsaw. It would appear that during this period a maximum of only 500 copies were printed, a negligible figure when compared to the potential readers in Warsaw.

Hilary-Hillel Glatshtern, the editor and publisher of the *Varshoyer yudishe tsaytung*, had earlier been a collaborator on the Jewish-Polish *Izraelita*, which had openly called for the Polonization of the Jews. His Yiddish newspaper also tried to advance this goal. The newspaper however spoke to its readers in a restrained tone, trying to conceal its true aims, and not only with regard to assimilation. This restrained tone also had commercial motives. The editor and his newspaper were, however, very well-known in Orthodox circles in Warsaw, who took great pains to emphasize their disagreement with him. All this can be directly deduced from the declaratory final issue, with its clear statement of intent, where no words were minced regarding the true aims of the newspaper and those it considered its opponents. The restrained tone had clearly not helped. Similarly unsuccessful was Glatshtern's idea that the Tsarist authorities should compel every synagogue in Poland to buy regularly two copies of the newspaper, and thus guarantee its survival. Even the Tsarist authorities were not willing to meet his request to impose the newspaper on Jews.[17]

If the *Varshoyer judishe tsaytung* was commercially unsuccessful, its literary achievements were no greater. Certainly, one can find there names of new local writers, and there are some significant and interesting historical materials regarding Yiddish in Warsaw. Yet, not one single significant literary talent was revealed. The most important items of *belles-lettres* published by the newspaper were imported – two poems of the late Shloyme Ettinger from Zamość and some short stories of Ajzik-Mayer Dik from Wilno. The newspaper has left no lasting imprint on Yiddish literature.

One would have hardly expected the *maskilim* of Warsaw, with their open and sustained support of Polonization, to have tried to publish a newspaper in Yiddish for its own sake. Barely twenty years after the collapse of the *Varshoyer judishe tsaytung*, with *Izraelita* already established since 1866, and ten years after Chaim Zelig Słonimski brought back the Hebrew newspaper *Ha-Tsefirah* [The Dawn] from Berlin, the Polish writer Klemens Junosza Szaniawski criticized *Izraelita*, for its refusal to use

Yiddish as a weapon to promote Polish assimilation. He knew better than they:

> Not one single Jew among those whose eyes we wish to open and whom we wish to civilize, reads *Izraelita*. It therefore achieves none of its aims, since it fails to reach where it should reach . . . Meanwhile the Yiddish booklet finds its way into the hands of the Jew. There is a clear and totally un-Jewish lack of realism on the part of *Izraelita* in its opposition to Yiddish literature . . .[18]

We should mention that Aleksandr Tsederboym of Odessa was also far from being a Yiddishist. He had, however, a practical instinct which overcame all other possible obstacles, and it was not for their own sake that he produced his Yiddish weeklies with their massive contribution to Yiddish literature. At this time Warsaw still did not possess *maskilim* of Tsederboym's type and energy.

When some years later, the Yiddish translation of M. Pines' *The History of Yiddish Literature until 1890*[19] was published in Warsaw, Y. L. Perets attempted a brief summary of the situation in the period covered by the book. Although he was talking very generally, he clearly means Warsaw, and we can discern tones which are clearly personal in character:

> . . . In 1890 there was hardly the basis for a literature. Only a small bunch of people were involved in it. There was no previous agreement between them. They did not know each other. No one called on anyone else. Each one sprang from his own roots and set about working in his own corner. Already at work – they glimpsed each other, introduced themselves, stretched out a hand which, most often, was returned . . . Who was the master and who the assistant? Who the rabbi and who the pupil? Where was the school[20]

Thus in the second half of the eighteen-eighties in Warsaw, it already looked as though there were clear signs of something new. Warsaw had then a small, but important group of Yiddish writers who, within a few years, would come to play an important role in the new literary centre. A few of the writers who came there already had something of a name in Yiddish literature. At the end of 1885, Jankev Dineson came from Lithuania, and in 1887, Mordkhe Spektor from Uman.[21] Yitskhok Leybush Perets from Zamość had already settled in Warsaw in 1889. Spektor had already brought out his collection *Der familien-fraynd* [The Family Friend] in 1887, and continued until 1896 with the five volumes of his *Der hoyzfraynd* [The House Friend].[22] In 1888, Heshl Epfelberg, who came from Łomża in 1880, began to issue his *Varshever yudishen kalender* [Warsaw Jewish Calendar], in which he also published modern Yiddish works. Epfelberg kept up his calendars for almost twenty years.[23] Both Spektor's and Epfelberg's publications, constituted a new departure in Yiddish publishing, based on the Warsaw Hebrew typography, with an eye on a mass readership. Their ventures were crowned with success, since both continued for a number of years. Spektor's *Hoyzfraynd* was sold and reprinted. With these publications, modern Yiddish literature, for the first time, penetrated middle class conservative circles in Warsaw.

In the formation of Warsaw as a literary centre from the eighteen-eighties, the commercial success of publications such as these literary anthologies and calendars, played a most important role. The modernizing influence of the big city had broken down many barriers, even in the traditional Jewish environment, which created new reading habits. This development went along with the emergence of new ideological currents, social and national, which, at least until the eighteen-nineties, continued to see Yiddish as nothing more than an effective means of propaganda, although later they were to recognize the language and its literature as having a value of its own. It is difficult to present Spektor and Epfelberg as conscious spokesmen for these new politico-ideological currents. They do, however, find some expression and partial realization in Perets' publications of the eighteen-nineties, in his *Di judishe bibliotek* [The Jewish Library] (1891–1895 – 5 Volumes), in his *Literatur un lebn* [Literature and Life] (1894), and most notably in his famous *Yontev-bletlekh* [Festival Pages] (1894–1896). All these publications came out in Warsaw.[24]

These publications show us that a wide Yiddish readership had already been formed in Warsaw along with a group of Yiddish writers, who had no difficulty whatsoever in satisfying the needs of that readership. It is indeed a paradox that just when a market had emerged in Warsaw for modern Yiddish newspapers, the Tsarist government began to turn down all applications and requests for permits to issue a Yiddish newspaper in the city. Such rejections occurred both in the eighteen-nineties and in the first years of the twentieth century.[25] From 1899 Yiddish readers of Warsaw had thus to be satisfied with periodicals in fact edited in Warsaw but printed in Kraków, and then imported to the Congress Kingdom[26] or later, after 1903, with the St. Petersburg *Fraynd* [Friend], a newspaper which was published in a city with a very small Yiddish readership.

The Tsarist government was not so severe with regard to Hebrew as it was with regard to Yiddish. In the years 1902–1904, a Hebrew daily newspaper – *Ha-Tsofeh* [The Observer] – appeared in Warsaw. Grouped around it were a group of bilingual writers, who later worked for the Warsaw Yiddish press. Perets, too, was a regular contributor to *Ha-Tsofeh*.[27] In these years *Ha-Shilo'akh* [Ahad Ha-Am's Journal] was edited and published in Warsaw. The achievements of the Hebrew literary centre, headed by Bialik and Klausner are well known.[28] Research on the Yiddish literary centre in Warsaw cannot avoid the close and very often personal and intimate links with Hebrew literature here, both before and after the famous Czernowitz conference of 1908 in favour of Yiddish.

It was in 1905, when Zvi-Hirsh Prilutski began to issue *Der veg*,[29] that Warsaw first began to become the metropolis of the Yiddish daily press in Eastern Europe. The official statistics of 1906 demonstrate just how quickly that daily press developed. Five Yiddish newspapers, published in Warsaw – *Der veg* [The Way], *Der telegraf*, *Yidishes tageblat* [Jewish Daily Paper], *Morgenblat* [Morning Paper] and *Di naye tsaytung* [The New Newspaper] – had a combined daily circulation of 96,000. In the same year three Hebrew daily newspapers appeared – *Ha-Yom* [The Day], *Ha-Tsefirah* [The Dawn] and *Ha-Tsofeh* – with a combined circulation of only 12,000. The single Polish-Jewish newspaper – *Gazeta Nowa; Ludzkość* – had a circulation of barely 10,000. The three Yiddish weeklies which were also published in Warsaw in 1906 – *Dos fraye vort* [The Free Word], *Yidishes vokhenblat* [Jewish Weekly Paper] and *Di bihn* [The Bee] had a combined circulation of 38,000.[30] From 1905 until the First World War, a many-branched Yiddish daily press and a multi-faceted periodical press emerged. After a brief period of stagnation during the German occupation of Warsaw in the war, the growth of the Yiddish press continued. But the Warsaw Yiddish press had, even before the First World War, already put into the shadows the older Hebrew and Jewish-Polish press. The two biggest Yiddish newspapers in Warsaw, *Haynt* [Today] and *Der Moment*, were founded in the period before 1914, and were part of rapid growth of the Yiddish press after 1905. These were the daily newspapers of Warsaw Jewry and indeed of all Poland for the next thirty years until the Holocaust.

Our discussion here of the Yiddish press and periodicals is not primarily concerned with the press itself and its dynamic development after 1905. The Yiddish press in all its manifestations, political, ideological and commercial, is rather an indication both of the emergence of a massive Warsaw readership and of the output of the writers who wrote for it. The Yiddish press in Warsaw gave a very important place to Yiddish literature in its various levels and forms, from fragments of Perets' complex drama *Bay nakht oyfn altn mark* [At Night in the Old Market] to primitive *shund* [trash] novels, designed to increase circulation. In addition, day-to-day work on the Yiddish newspapers allowed Yiddish journalists and magazine writers to practise their craft, and for the first time in the history of Yiddish literature in Eastern Europe, created a real and *stable* source of livelihood for the Yiddish writer. The growth of the Yiddish press established the economic base for a modern Yiddish intelligentsia and for the Yiddish writer. It was also able to widen its readership by appealing to various levels of literary taste and receptiveness. The extremely sharp competition between newspapers and their struggle for readers, only accelerated this process, and also broadened the possibilities for publishing literature in daily newspapers. Every newspaper endeavoured to see that amongst its contributors should figure the most resonant names of contemporary Yiddish literature.

It should be mentioned here, in passing, that similarly, at the very same period, between 1908 and 1918, a commercial Polish press developed, which was able to provide a source of livelihood for contemporary Polish literature.[31]

A detailed comparison of the Warsaw Yiddish-Hebrew literary centre with those of Odessa and Wilno up to the First World War could be attempted. It would seem, though, that however important Odessa might have been in this period, with Bialik and Mendele, Warsaw overtook it not only in terms of size, but also in its dynamism, especially after 1905. The same could be said of New York. Certainly, although it already possessed a multi-faceted daily and periodical press and a significant group of writers, including, since 1907, ***Di yunge*** [The Young Ones], the New York centre was still, in essence, no more than an admittedly very large offshoot of Eastern Europe. The New York writers still sought critical approval from Warsaw. Apart from those advantages to be found in all Yiddish literary centres, Warsaw was privileged to have a great personality – Y. L. Perets – whose strength and impact were apparent wherever Yiddish literature had spread. It was thanks to the personality of Perets that Warsaw became the centre of all the centres of Yiddish literature.

At present, it is not yet possible to decide when Warsaw became this centre. Further research could perhaps help in this respect. We must meanwhile be satisfied with the thesis that this occurred between the mid-eighteen-nineties and 1905. For if Perets was right that, in 1890, no one knew in Warsaw 'who was the master and who the assistant, who the Rabbi and who the pupil', it is clear that, in the course of the eighteen-nineties, Perets' home on Ceglana now Pereca Street became the address of the master and rabbi of virtually the whole of Yiddish literature. To Perets would come pilgrims from all corners of the realm of Yiddish in Eastern Europe, from the Ukraine, from Lithuania, but above all from all over Congress Poland. [32] Let us also mention in passing that Perets was the only one of the three classical Yiddish writers from whom the American ***Yunge*** were to claim a literary lineage.[33]

The doors of Perets' home opened up a range of new possibilities, some of them illusory, for the modernised traditional intelligentsia, in the dynamic and effervescent centre which had developed in Warsaw. Let us now pause to consider a very significant phenomenon to which we have already alluded. The colourful and many-faceted Warsaw Yiddish centre was the creation of generations of non-native writers and cultural activists, not only at its beginnings, but also in the eighteen-eighties. The significance of this phenomenon has not yet been fully investigated. One can nonetheless assert, with some certainty, that it continued to apply to Warsaw until the Holocaust.

Two later examples will illustrate this clearly. Firstly, in the well-known and significant flourishing of 'expressionist' Yiddish poetry in the early nineteen-twenties, which is to be found in the Warsaw journals *Ringen*, *Khaliastre* [Gang], *Albatros* and *Di vog* [The Scales], not one resident or native of Warsaw took part. Uri-Zvi Grinberg and Melekh Ravitsch came to Warsaw from Galicia, Perets Markish came from the Ukraine. Again, of the 32 Yiddish writers in Trunk and Zeitlin's *Antologie fun der yidisher proze in poyln tsvishn beyde velt-milkhomes (1914–1939)* [Anthology of Yiddish Prose in Poland between the Two World Wars][34] there is only one native of Warsaw – Efroim Kaganovski.

We can indeed see before our eyes the image so widely depicted in memoirs of the generally provincial youth or young man, usually from the provinces and often wearing the small circular cap and long coat typical of Polish Jews, knocking on Perets' door on Ceglana street with a bundle of manuscripts in his hand or in his coat pocket.[35] This image persists like an obsession, even though in his later years, Perets had already moved to Aleje Jerozolimskie. It tells us more than any research of the power and importance of Perets and of Warsaw as a literary centre. There is great doubt whether any other Yiddish writer in Warsaw, or anywhere else, could have either then or later been compared to Perets. With Perets' stamp, Yiddish literature in Warsaw continued to develop until the Holocaust. Over the whole Yiddish literary world, his approval was cited as the principal justification for any writer's claim to fame. Perets' Warsaw authorisation was carried over the seas and in New York, too, his spiritual legacy was felt. It is true that Perets was not always understood, and that people did not always want to understand him. A part of his legacy was even rejected. Nevertheless, all agreed that his reputation had to be upheld and that one could indeed find in his legacy the basis for every politico-ideological banner. One wonders whether, without Perets' personality and the Perets address, Warsaw could have remained the centre of Yiddish literature in the decades before the Holocaust.

The aspects of the history of Warsaw as a Yiddish literary centre we have described can only inspire wonder. This history is very short, lasting up to the Holocaust perhaps 35, at most 40 years. It is scarcely believable that the well-established and dynamic literary Warsaw of the immediate pre-Holocaust period, had behind it no more than two generations since its emergence. In the time-scale of Jewish history, this is no time at all. In spite of these short cuts, Yiddish literature in Warsaw achieved a great deal, and its legacy is one of lasting worth, to which we today still accord great value. Let us hope that the memory of that great Yiddish literary centre will remain alive in the future, even though there remains in Warsaw, to our deep sorrow, nothing more than the orphaned graves of our fathers on Gęsia Street, with Perets in their midst.

NOTES

1 See, e.g. Elkhonon Tseytlin, *In a literariser shtub* (Buenos Aires, 1946); Z. Segalovitsh, *Tłomatskie 13* (Buenos Aires, 1946); B. Shefner, *Novolipie 17* (Buenos Aires, 1955); Efroim Kaganovski, *Yidishe shrayber in der heym* (Paris, 1956). Especially important for this period are M. Ravitsh's *Mayn leksikon*, Vol. 1 (Montreal, 1945), Vol. 4 (Tel-Aviv, 1982) and especially the third volume of his *Dos mayse-bukh fun mayn lebn, yorn in varshe 1921–1934* (Tel-Aviv, 1975). Very rich in material on this period is Bashevis Singer's multifaceted memoirs. See: Ch. Shmeruk. 'Bashevis Singer – In search of his autobiography' *The Jewish Quarterly*, no. 4 (108), 1981/82, pp. 28–36.

2 The statistics according to S. Kieniewicz, *Warszawa w latach 1795–1914* (Warsaw, 1976), pp. 76, 145, 255, and for 1882 according to the article on Warsaw in *Ha-Entsyklopedia Ha-Ivrit*, vol. 16, p. 545.

3 Regarding the newspapers see the book by M. Fuks, *Prasa żydowska w Warszawie, 1823–1939* (Warsaw, 1979), and in my review of the book in *Soviet Jewish Affairs*, vol. 11, no. 3, November 1981, pp. 35–53.

4 Yankev Shatski, *Geshikhte fun yidn in varshe* (hereinafter abbreviated to: Shatski), vol. 2 (New York, 1948), p. 137.

5 Y. Kornfeld-Dagny, *Le-korot hotsa'at ha-sefer ha-ivri be-ir Varsha mi-hatkhalah ha-defus bi-shnat 5556 ad ha-hurban ve-ha-shoah bi-shnat 5699*, *Perakim*, *Bita'on ha-akademia ha-ivrit be-Amerika* (New York, 5726 [1965/6]), p. 361.

6 The chapter on Warsaw in H. D. Fridberg's *Toldot ha-defus ha-ivri be-Polania* (Tel-Aviv, 1950), pp. 109–115. Although considerably out of date, it is still the only comprehensive treatment. For Jewish presses in Warsaw see also all three volumes of Shatski's *Geshikhte fun yidn in varshe*. The work mentioned in the previous footnote is of a complementary character. Regarding the beginnings see H. Liberman, 'Ha-defus ha-ivri be-Varsha' in his *Ohel Rakhel* (New York, 5740 [1979/80]), pp. 203–207. Regarding the attempt to establish a Jewish press in Warsaw from the seventeen-seventies to the seventeen-nineties see the article recently published in Warsaw: J. Szczepaniec, 'Próby założenia drukarni hebrajskiej w Warszawie w latach 1776–1794', *Rocznik Warszawski*, 1981, pp. 164–208. See also the bibliographical citations in the above works.

7 N. Prilutski, 'Mikoyekh di yidishe Robinzon-oysgabes', *Yivo Bleter*, 3 (1932), pp. 36–48.

8 'Varshever mekhabrim in di 50er un 60er yorn (notitsn tsu der kharakhteristik fun der burzhuazer rikhtung in der yidisher literatur)', *Bibliologisher zamlbukh*, 1 (Moscow-Kharkov-Minsk, 1930), pp. 164–197.

9 Volume 3, pp. 264–266. See also, according to the index in Y. Tsinberg's *Di geshikhte fun der literatur bay yidn*, vol. 9, *Di bli-tekufe fun der haskole* (New York, 1966).

10 See Ch. Shmeruk, 'Le-toldot ha-"shund" be-Yidish', *Tarbiz*, 55 (1983), p. 342, footnote 43.

11 D. G. Roskies, 'An Annotated Bibliography of Ayzik-Meyer Dik', *The Field of Yiddish*, Fourth Collection (Philadelphia, 1980), pp. 138–42.

12 On him, see Shatski, vol. 3, p. 281 and also his foreword to Gordon's booklet, which is not mentioned in Shatski.

13 On the Lebensohns, see Fridberg's work (cited above in footnote 6) and in Shatski, vol. 3, p. 137.

14 On the Morgenshtern family, see Shatski, vol. 3, p. 33. Stefan Lewandowski, *Poligrafia warsawska 1870–1914* (Warsaw, 1982); Marianna Ulekicka, *Wydawcy Książek w Warszawie, w okresie zaborów*, (Warsaw, 1987). In both books the part of the Jews is

very evident. In Ulekicka's book pp. 163–186 are devoted to 'Wydawcy pochodzenia zydowskiego' but mainly in the Polish book trade.

15 See the chapter 'Sifrut Yidish ve-reshitah ha-itonut ha-modernit be-Yidish' in my book *Sifrut Yidish; Perakim le-toldoteha* (Tel-Aviv, 1978), pp. 261–93.

16 On this newspaper see M. Fuks, pp. 21–41 and my review, both cited in footnote 3 *supra*. Refer also to the earlier works.

17 The most comprehensive and accurate treatment of the newspaper is Y. Lifshuts' 'Di "varshoyer yudishe tsaytung"', *Yivo-bleter*, 44 (1973), pp. 107–37. There is new, hitherto unknown archival material in M. Fuks, pp. 62–84. There on pp. 67–69 Glatshtern's plea, mentioned above, is reprinted.

18 The quotation is from 1885. It is a translation of Klemens Junosza, *Donkiszot żydowski* (Warsaw, 1899), p. 240. See also a further quotation of a similar kind from the same book, Shatski, vol. 3, p. 273.

19 Published in 5672/1911.

20 Also cited in Shatski, vol. 3, p. 275, but without any reference to the context. A continuation from the quotation: 'who stems from whom, perhaps Sholem-Aleykhem from Mendele – perhaps!' Here quoted from the volume *Gedanken un ideen* Y. Y. Perets, *Ale Verk*, vol. 9 (New York, 1947), pp. 154–155. The feuilleton was published for the first time in the newspaper *Fraynd*, no. 295 of 1911 and no. 23 of 1912.

21 For both of them see Shatski, vol. 3, p. 283.

22 A.Kirzhnits, *Di Yidishe prese in der gevezener rusisher imperie (1823–1916)* (Moscow-Kharkov-Minsk, 1930), (hereafter abbreviated: Kirzhnits), nos. 286, 293.

23 Kirzhnits, no. 296. On Epfelberg, see Z. Reyzin's *Leksikon*, vol. 2, p. 793. Spektor also published his *Familien kalendar* in Warsaw from 1893–1897 (Kirzhnits, no. 315).

24 Kirzhnits, nos 9, 327, 318–324, 331–338, 341–342.

25 See further references in my review of M. Fuks, *op.cit.*

26 *Der Yud* and other publications. See my review, *supra*.

27 His publicistic literary series 'Ha-Yahid be-reshut ha-rabim' and 'Be-olam ha-otiot ha-mahakimot' were published in *Ha-Tsofeh*. They were not printed fully in *Kol Kitvei, Y. L. Perets*, vol. 7, *Even ve-Even* (Tel-Aviv, 5721 [1940/41]).

28 On Bialik's Warsaw period see F. Lakhover, *Bialik, hayav ve-yetsirato* (Jerusalem-Tel-Aviv, 5704 [1943/4]), pp. 444–519.

29 Kirzhnits, no. 68. On this newspaper, with which Perets was a close collaborator, see its editor, Zvi Prilutski's *Mayne zikhroynes*, which were published in series in the Warsaw *Folks-shtime* beginning with 25–31st December 1982.

30 All details and figures according to the most important statistical document of the censor, reprinted in M. Fuks' book, p. 298.

31 One should on no account allow this most interesting parallel in the same city to pass one by. On this see, e.g., Z. Kmiecik, *Prasa warszawska w latach 1908–1918* (Warsaw, 1981), pp. 14, 16, 36, 38.

32 See below.

33 See Y. L. Perets, *A zamlbukh tsu zayn ondenken* (New York, 1915). This is, in fact, identical with the 'Perets number' of *Literatur un lebn. Di naye idishe velt*, II, no. 5, May 1915.

34 New York, 1946.

35 See the following randomly selected memoirs: Shloyme Mendelson, 'Perets in Varshe', in Shloyme Mendelsohn, *Zayn lebn un shafn* (New York, 1949), pp. 151–59; Y. Trunk, *Poyln* (New York, 1949), Vol. IV, pp. 279–297; vol. V, pp. 15–19; Perets Hirshbein, *In gang fun lebn*, vol. I (New York, 1948), pp. 29–35; Der Nister, 'Perets hot geredt un ikh hob gehert', in his *Dertsteylungen un eseyen* (New York,

1957), pp. 279–289; E. Kaganovski, *Yidishe shrayber in der heym* (Paris, 1956), pp. 202–91; in the New York anthology prepared in Perets' honour (see note 33) are printed memoirs of the first encounters with Perets of Menakhem (pp. 21–22) and Opatoshu (pp. 44–5). No less symptomatic here are Herman Gold's 'Perets-bleter', which begin with the words, 'I was in Warsaw for five years and did not see Perets' (p. 97). There is also mention of D. Bergelson's unwillingness to visit Perets in R. Rubin *Aza min tog* (Moscow, 1982) p. 263.

10

NON-JEWS AND GENTILE SOCIETY IN EAST EUROPEAN HEBREW AND YIDDISH LITERATURE 1856–1914*

Israel Bartal

The evolution of Jewish literature in Eastern Europe was closely related to the social, economic and cultural changes which took place in the contacts between Jewish society and the non-Jewish population. These changes, which were part of the 'modernisation' process in Eastern Europe, influenced literary creation, whether in Galicia under Austrian rule or in the Congress Kingdom, Lithuania or Volhynia under Russian rule. This extra-literary reality not only found expression in the literary material, but also determined the manner of characterisation and form, for the world of the ideas of the writers and their emotional load mingled with the literary traditions and determined their use of conventions, literary patterns and modes of formation. An analysis of the changes which took place in the image of the non-Jews and their society in relation to the historical background has to be an inter-disciplinary study which touches the realms of sociology, linguistics and folklore.

The changes which took place in the way the non-Jewish environment and its socio-historical background was described in literature are a part of a cultural-linguistic polysystem which evolved over a specific period. In this sketch, I want to deal with the period which begins with the reign of Tsar Alexander II (1856) and which ends with the outbreak of the First World War. During this period there was an intensification of contact between the Jews of Eastern Europe and the non-Jewish population. Social and cultural processes which had already begun in the first half of the nineteenth century were accelerated, and literature evolved in Hebrew, Yiddish, Russian, German and Polish, in which expression was given to the image of the non-Jewish environment in relationship to these changes. This was a transitional period at the start of which a system of contacts and

*This article is a summary of the main themes set out in my forthcoming book on this subject, to be published shortly by Hebrew Union College.

relationships of a medieval character was dominant between Jews and Gentiles. By its end, a number of different views of the relations between Jews and Gentiles competed for dominance in the Jewish environment. These ranged from the acceptance of the conceptual and literary influences of the outside world while rejecting assimilation, to the negation of a specific Jewish identity.

The Jewish literature produced in this period is a prime historical source for the clarification of the sociological phenomenon involved in the changes in the relationship of the Jews to their environment in Eastern Europe. It is possible to learn from this literature how non-Jewish society came to be seen as a model for those absorbing its cultural and intellectual influences, to elicit from it the image of the various ethnic layers or social *strata* which made up the surrounding society, to examine the abstract conceptual view of the world which underlay trends toward integration or separation and to observe how a group of writers, all of whom were born within a traditional Jewish environment, underwent a similar process of estrangement from this environment, but failed to integrate into the non-Jewish environment, whether Russian or Polish. The acquaintance of these writers with non-Jewish society was, of course, mainly literary and abstract, and they treated only the social sectors familiar to them. Moreover, they relied upon literary models and conventions which, in themselves, and in the way they were used, were a product of their spiritual attitudes. These Jewish writers were 'transitional' writers, sociologically speaking: they observed the passage from Jewish traditional society, with its long-established relationship with the world of the 'goyim', to the 'maskilic' or 'national' society of the future. There is a strong continuity between the writers of the 1860s and those of the 1880s or of the early 1900s. Their reliance upon fixed literary models built on conceptual analyses or common traditional images, led to the preservation of such models for the figure of the Russian or Polish hero, even though the ideological and political background changed continually.

This literary phenomenon, which is of central sociological significance for the understanding of the spiritual world of the Jewish intelligentsia in Eastern Europe, is not peculiar to the society we are discussing or to any specific period. There is a typological similarity between the subject we are examining here and the form of the 'Jewish figure' in European literature during the seventeenth and eighteenth centuries. The transition from an essentially religious stereotype to new models, whether an essentially negative socio-economic stereotype, or the positive exemplary figure based on the principles of rationalism, was one of the reflections of the changing character of social contacts between Jews and their environment. In Eastern Europe, a similar phenomenon can be observed in Russian and Polish literature in the nineteenth century. Jewish society, too, when it found itself in a situation in which it was forced to make contact with the

Gentile environment at various levels of intensity, revealed its expectations, suspicions and familiarity through literary modes. In traditional Jewish society, there were defined patterns of thought and behaviour for explaining and dealing with phenomena and individual types in the non-Jewish environment. In Eastern Europe, these were preserved until the twentieth century and found expression in language, folklore, *halakhic* literature and other facets of human behaviour. Deviations from these patterns, one of the obvious signs of the disintegration of the traditional social systems, evolved mainly as a result of conscious conceptual justification. But alongside this consciously new pattern of thought, the older patterns in language and literature were preserved for a time, and sometimes came to the fore as authentic, complex manifestations of Jewish attitudes, as the Jew emerged from his traditional environment and encountered Gentile society. Thus, in Jewish literature, there existed, side by side, both a rational-universal trend and a deeply rooted heritage of traditional characterisation. The relative strengthening or weakening of these two components, the rational-universal trend and the traditional characterisation, can be compared to the historical model proposed by Shmuel Ettinger for explaining the extent of openness on the part of Russian society to the integration of the Jews. In his view, this was related to the strengthening or weakening of 'westernising' influences as against the Christian-Slavic components in the Russian tradition. The period between 1856 and 1914 extends between two high points of increased 'westernising' influence: the reforms of Alexander II in the first years of his reign and the political ferment of the beginning of the twentieth century.

The Jewish attitude toward the non-Jew in literature can be examined simultaneously on three planes, interrelated and of mutual influence:

(a) the non-Jewish figure as a *literary* problem;
(b) the non-Jewish figure and his society as an *anthropological-sociological* problem; and
(c) the form of the non-Jewish figure and his society as a *historical* problem.

The emergence from traditional society in modern Jewish history involved an actual relationship, or at least an abstract-ideal one, with a specific sector of the surrounding society. This relationship also found literary expression, whether directly or through the adoption of formal and linguistic features and their association with the integrated or assimilated Jewish character. Whereas in Central Europe, the bourgeoisie was the only social class which served as a model for integrated Jews in the eighteenth and nineteenth centuries, this class occupies only a marginal position in Eastern European literature. Of the sectors of the population living alongside the Jews, or coming into contact with them, in the Jewish literature of our period, a relationship exists only with three basic groups, whose literary form depicts the full range of attitudes toward the non-Jewish historical reality: the *authorities*, whose literary manifestation can be seen in the depiction of Russian or Austrian officialdom; the *Polish nobility*, whose principal literary manifestation is the image of the *porets*; and the *peasantry*, which is made up of various ethnic elements (Ukrainian, Polish, Byelorussian, Lithuanian). The changes in the depiction of these three groups should be discussed not on the one-dimensional, apologetic-national plane, which is still occasionally found in scholarship, but in a broader socio-historical context.

The Jewish literature of this period, whether in Yiddish or in Hebrew, contains partial manifestations of other trends of development and further possibilities, which were sometimes realised in the creation of literary works. It is particularly in literary creation that the complexity of spiritual attitudes toward figures and situations within Gentile society can be detected. The mode used by writers to deal with the raw material of reality is often more significant than their declared attitudes in digressions within a given work or in journalistic writing. The large gap between the *centrality* of the confrontation between Jews and surrounding world, and the *marginality* of the literary involvement which depicts that encounter, is obvious to the reader of the literature we are discussing. Calls for integration with the environment are rarely accompanied by the presentation of a literary picture of that society. Indeed, negation and contrast are usually perceptible not in a rich, detailed literary reality, but rather by symbolic form or by digression.

Despite the infrequent treatment in literary criticism of the question of the image of the non-Jews in Hebrew and Yiddish literature, it is possible to find a certain 'image' of the non-Jewish image in criticism: there is almost no treatment of its historical development, whereas the 'traditional' context of the relationship of Jewish society to the outside world or its neo-romantic and symbolistic metamorphosis is emphasised. The reason for this seems to be connected with an anachronistic attitude toward nineteenth century literature, influenced by the impact of the pogroms of the beginning of the century and the massacres in the Ukraine following the First World War. The beginning of the twentieth century provides a clear chronological limit for studying the literary depiction of non-Jews and their society; on the one hand, the relationship between Jews and their surroundings was intensifying, as was their familiarity with the surrounding cultures and even their identification with conceptual trends and political parties. Yet, on the other hand, pogroms were taking place, supported by broad segments of non-Jewish society. Familiarity was increasing, as were withdrawal and suspicion. This was the backdrop to the zenith and decline of the use of certain literary patterns and modes of characterisation which had already begun in the 1860s, alongside new modes and different thematics, the appearance of which also constitute a borderline.

The key Jewish writers of the years 1856 to 1914 link, both historically and literally, the period of the beginning of the changes in the contacts of the Jews with their environment and the high points of intensive contact on the eve of the First World War: Gottlober, Dik and Mapu represent, in their anachronistic mode of writing, the conceptual world of the *maskilim* of the first half of the nineteenth century, whereas Sholem-Aleichem and Peretz are confronted with the Revolution of 1905, the pogroms of the beginning of the century and the spiritual and political trends within Russian and Polish society on the eve of the First World War. The centrality of the three classic writers, Abramovitz (Mendele Mokher Seforim), Sholem-Aleichem and Peretz, who all wrote in both Yiddish and Hebrew and who all derived from the *haskala* traditions while also rejecting much of their central concerns, enable us to find, within their *oeuvre*, texts which represent either a pessimistic assessment of social development in relation to the external environment or modes of literary struggle with the non-Jewish world. Their literary creativity extends beyond the limits of the two chronological and literary 'generations' which began in the years when Mapu's *The Hypocrite* and Abramovitz's *Fathers and Sons* were written and ends with the literary works of the period prior to the First World War. As a result, their absorption of influences stemming from the central spiritual trends both within Jewish society and within the neighbouring cultural environment, enables us to see clearly the way the literary picture of the non-Jewish world developed in this period.

The literary works of the period of Alexander II are concerned principally with the image of the higher social *strata* of non-Jewish society and, only to a much lesser extent, that of the lower classes. The Ukrainian peasants, the Byelorussians or the Lithuanians came into close daily contact with broad strata of the Jewish population, but the literary and ideological interest of Jewish writers in these *strata* was rather limited. They were depicted as part of the existing Jewish social milieu, serving as a part of the landscape, as a backdrop for the plot. Only toward the 1870s is there an increasing interest in them, an ideological attitude in which the impact of the positive image of the Russian 'people', as it appears in Russian literature and journalism is evident. Most of the descriptions of the non-Jewish environment are built on two ethnic-social groups which, for the Eastern European Jew, were the politically, culturally and economically élite *strata*; the Polish nobility and the Russian cadre of officials. The depictions of these *strata* underwent changes and developments which were related to political and social processes within Polish society in the areas of Jewish settlement. But an examination of the formation of the images and situations clearly indicates that the ideological element – and, in its wake, the literary conventions of the *maskilic* tradition, whether in Hebrew or Yiddish – was decisive in the development of the image of the Russians and Poles. The various images which appear in these works, repeat almost constant character traits and are integrated within plots in similar modes. Despite the fact that these images are sometimes represented negatively and sometimes almost entirely positively – the logic of the ideological form can clearly be seen.

The depiction of the Russian official as a positive social exemplar, in Hebrew and Yiddish literature of the 1860s and early 1870s, is related to the continuation of the literary conventions within *haskala* literature from the days of Perl on; the alliance of Jewish *maskilim* with '*maskilim*' within the upper classes of the non-Jewish society, against the vices of the traditional society. This theme recurred in the works of Gordon, Gottlober and Linetzky. Thus Gordon's Hebrew short story 'Two days and one night in an inn', written in 1871, contains a highly stylised eulogistic description of a Russian government official:

> Out of the carriage stepped a man dressed in an official uniform, looking like an army officer. I heard him speaking the language of Russia and I felt secure enough to approach him. The Russians are a people of modest mien and genuine feeling and they adhere to the tradition of their Slavic ancestors of making foreigners welcome and receiving them hospitably . . . The Russian responded to me with a smile and answered me politely. 'I am going to Warsaw, Sir . . . Very good, Sir,' continued the good-hearted official. 'I will be happy to keep you company because I am travelling alone . . . I know you are a Hebrew (Evrei).' He said to me, 'You cannot go on your way because it is still the Sabbath. I shall wait for you until nightfall.'

In the 1870s, one notices the disappearance of the image of the positive official, as is evident in the novels of Smolenskin and Braudes. But the change is ambiguous, except in *The Nag* (*Di Kliatshce*) by Abramovitz in which the abandonment of this literary convention is implicitly presented as a consequence of concrete historical reality. Similarly the literary characterisation of the Polish nobility, between the 1860s and the 1870s, ranged from the unreservedly positive to the complete negation of the ethics and morals of this social class. The absolutely positive manifests itself as an outcome of the *haskala* ideology of exemplary images, which are identified with historical examples of enlightened Polish nobles who were in accord with the trends of enlightened absolutism in Russia and Austria. Thus in his Hebrew novel, *The Hypocrite* (1854), Mapu depicts the salon of a Lithuanian magnate, in which enlightened Poles and Jews meet and discuss Voltaire, philosophy and the Jews. 'The Count's wife and her daughter are well-disposed: they do not distinguish between members of different nations but only between good and bad people.' The Countess introduces the Jewish hero and heroine, 'These are the young people of the new generation, filled with knowledge and reason.'

In sharp contrast to this idyllic picture is the negative characterisation of the aristocracy derived essentially from the traditional Jewish milieu and reflected in the folkloristic depiction of the *porets*. A good example is contained in Gordon's story 'Two days and one night in an inn' where the arrogance and condescension of a Polish nobleman contrasts strongly with the idealised picture of the Russian official we have already cited. In this incident, the aristocratic Pole is receiving a Jewish pedlar:

> The nobleman sat on his chair, like an officer in front of his regiment. He sipped from the full glass in front of him and shook his head at everything the pedlar took from his basket to show he did not want his wares . . . The Jew showed the Pole all his treasures, exhausting his soul by his efforts and trying to induce him to buy with all the adjurations in the *Torah*. But the nobleman did not choose any of his wares. He criticised and cursed him and all the Jews, and when he was wearied with all the trinkets set before him, drove the pedlar away.

The last positive *maskilic* image appears in the works of Smolenskin, whereas the negative characterisation – the 'national' one – can be encountered in the literature of the 1880s and, albeit with modifications, becomes linked with social-radical influences in the depiction of Polish society and its attitude toward the Jews.

The literary formation of peasants in the 1860s and 1870s is strongly influenced by the literary criteria of Russian criticism in the 1860s, which made its impact on Jewish literature through the writings of Kovner, Abramovitz and Paperna. Beyond revealing understanding and sympathy for the reasons underlying the economic and social conditions of the peasants, their characterisation is linked to their image within traditional society and to a limited and fixed repertory of realia of contacts between Jews and peasants in the *shtetl* environment. Thus, for all the sympathy he would like to display towards the peasants, they remain for Abramovitz primitive and prone to violence. His novella *The Nag* is an allegory, in which the peasant's broken-down horse represents the suffering Jewish people, the peasant, the popular persecutor of the Jews, the narrator a typical Jewish radical of the '70s, and the Devil, who rides the nag, the Russian government. The encounter between the narrator, Yisrolik and a peasant is described as follows:

> A few minutes later, a peasant came out of the woods with a large cart, which was being pulled by a broken-down nag. He shouted and screamed, cursed and hit the horse, which could barely drag along

> the heavy cart, as if he wanted to kill it. From time to time, unable to go on, the horse stopped . . .
>
> I went to the peasant and said, 'Listen, why are you hitting the horse like that. Have pity. You shouldn't hit him like that.' 'Why do you say I can't,' the *goy* [*orel* – an even more derogatory term. The reply is also clearly shown to be in Ukrainian] responded, rather surprised, and again attacked the horse . . . A peasant always remains a peasant. He wanted to beat me.

Abramovitz's literary activity had begun early in the reign of Alexander II. In his novel *Fathers and Sons*, he continued the well-known *haskala* convention of the *maskil* struggling against traditional society and its institutions, assisted by a Russian official. This convention enjoyed a life-span corresponding almost exactly to that of *haskala* literature itself in Eastern Europe, from Perl to Gordon, Gottlober and Smolenskin. The first version of this novel (1862) was, in general, steeped with a passionate love for Russia and for the Russians. In the late 1860s and early 1870s, the more Abramovitz abandoned his former optimism about government intentions, the greater was the change in his literary stance vis-à-vis this particular convention. In *The Nag*, as we have seen, the Russian government is depicted allegorically as the Devil who exploits the people of Israel. Cooperation between a Jewish *maskil* and the authorities is now presented as something indecent and quite unacceptable. Yisrolik, the narrator, strongly objects to serving as a *baal toyve* ('benefactor' or 'informer' for the authorities), a position which, in much *maskilic* literature, would have been looked on with understanding and even with favour. 'I will not do it,' he protests. 'I cannot cooperate with them.'

This change, which led Abramovitz to regard the officials as an element hostile to the Jews and to Russian society, finds its literary expression in the refusal of the *maskil* to serve the authorities. Similar examples could be adduced from other *haskala* writers of the late 1870s. As far as Abramovitz is concerned, he now develops a preoccupation to depict the typical non-Jewish character from a *shtetl*, who is to be seen as part of the literary picture of that environment. A single central non-Jewish type now becomes dominant in his works between the 1870s and the Hebrew reworkings of his material: the peasant 'goy' from *shtetl* or village. This characterisation is derived from two main sources: Abramovitz's social world-view, expressed in digressions in the style of Russian populism and in positive elements in the image of the peasant, and in contrast, the image of the peasant and the *shtetl* 'goy' in the traditional Jewish model – stereotypic, comic and typified by peasant traits (crudeness, drunkenness, violence, dullness and the like). The image of the peasant serves Abramovitz as an element in Jewish social criticism, and the point of contact with the 'goy' emphasises also the author's ambivalent attitude toward Jews.

His story *The Secret Place of Thunder*, (*Be-Seter Ra'am*, 1886), written in reaction to the pogroms of 1881–82, contains most of the components of his image of the peasant and his contact with Jews. The conceptualisation of the 'setting' with all its typical components does not, in the first instance, castigate the violence against the Jews, but rather the social and political conditions which Abramovitz continued to oppose, in his manner of the 1870s. It is clearly a characterisation much more favourable than that to the found in *The Nag*. Thus, in this story, the narrator asks a group of peasants, 'Why do you blame the Jews for what are in fact the consequences of the economic system?' One of them, Vlas, replies as if from a text book of Marxist political economy,

> There is no work and no demand for production and the wages in our town have fallen to miserable levels since men have begun to dominate men to do them wrong [i.e. since the introduction of capitalism]. Many of the merchants are impoverished and go hungry. When men are idle, what have they to do but drink?

Sholem-Aleichem considerably expanded the social backdrop and filled it with a broader range of the non-Jewish characters. At a certain stage in his work, he abandoned the ideological-*maskil* tradition in describing the social milieu and brought greater unity to the Jewish traditional and literary images of the *shtetl* and peasant 'goy'. The conflict between Jew and 'goy' in his writings is much sharper than in the works of Abramovitz and the stereotypic traits of the non-Jew within the milieu – the quantitative and qualitative richness of which is also greater – are more absolute and are not blurred by ideological digressions or by traits imposed upon the characters. But Sholem-Aleichem sought to come to terms with the changing reality, which Abramovitz consciously and openly ignored, and he abandoned the image of the 'goy' of the *shtetl* milieu. In his novelistic and dramatic *oeuvre*, he created several images of non-Jews from the 'young intelligentsia' of the early twentieth century. These characters, such as the Ukrainian lover of Chave, Tevye's daughter, or Romanienko, the revolutionary in the novel *In Shturm*, are constructed in a shallow manner around social, ideological models derived from Sholem-Aleichem's world-view and the literary-political images of reality as he saw them. The shallow, positive model of the non-Jewish revolutionary – set in antithesis to the shallow, negative model of the non-Jewish anti-semite – was a sort of return to the commonplace gentile '*maskil*' as depicted by Abramovitz in the 1860s. The only difference is that instead of the enlightened Russian official, we find the radical member of the intelligentsia.

Sholem-Aleichem's portrait of the radical Romanienko is hardly less idealised than Gordon's view of the enlightened Russian official, willing to wait until the end of the Sabbath to accompany a Jew to Warsaw. Romanienko is half-Polish and half Ukrainian. His mother is a well-meaning, distinguished and liberal Polish lady, his father a brutal Ukrainian anti-semite. Sholem-Aleichem describes him as follows:

> Anyone who knows the events of recent times will understand the meaning of the phrase 'eternal student'. He is, indeed, one of the best children of this land, he has in his heart a warm love, a pure conscience, lofty ideals and was full of goodwill to do everything possible for the hungry and unhappy people . . . In short, not only does he hold revolutionary and socialist views, he is also an organiser and activist, the creator of a whole group.

Peretz, too, fluctuated early in his writings between the ideal image of the Pole of the 'intelligentsia' with a radical-social world-view (and the obverse of the negative, stereotypic anti-semite) and the image of the Polish peasant, whose formulation was also influenced by ideology. Most of the common ground with the peasants in his social stories in realistic style is economic, and the contrast between Jew and peasant is blurred and almost non-existent. The character of the provincial professional is tailored according to the cut of the positivist trend in Polish literature, and served Peretz as an antithetic figure to the provincial Jew, whose life and opinions are subjected to penetrating social scrutiny. Thus the story, *In the Post Carriage* (*In postvogn*, 1891), is a sympathetic portrait of Janek Polyniewski, a radical member of the intelligentsia who has abandoned the study of medicine to become a provincial pharmacist. The character owes much to Konopnicka, Prus and Żeromski and his largely positive depiction is used to set off the aesthetic and moral flaws in Jewish society. Peretz cannot, however, stop himself from recoiling instinctively when Polyniewski displays interest in a Jewish woman. He observes: 'A Jewish woman? Why not? Once it was a religious duty to baptize them, now they aim merely to make a Jewish woman rebel against her God, her parents, her husband and her whole life.'

In his later folk-like stories in neo-Romantic style, Peretz created a Jewish reality, supposedly historical, in which the antagonism between Israel and the Nations is absolute and unbridgeable. Much of these stories is built on the constellation of relationships between the Polish nobility and their Jewish lessees: the Polish nobleman represents the uncleanness, the lust and the violent nature of the gentile world. The Polish noble-woman is the epitome of sexual attractiveness and lasciviousness, and can be resisted by the Jew only with difficulty:

> On market days, especially on the days of their festivals, they drive about in their carriages, all decked out, splendid, and accompanied

> by the cossacks of their courts, through the towns and villages. When they see a handsome and comely Jew, they call the cossacks . . . [And the Jew] is filled with fear and awe before the lady whom he had glimpsed and seen that she was very beautiful, splendidly dressed and ornamented.

In most of Peretz's stories, the Polish peasant appears in a more positive light, sharing the suffering of the Jews. In *The Fur Hat* (*Dos shtrayml*, 1893), a Jewish tailor feels sympathy for his peasant clients:

> I used to enjoy making peasant coats.
> First, why not?
> Second, I thought to myself, 'The peasant gives us bread, he does hard and bitter work in the summer and he cannot protect himself against the sun, so he should at least be protected from the cold, during the winter, when he rests'.

Indeed, the non-Jewish characters in Peretz's stories are mostly stereotypic, whether they are constructed according to ideological conventions or based mainly in the social milieu or representative of the impure gentile world which is to be totally rejected. In their stereotyped essence, they stand in ironic contract to Peretz's literary criticism of the one-dimensional depiction – lacking in internal comprehension – of the Jewish character in Polish literature. Yet, as he shows in his writings, he was not over-keen to dispel this ignorance. In one of his reviews, he wrote:

> From time to time, the Polish press complains 'We don't know the Jews at all. The Jews are familiar with us and with our life. Polish literature is known to every member of the Jewish intelligentsia, while we hear from the Jews only what they want to tell us. The Jew, who has lived with us, in our neighbourhood, for centuries is a closed book, an unsolved riddle'. When this gap is mentioned, there rush in writers who have been sitting on the fence, Poles who (with the help of a little Jew) know some Yiddish, like Klemens Junosza. The Jews also write in Polish, but not all of them. Those who have any talent or gift do not want to sell their Jewishness. On the contrary, they try to purify it with holy water, or at least to throw away the Jewishness, lest it be used against them.

Several central trends are common to the position of the non-Jew and his society within Jewish literature throughout the period under discussion. The social *strata* which were best represented in literature are those which had traditional ties with the Jews and their environment: the

Polish nobility; the Slavic and other ethnic villagers; the Russian or Austrian authorities. Attempts to form other images from social realms outside the recognised system of contacts do not diverge in most cases from a simplistic ideological mode or from adherence to known material. Even though most of the writers were long resident in the larger cities (St. Petersburg, Odessa, Kiev, Warsaw, Wilno), they were close to the *shtetl* milieu and the associated surrounding society. The social class of which the Jews were a part-the various sub-groups of townfolk – occupied a marginal position, both as a group embodying a cultural mode and as an entity which was in daily contact with the Jews. Yet the description of this group is less stereotypic and its literary application is less loaded with symbolism and ideological meanings, apologetic or mythical. Adherence to a basic ethnic-class group was a result of the social-demographic structure of Eastern Europe and of the role of the Jews within it. Yet changes in this structure are largely interpreted and distorted through its own concepts and terms, as can be seen *inter alia* in the facility in which the writers depict the 'milieu', in contrast to the constant difficulties created when they attempt to go beyond the small town or *shtetl* environment.

Socio-cultural change is conceived in terms of the traditional environment or, conversely, through the application of ideologies which demand an approach to the environment. These find expression in fixed models whose relationship to historical reality is weak or even contradictory. Traditional situations involving the contact between Jews and their environment, which had been part of a fixed and defined system, also evolve toward attempts to define the changes, and are revealed in the continued application of earlier patterns and conventions. The literary encounter with the 'goy' in the city is often the continuation of the familiar encounter in the *shtetl* or in its environment. When a new social possibility emerges, such as the meeting of youth of various ethnic origins in the context of radical activity, national or social, similar patterns recur, from Smolenskin to Sholem-Aleichem. These have at their base the tension between the rationalistic-universal concept and the persistence of the traditional aversion to direct contact between Poles, Ukrainians, Russians and Jews.

These repeated literary patterns are typical of the range of contacts between Jewish society and the non-Jewish environment. They are closely tied to the geographical, historical, economic and linguistic reality. In this sense, there is no difference between the *haskala* literature of the 1860s and 1870s and the works of the 1880s and later. The meanings, the modes of characterisation, the style and language change – but the fixed models of the Jewish-Gentile encounter remain intact, from Mapu and Dik almost to the last works of Abramovitz, Peretz and Sholem-Aleichem.

The ideological changes modify meanings, but the possibilities of contact with the environment remain limited. The *haskala* conventions of the struggle of an enlightened government and its officials with a backward traditional society lose their force during the 1880s. An encounter of the police with the *Hasidim*, a frequent occurrence in *maskilic* literature, intended to display Hasidic backwardness, evolves into Peretz's story *Khsidish,* which depicts Hasidism in a much more favourable, neo-romantic manner. A Jewish youth in the 1870s turns to Polish liberal nationalism, which he associates with the idealised literary image of a Polish girl-friend. In the 1880s and 1890s, the Jews seek Liberty, Art or Self-Identity in the companionship of a nobleman or official. At the beginning of this century, they are carried away by revolutionary-radical fervour and join the Russian revolutionary movement. Yet, in all these instances, the meeting is formed on similar lines, partly derived from Jewish popular writing, the repetition of an almost fixed pattern. The Polish nobleman who tempts the Jewess, in a tavern in Smolenskin's novel *The Reward of the Righteous* (1876), behaves like the nobleman who wins the heart of the daughter of the Jewish landowner in Ben-Avigdor's *Eliakim the Madman* (1889) and like the customs official who courts the Jewess in Sholem-Aleichem's *Moshkale Ganev* (1903). The possibility of replacing each text with another (taking into account the differences in language), reveals just how strong is the one-dimensional adherence to an almost inflexible form.

The demographic situation of the Eastern European Jews – a large population centred in areas of settlement in which they often comprised a decided majority or at least, a large sector of the population-finds expression throughout the period under discussion. The sense of the Jews as a weighty demographic entity with an autonomous socio-cultural existence, almost entirely independent of its immediate surroundings, is typical both of the *haskala* attitude and of the changing characterisation of the 'milieu'. Even when the 'autonomous' Jewish milieu is rejected, the historical reality of a large social body is recognised, one in which the non-Jews are numerically insignificant, and culturally of no influence. Models for 'departure' from this traditional realm are also literary projects of a historical-biographical situation linked with a consciousness of the strength and the size of traditional Jewish society.

The non-Jewish socio-cultural model with which the Jewish writer in Eastern Europe was faced, constitutes a continuing problem. The gap between the abstract idealisation of social *strata* and direct familiarity with them within the reality of the Congress Kingdom, Lithuania or the Ukraine constitutes a literary *problem* and a *subject* for developing conflicts. The solutions, in most instances, involve reservations about the ideal model of depiction of non-Jewish figures or frustration of any approach to them by literary means within the plot. In any event, the ideal model of the images from the upper social classes (up to the 1880s) is related to Gentiles whose culture is dominant in the Jewish environment – Russian or Polish – and not to the peoples living in that geographical environment and maintaining daily economic contacts with Jews. Until the beginning of the twentieth century, at least, the positive ideological relationship was connected with 'the Russian people', as a general concept, with no other, specific national designation noted. It is only from the linguistic reality that the non-Russian identity of the non-Jew is revealed.

The linguistic differentiation between the various national groups - which is well developed in Yiddish prose but which penetrated Hebrew writing only belatedly - in *haskala* literature simultaneously serves a didactic purpose and is a literary means making possible the 'realistic' characterisation of the non-Jewish figures. The first trend is weakened, though it does not disappear, in the various language transitions, while the second trend is expanded (less so in the works of Peretz, more so in those of Sholem-Aleichem), and reveals the very wide possibilities existing in the multi-lingual system. The general model related to the socio-ethnic structure of Eastern Europe is preserved from the 1860s until the beginning of the twentieth century; the 'high' non-Jewish language, that of culture and the authorities (Russian, Polish); the 'low' non-Jewish language, that of the peasants and the *shtetl* 'goyim' (Ukrainian-Byelorussian); the Jewish diglossia in its relationship to the non-Jewish languages ('Holy language' i.e. Hebrew; Yiddish). Both because of the direct relationship with the 'milieu' and because of the literary addressee of the Jewish *oeuvre*, the 'low' non-Jewish language occupies the principal quantitative position in the texts examined. A large part of the use of Polish, Russian, Ukrainian or Byelorussian is limited to a vocabulary typifying the regular contacts between Jews and their environment and related to the fixed figures characterised in it.

In Sholem-Aleichem, there is a special language used by the *shabbes-goy*, by the non-Jewish maid who serves in a Jewish house, by the non-Jewish healer in the *shtetl*, by the village policeman, by the anti-semitic postman, by the Justice of the Peace and by the village priests whether Catholic or Orthodox. All of them use a fixed vocabulary with many Ukrainian or Russian words, when talking to Jews or about Jews. Thus, Sholem-Aleichem writes of Hapke, a Ukrainian maid in a Jewish household that, 'Hapke spoke Yiddish like a Jew and used in her speech a mass of phrases in *loshn-koydesh* [literally 'holy language' - Jewish religious terms, usually Hebrew or Aramaic derived]. When she spoke of Hveydor [another servant], she referred to him as a *kapoemik* [a derogatory term for non-Jew].

A decidedly negative stance toward Christianity, both Polish Catholicism and Greek Orthodoxy (Russian, Ukrainian or Byelorussian) is revealed in the characterisation of the clergy. Deviations from this attitude occur only when a priest (exclusively Catholic!) is characterised as enlightened, with a universal attitude differing from the medieval posture of the Church toward the Jews; or when 'realistic' figures are depicted derived from the realm of economic contacts between Jews and clergy.

Izaak Meir Dik's story *Zafrona* illustrates maskilic attitudes to enlightened churchmen. Writing of a senior figure in the Catholic hierarchy, he observes:

> He was one of the most distinguished of all the priests of the region, he knew oriental languages, Hebrew and Arabic, was a great engineer and scientist and knew history. His wealth corresponded to his wisdom, since, the descendant of great ancestors, he owned much property. Despite his wealth he was modest with all people of the town . . . They [the bishop and the Jewish narrator] both had benevolent feelings for both Jews and Christians. At one table they, each for his part, spoke peace and truth [traditional *haskala* catch-phrases]. The difference of religion did not separate their hearts.

Peretz distinguished between the pre-modern setting in which Catholic priests were a positive force and friendly towards the Jews, and the modern period, when the priest is frequently an anti-semite. Peretz depicts more than once the transition from a 'positive' to a 'negative' priest. Thus in *The Stake* (*Der drong*):

> Previously there had been a good priest, roly-poly, smiling, with red cheeks and laughing grey eyes . . . He was friendly with the Jews . . . He used to lend a ruble from time to time against some pawn and without high interest . . . Before the Sabbath and holidays he was a redeemer and saviour . . . 'Take pity on Moyshe Khaym, an abhorred Christ-hater, but who has a wife and children, and lend him a few coins . . .'
>
> While the old priest had maintained good economic relations with the Jews, the new one was active in boycotting them. The new priest was infected with anti-semitism and preached against economic contacts with the Jews. He often referred to that story, the old tale of the hanged man [i.e. Jesus] . . . 'Be careful,' he says, 'you should not deal with any Jew, neither buy nor sell.' If they don't listen, he refuses confession, won't grant absolution. 'Let their souls burn in hell for ever,' he says.

Jewish hostility is also evident in the anxiety provoked by Christian worship and its symbols, by churches, by monasteries and by the objects connected with them. The transfer of the Jewish-Christian encounter to the plane of an ideal confrontation or the symbolic link with materials derived from Jewish mysticism expresses this attitude. Christian themes, even at the beginning of the twentieth century, were regarded as taboo, beyond the realms already depicted in literature, and outside the frame of reference of *maskil*-radical attitudes, which linked the Church with reaction and modern anti-semitism.

The rise of this modern anti-semitism in Eastern Europe had a decisive influence on the literary depiction of non-Jewish society and on its image. The struggle with modern anti-semitism, in the works we have described, was also carried out with *haskala* conceptual tools, according to which this ideology was conceived as the reactionary antithesis of the progressive elements in Russian and Polish society. The apologetic element was still central in Jewish writing and, parallel to it, literary conventions were developed to describe the anti-semitic non-Jewish figure, which are the exact opposite of the traits and concepts which characterise the enlightened non-Jew, whether *maskil* or revolutionary. There seem to be only two ideological possibilities for characterising the modern non-Jewish figure: the revolutionary philo-semite or the reactionary anti-semite. These figures perpetuate ideological attitudes and literary analyses from the 1860s and 1870s. The difference between Abramovitz and Sholem-Aleichem, in their application of these patterns, is related *inter alia* to the extent of their attachment to particular *strata* within non-Jewish society. Abramowitz derived his universalism from the influence of Russian literature and criticism of the 1860s and 1870s, but his contacts with the radical Russian intelligentsia were quite limited. Sholem-Aleichem, on the other hand, came into contact at the beginning of the twentieth century with several radical Russian writers, and even absorbed something of the 'optimism' which typified the Russian intelligentsia of the period. Peretz, in contrast, was influenced by Polish positivism and absorbed something of the pessimistic spirit. Yet he also stood apart, early in the century, from the unambiguous assimilatory trend with which radical Polish philo-semitism was marked. Certainly, some of the most striking differences between the image of non-Jews in the works of Sholem-Aleichem and those of Peretz are related to their different relationships to the two sources of literary ideological influence – Russian and Polish. In spite of these differences, what is striking is the persistence of literary images derived either from the *haskala* or from the traditional Jewish view of the non-Jewish world, which retained their force on the eve of the First World War. Neither modern ideologies, nor modern literary trends could erase these deeply-rooted images. This was, of course, not only a literary but also a social and political phenomenon, the reflection of the ambiguous character of the Jewish encounter with the modernising societies of Eastern Europe.

The ambivalent feelings widely felt about this process in the Polish environment were well articulated by Peretz in his article 'I give up', written in 1911:

> It was not I who allowed Poland to be partitioned, because of family intrigue and hope of material gain. It was not I who put foreign rulers

on the Polish throne . . . It was not I who brought modern civil law from Paris. It was not I who brought religion and the Jesuits from Rome. It was not I who delayed the emancipation of the peasants, so that it had to come from Petersburg. Dear nobleman, this culture, with all its virtues and mistakes, is *yours* [. . .] my only sorrow is that in this Poland which is *yours*, besides me, who works and trades in the town, so, also, the peasant, who ploughs and sows had no share! There is also no place in *that* culture which you have created with foreign ideologies and laws for those who feel and act in a human (*menshlekh*) and not in an aristocratic (*pritsish*) way. I know, too, that in the Poland that is coming, there will be a place for the humanist, for the peasant and for me.

11

TRENDS IN THE LITERARY PERCEPTION OF JEWS IN MODERN POLISH FICTION

Magdalena Opalski

1. TOWARD LITERARY EMANCIPATION OF THE JEW. CLASSICIST AND ROMANTIC TRADITIONS

In the early 1840s Michał Grabowski, a conservative literary critic, deplored a Polish writer's 'serious' that is, non-comical that is, non-comical, treatment of his Jewish characters. Grabowski blamed the romantics, against whom he campaigned on a number of ideological fronts, for much of this new 'seriousness' in depicting the Jewish world. Specifically, he linked this new approach to the figure of Jankiel in Adam Mickiewicz's *Pan Tadeusz*. Although Grabowski devoted only limited space to comments on Polish literary perceptions of the Jews, he was in fact responding to a major socio-literary trend.[1]

In the mid-nineteenth century, the social horizons of Polish literature were rapidly widening. This process expressed itself in the massive introduction of lower-class themes which were until then regarded unfit for artistic treatment. The literary advancement of peasant, bourgeois, Jewish and other plebeian motifs was accompanied by the gradual abandonment of comicality as the standard approach to non-noble characters. The appearance of 'serious' Jewish characters in non-satirical contexts, an approach offensive to Grabowski's understanding of literature, echoed the emergence of new literary perceptions of non-noble groups in Polish society.[2]

In other words, the classicist convention in depicting social reality was crumbling. The Jew's place in this convention was determined by the role which classicist aesthetics assigned to literary characters in general. Treating them as mutations of a basically unchangeable 'human nature', classicist writers credited fictional figures with features which, while universal, were 'typical' of groups rather than individuals. As an element in the classicist panoply of plebeian types, the Jew was to remain on the periphery of high culture. The collective features which he personified such as greed, shrewdness and social exclusivism made him instrumental in the classicists' selective criticism of the basically immutable social order. Although this enlightened didacticism became less pronounced in the following period, the comical Jewish villain established himself as a stock figure in Polish literature and folklore.

Grabowski was correct in blaming the romantics for altering this classicist pattern. They did so by establishing a link between the degradation of the contemporary Jew and the glory of his biblical ancestors. The biblical connection increased the dramatic potential of Jewish characters and cleared the way for their selective literary 'rehabilitation'.[3] This growth in stature, occasionally reaching pathetic dimensions, and the more prominent roles assigned to Jewish characters, coincided with a gradual shift away from group stereotypes, and toward a more individualised approach. Indeed Jankiel in *Pan Tadeusz* (1834), Judyta in Słowacki's *Ksiądz Marek* (Father Marek) (1843), Rachel in Hołowiński's *Rachel* (1847) and Jews appearing in the works of Jan Czyński, Teodor Tomasz Jeż, Józef Ignacy Kraszewski – were full-fledged romantic heroes who drew much of their spiritual resources from the past greatness of the Jewish tradition. However, the new emphasis on Jewish spirituality, and the resulting marked psychological dualism of the Jew, were instrumental in both ennobling and demonising Jewish characters.

From the sociological point of view, early and mid-century Polish writers typically focused on the economic role of the Jew in the life of Poland's landed nobility. The relationship between the landlord and his Jewish tavern-keepers and creditors, loyal or disloyal to the noblemen in managing his finances or dealing with his peasants, remained the single most common 'Jewish' theme.[4] If this approach mirrored the prevailing feudal pattern of the Polish-Jewish encounter, the new stereotype emerging in mid-19th century emphasised the Jews' link to the expanding capitalist economy and the modernisation of their way of life. Mid-century writers focused on the upward mobility of the assimilating *stratum* of Jewish society and the increasingly visible process of osmosis between Polish and Jewish societies. While romantic literature dealt with the traditional Jews, its more realistic successor stressed the growing cultural and social differentiation of Jewish society. This diversification, complicated by the emergence of a sphere of mixed Polish-Jewish cultural influences, further undermined the classicist concept of the Jews as a social 'type'.

In the mid-nineteenth century, the proliferation of Jewish themes was not limited to literature. In many other spheres of cultural life, Jewish themes as well as Jewish contributors to Polish culture dramatically increased their visibility. Both these forms of Jewish cultural 'invasion', which intensified in the following decades, are crucial to our understanding of the subsequent transformations of the Polish image of the Jews.

Mid-century literature took note of the appearance of the Jew in many new social roles. For example, in *Sfinx* (Sphinx) (1846), Kraszewski introduced the first figure of a Jewish painter to appear in Polish fiction. The arrival in Wilno of this highly idealised character causes a sensation in the city's artistic community: 'A Jewish painter! – said Jan with amazement – something strange indeed! Indeed, an uncommon phenomenon!'[5] To understand the novelty of the phenomenon over which Kraszewski's interlocutors marvel, we should remember, that in the mid-nineteenth century not only Jewish painters but also non-biblical Jewish themes in the fine arts were an unheard of violation of the artistic conventions of the time. Nineteenth century Polish reviews of art exhibits illustrate the Polish audiences' ambivalent responses to the proliferation of Jewish themes, not to mention works by Jewish painters.[6] The resistance which this increased Jewish presence met, and the clash between the traditional and modern approaches, was echoed in Daniel Zgliński's play *U wspólnego stołu* (At the Common Table) (1833). In the play, a noble woman who watches her daughter draw a figure of a lamenting Jew, makes the following comment:

> I must admit, I am surprised by your choice of topic. In the final analysis, despite the great sorrow expressed in the features of your Israelite, your picture as a whole makes a comical impression. The looks of a Jew are always comical, even in tragedy. You would do better to leave drawing Jews and peasants to Kostrzewski. I am free of aristocratic prejudice and I share the democratic ideals of my husband, but this is not to say that I am delighted to see my daughter drawing lapserdak-wearing figures.[7]

The anachronism of the artistic conventions used to depict the Jewish world found its first critic in Józef Ignacy Kraszewski. Unusually sensitive to new cultural trends, Kraszewski contrasted the wooden vagueness of Jewish characters and the stereotypical situations in which they appeared with the picturesque richness of real Jewish life. In *Latarnia czarnoksięska* (The Magic Lantern) (published in 1843, simultaneously with Grabowski's essays), Kraszewski called for more realism in rendering contemporary social life, including Jewish society.

> Why, in depicting the Jew, do writers content themselves with hanging on beards and sidelocks and putting a *yarmulke* on the Jew's head . . ., portraying always in the same way and with the same monotony our Jewry, so diverse and full of character? There are Jews and there are Jews, as different as earth and sky.[8]

Kraszewski's 'Historia Herszka' (The story of Hersz), included in *Latarnia*, a picturesque story of a Jewish smuggler whose wife runs away with a nobleman, translated into literary practice Kraszewski's desire to break with the dominant convention by providing the reader with a 'photograph' of Jewish life. Kraszewski's theoretical remarks seem to be rooted in the emerging realist rather than the romantic worldview. However, they passed over in silence the predominantly negative or comical features attributed to Jews in earlier Polish fiction, a fact acknowledged by some contemporary intellectuals. Newer historical research confirms that nineteenth century writers were aware of that negative image, but held divergent views on how to interpret it.[9] Waleria Marrené, the first Polish writer to deal systematically with the literary perceptions of the Jew, characterised his prevailing image in pre-positivist literature in the following manner:

> For many years a Jew appearing in a literary work represented, with very few exceptions, the negative or the comical element. (. . .) Our writers depicted Jewish society mainly in its relationship to the Christians. Not surprisingly, then, Jewish middlemen, cheats and moneylenders were introduced as being representative of the Jewish population. Portraying the Jews in the standard role which they played in relation to the non-Jewish world, literature presented this role as either base or comical, but invariably humiliating. (. . .) In that way fiction exacerbated mutual irritation instead of diffusing it. After the country's prosperity decreased and the discussion of financial matters gradually came to be accepted in *belles lettres*, Jewish characters appeared more frequently. The more realistically the novel mirrored real life, the greater the frequency of these appearances.[10]

In a series of essays published by *Tygodnik Ilustrowany* in 1879 Marrené not only noted the negative stereotype of the Jew rooted in the classicist and romantic traditions, but tried to explain it in terms of the prevailing pattern of Polish-Jewish encounters. This pattern, according to Marrené, exposed the Poles to the least attractive elements of Jewish society, the more positive features of which remained hidden from Polish eyes. Marrené did not question the legitimacy of this perception. At the same time, however, she correctly observed the increasing visibility of the Jews in contemporary Polish literature and linked this growing visibility to the expansion of the capitalist economy on the one hand, and to changing literary trends on the other.

2. THE RISE OF A MODERN JEWISH HERO

The impact of these combined factors expressed itself in the confusion surrounding the Jew's place in the social structure, a confusion that intensified as the Jewish quest for improved social status grew stronger. Signs of diversification in Jewish themes in literature appeared sporadically in the 1840s. For instance, a number of ideologically diverse authors[11] dealt with the question of intermarriage, a theme that became one of the most frequently treated 'Jewish' motifs in the post-1863 period.[12] All of these authors discussed possible matches between a Pole of noble ancestry and a totally assimilated, well-to-do and sympathetic convert to Christianity, or a Christian-born child of converted Jewish parents. Although – characteristically enough – none of these love stories ends happily, the large-scale introduction of the intermarriage theme reflected major changes in the Polish-Jewish encounter. These new patterns could hardly be served by literary techniques which, by promoting the idea of the immutability of the social order, petrified obsolete feudal structures.[13]

The number of Jewish characters deviating from the stereotypical figure with *yarmulke* and sidelocks continued to grow rapidly in the two decades preceding the January uprising. In addition to Kraszewski's previously mentioned Jewish painter, an important role in Józef Korzeniowski's *Kollokacja* (The Liquidation) (1847) is played by a gifted young Jew, Szloma, the Polish-educated son of a well-known Jewish physician. Several Jewish doctors appeared in mid-19th century Polish literature, ranging from unscrupulous and money-minded figures in Kraszewski's *Metamorfozy* (Metamorphoses) (1856) and Korzeniowski's *Nowe wędrowki oryginala* (New Journeyings of an Eccentric) (1858), to the ideal of selflessness in August Wilkonski's *Szlachetny nieznajomy* (The Noble Stranger) (1846). A Jewish actress of extraordinary beauty and great spiritual richness, played a leading role in Kraszewski's *Powieść bez tytułu* (A Story without a Title) (1853–4). Among this first generation of emancipated Jews to appear in Polish literature were also Jewish landowners with freshly acquired aristocratic titles and considerable fortunes, and Jewish bankers such as the pretentious Baron Geldson and the more amiable Olkuski (a former 'Żydek z Olkusza': a little Jew from Olkusz) in Korzeniowski's *Krewni* (Relatives) (1856).

Individual departures from the traditionally Jewish way of life continued to attract Polish attention in the years preceding the January uprising, giving birth to a gallery of increasingly acculturated Jewish characters. In Kraszewski's *Jermola* (1856), for instance, a rich Jewish tavern-keeper in Eastern Poland, 'having filled his purse and feeling the importance of his condition, slowly began to suffer from lordly pretensions.'[14] Among the characteristic symptoms of the Jew's 'sickness' is his large, recently built tavern, whose architectural features and interior decor are clearly reminiscent of a typical nobleman's manor. In Ludwik W. Anczyc's *Flisacy* (Raftsmen) (1855), both of the play's Galician-Jewish characters deviate from the traditional stereotype of a rural Jew. The acculturation of the more conservative of them, Chaim, is symbolised by a red umbrella that he carries with his traditional black dress. The pitilessly ridiculed cultural ambitions of the second Jew in the play, Edelstein, reach much farther. They include attending the theatre and opera, subscribing to Viennese newspapers and art periodicals, reading the Polish-language *Czas*, playing the violin, having affairs with women from various social strata and, generally speaking, pursuing the way of life characteristic of a well-to-do Polish nobleman. In the novel *Powieść bez tytułu* (A Novel without a title) (1853–4), Kraszewski presents a complex and unbiased portrayal of a well-to-do Wilno Jewish family, whose three generations represent three different cultural worlds.

The literature of the 1850s recorded, in addition to individual attempts by Jews to break away from the ghetto, another important development: the rise of a rich, secular and assimilated Jewish bourgeoisie. Literary portrayals of this new élite soon became a major 'Jewish' theme of Polish fiction. The first depictions of this milieu appeared in the 1850s with the publication of novels such as Kraszewski's *Dwa światy* (Two Worlds) (1851), *Choroby wieku* (Illnesses of our Age) (1856), *Metamorfozy* (Metamorphoses) (1958), Korzeniowski's *Nowe wędrowki oryginała* (New Journeyings of an Eccentric) (1851), *Krewni* (Relatives) (1856) and Niemcewicz's *Rok 3333 czyli sen niesłychany* (The Year 3333 or a Nightmare) (1858). These works introduced the Jewish bourgeoisie as a standard element of the social landscape portrayed in literature and consolidated the Jewish banker's status as a villain in Polish fiction.[15]

These novels articulated, on the one hand, the accumulating resentment which the accomplishments of this highly visible group generated in various *strata* of Polish society. On the other hand, they betrayed a preoccupation with the upward mobility of Jews in general. In fact, in that time of accelerated social change, the upward mobility of the Jews attracted more attention than that of any other group. The concern with their increased 'pushiness' found its characteristic reflection in scenes such as the dramatic description of Warsaw's Saxon Gardens being 'invaded' by the public from the nearby Jewish quarters in a 'takeover' compared to the biblical siege and fall of Jericho.[16] An even more dramatic takeover, presented as a nightmare (*sen niesłychany*) from which the narrator awakens in terror, was recounted in Niemcewicz's *Rok 3333*. In the story, whose distinctly 'classicist' comicality derives from the reversal of the established social hierarchies, a mafia of superficially modernised Jews takes over Warsaw, now renamed Moszkopolis after its Jewish ruler. The preoccupation with the advancement of the Jews was also mirrored in expressions such as *Żyd szejne morejne*, referring to a Jew whose modern urban 'elegance' distinguished him from his more traditional coreligionists, and *chorować na morejnë*, meaning 'suffering from exaggerated lordly ambitions'. Jermola's tavern-keeper is not alone among the previously discussed characters in being described in terms of one or both of these expressions.[17] Both these and many similar terms which entered the mid-century Polish vocabulary were applied exclusively to Jews.

Many nineteenth century writers, and particularly Kraszewski, associated the capitalist transformations in Polish society, including the growing power of money, with the irreversible destruction of the old world. In *Choroby wieku*, *Wieczory wołyńskie* (Volynian Evenings) (1959), *Metamorfozy* and other writings of that period, he obsessively depicts the disappearance of the old civilization in catastrophic terms.[18] Kraszewski was not alone in perceiving the Jews – and more precisely the most modernised strata of Jewish society – not only as a force rising on the ruins of the old social order (whose fall it previously accelerated) but also as one which successfully imposed its own values upon European culture. Such ideas were echoed even by writers who showed a considerable understanding of economic matters and were more differentiated in their responses to capitalist changes in Polish society. But even Józef Korzeniowski, a writer commonly considered a forerunner of Polish positivism, unequivocally associates the Jews with 'easy' money, the morally ambiguous wealth generated by unproductive financial operations. The opposition between money created by productive and by unproductive labour, and the author's contempt for the latter, provides the plot structure for several of Korzeniowski's literary works.[19]

3. JEWS IN POST-1863 POLISH LITERATURE

The immediate post-insurrectionary and the following Positivist periods brought about crucial changes in Polish literary perceptions of the Jewish world.[20] The basic impulse behind these changes came from a new ideological scheme which became influential in the late 1860s, and found its most mature literary expression in the following decade. The political depression which followed the defeat of the January uprising turned the attention of a new generation of liberally-minded writers to the question of Poland's economic and social well-being. Post-1863 literature, characterised by a more down-to-earth approach to social reality, called for a Western-style modernisation of Polish society as the only means of ensuring the nation's survival. It advocated a re-channelling of social energy away from the dream of Poland's independence, which was considered utopian, towards attainable goals: the satisfaction of basic needs and human welfare.

These writers evaluated individuals and groups according to their productivity, and in order to promote the latter, advocated individual liberty and equality of rights, opportunities and duties within society. Overcoming the traditional anti-urban and anti-capitalist bias, the positivists looked for a way of strengthening the entrepreneurial and middle-class element in Polish society and assigned an important role in this process to the Jews. However, they saw no possibility of using their potential without the immediate and complete Polonisation of the recently emancipated Jewish masses. Overestimating both the readiness of the Jews to surrender their cultural distinctiveness, and the willingness and ability of the Poles to integrate them, they advocated the dissolution of Jewish 'separatism' while appealing to the Poles for compassion and tolerance. Intended to be bias-free, many works which this assimilationist ideology inspired were, in fact, *romans à thèse* promoting various enlightened 'solutions' to the Jewish question in Poland.

On the other hand, the positivists' perceptions of Jewish society were shaped by the actual patterns of Polish-Jewish relations, which in many instances ran counter to their ideologically-motivated expectations. They took shape at a time when the acquisition of civil rights in the 1860s abolished most of the obsolete social barriers between Poles and Jews, while creating new areas of tension between them. It is true that instances of co-operation during the January uprising improved the climate of inter-ethnic relations, generating hopes that the troublesome 'Jewish question' in Poland could be solved or at least substantially eased. This mood expressed itself, for example, in the popularity in the 1860s of the messianic motif of 'the two Israels' – a vision of the parallel destinies of Polish and Jewish nations, chosen by God for the accomplishment of crucial historical missions. In the long run, however, these gains were offset by the intensifying economic competition and Polish concerns about Jewish political loyalties at a time when Polish society faced strong denationalisation pressures. This climate was neither eased by the rise of militant nationalisms in the late 19th century, nor by multiplying indications that the dissolution of Jews in a sea of ethnic Poles was not likely to occur.

The positivists' massive literary 'discovery' of the Jewish world produced a body of writings dealing with various aspects of Jewish life which, marking the beginning of 'Jewish' topical specialisation in Polish fiction, further increased the overall visibility of the 'Jewish question' in Poland. Going far beyond occasional glimpses of Jewish life, the positivist interest in Jewish matters widened to include all of Poland's Jewish society, whose internal structure and grievances became the subject of literary investigation. The most ambitious of them placed the plots of their Jewish stories in a purely or predominantly Jewish environment, enriching Polish literature with a hitherto unheard of variety of human types. Many of these works focused, as did the most famous 'Jewish' novel of that period, Eliza Orzeszkowa's *Meir Ezofowicz* (1878), on the struggle between traditionalists and the pro-Polish forces of progress in Jewish society. Others, such as Przyborowski's *Hinda* (1869), Asnyk's *Żyd* (The Jew) (1874), Lubowski's *Żyd* (The Jew) (1868), Bałucki's *Żydówka* (The Jewess) (1869) i *Za winy nie popełnione* (For an uncommitted fault) (1871), Jeż's *Urocza* (The Charmer)

(1866), Orzeszkowa's *Eli Makower* (1874), set in a mixed or predominantly non-Jewish cultural environment, explored the conditions which encouraged or discouraged the integration of Jews into Polish society. It is noteworthy that this preoccupation with acculturation and assimilation of Jews retained its prominence long after the assimilationist ideology of Polish positivism was declared bankrupt. Free of the unrealistic optimism of the 1870s, works such as Prus's *Lalka* (The Doll) (1995), Maciejowski's *Żyzma* (1896), Konopnicka's *Mendel Gdański* (Mendel of Gdańsk) (1893), continued to focus on the pattern of Polish-Jewish interaction along the lines established by positivist writers.

Emphasising the need for greater Jewish participation in public life, 'classical' positivist fiction depicted mutually-enriching encounters between Poles and Jews. In *Ogniwa* (The Links), for instance, Orzeszkowa brings together an old Polish nobleman and a Jewish watchmaker and makes them discover the amazing similarity of their respective human experiences. In *Gedali*, the wonderful Talmudic parables told by a poor village pedlar meet with the love and gratitude of his gentile audiences. In Prus's *Anielka*, a village tavern-keeper is the only constructive force in the troubled life of a bankrupt nobleman and his children. No justice can be done to these works without mentioning the genuine human warmth permeating many of these images, and their well-documented ability to move both the Polish and Polish-Jewish readers for whom they were intended.

On the other hand, the early realists developed and broadened the scope of 'Jewish' themes introduced in the 1850s. Their discussion of the social progress of the Jew and its implications for the non-Jewish environment, acquired new political undertones. The post-1863 images of Jewish life were also characterised by a gradual shift from rural to urban surroundings. The heavy emphasis on the Jew's role in the capitalist economy overshadowed other 'Jewish' themes which, like inter-generational conflict in Jewish families, mixed marriages, scenes from the life of the Jewish bourgeoisie and other aspects of the osmosis occurring between the two societies, still inspired a substantial literary output.

In literary terms, these developments were made possible by the continuing advances of realism, which from timid non-romantic subcurrents evolved into the dominant literary trend in the late positivist period. In fact, the most widely-read 'Jewish' novels, Eliza Orzeszkowa's *Eli Makower* (1874) and *Meir Ezofowicz* (1878) and Aleksander Świętochowski's *Chawa Rubin* (1879) also helped shape the model of a realist novel. Reaching maturity in the late 1870s, realism remained a constant factor in Poland's literary life to the end of the period under study. Its internal evolution progressed from the tendentiousness characteristic of the positivist period, to an objective and mature form of realism, contributing to the continuous widening of the social horizons of Polish literature.

As the 'invasion' of creative arts by popular themes and characters continued, the literary and journalistic exploration of lower-status groups became the centrepiece of the positivist programme.

> From the moment when journalism poked its head out of the salons of its sponsors and looked at the world around, the time of Arcadian articles was over. It became clear that, in addition to people living off their capital, which, as is generally known, helps keep up spirits and preserve virtue, in addition to serious matrons, innocent virgins and vigorous young men 'gracefully mounting their steeds', there existed a different form of mankind: the world of parvenus and starvelings, of swindlers and murderers, of malicious old ladies and licentious young women. In this ocean of misery and bitter struggle for survival the world of good tone and good manners, with its livery and optimism, constituted only a tiny island. Moreover, this island was not beyond the reach of the poisonous breath of the crowds, and it occasionally happened that some of the island's inhabitants rolled down to the common den.[21]

In general, for the remaining part of the nineteenth century, the growing visibility of the Jew in Poland's social life led to an increased demand for fictional and non-fictional literature dealing with Jewish matters, and the number of such publications rose considerably. In *belles lettres*, there was a significant broadening of the reading public. As the popularity of Jewish themes increased in Polish literature as a whole, much of this growing demand was satisfied by 'professionals', writers like Klemens Junosza-Szaniawski, Artur Gruszecki and Tadeusz Jeske-Choiński, who partially built their careers on the basis of their literary depictions of Jewish society. Junosza-Szaniawski's reception by contemporary critics indicates that his colourful depictions of Jewish life account for most of his considerable popularity with Polish readers.[22]

A bibliographical survey I have undertaken can provide the basis for a rough estimate of the rising visibility of the Jew in Polish literature. The survey includes slightly less than 700 fictional works written between 1820 and 1905. Imperfect as it may be, this sample clearly shows the growing frequency with which Jewish themes are treated in Polish fiction of the late 19th century. While the period up to 1863 accounts for less than 10 percent of the works listed, those published during the positivist period (1863–1885) comprise close to 30 percent. For the following two decades (1885 to 1905), the figure is slightly more than 50 percent of the total. If we consider the quality of the works surveyed, and the prominence of Jewish motifs in their plots, this increase is even more significant. While few lengthy 'Jewish' novels were published in the years 1820–1863, the abundant production of poetry in the early 1860s represents an important part of the 10 percent recorded for the first period. The positivist discovery of the Jewish world as a subject of literary exploration alters these proportions. In general, Jewish motifs move to the foreground while works devoted primarily to the Jews grow both in volume and in literary importance. The output of such 'heavyweight' fiction becomes more significant in the mid-1870s and reaches its peak in the last decade of the 19th century.

4. THE TURN OF THE CENTURY

The great novelty of the positivist period was undoubtedly its idealisation of capitalism, an approach which paved the way for a more positive evaluation of the Jewish role in Polish society. This idealisation of capitalism, however, turned out to be short-lived and ran against values deeply rooted in the national tradition. The pragmatism of positivist writers failed to address the painful issue of Poland's lost political independence. Moreover, the Warsaw anti-Jewish riots of 1881 eroded what was still left of the assimilationist hopes for the massive, quick and painless Polonisation of the Jewish masses. In the course of the following decade, opposition to the 'shamefaced materialism' inherent in the positivist ideology continued to grow. Looking back at the failure of this positivist ideal, Ignacy Matuszewski, a well-known literary critic of the turn of the century, observed:

> Alas! The golden age remained a dream: the heroic engineers, praised by contemporary writers, were transformed into legal bandits. [Organic] work, which was to raise the spirits of the individual and of the collective, changed into a nightmare which preyed on the sweat of the poor and the brains, nerves and hearts of the rich and those determined to become rich.[23]

The reaction against the 'materialist' orientation of the positivists, marked by the transformation of 'heroic engineers' into 'legal bandits', was bound to affect literary perceptions of the Jew. In fact, in the last two decades of the 19th century, the image of capitalism, including its specifically Jewish face, becomes darker and more threatening. This trend continued to prevail in the early 20th century. Klemens Junosza-Szaniawski's *W pajęczej sieci* (In the Spider's Web) (1896), *Pod wodę* (Under Water) (1899), *Pająki* (Spiders) (1894), *Czarnobłoto. Pająki wiejskie* (Rural Spiders) (1895), Kazimierz Laskowski's *Zrosli z ziemia* (They have grown from this Land) (1913), *Pamiętnik eks-dziedzica z dopiskami eks-pachciarza* (The Memoirs of an ex-Landlord, taken from the Notes of a Jewish ex-tenant) (1904), Artur Gruszecki's *Szachraje* (Swindlers) (1899), *Dla miliona*

(For a Million) (1900), Władysław Reymont's *Ziemia obiecana* (The Promised Land) (1899), Teodor Jeske-Choiński's *Na straconym posterunku* (At a Lost Outpost) (1891), Michal Bałucki's *W żydowskich rękach* (In Jewish Hands) (1884), *Przeklęte pieniądze* (Cursed Money) (1899), Jozef Rogosz's *W piekle galicyjskim* (In the Galician Hell) (1896) – this is just a small sample of turn-of-the-century works which stress the dark side of capitalist society. Most of them are lengthy novels which focus on the unsuccessful efforts of Polish characters to free themselves from the capitalist cobwebs that entangle them. In all cases, the 'flies' are ultimately strangled and become the prey of a swarm of Jewish 'spiders'.

Maria Konopnicka's short story *Nasza szkapa* (Our Nag) (1893) offers an example of this approach. Described with exceptional detachment, its Jewish hero is typical of Jewish figures found in most works of this group in his lack – if not a total absence – of any non-pecuniary traits. This petty merchant, characteristically nicknamed Handel (trade), appears on the scene in order to deprive a debt-ridden worker's family of yet another of its few remaining necessities. His appearances divide the plot into segments and mark consecutive stages in the family's realistically depicted physical, economic and social decline. The child who narrates the story does not resent Handel as an individual. He sees the Jew as a tool in the hands of impersonal forces which, destructive as they may be, appear to him to be self-explanatory, necessary and constant elements of life. The naivété and fatalism inherent in the narrator's perspective enable Konopnicka to pass over in silence the nature of the threat and to give it the appearance of invisibility. This literary trick, however, does not make the danger hanging over the boy's head less real. In the final analysis, the perspective of the narrator reinforces rather than tones down the naturalistic cruelty and sadness of *Nasza szkapa*.

It is noteworthy that in the post-positivist period interest in Jewish matters was particularly pronounced among writers with naturalist leanings. Although a distinctly naturalist school remained on the periphery of mainstream Polish realism, both currents absorbed-to varying extents and in various ways – the experiences of Zola and the French naturalists. In fact, all of the most prominent representatives of naturalism, such as Junosza-Szaniawski, Gruszecki, Gabriela Zapolska and Ignacy Maciejowski (Sewer), devoted substantial attention to the Jews. Jewish society appears to have provided them with a theme particularly fit to illustrate their pessimistic vision of social reality based on biological determinism.

As with the overall vision of capitalism, an optimistic interpretation of the bonds tying individuals and groups to their respective environments and backgrounds was gradually replaced by a more pessimistic view. The optimistic interpretation of determinism expressed itself in the form of a positivist faith in the magical power of education as a tool for the transformation of human societies. The positivist writers' emphasis on the harmonious and self-regulatory nature of social evolution accounts for their persistent reluctance to confront the issue of anti-semitism. A more pessimistic view of determinism is echoed in the previously quoted passage by Prus: a bitter struggle for survival governs the 'other mankind', the world of 'parvenus, starvelings, swindlers and murderers'. This vision of human relations as conflict-ridden is a typical feature of mature realism and naturalism. In general, the naturalists tended to view conflicts pitting various human groups against each other as an integral, 'natural' and necessary element of social life.

Analogies between the patterns of animal and human behaviour underlie many naturalist depictions of the tension between Poles and Jews. The following scene from Dygasiński's story of animal life, *Wilki, psy i ludzie* (Wolves, Dogs and Men) (1883), provides a particularly illuminating example of this way of thinking. It discusses the nature of the hostility between the narrator's dog and a young domesticated wolf. At first the narrator spontaneously intervenes in defence of the wolf, offering him protection against the dog's aggression. On second thought, however, deeper 'philosophical and historical' reflection makes the narrator refrain from interfering in the animals' affairs. Comparing the dogs' instinctive hostility towards wolves to the antagonism between Jews and non-Jews, he recognises the 'natural' character of human and animal aggression.

> Although anti-semitism did not yet exist at the time when I raised Buta (the wolf), even then the Christians held the Jews in contempt. Such and similar reflections cooled down my anger at the hound. How can you expect animals to achieve equality, I thought, if humans seem unable to achieve it? Let my wolf experience the bitterness of civilised life in his youth: let him have some tragic memories.[24]

From the 1890s onward the realist and naturalist depictions of Jewish society – now reaching their peak of popularity – were shaped by yet another literary factor. Individual psychology and the 'metaphysical essence' of the Jew became the focus of modernism, a current which placed the individual quest for the absolute, and devotion to pure art, at the heart of its artistic credo. The gloomy and decadent moods of the Polish modernists were fed by a strong perception of the decline of modern civilisation, a vision which was spreading throughout *fin-de-siècle* Europe.

The modernist taste for the esoteric and the irrational is exemplified by the psychological portrayals of Jewish women at the turn of the century. Thus Rachela, a thoroughly acculturated young Jewess with a deep interest in Polish literature, personifies the magic power of poetry in Stanisław Wyspiański's *Wesele* (The Wedding) (1901). At a wedding party which brings together all strata of Polish society, Rachela establishes contact with the world beyond. At her invitation the spirits of Polish history join the living, thereby initiating a confrontation between Poland's present and past which is at the very heart of Wyspiański's masterpiece.

But while Rachela's poetic visions play a constructive role in *Wesele*, dark and destructive sensuality is the dominant feature of Jewish heroines in Kazimierz Tetmajer's *Panna Mary* (Miss Mary) (1899), Zofia Nałkowska's *Węże i róże* (Serpents and Roses) (1913) and Jozef Weyssenhoff's *Hetmani* (The Hetmans) (1911). All these rich and spoiled young women emanate a striking lack of moral sensitivity. The two former characters' obsessive love of riches is equalled by the latter's hunger for political power. Although on the surface their alienation from the Jewish tradition is complete, the 'southern blood', the mysterious power of heredity, ties these three women to various aspects of Jewishness. In *Hetmani* this atavism expresses itself in the form of Hala's political support for the Jewish cause, which ranges from diplomatic intrigue to political terrorism. The Jewish roots of the two other heroines, who live in the twilight zone between the realities of contemporary Poland and biblical Palestine, are far more esoteric. The key to their psychology lies in the latter world, full of strange animals, of exotic plants and precious stones, and permeated by an intense eroticism.

On the whole, post-positivist Polish literature legitimised greater brutality in the depiction of conflicts between Jews and their gentile surroundings. This phenomenon can be explained in terms of the trends which marked the evolution from positivism to mature realism and naturalism. Among these features were the shift from a materialist to an idealist trend and the evolution from an optimistic to a pessimistic interpretation of determinism, a vision which reached fatalist dimensions in the literary output of the Polish naturalists. This evolution was also encouraged by a shift of emphasis from the harmony between the interests of an individual and his community to the vision of society as conflict-ridden and, finally, from the tendentiousness of positivist literature to an objective and more mature form of realist.[25]

At one pole, we have Orzeszkowa's *Eli Makower*, a novel depicting the conflict of economic interests with a realism and explicitness rarely found in the positivist *romans à thèse*. Ideological considerations, however, imposed an artificially happy ending on Orzeszkowa's realistically depicted conflict. By uniting Poles and Jews around common goals, the author restores the natural harmony of the social organism. At the other pole we have the basically conflict-ridden social reality of the 'cobweb' novels. All of them depict confrontations between two antagonistic human species, presented in their respective roles of 'flies' and 'spiders'. Together with the modernist exploration of Jewish spirituality, which removed much of the previous restraint on fantasising about Jews and their culture, these trends reinforced the perception of the Jews as an alien and threatening group.

5. CONCLUSIONS

The highly eclectic image of the Jew in modern Polish literature can only be studied as a complex interplay of social, literary and ideological factors. Its relatively short formative phase was marked by a rapid succession of diverse, sometimes conflicting, trends. The lives of writers who shaped Polish perceptions of the Jew stretched over several periods dominated by 'romantic', 'positivist', 'realist' and other literary conventions, techniques and topics. Formed under the combined impact of rapid social change and political instability, their views of Jewish society went through several equally distinct phases. While the erosion of liberal values and the failure of an integrationist ideology characterised the post-positivist period as a whole, the evolution of Swiętochowski's or Bałucki's views illustrates what radical forms such a reorientation of Polish intellectuals could assume.

While the literary image of the Jew grew out of contributions made by various literary currents, periods marked by an unquestionable dominance of one of them were few and short. Rather, it reminds one of a *pot pourri* in which old and new elements, integrated around some obsessively recurring social themes, constantly change their place and functions within the broader framework of a literary tradition. For example, the appearance of 'serious' Jewish characters noted by Grabowski did not eliminate their classicist predecessor, the 'comical' Jew. Rather, it relegated it to the periphery of mainstream Polish literature, where it continued to thrive, indeed blossom, in second-rate fiction, mass-produced popular literature and folklore. Also, the longevity of some artistically and socially obsolete themes was due to the political connotations which they acquired. This politicisation of certain positivist and romantic themes is best exemplified by the figure of Jankiel in Mickiewicz's *Pan Tadeusz*. Countless imitations of Jankiel, a symbol of the retrospectively idealised golden times of Polish-Jewish relations, as well as his vicious caricaturing by writers supporting or opposing various 'solutions' to the Jewish question, Poles and Jews alike, indicate his continuing importance as a political symbol in the late 19th and early 20th century.

NOTES

1 Michal Grabowski, *Korespondencja literacka M..G..*, Wilno 1842, part I, pp. 75–78. Grabowski's views are discussed by Eugenia Prokopówna, in 'Śmiech szlachecki w

satyrycznych obrazach żydowskiego świata', in *Studenckie Zeszyty Polonistyczne*, no.4, *Ironia, Parodia, Satyra*, Krakow 1988, pp. 131–135.

2 See W. Wolk-Gumplowiczowa, 'Chłopi, mieszczaństwo i szlachta w powieści polskiej w pierwszej połowie 19–go wieku', *Przegląd Sociologiczny*, 7 (1938), p. 226; R. Czepulis, 'Uwarstwienie społeczne Królestwa Polskiego w świadomości współczesnych', in *Społeczeństwo Królestwa Polskiego*, Warsaw, vol. 1, pp. 356–376.

3 A characteristic example of such romantic ennoblement is the motif of the Sabbath and, in general, of the praying Jew. See Eugenia Prokopówna, 'The Sabbath Motif in Interwar Polish-Jewish Literature', in *The Jews of Poland Between Two World Wars*, University Press of New England, Hanover, 1989.

4 See Madgalena Opalski, *The Jewish Tavern-Keeper and His Tavern in Nineteenth-Century Polish Literature*, Center for Research on the Culture and History of Polish Jews at the Hebrew University of Jerusalem, Jerusalem 1986.

5 J.I. Kraszewski, *Sfinx* (1846), Poznań 1874, pp. 127–128.

6 An extensive discussion of the emergence of Jewish themes in Polish fine arts, and of Polish reception of the first Jewish contributors to Polish visual arts, can be found in an unpublished essay by Aleksander Żyga, 'Kraszewski and the Jewish Iconography'.

7 Daniel Zgliński, *U wspólnego stołu*, Warsaw 1883, pp. 7–8.

8 J.I. Kraszawski, *Latarnia czarnoksięska*, Kraków 1978, vol. 1, p.219.

9 Such opinions were expressed by Warsaw Jewish assimilationists centred around Daniel Neufeld's *Jutrzenka*. Aleksander Kraushar, 'Wspomnienia. Kartka z niedawnej przeszłości', in *Książka jubileuszowa dla uczczenia pięćdziesięcioletniej działalności J.K. Kraszewskiego*, Warsaw 1880, p. 508; W. Marrené, 'Kwestia żydowska w powieści współczesnej', *Tygodnik Ilustrowany* 199 (1879), p. 253; H. Galle, 'Żydzi w belletrystyce dzisiejszej', *Biblioteka Warszawska*, vol. 1 (1905), pp. 138–150: see also Czepulis, op.cit., pp. 275–380.

10 W. Marrané, op.cit., p. 253.

11 A. Wilkoński, *Szlachetny nieznajomy* (1846), J. Korzeniowski, *Żydzi* (1843); I. Hołowiński, *Rachel* (1847).

12 J. Szacki, 'Asnyk a Żydzi', *Nasz Kurier*, 22 August 1922.

13 On the socially conservative character of the classicist typology of literary figures in Polish literature, see S. Pietraszko, *Doktryna literacka polskiego klasycyzmu*, Wroclaw 1966, pp. 615–17.

14 J.I. Kraszewski, *Jermoła* (1856), Wrocław 1948, p. 49.

15 R. Czepulis, op.cit., p. 358.

16 *Szkice i obrazki. Fizjologia Saskiego Ogrodu*, Warsaw 1858, p. 77.

17 The importance of the socio-cultural information conveyed in these terms is best illustrated by Korzeniowski's introduction of Szloma in *Kollokacja*: 'Closer to the door stood Szloma Krzemieniecki. Szloma was an educated and *szejne morejne* (type of) Jew.'

18 A discussion of this vision in Kraszewski's *Wieczory wołyńskie* (1859) can be found in W. Danek, 'Kraszewskiego droga do pisania *Rachunków*', in *Pamiętnik Literacki*, vol. 1 (1956), pp. 27–30: for Kraszewski's view of the Jewish role in this process see also A. Eisenbach, *Kwestia równouprawnienia Żydów w Królestwie Polskim*, Warsaw 1971, pp. 263–265.

19 See J. Bachórz, *Realizm bez 'chmurnej' jazdy. Studia o powieściach Józefa Korzeniowskiego*, Warsaw 1979, pp. 75–76.

20 My discussion of the positivism is to a large extent based on my earlier essay, 'The Concept of Jewish Assimilation in Polish Literature of the Positivist Period', *The Polish Review*, vol. 32, no.4 (1987).

21 Bolesław Prus, *Kroniki*, vol. 7, p. 103; the column was originally published in *Kurier Warszawski*, no.123 (1894).

22 (A. Świętochowski), 'Klemens Junosza-Szaniawski. Wspomnienie pozgonne', in *Prawda* no.13 (1898); 'Liberum veto', *Prawda* no.39 (1893). See also A. Dąbrowski, 'Klemens Junosza-Szaniawski. Portret literacki', *Świat*, nos.3 and 5 (1899); M.b. (M. Blumberg), 'Klemens Junosza-Szaniawski jako żydoznawca', *Izraelita* nos.17–19 (1911) and T. Jeske-Choiński, 'Klemensa Junoszy nowele i opowieści żydowskie', in *Żyd w powieści polskiej*, Warsaw 1914, pp.61–68.

23 I. Matuszewski, 'Przemyśl w powieści', *Tygodnik Ilustrowany* no.48 (1899).

24 A. Dygasinski, *Wilki, psy i ludzie* (1883) in *Wybór nowel*, Warsaw 1973, p. 65. The wolf was found by the narrator in 1866.

25 H. Markiewicz, 'The Dialectic of Polish Posivitism', in *Literary Studies in Poland. Études littéraires en Pologne*, vol. 6, *The Positivism. Le positivisme*, Wrocław 1980, p. 27.

12

EROS AND ENLIGHTENMENT: LOVE AGAINST MARRIAGE IN THE EAST EUROPEAN JEWISH ENLIGHTENMENT

David Biale*

In the winter of 1810, only a few months after his fourteenth birthday, Mordecai Aaron Guenzburg departed from his parents' house in the Lithuanian town of Salant and began his wedding journey to the house of his new in-laws in Shavel. Engaged two years earlier, at the age of twelve, Guenzburg was following in the footsteps of generations of young Jewish boys from Eastern Europe before him: engaged and married in their early teens, they left their parents' houses to spend their years of adolescence under the roofs of their in-laws. But unlike his silent forebears, Guenzburg rebelled publicly against his early marriage, penning a devastating condemnation of Jewish marital practices in the form of an autobiographical confession. With Guenzburg, the nascent Eastern European Jewish Enlightenment or *Haskalah* turned its sights on the Jewish family as part and parcel of its attack on the medieval practices of the Jews.

In the period from the early part of the nineteenth century to about 1870, the *Haskalah* was a tiny movement, persecuted by the Jewish communal authorities. Yet it was during these years, perhaps even as a result of persecution, that the *maskilim* or disciples of the *Haskalah* evolved the fundamental arguments of their movement. The ideology of the Eastern European *Haskalah* has been studied exhaustively by historians.[1] A new educational system emphasizing European languages and sciences, changes in Jewish dress, moderate religious reform and a wholesale critique of the unproductive Jewish economy were all the stock-in-trade of the *maskilim*. But this ideology did not emerge from a vacuum; it stemmed from the personal lives and experiences of the *maskilim*, especially from the struggles for identity that marked their adolescent years. For it was typically during those years that they became converts to the cause. While the *maskilim* shamelessly borrowed their ideas often word for word from the European Enlightenment, they integrated them into a peculiarly

*This essay is a revised and expanded version of a lecture entitled, 'Childhood, Marriage, and Family in the Eastern European Jewish Enlightenment' (American Jewish Committee, 1983). The lecture has been reprinted in Steven M. Cohen and Paula Hyman, eds., *The Jewish Family* (New York, 1986).

Jewish framework, that is, into their own reality. My remarks here will therefore focus on the conjunction between ideology and identity in the early *Haskalah*, for what is most interesting in the thought of this movement is not so much the ideas themselves but how they resonated against the problems of Jewish adolescence: early marriage and the teen years spent in the house of one's in-laws.

According to Erik Erikson, every generation experiences a struggle during adolescence for a viable adult identity, a struggle that necessarily entails a certain rebellion against the parents' generation.[2] Societies have always tried to control the potentially dangerous and rebellious energies of their young; Natalie Davis and Richard Trexler, for instance, have shown such mechanisms at work in Renaissance France and Italy.[3] In the Jewish world of Eastern Europe, marriage during early adolescence and a period of *kest* or board in the in-laws' house sought to cut off adolescent rebellion and channel such energies into traditional occupations.[4]

The late-eighteenth and early-nineteenth centuries were a period in the history of the Jews of Eastern Europe when old institutions began to fail. As a result of the crisis of the Kingdom of Poland, the authority of the Jewish community disintegrated in the late eighteenth century. The supracommunal governing body, or *Va'ad Arba'at ha-Aratsot*, was disbanded in 1764 and as increasing numbers of Jews moved from the towns into small villages, the traditional communal institutions were unable to extend their authority. Under the impact of this breakdown in traditional authority and the influence of both enlightenment ideas from the West and mystical ideas from the Mediterranean, a host of new movements emerged to challenge the regnant institutions. Hasidism, the *yeshiva* movement begun in Volozhin, the *musar* movement of Israel Salant and, finally, the *Haskalah* itself were all products of the period from 1750 to the 1840s.

What has not been sufficiently noticed is that all these movements, regardless of their radical differences in ideology, typically attracted their followers as adolescents. I should like to offer a demographic argument as one possible explanation for this fact.[5] From the period after the massacres of 1648 through the nineteenth century, the population of the Jews of Eastern Europe increased dramatically. Although our statistics are not particularly reliable, especially for the early part of this period, it would appear that the Jewish population explosion was somewhat greater than that of the Russian or Polish population as a whole, which was also undergoing a phenomenal increase. From 1648 to 1765, the Jewish population of Poland grew 3.2 times, to more than half a million. By 1825, the Jews of that part of Poland partitioned to Russia numbered some 1.6 million. In the census of 1897, this figure had again risen 3.2 times, to well over 5 million. One result of the higher rate of population increase among the Jews is the relatively greater number of youth, defined as those under the age of twenty. By the census of 1897, which is the most detailed and reliable of the Russian statistics, over 52 per cent of the Jews were under twenty, compared with 48.4 per cent of the population as a whole. Would it be possible to argue that the restless search for new intellectual and religious identities was in part due to this youth explosion, which lasted perhaps a century and a half?

One reason for this demographic boom, in addition to the other causes historians have adduced for Europe in general, was the very early age of Jewish marriage in Eastern Europe. I have examined the biographies of several dozen writers, and the overwhelming majority were married by age sixteen or seventeen, most by age thirteen or fourteen.[6] Abraham Ber Gottlober, whose memoir includes a kind of anthropology of Jewish marriage, states flatly that everyone he knew was engaged by the age of eleven.[7] This is probably not reliable evidence for the Jewish community as a whole since the *maskilim* typically came from the class of merchants and scholars which formed the elite. But there is a variety of evidence to suggest that even the lower classes were marrying at exceptionally early ages: if not thirteen or fourteen, then perhaps fifteen and sixteen. For instance, non-Jewish enlighteners in Poland in the eighteenth century who sought to reform the Jews commented unfavourably on the early age of Jewish marriage.[8] Laws passed in a number of European countries, including Russia in 1835, sought to compel the Jews to marry in late adolescence, thus suggesting that many Jews were marrying earlier.[9] At the same time, a number of rabbis in Central Europe, where the age of Jewish marriage was much higher, made similar observations about their brothers to the East, writing as if these Jews were from some exotic African tribe.[10]

The census material from Russia suggests similar conclusions.[11] The age of marriage only began to rise above adolescence in the last third of the nineteenth century. In 1867, some 43 per cent of bridegrooms and 61 per cent of brides were under the age of twenty. By 1897, the figures were only 5.8 per cent and 27.7 per cent, a rather dramatic drop in teenage marriages. In this respect, the Jews resembled the early marriage patterns of Eastern Europe in general.[12] If anything, male Jews were marrying younger than male peasants, who were forbidden by Russian Orthodox canon law from marrying before the age of fifteen.

This large youth cohort and the pressures of early marriage may help us explain the rise of the new religious, intellectual and political movements of the nineteenth century. We should not imagine, however, that the problems of growing up Jewish were discovered by the intellectuals of whom we shall speak. In the traditional world of the Jews of Eastern Europe adolescent rebellion certainly occurred, but it remained an individual and private matter. Consider, for instance a celebrated case from the 1760s reported in the responsa of Yehezkel Landau from Prague.[13] A twelve-year-old boy was married to a girl of the same age and forced by family pressure to have sexual relations with her in order to consummate the marriage. During the act, a member of the household, presumably waiting with bated breath outside the room, knocked on the door, thus causing the young boy to have a premature ejaculation. Their attempt at sex thus aborted, the two refused subsequently to approach each other and, shortly before his fourteenth birthday, the boy disappeared. Although reported in the terse style of the responsa literature, such a case eloquently conveys the pathos and humiliation that must have made the boy run away from his in-laws' house.

If escape and disappearance were time-honoured responses in the past to the pressures of adolescence, the new movements of our period furnished their own avenues of escape for the disaffected. Generational conflict was the fuel that propelled all of these vehicles for change, with problems of marriage often mixed in as a potent additive. This battle of the generations in the formation of the Jewish intelligentsia closely resembles the familial warfare characteristic of the rise of the Russian intelligentsia at roughly the same time.[14] Here is an example from the memoirs of the Yiddish writer Yehezkel Kotik, born in 1847.[15] Kotik tells how his father, a newly married thirteen-year-old, rebelled against his grandfather by becoming a *Hasid*. Kotik himself rebelled against his Hasidic father by imitating his grandfather: he became a *misnaged*, an adherent of the intellectualist movement that opposed Hasidism. Kotik's father tried to win him back to the true religion by arranging a Hasidic bride for him, but after two months of marriage, Kotik fled his wife and father to study at the Volozhin *yeshiva*, a stronghold of the *misnagdim*. Notice that although Kotik later became a *maskil*, this whole battle was fought out between the new movements of the orthodox world.

Kotik is not the only example of how the problems of marriage played a role in the emergence of new movements within orthodox society. There are numerous stories like Kotik's of young bridegrooms escaping to the great Lithuanian *yeshivot*, including those like Kalman Shulman (1819–1899), Shlomo Mandelkern (1846–1902) and Isaac Kaminer (1834–1901), who would ultimately end up in the *Haskalah*.[16] One such figure who remained part of the orthodox world was Moshe Feivish, born in 1817 and married at age fourteen.[17] When his in-laws refused to let him study, Feivish ran away with his wife to Wilno where he entered a *yeshiva*. Later, in 1858, he published a popular treatise on marriage in which he argued that boys should delay marriage until they had completed their studies, a position rooted in a talmudic teaching typically ignored in Eastern Europe.[18]

Similar tendencies can be found in eighteenth-century Hasidism. For instance, Nachman of Bratslav, as a young bridegroom at thirteen began to gather around himself a group of *Hasidim* of around the same age, all similarly newly married. It is not unlikely that the profoundly ascetic attitude toward sexuality which Nachman preached was directly related to the tensions produced by early marriage.[19] Yet, even if early marriage prompted adolescents to turn to these new movements, it did become an explicit focus of the ideologies of either the *Hasidim* or their talmudic opponents.

It was the *maskilim* who first turned these private dilemmas into the subject of public polemic. Adam Hacohen Lebensohn, one of the outstanding poets of the first generation of the Russian *Haskalah*, was born in 1794 and married in 1807 at age thirteen. In his later memoirs, he wrote: 'I had not yet had a chance to become a young man when they already made me a husband and father while I was still a child.'[20] In the 1840s, Lebensohn wrote an important memorandum to Moses Montefiore, the English Jewish philantropist who undertook a mission to investigate the condition of the Russian Jews.[21] Lebensohn listed four reasons for the impoverished and degenerate state of the Jews, the second of which was early marriage. Lebensohn blamed early marriage for preventing the fathers from gaining productive professions and also for causing Jewish children to be born with physical weaknesses, an argument borrowed from eighteenth-century medicine.

The *maskilim* wrote their memoirs as conscious attempts to define the personal problems of Jewish childhood and adolescence as social issues. The most striking of these were the memoirs of Abraham Ber Gottlober, Moses Leib Lilienblum and Guenzburg himself whose *Aviezer* became a kind of model for the genre in the fashion of Rousseau's *Confessions*.[22] These memoirs follow certain conventions, partly influenced by European literary traditions, and they must be treated more as works of literature than as objective accounts. Indeed, we learn less about the reality of Jewish life in Eastern Europe than about the image of that life consciously created by the *maskilim*. The *maskilim* typically generalized from their own experience and thus created a distorted picture of the nature of Jewish childhood and adolescence: certainly many of their blanket statements about the devastating impact of early marriage and resulting divorce should be seen more as measures of their own lives than as accurate for the Jewish population as a whole. They also composed their memoirs long after the events described and under the influence of an already crystallized ideology, thus fulfilling Erikson's dictum that autobiography is an attempt at 'recreating oneself in the image of one's own method in order to make that image convincing'.[23] Yet the writings of the *maskilim*, whatever their shortcomings as social history, created the first modern Jewish definitions of childhood and adolescence and thus constituted an important critique of how these periods of life were traditionally understood.[24]

The *maskilim* typically viewed childhood as a period of innocence and of unproblematic relationship to one's biological parents. Both Guenzburg and Gottlober speak of it metaphorically as like the garden of Eden or as the 'springtime of life'. In most of the memoirs, the writers portray their parents in thoroughly positive and unambivalent colours. They describe their fathers as *maskilim*, although this is really a play on the traditional meaning of the word, namely 'learned in Torah', since most of the fathers of this generation were not *maskilim* in the sons' sense of the word. We shall see how this exaggeratedly rosy picture of the family was a product of the contrast with the family of the in-laws.

But an early intimation that the idyllic atmosphere of the family could not last came when the young boy was sent off to the *heder*, the one-room school, at the age of five or six. In memoir after memoir, both the *heder* and the *melamed*, the teacher, are presented as the very antithesis of home and parents: the boy is beaten and abused and his love of learning squelched. The brother of one of the early *maskilim* was actually beaten to death by the *melamed*. Whether or not the thoroughly negative image of the *heder* corresponded to real life, it played a crucial role in the pedagogical ideology of the *maskilim* in which traditional Jewish education was denounced in favour of new government schools based on European languages and modern sciences. Here is the first instance where experience, or at least a later memory of experience, formed the basis for ideology.[25]

In most of the memoirs, the writers never admit to having been beaten by their parents, while the *melamed* invariably metes out corporal punishment. Whether this memory of the parents is accurate or not, it is significant that our writers typically perceive brutality as external to the family, which is quite a contrast to what historians of the family argue about child rearing in early modern Europe when such harsh punishment was the province of the family patriarch.[26] In the Jewish experience, this sort of discipline is associated with an agent outside the family.

There is a persistent tension in these works between the 'good parents' and the cruel outside world. The literature of ego psychology calls this phenomenon 'splitting' and argues that it results from a very early inability to separate properly from the mother.[27] Those who split the world in this fashion typically idealize certain people while exhibiting aggression towards others. In addition, such personality types often have considerable difficulty in achieving mature love relationships. We shall see that many of these characteristics are relevant to understanding the *maskilim*.

If the *heder* was the first experience of separation from the parents, it was only a premonition of the more traumatic break that would come with marriage. The vast majority of Jewish marriages were arranged. For the *maskilim*, arranged marriage constituted the worst symbol of the mindless tyranny of traditional Jewish society. Some rebelled against their arranged marriages, such as Reuven Braudes, who was to become one of the important Hebrew novelists of the second half of the nineteenth century.[28] When his mother arranged a match for him in 1868, Braudes ran away from home and only ended up marrying at age forty-six. But Braudes was seventeen when he was engaged and was already a *maskil*. Many of the younger boys who were to become *maskilim* later responded quite differently to their engagements at the time, experiencing feelings similar to romantic love toward their prospective brides, usually before they actually met them. Clearly, for these people, the arranged marriage only became repugnant later, when the marriage itself became problematic. For instance, Isaac Ber Levensohn, one of the first Russian *maskilim*, wrote a love poem to his fiancée, even though when he married her some three years later, their relationship immediately turned sour and ended in divorce.[29]

These cases raise the fascinating question of the status of love in traditional Eastern European Jewish society. The *maskilim* hasten to assure us that love plays no role in marriage and, indeed, much of their polemic is designed to introduce love and romantic free choice into what they perceived as a cold and calculating business deal arranged by the parents. Historians such as Jacob Katz have largely accepted this picture of traditional Jewish society.[30] But even though the traditional Jewish marriage was arranged by the parents based on the criteria of learning, wealth and pedigree, there was an expectation that the young couple would develop romantic feelings for one another within the constraints of the arranged marriage.[31] For even though the *maskilim* report these romantic feelings many years later when they had already been exposed to a European vocabulary of love, the fact that many of their marriages ultimately failed would lend credence to the authenticity of their original feelings: a failed marriage would tend to sour one's memories of the engagement period and, therefore, the persistence of more positive memories suggests that they were genuine and not later retrojections.

If the period of engagement appeared to be a kind of puerile romance from a safe distance, for many of the *maskilim* the marriage itself seemed literally a death knell for all erotic feelings. Gottlober speaks of the child snatched out of the paradise of childhood and forced to eat prematurely of the apple of love which he calls 'honey mixed with poison'.[32] In this version of Adam's fall, early marriage was the kiss of death. Indeed the *maskilim* typically portray their adolescence as premature old age. Lilienblum, writing at age twenty-nine, sees himself already as an old man, a tragedy he attributes to his premature marriage. This feeling that one has already failed at the outset of life was not unique to the *maskilim*, for, as Henri Brunschwig argued, it was characteristic of the eighteenth-century German intellectuals as well.[33]

Was the experience of *maskilim* generally true, as they themselves insisted? Or were they merely representatives of a small, disgruntled minority? Although it cannot be proven, it appears possible that the social expectations inculcated in Jewish children made the system of early marriage work for most people, in part because the young couple were not treated as fully autonomous adults, but as half-grown children still under parental supervision. While this period was to be spent in a married state, the couple were regarded as apprentices for the full-fledged occupation of adulthood. Rather than thumbing its nose at the laws of biology, as the *maskilim* would have it, traditional Jewish marriages effected a shrewd compromise between biology and culture.

But for many of those who ended up in the *Haskalah*, this system did not work. Many of the *maskilim* focused understandably enough on the trauma of sex. Guenzburg is the most explicit on this subject. He tells us that he married before he was sexually mature, when he still had no interest in members of the opposite sex. To make matters worse, he describes his wife, who was older than he, as a 'masculine female', while he was a 'feminine male'. The wedding night, needless to say, was a sexual catastrophe and the second night no better. What followed tells us a great deal about sexuality in traditional Jewish culture. Although public displays of sexuality were thoroughly forbidden, a sexual dysfunction such as Guenzburg's impotence became the subject of intense scrutiny by his in-laws' family. It was obviously discussed by one and all and the poor boy's mother-in-law concocted some home-brewed medicine that almost did him in. In the end, Guenzburg was sent to a doctor who temporarily cured him with techniques that seem to resemble today's behaviour modification. While no other memoir quite matches Guenzburg's for sexual explicitness, a number of others allude in more circumspect language to sexual problems. For these writers, the trauma of premature sexuality seems to have made a mature relationship with the new wife extraordinarily difficult and, in some cases, contributed to a later divorce. Later, when the *maskilim* came to adopt European ideals of romantic love, their own premature encounter with eros created a bitter tension between ideology and reality.

But not only the problem of relating to their new wives plagued these memoirists. The separation from their parents and adaptation to new in-laws was just as difficult. Virtually all wedding contracts stipulated that the in-laws would support the young husband as a student for a number of years while he and his wife lived in their house. The length of the period of *kest* varied according to the wealth of the parties, but it typically covered a substantial portion of adolescence. Thus, during this critical stage of life, the boy lived with his in-laws and not with his biological parents. From the literature on the English public school, we know what it meant to spend one's teenage years away from home, or – closer to our subject – what was the experience of apprentices and house servants separated from parents at an early age. While young Jewish boys experienced many of the same problems, their situation as sons-in-law was at once better and worse. They could be pampered as prize possessions, or, as Solomon Maimon, Guenzburg and Lilienblum attest, the in-laws could take over the office of external persecutor, previously held by the *melamed*.

Solomon Maimon's autobiography, written in Germany after he had fled Poland, provides one of the most hilarious accounts of relations with in-laws, in his case, and, in fact, in many others, with the mother-in-law.[34] Maimon describes the brutal beatings his mother-in-law inflicted on him, for which he amply repayed her with a variety of cruel practical jokes. Lilienblum states 'it was my mother-in-law who in a real sense was the creator of this biography, that is, of the tragic part of it.'[35] These youths experienced a distinct tension here between their new status as married men and the infantilizing and sometimes violent treatment visited on them by their in-laws.

As the memoirs we have been discussing were all written by men, we might wonder about the experience of the young wives, caught between their parents and their new husbands. The autobiography of Pauline Wengeroff, one of the very few written by a woman in the nineteenth century, suggests that the problems of growing up in such a family situation were perhaps as difficult for girls as for boys.[36] A fascinating case from the nineteenth-century responsa literature tells of a young town girl who goes to live with her husband's family in the countryside, the reverse of the usual arrangement where the boy comes into the girl's household.[37] Not only is she disconsolate at leaving her family and lonely in the unfamiliar rural setting, but she is seduced by her father-in-law while her husband is off at school. Unfortunately, I have no such racy tales about the young *maskilim*, but it is interesting to note that the Talmud was so concerned about possible relations between young bridegrooms and their mothers-in-law that it forbade them from dwelling in the same house. As we have seen, in Eastern Europe, this rabbinic dictum was universally ignored.

Thus, for most males in traditional Jewish society, the natural battles of adolescence were not waged with their biological parents but with their in-laws. When the *maskilim* turned this situation into an ideological struggle; they bifurcated the family into the 'good' biological family of childhood and the 'bad' family of their marriages. Their entrance into the family of the in-laws spells the end of paradise and the beginning of hopelessness, despair and senescence. And it is during this period that they typically discover the ideas of the *Haskalah*, a discovery which frequently brings them into severe conflict with their in-laws. Gottlober, for instance, was forced to divorce his wife, whom he loved deeply, when his father-in-law learned that he had fallen into the heretical clutches of the Enlightenment.

For the *maskilim*, the Enlightenment provided an avenue of escape from the pressure cooker of the adoptive family. It allowed them to attack the very social system that had torn them out of their parents' arms, to subject them first to the *heder* and then to the graveyard of an early marriage. If Hasidism and the *yeshivot* also offered a means of escape from the life of the traditional family, they did not provide the weapons of direct criticism.

Little wonder that some of the *maskilim* found their way to the *Haskalah* through the court of the Hasidic *rebbe* or the study hall of the *yeshiva*. We cannot resolve the eternal question of whether ideology appeared here as the egg or the chicken; undoubtedly, the *Haskalah* found those whose marriages were already less than successful as much as it actually caused the prospective *maskilim* to become disaffected.

But as a result of this interplay of ideology and identity in their adolescent years, the *maskilim* tied the system of arranged early marriage into their critique of traditional society and their programme for reform. As Lebensohn's memorandum to Montefiore demonstrates, the *maskilim* argued that early marriage contributed to the unproductive nature of the traditional Jewish economy. Instead of gaining a worthwhile profession, the young married man was expected to study, a parasite supported first by his in-laws, and later by his wife. In Peretz Smolenskin's novel *Ha-To'eh be-Darkei ha-Hayyim* (Wanderer in the Paths of Life), for instance, a young Hasid tells a *maskil* who wants to know how he supports himself: 'Is my mother-in-law paralyzed that I should have to earn a living? Until the day the worms take up residence in her corpse, she will go on working and supply our needs.'[38] The *maskilim* advocated destroying this system by urging that adolescence be devoted to gaining a productive occupation. Marriage would only come later, when the boy could himself support a wife. Adolescence would be re-defined as a period of some autonomy, or at least a period when the constraints of family life would be delayed.

Interestingly enough, the orthodox Jewish world, which was unremittingly hostile to the *Haskalah* on the ideological plane, was beginning to come to similar conclusions. While the general opinion in the Middle Ages held that a youth might dedicate himself more energetically to study if he was married, a number of rabbinic authorities in the nineteenth century, such as Moshe Feivish mentioned earlier, argued that study must precede marriage, a position supported by the talmudic dictum, 'can he have a millstone around his neck and study Torah?' Naphtali Zvi Berlin, the head of the Volozhin *yeshiva*, claimed that early marriage was medically unsound, even if young people in earlier generations had been able to cope with it.[39] This view was echoed by Yehiel Michael Epstein in his authoritative legal synposis, *Arukh ha-Shulhan*, published at the beginning of this century.[40] Toward the end of the nineteenth century, the age of marriage of students at the great Lithuanian *yeshivot* rose to around 25 though it probably remained much lower among *Hasidim.*[41]

The connection between productivization and marriage in *Haskalah* ideology had a further dimension. For the *maskilim*, traditional marriage was a commercial transaction unsuited to the modern world. Instead of money being earned by productive labour or capitalist initiative, the highlight of Jewish financial transactions was the *shiddukh* or engagement. The *maskilim* were particularly hostile to the institution of the *shadkhan* or matchmaker whom they considered an unproductive parasite, living off marriage commissions and whom they suspected – rightly, in my judgment – of playing a major role in keeping the age of marriage inordinately young. This portrait of marriage as a financial transaction was largely correct, as we can learn from the autobiographies of Glueckel of Hameln, who lived in the seventeenth century, and Jacob Emden, who lived in the eighteenth, both remarkable testimonies from the traditional world.[42] For many Jews, these transactions must have been economically among the most significant of their lives.

It is interesting that despite the hostility which the *maskilim* had for the traditional method of arranging marriages, they themselves sometimes resorted to the same practices. The scholar David Kahane and the Yiddish writer Y. L. Peretz were both sons of *maskilim*, yet in both cases their fathers arranged the sons' marriages. Abraham Mapu, the first Hebrew novelist, wrote a series of letters to his widowed brother filled with involved descriptions of the wealth of various eligible women. Even Moses Mendelssohn, the father of the Berlin *Haskalah*, who boasted that his own marriage did not require a *shadkhan*, is said to have taken a matchmaker's commission and to have used matchmakers for his own daughters.[43]

But if the *maskilim* did not live up to their own ideology, in theory, at least, they wanted to take marriage out of the market-place. Two didactic *Haskalah* novels make this point. Israel Aksenfeld's Yiddish novel, *Dos Shterntikhl* (The Headband), written in the 1840s, is an allegory about the conflict between the old commercial values, represented by the marital headband with its valuable stones and the new values of capitalist commerce. As Dan Miron has pointed out, the former is based on fixed wealth and the latter on liquid. Women here represent medieval values and are portrayed with an utter lack of sympathy. The novel's hero, Mikhl, triumphs over these values by marrying the heroine but presenting her with a *shterntikhl* made of false pearls. Once the *shterntikhl* and the values it represents are shown up as bogus, the new capitalist spirit that Mikhl has acquired in Germany can prevail.[44]

Similarly, the first Hebrew novel of Mendele Moykher Sforim, *Ha-Avot ve-ha-Banim* (Fathers and Sons), published in 1868, joins new commercial values with free choice and love in marriage.[45] Women, says Mendele, should no longer be treated as commodities to be bought and sold by their parents; instead, Jews must learn to deal in true commodities. Based explicitly on Turgenev's *Fathers and Sons*, the novel describes the generational conflict provoked by the *Haskalah*. For Mendele, this conflict is an essential ingredient of progress. The novel ends with the engagement of the hero and heroine after numerous misadventures. The match is blessed by the patriarch Ephraim whose death eight days later symbolizes a *brit milah* or circumcision in reverse: the birth of a new set of values and the triumph of a new generation.

Just as the *maskilim* advocated removing marriage from the market-place, so they preached taking women out of commerce, a role quite common for married women in Eastern Europe. While a moderate *maskil* like Mapu could still trumpet the business skills of prospective matches to his brother, more radical writers like Guenzburg and Isaac Meir Dik were not so compromising. In one of his didactic letter formularies, Guenzburg praises the customs of countries where men work and women stay at home; in his own country, he complains, the women engage in business and their morals have deteriorated.[46] In the same vein, Dik, the best-selling writer of Yiddish pulp novels, considered the market-place a disaster for feminine morality. With a characteristic lack of subtlety, he writes in one of his novels: 'The women of Israel and their daughters sit selling all kinds of silk and linen and everyone who comes to buy wants to try out the taste of a virgin and to possess her.'[47] Commerce was the pimp of female promiscuity. For the *maskilim*, both marriage and women had to be decommercialized.

Influenced by the nascent Russian feminist movement, Jewish writers of the 1860s and the 1870s such as Y. L. Gordon and Lilienblum sought to liberate the Jewish woman from the yoke of traditional marriage. Gordon's poem, 'Al Kotso shel Yod' (The Dot on the I) probably remains the most eloquent literary denunciation of the oppression of women by Jewish law and is certainly the first attempt to write from a woman's point of view.[48] Lilienblum, too, wrote several manifestos against the traditional view of women, denouncing in particular what he rather crudely labelled the wife as 'chamber pot' (*avit shel shofkhin*).[49] Lilienblum argued that the tasks assigned to the wife by traditional Judaism could as well be discharged by a servant and he advocated a version of companionate marriage to take the place of traditional marriage.

Those familiar with the history of the European family will immediately recognize in this treatment of women the Jewish variant of the bourgeois notion that in a modern marriage born of romantic love, a woman's place is in the home. While the *maskilim* directed their polemics against a specifically Jewish system of marriage and family, their goal was the same as that of other nineteenth-century advocates of domesticity, upholding such bourgeois values as privacy and chastity. The *maskilim* envisioned a family in which the position of women was at once better and worse than in the traditional family, or at least, in their image of the traditional family. While the *maskilim* experienced their mothers-in-law and, to a lesser extent, their wives, as powerful and domineering, they constructed a family in which power implicitly lay in the hands of the husband. Their revolt against the traditional family was a revolt against a perceived matriarchal family. If the wife was to be liberated from the yoke of traditional marriage, she would also be divorced from the perceived power which women wielded in the old system.

The *maskilim* posed not only as critics of the family, but also as its defenders against disintegration and promiscuity. In addition to their criticisms of the general practice of early and arranged marriages, some like Joseph Perl specifically attacked Hasidism for destroying the family by focusing all attention on God and the *rebbe*. Perl also attacked Hasidism for destroying the sexual morals of the Jews. For instance, he particularly criticized the allegedly pornographic language of Hasidic theology and deliberately distorted Hasidic texts in order to make them more explicitly erotic.[50] In his novel *Megalleh Temirin*, two of the many interwoven plots involve promiscuous behaviour by the *Hasidim*.[51] In one, two of them rape and impregnate a Gentile woman, while in another, the son of the rebbe sleeps with a Jewish woman. Perl seems to suggest that Hasidism has broken the bounds of sexual propriety on two counts: its theology is obscenely erotic and its followers' behaviour is promiscuous. The first, he implies, leads to the second. Both religiously and socially, all morality has collapsed and the family is on the road to destruction.

It is, of course, curious that Perl should have attacked Hasidism for unbridled eroticism. Hasidism was arguably much more puritanical toward sexuality than was rabbinic Judaism in general.[52] While Hasidism celebrated the emotions over the intellect, it redirected erotic feelings toward God. This is a classic case of control and displacement of eroticism through theology. Perhaps the *maskilim* saw in Hasidism something uncomfortably close to home. Coming from the same general background as the *Hasidim*, these adolescents no doubt experienced the same erotic tensions arising from early marriage. But where the *Hasidim* addressed these problems by directing eros toward God, the *maskilim* tried to neutralize eroticism in the confines of a chaste, bourgeois family.

The escape from eros and to the family ultimately proved a failure for the *maskilim*. This failure can be found first in the literature they created. If their own lives were ruined by early marriage, they felt that they could at least create a different world by acts of the imagination. In poetry and prose, they searched for biblical idioms to express values of romantic love. The early romantic novels of the *Haskalah*, such as those of Abraham Mapu, were often set in biblical Israel since it seemed impossible to imagine romantic love in the Eastern European environment.

By the 1860s and 1870s, the settings shifted to Eastern Europe where the typical plot involved the conflict between traditional society and the romantic love between a *maskil* and a *maskilah* (the latter being more a creation of the writers' imaginations than a real species). Society tries to undermine romantic matches or otherwise perpetrates horrors on the young couple. Among these works, one might mention the Mendele novel we have already discussed, as well as Reuven Braudes' *Ha-Dat vĕhā Hayyim* (Religion and Life), M. D. Brandstadter's *Ma'ase Nora'* (A Terrible Deed) and Manus Manassewitz's *Hata'at Horim* (The Sin of the

Parents). But these were by and large didactic works devoid of literary merit, detached from real life and based on apocalyptic divisions between the children of light and the parents of darkness.

By the end of the century, Hebrew literature went through a renaissance in which autobiography and fiction were fused in the works of authors such as Berdichevsky, Feirberg, Gneissin and Brenner. They cast their unhappy youths into story form, thus allowing them to wallow in self-pity through fictional *alter-egos*. But as the critic Baruch Kurzweil has pointed out, the characters of this fiction remain mired in a kind of perpetual adolescence, unable to mature and enter the adult world.[53] The *Lebensphilosophie* of the end of the century demanded that eros become the essence of life, yet the tortured and unsuccessful attempts at love one finds in this fiction belie the bombastic philosophy it sought to serve. In a sense, this depressing development in Hebrew literature was an ominous sign of the failure of art to solve the problems of life.

And, indeed, the biographies of the *maskilim* reflected the literary themes of sexual frustration and alienation. Frequently, the trauma of adolescent marriage was followed by divorce. I would estimate that the divorce rate among those for whom there is evidence was around 30 per cent.[54] Some of these fled their arranged marriages in pursuit of enlightenment while others were forced to divorce their wives after they had become infected by heresy. Years of wandering in search of a meagre existence was frequently the lot of these persecuted literati, including those who remained married. But the break-up of their marriage did not always lead to more successful second marriages. For many of these intellectuals, mature eroticism seemed unattainable. The only extramarital affair I know of from the *Haskalah* – that of Lilienblum – remained platonic and largely epistolary.

In life as in their literature, the *maskilim* could not create the kind of family which was their ideal. Small wonder that Abraham Mapu, in a letter to his brother, denounces family life. At a time when the myth of the Jewish family was becoming the stock in trade of Western European rabbis, he wrote: 'Only one in a thousand will derive joy from family life and even that will only be a facade.'[55] Eliezer Zweifel expressed similar sentiments in a poem entitled 'The Woman'. Zweifel, who was married off at age twelve or thirteen, fled his wife, who refused for many years to accept a writ of divorce from him. In his lament, which is patterned on the Book of Lamentations, he resolves that rather than marry, it would be better to follow the example of Ben Azzai, the second-century rabbi who according to tradition preferred to be married to the *Torah* than to a wife.[56]

Small wonder, too, that the *maskilim* should turn to male friendships for comfort in their shattered personal lives. Mapu writes to his brother: 'Yes, the love of women is strong, but as its price, it takes the souls of the husbands. . . . Not so is brotherhood whose candle will never be extinguished.'[57] Time and again, Mapu, like other *Haskalah* writers, uses frankly erotic language to describe male friendships. Would it be too bold to suggest that the erotic energies that some of the *maskilim* failed to direct toward women found their targets in men? Perhaps this speculation may help us understand the almost sectarian comradeship and ideology of friendship we find in the *Haskalah*.[58]

It would also be of interest to examine the relationship between the erotic problems of the *maskilim* and the later asceticism of the Zionist pioneers to Palestine in the early part of this century. Here was a movement that preached free love on the one hand but also regarded sexuality and love as dangerous to the collective effort of building a new Hebrew society. Might the problems of the Eastern European Jewish family pointed out by the *maskilim* perhaps have contributed to this later ideological tension?

We have come to the end of the historical journey that began with the passage of Mordecai Aaron Guenzburg from his parents' home to that of his in-laws. This small group of intellectuals revolted against traditional society and wanted to revolutionize the politics of marriage and the family along the lines of romantic love and bourgeois marital relations they borrowed from Western literature. They themselves could never realize these ideals in their own lives; like the generation of the desert, they remained in the grip of their own childhood and adolescence. I have suggested that the tendency to split the world into ideal versus evil archetypes, which informed both their artistic and biographical failures, may have been the product of childhood and early marriage in Jewish Eastern Europe. But even if the *maskilim* failed to successfully wed eros to enlightenment, they did radically alter the perception of the Jewish family and create the ideals which other, larger developments ultimately forced upon the Jewish world.

NOTES

1 See Mordecai Levin, *Arkhei Hevrah ve-Kalkalah be-Ideologiyah shel Tekufat ha-Haskalah* (Jerusalem, 1975); J. S. Raisin, *The Haskalah Movement in Russia* (Philadelphia, 1913); and Raphael Mahler, *Ha-Hasidut ve-ha-Haskalah* (Merhaviya, 1961).

2 Erik Erikson, *Young Man Luther* (New York, 1958), pp. 14, 41–2.

3 Natalie Z. Davis, 'The reasons of misrule', *Past and Present*, no. 50 (1971), pp. 41–75; Richard Trexler, 'Ritual in Florence: Adolescence and salvation in the Renaissance', in Charles Trinkhaus, ed., *The Pursuit of Holiness in Late Medieval and Renaissance Religion* (Leiden, 1974), pp. 200–64.

4 Jacob Katz, 'Nisuim vé hayei ishut be-motsai yamei ha-beinayim', *Zion*, vol. 10 (1944–45), pp. 21–54. See also his 'Family, kinship and marriage among ashkenazim in the sixteenth to eighteenth centuries', *Jewish Journal of Sociology* 1, pp. 4–22, where he extends his earlier analysis to include Eastern Europe. These

arguments are also summarized in his *Tradition and Crisis: Jewish Society at the End of the Middle Ages* (New York, 1961), chs. 14 and 15.

5 *Encyclopedia Judaica*, s.v. 'Population', vol. 13, cols. 866–903 and the bibliography found there. See additionally, J. Reinharz and P. Mendes-Flohr, *The Jew in the Modern World* (Oxford, 1980), pp. 525–42 and Jacob Lestschinsky, *Dos Yidishe Folk in Tsifern* (Berlin, 1922), pp. 29–82.

6 For sources of the biographies of *maskilim*, see Israel Zinberg, *History of Jewish Literature*, trans. Bernard Martin (Cleveland, 1972–78), esp. vol. 11, and Joseph Klausner, *Historiya shel ha-sifrut ha-ivrit ha-hadasha* (Jerusalem, 1953).

7 Abraham Baer Gottlober, *Zikhronot u-Masa'ot*, R. Goldberg, (ed.) (Jerusalem, 1976), vol. 1, p. 85. The typical goal was to celebrate the *bar mitzva* and the marriage at the same party. Since a two-year engagement was frequently considered necessary, the *shiddukh* (engagement) was often concluded when the boy was eleven.

8 On the Polish enlighteners, see Jacob Goldberg, 'Nisuei ha-Yehudim be-Polin ha-yeshena be-da'at ha-kahal shel tekufat ha-haskalah' *Gal-Ed* 4–5 (1978), pp. 25–33.

9 On legislation to set the minimum ages of marriage and its effect on the Jews, see Israel Halpern, 'Nisuei behalah be-Mizrah Eiropa', *Zion*, vol. 27 (1962), pp. 36–58. Governmental decrees may have contributed to the rise in marriage age in places like Bohemia, as Halpern contends, but not in Russia, where the legislation of 1835 does not seem to have been enforced.

10 See Jacob Emden, *She'elat Yavetz* (Altona, 1738–59), Q. 14, p. 18 and Yehezkel Landau, *Noda be-Yehuda*, Part 2 (Prague, 1811), Q. 54, p. 63.

11 For the census data of the late nineteenth century, see *Die sozialen Verhaeltnisse der Juden in Russland* (Veroeffentlichungen des Bureaus fuer Statistik der Juden, Berlin, 1906), Heft 2. See further Andrejs Plakans and Joel M. Halpern, 'An historical perspective on eighteenth-century Jewish family households in Eastern Europe', in Paul Ritterband (ed.), *Modern Jewish Fertility* (Leiden, 1981), pp. 18–32 and Jacques Silber, 'Some demographic characteristics of the Jewish population in Russia at the end of the nineteenth century', *Jewish Social Studies*, vol. 42 (Summer–Fall, 1980), pp. 277–8.

12 The classic model for the division between Eastern and Western Europe in terms of age of marriage is by J. Hajnal, 'European marriage patterns in perspective', in D. V. Glass and D. E. C. Eversley (eds.), *Population in History* (Chicago, 1965). Hajnal's work on Eastern Europe has now received detailed confirmation for Russian peasants by Peter Czap, Jr., 'Marriage and the peasant joint family in the era of serfdom', in David Ransel (ed.), *The Family in Imperial Russia* (Urbana, Ill., 1978), pp. 103–23.

13 Landau, *Noda be-Yehudah*, Part 2, Q. 52, pp. 45–6 (for the description of the case).

14 See Vladimir C. Nahirny, *The Russian Intelligentsia: From Torment to Silence* (New Brunswick, 1983), pp. 158–71 and Barbara Engel, 'Mothers and daughters: Family patterns and the female intelligentsia', in Ransel, *The Family in Imperial Russia*, pp. 44–59.

15 Yehezkel Kotik, *Mayne Zikhroynes* (Warsaw, 1913), vol. 1, pp. 110ff.

16 On Shulman, see Klausner, *Historiya*, vol. 3, pp. 362–75; on Mandelkern, ibid., vol. 5, pp. 282–96; on Kaminer, ibid., vol. 6, p. 209.

17 For Feivish's biography, see Jacob Galis, *Encyclopedia Toldot Hakhamei Erets Yisrael* (Jerusalem, 1977), vol. 2, pp. 317–20.

18 Moses Feivish, *Netivot Shalom* (Königsberg, 1858), sec. 1, para. 2.

19 For a brilliant discussion of Nachman's adolescent years with relevant texts, see Arthur Green, *Tormented Master* (University, Alabama, 1979), pp. 33–52.

20 See Klausner, *Historiya*, vol. 3, p. 175.

21 Ibid., p. 180. The memorandum can be found in *Kol Shirei Adam*, vol. 3, pp. 68–70.

22 Mordecai Aaron Guenzburg, *Aviezer* (Wilno, 1863), Avraham Baer Gottlober, *Zikhronot* and M. L. Lilienblum, *Ketavim Autobiografim*, 3 vols. S. Breiman (ed.) (Jerusalem, 1970). Guenzburg (1795–1846) began his memoir in 1828 but did not complete it. Gottlober (1810–1899) published the first part of his autobiography in 1881 and the second in 1886, but the section on his youth seems to have been written in 1854. Lilienblum (1843–1910) lived a generation later and published his *Hatte'ot Neurim*, the relevant part of his autobiography, in 1876 (it was written in 1872–3). Thus, Lilienblum was the only one of the three to have written the memoir close to the period of life described. For secondary literature on these memoirs, see Alan Mintz, 'Guenzburg, Lilienblum and the Shape of Haskalah Autobiography', *AJS Review*, vol. 4 (1979), pp. 71–110 and S. Werses, 'Darkei ha-autobiografiyah be-tekufat ha-Haskalah', *Gilyonot*, vol. 17 (1945), pp. 175–83.

23 Erik Erikson, *Life History and the Historical Moment* (New York, 1975), p. 125.

24 The classic study of these questions in European history is still Phillipe Aries, *Centuries of Childhood*, trans. Robert Baldick (New York, 1962).

25 See, for instance, the autobiographical notes of Adam Ha-Cohen Lebensohn, and Shmarya Levin, *Forward From Exile*, trans. Maurice Samuel (Philadelphia, 1967), pp. 51–2. A recent study of the Scottish Enlightenment attempts to correlate youthful experience and ideology in an approach similar to the one taken here. See Charles Camic, *Experience and Enlightenment* (Chicago, 1984).

26 See Erikson, *Young Man Luther*, pp. 63–79; Lloyd deMause, 'The evolution of childhood' in his *The History of Childhood* (New York, 1974), pp. 1–74; and David Hunt, *Parents and Children in History* (New York, 1970), pp. 133–48.

27 See Otto Kernberg, 'Barriers to falling and remaining in love', *Journal of the American Psychoanalytic Association* 22 (1974), pp. 486–511. On the concept of splitting in general, see Gertrude and Rubin Blanck, *Ego Psychology*, vol. 2 (New York, 1979), *passim*.

28 For Braudes' memoirs, see *Zekanim im Na'arim* (Vienna, 1886), p. 65. See further Klausner, vol. 5, p. 402.

29 On Levensohn, see Klausner, vol. 3, p. 36. For Guenzburg, see *Aviezer*, p. 54. For Gottlober, see *Zikhronot*, pp. 94–5.

30 See Katz, 'Nisuim', pp. 47–9.

31 For this argument, see my 'Love, marriage and the modernization of the Jews', in Marc Raphael (ed.), *Approaches to Modern Judaism* (Chico, Calif., 1983), pp. 1–19.

32 Gottlober, p. 93.

33 Henri Brunschwig, *Enlightenment and Romanticism in Eighteenth-Century Prussia*, trans. Frank Jellinek (Chicago, 1974), pp. 147–55.

34 Solomon Maimon, *An Autobiography*, (ed.) Moses Hadas (New York, 1947), pp. 31–3. The work was first published in 1792–3.

35 Lilienblum, *Ketavim*, vol. 1, p. 108.

36 Pauline Wengeroff, *Memoiren einer Grossmutter* (Berlin, 1913), pp. 100ff. Wengeroff's own marriage was a combination of old and new value systems. Although she was engaged in the traditional way in the late 1840s, she wrote love letters to her fiancé and spent time with him unchaperoned. Her sister, engaged only a few years earlier, had an entirely traditional engagement. Wengeroff speculates that Nicholas I's edicts requiring Jews to adopt modern clothing influenced marriage customs, at least in her native Lithuania. Wengeroff's family was already partially russified and all her children went on to convert to Christianity. Thus, her testimony cannot be regarded as representative of the *maskilim*, but rather as evidence of changes among the assimilating merchant class.

37 Hayyim Halbershtam, *Divrei Hayyim* (Lemberg, 1875), Q. 28, p. 97. Halbershtam (1793–1876) was the founder of a Hasidic dynasty in Zanz, Galicia.

38 (Warsaw, 1905), part 3, pp. 22ff. Translated in David Patterson, 'Hasidism in the nineteenth-century novel', *Journal of Semitic Studies*, vol. 5 (1960), pp. 367–8.
39 Naphtali Zvi Berlin, *He'amek Davar* (Wilno, 1879–80), commentary on Exodus 1:7.
40 Yehiel Michael Epstein, *Arukh ha-Shulhan Even ha-Ezer* (1905–6), Sec. 1, p. 11:3. Epstein claims that by his day (the beginning of the twentieth century), the custom of child marriage had virtually disappeared. The main reason for early marriage was to prevent masturbation, but Epstein holds that 'in these generations the instincts have decreased', so that such measures are no longer necessary.
41 See Shaul Stampfer, Shelosh Yeshivot Lita'ot be-Mea ha-19, unpublished doctoral dissertation (Hebrew University, 1981), appendix. My supposition about Hasidism comes from the observation that the only cases of nineteenth-century child marriage (i.e. below age thirteen), which may be an indicator of young marriage in general, are to be found in Hasidic responsa, while in the eighteenth century, such cases were much more common in all the responsa literature of Eastern Europe.
42 Jacob Emden, *Megilat Sefer*, (ed.) David Kahana (Warsaw, 1897). Emden wrote his autobiography around 1752. *The Memoirs of Glueckel of Hameln*, trans. Marvin Lowenthal (New York, 1977). Glueckel wrote in the second decade of the eighteenth century.
43 On Kahane, see Klausner, vol. 5, p. 298; Y. L. Peretz, 'Zikhronot', in *Kol Kitvei Y. L. Peretz* (Tel Aviv, 1957), p. 146; Ben-Zion Dinur (ed.), *Mikhtevei Avraham Mapu* (Jerusalem, 1970), pp. 184ff. On Mendelssohn's marriage, see his *Gesammelte Schriften Jubilaeumsausgabe* (Berlin, 1929–38), vol. 16, 15 May 1761, letter 103, p. 205 and 27 April 1762, letter 200, p. 324. See further, Katz, 'Nisuim', p. 50, and Alexander Altmann, *Moses Mendelssohn* (University, Alabama, 1973), pp. 92–100.
44 See the excellent translation by Joachim Neugroschel in his *The Shtetl* (New York, 1979), pp. 49–172. The novel was probably written in the 1840s but Hasidic pressure prevented its publication. It appeared in Leipzig in 1862. See further Dan Miron, *Bein Hazon le-Emet* (Jerusalem, 1979), pp. 177–216.
45 *Kol Kitvei Mendele* (Tel Aviv, 1935), vol. 6.
46 M. A. Guenzburg, *Kiryat Sefer* (Vilna, 1847), p. 59.
47 Quoted in Levin, *Erkhei Hevra*, p. 152. For a fuller treatment of this theme in Dik and other Yiddish authors, see David Roskies, 'Yiddish popular literature and the female reader', *Journal of Popular Culture*, vol. 10, (1977), no. 4, pp. 852–8. Roskies quotes a similar passage from Dik's *Royze Finkl* (1874): 'Our Jews only consider it shameful for [a Jewish woman] to flirt with a young Jewish fellow, but not with a Christian, because in the latter case, it is a matter of business.'
48 Y. L. Gordon, *Kol Shirei Yehuda Leib Gordon* (Tel Aviv, 1930), vol. 4, pp. 4–34.
49 Lilienblum, *Ketavim*, vol. 2, pp. 89–93.
50 Joseph Perl, *Ueber das Wesen der Sekte Chassidim*, ed. Abraham Rubinstein (Jerusalem, 1977), pp. 41–3, 125 and 146.
51 *Megalleh Temirin* (Vienna, 1819).
52 These contentions about Hasidism form the hypotheses of my current research.
53 Baruch Kurzweil, *Sifrutenu ha-Hadashah: Hemshekh o-Mahapekhah?* (Tel Aviv, 1971), pp. 234ff.
54 Guenzburg claims that early marriage produced a very high rate of divorce: of every two women, one had two husbands. See *Aviezer*, p. 104. His testimony is suspect because of his own unhappy marriage, but when compared to a survey of the biographies of other *maskilim*, if not the population as a whole, his observation is not far from the mark.
55 Mapu, *Mikhtavim*, 29 October 1860, p. 133.
56 For Zweifel's biography, see Klausner, vol. 6, p. 14. The poem appeared in *Mahbarot le-Sifrut* 1 (September, 1941), 96–102.
57 Mapu, *Mikhtavim*, 12/26 January 1861, p. 138. See also his letter to his brother of

7 November 1857 (p. 23): 'My right hand embraces you and my lips kiss your lips.' See further his letters to Shneur Sachs from 1843 (pp. 3–7) which include a 'love' poem to friendship. One must be careful not to impute too much to these conventions of epistolary style. What is significant is that such language seems appropriate between men but not between men and women. Whatever the particular emotional valence of these friendships, they provided emotional outlets inconceivable within marriage.

58 The *maskilim* may well have taken their conventions of male friendship from the German enlightenment. See Brunschwig, *Enlightenment and Romanticism*, pp. 208–13 and George Mosse, 'Friendship and nationhood: About the promise and failure of German nationalism', *Journal of Contemporary History*, vol. 17 (April, 1982), no. 2 pp. 351–67.

13
GENDER DIFFERENTIATION AND EDUCATION OF THE JEWISH WOMAN IN NINETEENTH-CENTURY EASTERN EUROPE

Shaul Stampfer

An assessment of the role, function and extent of women's education in nineteenth-century East European Jewry requires a substantial effort to distinguish facts from images. Our picture of the past is affected, of course, by present-day attitudes and stereotypes but even at the time, the contemporary reality was seen in light of assumptions based on cultural postulates. There were a variety of images of the Jewish woman and her education – and they were not necessarily consistent. Therefore, pointing out the differences between the realities and the images not only adds to an understanding of women's education in Eastern Europe but also clarifies the value system of the Jewish community in the previous century. It will be necessary to consider the image of women's education as well as relevant quantitative and qualitative data in order to understand the realities of women's education, the way this education was integrated into broader gender classifications and the implications and consequences of women's education.

THE IMAGE AND FRAMEWORKS OF WOMEN'S EDUCATION

There is a widely held misconception that, in nineteenth-century Eastern Europe, Jewish women were relatively ignorant from a Jewish point of view while many received a good general education.[1] A classic expression of this view is that of Zvi Scharfstein who wrote a number of widely used studies on the history of Jewish education and who stated in the opening to a (short) chapter on the education of girls:[2]

> The education of the Hebrew daughter – if we measure education as the degree of knowledge of Torah and books – was on a very low level

> in our midst. So low as to be a disgrace for the people . . . The Hebrews held that women are just for children and the kitchen and that he who teaches his daughter Torah taught her worthlessness . . . Only the national revival saved the Hebrew daughter from the shame of her ignorance – ignorance from the point of view of Judaism.

A typical portrayal of sex differences in Jewish and general education is that of D. Flinker.[3] While discussing education in Warsaw he noted that, compared with the education of boys, the education of girls was backward. At best, the elementary teacher would teach the girl to read Hebrew and Yiddish and with that all the Jewish education of the Jewish daughter came to an end. At the same time:

> In the small towns the men would study and acquired a broad and deep Torah education and their wives and daughters were uneducated and absolute boors. However, in the cities in the most recent generations, the girls as well were educated and cultured but their culture was different and alien to that of their parents and husbands.

It is not hard to find justification of such a situation in classical Jewish texts. The classic prooftext is 'anyone who teaches his daughter Torah taught her *tiflut*' (usually translated as indecency or frivolity).[4] This statement clearly indicates that women do not need any Jewish education at all. However, the existence of such statements does not mean that they were accepted, and even if accepted, that they were realized. Students of the history of Jewish education have often tended to see them as a true reflection of reality. However, this cannot be taken for granted. It is necessary to check the accuracy of this image by examining the education girls actually received.

A number of frameworks existed in which girls could, and did, study, but there was no standard pattern for women's education as there was for boys. This variety might well be a product of the lack of interest evoked by women's education. In many locations special *hederim*[5] operated for girls. In Tyszowce, a girls' *heder* operated in the same house as the boys' *heder* but in an adjoining room. The girls were taught by an old widow, Binele the '*rebitzin*'.[6] The programme of study consisted of prayers, reading and writing Yiddish, arithmetic and writing addresses in Russian. The text books were the prayerbook and three Yiddish texts tekhines (women's prayers), *Tse'ena Ureena* (on this see below),[7] and *Nachlas Tsvi* (a Yiddish ethical and kabbalistic tract). Sewing was also taught. The young students spent most of their time at play and were called when it was their turn for recitation.[8] Many other girls' *hederim* were probably no different.

Other girls were tutored at home. The tutor was often a 'learned' woman who would teach both reading and writing, though at times specialists were hired to teach each skill. Inevitably, such tutoring was for short periods during the day and probably did not amount to more than an hour a day. Since it was expensive, it was limited to the well-off:

> The well-off who gave any education at all to their daughters limited it to prayer and religious matters. Even they didn't send their daughters to school but they were satisfied with a house teacher and the curriculum was limited to reading and writing in Yiddish.[9]

Girls' education was a practical one. Writing was taught by copying business letters and not authoritative religious texts. Countless Jewish girls began their studies with the deathless words 'I went to Odessa to purchase merchandise' – which reflected the utilitarian nature of their education.[10] Their education was seen as the antithesis of that of boys' which was devoted to Torah study, or in other words, cultural education. This is illustrated in the following anecdote about a little boy who wanted very much to write (and ultimately did).[11]

> In our house it was seen as unnecessary for a boy to learn how to write. My sister was sent to Avrom Note the *Shrayber* (writing teacher) but I wasn't. I was supposed to study just Gemara with the Rabbi and not to trouble my head with silly ideas like writing . . .

For some girls, the question of where to study was resolved by their being sent to a *heder* along with the boys. The mixing of the sexes apparently was not considered worthy of note or reaction[12] and the decision to send a girl to a *heder* was usually based on convenience and cost. A *heder* was less expensive than a tutor. As Khaya Weizman-Lichtenstein wrote:[13]

> In the town it wasn't customary to send girls to *heder*, rather a rebbe would come to the house for an hour and teach the girls. In this manner, they would manage to acquire very little knowledge of the Torah and few of them knew Hebrew. For my older sister Miriam my parents hired a private tutor and he taught her all of the curriculum. However, this was impossible to do for the rest of the daughters because the family was too large. Therefore I was sent to (a boys') *heder*.

After basic reading was mastered, boys went on to study classical Jewish texts, the Bible and then Talmud, while girls dropped out.

QUANTITATIVE DATA ON WOMEN'S EDUCATION

The clearest quantitative picture of the educational realities of East European Jewry at the end of the nineteenth century is provided in a comprehensive survey of Jewish life in Tsarist Russia conducted by ICA (Jewish Colonization Association) at the time.[14] The total number of female *heder* students, whether with boys in a regular *heder* or in special girls' *hederim* was, not surprisingly, low when compared with the number of boys. In 1894, out of 13,683 *hederim*, (which were probably less than half of the *hederim* in the Tsarist empire), 191,505 male pupils were enrolled and 10,459 female pupils.[15] This figure includes girls in special *hederim* for girls as well as girls in boys' *hederim*. These statistics yield a ratio of about one to eighteen. However, this ratio is deceptive with regard to the number of girls *exposed* to education because female students studied for fewer years than males. If we can assume that girls studied at the most four years and boys an average of nine, the ratio for the first four years would be about one to eight. There was some regional variation, with the ratio of female students three times as high, for example, in the south west (which included Odessa) as in Central Poland.[16]

Despite the various opportunities for formal education for girls, it seems that many girls, and probably most, did not get a formal education, and if they did, they studied fewer years than boys. This fits the accepted picture of the education of women. However, if we look at educational achievements and not at schooling, then the stereotype becomes problematic. Women, as a group, were far from being illiterate or uneducated. An indication of the level of women's education can be seen by the distribution of Russian language literacy among the various age cohorts of the Jewish population as recorded in the 1897 census.[17]

Starting from the cohort of men and women born in the 1850s (i.e. ages

TABLE 1: JEWISH LITERACY AND POST ELEMENTARY EDUCATION IN EUROPEAN RUSSIA IN 1897 BY AGE AND SEX

Age Group	*Literacy in Russian (%) Male/Female*		*Post Elementary Education (%) Male/Female*	
1–9	6	5	–	–
10–19	41	30	1	2
20–29	51	28	2	2
30–39	47	17	2	1
40–49	40	9	1	–
50–59	31	6	–	–
60+	22	4	–	–

40–49), the levels of male and female Russian language literacy begin to converge. This suggests an advance in women's education. However, these data are only for literacy in Russian, while much of women's education, as noted above, was in Yiddish.

The levels of elementary ability to read Russian are surprisingly high. It is of course impossible to determine how careful the census takers were in accepting statements about literacy. When the data are broken down in Table 2 to urban and non-urban populations, the results indicate that urban populations were more literate than non-urban populations, which makes sense. Moreover, the gaps were larger between urban and non-urban females than among males. If the surprisingly high level of female literacy was simply the result of sloppy record-keeping by census takers, the sloppiness should have applied equally to town and country. Hence there is good reason to take the census data seriously.

TABLE 2: JEWISH LITERARY IN PERCENTAGES IN TWO AGE COHORTS IN EUROPEAN RUSSIA IN 1897 BY LOCATION AND SEX

	10–19		*20–29*	
	male/female		*male/female*	
urban	49	36	53	33
non urban	33	24	48	22

Unfortunately, the census material does not state in which non-Russian language individuals were literate. The questionnaire of the 1897 census did include a question on literacy in any language which theoretically should have included Yiddish. However, apparently Yiddish was not given the status of a language and the census statistics are clearly unreliable on this score. To learn about literacy in Yiddish we need to turn to other sources.

One of the most useful sources on women's literacy is a survey of the literacy of sample groups of Jewish immigrants carried out in 1913 in the USA.[18] It was conducted by a Jewish organization which was interested in dispelling the image of Jews as illiterates, but with a commitment to objectivity as well. In one sample, consisting of a group of 110 women that arrived in New York, 28 women were recorded as illiterate (25 per cent) but of these, eight of them were able to read the prayerbook leaving only 18 per cent totally illiterate. In a similiar study conducted at the same time in Houston, much higher levels of illiteracy for female immigrants (40 per cent) were recorded but this second study apparently did not take into account an ability to read a prayerbook. These data cannot be taken as irrefutable evidence for the educational level of the East European Jewish woman. Migrants to America were not only younger on the whole than the general Jewish population in Eastern Europe but they were also made up of the lower status elements of Jewish society, were less educated and less traditional.[19] Hence it would be quite likely that the higher class contemporaries who stayed behind in the Tsarist empire had even higher levels of literacy.[20]

Within Eastern Europe, the differences were almost certainly not just a question of socio-economic class. There appear to have been significant differences between levels of female literacy in cities and in towns. A study of Jewish workers in Wilno, Warsaw, and Berdichev in 1913 found that in Wilno less than 1 per cent of female workers surveyed were illiterate and less than 7 per cent in Berdichev and Warsaw.[21] At the same time, Lestchinsky found that in the town Horodisht (in the region of Kiev) many of the Jewish factory girls were absolutely illiterate and that almost half of the female population was illiterate, though it is not clear how typical a small town this was.[22]

Given the low figures on school attendance by girls, it appears that most of the literate women learned how to read on their own or with the help of friends or relatives. However, women who learned how to read in this fashion were not necessarily drilled in writing and received, of course, a less systematic course of study than the women who studied in school. Women who learned informally how to read were therefore not likely to write autobiographies, so testimony about this kind of education is difficult to cite. However, the gap between the number of women who read and those who could have gone to school cannot be explained otherwise.[23]

QUALITATIVE EVIDENCE FOR WOMEN'S EDUCATION

One can often question the accuracy of statistical data and wonder if there were overstatements or understatements of literacy in Yiddish or how representative a sample of the total population was taken. However, one can bring additional strong evidence for significant literacy among women. A long tradition exists regarding the printing of romances and popular literature directed to women.[24] To be sure, this literature was read by many men, who also found it appealing. What is significant is that addressing these books to women, irrespective of who really read them, presumes a reality in which many women could read and were in effect educated – even if they were not recognized as such. As we shall see below, the religious literature for women also played an important role in their lives and reading it was seen as significant behaviour. The Gaon of Wilno called on his female descendants to read this literature,[25] apparently instead of frivolous literature, and he took for granted their ability to read.

One could argue that his daughters may have been exceptional, but the publicity given to the Gaon's views indicate that they were regarded as role models for the general Jewish population.

The discrepancy between statistics on schooling and on literacy makes it necessary to carefully consider what the term 'women's education' means. Education usually relates to two important activities. One is the teaching of practical skills which can aid a person in earning a living or be useful in day-to-day life. The other function involves the study of the cultural tradition of a society.[26] All societies have to meet cultural and practical needs whether formally or informally. The specific determination of what is taught and how, is of course the product of traditions, needs and resources.

Among Eastern European Jewry, as in many societies, formal schooling (such as the *heder*, *bet midrash* and the *yeshiva*), the most visible aspect of education, concentrated on males and was devoted solely to the cultural tradition of the community. Occupational training for both males and females was carried out within the framework of informal education. Crafts were learned by apprentices on the job under the supervision of skilled individuals. Preparation for commerce or business was also learned on the job – though private teachers for specific skills like arithmetic were often used. As long as Jews did not enter occupations which required academic credentials or highly technical expertise, there was no need to include career preparation in the curriculum. The setting up of commercial and trade schools for Jews starting from the latter part of the nineteenth century with programs like that of ORT were important innovations in the Jewish educational systems and they drew on foreign, non-Jewish models and not on precedents within the local educational tradition.[27] The study of Torah was different because it was not practical, and obviously, it did not yield direct economic benefits.

Even *heder* did not emphasize applied knowledge. In a society which saw personal salvation, and possibly also group redemption, as the product of correct ritual behaviour, one might have anticipated that the goal of study would be to ensure that males were familiar with all the fine points of the law. This was not the case. *Halakha* (Jewish Law) was not on the curriculum of either the *heder* or the *yeshiva*. As with other practical skills, Jewish law was generally learned by example, a system possible in a context where most Jews observed law.[28] Since women were not regarded as obligated to study Torah, it was easier to justify formal study of secular topics on their part. Rabbi Elijah Rogoler, the rabbi of Kalisz, boasted in a letter written in 1840 that his younger sister (a candidate for a match) is not only beautiful but knows grammar and how to write Hebrew, Polish and German perfectly, and also has a knowledge of Russian. Her sister (also a candidate for a match) is described as beautiful as well, but no details are provided on her linguistic skills. Apparently such a knowledge of languages was desirable but not standard – even in circles where provisions were made for their study.[29]

In reality, while males and females were provided with very different frameworks for acquiring literacy education, women were not necessarily inferior to men in Jewish knowledge. Women not only knew how to read but read often. The image of the uneducated woman of the masses coexists with that of the Jewish woman who sat down at home in her chair every Saturday afternoon and read the weekly Torah portion – in Yiddish. It is quite possible, that of all the books sold in Eastern Europe, the two best-sellers were books specifically intended for a female audience and read only by women – *Tse'ena Urena* and *tekhines*. The *Tse'ena Urena* is a Yiddish text consisting of a free retelling of aggadic material. While originally written (around 1600) for both men and women it quickly became the classic women's text. Khone Shmeruk counted 110 editions printed between 1786 and 1900, and he affirms that there were no doubt many more.[30] While the regular reading of *Tse'ena Urena* was seen as an act of piety, the ability to read it was clearly not seen as exceptional. The repeated reading of *Tse'ena Urena* gave a woman a good picture of the biblical narrative as seen through the eyes of rabbis. In terms of knowledge of the biblical narrative women who read *Tse'ena Urena* regularly should have known at least as much of the biblical narrative as a male who had finished the *heder* curriculum.

One could cite the custom of having *zogerkes* or prayer prompters for women in the synagogue, who told women what to say and when to cry, as evidence for female illiteracy and ignorance. This would not be accurate. An ability to peruse a Yiddish text is not the same as being able to catch the Hebrew of the prayer service, and reading in the quiet of the home is not the same as finding one's place through the din of the women's section of the synagogue.

There were of course significant differences between the ways men studied classical Hebrew texts and women studied *Tse'ena Urena*. Male study usually took place in the *Bet Midrash* (communal study hall), in the company of peers, and therefore this study was a public demonstration of religious devotion and piety. *Tse'ena Urena* was read in the home and it was family members who served as an 'audience' for the woman's study activity. Males often had additional reasons for studying in public. The many males who were not capable of independent study participated in study societies (*hevrot*) and heard regular classes and lectures on classical texts. Even more advanced individuals who could study on their own anticipated an occasional need for assistance or to consult in order to understand the difficult texts studied, and therefore preferred to study in *Bet Midrash*. Since *Tse'ena Urena* was a Yiddish text it did not present linguistic problems. Moreover, since it lacked the status and classical character of a rabbinic book, it could be and was continually updated from a linguistic point of view, as Shmeruk's work points out. This meant that the *Tse'ena Urena* was easy to understand and it could be studied in private without the necessity of anticipating a need for assistance in understanding a difficult passage. Perhaps the most significant difference between the evaluation of male study of classical Hebrew texts and female study of *Tse'ena Urena* was that only the former was regarded as true study of the Torah while the latter was merely an act of piety.

The world of prayer also exhibited differences between patterns of male and female behavior. An examination of the role of *tekhinot*[31] makes this clear. *Tekhinot* were prayers written in Yiddish and organized around the weekly routine and life cycle of the East European Jewish woman. The *tekhine* literature reflects similar religious values and activities to those of men but radically different frameworks. The *tekhinot* were read by women individually and usually not in a synagogue. They were not chanted nor said in public. They were said therefore only by literate women. Women were free to choose which *tekhin* book to use, which *tekhinot* to say and when. Many of them were presented as having been written by women for women and were adapted to new realities and needs. The covers of *tekhin* books advertised the contents as including 'nice new *tekhines*' – even when that was not the case. A value was placed on the relevance and novelty of the *tekhinot*. All of this was very different from male prayer. Men prayed out of the fixed Hebrew text of the prayerbook. The sanctity of male prayers was closely tied to their ancient origins and novelty was disguised. Men prayed according to a ritual calendar and not according to the needs they felt. The writers of male prayers were figures out of the distant past, and not individuals with whom one could easily identify. What was common to both men and women was that prayer was said from a written text and that literacy was taken for granted.

GENDER DEFINITION IN TRADITIONAL JEWISH SOCIETY[32]

The use of *Tse'ena Urena* and the *tekhine* literature by women instead of the *Humash* (Pentateuch) and *Siddur* (Hebrew prayer book) were just two elements of a much wider range of distinctive gender-defined expressions for similar functions. Jewish men and women could be seen as occupying adjacent but different cultural worlds in Eastern Europe, in which the expression of a function in one gender was the mirror image of its expression in the other gender. Men and women shared a common spoken language and a common religious/national identity. However much else was radically different. Socially, men and women had no direct relationships unless they had common family ties. In the synagogue or *bet midrash*, the holiest place in the community, the seating of men and women was separated. Men came daily to the synagogue for prayer and study, often more than once a day, while women came less often and just for prayer. Men belonged to formal associations (*hevrot*), whereas for women, social life was informal. To a large extent men and women also did not share a literary language. Men were supposed to read Hebrew and if they could, wrote Hebrew, while if women were literate, it was generally in Yiddish. While Yiddish is of course written in Hebrew letters, up until the mid-nineteenth century there was generally no mistaking of a book written in Hebrew – e.g. directed solely to men, and a book written in Yiddish and ostensibly directed to women, because different fonts or types of letters were generally used for Hebrew and Yiddish.[33] When men gave charity it was usually in the synagogue while women gave charity into the 'pushke' or home charity box.[34] Even the concepts of beauty were different. The ideal man was the retiring, pale, delicate Talmudist with sensitive hands and long white fingers, while the ideal woman was an active, even aggressive, full-bodied woman with multiple chins.[35]

To be sure, there were many exceptions to this gender division and they did not extend to every sphere of life. Both men and women generally worked and contributed to the family income, so that there was no clear distinction between the males as breadwinners and the women as home-makers, as was common in many other societies. The economic conditions did not allow for that. Of course, the women's responsibilities for the home were clear – hers was the responsibility of running the house – even if she was the main breadwinner.[36] Generally, the occupational distribution of men and women was such that there was little direct competition between them. Even in the late nineteenth century when factory work became more common, men and women still did not work side by side in factories. To be sure, many men read Yiddish material, while there were also women who could read literature published in Hebrew. However, men were expected to read Hebrew while Yiddish works were generally, if not for the women, specifically directed to the unlearned. Similarly, the number of women who could understand a Hebrew text was probably statistically insignificant.

THE EDUCATIONAL REALITIES OF JEWISH WOMEN

In light of the fact that gender differences often concealed similar functions, it is worth re-examining basic educational institutions among Jews with the intention of distinguishing between the image and the reality. From this perspective, it is clear that the differences between the educational achievements of boys and girls on the level of elementary education, were more perceived than real – just as the differences in knowledge and prayer experience between men and women were more apparent and linguistic than real. Boys spent all day in the *heder*. However, much of their day was spent in play and story-telling, while the *melamed*[37] sat down for short periods of time with individuals or groups of two and three.[38] Thus the result of a boy's full day of non-intensive study in a *heder* was not necessarily much more than those of tutored girls who may have studied an hour or two a day. Women's education was certainly less stressful, which may explain in part why female education was not usually accompanied by the violence which so often characterized heder education. It was considered right for boys to be beaten but not for girls – though there were exceptions. Esther Rosenthal-Schneiderman (b. circa 1900) recalled never being beaten by her teacher, the *rebitzin* – but got plenty of slaps and pinches from the teacher's husband, the rabbi![39]

The low pressure and often informal elementary education of women was made possible by limitation to Yiddish. Among the many virtues of the Yiddish language is that, in written Yiddish, each letter has one sound and vowels are represented by letters – with the exception of words of Hebrew origin which are limited in number. In Hebrew, letters also have one phonic meaning, but vowels are represented by dots (often smudgy) in vocalized Hebrew texts and by nothing at all in unvocalized texts – and most printed Hebrew texts were unvocalized. Since Yiddish was the spoken language, the beginning reader could anticipate words and sounds from the context, which further facilitated learning to read Yiddish. As a result, while it sometimes took well over a year of *heder* study for a little boy to learn how to read Hebrew freely, a young woman should have been able to learn to read Yiddish in a short time – perhaps only a few weeks. Moreover, as soon as she could read she could understand what she read – which was an achievement not every *heder* student reached even after years of study. In short, women had an easier time than men in reaching functional literacy. Moreover, most men did not get much further than functional literacy in Hebrew despite all their years of study. While advanced Talmudic study was the goal of male study, it must be remembered that only a minority of students went on to such study.

Women could also go on 'past' *Tse'ena Urena* to acquire additional Jewish knowledge. A wide number of aggadic texts (texts of the non legal rabbinic literature) were also available in Yiddish and even much of the Zohar (the classic kabbalistic text) was, theoretically at least, available in Yiddish. In the early nineteenth century no general works in Yiddish on Jewish law were available and certainly no adaptations of classical rabbinic texts (such as the Talmud) into Yiddish for women.[40]

There were a few books of Jewish law in Yiddish that were specifically directed to a female audience. These were limited to topics which were relevant specifically to women, such as the laws dealing with kosher food and the laws relating to the times when intercourse after menstruation was permitted. The publication of such literature had been a topic of controversy when these books were first printed, and at least one important rabbi in Eastern Europe regarded this literature with misgivings and praised women for not relying on it.[41] This was apparently too close to the men's 'territory'. At the same time, since the study of Jewish law – in any form – was not part of the standard *heder* curriculum, there was no significant difference, in fact, in the way most men and women learned Jewish law. What should be noted is that, given the amount and variety of sources available in Yiddish, a reader limited to Yiddish could still become quite familiar with most areas of Jewish knowledge.[42]

Women's life contained functional equivalents to male activities which required reading, but these activities lacked the same status. For women these activities were voluntary, whereas for men they were obligatory. However, while women recognized the value of male activities such as prayer and study, men did not place similar value on the parallel activities among women or demand that women devote their time to these activities. The image of female ignorance made it possible to regard women as inferior to men, even though the image had little truth to it. The function of limited access to knowledge as a means of social repression was not unique to women in Jewish society. Among men as well, knowledge of Talmud, which was restricted to a socio-economic élite, served as a means of proving to the ignorant masses that they deserved their inferior position in society.[43]

ACCEPTANCE AND REJECTION OF WOMEN'S ROLES IN EDUCATION

In most cases, this system of limited formal education for most women was appropriate for the realities of traditional Jewish society in the early nineteenth century. Most women worked, either independently or helping their fathers or husbands, because their families could hardly make a living otherwise. Moreover they were also burdened by family responsibilities. With a high birthrate and without technologies to save time in housework, even most non-working housewives had few leisure moments or time to study difficult Hebrew texts. An education that trained them to devote hours every day to the study of the Talmud would have been an education designed to maximize frustration. Lack of 'school education' was part of a system that functioned to condition women to accept their role in the family and society with a minimum of conflict – just as the fact that most men were unlearned (and knew it!) was one of the ways that led them to accept communal authority. While most women apparently accepted this role and found fulfilment in the parallel culture that was theirs – and was meaningful to them,[44] that does not mean that all did. The daughter of the famous Yiddish writer Shomer wrote of her mother:[45]

> My mother in all the days of her long life bitterly resented the meagerness of her youthful education and cordially despised the three special duties [incumbent on women – candle lighting, ritual bathing and baking bread in accordance with Jewish law – S.S.] even if she did, in a manner of speaking, observe them . . . According to my mother, her father spent thousands of rubles on every cause and every charity in the town but denied her a ruble with which to pay for instruction in the Russian or Hebrew she had desired so much.

In her case, economic pressure could not justify the lack of investment in her education and this may have contributed to her frustration.

That this dissatisfaction could exist in the circles of the rabbinic élite as well, we learn from a description, written by the well known Rabbi Boruch Epstein about his aunt, the wife of the Rosh Yeshiva of Volozhin, Rabbi Naftali Zvi Yehuda Berlin[46]: The events described took place around 1875.

> . . . she was worried and vexed about the defiled honour of the women and their lowly status due to the fact that the Rabbis forbid teaching them Torah. One time she told me that if Eve (meaning the female sex) was cursed with ten curses, the prohibition of learning Torah, is equivalent to all the curses and is even more than all of them. There was no end to the grief. One time, while she was speaking excitably on this subject, I said to her, 'But my aunt, you women are blaming the men for this prohibition when they are not at fault. You yourselves caused this and you are guilty in the matter', and I explained my words. Our sages said (at the end of the second chapter of *Avot de Rabbi Natan*) that Torah should only be taught to a humble person. About women, our Sages decided in *Yerushalmi Shabbat*, Chapter 6, that 'they [women] are ostentatious' meaning conceited beings. If so, isn't it forbidden to teach them Torah because of their character traits, and who is to blame if not they themselves, and why do they complain? . . . She said to me: 'When I have free time I will do research on the word and find out the exact meaning. In the meantime bring me *Avot de Rabbi Natan* and I will look for the words which you mentioned from them.' I went and brought . . . and fell right into the trap! In *Avot de Rabbi Natan* the wording is as follows: Bet Shammai says: 'A person shall only teach to one who is clever, humble and rich' and Bet Hillel says: 'We teach to everyone because there were many sinners in Israel and they started learning the Torah and became righteous, observant men'.

> As she finished reading these words, she raised her voice in anger and said, 'How did you do this evil thing, or was it because you wanted to trick me that you took the opinion of Bet Shammai as the basis for your word? Every boy who has studied even a little Talmud knows that when there is a disagreement between Bet Shammai and Bet Hillel, the law is in accordance with Bet Hillel, and Bet Hillel permits teaching Torah to everyone!!' . . . As she was in good spirits at her victory over me, she was no longer angry with me, and when she saw that I had taken it somewhat to heart, she comforted me . . . and began to talk about this topic in a general manner . . . I remember that when she mentioned the name of Bruria, the wife of Rabbi Meir, I told her that a wrongdoing was found against her – that she mocked the words of our Sages, for 'women are light-headed.' In the end she herself was guilty of light-headedness, as is brought out in the story of Rashi on *Avoda Zara* 18b. She answered me, 'In truth, I know of this legend, but did our Sages find all men guilty because of the sin of Aher, who left the right way (*Hagiga* 15a)? Furthermore, Bruria did not mock with contempt and derision. She only thought that our Sages did not fully understand the rationale of women. According to her view, women are also strong-minded. This was the entire incident and nothing more.

There is no reason to take cases as evidence for widespread dissatisfaction among women. Indeed, there were probably as many boys who envied their sisters who were free of the *heder* as vice versa. However, they do indicate the tensions inherent in the educational system for women and the potential for change even in the most conservative circles.

CHANGING PATTERNS OF EDUCATION OF THE JEWISH WOMAN

Changes in women's education can be traced back to early in the nineteenth century. While almost no attention has been given to the fact, in two important centres of modernization in Eastern Europe – Warsaw and in Wilno – secular schools for girls were founded before secular schools for boys. In 1818, a 'modern' girls' school which taught secular topics was organized in Warsaw and almost immediately there was an initiative to open up a second school for girls. The first secular school for boys in Poland was set up only the following year by Jacob Tugenhold.[47] The first school for girls in the Pale of Settlement was founded in Wilno in 1826. It was succesful and continued to function through the 1840s. The famous Talmud Torah in Odessa was founded seven years later and the first school for boys in Wilno which included secular studies was founded only in 1841.[48] These developments were of course exceptions. However, by the

1860s, the traditional patterns of women's education began to erode and increasing numbers of women were studying in the modern schools, public and private, that were appearing, especially in the large cities.[49] However, the high cost of such an education makes it clear that the female students could have come only from families that were well off – which was not typical for the Jewish community.[50] This shift was related to many factors of which the most important were probably the influence of 'modern' values and models as well as a rise in the average age at marriage among the upper class of the Jewish community. While the first is generally well known, the second deserves some attention.[51]

Early in the nineteenth century, and long before as well, high status was demonstrated in Eastern European Jewry by marrying off the children at an early age.[52] Before reaching her teens, a girl from an élite home would become a '*baalebosta*'[53] with all of the duties that it entailed. For her parents, this meant undertaking to support an adolescent son-in-law (who often had a very healthy appetite) as well as potential grandchildren, for a number of years. For a variety of reasons, this pattern shifted in the course of the nineteenth century, as is shown by the following table:[54]

TABLE 3: AGE AT MARRIAGE IN PERCENTAGES OF ALL JEWISH WOMEN MARRYING IN THE TSARIST EMPIRE

Age	*1867*	*1885*	*1902*
20 and below	60.8	47.0	23.9
21–25	21.2	37.1	52.5
26–30	8.1	8.0	13.0

This rise in the age of marriage created, by the late nineteenth century, a population of teen-age girls from well-off families who had to pass time until marriage. It was necessary to find legitimate ways for young women to spend this time until they got married. Study was an ideal solution because it was consonant with contemporary non-Jewish elite views that women's education was desirable. One option was tutoring for women. However, this was expensive and, moreover, was becoming outmoded. Schools were the answer – whether government-sponsored or under Jewish auspices. The number of women in these schools was constantly on the rise from the mid-nineteenth century on.[55]

To justify devoting a few years to its study entailed having a sufficiently respectable syllabus. What was to be studied? The traditional rabbinic literacy corpus in Hebrew was regarded of course as suitable only for males. Yiddish texts, intended for independent study, were too 'easy' to justify a formal education. There were a number of options. One possibility was to provide a commercial education. This fitted the ideal of the working woman who supported her scholarly husband, an ideal that co-existed with that of the rich merchant, and a reality where many women worked. However, many young women and their parents preferred a cultural education. Such an education was of course testimony to the wealth of the household. Among the standard elements adopted were the study of French and the playing of piano – both suitably esoteric and non-utilitarian – and valued by the surrounding society as well. At a time when secular studies were traditionally seen in Jewish circles as irrelevant but not evil or harmful, such an education, which was typical for the non-Jewish élite, could easily be seen as not only permissible but even desirable for Jewish women.

However, what men thought general education was about, was not always what women found. Even without social contacts with non-Jewish society, a woman who received a general education was introduced to a world, even if only a literary one, which promised not only status but a very different set of values. Women often accepted these values and made radical changes in their life-style which led to estrangement from traditional forms of Judaism. Thus by the mid-nineteenth century there was no lack of families in which boys studied Talmud and their sisters French literature. This looked incongruous in later generations which viewed secular studies as evil or leading to evil. It can not be overemphasized that only a small minority of Jewish girls grew up in such homes. None the less, this secular situation attracted attention and began to be seen as typical – even though most Jewish homes were far too poor to provide either sons or daughters with higher education.

While only a minority of women went to modern schools, the number who did was not insignificant by the end of the nineteenth century. In 1899, a survey of such schools in the Tsarist empire found 193 girls' schools and 68 schools for both boys and girls (usually in separate classes) as opposed to 383 boys' schools.[56] This yields very different ratios between males and females than the *hederim*. Of the 50,773 students enrolled in such schools, about a third were girls. When population is taken into account, one finds that the most favourable ratio of female students to the total Jewish population was in the south (one female pupil for every 109 Jews) followed by the northwest (one per 208) with the least favourable the southwest (one per 458). The vast majority of the girls' schools were private (172), while of the boys' schools only 187 were private, and the rest were government or communal schools. In Eastern Europe the cost of tuition of girls in private schools was 50 per cent higher than that of boys. The large number of private girls' schools clearly indicates widespread interest in girls' education and willingness to pay for it along with an unwillingness or lack of interest on the part of the communities or government to invest in women's education. The girls' schools, it should be noted, were not just finishing schools with lots of glitter and little content. The academic level of the teachers in the girls schools was significantly higher than the average in the boys' schools and many of the teachers were women – positive role models.

These figures do not come near to fully reflecting the hunger for knowledge among the Jewish women of the Tsarist Empire – or of their parents. A study in 1894 showed that for almost every girl who applied for admission to a private school and was accepted – another was turned down for lack of space. It was equally difficult for a girl to gain admission to a coeducational school. The highest level of refusals was for admission to communal schools which enrolled mainly males. These schools had the advantage of being inexpensive and also under Jewish administration. In addition, Jewish girls tended to remain in private schools much longer than Jewish boys did.[57]

The pressure for admission to girls' schools in the Tsarist empire probably explains the differences between the enrolment of Jewish boys and girls in government schools. Reports from 1898 dealing with public elementary schools in the Wilno and Kiev districts indicate that in Wilno more Jewish girls went to public non-Jewish schools than did Jewish boys. About 14 per cent of the female students in the Wilno schools were Jewish while the Jewish boys made up 2.7 per cent. In Kiev the male Jewish pupils outnumbered the females by five to one, but both males and females made up about 4 per cent of the pupils of their respective sexes.[58] One must be careful about drawing conclusions from these data because attendance at these schools was hindered both by administrative hurdles designed to keep out Jews, especially boys, and by a policy which demanded that Jewish children attend classes on the sabbath and on holidays and violate the Jewish sabbath laws by writing.

The situation in Galicia, in the Austro-Hungarian empire, which had a far more effective program of public schools for Jews than existed in the Tsarist empire, was quite different and illustrates the potential for change in an East European Jewish population.

Unfortunately, we do not have detailed age breakdowns of the base population which would enable us to assess the exact percentage of school-age children actually attending school. However, there are rough figures on the age breakdown of Galician Jewry in 1890.[60] There were about 230,000 children under the age of 10 in Galicia in 1890 and 180,000 in the 10 to 20 year olds. Thus school age yearly cohorts were probably roughly 20,000. Assuming elementary schools had 6–8 grades, in 1890 the number of school-age children was about 150,000 and roughly 25 per cent of school-age boys and 40 per cent of school-age girls were in these schools. A decade later (assuming no dramatic changes in the size of the cohorts) roughly 45 per cent of the boys were in these schools and 60 per cent of the

TABLE 4: ATTENDANCE OF JEWS IN MODERN ELEMENTARY SCHOOLS IN GALICIA[86]

Year	Government Schools		Private Schools		Total	
	Boys	*Girls*	*Boys*	*Girls*	*Boys*	*Girls*
1880	10599	18271	1910	2620	12509	20891
1890	15497	29573	2555	2666	18052	32239
1900	22666	43855	10298	1647	32964	45502

girls. It is clear that the number of girls who received a modern education was increasing rapidly at the end of the nineteenth century. The masses of the Jewish population still retained traditional distinctions between what was proper for boys to study and for girls – though this was changing. However, in secondary and higher education, which was directly geared to careers and was common only among the socio-economic élite, the sexual balance was sharply reversed and boys far outnumbered girls.[61]

THE BACKGROUND OF THE STEREOTYPE OF WOMEN'S EDUCATION

The fact that women did not study in formal institutions contributed to the stereotype of East European women as having very limited education. Studies of educational history or descriptions of educational realities tend to centre on the development and growth of schools – whatever their function. Schools are highly visible institutions and make easy topics for research and description. However, limiting the history of education to schools is justifiable only to the degree that education is concentrated in formal frameworks. For example, in studying American student societies in the eighteenth and nineteenth centuries, James McLachlan found this to be the case in the formal classroom and justifiably claimed that 'the study of the formal curriculum of the early 19th century American College cannot be carried on in isolation from an equally intense study of the students' extra curriculum. To do so produces a completely misleading – in fact, downright false – impression of the history of American higher education.'[62] The same is true for Jewish women's education in Eastern Europe.

The traditional image of the extremely low level of women's education in traditional Jewish society can be accepted only if one adopts a very narrow definition of education which limits it to schooling and assumes that a religious text written in Hebrew is significant, whereas one written in

Yiddish is not. This distinction is artificial and misleading. To be sure, precisely such an identification of education with schooling was actually held by both men and women in the past. Their attention, like that of later observers, was caught by the fact that, in sharp contrast to the situation among males, few educational institutions were available for Jewish women and those which existed were elementary, poorly documented, and not well developed. However, since only males were really expected to go to school, concentrating on schools means in effect squeezing women into male categories, rather than seeing the full educational life of women. Far more significant is the fact that large numbers of women could read and did so – despite the fact that they hardly went to school. They acquired knowledge through reading and in this respect they were more self-sufficient than men who learned by listening to lectures and sermons! This behaviour was regarded as standard and desirable and not as deviant. It was also not categorized as Torah study, since women studied in Yiddish and mastered different texts from those which men did. However, these are not grounds for characterising these women as uneducated – despite the fact that at the time that is how they were viewed by others and also how they saw themselves. To accept this assessment is to assume male-oriented values as having absolute value and to miss the far more complex manner in which women's achievements were devalued. In short, to understand the past it is not sufficient to rediscover what was known in the past. It is also necessary to point out that which people in the past were not always aware of.

CONSEQUENCES

By the beginning of the twentieth century, women's education among East European Jewry was in a state of ferment. Significant numbers of women were exploring new educational frameworks. Traditional patterns, such as the regular reading of *Tse'ena Urena* and other religious texts, had exposed women to reading and accustomed them to turn to the printed text as a normal way to knowledge. At the same time, the traditional attitudes which had denied women access to classical Jewish literature, had allowed women to read Yiddish *belles lettres*. However, for males, reading for pleasure was a problem because, in theory at least, men were supposed to spend as much time as possible on Torah study.[63] Men had to justify not spending time in study either on practical grounds, such as the need to earn a living or on theological grounds such as involvement in other pious deeds. Reading literature does not fall into either category. However, women, who were not expected to study Torah, did not have to justify how they spent their time and hence their freedom to read for pleasure. Thus, inadvertently, the traditional Jewish patterns themselves facilitated change and developement in the lives of women. Women, even in traditional circles, were easily exposed to new bodies of literature. The *Haskala* literature and the Hebrew newspaper which served in the second half of the nineteenth century as agents of change in the intellectual world of men had their contemporary parallels in the developing Yiddish press and literature which was more directed to women – and the uneducated men.[64] Tsederbaum's influential newspaper *HaMelitz*, directed to a Hebrew-reading male public, was outsold in the 1860s by the emerging Yiddish press with its start in works directed to female readers. There is no question that there was a larger body of female readers. As Roskies points out in an article on this topic, the Yiddish popular writer Isaac Meir Dik could boast in 1860 that, after only five years of writing, 100,000 copies of his works had been sold.[65] The whole development of Yiddish literature was possible only because even in traditional Jewish society, a high proportion of the female Jewish population was literate, knowledgeable and accustomed to the written word.[66] The female immigrants to the United States and their daughters displayed an exceptional thirst for education and their educational achievements were far above those of other immigrants.[67] No single factor can explain the success of first and second generation American Jewish women in the American educational system. However, the fact that in East European Jewish society, the ideal mother read regularly and studied from books certainly did not have a negative effect. Here, as in many other cases, a careful consideration of the realities of Jewish life allows for a significant correction of stereotypical views.

ACKNOWLEDGEMENTS

* My thanks to Israel Bartal, Menahem Blondheim, Lisa Epstein, Michael Silber, Deborah Weissman, Zvi Wolf and Sarah Zfatman, for their constructive comments and criticisms. As usual, I am responsible for the results.

NOTES

1 One notable exception is a very perceptible unpublished paper by Jeffrey Shandler, currently at the YIVO Institute, titled 'Towards an Assessment of the Education of Women in Ashkenaz'(1985). The author very generously shared his paper with me, and, independently, we reached similar conclusion. The scope of his paper is much broader and it is very suggestive on a number of topics which are not dealt with here. For a useful and enlightening survey of realities and developments in women's education in Central European Jewry in the enlightenment period see Mordechai

Eliav *Jewish Education in Germany in the Period of Enlightenment and Emancipation* (Jerusalem, 1960) Ch. 11 'Education of Daughters' pp. 271–9.

2 *Hadeher Bekhayei Amenu*, 2nd ed. (Tel Aviv, 1951) p. 127.

3 D. Flinker, 'Warsaw' (in *Arim ve-Imahot Be-Yisrael* pt.III ed. J.Fishman) (Jerusalem, 1948) (in Hebrew) p. 163.

4 *Talmud Babli Sota* 20a.

5 A Hebrew term for a private one-room/one-teacher school.

6 The term literally means rabbi's wife – though it may have been used for learned women in general.

7 On *Tse'ena Urena* see below.

8 Yekhiel Shtern, *Kheyder un Beys-medresh* (NY, 1950).

9 Shlomo Zaltsman, *Ayarati* (Tel Aviv, 1947), p. 45.

10 P. Sharagrodska, 'Der Shura Gruss' *Filologishe Shriften fun Yivo* I (1926) pp. 67–72.

11 Mordkhe Spektor, *Mayn lebn* (Warsaw, 19..), p. 159.

12 This may be a bit surprising to readers today, given the contemporary concern (or obsession) in certain very orthodox-Jewish circles about co-educational education even in elementary grades, but it should be emphasized that a century ago, sending a girl to a boys' *heder* was not considered as having symbolic significance or reflecting an ideological commitment. *Hederim* were not competing with a co-ed system.

13 *Betsel Koroteynu* (Tel Aviv, 1948), p. 19.

14 *Recueil de materiaux sur la situation Économique des Israelites de Russie* (Paris, Felix Alcan, 1906). This is the source for all the following data up until references to the 1897 census.

15 Ibid. p. 279.

16 Ibid. P.294–5. It would be premature to attribute this to modern attitudes in the south-west or differing approaches to women's education. This variation was very possibly due to the fact that many of these *hederim* were in small towns where patterns were more fluid and where there were no alternatives for little girls, and not necessarily to a regional interest in reform. Most modernisers sent their children to a very different kind of school – coed or otherwise – and not to a *heder*. The attempt at the end of the nineteenth century to set up a new modern type of *heder* which emphasized Hebrew and was known as the *heder metukan* was a small-scale phenomenon which would not have affected these figures. On this new type of *heder* see Yossi Goldstein 'The Heder Metukan in Russia as a Basis for the Zionist Movement' *Iyunim Bechinuch* 45 (June 1986) pp. 147–57 (in Hebrew).

17 *Obshchi Svod Po Imperii Rezultatov Razrabotki Dannix Pervoi Bceobshchi Perepisi Naselenia* I (St. Peterburg, 1905) Table XVI In this census, literacy was defined very broadly, as compared with later censuses, as has been pointed out. 'In 1897 . . . people who stated that they could read were considered literate; in 1926 people were considered literate if they were able to write their last name; by 1959, the questionnaire asked whether respondents could read and write . . . 'Ralph Clem *Research Guide to the Russian and Soviet Censuses* (Ithaca, 1986) p. 167.

18 *Jewish Immigrant/Report of a Special Committee of the National Jewish Immigration Council Appointed to Examine into the Question of Illiteracy Among Jewish Immigrants and its Causes* Senate Document 611 63rd Congress 2nd Session (Washington DC Government Printing Office, 1914).

19 See S. Kuznets, 'Immigration of Russian Jews to the United States: Background and Structure', *Perspectives in American History* 9 (1975), pp. 35–126 and Z. Halevy, 'Were the Jewish Immigrants to the United States Representative of Russian Jews', *Migration* 16:2 (1978), pp. 66–73.

20 These data are of course very revealing about the make-up of the immigrant community. If the sample was typical for the immigrants, and there is no reason to suspect that it was not, it shows that most women who came knew how to read even though most of them came from the 'lower classes' of East European Jewish society and the less traditional element.

21 S. Rabinowitsh – Margolin, 'Zur Bildungsstatistik der Jüdischen Arbeiter in Russland', *Zeitschrift fuer Demographie und Statistik der Juden* IX:11 Nov. 1913 pp. 153–61.

22 J. Lestchinsky, 'Statistics of a Town', *The Jewish Dispersion* (in Hebrew) (Jerusalem, 1961), pp. 17–38, especially 34–5.

23 Being able to read does not mean that women knew how to write. A survey of signatures on marriage contracts in Warsaw in 1845 and 1860 indicates that only a third of the Jewish men and a similar percentage of Jewish women could sign their names. S. Kowalska-Glikman, 'Ludność Żydowska Warszawy ... w Świetle Akt Stanu Cywilnego', *BZIH* 1981:2 (118), pp. 37–49.

24 For information in English on this topic see David Roskies, 'Yiddish Popular Literature and the Female Reader', *Journal of Popular Culture* (1979), pp. 852–8 and 'The Medium and Message of the Maskilic Chapbook', *Jewish Social Studies*, XLI: 3–4 (1979), pp. 275–90, and see the forthcoming study of Chava Weissler, 'For Women and For Men Who Are Like Women', in *Journal of Feminist Studies in Religion*.

25 See the letter he wrote to his family on his way to Eretz Israel. It was first printed in *Alim Litrufa* (Minsk) and often reprinted. This was by no means unique. The Hatam Sofer in Pressburg, Hungary (= Bratislava) also called on his daughters to read religious works written in Yiddish – but no more. See his will, which has been translated into English in J. Reimer, and N. Stampfer, *Ethical Wills/A Modern Jewish Treasury*, (New York, 1983), pp. 18–21.

26 This does not mean that there are not other functions to education as well. For example, schools are often expected to encourage the development of proper character or personality among their students. However in practice, these are usually secondary to one or both of the two main functions.

27 On trade education among Jews in Germany see Mordechai Eliav, *Jewish Education in Germany in the Period of Enlightenment and Emancipation* (Jerusalem, 1960), Ch. 12. On ORT in Russia see Leon Shapiro, *The History of ORT*, (New York, Schocken, 1980). On vocational training in general see Bernard Weinryb, *Jewish Vocational Education* (NY, 1948), esp. part 2.

28 The tractates of the Talmud that were most often studied were not related to everyday life and even when relevant ones were studied, the halakhic implications and the legal conclusions were often ignored. When questions of practice came up, recourse was had to written guides on occasion, but in most questions of doubt, the rabbi was asked. To be sure, convenient summaries of Jewish law such as *Khayei Adam* were very popular and many study circles studied them regularly. However, in quantitative terms, the number of circles devoted to popular halakha was far smaller than those devoted to the saying of Psalms or the study of Aggada, Mishna, Talmud or similar texts.

29 See 'A Collection of Letters of R. Elijah Rogolier' ed. Efraim Urbach, *Kobez Al Yad*, VI (XVI), Pt. II (Jerusalem, 1966), p. 549. I thank Michael Silber for the reference.

30 Khone Shmeruk 'East European Versions of Tse'ene-Rene 1786–1859', *For Max Weinreich on the Seventieth Birthday* (Hague, 1964), pp. 320–36. On *Tse'ena Urena* see also K. Turniansky, 'Translations and Adaptations of the Tse'ena Urena' in the *Dov Sadan Jubilee Volume* (Tel Aviv, 1977), pp. 165–90. In the opening of her article she

mentions that it was an 'integral part of the 'oneg shabat' (shabat joy) in every Jewish home in Western and Eastern Europen and that it was the most popular Yiddish book'. On the *tekhinot* see the important articles of Chava Weissler: 'The Traditional Piety of Ashkenazic Women' in *Jewish Spirituality from the Sixteenth-Century Revival to the Present* ed. Arthur Green (New York, 1987), pp. 245–75 and 'The Religion of Traditional Ashkenazic Women: Some Methodological Issues', *AJS Review* XII:1, (Spring, 1987), pp. 73–94.

32 This topic has not received a great deal of attention in the literature, and much of what there is has hardly gone past the descriptive. See, for example, M. Zborowski and E. Herzog, *Life is with People* (NY, 1952), Part II Chapter 4. An example of what can be done by means of careful analysis in Chava Weissler's article 'For Women And For Men Who Are Like Women' forthcoming in *Journal of Feminist Studies in Religion*.

33 See M. Weinreich, *Oisgeklibene Shriftn* (Buenos Aires, 1974), p. 66. I am grateful to Prof. Turniansky for the Reference.

34 On the social history of the *pushke* see my article 'The Pushke and its Development', (in Hebrew) *Katedra* 21 (October 1981), pp. 89–102.

35 T. Somogyi, *Die Scheinen und die Prosten* (Berlin, 1982).

36 Michael Silber has found references in literature dealing with Hungarian Jews of men who were supported by their wives and were expected to do household chores. I have not found any such cases in Eastern Europe.

37 teacher.

38 See the vivid description of Yekhiel Shtern, 'A Heder in Tyszowce', *YIVO Annual* V (1950), p. 164. The article was reprinted in *Studies in Modern Jewish Social History* ed. Joshua Fishman (NY, 1972). The citation there is on p. 36.

39 *Naftulei Drakhim* (Tel Aviv, 1970), p. 31.

40 Works such as *Lekah Tov* – a Yiddish crib of the Talmud for *heder* teachers and students, was not part of the woman's library. There was no translation into Yiddish of a comprehensive guide to Jewish law, such as the *Shulkhan Aruch*, in the pre-modern period. The creation of popular guides to Jewish law, even in Hebrew, is itself a modern innovation. *Khayei Adam*, a very popular summary of Jewish law directed to non-learned readers, appeared in 1810, while the first Yiddish translation found in the National Library in Jerusalem dates to 1865. On this book see A. Goldrat 'On the Book "Khayei Adam" and its Author', in *Sefer Margaliot*, (Jerusalem, 1973), pp. 255–78. The first Yiddish translation found in the National Library of the *Kizzur Shulkhan Aruch* (a similar summary published in Hebrew in the 1860's) appeared in 1882. In short, general guides to Jewish law became available in Yiddish in the second half of the nineteenth century. On aspects of Jewish law specifically related to Jewish women there were Yiddish publications. See Agnes Segal, 'Yiddish Works on Women's Commandments in the Sixteenth Century', in *Studies in Yiddish Literature and Folklore* (Jerusalem, 1986), pp. 37–59 and Simcha Asaf, 'A Responsum Against the Writing of Law Books in Yiddish', in his *Mekorot Umekhkarim* (Jerusalem, 1946), pp. 249–51 (in Hebrew).

41 'It was never the custom to teach women from books and I never heard of such a practice. Rather the known (e.g. relevant) laws are taught by each woman to her daughter and daughter in law and recently books of womens' law have been printed in the language of the nations (e.g. Yiddish!) and they can read them and our women are energetic in every case of doubt and ask and do not rely on their (book) knowledge in even the slightest matter.' Yechiel Michel Epstein, *Aruch Hashulchan*, Yore Death, 246:19.

42 See Yosef Yerushalmi, *From Spanish Court to Italian Ghetto* (NY, 1971), for an example of what a marrano could learn from translations into Spanish.

43 See Amos Funkenstein, and Adin Steinsaltz, *Sociology of Ignorance*, (in Hebrew, Tel Aviv 1987), and my 'Heder Study, Knowledge of Torah, and the Maintenance of Social Stratification in Traditional East European Jewish Society' in *Studies in Jewish Education* III (Jerusalem, 1988), pp. 271–89.
44 S. Zaltsman, *Ayarati* (Tel Aviv, 1947), p. 47.
45 Miriam Zunser, *Yesterday* (NY, 1978), p. 66.
46 Borukh Epstein, *Mekor Boruch*, selection trans. by Malka Bina in *Petach* II (Jerusalem, 1975), pp. 98–100.
47 Jacob Shatzky, *Jewish Educational Policies in Poland from 1806 to 1866* (NY, 1943) [Yiddish], p. 210–12. See also Sabina Levin, 'The First Elementary Schools for Children of the Mosaic Faith in Warsaw 1818–1830' in *Galed* I (1973), pp. 63–100, esp. pp. 78–9.
48 See Israel Klausner, *Vilna, Jerusalem of Lithuania/Generations from 1495–1881* (Ghetto Fighter's House, Israel), pp. 207–8 [in Hebrew].
49 This phenomenom will be discussed by Semyon Kreis in a Ph.D thesis now in progress at the Hebrew University.
50 See Kh. Kazdan, *From Kheder and Shkoles to CYSHO* (Mexico City, 1956) [Yiddish], p. 202. He also brings interesting material on calls for reform.
51 See Deborah Weissman, 'Bais Yaakov: A Historical Model for Jewish Feminists' in Elizabeth Koltun ed. *The Jewish Woman: New Perspective* (NY, 1976), pp. 139–48.
52 See Jacob Goldberg, 'Die Ehe bei den Juden Polens im 18. Jahrhundert' *Jahrbücher fuer Geschichte Osteuropas* XXXI (1983), pp. 481–515 and my study 'The Social Significance of Premature Marriages in Eastern Europe in the Nineteenth Century' (in Hebrew) *Studies on Polish Jewry/Paul Glikson Memorial Volume* (Jerusalem, 1987), pp. 65–77.
53 Homemaker.
54 Based on S. Rabinowitsh-Margolin 'Die Heiraten der Juden im europäischen Russland vom Jahr 1867 bis 1902' *Zeitschrift für Demographie und Statistik des Juden* V (1909) issues 9, 10, 11, 12.
55 The best study I know of on the topic is an unpublished paper of Naomi Shiloah written at Haifa University.
56 See the ICA report cited above, note 14, p. 318, 314.
57 Ibid., p. 324.
58 I do not have an explanation for the differences between the two cities.
59 This table is based on data provided by Jacob Thon, *Die Juden in Oesterreich* (Berlin, 1908), pp. 81–8. I am very grateful to Michael Silber for having brought this important source to my attention.
60 Ibid., Table XXIII on page 46.
61 Thon does not provide data on the sexual breakdown of students in secondary and higher education. However, Michael Silber found that in Hungary boys by far outnumbered girls in advanced education and there is no reason for the situation in Galicia to have been different. Indeed, had this been the case, Thon would have no doubt noted it. See Michael Silber, *Roots of Schism in Hungarian Jewry*, unpublished Hebrew University Ph.D thesis (in Hebrew) (Jerusalem, 1985), esp. p. 226 Table III.8.
62 James McLachlan, 'The Choice of Hercules: American Student Societies' in L. Stone ed. *The University in Society* II (Princeton NJ, 1974), p. 485.
63 Jakob Katz, *Tradition and Crisis* (Glencoe, 1961), ch. XVI 'Associations and Social Life'.
64 On *Kol Mevaser* see Khone Shmeruk, *Sifrut Yiddish* (Tel Aviv, 1978), Ch. VII and Alexander Orbach, *New Voices of Russian Jewry*, Leiden 1980, Chs. V, VII.

65 David Roskies, 'Yiddish Popular Literature and the Female Reader, *Journal of Popular Culture* (1979), pp. 852–8.

66 The world of the female readership is explored in depth by S. Niger *Bleter geshikhte fun der yiddishe literatur* (NY, 1959), in section 'Di yiddishe literatur un di lezerin' pp. 35–108.

67 Thomas Kessner, *The Golden Door*, (NY), pp. 90–1; and see his sources there.

14

POLISH SYNAGOGUES IN THE NINETEENTH CENTURY

Maria and Kazimierz Piechotka

The fall of the Commonwealth of Poland and Lithuania and the partition of the state weakened the institutions which had kept the Polish Jews communally united. These had existed until the end of the eighteenth century despite the abolition of the Council of the Four Lands in 1764.[1] New integrating factors emerged because of the changes in state dependence and the legal and economic position of the Jews, their relations with the Polish population and the administrations of the partitioning powers, as well as the emancipation processes and acquisition of real and formal equality, assumed different forms in the three areas of partitioned Poland. Of great relevance, as well, were the internal factors – Jewish attitudes toward inherited forms of communal organization and the distinctive features of this religious and cultural life. In the nineteenth century, processes developed which were already evident among the Polish Jews in the pre-partition period. Economic, social and cultural stratification accentuated. But it is chiefly religious divisions which are important to us here, since they affected how and why synagogues were built.

In the first half of the nineteenth century, *mitnagdim*, the followers of classical rabbinical Judaism, were largely recruited as members of the superintendence of synagogues.[2] (This institution was introduced in the 1820s in the Congress Kingdom of Poland and Galicia, to replace the *kehillah* organization.) It was *mitnagdim* who were typically put in charge of communal property, which included synagogues, *batei midrash* (study houses), ritual baths and the like, and who made decisions concerning their management.

Hasidism grew in opposition to rabbinical Judaism. Originating in the eighteenth century in Podolia, during the nineteenth century it spread across Galicia, the Congress Kingdom of Poland and the Russian partition zone, becoming increasingly dynamic and popular among the Jewish masses. The religious life of the Hasidic Jews was centred around the homes of their spiritual leaders or *tsaddiks*. The *hasidim* did not normally take part in religious services held in the synagogue, and they prayed in their usually small *shtibels*, frequently located in private houses. Occasionally a few *shtibels* were situated in the same town, each one attracting the followers of a different *tsaddik*. *Hasidim* also erected their own large synagogues (for instance, Glancer's synagogue in Lwów, the synagogues at Kowno, Sadagóra).

The Jewish Enlightenment movement (*Haskalah*) grew mainly in large towns.[3] Its followers, the *maskilim*, were supported by the new Jewish intelligentsia and bourgeoisie. Polish *maskilim* were inspired by the German Jews. The influence of German culture on them is *inter alia* reflected in the names of the first, so-called 'progressive' synagogues (*die dajcze szul*) built at the time and also by the fact that German prevailed for a long time as the language used in sermons preached in these synagogues.[4] There were relatively few East European *maskilim* and especially at the beginning of the nineteenth century their activities were resisted by the traditionalist Jewish masses; indeed, the *mitnagdim* and *hasidim*, who were traditional enemies, united in the hatred of the *maskilim*. Moreover, the 'enlightened' received little official support.[5]

After 1815 the bulk of the Jewish population found themselves in the territories acquired by Russia. They lived in two areas which were administratively distinct – the Russian zone, which included the former provinces of Byelorussia, Lithuania and the Ukraine and which were annexed directly by the Russian Empire, and the Congress Kingdom of Poland. Together with the Jewish population of Galicia they constituted the largest, and most expanding concentration of Jews in Europe.

In the territories that belonged to Russia and Austria the Jewish population not only increased in size but also as a proportion of the overall population. During the nineteenth century the number of Jews in Galicia increased more than fourfold – from 200,000 (5.5 per cent) in 1816 to 872,000 (11 per cent) in 1910, despite emigration to the Congress Kingdom, which had begun in the 1840s, and to the West and America in the 1870s.[6] In the Congress Kingdom the growth rate was even more dynamic – from 213,000 (7.8 per cent) in 1816 to 719,000 (13.5 per cent) in 1865, reaching 1,320,000 in 1897 (14.5 per cent of the overall population and 28.3 per cent of the urban population)[7] which practically meant a sevenfold population increase. There was a relatively small number of Jews in the provinces which belonged to Prussia; the majority of them inhabited the territories of the Grand Duchy of Poznań (around 50,000 in 1816). The Jewish population was much smaller in Silesia (around 16,000), and there was only a tiny number in Pomerania (2,800).

Attachment to traditional forms of worship, which prevailed in Russian and Austrian Poland, together with the poverty of Jewish communities in small towns, helped to preserve a considerable number of synagogues built in the pre-partition period. Though they had to be rebuilt frequently or enlarged, they often still served communities. The Jewish demographic increase required that additional rooms be added to accommodate women or as prayer rooms for brotherhoods and guilds. Interiors were often modernized, galleries for women were built into the older structures. Occasionally the exterior was modernized. Most frequently sunken roofs, which were difficult to maintain, were removed and replaced with sloping ones. In such cases parapets were demolished and the more prosperous communities had elevations decorated. The finest synagogues of the sixteenth, and especially the seventeenth and eighteenth centuries survived in the eastern and central provinces of the Polish Commonwealth until the Second World War. Elsewhere, in the former Prussian territories, such buildings were not preserved by the turn of the century. Jewish mass emigration further discouraged the erection of new synagogues and was unfavourable for the preservation of the old ones. This was noted in 1939 by Sz. Zajczyk[8] when he wrote about the paucity of examples of synagogue architecture in the western provinces of Poland. It was only in the nineteenth century that huge synagogues, designed by German architects and modelled on German synagogue architecture, were erected in Silesia and the big cities of Great Poland and Pomerania (such as Gliwice, Racibórz, Bytom, Katowice, Gdańsk, Bydgoszcz, Poznań).

The rapid increase in the number of Jews, along with interval migration patterns, created a need for new synagogues, *batei midrash*, ritual baths and slaughterhouses. The authorities of the Congress Kingdom were aware of this. Correspondence between the presidents of the Kalisz and Mazovian provinces and the Government Board for Instruction and Public Worship has survived from 1818 on how to grant permission to erect new synagogues 'where they had never been built before' because of the 'growth of the resident population of the Judaic Faith in the Kingdom'.[9] Attempts were also made to regulate organisational dependence of those new communities. The increasing Jewish populations of small towns tried to escape from dependence on the *kehillot* elsewhere. Complaints were occasionally lodged of excessive taxation and of the accumulation of wealth by the synagogues of dominant *kehillot*. Such a complaint was made in 1822 by the Jews from Serock and Nowe Miasto Pułtuskie against the Nasielsk *kehilla*.[10] The Jews of Wyszków also struggled for independence from Maków Mazowiecki (correspondence about this dates from 1837 to 1859). They tried to create the conditions necessary for each community to act independently. It was decided that, until a new synagogue could be built, rooms would be rented for common prayer and the synagogue service accommodated in this way. Though these efforts failed to produce the expected results, the community did act independently and eventually built a synagogue without official permission.

The rise of new communities was generally encouraged by the owners of private towns, who would provide sites for synagogues, and often established them themselves (for instance, in Aleksota, Izbica Kujawska). Their ability to do so decreased over time.[11] First, *kehillot* and, from 1821, the superintendence of synagogues was subjected to the control of both provincial and central authorities. Under these conditions the cost of the normal maintenance of existing structures was ensured but not money to erect new buildings. Synagogues and other buildings necessary for the religious needs of the community therefore usually had to be built out of the funds collected especially for that purpose from Jews, and occasionally with the help of large donations. If a community wanted to undertake a building project, the authorities would examine how it was to be financed. They evidently feared in such cases that the 'elders' of the community, who usually figured among the more affluent members, would undertake excessive financial obligations which they would then impose on the Jewish poorer elements, who made up the bulk of the Jewish population. Such control was exerted in 'national' as well as private towns.[12]

The Prussian and Austrian authorities carefully supervised the construction of all sorts of buildings including religious ones, and comparable supervision was later adopted in the Duchy of Warsaw, and the Congress Kingdom. New laws forbade the erection of buildings, including synagogues, *batei midrash*, ritual baths or slaughterhouses, without the approval for the construction of these designs. These procedures were identical to those for other religions. District and provincial architects were responsible for drawing up plans and helping to execute them.[13] Final projects were then approved by the provincial authorities, checked by the architects from the Government Board for Internal Affairs, and accepted by the Government Board for Instruction and Public Worship and the bodies which replaced them. Therefore the comments and signatures of architects who worked in the Warsaw offices (including H. Marconi's) are often found on the plans beside the authorities' decisions.

There was inevitable conflict between the economic restraints imposed by the authorities responsible for the distribution of funds and the desire for appropriately 'magnificent' synagogue exteriors from the architects who commented on the plans.[14] To satisfy the architects, the Government Board for Instruction and Public Worship thought it necessary to lay down a suitable architectural formula for synagogues and other buildings, and it therefore promoted model plans.[15] Many complications arose, of course: communities might also have particularly pressing needs for a new building, such as after a fire, while in other cases the indolence of officials encouraged builders to erect synagogues without offical permission. When this was discovered, enquiries were held, the building site was visited, lengthy negotiations conducted and letters exchanged. Typically these led to an acceptance of the status quo, for despite the protests of local authorities to higher ones, it was impossible to pull down buildings. This state of affairs had a deleterious impact on building and frequently hampered rational planning and regulation of the urban environment.[16]

At the end of the eighteenth century both wooden and masonry synagogues ceased to be designed with a high main hall, covered by a multi-tiered roof, and surrounded by rooms with galleries and corner pavilions. This design disappeared, together with the Baroque way of arranging space. At the same time the widespread general impoverishment and decline of patronage created unfavourable conditions for building in the previous sometimes lavish way. The synagogues' interiors were now also poorer. The main hall, which was still very lavish, especially in wooden synagogues into the late-eighteenth century, was simplified. The multi-tiered, false vaultings, built into the roof framework, disappeared – the last known instance of such vaulting is the wooden synagogue at Warka, built in 1813. Vaulting gave way to flat ceilings or mirror vaults (flat ceilings with a high concave cove running around the hall). As well as halls without internal supports, nine-bay and three-nave arrangements were still employed, the piers, however, being used to support key beams. Similar ceilings also appeared in masonry synagogues. The introduction of roofing paper and sheet metal made it possible to reduce the roof pitch. The high-pitched, multi-tiered, gabled or half-gabled roofs with four slopes started to be replaced by ones with low, two or four slopes.

The nineteenth century brought a change of attitude towards timber as a building material. Its specific properties had allowed such shapes as false vaultings or hanging galleries, which were impossible to execute with other materials. But it was now no longer used. Because of the risk of fire and because it had a short life, timber was reserved for building more modest buildings intended for the poorer classes. Consequently it was primarily employed as a building material in villages and small towns, where its availability and the ease with which it could be worked encouraged its wide use. Timber was also now of poorer quality – sawmill timber appeared, cheaper and in short lengths. The building authorities moreover pressed for masonry synagogues to be built. They had practical and aesthetic advantages – masonry synagogues were considered more 'monumental'. But they required larger funds and the use of larger numbers of skilled workmen. Consequently masonry synagogues, often replacing wooden ones, were built in the big cities or towns where the communities were older, more prosperous and better established, or where the donors were particularly generous. On the other hand the poor communities in the small towns struggled to be allowed to build in timber, which was cheaper and readily available. Often it was possible to get hold of it free from the local landowner and have local carpenters erect simple and modest buildings.[17]

The nineteenth century synagogues on a traditional lines were usually erected on the 'longitudinal' plan. The main hall, intended for men, was square or squarish, with the holy ark up against the east wall and the *bimah* in the centre, and was entered from the west through the vestibule, with a prayer room above it for women. The latter was occasionally extended by galleries built into the hall. In both masonry and wooden synagogues the 'longitudinal' plan was normally employed in its basic form: the height of the walls of the main hall was equal to that of the vestibule and the women's section added together. All these made up a compact structure, under one roof, with eaves all around at the same level. A variation on the 'longitudinal' plan was occasionally used in small, poor synagogues and *batei midrash* (called *przyszkótki*). Here the walls of the main hall were lower than those of the vestibule and the women's section; the latter was above the vestibule, and was completely, or partially, built into the loft. One-storey synagogues and *batei midrash* were built as well, resembling the small single-storey town buildings, that surrounded them. They consisted of a porch, and the hall for men, joined by small openings in the wall to the smaller hall for women, which was accessible directly from the outside. All the rooms were low (240–250 cm), with a ceiling at the same level; the roof was shingled, tiled or even thatched. *Batei midrash* and occasionally even small synagogues were attached to the rabbi's or scholar's rooms, or the ritual bath and under the same roof. A plan from 1865 has survived from the House of Prayer at Bielawy and this shows that the same building was to house a small synagogue, the rabbi's home and a ritual bath. The project was drawn up by K. Pelletier, an architect from Łowicz district. Because of lack of money only a small synagogue was built.[18]

Houses of prayer were also set up in private dwellings, and were supported by groups of the faithful. In 1826 the Municipal Office of Warsaw informed the Government Board for Instruction and Public Worship that because of the lack of a synagogue in the capital 'the services are only held in private dwellings, where the neighbours gather for common prayers, sharing the cost of rent, fuel and light', and that 'it [the office] granted temporary permission for their further activity.' The letters enclosed listed 101 houses of prayer in Warsaw and ten in the Praga suburb, and also included the addresses and names of 'supporters'. Depending on their size the houses could take twelve to one hundred worshippers; the majority consisted of two rooms, but as many as twenty-nine had only one, and only two had three rooms.[19] Throughout the nineteenth century the number of such prayer houses was increasing, especially in the large cities. In Warsaw there were already 217 by 1891.[20] The situation was analogous in other towns.[21]

The basic version of the 'longitudinal' design, worked out at the turn of the sixteenth and seventeenth centuries, was employed until the inter-war period. Its simplicity allowed different architectural styles to be used in synagogue building while conforming to the traditional arrangement and shape of rooms, determined by the rules of worship. This was of special importance in the nineteenth century because of contemporary historical thinking, which led to stylistic pluralism.

The elevation at the entrance was the main one. It screened the fact that the western part of the building was divided into two storeys, which could, but need not be, reflected in the elevation: light could enter the women's section in the upper storey through windows in side walls too. Similarly the stairs could either be placed against the elevation (outside stairs) or remain hidden inside the building. The size and position of windows on side elevations depended on the arrangement of the interior. Usually they were different in the two-storey western part and in the high main hall. In synagogues with side galleries turning along the whole wall, there were usually two tiers of windows. Since the Holy Ark was placed inside the synagogue, against the eastern wall, this consequently determined how the eastern elevation would be built. The central part of the wall could not have windows up to the level of the ark. The shape of roofs in the nineteenth century, once the practice of building vaults into the lofts had been abandoned, depended on their framework and the material used to cover them.

In the first half of the nineteenth century architecture was dominated by classicism. In the constitutional period of the Congress Kingdom the authorities enforced the use of the classical style when edifices were built or rebuilt for them, and it also tended to be imposed on government architects, who designed sacred buildings among others. Classical forms continued to be employed throughout the nineteenth century until the end of the 1920s. They ensured that the plans employed would be generally approved: architectural rules were viewed as a reflection of eternal ones which contributed to the imperishable grandeur of the edifice.[22] In the case of sacred buildings, they expressed the timeless character of religious truths. The principles of 'ordered' architecture were taught in every architectural college. They made it easier to draw up projects. Rules were followed which almost automatically determined the proportions of a building, its architectural divisions, the position of openings and the choice of detail. In the first half of the nineteenth century architectural orders were associated with the social 'position' of its founder or of the class the building was designed to serve.[23] The use of columns, together with Ionic and Corinthian orders, was considered proper for upper classes, whereas the urban middle classes were entitled to either pilasters of Doric or Tuscan orders, or else to not using orders but architecture based on classical canons. When government edifices were erected, their architectural style had to correspond with the position of the city in the administrative hierarchy. Albums filled with designs, for churches as well, were used for this. Piotr Aigner, professor of architecture at the University of Warsaw, who was employed by the Government Board for Internal Affairs and Police and was one of the most outstanding architects of the first quarter of the nineteenth century, published a book in 1825 called, *Budowy kościołów część pierwsza zamykająca cztery Projekta Kościołów Parafialnych różnej wielkości w dziewięciu tablicach* (Church Building. Part I: Four Designs for Parish Churches of Different Size in Nine Plates).[24]

As far as synagogue architecture was concerned, it was considered proper to follow the designs ascribed to urban middle classes, though this rule was not strictly observed. Usually the 'grand order' was employed: the pilasters articulated all the elevations, or only the front one along the whole height of the wall. The front elevation could occasionally be emphasized by a columnar portico (most frequently three-axial, added, recessed or only blind), crowned with a triangular pediment, set against the background of a stepped gable, screening the high-pitched roof (Kuźniczka, Pabianice, Wieniawa near Lublin, Płońsk, and others). There is a striking resemblance between these elevations and the model churches designed by Aigner. They were a continuation of the Palladian tradition, which appeared in palace and church architecture in the last thirty years of the eighteenth century. Then the palace at Tulczyn, owned by the Potockis, was built, and the synagogue as well, whose front elevation imitated the Venetian church of San Giorgio Maggiore.[25] Porticoes with pediments were added to synagogues with roofs with four slopes (Kępno,1815). At Klimontów (1851) a portico of this type screens the outside stairs. The synagogue at Działoszyce (designed by I. Frankowski in 1852) has a saddle roof, crowned with pediments, and pilasters articulate all the elevations; it is worth noting that the Tuscan style was correctly designed. The synagogue in Biała Podlaska, rebuilt after a fire in 1826, had a recessed portico hiding a gallery in the storey, and flanked by two square towers, reminiscent of former pavilions.

The revival of classical forms was seen in wooden synagogues too. The synagogue at Mogielnica had a columnar portico; at Raków the pillars of the outside gallery were crowned with small Tuscan capitals. Similar heads were put on the pillars of the gallery at Zabłudów which at that time was added above the vestibule of the seventeenth century synagogue. A columnar portico, set against a stepped, boarded gable appeared as well in the unexecuted plan of 1825 for the synagogue at Aleksota. Walls were decorated with the pilasters, rustications and cornices, characteristic of masonry architecture.

The use of 'Gothic' styles dated back to the third quarter of the eighteenth century. They were believed to show the ancient lineage or, as it was called, the 'antiquity' of the family, social group or institution for which the building was designed. It recalled the splendour of the monarchy of Casimir the Great, the royal law-maker, who was associated with 'bringing the Jews to Poland'. In the nineteenth century Gothic styles were used to rebuild castles, erect buildings intended to house the relics of the nation's past, and from the 1820s they were adopted widely in Christian sacred architecture.[26] Similarly there are a few instances known of synagogues built on the traditional, longitudinal plan, as well as *batei midrash* where neo-Gothic styles were employed. In the synagogue at Chomsk a high-pitched, stepped gable was added to the western elevation (narrower than the elevation itself), buttresses were built, and the windows acquired an ogival shape. Often, however, the builders confined themselves to the shape of the openings, which were occasionally combined with details borrowed from various styles (for example Szawle, the portico in Witebsk). Gothic styles were also imitated in wooden synagogues. When the synagogue at Wyłkowyszki was renovated in 1839 or 1852, an ogival door was introduced into the vestibule. Presumably at the same time ogival windows were constructed at Szawlany. Although the synagogues with neo-Gothic elements appeared across vast territories throughout the nineteenth century, there were few of them. This situation was because the neo-Gothic style was becoming widespread and typical in church architecture, with which Jews did not want to identify. In the cases described above the inventiveness of architects was reduced to adding to the traditional scheme; they were primarily classical, but Gothic as well, and later 'oriental' and neo-Romanesque ones also appeared. The faithful accepted them, provided the traditional arrangement of rooms and location of the holy ark and the *bimah* were preserved. Any attempts to alter this layout encountered opposition. The synagogue at Terespol was not built according to the plan accepted by the provincial authorities in 1856, but a traditional synagogue was erected instead on the longitudinal plan, with an outside gallery supported by pillars.

In the 1830s the first attempts were made to abandon the longitudinal layout. Such a synagogue was built about 1830 at Praga in Warsaw, and for many years this was the only community synagogue in the capital. The structure was designed by J.Lessel as a rotunda. That the synagogue was executed with so little respect for traditional solutions seems to have been possible because of the approval and support of its founder, Berek Szmulowicz (Bersohn). H. Marconi's synagogue plans have also been preserved.[27] In 1832 he drafted the first version of the project for the synagogue in Łomża. It was planned as a central building and was based on five squares with bevelled corners. The same layout was designed for the main hall and four corner pavilions adjoining it, connected by rectangular joins. The galleries above for women ran around the hall. Both the high hall and lower pavilions had flat octagonal cupolas over them. This version, however, must have been rejected, for a new plan was produced in 1835 which followed the traditional arrangement of rooms and masses but which were interpreted in an oriental fashion. The square hall with nine bays and two projecting corners on the west side, which were partly modelled on eighteenth century pavilions, had quadrilateral domed roofs, looking like a flattened 'donkey's back', and the windows were finished with horseshoe arches. The front elevation of the synagogue at Kolno, designed by Marconi in 1847, also had an arched horseshoe portal and similar windows. Marconi, who had already employed oriental forms in palace interiors, the 'Moorish' hall in the Pac palace in Warsaw, and the palace at Jabłonna,[28] presumably used them to emphasize that 'Jews are eastern people'. The synagogue at Łomża seems to be one of the first in which 'Moorish' forms appeared. They were further embellished and elaborated by Marconi in the two versions for the unexecuted vast synagogue in Franciszkańska Street in Warsaw in 1850. In the first version the square hall was surrounded on three sides by galleries in the first and second storey, and light was additionally provided by a 'lantern'. The second version provided for three naves with side galleries. In both versions the Moorish motifs were consistently used on the elevations and in the interiors. Marconi's plans were drawn up when the supporters of the 'Enlightenment' were increasing in number and beginning to play an important part in the economic life of the Congress Kingdom.

The supporters of the reforms believed that the basic aim of religion was to improve the morals of the faithful. This was to be achieved by teaching and sermons, which, together with prayers, became central elements of the services. The rabbi-preachers not only required religious knowledge but now had also to be talented speakers. The faithful were expected to participate in the service. To achieve this a few innovations were introduced into the Reform synagogues: the services were conducted in German and eventually in Polish; well-trained cantors were employed, choirs and, later, organs.[29] This led to changes in the layout of synagogues. A spot had to be found for the preacher so that he could face the faithful and so that they could focus their attention on him. Supervisors of the synagogue wished, moreover, to highlight their own importance by placing their seats in prominent locations. There was also a need for a spot for the choir, and possibly the organ. Unlike in the traditional interiors, where Jews could shift their pews to concentrate on the Holy Ark against the eastern wall or the *bimah* in the centre of the hall, in the Reform synagogue the fact that attention should be focussed in one particular direction was emphasized. The *bimah* was moved directly in front of the ark and lost its 'canopy'. A pulpit or rostrum for the speaker was put between the *bimah* and the ark, and benches were placed next to it for him and the synagogue supervisors. Consequently, a kind of a presbytery emerged – one raised above the floor of the hall and occasionally emphasized, as in Christian churches, by the apse. The interior, as in Protestant churches, was surrounded by galleries for women. These, unlike in former synagogues, could now watch the service and be seen from below. The isolation of galleries was becoming increasingly token and eventually entirely disappeared.[30] Undoubtedly reform of worship and the layout of progressive synagogues were influenced by the forms of services introduced by Protestantism.[31] This influence was already evident in the eighteenth and the first half of the nineteenth centuries in some traditional synagogues, where benches invariably were directed towards the ark, and especially with the introduction of galleries for women in the main hall along one or both side walls.

Such reform was initiated by German Jews.[32] Their assimilation and rising social status encouraged them to erect synagogues of a size and architectural style reflecting their social, economic and cultural position. But attempts were made to make Jewish sacred architecture look different from religious buildings of other faiths throughout the nineteenth century not only in Germany. The building of a new synagogue stimulated architectural competition and encouraged heated discussions, in which the most outstanding architects took part. These, however, did not lead to any unanimously accepted solutions.[33] The structures built at that time conformed to contemporary eclectic ideas and were usually a compilation of forms borrowed from different styles and cultures. The break in the tradition of synagogue building, which occurred in the majority of German countries (in some it had already begun in the Middle Ages), resulted in attempts to find the origins of synagogue architecture within Jewish history. Some were attracted to the architecture of countries where the Jews originated (Egypt or Arab lands); others to that of those countries in western Europe inhabited by Jews for long periods of time and where Jewish culture had flourished (Spain, Italy and Germany). Consequently inspiration frequently came from both Moorish and early-Christian architecture as well as from that of the Italian Renaissance and German Romanesque. The adherents of the latter declared, in the words of E. Oppler, who designed numerous synagogues himself, including those in Głogów and Wrocław, 'In Germany a German Jew must build in the German style . . . The Romanesque style is completely German'.[34] Both this view and Bałaban's comment on the Germanization of Jews under Prussian rule are well illustrated by the Great Synagogue in Poznań, which was built in 1910 in the same style as an emperor's 'Romanesque' castle.

The *maskilim* in the Congress Kingdom and Galicia came from a similar *milieu* to German Jews: they were recruited from the Jewish intelligentsia as well as bourgeoisie and plutocracy, whose economic importance was gradually increasing. The first Reformed house of prayer in Poland was the *minyan*, founded in Warsaw in 1802 by Flattau, a banker from Germany, in his own home, and the orthodox Jews called it the 'German *shul*'. The *maskilim* attached to it in 1843 built the first progressive synagogue in Warsaw in Daniłowiczowska Street. It survived until the 1870s, and was then replaced by the great synagogue at Tłumackie.[35] From the 1830s, the *maskilim* in Lwów tried to build a progressive synagogue. They followed the example of the 'progressive' Viennese with

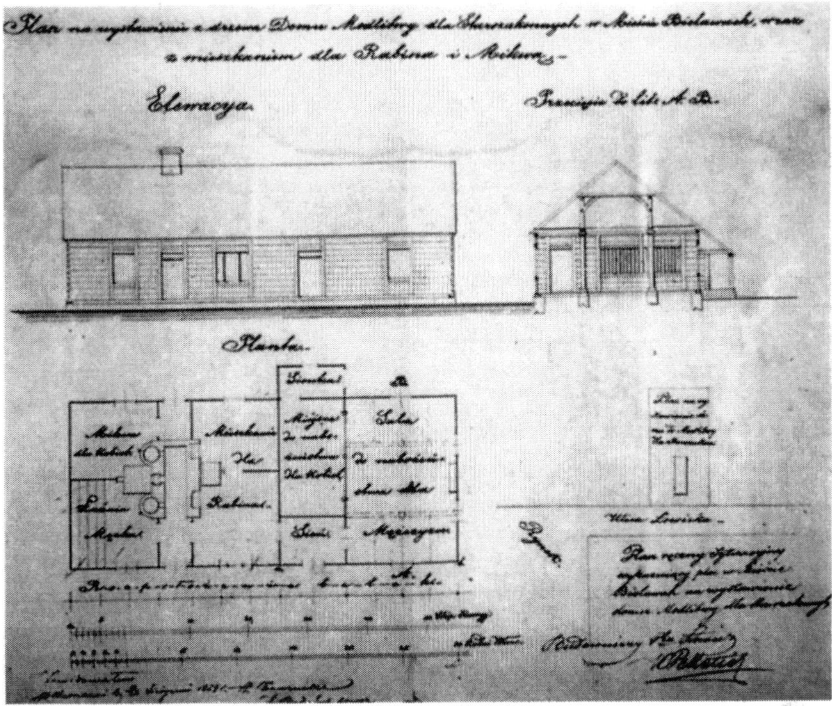

1. Bielawy: synagogue with rabbi's dwelling and *mikve*; designed by T. K. Pelletier, 1856. (AGAD-CWW)

2. Kuzniczka: first half of the nineteenth century. (photo: Czubrykowski, before 1939; photo archives of IS-PAN)

3. Działoszyce: designed by F. Frankowski, 1852.
(photo: Dobrowolski, 1950; photo archives of IS-PAN)

4. Klimontow: built *c.*1851. (photo: T. Przypkowski, 1952)

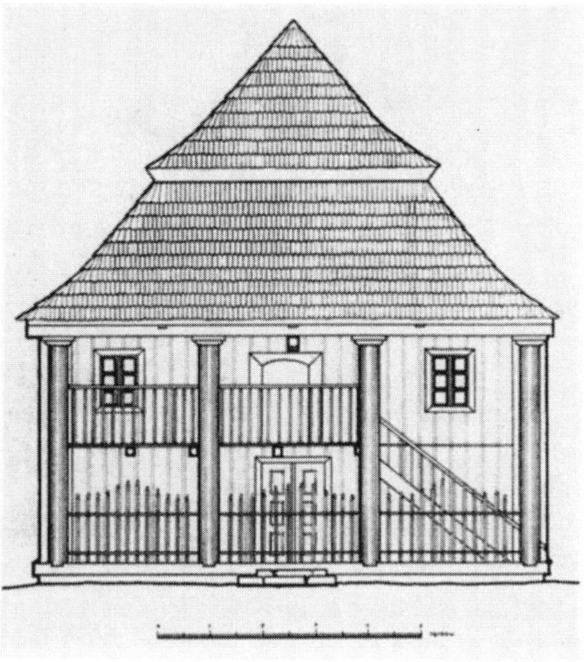

5. Mogielnica: first half of the nineteenth century.
(surveyed by ZAP before 1939)

6. Chomsk: first half of the nineteenth century.
(photo: T. Bochnig, 1929, photo archives of IS-PAN)

7. Warsaw: Praga, Szeroka Street; designed by J. Lessel, *c.*1830; pulled down, 1961. (photo: K. Beyer, *c.*1860; photo archives of IS-PAN)

8. Łomza: version 1, unexecuted; designed by H. Marconi, 1832. (AGAD–Marconi Collection)

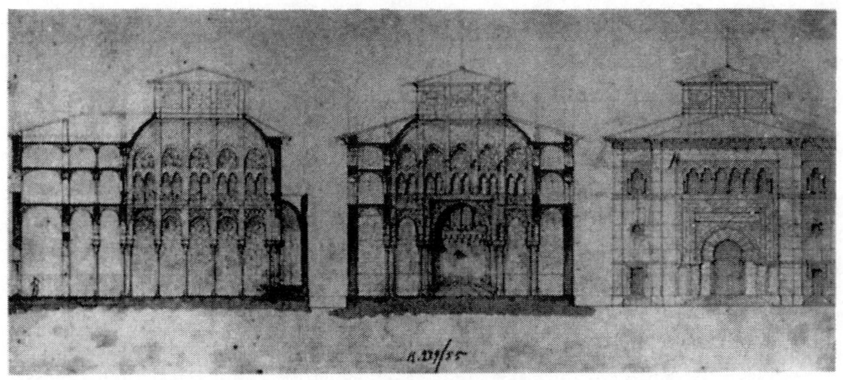

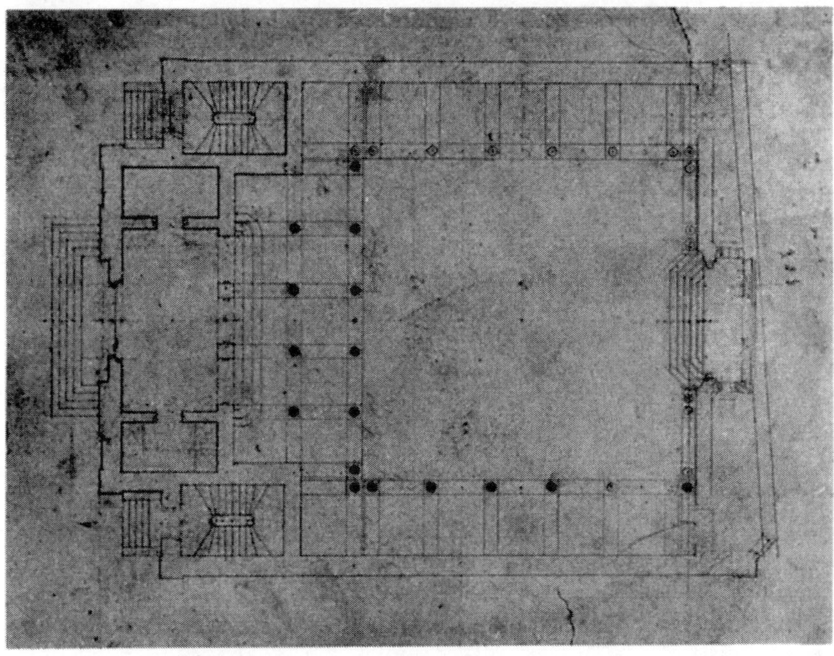

9. Warsaw: Franciszkańska Street, version 1, unexecuted; designed by H. Marconi, 1850. (AGAD–Marconi Collection)

10. Lwów: Progressive synagogue, 1846.
(after M. Bałaban, *Historia Postępowej Synagogi we Lwowie*; photo: J. Morek)

11. Lwów: Progressive synagogue, interior. (photo: as pl. 10)

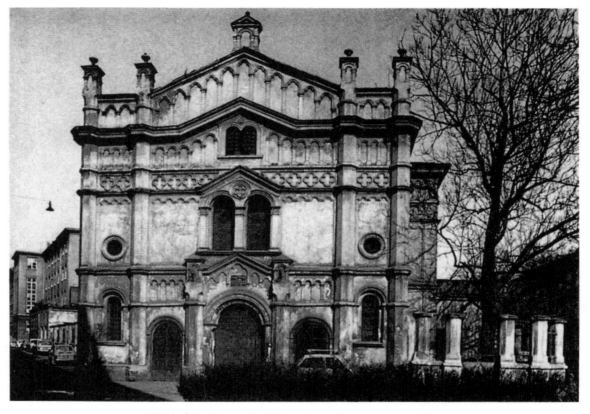

12. Kraków: Tempel, 1862. (photo: M. Krajewska, 1985)

13. Kraków: Tempel, interior, 1862. (photo: M. Krajewska, 1985)

14. Warsaw: the Great Synagogue at Tłómackie, designed by H. Marconi, 1875.
(photo: H. Poddebski; photo archives of IS-PAN)

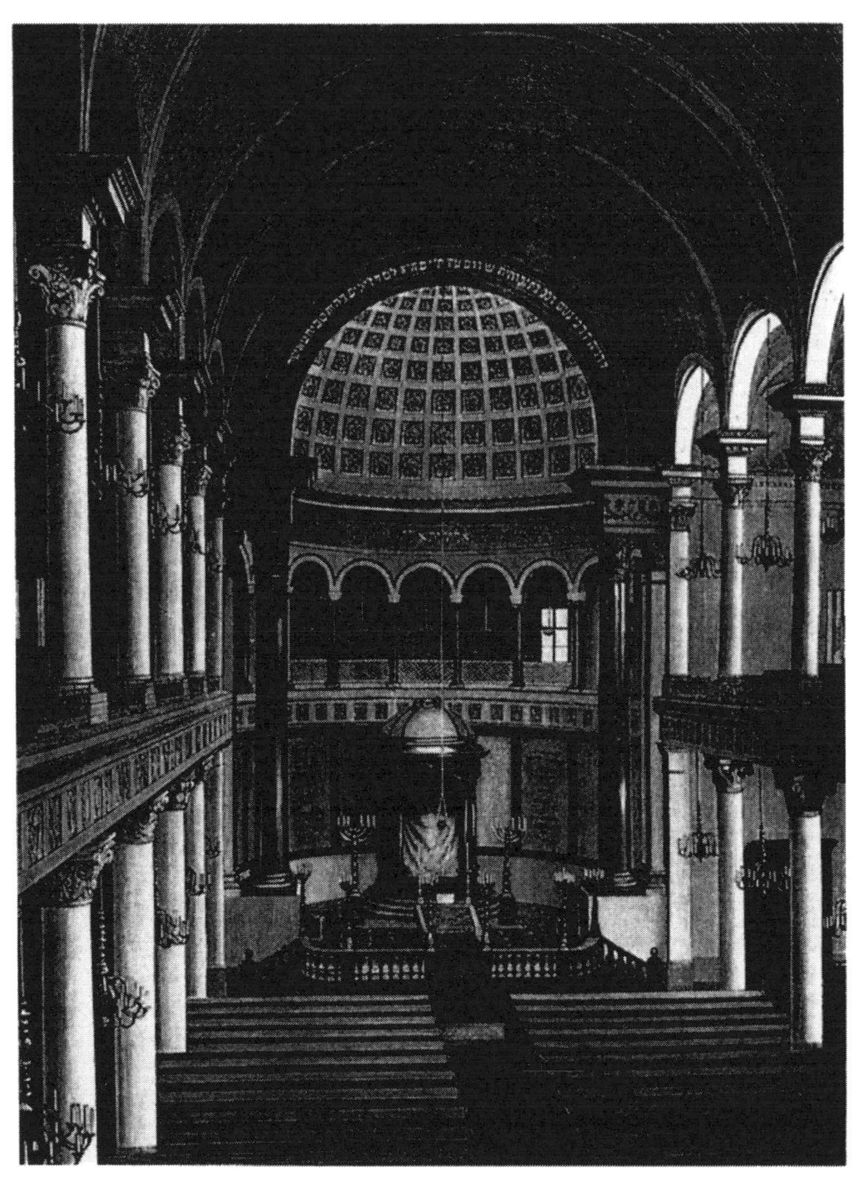

15. Warsaw: interior of the Great Synagogue, 1875.
(engraved by Witoszewicz; *Klosy*, 1,183 (1888), p, 139)

16. Będzin: second half of the nineteenth century. (photo archives of IS-PAN)

17. Włocławek: designed by F. Tournelle, 1847.
(engraved by A. Kozarski, *Tygodnik Ilustrowany* (1872), pp. 254–5)

18. Stanisławów, *c.*1879. (photo archives of IS-PAN, before 1939)

19. Łódź: 'Italian' synagogue, designed by H. Majewski, *c.*1880. (after *Architektura Łodzi Przemysłowej*, reproduced by G. Russ)

20. Przemyśl: Szajnbach's synagogue, *c.*1910. (photo archives of ZIH)

21. Radymno, *c.*1910. (photo: J. Zurowski, 1961; photo archives of ZIH)

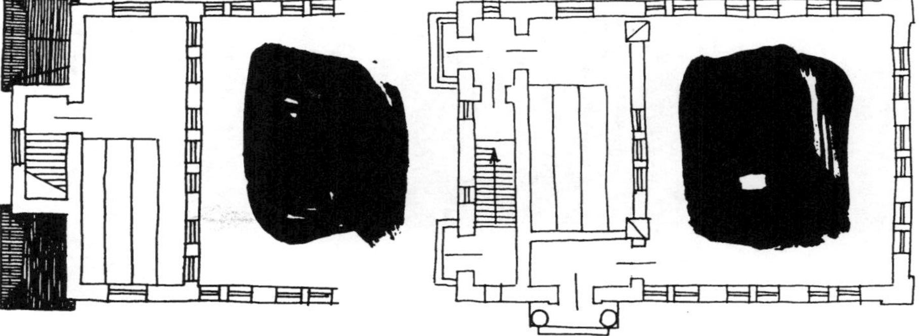

22. Wilno: Subocz Street, designed by A. Dubowik, 1927. (AAN.23)

23. Wielkie Oczy: nineteenth-century synagogue. (photo, *c.*1950; photo archives of IS-PAN)

their synagogue in the Seitenstettengasse, built in 1826. In 1846 the synagogue in the Rybi Square in Lwów was ceremoniously opened. It was initially called *Deutsch-Israelitisches Bethaus*, and the sermons were preached in German until 1903, when its name was changed to the Community Progressive Synagogue and Polish was introduced as well as German.[36] Its spatial aspects did not follow traditional arrangements: it was modelled on the central Protestant churches. The synagogue was based on the plan of a cross with arms of the same length and its octagonal hall had a high cupola above with a lantern. The central character of the interior was emphasized by at first two, and then three, tiers of galleries running along the hall. To meet the needs of the Reformed worship the *bimah* was placed near to the ark against the east wall. The arrangement of the exterior architectural shape was characteristic of the trend to not using orders but classical architecture which developed at the turn of the eighteenth and nineteenth centuries. In Kraków from 1845 the Progressive Synagogue was housed in a school building. It was only after opposition from the *mitnagdim*, who ran the community, had been overcome, that permission was granted to erect the *Templum*. The construction of the *Templum* was finished in 1862, and it has survived to the present day and continues to fulfil its purpose. As a result of successive rebuildings (1868, 1883, 1893, 1893–94, 1924) the main hall, originally on the square-shaped plan, has been extended to the east by two bays; the apse, aisles and staircases have been added, and the front elevation been transformed, retaining, however, its original neo-Romanesque character.[37]

The construction of synagogues in Lwów and Kraków was opposed by the communities' boards, which had controlled their own synagogues for centuries. In Warsaw the situation was rather different. The municipal authorities had, for many years, blocked the organization of the community.[38] It was only in 1830 that the synagogue at Praga, founded by Berek Szmulowicz (Bersohn), was built. In Warsaw itself prayers were conducted in numerous small synagogues. As late as 1900 the synagogues founded by the Nożyks (6 Twarda Street) and Sardiner (4 Twarda Street) were the property of the community.[39]

In 1859 the *maskilim* attached to the synagogue in Daniłowiczowska Street, realized that their building was too small and started plans to build a new and vast Progressive synagogue. However, it was not until the 1870s that it was possible to put this idea into practice. The members who built it were representatives of the growing number of assimilated Jewish plutocracy and intelligentsia. Their synagogue committee included Jews who played an important role in Polish culture. In order to obtain the best design a competition was announced in 1873 in which noted architects participated. The projects of Br. Żochowski, T. Lemke and J. Heurich, were awarded prizes in the competition, but not accepted by the synagogue committee. Eventually the synagogue was built to the plan of

Leander Marconi (Henryk's son).[40] It had a three-nave hall; the nave was enclosed by the apse, and galleries for women were located in the storey over the aisles. It housed around 1,500. The use of the 'grand order' in a portico, and the accumulation of structures, crowned by a cupola, produced a monumental building modelled on the classical and neo-Renaissance traditions of Warsaw architecture, begun by the neighbouring edifices in Bank Square (now the seat of Warsaw's People's Council). The combination of a cupola and a crown emphasized the character of the structure as a Jewish sacred building and must have fulfilled the intentions of the Synagogue Committee, whose members participated actively in both Jewish and Polish social life. This also accounts for the rejection of St. Adamczewski's design, as he borrowed ideas from other sources. His views are described in the literature as representing contemporary ways of thinking.[41] Adamczewski wrote: The edifice is designed in the monumental Egyptian style for historical reasons: the principles in Moses's laws for the Chosen People came from Egypt, and moreover, that way of building, emphasizing dignity and power, is a reminder of the dignity and power of ecclesiastical dogmas, that is of the law at that stage of struggle.' In fact the structural arrangement was classical and its 'Egyptianness' lay in the use of certain details, but, above all, in the symbolic meaning ascribed to particular elements of the building – for instance, in the twelve columns that represented the twelve tribes of Israel, two columns with stars for the past triumphs of the Israelites, the cupola for the power of the law over the nation.[42]

The general economic prosperity in the rapidly industrializing towns of the Congress Kingdom and the larger cities of Galicia in the 1870s and 1880s, resulted in the building of many substantial synagogues, both traditional and progressive. They were erected by communities and religious societies as well as by private persons. Ample funds were provided by the Jewish bourgeoisie and plutocracy with the equality of rights. Additional rooms were designed to serve the community's social life. The buildings were occasionally crowned with cupolas or tall, domed roofs (Częstochowa, Łódź, Płock, Tarnów, Słonim). Small cupolas and towers also appeared (Będzin) as well as turrets like minarets, which flanked the western elevation or emphasized the corners of the building (Stanisławów). These structures became part of the urban skyline, and occasionally even dominated it (Tarnów, Będzin).

Synagogue architecture ran the whole gamut of neo-styles, except perhaps neo-Gothic, and were frequently mixed. Large neo-Renaissance synagogues were erected in Łódź and Częstochowa – the so-called Italian Synagogue, designed by H.Majewski in 1880 in the former, and the New Synagogue in the latter. In the way the nineteenth century interpreted architectural styles, they were designed to demonstrate the links between Jewish and European culture, like the neo-Romanesque synagogues in

Warsaw, founded by Nożyk, Łowicz, Węgrów, Sosnowiec, Kałuszyn. The oriental trend, begun by Marconi's designs mentioned above, emphasized the Jews' connections to the East. This tendency persisted in the synagogue erected at Włocławek in 1854, designed by Marconi's disciple, F. Tournelle, and afterwards in numerous synagogues built in the Congress Kingdom and Galicia until the First World War, including the synagogues at Stanisławów (1870), Wołkowysk, Łódź, Kielce (1901–2), Białystok (1909–13), and elsewhere. Such elements as cupolas, horseshoe, trefoil and 'donkey's back' arches, borrowed from Islamic architecture and occasionally combined with neo-Romanesque, neo-Gothic, neo-Renaissance, and even neo-Baroque (Wołkowysk) styles, identified a synagogue in much the same way as the Star of David, the tablets of stone of Moses and the seven-branched candlestick placed on the front elevation.

Elements borrowed from various historical styles, such as towering gables, pinnacles, arcaded friezes, semi-circular and horseshoe arches, were eagerly employed in small synagogues as well, and here generally adopted traditional layouts. Many of them were erected at the same time in small urban centres in the Congress Kingdom and Galicia; around 1910 in Galicia *art nouveau* forms also appeared (such as in Radymno). The final effect produced by the building of course depended on the inventiveness and skill of an architect but also on the funds provided by those who commissioned them and the technical possibilities allowed them. Since these were frequently limited, many buildings appeared lacking style or with their stylistic provenance merely hinted at and often in simplified forms by the shape of openings, their frames, and the profiles of cornices. Similarly, throughout the nineteenth century, wooden synagogues continued to be built in small towns throughout central and eastern Poland. There were in 1910 at least 90 such buildings existing in Galicia only, 20 of them being classified as 'recently built'.[43]

Contrary to the eclecticism, which borrowed and combined elements from different styles and epochs, attempts were made to create a Polish national style.[44] While such aspirations were not limited to Poland, they were particularly understandable in a nation deprived of its own state, and living in a divided country. The desire to stress national identity and unity had its impact on all spheres, including architecture. Research into the Polish architectural past as a source of inspiration, began in the 1860s and then developed extensively in the 1880s, and was to affect small towns and villages as well. It was discovered that a number of elements which had been traditionally recognized as specific to Polish architecture had also been employed in synagogue building: these were, for example, the high-pitched, multi-tiered roofs, arcades and pavilions in wooden synagogues, and parapets in masonry ones. In 1903, at the same time as eclectic synagogues were being erected, and when *art nouveau* was beginning to appear, the synagogue was built at Oszmiana, whose huge, cuboid shape, with the traditional arrangement of interiors, was covered by a high-pitched, three-tiered, shingled roof with an octagonal wooden cupola built into it.[45] It almost precisely copied the traditional layout of Polish eighteenth century synagogues. In 1910 A. Szyszko-Bohusz published his own plan for the synagogue in Charków, modelled on styles characteristic of Polish provincial Baroque.[46]

The outbreak of the First World War ended the period of building vast synagogues. Architects began to rebuild the towns and villages destroyed by the war. An exhibition was organized in 1915, which resulted in the publication in 1916 of 'The Village and the Small Town'.[47] This included photographs of Catholic and Orthodox churches, manors, town and village houses, granaries and inns, as well as sixteen synagogues built in the territories of the Polish Commonwealth. They were not intended to serve as models, but as a source of inspiration. After independence, especially in the early years, architects found inspiration in this collection. Similarly continuity of tradition was emphasized with pre-partition Poland. Numerous plans have survived of wooden and masonry synagogues designed between 1921 and 1928.[48] Many of them repeated the traditional arrangement of interiors and structures. The halls were unispatial, nine-bay or three-nave. High-pitched, multi-tiered roofs reappeared, and even false vaults built into them (Lachwa), as well as reminders of corner pavilions, outside galleries (Bielsk Podlaski), lofts (Łuck, the so-called 'Purycówka'), gables modelled on Baroque ones (Pustelniki), and small cupolas (Wilno-Subocz). Moreover, the schemes not directly modelled on traditional forms (Otwock, Młądzka Street, designed by M. Weinfeld) were actually based on the well-established spatial arrangements. In the period between the wars, buildings were also constructed with no architectural style or pretence, occasionally naively imitating so-called 'modern architecture'.

Most Polish synagogues dating from the nineteenth and early twentieth centuries, like those dating back to earlier periods, have been destroyed. The structures destroyed first were those that attracted attention by virtue of their style and grandeur. Some were rebuilt and given new use. This entailed changing the arrangement of interiors, and occasionally altering their original architectural shape. Others were demolished. Undoubtedly, this architectural value (and this applied not only to synagogues), was not properly appreciated. They were considered of little value and were not given due care and attention. This is still partly the case. Interest in the architecture of this period did not develop until the late 1960s, while research on synagogues has hardly begun. In the historical or architectural literature they are typically mentioned only in passing.[49] We do not even possess a complete list of surviving monuments and their survey. Archival research is still at a very preliminary stage. The few publications devoted to particular buildings deal primarily with the history of communities and congregations connected with them; those that examine architectural problems specifically, are exceptional.[50] Consequently it is impossible to present a full range of problems connected with the Polish synagogue architecture of the nineteenth and twentieth centuries in their complicity. This will be possible only after completing the investigations initiated two years ago by the Institute of Art PAN. The authors of the present paper are fully aware of this state of affairs and the present paper is intended to draw attention to the value of those structures and urgent necessity to preserve the existing ones and to provoke discussion rather than serve as a comprehensive or conclusive investigation.

NOTES

1 The dissolution of the Council of the Four Lands in 1764 did not entirely destroy the internal organization of Polish Jews. The Jewish question continued to be discussed by Poles and Jews. Jewish plenipotentiaries were active during the Four-year Diet. Royal permission allowed representatives from over 100 communities to meet; memorials and projects were worked out, and there were negotiations between Jewish plenipotentiaries, members of the Polish Diet and royal deputies. See A. Eisenbach, *Z dziejów ludności żydowskiej w Polsce w XVII i XVIII w.* (Warsaw, 1983), particularly the chapter entitled 'Sprawa żydowska w Polsce w okresie stanisławowskim'.

2 'Supervision' was ordered by a letter of the Government Board for Internal and Religious Affairs in 1856 because of the unfortunate accident in Lublin. They were intended to control the safety of existing synagogues. During a 'supervision' the number of Jews who attended synagogues was specified as well. AGAD Acts CWW, vol. 1441.

3 S. Łastik, *Z dziejów oświecenia żydowskiego*, (Warsaw, 1961).

4 M. Bałaban, *Historia Synagogi Postępowej we Lwowie*, (Lwów, 1937); S. Silberstein, 'Postępowa Synagoga na Daniłowiczowskiej w Warszawie', *Bulletin of ŻIH*, no. 47; H. Kroszczor, 'Wielka synagoga na Tłumackiem', *Bulletin of ŻIH*, no. 95.

5 A. Eisenbach, op. cit., 'Problem praw obywatelskich Żydów w dobie porozbiorowej'.

6 M. Bałaban, *Dzieje Żydów w Galicyi i Rzplitej Krakowskiej 1772–1868*, (Lwów); A. Eisenbach, op.cit., 'Rozwój i urbanizacja ludności żydowskiej'; J. Tomaszewski, *Rzeczpospolita wielu narodów*, (Warsaw, 1985), see particularly the chapter 'Żydzi polscy w Niemczech'.

7 R. Kołodziejczyk, 'Miasta Polskie w okresie porozbiorowym', *Miasta Polskie w 1000-leciu*, (Wrocław, 1965), vol. 1; A. Eisenbach, op. cit.

8 Sz. Zajczyk, 'Bożnica w Kępnie', *Bulletin of History of Art and Culture* [BHSiK], (June 1939), no. 2 – reprint *Bulletin of ŻIH*, no. 43–44.

9 Archiwum Glówne Akt Dawnych, Warszawa – Akta Centralnych Władz Wyznaniowych [AGAD – Acts CWW], vol. 1441.

10 AGAD – Acts CWW, vol. 1679.

11 AGAD – Acts CWW, vols. 1821, 1715.

12 AGAD – Acts CWW, vols. 1441, 1715.

13 AGAD – Acts CWW, vol. 1441: The Committee of the Kraków province raised on

29 November 1827, the matter of costs for making the plans and *anszlagi* of 'neglected synagogue houses'. In response the Government Board for Internal Affairs and Police stated that making them was part of the professional duties of district builders, who were obliged to prepare plans and *anszlagi* and were to be repaid only for the costs of travelling and stationery. 'Synagogue houses, as they are public and devoted to the service of an officially tolerated faith, will remain under government protection, like churches and church houses' – the term 'church houses' in the letter applied to synagogues, baths and churches.

14 The plan for a small synagogue at Bielawy, when presented to the architectural authorities, was objected to on the grounds of its being too poor. It was declared that the synagogue, despite the modest means available, should be more impressive and 'different from the simple hut that had just been planned'. AGAD – CWW, vol. 1752.

15 The Board for Instruction and Public Worship rejected the plan for a synagogue presented by the owner of the estate of Aleksota, who intended to have it erected at his own expense. It recommended instead the use of the plan it had previously commissioned for Filipowo, 'which would probably be more suitable', since 'a synagogue constructed according to this plan would be decorative and truly beautiful'. AGAD – CWW, vol. 1821. Unfortunately we do not know the plan for Filipowo.

16 A fascinating exchange of letters on the building of a Jewish school at Działoszyce (Działoszyn) without official permission, in a place formerly designated for a new street, lasted from 9 February 1836 until September 1840. AGAD – CWW, vol. 2306.

17 The letters of the Jews from Działoszyce, who wanted to build a school out of timber, as it was available 'everywhere' and much cheaper. AGAD – CWW, vol. 2306. Z. Gloger in *Encyklopedia Staropolska*; the entry 'Synagogue' stated that 'elaborate building was much easier for them, as in the majority of cases they did not need to purchase timber: an ancient custom, preserved until our times, was that when a synagogue was to be built, the *kehillahs* would visit the neighbouring manors of nobles and landowners to collect timber; often they were given more than they actually needed'.

18 See note 14.

19 AGAD – CWW vol. 1441.

20 H. Kroszczor, op. cit.

21 L. Infeld, *Szkice z przeszłości*, (Warsaw, 1964); M. Bałaban, the introduction to *Historia Synagogi Postępowej we Lwowie*.

22 W. Krassowski, 'Problemy architektury polskiej między trzecią ćwiercią XVIII w. drugą XX w. dwudziestego wieku', *Architektura*, (1978), no. 11–12; A. Miłobędzki, *Zarys dziejów architektury w Polsce* (3rd ed. Warsaw, 1979).

23 W. Krassowski, op. cit., after S. Sierakowski.

24 P. Biegański, 'Teoretyczne projekty Kościołów Aignera', *BHSiK*, (1938), no. 4, file 6; A. Miłobedzki, op.cit., (1st edition, Warsaw, 1963), 213–214; T. S. Jaroszewski, *Christian Piotr Aigner – architect warszawskiego klasycyzmu*, (Warsaw, 1970). Aigner's work was not the only publication. It was preceded by standards and 'model plans' (*Musterpläne*) published in Galicia (*Einhundert und vierzig Kupfertafeln zum praktischem Baubeamten vom Jahre 1800*). See T. Mańkowski's review in *Dawna Sztuka* (1939), no. 3, file 2. In 1824 Hilary Szpilowski, a builder in the Mazovian voyevodship, published *Wzory Kościołów parafialnych*.

25 T. S. Jaroszewski, op. cit., contended that *Budowy kościołów* would only serve as a practical guide for the less independent provincial architects. To satisfy the need for recognized models, necessary for the government enterprise of building churches, Aigner used his own and other architects' experience. The plans in his

publication are a product of the eighteenth century spirit in architectural planning. T. S. Jaroszewski lists a number of churches, built before and after Aigner's work, which were inspired by the facade of St. Ann's Church in Warsaw, built in 1786–8 and designed by St. Kostka Potocki and Ch. P. Aigner on Palladian models. This list could be enlarged to include numerous synagogues. This is understandable, if one remembers that they were probably planned by the same architects who worked for the government. R. Wischnitzer, *The Architecture of the European Synagogues* (Philadelphia, 1964), includes T. Loukomsky's drawings. Although the author is right to draw attention to the links between the elevation of the synagogue at Tulczyn and the Palladian churches of St. Giorgio Maggiore and San Andrea della Vigna in Venice, she has misinterpreted them as being influenced by the Russian translation of *I quattro Libri dell Architettura*, published in 1798. For, as St. Lorentz has contended in *Efraim Szreger* (Warsaw, 1986), already at the end of the 1770s and the beginning of the 1780s a few palaces had been built in the south-eastern territories of the Commonwealth in the style of Palladian classicism, including the palace at Tulczyn (1775–82). In St. Lorentz's opinion it was E. Szreger who 'transferred great classical conceptions to the Ukraine'. See also T. S. Jaroszewski, 'Materiały do dziejów pałacu Potockich w Tulczynie', *The Annual of the National Museum in Warsaw*, (1982), no. 26.

26 W. Krassowski, op. cit.; P. Krakowski, 'Teoretyczne podstawy architektury XIXw', in *Zeszyty Naukowe Uniwersytetu Jagiellońskiego*, (Warsaw-Kraków, 1979).

27 AGAD – the Marconi collection.

28 T. S. Jaroszewski, 'Orient w architekturze polskiej XIXw', in *Orient i Orientalizm w Sztuce*, (Warsaw, 1986).

29 M. Bałaban, *Historia Synagogi Postępowej we Lwowie*, pp. 142–51. In 1887 a harmonium was purchased, in 1893 a mixed choir with professional female singers was introduced – it was located in the gallery. The organist, Prof. Wojnowski, was employed – according to the record book the organist should be non-Jewish. In 1897 organs were bought.

30 M. Bałaban, op. cit., pp. 44–5, quotes the description of the synagogue and its consecration from *Gazeta Lwowska*, 24 September, 1846, no. 11:

> . . . basically it is a synagogue like many others, though with a few alterations which are now being adopted in Vienna and Germany. The interior looks magnificent enough, owing to the elevated, spherical dome, although the positioning of benches, as in an amphitheatre opposite the gallery erected for the elders, spoils slightly the impression usually produced by any holy place devoted to prayers. The sight of the whole congregation was both interesting and absorbing . . . The most favourable impression, however, was produced by the upper galleries, surrounded with grilles, and filled with the beautiful faces of the daughters of Israel, whose dress, as we have noticed, has gradually come to resemble our own.

31 M. Bałaban, op. cit., 'Reforma czy oświata'. Dr Jezechiel Lewin, a rabbi, in his opening sermon on 8 September, 1928 compared styles and doctrines, reform and education. He contended: 'So the work and efforts of a century of Jewish history led to the ultimate overthrow of reform, which aimed at Protestantizing our religous life, our houses of worship. The sound instinct of the nation triumphed. Having to choose between reform and education, it decided to favour education. This has already started to breathe new life into Jewry and to penetrate all aspects of our culture, in all stages of its evolutionary development.'

32 M. Bałaban, op. cit.

33 H. Eschwege, *Die Synagoge in der deutschen Geschichte*, (Dresden, 1980); Brien de Breffny, *The Synagogue*, (Jerusalem-Tel Aviv-Haifa, 1978); P. Krakowski, op. cit.; H. Hammer-Schenk, 'Ästetische und Politische Funktionen historisierender Baustile in Synagogenbauten des ausgehenden 19 Jahrhunderts', *Kritische Berichte* (1975), no. 14.
34 H. Hammer-Schenk. op. cit., trans. by P. Krakowski, op. cit.
35 H. Kroszczor, op. cit.; S. Silberstein, op. cit.
36 M. Bałaban, op. cit.
37 M. Bałaban, *Historia Żydów w Krakowie i na Kazimierzu*, (Kraków, 1936), vol. 2; M. Bałaban, *Przewodnik po żydowskich zabytkach Krakowa*, (Kraków, 1935); H. Kozińska, 'Typy architektoniczne synagog w XIXw. w Polsce (ze szczególnym uwzględnieniem Galicji)' the typescript of an MA thesis of the Jagiellonian University.
38 A. Eisenbach, op. cit., particularly the chapter 'Ludność żydowska w Warszawie na przełomie XVIII i XIX w'.
39 M. Bałaban, *Zabytki historyczne Żydów w Polsce*, (Warsaw, after 1929).
40 H. Kroszczor, op. cit.
41 W. Krassowski, 'Aestetyczna ozdoba w architekturze drugiej połowy XIXw.' in *Sztuka II poł. XIXw.*, (Warsaw, 1983); *Inżynieria i budownictwo* (1880), no. 39, p. 158; P. Krakowski, 'Teoretyczne podstawy architektury XIXw.', op. cit.
42 An example of drawing inspiration from ancient traditions was J. Zachariewicz's project to rebuild a progressive synagogue in Lwów. M. Bałaban wrote in *Historia Synagogi Postępowej we Lwowie*, p. 142 ff:

> Zachariewicz, having started from the erroneous assumption that Jewish synagogues were the successors of the Lord's Temple on Moria (that of Solomon and Herod), began to study construction and preservation, and conceived the plan for the reconstruction of the *templum*: the vestibule and the apse were to be enlarged, and two massive towers in the eastern style, as high as the apex of the dome, were to be placed over the vestibule. New appendages were to house the council's assembly hall, or possibly a prayer room for winter, a rehearsal room for the choir, and the like . . . Fortunately, there were not enough funds for the major restoration, and the community was satisfied with minor rebuilding, which did not alter the outward appearance of the *templum*, which was so admired for half a century.

The plan was published in *Czasopismo Techniczne*, (Lwów, 1896).
43 Warsaw National Library, to Czołowski's Archives, MS 5635, 'Wykaz drewnianych synagog w Galicji', drafted by K. Notz in 1910.
44 Andrzej K. Olszewski, 'Przegląd koncepcji stylu narodowego w teorii architektury polskiej przełomu XIX i XX w.' in *Sztuka i Krytyka*, (1956), no. 54; A. Miłobędzki, op. cit. W. Krassowski 'Problemy architektury', op. cit.
45 The date for the building of the synagogue has been taken from *Encyclopaedia Judaica* (Jerusalem, 1972), vol. 12, p. 1496.
46 T. S. Jaroszewski, 'Architektura neobarokowa w Polsce' in *Sztuka I poł. XVIII w.*; materials from the meeting held by *SHS* (*Stowarzyszenie Historyków Sztuki* . . .) in November 1978, in Rzeszów (Warsaw, 1981). A. Szyszko-Bohusz's plan was published in 1910 in the annual *Architekt*, (1910), no. 9, file 11, plates 33–4.
47 *The Materials for Polish Architecture*, vol. I, *Wieś i Miasteczko*, (Warsaw, 1916).
48 In AAN (Archives of New Acts) in Warsaw; in the Acts of the Ministry of Internal Affairs, there are twenty-four projects for synagogues accepted by the Ministry of Civil Engineering in 1921–8.
49 W. Krassowski, 'Aestetyczna ozdoba', op. cit.; P. Krakowski, op. cit.

50 M. Bałaban, *Historia Synagogi Postępowej we Lwowie*; S. Silberstein, op. cit.; H. Kroszczor, op. cit.; A. Penkalla, 'Synagoga w Klimontowie', *Bulletin of ŻIH*, (1980), no. 4, p. 116; A. Penkalla and J. Szczepański, 'Synagoga w Kielcach' *Bulletin of ŻIH*, (1981), No. 4, p. 120.

51 The history of the reconstruction and rebuilding of the synagogue at Piotrków Trybunalski is an exception. J. Baranowski and H. Jaworowski, 'Historia i rozwój przestrzenny synagogi w Piotrkowie Trybunalskim', *Bulletin of ŻIH*, (1966), no. 57.

ABBREVIATIONS

AAN – Archiwum Akt Nowych, Warszawa . . . Archives of New Acts, Warsaw

AGAD – CWW – Archiwum Główne Akt Dawnych, Warszawa – Akta Centralnych Władz Wyznaniowych . . . Main Archives of Old Acts – Acts of Central Denominational Authorities

IS – PAN – Instytut Sztuki Polskiej Akademii Nauk . . . Institute of Art of Polish Academy of Sciences

WAPW – Wydział Architektury Politechniki Warszawskiej . . . Department of Architecture of the Polytechnic of Warsaw

ŻIH – Żydowski Instytut Historyczny . . . Jewish Historical Institute

ZAP – Zakład Architektury Polskiej . . . Institute of Polish Architecture

PART III

Between the Two World Wars

15

ETHNIC DIVERSITY IN TWENTIETH-CENTURY POLAND

Norman Davies

This essay aims to outline some of the main features of Poland's pre-war society, and to relate them to the study of Polish-Jewish relations. It is not a research paper, and does not present any facts that are not widely known. What it does is to stress the multinational character of old Poland, and to place the bilateral problems of Poles and Jews within the multilateral complexities of ethnic relations as a whole. It warns against the tendency of some modern historians to view the past anachronistically, or to reduce the complex realities to a simple confrontation between Poles and Jews.

Nowadays, the ethnic make-up of modern Polish society is remarkably, and artificially homogenous. Contemporary Poland is overwhelmingly Polish. As a result of the mass murders, mass deportations and comprehensive frontier changes of the Second World War and its aftermath, young Poles can grow up without ever hearing their neighbours speak a different language or practise a different religion. Very few Poles under the age of 45 or 50 – i.e. the great majority of the population – can ever remember having a German or a Jewish or a Ukrainian classmate or neighbour, or can remember seeing a recognisable 'resident foreigner' in their midst. Although they know, of course, that pre-war Poland contained many so-called 'minorities', the present state of affairs has inevitably strengthened traditional nationalist mythology linking the Polish 'land' exclusively with the Polish 'nation'. Government propaganda has undoubtedly played its part: but it was perhaps inevitable that an uprooted post-war generation of Poles should yearn for a national past in which their own antecedents held pride of place and where the 'minorities' played only a marginal role. Post-war historiography has certainly reflected this feeling.

Similarly, it is entirely natural that post-war Jewish opinion, traumatised by the Holocaust and properly impressed by the creation of the Jewish state of Israel, should be dominated by the Zionist perspective. Zionism (in the sense of modern Jewish nationalism) naturally stresses not only the existence but the distinctness of the Jewish nation in the past, as in the present. The thousand-year sojourn of the Jews in Poland is viewed less as an integral part of Polish history; but rather as a lengthy stage of the Jewish nation's Long March through the world's wildernesses, begun in Zion and ending in Zion.

The starting point of this discourse must obviously lie with the extremely complex kaleidoscope of ethnic settlement which developed in the Polish lands over a thousand years and more. Contrary to the picture painted by the Polish nationalist 'Autochtonous School', it is doubtful whether one can fairly talk at any period of history of a broad Polish heartland inhabited exclusively by Poles and overlapping with areas of non-Polish settlement merely on the outer fringes. In reality, the areas of mixed settlement both in West and East formed by far the largest part of the whole. By the late nineteenth century the cradle of historic Poland in Posnania (Wielkopolska) contained a large and growing German element. The *Kresy* or Borderlands in the East, with their mixed populations of Poles, Lithuanians, Byelorussians and Ukrainians were more extensive than the provinces which form the 'centre' of modern Poland today. The whole country, from Silesia in the west to deepest Ukraine in the east, was overlaid by what elsewhere I have called 'the Jewish Archipelago'. Jewish settlement was naturally very thin in the rural countryside. But it was concentrated in the small towns, the *shtetlach*, in the provincial centres, and in the growing cities, where, as often as not, the Jews would form an absolute majority in their particular ward or locality. In addition, the imperial régimes of the nineteenth century imported large numbers of foreign bureaucrats – Prussian Germans from Berlin, Austrian Germans from Bohemia or Vienna and Russians from St Petersburg – to administer their Polish provinces.

Given these complex patterns, I often think that it is misleading to describe Poland's multinational society in terms of the statistical 'Polish majority' on the one hand, and of the so-called 'national minorities' on the other. In a very real sense, most people in early twentieth century Poland lived in conditions which nourished their perception of being an exposed minority, surrounded by potentially hostile foreigners, and wearied by the universal feelings of insecurity. In particular, it would be wrong to identify automatically the majority population as the social oppressors, and the national minorities as the oppressed. Both the Polish and the Jewish communities displayed a wide range of social and economic standing, and in various times and locations different groups of Poles and Jews could sometimes be regarded as advantaged, sometimes as disadvantaged, elements of society. The lines between rich and poor, or between privilege and underprivilege, did not follow the ethnic divide.

If one examines the distribution of the Polish 'majority', for example, – say in 1921 at the first independent census – it soon becomes clear that there were not many provinces or towns of the reborn Republic which ethnic Poles could feel were exclusively 'theirs'. Having passed the entire nineteenth century as a minority group within Russia, Prussia or Austria, and having developed all the complexes to match, the nationalistic element within the Polish community now realised with no small sense of frustration that the new Poland did not measure up to their dreams. All too often, from their point of view, the Poles were still a minority, or at best an embattled and marginal majority, within their own land. In many of the former Prussian districts, the German element still maintained an economic, if not always a numerical supremacy. In the east, although the Polish landowners still dominated the social scene, the Poles were heavily outnumberd by Byelorussians and Ukrainians. In the urban centres, the Jewish presence was strong, and sometimes dominant. In Warsaw, the capital of Poland, the Jewish element, which was set to decline in relative terms, nonetheless stood only slightly below the 50 per cent mark.

For Jewish readers, especially in America, the picture of an isolated Polish minority living in a predominantly Jewish town and feeling uneasy at their predicament, may seem to be standing history on its head. And, of course, it wasn't the norm; but it was common enough in the eastern provinces. Memoirs and personal reminiscences of life in the former East Galicia, for example, in towns such as Buczacz, or Brody, or Podhajce in the late 1930s, recall Polish apprehension as the ***Betar*** movement marched its young people round the market square to chants of 'We will conquer Palestine' or 'We're not scared of Arabs'. In this case, Polish-Jewish tensions were tempered by the shared fears of local Ukrainian activists who tended to view both Poles and Jews as fair game for harassment. After all, there was a long history in those parts dating back to Chmielnicki's Revolt (1648) and the Massacre of Human (1768), when vengeful peasants on the rampage had slaughtered both Poles and Jews indiscriminately.

On the other hand, one needs to remember that the interests of the Polish community were supported by the full panoply of state power: whilst the interests of the 'minorities' were not. The reigning mood of Poland's state authorities in the inter-war period was 'unremittingly nationalist'. The prevailing convention, especially among the lower levels of the bureaucracy, was to view the Second Republic as a Polish state. As a result, the dealings of the Polish community with the other nationalities could not be conducted on the basis of equality. In terms of attitudes, the imbalance could only increase the embitterment of the 'minorities', which in turn fuelled the fears and suspicions of the Poles. In terms of political power and action, however, it gave the Polish community a commanding position. In the 1930s, there was no way that Polish Jewry could have properly defended itself against discriminatory legislation or against petty harassment by officialdom: no way that Poland's Ukrainians could have matched the firepower and resources of the army and the state police in their murderous campaigns of 'pacification'.

In my view, it was these specific conditions, where each of the ethnic communities had reason to feel insecure, that fostered the rise of rival nationalisms on all sides, and the growing threat of intercommunal violence. Nationalism – with its mission for strengthening the separate identity of each community, and its later stage of demanding a separate homeland for each nationality – fed on the tensions and flourished in proportion to people's anxiety. Regrettably, it also diminished the chances for maintaining mutual toleration and intercommunal harmony. Yet one glimpse at the maps shows that the nationalists' hopes for creating national homelands for each of the nationalities of the region could never have been achieved by natural evolution. To create a Poland exclusively for the Poles, a Ukraine for the Ukrainians, a Lithuania for the Lithuanians, or an Israel for the Jews required the unscrambling of a thousand years of social development, together with a degree of brute force and political compulsion which no one in pre-war Poland possessed, or even imagined.

During the Second World War, of course, the situation changed radically. The arrival of the Nazis and the Soviets, both of whom possessed the political will and the logistical capacity for social engineering on a mass scale, sounded the knell for Poland's multinational society. The Nazis with their plans for German *Lebensraum* and their predilection for mass murder, the Soviets with their practice of mass deportation, and the Allied Governments with their acquiescence in wholesale territorial and demographic changes, combined to bring Poland's traditional society to an end. The ethnic conflicts of pre-war Poland were not so much solved as destroyed (together with millions of people whose existence or address had not suited the plans of the Nazi and Soviet social engineers).

In the meantime, and especially in the rising tensions of the 1930s, each of Poland's ethnic communities increasingly felt itself to be caught in a trap from which there was no obvious escape. The Poles, inflamed by nationalistic elements with growing influence, felt that all the 'minorities' were ever more 'anti-Polish'. The Germans of Poland, won over by Nazi propaganda, felt that they were under attack by 'anti-German' oppressors. The Ukrainians, whose nationalist movement had sprouted an active terrorist wing, increasingly felt that their Polish, Jewish (and Russian) neighbours were 'anti-Ukrainian'. The Polish Jews, who in their scattered settlements were least able to defend themselves increasingly felt that all other groups in Poland – Poles, Germans, Lithuanians, Byelorussians, Ukrainians – were 'anti-semitic'. It is no simple matter to determine how far these mutual fears and hatreds were subjective, and how far they were based on cold, rational analysis. Yet it is impossible to deny that they were on the increase on all sides.

In the 1930s, each of the communities spawned activist groups who in their different ways were all beginning to think of radical solutions to (what they considered) an intolerable dilemma. The Polish National Democrats, and even more their radical and illegal offshoot, the *ONR-Falanga*, began to talk not merely of compulsory Polonisation of the minorities, but also of assisted emigration, even of expulsion. The Nazi 'Fifth Column' began to plan, and to arm, for a German invasion. The Ukrainian *O. U.N.*, apart from its terrorist campaign against the Polish authorities, aimed to attach themselves to the Nazis' bandwagon. The Polish Zionists were training young Jews in agriculture, with emigration to Palestine in view; and the Zionist-Revisionists were organising Jewish self-defence units. None of these radical groups had the means to put their wider schemes into operation.

Not everyone in Poland, however regarded the ethnic mix as a recipe for disaster. The entourage of Piłsudski, a native of the Wilno region whose inhabitants were familiar with particularly complicated patterns of ethnic settlement, had no sympathy for ethnic nationalism, tending instead to look for a revival of the multinational traditions of the old, pre-Partition Commonwealth. Piłsudski's outlook prevailed in the upper echelons of the Polish Government until his death in 1935. Similarly, each of the 'minority' communities contained groups and individuals resolutely opposed to the nationalist trend amongst them, dreaming instead of turning Poland into a 'Switzerland of the East'. Within Polish Jewry, for instance, the Zionist movement met stalwart opposition both from conservative, religious groups and, on the Left, from the ***Bund***.

The ***Bund***, though it was actively nationalist in the cultural sphere – especially in the promotion of Yiddish education and literature – would have nothing of the Zionist plans for a separate Jewish homeland. The vision of the ***Bund***, as of Polish socialists in general, was of a multinational Poland, where each ethnic community could preserve its identity, but live with its neighbours in harmony and justice. Later apologists for the ***Bund*** have claimed that by the late 1930s it had assumed 'the leadership of Polish Jewry'.[1]

As things worked out, Poland's ethnic cauldron was knocked over by the Second World War before it ever reached spontaneous boiling point, and it is difficult to say whether, if left to itself, the situation would have developed into a generalised ethnic conflagration of the sort which has erupted elsewhere in the world – say in partitioned India, or in the Lebanon. All one can say is that the prospects were not favourable. As it was, Polish-German antagonisms led to terrible local blood-lettings and mutual reprisals that did not end until Poland's Germans were forcibly expelled in 1946–7. Polish-Ukrainian antagonisms led during and after the war to genocidal massacres on both sides, with thousands of Ukrainian civilians being killed in central Poland and tens of thousands of Poles killed in Volhynia and Podolia. In that context, where existing ethnic hatreds had been further inflamed by the overt racism of the Nazi Occupation, it is doubtful whether Polish-Jewish relations could have escaped unscathed. But, as it was, by constructing hermetic Jewish ghettoes at the start of the occupation, the Nazis forcibly separated Poland's Jews from the general population at an early stage, and proceeded to murder them from 1942 onwards in isolation. By that particular arrangement, the attitudes of Poles to Jews and of Jews to Poles, were for practical purposes rendered largely irrelevant.

After 1945, Polish society was transformed. Polish Jewry had been literally decimated by the Holocaust and most of the survivors were intent on leaving for western Europe, America or, when possible, Palestine. Individuals apart, the only Jewish groups who chose to stay were those who for one reason or another felt committed to the new communist-led régime.

It is ironic that it was in this phase of Polish-Jewish disengagement that the Kielce Pogrom of July 1946 produced an act of more flagrant and shameful anti-semitism than anything which had occurred in the critical years preceding the outbreak of war. Poland's Germans had either fled, or in 1945–7, were forcibly expelled. Poland's Ukrainians were either incorporated into the USSR by frontier changes, or forcibly deported or dispersed following the civil war of 1945–7. Moreover, throughout the war, the Soviet authorities had observed a narrow definition of Polish nationality – which excluded all non-Catholics, and/or non-Polish citizens before 1939. As a result, large numbers of non-Poles who might otherwise have take up residence in Poland were prevented from leaving the Soviet Union, even during the post-war 'repatriation' campaigns. The outcome was the ethnically 'Polish Poland' which we know today.

The implications of this multinational context for the study of Polish-Jewish relations are considerable. I wouldn't claim that the following observations are completely original but they may help to throw some new light on the subject, and to keep it away from the confrontational posture, which can still be encountered in some quarters.

I

> Before the Second World War, Polish-Jewish relations formed but one aspect of a much more complicated ethnic mix, and cannot be judged in isolation, or simply as a bilateral issue.

As often as not, Polish-Jewish relations formed one axis of a trilateral ethnic framework. In Silesia, for example, where the Jews were assimilating fast into German culture, Poles, Jews, and Germans all contributed to the ethnic pattern. In Wilno, or in Lwów, the Jewish community held the middle ground in the complicated relations of Poles and Lithuanians, or of

Poles and Ukrainians. In Łódź, the Polish-Jewish-German triangle – so eloquently reconstructed in the main protagonists of Reymont's novel, *Ziemia obiecana* (The Promised Land) – requires that consideration be paid to all three sides of the problem.

The events in Lwów (Lemberg) in November 1918 provide a concrete example of the odd conclusions that can be reached if the Polish-Jewish relationship is artificially extracted from the wider, multi-ethnic context. At the end of a week-long battle for the city between Polish and Ukrainian forces, elements of the victorious Polish soldiery went back into certain streets, where they claimed to have been fired at by civilians, and massacred the inhabitants. An estimated 340 innocent persons were killed. Some two-thirds of the victims were Ukrainians. The remaining seventy or so were Jews. Many history books refer to these events as the 'Lemberg Pogrom', and cite it as one of the worst instances of Polish anti-semitism in action. Yet one has to wonder whether a massacre in which the majority of victims were Christians can fairly be described as a 'pogrom'. It is conceivable, of course, that two distinct atrocities occurred – one a pogrom of Jews inspired by Polish anti-semitism; the other a military massacre, four times as large, inspired by Polish anti-Ukrainianism. Or perhaps, a gang of embittered soldiers, brutalised by a vicious local war, simply went on the rampage, and killed every 'foreigner' they could find. Some clarification is necessary.[2]

II

> The condition of any one of Poland's numerous ethnic communities can only be fairly described in relation to other elements within Polish society. Comparisons with western Europe, or with North America, are not very relevant.

For example, it is very understandable for present-day Americans to study the condition of their forebears in Poland, and to feel indignant at the poverty and oppression which they had to endure. Polish Americans, American Jews and others are all apt to undertake the same exercise, and to reach the same conclusions with respect to *their* own particular forebears. The greatest wave of emigration from Poland to North America took hundreds of thousands of starving people of various nationalities from Galicia – Poles, Jews, Ukrainians – in the decade or so before the First World War; and it is a sobering thought for their descendants living comfortably in the suburbs of Chicago, New York, or Toronto to compare their grandparents' life with their own. However, if the aim is to understand the realities of early twentieth-century Polish society, as opposed to the consequences of migration, one should be studying, above all, the interdependence and mutual hardships of all elements of Galician society, where the Jewish masses no less than the Polish and Ukrainian peasantry, were forced to live on the hunger line. In this way, one might learn that the various ethnic communities, despite their differences, had much in common. What is not in order, I think, is for a historian to take the misfortunes of his own group in isolation and to pretend that their misfortunes were somehow unique or isolated.[3]

III

> Regional variations were very marked. Polish-Jewish relations in western districts, where Germans often predominated, could not be the same as in certain eastern districts, where the Poles formed a small but powerful landed élite surrounded by a largely Lithuanian or Ruthenian peasantry.

The same might be said of the Jewish community which in the western provinces was largely associated with the prosperous 'modernised' German bourgeoisie, but in the east consisted largely of an impoverished, traditionalist society. Arguably, in cultural no less than in economic terms, the Jews of Posnania or Silesia were separated from the *Ostjuden* of Lithuania or East Galicia by a gulf even wider than the barriers which separated them from their Polish and German neighbours. Ethnic divisions alone cannot begin to explain these variations.

IV

> In so far as the ethnic divisions were correlated, at least in part, with social structures, it is essential to identify the socio-economic interests which underlie many of the traditional attitudes of the various communities to each other. Polish Jewry was the one major group which had never been subjected to serfdom, and comparisons between the lot of Polish Jews with that of black slaves in America are misconceived.

In the feudal society of the Old Polish Commonwealth, the Jews had formed a separate social and legal estate, but one which, through the *arenda* system, worked closely with the nobility. Attitudes deriving from former centuries often persisted long after the destruction of the Commonwealth in 1795, or the final abolition of serfdom in 1864. The Jews continued to fulfil many of the same social and economic functions which they had carried out in feudal times – being very strongly represented in the professions, as doctors and lawyers, in urban services and in trade and commerce. Of course, from the Jewish perspective, the changes wrought by a modernising society which saw the rise of an aggressive, and frequently anti-semitic Polish bourgeoisie, and in the inter-war period, the establishment of an expansive Polish state bureaucracy, were often seen in a negative light – even as a concerted 'anti-semitic' attack on the Jewish community. From the perspective of the peasants, however, and especially of the Byelorussians and Ukrainians of 'Polska B', who saw little escape route from their life of illiteracy and provincial backwardness, the Jewish community could easily be seen as a continuing agency of their former servitude, and as an obstacle to progress. None of these 'perspectives' is necessarily impartial, or scientifically accurate; and all viewpoints need to be weighed in the balance. But for anyone familiar with Polish social history, the fashionable transatlantic perspective which tries to liken the position of the Jews in Poland to that of the descendants of black slavery in the USA must surely be the least convincing.[4]

V

> Nationalism is a force which has afflicted every ethnic community in Eastern Europe, and Zionism, with its goal of building a separate Jewish homeland in Palestine, should probably be seen as a variant of the other nationalisms prevalent in the area, rather than a phenomenon *sui generis*. The divisions and conflicts which the rise of Zionism provoked within Polish Jewry, as well as with their neighbours, could be profitably explored in the light of similar developments provoked by the rise of ethnic nationalism in each of the other communities of the Polish lands.

At this point, I should probably declare my own interest. In my studies of Polish history, I have always felt that 'Nationalism', though all-pervasive, is a phenomenon which on balance has done more harm than good. One of the minor upsets of my early career occurred when *Myśl Polska*, the organ of the Polish National Democrats in London denounced me as a communist agent. Later, having written one of the first non-nationalist histories of Poland, which pays due attention to all the non-Polish elements of the story, I received the applause of all sections of Polish opinion, except the Nationalist one. Before falling foul of certain distinguished and undistinguished commentators in the USA, I had the honour to be attacked as 'anti-Polish' in that fount of wisdom, the *Tydzień Polski*.[5]

With this background, I tend to look at Zionism in the light of my understanding of the parallel Polish experience. I see Zionism (meaning Jewish Nationalism in the broad sense) as encompassing both the national independence movement of the Jews, on the one hand, as well as the narrower or 'integral' ethnic Nationalist element on the other. In this line of reasoning, the broad and tolerant concept of Zionism, as practised by the founding fathers of Israel, strikes me as a cousin of the Polish Independence Movement of the early twentieth century; and David Ben-Gurion as a fellow-spirit to Józef Piłsudski. By the same token, the narrower, militant and nationalistic concept of Zionism, as practised by say the Zionist Revisionists and others, I take to be a relative of the Polish National Democrats. In this connection I was encouraged to read a recent comment along these lines by my colleague, Neal Ascherson, an author well versed in the history of Poland in the twentieth century: 'Perhaps, to be really pessimistic, the lasting legacy of pre-war Jewish politics in Europe is not democracy, but the blind 'national egoism' which some Zionists in Poland learned from the Nationalism preached by Roman Dmowski.'[6] Further to the Right, on both the Polish and the Jewish spectrum,I see further similarities between the extreme *fascisants* of both sides. In the continuing debates between the advocates of Piłsudski and Dmowski – as between those of Ben-Gurion and Begin, (though I know much less about it) – I do not conceal my critical but committed adherence to the cause of the non-Nationalists.

Of course, despite the accusations of careless critics, I have never advocated any exact equivalence between the characteristics of Polish and Jewish Nationalism: but I do maintain that it is a fruitful line of enquiry. I do not believe that the intense antipathy which Polish and Jewish Nationalists have tended to feel towards each other should blind us to the common mentality and philosophy which underlies each of their positions. The same would apply, in my view, to the relationship of Polish and German, or Polish and Ukrainian Nationalists. Just because Roman Dmowski saw German nationalism as Poland's prime enemy and campaigned against it throughout his career as the principal threat to Poland's survival, we are not entitled to conclude that Dmowski did not borrow many of his ideas from Germany, before transposing them for his own intensely Polish purposes. One of the themes of my writings which has won least approbation from the admirers of Dmowski, is that where I suspected Pan Roman of 'wanting to build a new Poland in the image of Prussia'.[7] This is not the place to explore the phenomenon in detail but I have long ruminated on the truth of a half-remembered aphorism by Oscar Wilde to the effect that 'excessive hostility is often the mask of secret affinity'.

VI

Xenophobia – the hatred of foreigners – is one of the deplorable features of all nationalist movements, which, in their eagerness to

> strengthen the separate identity of their own group, inevitably weaken the sense of solidarity with other groups. All nationalities complain of persecution and oppression by their neighbours; and it would be pertinent to enquire how far the antipathies, which undoubtedly increased between Poles and Jews, reflected the painful, but predictable tensions of an impoverished multinational society beset on all sides by Nationalist fervour.

In its extreme form, I suppose, the question being asked is: can anti-semitism be regarded as a variant of other forms of xenophobia, with essentially similar well-springs and characteristics, or is it something of an entirely specific and unique nature? In the context of Polish-Jewish relations, one has equally to ask whether the 'anti-semitism' which Jews often see among Poles is the same sort of phenomenon as the 'anti-Polonism' which Poles often see among Jews? Or perhaps, are not *all* the dialectical 'anti-Usisms' a reflection of the insecurity which all ethnic groups experience in turbulent, multinational societies and which strengthen the distinction between 'us' and 'them'.

Obviously, one of the difficulties lies in the elastic definition of the term anti-semitism, which in modern usage has been turned, especially in America, to all sorts of inappropriate uses. Along with others, I am one of the people who has tended to restrict my use of the term, not because 'an irrational hatred of Jews' is not a very real and deplorable fact of modern history but because it has been confused with all sorts of non-pathological positions, from 'a dislike of bagels' to well-intended criticism of Israeli Government policy.[8]

I would also count it essential to distinguish between attitudes which are the product of real political, cultural and socio-economic rivalry between nationalities (and in that case, however deformed and exaggerated, possess some sort of genuine rationale) and other attitudes which derive from thorough-going racist ideology. For example, I thought it distasteful to listen the other day to a BBC interviewer asking the Israeli Ambassador whether the attitude of the Israeli Government towards the Palestinian Arabs was not reminiscent of the Nazis' attitude towards the Jews. The answer, obviously, is that there is no comparison. It follows, however, that the tensions between Jews and Poles in pre-war Poland, emanating from the long-standing rivalry of two communities inhabiting the same country, also bear little resemblance to the relationship of the Jews and the Nazis during the Holocaust. The two relationships are different in kind, and not simply in degree.

Incidentally, one of the most paradoxical aspects of Polish-Jewish relations during the war concerns the parallel efforts of Poles and Jews to win the support of the British. It so happened that in 1942–3, at the height of Britain's life and death struggle with Nazi Germany, the British forces in

Palestine found themselves under attack from militant Zionists. As a result, when Zionist delegations in London were trying to persuade HMG that the Jews were a member of the Allied nations, the British were not disposed to agree.[9] At that same juncture, the Polish Army of General Anders made its appearance in Palestine, en route from Persia and the Soviet Union, and immediately found itself embroiled in the British-Jewish contest. Several thousand Jewish soldiers from Anders's Army deserted the Polish ranks and promptly took up arms against their erstwhile British patrons. To the Poles, such events can only have strengthened their claim to be Britain's first and most loyal ally. Yet they were not repaid in kind for their loyalty. When the chips were down at the end of the war, the British did not speak out for Poland's independence, in whose defence the War had originally been declared. Instead, in line with the USA, they conceded Poland's interests to the demands of the most recent, and their most powerful ally, the Soviet Union.

Naturally, one cannot deny that some sort of link exists between Nazi ideology and the ethnic conflicts surrounding the Jews in Central and Eastern Europe. In order to spin their hideous, pagan fantasies, the Nazis had first to draw on the existing body of German and especially Austrian anti-semitism, and on earlier conflicts between Jews and Christians, as well as on other hatreds born of the German nationalists' contempt for Germany's neighbours. On this score, one might only add that Nazi ideology did not consist merely of a monstrous, inflated version of anti-semitism. It was a theory of Master Racism, which was directed not only against the Jews but in different degrees against many other groups as well.[10] Nazi policies against the Poles, for example, were no less genocidal for the fact that they aimed to eliminate particular political and cultural classes rather than the Polish nation as a whole.

VII

> Although the goals of Nationalism have been achieved in Poland, and the Nationalities separated out into their respective homelands, a balanced view of history requires an equal appreciation of those individuals and movements who opposed Nationalism in all its forms, striving instead for the multinational harmony which was destined not to be.

It is one of the ironies of modern Polish history that the Nationalists' goal of an ethnically 'Polish Poland' was achieved not by Dmowski's right-wing National Democrats but by the allegedly left-wing Communists. Since 1945, in order to legitimise Poland's new territorial arrangements, the ruling Party has propagated an ideology where old-fashioned Polish

Nationalism has been mingled with 'revolutionary' Marxism-Leninism.[11] The whole post-war generation has been schooled in an ultra-nationalist, intellectual framework where the eternal Polish nation and the eternal Polish *macierz* (homeland) between the Oder and the Bug have been taken for granted. In such a system, an awareness of Poland's links with the various non-Polish peoples of Poland was not necessary. The memory of Poland's multinational heritage, when not actively suppressed, was ignored. Yet one of the features of the Polish 'Revolution' of 1980–1, when respect for the official ideology was cast to the winds, was the marked resurgence of interest in ethnic matters, including Polish-Jewish history. Since then, the authorities have not cared to reverse the trend and, as recent conferences have testified, Polish-Jewish studies have become a subject of widespread, and serious concern in Poland. Even more heartening to my mind is the newfound readiness of Polish scholars to re-examine some of the moral implications of Polish Nationalism and not to flinch before a discussion of even the most shameful episodes and attitudes. It is in this context, in my personal view, that the initiative of Professor Jan Błoński in *Tygodnik Powszechny* at the beginning of last year, must be most warmly applauded. Błoński's compatriots need not agree with every detail of his argument; but they must recognize the fine mixture of courage, modesty and self-criticism which raised the debate onto a higher plane. In my view, Błoński has set an example which all parties to the Polish-Jewish debate could profitably follow.[12]

On the Jewish side it is also clear that Zionism triumphed at the end of the war, and that in the last twenty years or so, the more nationalistic elements within Zionism have risen to prominence. (This in itself is an interesting parallel with the shift of political attitudes within independent Poland between the wars – a marked shift to the right occasioned by continuing tensions at home, and unresolved threats from abroad.) Certainly, the political atmosphere is bound to affect the conduct and direction of academic studies and debates, in the Diaspora no less than in Israel. In which case, one might conclude that in prevailing circumstances, if we are to understand the rich variety and achievements of pre-war Polish Jewry, there may be a special need to emphasize the non-Zionist and non-nationalist elements of the story and to explore in greater depth, and with greater sympathy, the aims and aspirations of those numerous Jews who were committed to life in Poland and who strove to improve the lot of all nationalities in the land of their birth. I am well aware that interventions of this sort may not meet with universal approval. Having myself made a minor foray in that direction, I know only too well that one can be rewarded with a nasty bout of earache.[13] But the outcry only convinces me all the more that the attempt is worth the making.

One positive aspect of the present situation, which enables us to take an optimistic stance in the wake of former tragedies, is the fact that Polish-

Jewish relations are very largely the concern of historians. For better or for worse, Poles and Jews no longer inhabit the same multinational society where their various aspirations were constantly interrupted by everyday fears and alarms. As a result, Polish and Jewish scholars, and rash interlopers like myself, have a real opportunity to study the past in relative tranquillity, and to recreate that international harmony of purpose which many people in former Poland longed for, but few enjoyed.

NOTES

1 See Bernard Johnpoll, *The Politics of Futility: the General Jewish Workers' Bund of Poland. 1917–43*, (Ithaca, 1967), p. 195.

2 One of the first reports to reach the west described the events in Lemberg as 'one of the worst pogroms in Polish history' *Manchester Guardian*, 30 Nov. 1918. Later, in 1919 in a series of articles written by Israel Cohen and entitled 'Pogroms in Poland', the *Times* followed the same line. See Israel Cohen, *Travels in Jewry* (London, 1952). Independent investigations by British and American missions, however, could not establish any clear conclusions. The British Embassy in Warsaw in particular thought that press reports had been inaccurate. In his covering letter to the Samuel Report in June 1920, Sir Horace Rumbold wrote: 'It is giving the Jews very little real assistance to single out . . . for reprobation and protest the country where they have perhaps suffered least.' Norman Davies, 'Great Britain and the Polish Jews. 1918–20', *Journal of Contemporary History* vol. 8, no. 2, 1973, pp. 119–42.

3 A persistent offender in this regard is Martin Gilbert, whose *Jewish History Atlas* (London, 1976), is one of the most popular introductions to the subject. Gilbert would argue no doubt that his atlas is limited by definition to the Jewish experience. But that does not save it from numerous misleading statements. For example, when, on his map of 'The Chmielnicki Massacres' (p. 530) he writes, '. . . his followers joined with the Polish peasants in attacking the Jews . . . Over 100,000 Jews were killed; many more were tortured or ill-treated; others fled . . .', the reader might easily get the erroneous impression that the Chmielnicki massacres were directed mainly, if not exclusively at the Jews. In fact, there were virtually no Polish peasants at that period in the areas marked on Gilbert's map, and the attacks on the Jews were but one part of the terrible vengeance wreaked by the Cossacks and their associates on everyone whom they regarded as the agents of feudal oppression. Similarly, on his map of 'The Jews of Austria-Hungary, 1867–1914' (p. 73), Gilbert marks a wide area of Galicia 'in which 5,000 Jews died each year through starvation, 1880–1914'. Again, the unsuspecting reader might be led to assume that the Jews of Galicia were the main or even the only victims of starvation. There is nothing in the text to indicate that the Polish and Ukrainian peasants of Galicia were starving in even larger numbers. Indeed, it was the desperate condition of the peasantry, on whom most of the Jews depended for their livelihood, which drove up to a quarter of the surviving population of the province to emigrate to the United States in those last two decades before the First World War.

4 Even Ezra Mendelsohn, whose brilliant article 'Interwar Poland: good or bad for the Jews?' avoids any direct equation between American racism and Polish anti-semitism, cannot entirely resist the analogy. 'Few, if any American intellectuals,' he claims, 'would deny that America was (and still is) an anti-black country. Possibly one reason why Polish scholars are reluctant to state that Poland was an anti-Jewish country is that they are accustomed to regard Poland as a victim and victims are

extremely reluctant to admit that they have victimised others. But such things are possible.' (In *The Jews in Poland*, ed. C. Abramsky *et al*, Oxford 1986, p. 138). To which, Amen. This is the heart of the matter. The study of Polish-Jewish relations is constantly bedevilled by the fact that both sides have had good reason to think of themselves as victims and underdogs. Both sides are reluctant to admit that they have victimised others; and it is only the exceptional scholar who can rise above the recriminations and admit that attitudes among his own people have sometimes been less than charitable. (See Note 12.)

5 See *Tydzień Polski*, (London) 6 September 1986, p. 6 and references.

6 Neal Ascherson, 'Peace Now and Israel's Nemesis', *The Observer* (London) 3 January 1988.

In their common opposition to Nationalism, both Polish and Jewish, the pre-war Bundists made no bones about what their opponents had in common. 'Zionism has become an ally of anti-semitism,' wrote Henryk Erlich in a polemic against the historian, Szymon Dubnow, in 1938. 'The worsening situation of the Jews throughout the world is exploited by the Zionists. The Zionists regard themselves as second-class citizens in Poland. Their aim is to be first-class citizens in Palestine, and to make the Arabs second-class citizens . . .' (Quoted by Antony Polonsky, 'The Bund in Polish Political Life, 1935–39', draft paper for the Jerusalem Conference, January 1988.) Fifty years later, Ehrlich's words sound almost uncannily prophetic.

7 On Dmowski's ambivalent attitude to Germany, see Norman Davies, *Heart of Europe: a Short History of Poland*, (Oxford, 1984), pp. 138–9. 'Although Dmowski would have been the last to admit it, his model for this ideal [Poland] derived from the earlier German nationalists of the Blut und Boden school, the original purveyors of the mystical link between 'the blood and the soil'. By the same token, one might fairly suspect Dmowski of subconsciously wishing Poland to resemble that powerful, prosperous, ethnically cohesive and reunited imperial Germany, which consciously, he so much feared and hated . . .'

8 For a summary of my views on the uses and abuses of the term 'anti-semitism', see 'Poles and Jews: an Exchange', in *New York Review of Books*, 9 April 1987.

9 When a Zionist delegation headed by Lewis Namier approached the Colonial Office in London in 1943 with a plea to admit Jewish children to Palestine, and 'to regard the Jews as an Allied people suffering more than any others at the hands of the oppressor,' a British official minuted: 'This is a major fallacy'. Martin Gilbert, *Auschwitz and the Allies*, (London, 1981), p. 98.

10 See, for example, Max Dimont, *Jews, God, and History*, (New York, 1978), p. 389. 'We must realise the fact that Nazism was not just anti-semitic, but anti-human. . . . If the Christian reader dismisses what happened in Germany as something which affected a few million Jews only, he . . . has betrayed his Christian heritage . . . And if the Jewish reader forgets the 7 million Christians murdered by the Nazis, then he has not merely let 5 million Jews die in vain but has betrayed his Jewish heritage of compassion and justice.'

11 On the post-war marriage of Polish Nationalism with Marxism- Leninism within the ideology of the ruling Party, see *Heart of Europe*, op cit. pp. 149–151; also *God's Playground*, op.cit., Vol.II, p. 551: 'The exclusive, intolerant approach to the problem of national identity, which among other things had distinguished the *PPR* and the *PZPR* from the pre- war *KPP*, marks the ultimate victory of the basic ideas of Dmowski's National Democracy.'

12 Jan Błoński, 'Biedni Polacy patrzą na Getto', *Tygodnik powszechny*, (Kraków), 11 January 1987.

13 Norman Davies, 'The Survivor's Voice', being a review of Hanna Krall, *Shielding the Flame: an Intimate Conversation with Marek Edelman, the Last Surviving Leader of the*

Warsaw Ghetto Uprising. (Translated by Joanna Stasińska and Lawrence Weschler. Preface by Timothy Garton Ash. New York, 1986), in *New York Review of Books*, 20 November 1986. This review, which expressed a positive view of Edelman, of the Bund, and of Hanna Krall's book, has inspired three lengthy, and less than positive responses: from Abraham Brumberg, in *New York Review of Books*, 9 April 1987; from Lucy S. Dawidowicz, 'The Curious Case of Marek Edelman', in *Commentary*, vol. 83, no. 3, March 1987; and from Jon Wiener, 'When Historians Judge Their Own', in *The Nation*, 21 November 1987. Each response has in turn provoked extensive correspondence, notably in the *New York Review of Books*, 9 April 1987; in *Commentary*, vol. 84, no. 2, August 1987; and in *The Nation* (5 March 1988).

16

SOME METHODOLOGICAL PROBLEMS OF THE STUDY OF JEWISH HISTORY IN POLAND BETWEEN THE TWO WORLD WARS*

Jerzy Tomaszewski

The growing public interest in the history of Polish Jews between the wars has been the reason for the publication of many books and articles. Some are based on only a superficial survey, others present a deep and penetrating analysis of specific problems. This body of literature deserves methodological consideration, together with a critical review of the most important sources, so that some queries, doubts and suggestions can be raised.

During at least the past hundred years, a tradition developed in some Jewish and Polish political circles of treating the Jews as a kind of alien body within Polish society. This attitude can also often be observed in contemporary historical studies, despite the authors' declared intentions. This can partly be explained in terms of the distant past, when Jews constituted a distinctly different class of people with its own legal status and institutions, but there is no reason to maintain such an approach when investigating the history of the twentieth century.

In every country, especially in Poland with its complex social and ethnic structure, different classes and groups (ethnic groups among them) have their specific interests. But there are also other interests, common to some or even all of these groups and classes. A good example of such an interest, common to almost all Polish citizens, was resistance against the Third Reich in September 1939. Even some Polish citizens of German origin volunteered to defend Warsaw against the *Wehrmacht*. If we consider the Polish Jews to be an important part of Polish society and not an alien body inside it, we must discuss those common as well as particular interests, having full regard for the differentiated structure of the Jewish population. In some cases those particular interests separated Jews from Poles, from Ukrainians, and from other groups. In other cases, there were common interests that united, for example, workers, shopkeepers, or other professional and social groups, regardless of their ethnic divisions. A good example of such an interest was the attitude of all commercial professional associations, irrespective of their ethnic character, to the tax reform introduced on the eve of World War II.

In most of the studies – and, it seems, in all studies concerning the inter-war period – historians present a pattern which can be termed 'Jews *contra* Poles' or 'Jews *contra* the Polish state', if we use the terminology of civil law. However, these words must not be considered as criticism of any particular writer.

Such an attitude can be understood – and excused – in the parliamentary speeches of Itzhak Grünbaum and other Jewish members of the Polish parliament. They defended Jewish interests and rights in the way they interpreted them. They analysed their situation in terms of an old question: what is good for the Jews? Such a standpoint is almost similar to the view mentioned above that regards the Jews as an alien body in Poland. Even then some politicians and writers did not agree with such an approach. A scholar today should be objective and avoid involving his personal feelings in past conflicts in an attempt to find more general criteria.

There is no doubt that in many cases the answer to the questions 'what was good for the Jews' and 'what was good for the society as a whole' will be the same. A good example is the issue of constitutional rights and the equality of all citizens irrespective of their nationality and religion. In other cases, however, the answers may differ, and it is often not easy to find them. An example is the problem of the compulsory Sunday rest day introduced by Polish law. It is true that this was a difficult dilemma for Jews: according to the law, workshops and factories had to be closed on Sunday, whereas according to God's commandment Sabbath was the day of rest. Jews faithful to their religion had to rest two days in a week while the Christians had only one day of rest. This situation had important economic consequences.

The contemporary historian cannot neglect another side of the problem. In a country with a very weak tradition of social legislation and (especially in the former Russian part of the Polish state) with a strong tradition of breaking the law, it was necessary to create a simple and obvious legal system. The solution proposed by some Jewish politicians – the freedom of choosing which day of the week, Saturday or Sunday, was to be the day of rest – could create a convenient excuse for a seven-day working week in many factories. We know of many cases when the workers, for fear of being fired, helped the entrepreneurs by concealing breaches of social legislation. In a country as poor as inter-war Poland, the workers fought mainly for their wages and rarely defended other social rights. Therefore most trade unions supported the compulsory Sunday rest day, which was relatively easy to control and defend, despite the fierce arguments of many Jewish politicians.

I do not intend to suggest which was the best solution to this problem. What is important here is that the question 'what was good for the Jews' cannot be the only approach to studying the history of Polish Jews.

The attitude 'Jews *contra* Poles' has some important consequences. When analysing past and present developments it leads to the assumption that ethnic groups must be irreconcilably alien or even hostile. Such an attitude is dangerous, for the same arguments may be used to defend the nationalist policy of the National Democrats directed against the Jews and other national minorities in Poland. If in any state there were different national groups with unavoidable hostile interests, then a constant fight against the 'aliens' would be inevitable. These 'alien' ethnic groups could be dangerous for the national interests of the majority. The arguments against such an ideology are not the subject of this paper. I can only state that in my opinion the theory of eternally alien ethnic groups cannot be maintained. It may lead towards permanent conflict between nations, fatal for the future of us all.

Let us return to the history of inter-war Poland. The attitude 'Jews *contra* Poles' and the theory of hostile ethnic groups can be used to support some aspects of the anti-Jewish policy of the Polish authorities. If there was such a rivalry or such a conflict, the Polish authorities – at least in some cases – would have to protect the Polish population against the Jewish associations and propertied classes. However, one should not discuss economic and political questions from the point of view of only one ethnic group in a state. There is no society or state which can – without fatal consequences – carry out a policy based on the interest of only one such group, even the most numerous one.

This is the reason why I have reservations about the title of the brilliant paper by Ezra Mendelsohn, presented in Oxford at the Conference on Polish-Jewish Relations in Modern History in September 1984: 'Inter-war Poland: good for the Jews or bad for the Jews?'[1] I understand that the author did not mean this proposition literally, but even in a somewhat hyperbolic sense there is some danger in it. After studying many documents and memoirs of Polish citizens I could suggest a topic for another paper: 'Inter-war Poland: good for the Poles or bad for the Poles?' Many people in Poland considered the 1930s the most tragic period in their lives (if we do not take into consideration the years 1939–45). In the memoirs of Polish peasants published before the war, we can find the view that conditions were better under Tsar Nicholas II. Some Polish workers who fought against the Germans in Silesia emigrated to Germany after 1929 in search of work. Many people in Galicia longed for the times of Emperor Franz Joseph. Poles, who in the past dreamed of an independent Polish state, then recalled with regret the 'good old days' of foreign rule!

It would be dangerous to draw too far-reaching conclusions from the facts mentioned above and from many other opinions found in the documents. Many factors – internal as well as international – caused the very difficult situation in the Polish Republic between the wars. In a hyperbolic sense we can risk claiming that the Republic 'was bad' for all its citizens. It created growing internal tension in various areas of life and affected the situation of national minorities, including Jews. These conditions were, I believe, the most important reason for the very difficult situation of the Polish Jews and its deterioration in the thirties. At the same time, in other spheres of life, the Republic 'was good' for them. Ezra Mendelsohn, I hope, will agree that legal equality for Jews was an important step forward.

I do not deny the existence and consequences of anti-semitism, but only as one kind of nationalism in Poland. A special kind, it is true, since it was a mixture of national, social and religious conflicts with the addition of some old prejudices and – in the thirties – an imitation of Nazi policy. However, the development of anti-semitism was affected by unsolved social and economic problems. An even more important question is how far anti-semitism influenced Jewish life and whether some of the unhappy changes were not perhaps a result of growing economic and international difficulties. The relative importance of particular factors cannot of course be estimated by any strict formula. However, it is often easy to trace the immediate effects of the anti-Jewish policy while there are no similar direct data that would permit an assessment of the influence of various hidden social trends unconnected with nationalism. For instance, it is very easy to study the organized settlement of Christian shopkeepers and artisans in the predominantly Jewish *shtetls* of the Eastern provinces. It is much more difficult – if at all possible – to study the general worsening conditions of trade and the effects of migration from villages to towns. Some data seem to indicate that this latter problem was of prime importance and the famous settlement movement only a noisy political affair.

An old definition of what makes front-page news is: dog bites man is not worth mentioning; the real news is when man bites dog. Something similar can be observed in archives. The documents describe conflicts, special cases when the administration had to intervene, or trade-union activity that was undesirable from the government point of view. In most cases, everyday life does not interest the administration. Events that cause no trouble are not recorded. Thousands of men returning quietly to their homes go unnoticed, but a single drunkard can be registered in police records, newspapers and diaries. This is why we can find documents recording every anti-Jewish riot, but the many more cases of peaceful Polish-Jewish coexistence left no documents in the government files.

This is true not only for the history of Polish-Jewish relations. Polish archives are full of documents describing the fate of Polish emigrants, mainly workers, in Germany. In most cases they concern maltreatment and abuses, wage cuts, discrimination etc. This does not mean that the story of the Polish emigration to Germany was composed only of such facts. The Polish emigrant who was satisfied with his work and wages did not inform the Consulate about it. The worker looked for help when he suffered maltreatment; he then asked the Polish representative to intervene and the document is now there for the contemporary scholar to find.

The same happened with Polish citizens of Jewish origin living in Germany. When they led a normal life, earning money without suffering any special discrimination, they had few reasons to contact the Polish Consulate. It was necessary only on rare occasions. Young people had to perform their military service; sometimes there were problems connected with commercial affairs; Jews sometimes attended official ceremonies organized on Polish state holidays; some associations of Polish Jews maintained – from time to time – contact with Polish officials. Only a few documents inform us of these facts. But Polish citizens asked for help when they faced discrimination. Therefore the files of the Polish Consulates, the Embassy and the Ministry of Foreign Affairs contain many documents concerning the life of Polish Jews in Germany after 1933. Polish Consulates tried to protect Polish citizens against Nazi policies, settled various personal affairs, and presented reports to the Polish Ministry of Foreign Affairs.

A similar situation appeared in many other cases. Every historian has to remember that the documents reveal only part of what happened in the past. Many problems, important for the study of history, left no documentary record. A study of archives and newspapers can therefore provide a distorted picture. One can write about conflicts relatively easily, whereas normal everyday life can pass unnoticed. This is one of the main reasons why Frank Golczewski, leaning as he does primarily on the press, has described the history of Polish-Jewish relations as only a history of anti-semitism.[2] A complete and vivid picture of past events can only be revealed after finding a way to fill the gap in the archival records. It is by no means an easy task.

Similar difficulties arise when studying the economic activity of the Jewish population in Poland. A significant number of Jews was employed in small enterprises: shops, artisans' workshops, small factories. The average shopkeeper or artisan did not leave any documents connected with his work. It is possible to find – more or less easily – documents concerning big industrial companies. They were obliged to present reports for the shareholders; they maintained business relations with banks, which required certain documents; they were in contact with the administration; they were obliged to keep regular accounting books. The average shopkeeper or artisan did not need to do this. They paid taxes according to basic principles. They did not have contact with big banks. The state authorities were interested in a particular shopkeeper only when there was something wrong: when he acted against the law, when he was a victim of some crime. All these cases are exceptions in everyday life. Of course, the same can be said about the broad social stratum of the petite bourgeoisie irrespective of its ethnic structure. The historian does not have enough sources at his disposal to study this social group.

There are some exceptions. First of all, there were important professional journals published by some associations of artisans or tradesmen. Secondly, the scholar can use political documents, such as shorthand records and other parliamentary materials. But all these sources are defective in some respects since they present only one side of events.

Quarrels concerning taxes are a good example of this problem. I have never met a taxpayer who was glad to pay tax. I have not heard of a taxpayer who did not try to gain some allowances or reductions or shift his financial burden onto other social groups. Therefore the professional journals of tradesmen – irrespective of their religion or nationality – were full of protests against taxes, and recorded the arbitrary and cruel demands of the financial authorities, arguing that commerce and industry were discriminated against compared with agriculture. At the same time, peasants maintained that agriculture was overburdened with taxes and that the interest of the national economy required the tax system to be altered in their favour.

Most historians take all these arguments at their face value. Those who are interested in the history of agriculture argue that there was discrimination against this branch of the Polish economy. Others, interested in the history of Polish Jews, maintain that artisans and shopkeepers were overburdened with taxes and that agriculture was in a much better situation. Some of them even formulate the opinion that this resulted from the anti-Jewish policy of all Polish cabinets. Even so distinguished and experienced a scholar as Isaiah Trunk was misled, and considered the tax system to be a symptom of Polish anti-semitism.[3]

It is impossible to resolve this problem if one considers only one particular branch of the Polish economy. The documents I have seen cannot prove any nationally-biased tax policy. There is no evidence that the taxes were constructed to reflect the national structure of people employed in agriculture, commerce or industry. Only at the end of the Second Republic were there plans to introduce some kind of national discrimination in the official taxation policy of the state. They were not realized.

Quite another problem was the activity of local administration. In the general framework of the legal system there was some possibility of hidden discrimination against certain groups of people. Scattered and rare data inform us of economic discrimination against Jewish professionals in some towns. Was it a general trend in the country? Were they only local abuses? I am afraid that it is not now possible to answer this question.

Besides, there is one more problem. Some data indicate that local administrations were corrupt in some cases and that the privileges or discrimination they exercised depended on the money (or other bribe) offered by interested businessmen. People who offered more bribes were treated better. I cannot formulate any hypothesis as to how often such cases occurred and if they were connected with ethnic discrimination.

Sometimes our most important, or even our only available source, is the press or parliamentary documents such as speeches and questions by Jewish members of parliament. Such documents are very difficult to analyse. Anyone involved in journalism can understand that the possibilities for research are limited. This is the case even with contemporary magazines that have archives within reach and plenty of money for financing investigations. The newspapers of inter-war Poland, especially those opposed to the government, often had no possibility of verifying the news obtained from a local correspondent. The speed needed to prepare a daily paper did not permit them to take care over details.

The same was true of parliamentary documents. Members of parliament had no staff to investigate particular cases. They used information received from their electors which was sometimes biased and sometimes distorted because of incomplete knowledge of the facts. On the other hand, there were certain independent sources of information available to members of parliament and to Jewish journalists and these could often offer much more complete data than official documents.

All these sources deserve careful and critical analysis. Sometimes it is possible to compare them with other documents and formulate certain conclusions. More often there are no other, more reliable materials. Thus the scholar studying the past can often be trapped in the old conflicts without the possibility of finding a clue to them. This is the case, I think, with some parts of the valuable book written by Frank Golczewski. Having no access to documents he based his account mainly on press reports and similar material. A comparison of some cases with the documents reveals the inadequacies of his book and shows the truth was more complicated. The merits of his work lie in that he has gathered a vast amount of material and formulated tentative conclusions; it is now necessary to continue his studies and present a more complex picture of events.

The dangers of depending on press reports are clearly revealed in Ezra Mendelsohn's book on the beginnings of Zionism in Poland (*Zionism in Poland: The Formative Years 1915–1926*, New Haven, Connecticut 1982). Discussing the problems associated with the fourth *aliyah* and the return of some emigrants to Poland, he quotes Jewish journalists and the opinions of some of the people who went to Palestine or returned. Those who returned presented an exaggerated view of the difficulties they met in Palestine and the economic crisis in that country. The author justly expresses his doubts as to the accuracy of these views. It can be added that some exaggeration was inevitable. The returning Jews wanted to find an explanation for their failure in Palestine, at least for themselves if not for their relatives and friends. The only argument was that conditions in Palestine were much worse than was believed in Poland, and that this was the reason for their failure.

Ezra Mendelsohn takes similar views about the situation in Poland at their face value. An analysis of the general economic conditions in Poland does not confirm all these theses. The crisis associated with the policy of stabilization was not so deep as it was presented in the press or in the opinions of emigrants. The real significance of the fourth *aliyah* was rather limited, at least from the point of view of the Jews living in Poland. It is true that in the years 1924–5 the number of Jews going to Palestine increased, reaching nearly 15,000 in 1925. Compared with about three million Jews living in Poland, the fourth *aliyah* was of very little importance. The contrary appeared to be the case from the point of view of the Jewish settlement in Palestine. At that time there were about 120,000 Jews in this country, and even ten thousand immigrants were important. The Palestinian Jewish press therefore presented the fourth *aliyah* as a significant step forward and emphasized the difficult conditions in Poland. This was an exaggeration that can be understood easily, but the contemporary scholar has to be very cautious about such opinions.

Ezra Mendelsohn justly records the rapid shifts of opinion presented in the Jewish newspapers. There were certainly important reasons, some of them psychological, for such changes. This, however, is an additional argument supporting my thesis that information presented in newspapers must be analysed critically because of possible over or understatement.

Some misunderstandings are involved with special features of other sources. Moreover, some historians either do not know, or choose to neglect, the documents about other problems besides the fate of the Jews.

No serious scholar can deny that some serious and tragic events occurred at the beginnings of Polish independence, deeply influencing Jewish society in Poland. The riots in Galicia and the cruelty of some of the troops are generally known. In many cases these facts are presented as a result of widespread anti-semitism in Poland. Such an opinion is based mainly on the data presented in the Jewish newspapers published in those years and on the reports of Jewish politicians sent abroad from Poland. It is obvious that the Jewish press and the Jewish politicians were mainly interested in the fate of Jews in Poland. They had justly demanded that the Polish government stop these crimes and punish the offenders. They considered the crimes to be directed almost exclusively against Jews.

A critical survey of documents gives a somewhat more complicated picture. In many cases, anti-Jewish riots were connected with strong social conflicts. The Galician agricultural regions were seriously damaged during the war and the peasant population lived under very poor conditions. There was a traditional conflict between the village and the town, existing from medieval times. The traditional image of economic life presented the idea that peasant labour was the only or the main source of new values and goods. A merchant could create no value; he bought cheap corn or cattle from the peasant and sold them at a much higher price. The townspeople, especially shopkeepers, were regarded as living at the expense of peasants.

One should also remember that, in the difficult time between war and peace, profiteering was widespread (for example, hiding the most essential goods in order to obtain a higher price in the future). Most peasants were Poles or Ukrainians, whereas shopkeepers were Jews. The social conflict changed into a national or religious one. This was not the first or the last occasion when social animosities and economic differences were to emerge as religious or national clashes.

There were some reports of atrocities by troops, and documents of the Polish military authorities confirm them; discrepancies occurring in particular cases do not change the general picture. It should be added, however, that other reports – those of no interest to the Jewish journalists and politicians – give evidence of similar atrocities or robberies against non-Jewish populations in the same regions. The war allowed the dark side of the human character to come to the fore. In many cases, soldiers used force against civilian populations unable to defend themselves. An old barrack-room joke – I do not know of which army – defines the 'right' pecking order: the first and the most important person is Colonel Sir, the next Mr. Corporal, the next Colonel Sir's mare, next there is nothing, next a common soldier, next there is nothing, and once again nothing, and many many times nothing, and at the end there is the lousy civilian.

The Jews frequently belonged to the most obvious group of victims because of their different clothes, traditions and language. They were by no means the only victims. The unhappy fate of the civilian population in some regions of Poland in the years 1918–21 cannot be treated as only a new chapter of anti-semitism. The problem is much more complicated. In this connection the memoirs of Jean Paul Sartre may be mentioned: he describes the unholy behaviour of the French soldiers in 1940 in the French provinces on the German border where there were no Jews.

Some hypotheses can be based on data concerning criminal offences in Poland. In 1937, from every 10,000 Roman Catholics, 113 persons were convicted; from every 10,000 Jews, 72 persons. There is no reason to think that the police or courts were more tolerant towards Jews. In addition, there were significant differences between the two groups over the kind of criminal offences. Among the Roman Catholics, 8.3 per cent were convicted for crimes of violence, 35.1 per cent for theft, 0.5 per cent for robbery, 3.1 per cent for offences connected with commercial or financial affairs. Among the Jews, the corresponding figures were: 2.1 per cent for crimes of violence, 11.8 per cent for theft, 0.1 per cent for robbery and

7.1 per cent for commercial offences. Thus Jews appear to have committed crimes involving the use of force much more rarely than Roman Catholics. On the other hand, the Jews were convicted more frequently for crimes of a more peaceful character. It is generally accepted that the traditional culture of the Jewish people was a peaceful one, and this was reflected in the kind of criminal offences. The traditional culture of the Polish people was more militant, and this could also be seen in the criminal offences.

These differences could be observed in many other fields. Polish literature contains important works of great artistic value connected with war or other kinds of aggression. Jewish literature does not typically possess novels, poems or short stories of this kind. When war is mentioned, it is usually from the point of view of a civilian victim. Similarly, many of the best Jewish writers were interested in the peaceful life of the small town. The traditional Jewish education of a child or young man emphasized the study of *Torah*; that of a Polish nobleman was associated with horsemanship and military training. We can find similar kinds of aggression in the traditional games played by Polish children irrespective of their social origin.

These important differences had their effects on Polish-Jewish relations. There are certain kinds of people who are the most likely victims of various offences. In general, people of a peaceful nature, who are unprepared, inexperienced in defending themselves by force, and lacking physical training, can be easily attacked by men with aggressive backgrounds. The Jewish shopkeeper was a very easy victim of aggression; the Jewish smith or porter was not. As we know, there were many more Jewish shopkeepers than there were smiths or porters.

In many cases, Polish-Jewish conflicts resulted from differences in their traditional culture and character. The primitive and malicious jokes made by village youngsters could not be treated as something unimportant by the peaceful Jewish townsmen. This added to the mutual tension induced by other, often more serious, problems.

Certain important questions were associated with the impact of ethnic and religious differences upon conflicts of quite another character. If people live closely together, differences inevitably occur on many issues. Sometimes it is trespassing on a neighbour's territory, sometimes there are hens destroying a neighbour's garden, sometimes more serious disputes involve curses or even a tussle. When such a conflict develops between people of the same language, religion and origin, it has no far-reaching consequences. However, when the antagonists belong to different groups (for example, if they live in different villages) the quarrel may be much more serious and may involve the revival of old prejudices or cause new ones: 'they' are always treacherous and God-forsaken. When the difference is much more serious, connected with religion, language and ethnic differences, the quarrel turns into one more case of a general conflict between two nations or two beliefs.

This could easily be observed in the case of the Czech-Polish conflict in the Cieszyn area. In about 1934 the Polish Consulate in Moravská Ostrava produced periodic reports entitled 'Chronicle of discrimination against the Polish people'. These reports included cases of political and economic pressure exerted on the Polish minority in the Czech lands. Much more frequently, however, they were focused on local conflicts of a traditional kind. A fight in a pub between a Czech worker and his Polish comrade became a case in the 'Chronicle'. No doubt, in an atmosphere full of tension between Czechs and Poles, ordinary drunken quarrels were transformed into national conflicts. It would be absolutely mistaken to take such reports at their face value and to consider them all as evidence of an old Polish-Czech conflict over the border that divides Silesia.

Taking into consideration the important differences between Poles and Jews over religion, language, traditional culture, and often their social and economic position, I am sure that in many cases personal quarrels and conflicts could develop into much more important disputes involving many others. This was especially likely when some organized group was interested in the development of a conflict. The documents relating to particular anti-Jewish riots in the thirties often indicate that they began as purely personal incidents. A Jewish thief who had wounded a Polish policeman, or a Jewish apprentice who had beaten his Polish comrade, was used by the Polish radical nationalists: a Jew had killed a Pole! At other times it was the Pole who had caused the trouble and wanted to beat a Jew who later became the victim of a fight. This was the case with a student, Stanisław Wacławski, who was killed in Wilno in an anti-Jewish riot. Wacławski became a kind of martyr for the radical nationalists, who organized a so-called 'Wacławski festival' at the beginning of each academic year, which took the form of anti-Jewish riots and propaganda.

Bearing in mind all the possible causes and consequences of local and personal conflicts it would be improper to consider them as a manifestation of nationalism, including anti-semitism. The problems were much more complicated. The newspapers published in this period discussed all such cases simply as evidence of the eternal antagonism between two nations. This was especially true of the Polish radical national press. It was also the case, and I can well understand the reason, with many Jewish journals. The contemporary scholar ought anyway to be much more careful in his conclusions.

The last problem dealt with here includes relations established between Jews and Poles in the Second Republic, especially in the economic sphere. The history of every national minority can be studied and presented separately from the evolution of the majority of the population. This is the case, for example, with the history of the Poles in Germany in the nineteenth century. At the same time, one should, however, remember the fact, a substantial one for the understanding of the development of the society under investigation, that their two histories cannot be fully independent. The Poles in the Prussian part of Poland were to some extent an independent society under German rule. In the Polish lands a full social and professional structure developed, together with a system relatively independent of Polish institutions. However, this society was under German law, and German administration had a strong influence on its life. Therefore the independence of Polish life was limited. The Polish minority groups living in Berlin or in West Germany did not enjoy even such relative independence. Poles were dispersed among Germans and their situation was strictly related to the situation of their German neighbours.

The connections between Jews and Poles in the Second Republic were even stronger. The important differences in the social and economic structure of the two societies resulted in their mutual dependence. Jewish merchants traded in goods produced by Polish, Ukrainian and other workers and peasants. Polish peasants and other producers sold their goods to Jewish tradesmen and bought other products from them. Many Poles used the services of Jewish tailors (most tailors in Poland were Jews) or shoemakers. The sudden removal of the Jews from Poland could produce immense economic difficulties. On the other hand, the Jews were dependent on their Polish suppliers and buyers. In the economic sphere the two societies were inseparable.

Mutual dependence in other fields was not so strong. The Jews – being a minority – felt this dependence much more strongly than the Poles, especially in political life. At the same time, however, the Polish political parties and the government could not disregard Jewish feelings and strivings. Therefore it is necessary to investigate not only Jewish life in Poland but its connections with Polish society. This cannot be simplified and treated only as a problem of government policy and anti-semitism.

The merit of Ezra Mendelsohn's book, *Zionism in Poland*, is that the author perceives these problems and tries to analyse Jewish political life in Poland in relation to the general problems of Polish history. Even here, and in the best other studies of the history of Polish Jews, there are some misunderstandings caused by inconsistent treatment of these questions. On the other hand, Polish studies that neglect Jewish history cannot explain all aspects of political and economic life in Poland.

The conflicts of the past have induced passionate accusations on the part of Poles and Jews and no less passionate defence. On occasion, it seems, the man who bit a dog became famous while all other men and dogs were forgotten. The task of the contemporary scholar is to try to explain situations where the past has left only conjective, mutual accusations, or nothing at all. There is a need for a thorough and critical investigation based on a variety of sources. There is a need to find new sources or to explain the real meaning of known documents. It is necessary to explain different sides of reality and understand the reasons for events.

I do not propose studying history without emotion and with indifference. This would be disrespectful to the human tragedies, strivings, hopes, achievements and disappointments of the past. The historian's emotions, however, should not cloud his thought or impair his critical faculties.

NOTES

1 Published in ed. C. Abramsky, M. Jachimczyk, A. Polonsky, *The Jews in Poland* (Oxford, 1986).

2 Frank Golczewski, *Polnisch-jüdische Beziehungen 1881–1922. Eine Studie zur Geschichte des Antisemitismus in Osteuropa* (Wiesbaden, 1981).

3 I. Trunk, 'Economic Anti-semitism in Poland between the Two World Wars' (in Yiddish), in *Studies on Polish Jewry 1919–1939. The Interplay of Social, Economic and Political Factors in the struggle of a Minority for its Existence*. Edited by J. A. Fuhman (New York, 1974).

* This paper was presented in 1985 during the International Congress of Judaica Studies in Jerusalem.

17

LUCIEN WOLF AND THE MAKING OF POLAND: PARIS, 1919

Eugene C. Black

Organized Jewry brought competing formulations to the Paris Peace Conference of 1919. The Balfour Declaration of November 1917, the disintegration of the old multi-national empires, and the emergence of competing East European and Middle Eastern ethnic nationalism inspired Zionists to make particularly extensive claims. Confident of their friends in high places, especially in the American and British delegations, they pressed their cases with enthusiasm, vigour, and tactlessness. Western Jewish assimilationists, particularly British and French, worked tirelessly and patiently to defuse the Jewish Nationalism, to contain it, and, insofar as possible, to substitute the assumptions upon which Franco- and Anglo-Jewish elites had framed their diplomatic programs for almost half a century as the 'Jewish *desiderata*' for the Peace Conference. For Zionists and Jewish Nationalists such an agenda was worthless; anti-Semitism was ingrained in Western culture and Christian habit, and inescapable in European politics. Jews could never assimilate and remain Jews.

Western acculturated Jews – the self-styled 'moderates' – accepted the assumptions of liberal civilization. While the process might be uneven, moving in fits and starts with occasional regressions, Jews were part of Western culture. The diaspora was a fact of life. 'Next year in Jerusalem' was a spiritual aspiration, not a social reality. Education and economic progress would ultimately produce harmonious societies in which Jews could realize themselves within enlightened national cultures while preserving their Jewish identity and religion. Harmonious, well-defined Jewish subcultures had evolved and could thrive in the liberal west. Since all mankind would ultimately see that its best interests lay in the creation of socially harmonious and peaceful national cultures modelled upon that of Western Europe, history was on the side of assimilation and acculturation.

Enlightenment, liberalism, economic development, and social opportunity had not yet, 'moderates' conceded, come to all of the European world. But come they would, and once Eastern Europe provided the same economic, social, and political scope that the West already did, Jews would be contented, effective participants in their various national states. Western Jews even sought to expedite the process. Baron de Hirsch spent millions and offered more in an attempt to create opportunities, not merely for Jewish immigrants in new worlds, but for Jews remaining in Russia. Anglo-French Jewry, proud of the world it had shaped for itself, saw that carefully honed and cultivated image threatened by the intrusion of poor aliens. British and French Jewish leaders adopted two strategies to deal with the problem. On the one hand, they processed as many migrants as possible onwards to new worlds as far removed from their own as possible. They worked assiduously at the same time to educate and socialize those who remained on their hands, teaching them western languages, assumptions, and values. On the other hand, Western Jewish establishments also worked in tandem with each other through diplomatic channels in an effort to bring pressure through their own governments, particularly on Russia and Romania, to secure political and social conditions in Eastern Europe which would help to stem the immigrant tide.

Leading western Jews actively promoted such views and policies within the Jewish community and in the nations of which they were a part by the middle of the nineteenth century. Adolphe Crémieux (1796–1880), by virtue of his ministerial service in French governments and his leading role in the *Alliance Israélite Universelle*, established intimate connections between and *Alliance* and the Quai d'Orsay that continued into the twentieth century. The relationship proved mutually beneficial. Jewish interests received a hearing, if not accommodation, in French foreign affairs. The *Alliance*, by virtue of its school system scattered through the Ottoman Empire and North Africa, could serve as a potential stalking-horse for French cultural imperialism.[1]

For Anglo-Jewry, a small group handled diplomatic initiatives with the Foreign Office. The Conjoint Foreign Committee consisted of equal representation from the Board of Deputies of British Jews, the recognized representative body of British Jewry, and the Anglo-Jewish Association, which originated as a part of the *Alliance Israélite Universelle*. The AJA, ironically, achieved its august status by being the body through which Reform Jewish leaders could participate in communal leadership, since Chief Rabbi Dr. Adler stood foursquare for Orthodoxy as he understood and defined it. Montefiores and Goldsmids, however, could scarcely be excluded from the great panoply of Jewish leadership: thus the special importance of the AJA.[2] The Conjoint Foreign Committee preserved a delicate and decorous balance. The presidents of the Board of Deputies and AJA chaired alternate meetings. The Conjoint Foreign Committee reported back to and took 'instructions' from the two parent bodies. The Committee, however, by virtue of existing and being the medium through which most transactions went to the Foreign Office, achieved an importance and independence recognized by permanent officials, even by ministers themselves.

The Damascus Affair of 1840 and the Mortara case in 1858 had brought home to Western Jewry the need to create institutions to speak for their international interests, and the formation of the *Alliance* in 1860 established matters on a formal institutionalized basis. From their early days, the *Alliance* and AJA worked directly with foreign governments and through British and French diplomatic channels to secure full civic and religious freedom for Jews everywhere in East European and the evolving new Balkan states.[3] Adolphe Crémieux, president of the Alliance from 1863 to 1880, established that organization's forward position in foreign affairs. Never would the AIU play a more activist role in foreign affairs than it did during the Congress of Berlin in 1878.

Regular, organized Jewish activism in foreign affairs dates from that Congress. Having exerted themselves, particularly with Quai d'Orsay support, to secure civil and religious rights for Jews in Romania, Anglo-French Jews witnessed the systematic violation of those guarantees. They discovered, to their horror, that neither Britain, France, Germany, nor Austro-Hungary had any intention of enforcing such clauses so long as Russia remained hostile. Worse soon proved to be in store. Beyond the obvious diplomatic quandaries of the Bismarckian world, Anglo-French Jewry confronted an Eastern Europe appearing to go mad on the subject of Jews. The uncomfortably large number of Russo-Jewish immigrants moving westward in search of economic opportunity and cultural freedom exploded in the early 1880s as official and unofficial pogroms spawned panic flight. Both British and French Jewish leaders laboured assiduously, if unsuccessfully, to convince the Foreign Office and *Ministère des Affaires Étrangères* to intervene on behalf of persecuted Russian Jews.[4] Most organized Jewish international activity revolved around processing unprecedented numbers of human beings on the move, preferably to any country but their own. The British government, given its ostensible influence in Constantinople, suffered a Conjoint Foreign Committee barrage of Jewish Memorials and petitions from as far afield as Morocco and Persia, as well as a flood of grievances concerning Jewish refugees and settlers in Palestine.[5] After the death of Crémieux in 1880 and the problems of the Dreyfus case, the *Alliance* increasingly concentrated on educational, relief, civil rights, and anti-defamation work. The Conjoint Foreign Committee, although it often worked through the French, came increasingly to take the lead in matters of foreign policy.[6]

The Conjoint Foreign Committee saw Russian anti-Semitic policies at the heart of Jewish international problems. Romania's cynical violation of Jewish treaty rights infuriated Anglo-Jewry, but success in Romania still depended upon solving 'the Russian problem'.[7] No efforts were spared, but *Realpolitik* stood in the way. The French government, for which national security was wrapped up in its Russian alliance, was understandably cool to Jewish grievances. King Edward VII of England, who numbered Jews among his personal friends, attempted a personal intervention and actually chided his cousin, Tsar Nicholas II, for his anti-Semitic policies. Nothing changed, save possibly for the worse. And so the problem festered.

Before the outbreak of the first world war, Lucien Wolf (1857–1930) had become the secretary of the Conjoint Foreign Committee. Wolf, a journalist of consequence well connected with the Reuters News Agency, a scholar and distinguished historian, had his battle-scars of diplomatic experience. He edited *Darkest Russia*, a periodical that pilloried Imperial Russian abuse of Jews before the British public. The network of informants this nearly-blind diplomat developed, the clipping, translating services he arranged, his superb contacts in the Foreign Office, and the skill that he had already demonstrated, made him a central figure in the diplomacy of Anglo-Jewry. Although of relatively modest origins, he had moulded himself to and become a representative of the Jewish 'establishment'. An Anglo-Jew from hat to bootlaces, he shared the assumptions and values of the Jewish establishment. He enjoyed the confidence of those who mattered, particularly Claude J. Montefiore, president of the Anglo-Jewish Association, and David L. Alexander, president of the Board of Deputies. Through the intimate relations he developed through the war, particularly by early 1915, with Jacques Bigart, secretary of the *Alliance* Israélite, he also came to play a crucial role in Franco-Jewish diplomacy.

Both the *Alliance* and Conjoint Committee spent the first months of the war dealing with issues the war brought to the fore. Organized Jewry divided, flocking to their particular colours, demonstrating above all whether in London or Berlin, in Paris or Vienna, that they were English or German patriots, French or Austro-Hungarian. The cooperative network that had processed East European Jewish immigrants and refugees suddenly collapsed. Suddenly Jewish internees and prisoners of war demanded attention. Philanthropy and relief demanded reconstruction in the light of totally new circumstances.

Anglo-Jewry, perhaps because its international operating network had been less disrupted, also began to contemplate the ways in which the war might be turned to diplomatic good account for East European Jews. Poland brought the Alliance and Conjoint Committee to act together in concerted policies. While Anglo-Jewry contemplated ways in which pressure might be placed upon Russia to ease its anti-Semitic policies and give Jews at least the same rights and privileges accorded other 'subject' peoples within the Empire, Yehiel Tschlenow and Nahum Sokolow appeared with news of Russian outrages against Jews in wartime Poland. Anglo-Jewry took these matters in stride (or, because of its alliance with

Russia, felt compelled to downplay the news) and paid little heed to the Zionist appeal that accompanied the tidings. Zionism, while enjoying popularity among some Jewish professionals and intellectuals, had not yet gained the broad support it would soon develop in the East End. Zionism remained anathema to most Anglo-Jewish leaders, as they saw it as antithetical to all that had been achieved during the previous century. Herbert Samuel had just been rebuffed in his first attempt to fly that flag before the British Cabinet, and Chaim Weizmann had not yet seized effective leadership of the extra-parliamentary Zionist campaign.[8]

When Tschlenow and Sokolow flew their atrocities and Zionism flags in Paris in February 1915, however, Jacques Bigart, the long-time secretary and chief administrative officer of the *Alliance Israélite Universelle*, sprang into action. While Bigart understood that the *Alliance* could never take an overtly anti-Zionist policy for a variety of prudential reasons, he believed that Zionist principles, if ever ascendent, would wreak havoc for Jews in Western Europe. Bigart pleaded for Anglo-Jewry, with its avowed anti-Zionist stance, to assume the leadership in developing and executing policies that would secure true Jewish interests as Anglo-French Jewish leaders understood them and resist this Zionist threat. From February 1915 to the Paris Peace Conference and beyond, the *Alliance Israélite* and Conjoint Foreign Committee (reconstituted in 1918 as the Joint Foreign Committee) worked hand-in-hand on all matters of foreign policy.[9]

That policy, however, contained little that was new. Locked as they were into the liberal assumptions of the past half century, Anglo-French Jewry had few options. They hoped that the circumstances of war would enable them, particularly as the Western Allies became increasingly dependent upon American aid, to persuade their governments to press the Russian government to end Jewish disabilities. Anglo-French Jewry appealed to Russian self-interest as best they could with a mixture of inducements and implied threats.[10] Jewish 'demands' were modest enough. While the details varied from one proposal to another, Western Jewry asked the Russians to end restrictions upon Jewish settlement and education, and to abolish invidious religious discrimination in matters of passports and visas. Efforts to move either the British or French governments proved unavailing. Neither government was prepared to risk the Russian ill will that such pressure would engender. Private negotiations with Russian officials were no more successful. Russian behaviour, in fact, aggravated rather than eased the problem. The war in Eastern Europe, while stalemated as was that in the West, had a fluid battlefront which flowed back and forth through Galicia and the traditional Jewish Pale of Settlement. Russian generals regarded Jews as security risks, charged some with spying for the Germans or Austrians, and even developed a plan for substantial deportations to the Don basin.[11] While Grand Duke Nicholas sought to scapegoat Jews for his own military incompetence, Germans 'liberated' Polish Jews, just as they were later to do in Romania, by granting enough concessions to win Jewish favour while retaining Jewish dependency. Germans never, for instance, granted liberties to Jews that compromised their ability later to play to Polish nationalist sentiment.

Lucien Wolf found that, first, Sir Edward Grey, then Arthur Balfour, as Foreign Ministers resisted pressure to remonstrate about Russian abuses on the grounds that they could not interfere in the domestic affairs of an ally. The more Wolf and the 'moderates' pushed their case, the more irritated the British government became. They could do nothing, and Anglo-Jewry should understand that. Their good offices, while they might help after the war, had availed nothing before 1914. Lord Robert Cecil, the British Coalition Government Undersecretary for Foreign Affairs, charged, among other things, with Eastern European affairs, contended that the Jews in Britain and the United States were constructing their political position on 'the Russian difficulty'.[12] Cecil's observation reflected British and French fears about American politics. Both governments depended upon continued American support to prosecute their war effort. Both recognized the delicate balance in American politics. Both overreacted to anything that might appear to threaten the stream of financial and material aid. American Jews were overwhelmingly anti-Russian, and the German background of much of the American Jewish élite could be and was represented as dangerous. Both the British and French governments attempted to recruit Jewish support at home to play a missionary role for the allied cause in the United States. Since neither government was in a position to make the Russians 'behave', other options, particularly Zionism, became attractive cards to play. The French, who thought that Allied agreements meant the ultimate creation of a French-dominated greater Syria, dispatched a Zionist on a Quai d'Orsay sponsored lecture tour in 1915, while simultaneously bringing assimilationist Jews into a special propaganda bureau under Foreign Ministry and Chamber of Deputies sponsorship.[13] Lucien Wolf and Lord Robert Cecil had private discussions to the same purpose, but Wolf took a much stronger line than his French colleagues about limiting Palestinian commitments. Wolf understood that American Jewish leadership was more divided than Anglo-Jewry on the subject of Zionism. Something must be offered American Zionist as well as anti-Zionist opinion were a propaganda campaign to succeed. Wolf suggested a declaration for unrestricted settlement, equal rights, and a degree of Jewish communal autonomy. Knowing that the Zionists had established contacts with the British and French governments, he also hoped such a program would meet the political needs of the moment and preempt the Zionist position.[14]

What Wolf did not appreciate was that his government would see in Zionism the least difficult concession it could make to Jewish opinion. A half century of Anglo-Jewish pressure backfired. Equal rights for Jews in

Russia were clearly unattainable. Even if some half measures were secured, they would not satisfy the 'moderates' and would be meaningless to the growing and vociferous number of Zionists. Anglo-Jewish support was scarcely at risk for the British government. A Zionist policy might annoy the assimilated, but they had no place else to go. A Zionist statement would counter any German gains in East European, American, or neutral Jewish opinion. Both the British and French had private ambitions in the Middle East with which Zionism did not appear, at that time, to be incompatible. Zionism could be, as it was, an indirect way of pushing British claims in a region where British imperial interests collided with French. Some British statesmen believed in the cause. Herbert Samuel certainly did. Arthur Balfour possibly did. David Lloyd George assumed most positions at least once in his life. Sir Mark Sykes definitely came to believe in Zionism as well as other more grandiose and less achievable Middle Eastern goals. The Quai d'Orsay, not suprisingly, did much the same analysis with hopes that an early commitment to Zionism might benefit French Middle Eastern ambitions. Endorsing Zionism was the grand gesture the Western Allies could make to Jews without apparent cost, and, ultimately, in the British case, some benefit to themselves.

The French and British governments moved further into the Zionist orbit, pressing on even after Wilson's reelection. The February Revolution of 1917 with its dramatic promulgation of full Jewish equality did nothing to stem the Zionist momentum. Now the Allies sought any means to keep Russia in the war, at least until American forces could be mobilized and trained. Once committed to Zionism, moreover, they also feared conceding any 'Jewish' advantage back to the Germans. The united front of Anglo-Jewry, moreover, had broken. The uncompromising anti-Zionists at the Jewish Board of Deputies were overthrown in the summer of 1917. The mass of Jewish aliens, activated by the threat of being conscripted into either the British or Russian army, increasingly turned to Zionism. Both domestic and international considerations offered the British an opportunity to serve principle and self-interest. The French, having publicly committed themselves even before the Balfour Declaration was issued, were in no position to retreat. Woodrow Wilson, weighing matters judiciously, brought America into line at a more leisurely pace.

The Allied commitment to Zionism also encouraged East European Jewish Nationalists. They, too, rejected the 'moderate' formula of treaty guarantees for equal rights, and demanded, instead, the right to be different – to manage their own affairs in a quasi-corporative mode within their new national states. The Romanian experience seemed to them to demonstrate that only constitutional recognition and guarantee of Jewish autonomy within national states could guarantee Jewish freedom. But the right to their own schools, their own language and control of their lives flew in the face of the West European liberal conception of the national state, and that conception appeared to Western eyes to triumph in November 1918. Since the East European multinational empires had all been defeated – Russian, German, Austro-Hungarian, and Ottoman – liberal western-style nations were to be created, whether appropriate or not, through the Succession States.

This ostensible triumph of liberalism ultimately outweighed the momentary ascendancy of Jewish Nationalists. Zionism had previously offered the simplest concession to Jews. Now as the peacemakers confronted the unnerving ethnic map of Eastern Europe in 1919, Lucien Wolf and Anglo-Jewish 'moderates' offered a carefully calculated appeal. For Western anxieties about the bacillus of Bolshevism, the ethnically homogenized state appeared to form the best *cordon sanitaire*. What Wolf and the 'moderates' proposed implied 'stronger' states, western-dependent and western-oriented nations. Wolf demanded guarantees in each instance for Jewish civil rights, but was as anxious to contain Jewish Nationalist ambitions in Eastern Europe and at the same time to limit commitments to Zionists in Palestine. From Finland through the Baltic states to Poland, Czechoslovakia, the Ukraine, Austria, Hungary, and Romania, Wolf had a minimal and an optimal agenda.

Wolf laboured under no illusions about the depth of East European anti-Semitism. Untutored and uncontrolled masses were dangerous. He understood that folk prejudices, unrestrained by authority, meant endemic pogroms. Hostility towards Jews would only wane, as it had done in Western Europe, when Jew and gentile fused in a common culture respecting one another's individuality but speaking the vernacular, sharing patriotism, identifying one another as fellow citizens first. Reflecting back in September 1919 on the treaties he had done so much to help frame, Wolf observed:

> We cannot pretend to have solved the Jewish Question in Eastern Europe, but at any rate we have got on paper the best solution that has ever been dreamt of. We have still before us the task of working out this solution in practice. It will be difficult and delicate because we shall be confronted by two kinds of mischief-makers – on the one hand the violent anti-Semites, and on the other the extreme Jewish Nationalists. We have, however, in the Minorities Treaties so solid a basis to work upon that I think we can look forward to the future with a great deal of confidence.[15]

While Wolf was not above playing the disruptive implications of Jewish Nationalism, what he sought to convey to the peacemakers was the viability of the 'moderate' formula. Wolf simultaneously sought out and cultivated 'reasonable' East European statesmen and leaders who understood the difficulties of state-making, who favoured 'constructive' solutions, who would 'protect' Jewish minorities through that necessarily long and difficult process of moulding a new national culture. Thus Wolf sought and found East European national leaders who shared his vision and values – Beneš and Masaryk in Czechoslovakia, Ionescu in Romania, ultimately Paderewski in Poland – with whom to negotiate the best 'practical' arrangements.

At one particularly tense moment at the beginning of June 1919, while negotiating the Polish minority rights clauses, Wolf reminded his distinguished American colleague, Louis Marshall:

> The question to my mind is a political, and not a legal one. In everything I have done here since the Peace Congress has been sitting I have endeavoured to bear steadily in mind the permanent interests of our brethren in Eastern Europe and not to allow myself to be deflected from that duty by the conflicts and bitternesses of the moment. I look beyond the pogrom-stricken fields and the passions and recriminations to which ephemeral political conditions have given rise, to a time when on the basis of Equal Rights the Jews of Poland will be full partners in a State to which they will be patriotically attached, and of which they may be legitimately proud. But if this prospect is to be realised we must see that we do not poison the new relations of Poles and Jews at their source. And this we shall assuredly do if, for the benefit of Jews alone, we abridge in any way the sovereign rights of Poland and humiliate her before the whole world.[16]

The stakes were considerable. Jewish rights must be effectively secured. Jewish lives must not be at risk. But all of this had to be accomplished in a real world.

Covert as well as overt agendas had to be respected. The United States, in spite of lip-service to advanced principles, could not tolerate the suggestion of general League of Nations intervention on behalf of abused minorities. That might mean outside intervention on behalf of abused Japanese in California or, even worse, of Blacks in the American South. Minority rights could not, therefore, be obtained through the League of Nations charter. Each case would have to be managed in the individual treaty defining the new state. That meant tortuous negotiations in each instance. Poland, for its part, was unwilling to grant full rights to all national minorities. In the instances of Ukrainians or White Russians, the minorities had clearly defined territorial bases. Jews, on the other hand, were scattered throughout Poland. Poles, moreover, had no intention of granting minority rights to Germans within the Polish state. To aggravate difficult enough problems, the United States, France, and Britain feared Bolshevism and social revolution. The alleged extensive Jewish involvement in Bolshevism rekindled embers of western anti-Semitism and was even used to justify the brutal slaughter of Jews in Pińsk. And, finally, Jews, sharply divided between Nationalists and Assimilationists, also divided on matters of personality. Many rough edges had to be made smooth were any viable settlement to be produced.

Any Jewish agenda also had, in the first instance, to accommodate itself to great power wants and needs. The defeat of both Germany and Russia, not to mention the disintegration of the Austro-Hungarian Empire, made possible the reconstruction of Poland. While Poland could be resurrected given this power vacuum, Polish survival depended upon Poland either coming to terms with its more powerful neighbours or somehow developing the capacity to maintain its independence. Polish nationalists sought the frontiers of 1772. So vast an appetite – reaching well into overwhelmingly German provinces in the north and west, White Russian and Lithuanian areas around Wilno, and White Russian and Ukrainian lands to the east and south-east – invited discontent, if not war, and squared ill with grand pronouncements about rights of national self-determination.[17] Even in modified form, Poland would have to concede substantial minority guarantees before the nation could be reconstituted.

Beyond the immediate problem of securing concessions for Jews that neither Poles nor the allied powers wished to concede to Germany, lay the ebb and flow of the Bolshevik crisis. British, French, and American aid flowed, in ill-considered driblets, to White factions seeking to overthrow Lenin's government. American troops occupied Vladivostok, British troops Archangel. By late March 1919, the Jewish task became even more complicated. Béla Kun's spectacular rise to power in Hungary jarred peacemakers' priorities. Bolshevists in Hungary, like Spartacists in Germany, threatened to bring revolution from Russia to the west. The Allied military commander, Marshal Foch, considered Poland and Romania the necessary military bastions for resisting revolution in Europe. Clemenceau concurred, but both Lloyd George and Woodrow Wilson were less certain, Lloyd George, in particular, seeking pacification for disorder and unrest both at home and abroad.[18]

Wolf's first 'Polish' work during the war had been anti-defamatory, countering various charges about Jews spying for Germany. He first directly confronted Polish nationalism in 1915 when the Papacy made overtures to the *Alliance*, the Conjoint Foreign Committee, and the American Jewish Committee. François Deloncle, a French journalist, sometime diplomat, and politician, acted for the Vatican Secretary of State. Deloncle suggested that Jewish organizations and the Papacy should make common cause and develop joint agendas for the peace and conference that would follow the war. The Alliance and the Americans considered these overtures seriously, but Wolf asked the French to restrain themselves. Appointing himself to speak for both nations' Jewish organizations, Wolf suggested that the Pope could demonstrate his good offices best by improving Roman Catholic attitudes and relations with Jews in Poland. The Alliance concurred, and the Deloncle affair appeared to be over. Deloncle, however, returned in 1916 with a more elaborate program, one with strong Zionist implications. Wolf warned against allowing Jews to become spokesmen for Papal representation at the Peace Conference or allowing Jewish interests to become entangled on matters of Papal territoriality. He cautioned the French that supporting any Papal territorial claims, even in Vatican City, by extension might imply an endorsement of Zionist claims for Palestine. The Papacy offered a pronouncement against anti-Semitism conditional upon Jewish endorsement of various Roman Catholic proposals. On Polish national independence, for instance, Jewish opinion was divided, and Jewish organizations should never actively endorse policies as Jews that did not affect Jewish interests.[19]

Jewish interests were, however, directly involved in matters of new Russian anti-Semitic regulations in 1915 and 1916, removed only after extensive Jewish pressure had been placed on the British and French governments. Such successes could scarcely be represented as great 'improvements'. Zionism promised action, emancipation from European persecution, something new and dramatic that could capture the imagination.[20]

When Russia granted 'autonomous' status to Poland, some 80 per cent of Russian Jewry, according to contemporary estimates, confronted ethnic Polish nationalism. Matters were bad enough under Russian overlordship, but Roman Dmowski's Polish National Democratic Party, stridently anti-Semitic, asked the British and French governments to recognize it as the 'government in exile' of the Polish nation. Only those of the 'Polish race', contended the National Democrats, qualified for citizenship, and a 'Pole' had to prove that he had not been Jewish for three generations. Such a definition embarrassed the Foreign Office, now busily attempting to paint British policy in enlightened liberal terms. The National Democrats gave way and agreed to allow token 'Jewish' representation on the National Committee.[21] That changed nothing. The National Democratic Party continued to pursue its publicly-avowed policy of 'the forcible elimination or reduction of the Jewish population', harassing Polish Jews and particularly preventing Jewish refugees and victims of the wartime 'barbarous deportations' from returning to Poland.[22] Wolf's Foreign Affairs Committee of the Anglo-Jewish Association, rebuffed on its resistance to Zionism, made Poland its principal European preoccupation by the summer of 1917. The Committee consulted 'representative' Polish Jews and began negotiations in London with representatives of the Polish Progressive Party and Polish State Council. Besides equal civil and political rights for Jews, the Anglo-Jewish Association sought guarantees for Jews as 'a substantial nationality minority' with cultural autonomy and proportionate political representation.[23] Left politicians of liberal views on the Jewish question were a small minority. Dmowski's Polish Nationalists, however, were another matter. Dmowski and Paderewski had failed to secure British support in 1915, at least in part thanks to Wolf's well-orchestrated Conjoint Committee campaign in the London press,[24] and the British government was moving closer to formal recognition. Lord Weardale discussed the problem with Balfour, at the request of the AJA, on 23 November 1917, and found the matter was still 'under consideration'. That encouraged Lucien Wolf to have a long interview the following day with Lord Robert Cecil. The *Alliance Israélite* took the same approach with the Quai d'Orsay. Keeping both the Petrograd Committee, composed principally of 'moderate' Jews seeking accommodation with the Russian government after the February Revolution, and the American Jewish Committee, created in 1905 to safeguard Jewish international interests, apprised, Wolf's committee attempted to ward off British government recognition of Dmowski while securing government approval for a conference in some neutral country of representatives of Western Jewish communities and delegates from the progressive and Socialist parties in Poland.[25]

In Poland, however, the program of economic boycott of Polish Jews begun under Russian administration and applied intensely after 1912 'to nationalize Polish trade and industry in a narrow racial sense' continued. Worse still in 'moderate' eyes, the boycott was working, squeezing more and more Jews into poverty and forced emigration. Poland was replaying Russia in the 1880s, raising for Western Jewry the spectre of Eastern pauper hordes descending on their countries, draining resources and rekindling anti-Semitism. Wolf and 'moderates' sought to modify Polish behaviour, end boycotts and pogroms, and develop within Poland those institutions and conditions that would sustain the peace and allow for economic and social development. Such Zionist partisans as Balfour and Brandeis agreed with Wolf, Bigart and the majority of 'establishment' Jews on the matter of Jewish migration. They did not want 'those people' in their countries. The 'moderates' hoped to liberalize Poland, rendering emigration unnecessary. 'Establishment' Zionists saw Palestine as an option, another place to deflect immigration, whether Poland 'liberalized' or not.

Poland, by 1919, became a testing ground for Wolf's ideas, diplomatic skills, and political sagacity. Poland was the opportunity to win the long, unavailing struggle with Russia and Romania for decades past. If Wolf could find a way to fuse Polish national ambitions with properly framed Minority Treaties and safeguards for Jews, then it just might be possible to begin to quest for economic viability and social stability in this potentially most volatile and troublesome Succession State.[26] Wolf, anxious to minimize the Jewish Nationalist and Zionist impact upon the Peace Conference, saw Poland as an issue upon which the Allied delegations would be inclined towards what they perceived to be the least disruptive settlement. Extreme proposals for Jewish autonomy could be both exploited and discredited to reach 'our moderate formula of cultural autonomy'.[27]

Wolf always relied on the well-documented case to prevail. His careful research and tightly argued conclusions almost invariably gave him an advantage in discussion. To establish his assumptions as the basis of discussion and negotiation, he furnished the peace conference staff with his *Notes on the Diplomatic History of the Jewish Question*, a careful compilation of British State Papers to which he had been given access in 1915.[28] The Green Book, as it was usually called, proved one of Wolf's most useful weapons. He distributed copies to all national delegations and the more important members of the conference staff. Wolf's next step was to open direct negotiations with the Polish Nationalists. He began by calling upon Count Ostroróg, one of the Polish diplomats, the morning of 20 February. Ostroróg seems to have reacted well to Wolf, and Wolf found the Count 'very charming', as well as precisely the person who could facilitate negotiations with the Poles. The discussions encouraged Wolf to move without consulting the Zionists, a step that created gratuitous tension within the Jewish delegations, but unquestionably simplified Wolf's task.

Wolf's parallel problem was to carry the key members of the British delegation. With unerring instinct, he singled out J. W. Headlam-Morley, who was to be the principal treaty draftsman. Headlam-Morley, an educator, an intellectual, and historian as well as a diplomat, was precisely the sort of person with whom Wolf worked best. They shared the same values and unspoken assumptions. They saw one another as sensible individuals pursuing reasonable and just causes. Headlam-Morley was not initially encouraging. He doubted on 1 March that Wolf's formula for Jewish rights could be put into the treaty. The League of Nations, in his opinion, would regulate matters between states but would not intervene in internal issues. Woodrow Wilson and the Americans, he reminded Wolf, had removed the statement about civil and religious liberty from Article XIX of the Covenant. Wolf's French colleagues were also pessimistic. Bigart of the *Alliance* feared that, since Britain had already recognized the independence of Poland without insisting upon safeguards, the 'moderates' were already too late. Baron Edmond de Rothschild thought that the great powers, having made their declarations on Palestine, no longer wished to be annoyed with Jewish questions.[29]

Wolf hoped to be able to take Oscar Straus, as a leading American Jewish delegate, with him when he opened formal negotiations with the Polish Nationalists. Influenza, however, took its toll, and Wolf found himself engaged in a three-hour 'unofficial' discussion alone. The two principal Polish spokesmen were not regarded as being particularly well-disposed to the Jews. Piłsudski and Kozicki, the Secretary General of the Polish Delegation to the Peace Conference, joined Count Ostroróg, who had generally assumed a conciliatory role, in pressing the Polish case. Wolf reminded them that the Conjoint Foreign Committee had no interests of its own in this matter, that British and French Jews saw matters very differently from Polish Jews, but that the long history of Polish Jewish appeals for assistance led Anglo-French Jewry to offer its good offices in the search for peace and amity. Wolf conceded that Polish Jews asked for much that British Jews would not, but the Jewish problem in Poland was different and demanded settlement on its own terms. Wolf conceded that, when the Joint Foreign Committee undertook to confer with Count Sobański, it was prepared to encourage Polish Jews to accept a program that 'would make for a happy and contented Poland', and Wolf suspected that an appropriate settlement 'would be supported by moderate men in all great Jewish communities in the world'.

Wolf then proposed the five points of the Joint Foreign Committee resolutions of 3 October 1918 on minority rights as a basis for discussion. Issues of citizenship, the first two resolutions, presented no problem, but Jewish claims for educational, political, and linguistic rights seemed to the Poles merely a disguised form of national autonomy, making the Jews a nation within the nation. Lithuanians and White Russians might make such claims, for they were concentrated in specific lands, but Jews were scattered throughout Poland. Piłsudski conceded that serious difficulties existed between Poles and Jews that presented a problem 'of extreme gravity' to the Polish state. Wolf seized upon the statement as a satisfactory basis for discussion. A 'serious problem' cannot be resolved on ordinary lines. It demands special treatment, and the Joint Foreign Committee proposal is extremely moderate, aimed solely at 'cultural autonomy'. That remained a sore point for the Poles, who found the continued use of Yiddish as a medium of instruction in state-supported schools the symbolic as well as practical sticking point. Wolf responded that Yiddish had been the Jewish vernacular for 700 years, that 'Jews had been forced by historical circumstances' to make the language their own. Yiddish 'had become endeared to them by such use and by a considerable literature'. Poles and Jews must realize that Jews existed in Poland as a separate body through no fault of their own and could not become assimilated by statutory enactment.

> To refuse to recognise their separateness would be to martyrise this very separateness and thus to prolong the Jewish question indefinitely. It would be better to make reasonable concession to them on the facts. This, at any rate, would make for friendly relations

> between the two races, and time and economic constraint might be trusted to do the rest in the way of bringing them still closer together.

The Poles took up Wolf's challenge to offer any reasonable amendment to this formula and agreed to consult the Warsaw government. At the same time, they asked Wolf about the Jewish problem in England. Wolf denied that such a thing existed. British Jews needed and had obtained certain legal concessions on matters relating to education and laws concerning Sunday trading. Wolf promised to furnish the Poles summaries of the English statutes on these points. English and Polish Jewish issues, he reminded the Poles, were not analogous. Yiddish was nowhere the permanent vernacular of any significant section of English Jews. Jews were less than 3/4 of one per cent of the English population, not the 14 per cent they were in Poland. Jews had not been in England for 700 years with their own language and institutions.[30]

Wolf, pleased that the Polish discussion had been more conciliatory in tone than he expected moved directly to the crucial issues and sought out E. H. Carr, the Foreign Office East European expert. He told Carr that Anglo-Jewry 'and practical politicians generally' considered the Polish question far more important than Palestine, for they understand that 'an amicable solution is essential to the stability of the new Polish State'. Wolf explained that the Zionists would themselves be organizing a bureau to deal with non-Zionist questions, and they would soon begin supporting the extreme Polish Jewish Nationalists. When Carr asked if Wolf would object to Carr alluding to Wolf's negotiations when talking to Polish delegates, Wolf suggested that it would be helpful and promised to furnish a copy of his report.

Wolf also continued privately to press Count Ostroróg to keep the negotiations moving. Yiddish remained the sticking-point, so Wolf reminded Ostroróg that Paderewski, speaking for the Poles, had suggested that Poland could make any concession that the United States did. Wolf believed that the Poles might ultimately accept Jewish 'control' rather than 'autonomy', a formulation that he realized would bother the Zionists, 'but they will have no real reason to complain, inasmuch as they will have the oysters while the Poles will only have the shells.'

Over the next several days, Wolf organized his campaign. On 18 March he laid out the Joint Foreign Committee case to H. J. Paton, the Foreign Office expert who was assigned particular responsibility for Poland, repeating his observation to Carr that 'moderate' success on Poland depended upon the degree of support that Allied Government would provide against the extreme demands of the Zionists. Paton promised his support. Wolf then approached Professor Sylvain Lévi, the French-Jewish orientalist of the Collège de France, whose Quai d'Orsay, *Alliance*, and Zionist connections made him an invaluable ally. Lévi, who had already broken the united Zionist front before the peace conference plenipotentiaries on 27 February, promised to secure Quai d'Orsay backing. Baron Edmond de Rothschild's representative thought that the baron might help. Wolf also went to the Ukrainians, who were anxious for any help they could gain in forwarding their own national claims, to secure their support for the Joint Foreign Committee formula. The Poles, Wolf felt, could scarcely afford to be behind the Ukrainians.[31]

The groundwork laid, Wolf then returned to his running struggle with the Zionists. The Americans were determined to make yet another effort to have all Jewry speak with one voice on issues of international policy. Louis Marshall, Cyrus Adler, Julian Mack, and Oscar Straus had their own differences of opinion, but they still hoped to be able to reconstruct a united Jewish front. Even the Zionists had internal quarrels. Weizmann, after all, quarrelled with Sokolow. On the nights of 5 and 6 April, the issue was fought out in the grand hall of the French *Consistoire*. Sokolow began by insisting that Jewish Nationalism was not revolutionary. Poland was hopelessly anti-Semitic, and Jews must have their ethnic and social rights preserved. This meant religious, cultural, and social autonomy, 'Jewish control of Jewish schools, with State aid, and a Jewish electoral curia which would elect Members of the Polish Parliament or any other Parliament in proportion to their numbers.' Subsequent Jewish Nationalist spokesmen swept away Sokolow's modest proposal. Menahem Ussishkin, in particular, announced that the privileges of a separate Jewish nationality within the succession states was but the first step. Jewish Nationalism would ultimately federate all Jewish communities everywhere in the world in one Jewish nation, argued the 'uncrowned King of Odessa', with a claim to be admitted to the League of Nations on an equal footing with all other nations. He warned assimilating Jews that this Jewish Nationality 'would set out to conquer them'. There were no French Jews, English Jews, or American Jews, 'but only Jews in France, England or America, who eventually would have to join the universal Jewish Nationality.' The Americans, with Judge Julian Mack in the lead, argued that the Nationalists must be allowed their way regardless of how Western Jewry felt about their ideas, 'even though we know they were mad and headed for self-destruction'. Louis Marshall attempted to secure a compromise by referring the matter to a small committee. Wolf, knowing the Alliance leadership was immovable, disingenuously stood aside, professing only his desire for 'unity', and allowed the French to veto the proposed accommodation.[32]

While allowing American tempers to cool, Wolf took the entire Anglo-Jewish delegation to the Czechoslovak Mission on the morning of 10 April. Beneš and Masaryk enthusiastically identified themselves 'with the best liberal traditions of Western Europe' and guaranteed Czech Jewish subjects with 'as happy and secure a position as their British and French co-religionists [enjoy] in their respective countries'. Sir Stuart Samuel invited the Czech government to seek loans from his bank and told Beneš that the British Government had entrusted Samuel Montagu & Co 'with several lines of the Credits opened for the Allies'. Such a happy resolution was a foregone conclusion, but Wolf realized that nothing could give the 'moderate' cause greater morale than such a clear triumph.[33] He could once again pick up the more difficult Polish issue, confident of support behind him. Wolf returned to lobby Headlam-Morley and Carr about Poland, warning them that the East European Jewish Nationalist delegations were readying memorials for a separate Jewish Nationality. All agreed on how 'very dangerous' it would be were such memorials to get into Polish hands. Headlam-Morley asked Wolf what they could offer Sokolow as an inducement to hold back the Nationalists. Wolf felt that a Polish government assurance that they would not gerrymander constituencies to the prejudice of Jews, and some liberal scheme of municipal self-government for all of Poland, not merely in White Russian and Lithuanian lands, would remove the justification for a Jewish Electoral Curia. At the same time, Wolf reminded them, the League of Nations must be made the special custodian for civil and religious liberty in Eastern Europe. Quite impossible as a general principle, contended Headlam-Morley with American reservations clearly in mind, but something might be managed on the specific treaty. All parted determined 'to promote a moderate compromise'.

Keeping both sides of his negotiations in tandem, Wolf lunched with Skrzyński, Prince Kazimierz Lubomirski, Count Ostroróg, and Jan Perłowski (the Parliamentary Secretary to Skrzyński) on 17 April. Skrzyński set the tone by denying the existence of Polish anti-Semitism and contending that special concessions to Jews depended upon Jews doing something special for Poland. Perhaps they might make a statement in favour of Poland acquiring Danzig and Teschen. Jews might also help to secure 'a conservative treatment of the Agrarian Question'. Wolf reminded himself that this was the Dmowski approach in slightly 'less aggressive' form. He responded coolly that Danzig and Teschen were international questions upon which Jews of different countries had different views. The Czechs had already asked Wolf for and been refused his support on Teschen, the Ukrainians on Lemberg. As to the agrarian question, surely that was one for Polish Jews themselves. When Skrzyński then trotted out the canards about Jews acting in harmony and controlling the press, Wolf firmly called him down. That myth lacked any foundation and was the source of much mischief. Turning the tables, Wolf added that 'kindness and generosity' would make Jewish Poles good citizens, ardent citizens, as conservative as they are in Western Europe. Radical anti-Semitism alone made them discontented and difficult.

Wolf declined to go further in discussions at that point, agreeing to see

Paderewski only after he had the opportunity to see the American Jewish delegation and demand its support. Oscar Straus and Cyrus Adler agreed. Straus specifically endorsed Wolf's 'equal rights' formula in preference to 'national rights'.[34] The Paderewski interview of 23 April went particularly well. The pianist-statesman acknowledged that Jews were very excited and discontented 'and that the problem was how to calm them and conciliate them'. The same was true of Poles 'who were also in an excited state and were disposed to look upon the Jews with anger'. The situation required patience. Wolf must understand, Paderewski continued, that his own desires 'to make great sacrifices in order to transform the Jews into good Polish citizens' were politically impossible in the present state of Polish public opinion. Of course they would be assured of equal rights. But what more could be done?

Wolf, as always, had a memorandum on hand. He was asking for no more than Jews enjoyed in Britain and France. The Diet must pass a Conspiracy Act 'which would be a tacit disavowal of the boycott', must secure religious and cultural minority rights, must pass an Electoral Law 'guaranteeing fair representation for the Jews', and deal with the issues of Sunday labour and trading for Jews. Paderewski was receptive. That brought Wolf to the Pińsk massacre. Paderewski did not deny the murder of Jews. He gave Wolf the official Polish reports 'which seem to show that the Poles had a measure of right on their side', while still conceding that 'the incident was deplorable'. Paderewski's welcome candour attracted Wolf. While pogroms and murder were intolerable, Wolf believed that Western Jewry confronted a difficult choice. Dmowski, the avowed anti-Semitic nationalist leader with whom Paderewski was at the moment on bad terms would clearly, if in power, make matters considerably worse. Paderewski surrounded himself with responsive, liberally-minded Poles, particularly Zaleski, whom Wolf felt to be the most warmly inclined towards accommodation with the Jews.[35] Impossible Jewish claims that might drive Paderewski from power would bring more dangerous leaders into authority and extend the already overlong nightmare of persecution and destruction. Leadership mattered. Were either the weak or ruthless, let alone both, to rule Poland, native savagery and political expediency would translate into endemic Jewish persecution.

Carr applauded Wolf's negotiations with Paderewski. He also reported that Sokolow and Mack, although they had considerably modified their terms, still were pressing for National rights, particularly separate Jewish Electoral Curiae. Carr felt, however, that some grounds for negotiation might be there. Wolf felt this was a testimony to the effectiveness of 'moderate' opposition to extreme Jewish Nationalism. Wolf's pleasure was even greater when he dined with Zaleski on the evening of 15 April. Paderewski was very satisfied with the Wolf interview and hoped to see him again soon. Zaleski was, in the meanwhile, to draw up a full report on the

Jewish question. Would Wolf supply him with documents relating to the various negotiations? Of course Wolf would. Zaleski also suggested that Wolf see Patek, leader of the Polish Parties of the Left, with whom Sokolow was already in negotiations. Wolf promised to do so as soon as he returned from London where he was going to 'be instructed' to stand firmly on the 1918 resolutions rather than 'National Rights'.[36]

Back in Paris on 3 May, Wolf found matters where he had left them. He gladly agreed to join Bigart and the *Alliance* delegation for a formal visit to Paderewski to present the French proposals when assured that they were essentially the same as his. He also found that Headlam-Morley had been appointed the head of a Committee of three to deal with the Jewish Question and Minority issues. David Hunter Miller sat for the United States, Philippe Berthelot for France, and E. H. Carr served as Secretary. Carr begged Wolf to furnish him useful documentation and reference material. Nothing could have pleased Wolf more.

> The appointment of this Committee is a great coup for us. It will probably postpone a settlement of the Jewish Question beyond the signature of the Peace Treaty, but it will be all the safer and solid for that. Instead of more or less banal Clauses in the Peace Treaty, we shall now have a detailed Statute of Minorities which will probably be the subject of special Treaties with the States concerned.[37]

Wolf believed that matters, once removed from the public glare of memorials, meetings, and presentations, would move into the hands of a handful of sensible people working to achieve reasonable, viable settlements. Behind-the-scenes negotiations, discreet diplomacy, were what he did best, and he had been at great pains in Paris and London to cultivate close personal relations and trust with those who mattered. From May to July, Wolf actually managed to shift the burden of negotiating with Zionists and Jewish Nationalists over to Carr, Headlam-Morley, Leeper, and the senior British peace conference staff. Keeping press contacts alive, to be used when needed, he cultivated Sir George Riddell, owner of *The News of the World*, one of Lloyd George's intimates, and information director for the British delegation.[38] Wolf was cordial enough when responding to individuals or groups who sought him out, but he had evolved a clear sense of priorities. Wolf covered his own rear by ascertaining that the Joint Foreign Committee and its parent bodies were kept appropriately informed, that Sir Stuart Samuel and Claude Montefiore were kept completely up-to-date, and that he was 'instructed' to do what he felt he should be doing. So successful was he in this tactic that Herbert Bentwich, his outspoken Zionist opponent and member of the Board of Deputies, unable to rein Wolf in from London through the parent committees, came to Paris on his own to disrupt Wolf's arrangements.

Bentwich arrived too late. Wolf had moved negotiations to circles Bentwich could not reach.

Wolf next ascertained that his allies were working in harmony with him. Jacques Bigart, Sylvain Lévi, and the Reinachs were in full accord with Wolf's views, so the *Alliance Israélite* was never a problem. The Americans, however, were another matter. Judge Julian Mack was an uncompromising Zionist and prepared to support any Jewish Nationalist position on the grounds that they were the best judge of their own problems. The unrepresentative nature of the East European Jewish Nationalist delegations bothered Mack not at all, for the cause he espoused was a minority position, and his commitment to it was total. Cyrus Adler, founder of the American Jewish Committee, while sympathetic to Zionist aspirations in Palestine, shared the 'moderate' view on European settlements. Henry Morgenthau, the financier and diplomat whose hostility to Zionism and Jewish Nationalism had led him to split with Stephen Wise, concurred completely with the Wolf position, but he had come to Europe to deal with issues of relief, not diplomacy. Louis Marshall, closest to President Wilson and the American delegation, stood somewhat between Mack and Adler. Never 'manageable', Marshall tended to think ill of solutions that did not appear to be his own. He had strong views on most people and things and an explosive temper that rendered him something less than an effective negotiator. Ultimately ground down, to some degree, between Wolf's unflappable persistence and the effective manoeuvres of the British peace conference delegation, Marshall tended, over time, to give way. While the American flank had an element of unpredictability and, at times, clear differences of opinion, Wolf attempted to see Marshall and other Americans almost daily, always conveying the same message of common purpose and cooperation.

Wolf simultaneously attempted to keep negotiations with the Poles on track. His candour, his openness, and his obvious sensitivity gave him a better reception and hearing than even he initially expected. He saw little hope in Dmowski and the extreme Polish Nationalists with their avowed anti-Semitic program and supported the Joint Foreign Committee policy of attempting to hold that faction in check through the Foreign Office. While warm to the Left, he was cautious to deal with it only after he had come to terms with President Paderewski and a spectrum of centre groups. Wolf's personal political preference, as a self-styled 'Manchester Liberal', were the Paderewski-Zaleski moderates. He also did well with Stanisław Patek, a Judge of the Court of Cassation in Warsaw, who was identified with the non-Bolshevik left and Piłsudski. Wolf and Patek had already taken the measure of one another in London in 1915, and they found it easy to work together. Patek had already encountered the Zionist-Nationalists at Paris. Sokolow attempted to persuade Patek to support Jewish National Autonomy. Patek knew that such a program would be political suicide and was delighted when Wolf indicated 'that I believed National Autonomy no longer had any practical importance . . .'.[39] Wolf began his Polish negotiations with Count Ostroróg and Foreign Minister Skrzyński's people, tripped lightly past the French Clerical-Polish Clerical political connections, and worked his way to the only people he trusted to be able to carry an acceptable treaty and give it effect. So Wolf returned repeatedly to Paderewski and Zaleski, conveying the importance of taking a firm public stand on those pressing political issues which validated extreme safeguards in Western eyes. Something must be done about pogroms, and the issue of boycott must be met head-on. Wolf effectively conveyed Western Jewry's hopes – and they were very real – that Polish Jews could find security and fulfilment as Polish citizens. Wolf could speak from conviction. Neither Americans, nor French, nor English wanted Polish Jews in 'their' countries.

Wolf's Fabian strategy worked. By late May, even the more unruly Americans were anxious to re-establish their 'moderate' ties. Louis Marshall, irritated with Zionist leaders and anxious for some accommodation, sought Wolf out to test the waters on 'ethnic rights' rather than 'national rights'.[40] A more representative Polish Jewish delegation, highly Orthodox, finally reached Paris in mid-May. The Zionists denounced them as 'impostors' for good reason. They rejected the secular state of the Zionists in which they claimed religion would be subordinated to 'Nationality and Politics' and sought rather a true *Eretz Israel*. Their first concerns, however, were Sabbath Questions and the fear that a rigid ban of Sunday Trading was about to be introduced in Poland in order to re-enforce the widespread Polish boycott of Jewish businesses. Observant Jews would be severely penalized by losing both Saturday and Sunday trade. Wolf snapped up that point, asked for a memorandum of facts, and agreed to place the issue before the Council of Four.[41] Meanwhile, however, the Pińsk murders required management. Paderewski agreed to write a general letter deploring them, promising investigation and punishment. Pressed by Wolf, he agreed to remove an exculpatory paragraph that sought to mitigate the blame by suggesting that the dead Jews were Bolsheviks. Pogroms, unfortunately, were spreading. Tales from Wilno multiplied their horrors in telling. Facts helped. The 2,200 initially reported killed shrank to 200, and a Jewish leader reported arrested showed up quite unscathed in Paris a few days later.[42] Matters were not improved when the American Minister in Warsaw, Gibson, sent ill-informed reports claiming no such attacks had taken place. Gibson repeated every libel Dmowski had used through the years, 'all the legends of Jewish pro-Germanism, treachery, espionage, profiteering and bolshevism. He describes the whole Jewish proletariat – indeed all the Jews who are not Assimilants or Chassidim – as 'criminals'. His later denials and feeble argument that his reports were garbled in transmission made

Gibson appear doubly foolish and cast doubts on American diplomatic intelligence.[43]

Would-be friends and allies occasionally provided unexpected problems. Baron Alexandre de Gunzburg sallied into Paris from Switzerland, having heard that Jewish delegations were in a state of disarray. The Baron shared the fears that Maxim Vinaver, one of the founders of the Russian Cadet party, also voiced to Wolf that dividing Jews among succession states with their unconstrained racial hatreds was a greater danger than having them under the rule of a greater Russia. Wolf demurred and reminded them in turn that should Kolchak and Denikin actually defeat the Bolsheviks, pogroms would be the order of the day.[44] While Marshall shared Wolf's views on this, he still baulked, as did Wilson, at specifically committing to the League the role of policeman for minority rights preferring, ultimately, to fall back on great power guarantees.

Lord Robert Cecil waded into the fray in May. An uncompromising champion of the League, Lord Robert and his aide, Baker, proved highly receptive to Wolf's formulations of the right of appeal. Cecil and Baker accepted articles granting the League the right to act on its own initiative in emergencies and defining minority rights of appeal to the League. Cecil was 'determined to do his best to make the Treaties a real living Charter of Liberties for the Jews'. Lord Robert, however, required some reassurance 'about the relations of Jews with Bolshevism and revolutionary movements generally'. Wolf, who had often had to deal with that canard, calmly settled Cecil's anxieties.[45] No sooner had Wolf begun moving matters forward with Cecil, however, than Louis Marshall exploded again. He categorically refused to allow Polish Jews to become enmeshed in Polish courts on issues relating to their treaty-guaranteed rights. Wolf responded:

> The question to my mind is a political, and not a legal, one. In everything I have done here since the Peace Congress has been sitting I have endeavoured to bear steadily in mind the permanent interests of our brethren in Eastern Europe and not to allow myself to be deflected from that duty by the conflicts and bitterness of the moment. I look beyond the pogrom-stricken fields and the passions and recriminations to which ephemeral political conditions have given rise, to a time when on the basis of Equal Rights the Jews of Poland will be full partners in a State to which they will be patriotically attached and of which they may be legitimately proud. But if this prospect is to be realised we must see that we do not poison the new relations of Poles and Jews at their source. And this we shall assuredly do if, for the benefit of Jews alone, we abridge in any way the sovereign rights of Poland and humiliate her before the whole world.[46]

Marshall finally agreed to support the British proposal were the American formula not to carry. By 17 June, the Council of Five opted for the British formula on Minority appeals. Lacking American or French support, the more extensive Sunday Trading clauses upon which Wolf and Marshall had agreed, were lost. The next day, however, the Poles rejected the minority treaty 'on the ground that it is an intolerable interference with the sovereign rights of Poland'. Without being overly specific, the Poles pointed at the education clauses, with Yiddish language rights, and Sabbath Observance clauses, as inimical to military discipline. To recover the treaty, all influence had to be brought to bear on the Council to stand firm. Headlam-Morley told Wolf that he and Marshall must rally all their friends to bring pressure upon Lloyd George and President Wilson. Japan and Italy, for their own reasons, would stand firm with the British. Headlam-Morley warned that clerical interests at the Quai d'Orsay, unknown to Clemenceau, were actually encouraging the Polish resistance.

Wolf immediately spurred Sir Stuart Samuel to bring all possible pressure to bear on Lloyd George. He also explained matters to Herbert Samuel, then in Brussels, asking him to appeal to Lloyd George. Morgenthau was pressed into service to write a strong personal letter to Wilson. Since Wilson had just asked Morgenthau to investigate the Polish pogroms, he could scarcely resist such a request.[47] Baron Edmond de Rothschild and Israël Lévi cornered Cambon at the Quai d'Orsay to beg his support in this crisis and hint about the clerical intrigues. Marshall stood firm against any compromises to soothe Polish *amour propre*, and the crisis passed. The Council stood firm, although the Poles had brought their own delegation of Jews headed by Stanislas Natanson to plead the Polish nationalist case. The delegation was not heard, as it happened, until after the Council had reached its decision. The Council responded firmly to the Polish protest, ending 'with what is virtually an ultimatum to Poland to sign it next Saturday when the main German Treaty will be signed'. Wolf relished the fact that the Council drew its historical argument from his *Diplomatic History of the Jewish Question*.[48]

So it was that, on 28 June, the Polish treaty was signed. The Poles made no objection, Dmowski signing immediately after Paderewski. Signatures to the Polish Treaty marked only the symbolic beginning of the process of attempting to fuse Jew and Pole into one national state. Even as a symbol, that agreement remained vital. Each subsequent treaty – with Czechoslovakia, Austria, Finland, the Baltic States, Hungary, Yugoslavia, Romania, and Greece – used the Polish precedent. Some negotiations proved relatively easy; others, predictably but not exclusively Romania, proved extraordinarily difficult. On none could there be retreat. If there were, the Poles could rightly demand renegotiation of their terms. Writing the Polish treaty was one thing. Making it work was another. As far as Wolf was concerned, that was what mattered most. Jewish blood was being shed on Polish soil even as ink was being placed on paper. Pogroms continued.[49] The boycott, still applied with unremitting severity, must somehow be broken. Until that happened no constructive bridges could be built within Poland.

Jews at Paris were still speaking with discordant and disruptive voices. Once a Polish treaty existed, all claimed credit for it, Wolf in his diary and reports, others in more public forums. In one sense, Wolf was fortunate quite as much as he was skilful. Polish territorial ambitions were so far-reaching that Lloyd George was ultimately able to tilt Woodrow Wilson to his side. Great power determination to avoid being dragged into the perpetual quarrels between Poles and subject ethnic groups meant Jewish rights would receive more careful attention and support than they otherwise would probably have done. Lucien Wolf, however, understood how to exploit Jewish Nationalist ambitions, Polish pride, and peacemaker anxiety for a reasonable settlement in quiet diplomacy. The *Alliance Israélite*, particularly Jacques Bigart, applauded Wolf. Wolf remained a tactful diplomat to the end. We owe the victories of 1919 to 'the complete loyalty with which we all worked together'.[50] That was true. Sylvain Lévi's close connection with the Quai d'Orsay provided essential access to Cambon and Berthelot at crucial moments. Clemenceau's general sympathies were important.[51] The timorous *Alliance Israélite* executive committee occasionally summoned up unexpected political courage and tipped the balance towards moderation. Even Louis Marshall, who so often worked at cross purposes to Wolf and the 'moderates', helped to carry the day. In spite of his overbearing ego and explosive temper, Marshall found himself bridging the gap between the strongly pro-Nationalist Judge Julian Mack and 'moderate' Cyrus Adler. Marshall also personally sustained the link between East European Nationalist delegations and their Western opponents. Marshall's ties to and influence upon Woodrow Wilson and key members of the American delegation were, at crucial moments, helpful and served the great common cause. His visit to Paderewski, a man he personally disliked and distrusted, just before leaving France, helped to contribute to that sense of cooperation that Wolf argued was the only basis upon which a viable future could be built. The *Alliance* executive, in its effort to part as friends, told Marshall that he was the principal architect of treaty success and invited him to a celebratory dinner. Marshall, temperamental to the last, declined to dine and flounced off to Le Havre only to find his ship back to the United States idled by a strike. Leopold Greenberg, powerful editor of the *Jewish Chronicle*, knew what Wolf had done and praised him for it in a private letter. But Greenberg was also a committed Zionist, so England's leading Jewish newspaper attributed treaty success entirely to the Zionist-Jewish Nationalist alliance and spoke of the Polish Treaty as a triumph for Jewish nationalism. Zionists, stalled although not rebuffed on their Palestine ambitions, had to mark time until a proposed peace conference commission investigated the situation in the Middle East and reported back. Financially pressed, Zionists needed to claim some major victory to launch a new fund-raising drive. They needed to claim the Polish treaty as their victory.

The Zionist assertion, however, created a serious political problem. Since the Zionists represented the treaty as a triumph of Jewish Nationalism, Zionist self-congratulation and publicity continued to threaten the tidy Wolf settlement. From the outset Wolf realized that the Polish treaty could only give scope for a settlement, not resolve the Polish-Jewish problem. Throughout his negotiations he sought safeguards tolerable to Polish nationalists. He worried about words or issues that might poison the subsequent relations of Jew and Pole. Poland in 1919 was a land lacking facts but strong on rumours, prejudices, and fears. Retreating Germans had warned Polish Jews that their only hope lay with the Russian Bolsheviks, even leaving arms with those who appeared convinced. Subsequent murders and pogroms, particularly those in Pińsk, were laid to the door of 'Jewish Bolsheviks', who allegedly started the violence. Tales of pogroms lost nothing in the telling, but the worst were not inflicted by Poles. The hopelessly unsettled Ukraine saw the massacre of thousands and the devastation of dozens of Jewish communities. Milling refugees attempting to avoid Red-White conflict in the Russian civil war found themselves victimized on all sides, whether Jew or gentile.[52]

Eastern Europe could not be made better by treaty. The settlement could do no more than create the necessary conditions through which time and mutual self-interest could bring Jew and gentile together in interwar Poland. Designing such an agreement required suspension of disbelief and mutual forbearance.

> The magnitude of the Jewish population makes it necessary that patience should be strained to the utmost in order to secure a stable social peace in that country. Moreover the alleged infractions while undoubtedly causing a widespread insecurity do not afford material for a reliable case before the League. Finally, the political situation was one which rendered great circumspection imperative.[53]

Lucien Wolf could never have accomplished that task alone. Jews, even speaking in complete agreement, could not do so. The leaders of the Western Alliance – Georges Clemenceau, David Lloyd-George, and Woodrow Wilson – saw their Jews as national patriots and believed Polish Jews could be the same. Wolf never strayed from his belief that they and every East European Jew must slowly merge into their individual national cultures. Even after the 'moderates' had returned to England from Paris, Wolf, rather than Leo Motzkin and the Jewish Nationalist Committee remained the person to whom diplomatists and Jewish lobbyists still turned. Wolf amused himself by reminding Greenberg of the *Jewish Chronicle*,

> It is rather amusing that although our Delegation is no longer in Paris, all the Jewish work there is still being done by us. Yesterday's post brought me frantic appeals both from the *Alliance* and the Roumanian contingent in the Committee of Jewish Delegations. I managed to tranquillise them before the day was out.[54]

Years later, in 1925, when Count Skrzyński, the Polish Foreign Minister, sought an impartial representative to come to Poland to discuss the serious Jewish problems, he turned to Lucien Wolf.[55]

NOTES

1 Aaron Rodrigues of the University of Indiana has been studying the Alliance school system in the Ottoman Empire and, in a forthcoming work, will argue that the schools did not, in fact, serve this purpose. The Quai d'Orsay, however, did not ignore their potential exploitation.

2 The AJA also served a vital function for the AIU. Under French law, the *Alliance* could not 'own' properties such as the shares in the Jewish Colonization Association and the Baron de Hirsch fund. The AJA, however, laboured under no such disadvantage.

3 The Goldsmid-Crémieux correspondence from 1863 illustrates the range of AIU-AJA concerns. [Archives de] A[lliance] I[sraélite] U[niverselle]. Angl[eterre] I/J/3. The Serbian files starting with Goldsmid à Crémieux, 15 mars 1863, and continuing through the 1870s are particularly interesting. The AJA petition to the King of Serbia, 29 Oct 1872 is in II/D/5/3892.

4 The leading Jews even tried personal diplomacy. See, e.g., Mocatta à Loeb, 10 jan 1882. AIU Angl II/D/34/631. Jews also attempted to make common cause with Christian groups. When an Anglo-American Protestant delegation visited the Kaiser in an effort to have him petition on behalf of Protestants in the Russian Baltic provinces, the AJA attached an address on behalf of Jews. July 1871. Angl II/D/2/1984.

5 See, Board of Deputies of British Jews Papers (hereafter cited as BDBJ) C 11/2/1 and particularly Pauncefot to the AJA, 19 June 1889. See also, B/2/9/8, C 11/12/54 and C/14 *passim*.

6 Issues of procedure, often crucial in diplomatic history, suggest that the British ascendancy began very early in the twentieth century. See, e.g., Montefiore's criticism of AIU protocol. Duparc to Bigart, 11 Apr 1902. AIU Angl I/D/18. Cf. Adler to Bigart, 28 Jan; Loeb à Adler 31 jan 1892. AIU Angl I/B/54 bis/7769.

7 BDBJ C 11/2/2 has the CFC record on Romania, 1901–1910. See particularly the Foreign Office responses and negotiations of 1902 and 1907 and the 'Private and Confidential Memorandum on the Treaty Rights of the Jews of Romania', November 1908.

8 For the communal politics, see S. A. Cohen, *English Zionists and British Jews* (Princeton, 1982) Samuel's 'The Future of Palestine', Jan 1915 was printed but probably not fully circulated. His second try, 'Palestine', March 1915 came before

the Cabinet on the 19th. See, M. Gilbert (ed), *Winston Churchill: Companion Volume, 1914–1916* (London, 1979), 713–716.

9 Bigart à Simonsen, 29 déc; Bigart à Montefiore, 30 déc 1914, 9 fév 1915; Bigart à Wolf, 4 mars 1915. AIU Cdc S238/136–137, 139, 186, 214. See also, ibid., 36–37, 86, 90–92. Bigart expressed his outrage with Zionism to Winz in Berlin in October 1913. Cdc S 236/10. The Conjoint Committee Confidential File, 11 Jan 1915. [Mocatta Library, AJA Papers] AJ/204/4 explains why Anglo-Jewry was less disturbed by the Zionist visitors. See also, Wolf to Bigart, 22 Feb 1915. When the aged Narcisse Leven, President of the AIU, died in January 1915, Bigart effectively ran the AIU. Sylvain Lévi, the eminent Orientalist, eventually assumed the presidency, but it made no fundamental difference. Bigart continued, well into the 1920s, to dominate the organization.

10 American Jews had persuaded the Wilson administration not to renew its Russian commercial treaty before the war. Jewish bankers, both English and German, had boycotted Russian government loans in the past in futile attempts to win concessions for Russian Jews. See, e.g., Grey to Revelstoke, 6 Apr; Asquith to Campbell-Bannerman, 7 Apr 1906. Grey Papers. [United Kingdom. Public Record Office.] F[oreign] O[ffice] 800/100/26–30. The AIU reminded the Quai d'Orsay that the French foreign ministry had promised in 1906 to remonstrate with the Russian government about restrictions placed upon Jewish visitors and businessmen travelling to Russia. Sée à MAE, 13 juin 1916. [France] M[inistère des] A[ffaires] É[trangères. Archives diplomatiques. Guerre.] A/1198/13–17; Wolf to Grey, 6 June 1916. AIU Angl II/D/26/5598.

11 Russian Foreign Minister Sazonov found the matter so embarrassing that he issued an elaborate explanation. Enclosed in Paléologue à Decassé, 15 Sept 1915. MAE A/1197/99–101.

12 Cecil to Spring-Rice, 29 Mar 1916. Cecil Papers. FO 800/196/141–144. Britain's Ambassador to the United States argued, 'If we make this demand from Russia we shall meet with a positive refusal and we shall not do the Jews any good. Some other means therefore must be taken of pleading their case and winning their sympathies'. Spring-Rice to Cecil, 17 March 1916. Spring-Rice Papers. FO 800/242/77–80.

13 On the Slousch lecture tour, see Jusserand à Briand, 17 déc 1915. MAE A/1197/115, encl 116–118. See also, *Appeal of the Consistory of the Jews of France to Jews of Neutral Countries* (Paris, 1915); Bigart à Wolf, 30 juil, 28 sept, 6 oct, 7, 10, déc; Wolf to Bigart, 28 July, 5, 12, Oct 1915; Bigart à Durkheim, 14 avr; Bigart à Sereni, 24 oct 1916. AIU Angl I/J/8/5311, I/G/4/5286; AIU Cdc S 239/35. 39, 233; S 240/15–16. MAE A/1198/100.

14 Wolf, Suggestions for a Pro-Allies Propaganda among the Jews of the United States, 16 Dec 1915. BDBJ C 11/3/1/3. See also, Wolf, 'Confidential Memorandum', 6 June 1917. BDBJ C 11/2/11; Wolf, Address to the American Jewish Congress, 1916. BDBJ C 11/2/8; de Bunsen to Wolf, 23 June; Wolf to de Bunsen, 29 June 1916. AIU Angl I/J/8/5649.

15 P[eace] C[onference] D[iary], 16 Sept.

16 Wolf to Marshall, 1 June 1919. [University College Library, London] Lucien Wolf, PCD, 1 June 1919.

17 Woodrow Wilson, although conscious of the considerable Polish-American vote and sympathetic to Polish nationalism, had quite enough of Polish pretensions before the negotiations began. 1 Apr 1919. P. Mantoux (ed), *Les Délibérations du Conseil des Quatre (24 mars–28 juin 1919)*, (Geneva, 1964), I, 112.

18 Paul Mantoux, *Les Délibérations du Conseil des Quatre*, I, 13 seq. Edwin Montagu, Secretary of State for India and, at the time, close to Lloyd George laid out so

restrained and perceptive a view of the Bolshevik problem that Lloyd George had it printed for secret Cabinet and peace conference circulation. Montagu to Lloyd George, 14 Feb 1919. GT 6861. CAB 24/75/275. A. J. Mayer, *Politics and Diplomacy of Peacemaking: Containment and Counterrevolution of Versailles, 1918–1919* (New York, 1967) advances the strongest case for anti-Bolshevism as a prime motive for the peacemakers.

19 Wolf to Deloncle, 17 July; Bigart à Wolf, 18 juil; Wolf to Montefiore, 16 July 1915. BDBJ C 1/2/6. Bigart à Wolf, 18, 22 juil, 22 août, 1 sept; Wolf to Bigart 20, 25 Aug 1915. AIU Angl I/J/8/5271; AIU Cdc S 238/375–376, 404–405. Successive lead stories in *Archives Israélites* on 27 avril and 4 mai 1916 reiterated the Wolf line. For an extensive file of both AIU and American Jewish Committee material, see MAE A/1197/121 seq. on the Deloncle mission and Benedict XV's statement for American Jews, see MAE A/1197/39, 44, and *passim*. See also, Le Sionisme et le Saint Siège, 19 juil 1917. MAE A/1199/98–101; CFC Conf, 16 July 1916. AJ/204/4. For 1916 discussions, see also Alexander and Montefiore to Marshall, 28 Apr 1916. AIU Angl I/D/13/5559; Bigart à Wolf, 15 mai, 5 juin, 5 juil; Wolf to Bigart 18 May, 18 Oct; Bigart à Duparc, 12 juin 1916. AIU Angl I/J/8/5559, 5738; I/G/4/5271; AIU Cdc S 239/298–299. 304, 320, 392; *Jewish Chronicle*, 9 June 1916; CFC Conf, 27 June, 16, 27 July 1916. AJ/204/4. See also Spring-Rice to Drummond, 30 Jan; Spring-Rice to Percy. 16 June 1916, Spring-Rice Papers. FO 800/242/28–29, 168–169.

20 Sée (AIU) à MAE, 13 juin 1916. MAE A/1198/13–17; Wolf to Grey, 6 June 1916. AIU Angl II/D/26/5598; Alexander to Bigart 28 Apr 1916. AIU Angl I/G/4/5529; LW to de Rothschild, 29 July; LW to Montefiore, 30 July 1915. BDBJ C 11/2/6.

21 Bigart à Wolf, 7 juin, 7, 13 nov; Wolf to Bigart 15 Mar, 21 May, 13 June, 16 Nov 1918. AIU Angl III/D/52/6181, 1403, 6344, 6424, 6830; Wolf to Bigart 5 Nov encl Sub-Committee on Negotiations, 28 Oct; Wolf to FO, 31 Oct 1917; Bigart à Wolf, 8 nov 1917. AIU Angl I/J/8/6/6183, 6193; Wolf, 'The Jewish Question', 14 June 1916. AIU Angl II/D/41/5731: CFC Conf, 27 July 1915, 17 May 1916, 3, 23 Oct, 11 Dec 1917; 31 Jan 1918. AJ/204/4.

22 L. B. N[amier], 'Poland', GT-2192. 4 Oct 1917. [United Kingdom. Public Record Office.] CAB[inet] 24/27/379 seq; GT-3912, 12 Mar 1918. CAB 24/45/34–41. See also, Sée à MAE, 18 juin 1916. MAE A/1198/18–19. For Wolf's files and cuttings, see [Mocatta Library] Wolf Papers ER-4(3).

23 The Russian February Revolution raised hopes overly high for settling the Polish-Jewish conflict. Jewish aspirations were 'sympathetically received', and further discussions planned. AJA/FAC Minutes, 22 Mar, 25 Apr, 3 Oct 1917. [Anglo-Jewish Association Archives. Mocatta Library.] AJ/204/4.

24 Stanislaw Patek and August Zaleski saw Lord Rothschild, Claude Montefiore, and Wolf to urge a 'liberal settlement'. They contended that Dmowski really only wished to drive 'Russian' Jews out of Poland. Wolf Confidential Memo, 30 June 1915; AJA/CC 27 July 1915. AJ/204/4. When Dmowski planned a 1916 lecture tour in Paris and London, the Alliance and Conjoint Committee brought government pressure to bear in view of his avowed anti-Semitism. Dmowski was not permitted to lecture in Paris, and his presentation at King's College in London, after a Foreign Office warning, proved innocuous. AJA/CC. 17 May 1916. AJ/204/4.

25 Polish political parties opposed to Dmowski meeting in Petrograd accepted national and cultural autonomy for minorities in principle. Jewish Nationalists, however, began to press for full 'national autonomy'. AJA/FAC 23 Oct, 11 Dec 1917, 31 Jan 1918. AJ/204/4; *The Times*, 20 Oct 1917; Wolf to Bigart, 31 Oct, 28 Nov 1917. AIU Angl I/J/8/6183, 6221. See also, Report of the Subcommittee on

Negotiations with Poland, 28 Oct 1917; Wolf to Balfour, 31 Oct; Wolf to Graham, 5 Nov 1917, ibid. 6193.

26 Joint Foreign Committee, *The Peace Conference, Paris, 1919* (London, 1920), 74; Blank to Wolf, 29 Nov 1918. BDBJ C 11/2/13; Wolf-Blank-Oliphant interview at FO, 2 July 1915. AIU Angl II/D/26/5271; Wolf's reflective report on the second meeting of the Assembly of the League of Nations, [16 Nov 1921]. AIU Angl III/D/52/9143; Wolf, Report to the JFC, 15 Dec 1920. AIU Angl III/D/52/8253. See also, FAC Confidential Minutes, 3, 23 Oct, 11 Dec 1917; 31 Jan 1918. AJ 204/4/54, 66, 71–72, unn. For the anxiety about emigration, see particularly Wolf to Bigart, 9 Feb; Bigart à Wolf, 9[!] fév 1920. AIU Angl III/D/52/8253.

27 Wolf, PCD, 19 Mar. Wolf returned to Paris from London on 9 February, having ascertained from the Joint Foreign Committee how much range he had for manoeuvre. While doing nothing to obstruct Zionist claims for Palestine, Wolf was determined to achieve his program in the European succession states. The Zionists, who however, having already stolen a march on the 'moderates' contended that their East European Jewish Nationalist delegations were fully representative of Jewish opinion. They were not, and a regular Polish Jewish delegation reached Paris in late April, but meanwhile Wolf had to fend off the Zionist-Nationalist claims of a delegation in being. See, e.g., PCD. 10 Feb.

28 Wolf to Oliphant, 15 June, de Bunsen to Wolf, 23 June, Wolf to de Bunsen, 29 June 1916. AIU Angl I/J/8/5649; Bigart à Wolf, 26 nov 1916. AIU Cdc S 240/68/6312.

29 PCD, 1, 3 Mar. the AIU and JFC had coordinated letters on the Polish question with their respective foreign ministries and conference delegations on 21 Jan. PCD, 21 Jan.

30 PCD, 5 Mar, 27 Feb; Henriques' summaries of the British statutes that Wolf furnished the Poles and British officials is in BDBJ C 11/2/14. See also the Minutes of the Joint Foreign Committee, 6 Mar, 14 Nov, 11 Dec 1918; Wolf to Marshall, 28 Nov 1918. BDBJ C 11/2/13.

31 PCD, 20 Apr, 19, 20 Mar; Sée & Bigart à MAE, 22 mai 1919. AIU Cdc S 243/3–5. The Ukrainians continued to seek Jewish support for their claims. See the circular letter to each Jewish organization asking for their participation in an investigation of reported pogroms from the President of the Ukrainian delegation, 11 Oct 1919. BDBJ C 11/3/1/3.

32 Wolf, Comité des Délégations, Report on the Visit of the Delegation to Paris [April, 1919]. BDBJ C 11/3/1/4; PCD, 24 Mar–16 Apr. The Joint Foreign Committee, including Lord Rothschild and Sir Stuart Samuel (both of whom favoured the Zionist formula in Palestine), approved of the refusal to accommodate Jewish Nationalism and instructed Wolf and the Paris delegation 'that they are not to agree to, or support the demands for Jewish National Rights'. 1 May 1919. BDBJ C 11/3/1/4. Sir Stuart Samuel, President of the Board of Deputies, initially toyed with accommodation, but by 11 April had shifted and 'deprecated' 'any Jewish political separatism in Poland'. PCD, 11 Apr. At the same time, the Joint Foreign Committee acted favourably on the Board of Deputies concern 'that Great Britain's intention to accept the mandate for Palestine will not be abandoned', since, as Claude G. Montefiore, the leading anti-Jewish Nationalist, added, 'any other arrangement would greatly hinder the immigration into that Country of those Jews who desire a new National Home'. BDBJ C 11/3/1/5. Woodrow Wilson, who felt that persecution of Jews was one of the problems most troubling world peace, when the Council of Four came to consider the issue of protection for national and religious minorities, took strong exception to any formulation granting autonomy to national minorities. 1 May 1919. Mantoux, *Délibérations*, I, 440.

33 PCD, 10 Apr. Sir Stuart Samuel had learned wisdom. At the *Consistoire* conference,

he had not opposed the Jewish Nationalists, but by this point he had shifted 'to deprecate any Jewish political separatism in Poland'. Ibid, 11 Apr. So had Headlam-Morley who, in utter frustration, asked Wolf what Polish Jewish Nationalists actually wanted. When Wolf told him that Jewish extremists were as mad as Polish extremists and that there was nothing to choose between Dmowski and Ussishkin, Headlam-Morley said, 'Well, they will all be murdered.' ibid, 14 Apr.

34 PCD, 17–22 Apr; Bigart à AIU, 25 avr; Bigart à Paderewski, 17 avr 1919. AIU Cdc S242/449; *Archives Israélites* LXXX/27, 29. 3, 17 juillet 1919.

35 Wolf's favourable impression of Paderewski outraged Louis Marshall. Morgenthau, however, although officially only working with the Red Cross, supported Wolf's position. PCD, 23–24 Apr.

36 PCD, 25 Apr.

37 PCD, 4–6 May; Mantoux, *Délibérations*, I, 440–442 (1 May) and 474–475 (3 May report from Berthelot, Headlam-Morley, and Miller and the Wilson-Clemenceau, Lloyd-George decisions).

38 Israel Cohen wrote a long article on behalf of the Eastern European Jewish delegates for *The Times* of 22 May 1919 in a desperate attempt to bring public opinion to bear and substitute the Jewish Nationalist for the 'moderate' formula in the Treaties. *The Times* editorially saved Wolf the problem of writing a response by coming out four-square for the 'moderate' position.

39 PCD, 17 May. By May 19th, the Big Three were attempting to restrain Poles from attacking the Ukrainians, who were rumoured to be slaughtering Poles wholesale in Galicia, not to mention their concern with stabilizing the situation in Hungary. Mantoux, *Délibérations*, II, 108–110.

40 Wolf, who had endemic quarrels with Marshall during the months of treaty negotiation, finally realized that Marshall was 'at heart a strong Tory', who allowed 'his views on general politics to affect his attitude on Jewish questions'. Marshall's personal, political detestation of the League as a danger to American interests, for instance, repeatedly led him to place the Jewish guarantees in the signatories to the Treaties rather than, as Wolf insisted, the League. Marshall's ego and temper, moreover, combined with his strong personal likes and dislikes to make him a most difficult and unpredictable colleague. PCD, 6, 27 June.

41 Montefiore agreed to ask Milner to present a letter to Lloyd George on the Sabbathy Question. Marshall successfully convinced President Wilson on the point. PCD, 18–22 May. H. S. Q. Henriques, barrister and chairman of the Board of Deputies Law & Parliamentary Committee, prepared a summary memorandum for Wolf to give Paderewski on Jews and Education in England. BDBJ C 11/2/14. See also the report on the Warsaw Jewish Congress in *Archives Israélites*, LXXX/22, 29 mai 1919.

42 PCD, 14, 16 June. Part of the problem, as Wolf repeatedly reminded the Poles, was prompt action, control, and investigation. The Zionists' Copenhagen Bureau needed such horror tales to promote the Jewish Nationalist cause and forwarded exaggerated statistics that inflamed opinion. The Jewish Information Bureau in Copenhagen continued generally to be reliable.

43 Gibson's incompetence served as the justification for the elaborate Morgenthau mission to investigate the Polish situation. Esmé Howard, the British Minister to Warsaw, happened to be in Paris at the time, and Percy Wyndham, the chargé, did not handle matters well. Wolf later prepared a story on the Morgenthau report and 'Jews and Bolshevism' for the *Daily Telegraph* of 6 Nov 1919. Copy enclosed with Wolf to Montefiore, 6 Nov 1919. BDBJ C 11/2/14.

44 PCD, 26 May, 6, 8 June.

45 PCD, 28 May. Weizmann, as one of his gambits, played the 'Bolshevik' card, arguing that without Zionism, Jews might become the shock troops of world revolution. Hogarth to Clayton, 30 Mar 1919. [St. Anthony's College, Oxford] Hogarth Papers 14 (iv). Sir Mark Sykes, for one, was absolutely convinced. Sykes to Balfour, 27 Feb 1918. FO 800/210/129. When Weizmann told Oscar Straus 'that a failure of Zionism would mean a great immigration of Russian-Jewish Bolshevists in America', Straus acidly replied, 'Well we shall hang them.' PCD, 25 Mar. Balfour also believed that Jews were 'to a large degree, leaders in such [revolutionary] movements'. He continued by passing on the preposterous rumour, popular in British genteel circles, that Lenin 'on his mother's side was a Jew'. Brandeis, to whom he was talking on that occasion, told him that was nonsense, that Lenin 'on both sides is an upper class Russian'. Paris, 24 June 1919. FO 800/217/187. Bolshevism as a Jewish conspiracy was promulgated in print, apparently on the initiative of Colonel Townshend, General Ironside's Intelligence Officer of the British Archangel expedition. PCD, 2 Aug. See also, Wolf, Memorandum on the Jews and Bolshevism, 2 Oct 1919. BDBJ C 11/2/14.

46 Wolf to Marshall, 1 June 1919. Copy in PCD, 1 June.

47 Wolf, however, found this request entangled him in American Jewish politics. Even Cyrus Adler criticized Wolf for involving Morganthau, likening him, for Wolf's benefit, to Bentwich as a chronic 'mischief-maker' PCD, 20 June.

48 PCD, 28 May–28 June; Mantoux, *Délibérations*, II, 92–94, 331–332, 340–341, 451–453, 470–471, 486–490, 544–547.

49 Wolf continually sorted out real and exaggerated claims. See, e.g., his discussions with Stuart Samuel and Cyrus Adler on the Częstochowa incident. PCD, 29–30 June.

50 Wolf to Bigart, 7 July 1920. AIU Angl III/D/52/7896. Wolf's consistent support from Claude G. Montefiore and Sir Stuart Samuel as well as most traditional Anglo-Jewish leaders gave him indirectly access to Lloyd George and his circle of advisers. Montefiore, for instance, had ready access through Lord Milner.

51 When Margolin was lobbying for his Ukrainian cause, he called Clemenceau's attention to the 'rabid anti-Semitism of the Polish Government. "Yes, I know", said Clemenceau, "they are all reactionaries and anti-Semites, but they are going to get an ultimatum from us."' PCD, 26 May.

52 See, particularly, R. Ullman, *Britain and the Russian Civil War*, II–III (Princeton, 1967–1973). See also, Wolf, 'Memorandum on the Danger of Anti-Jewish Excesses from the Army of Denikin', 30 July 1919. BDBJ C 11/2/14; Bigart à Simonson, 6 Nov; Wolf to Bigart, 31 Oct, 10, 11, 12, 13, 19 Nov; Bigart à Wolf, 3, 12, 21 Nov; Bigart à Wolfsohn, 20 Nov 1919. AIU Cdc S 243/7175, 7178, 7210, 7219, 7241, 7145, 7255, 7607, 7619, 7643, 7675, 7685.

53 Wolf, Report to the JFC, 15 Dec 1920. AIU Angl III/D/52/8253. See also Wolf's Report on the Second Meeting of the Assembly of the League of Nations [16 Nov 1921]. ibid/9143; Wolf to Bigart, 6 July 1920. AIU Angl III/D/53/7887; Samuel to Wolf, 1 Sept 1920. BDBJ C 11/3/2/3. See also, Wolf's reports on the mission of Professor Szymon Ashkennzy to undo the Minority clauses in Poland. Wolf to Bigart, 12 June, 18 Aug, 8, 28 Oct, 5 Nov 1920. AIU Anglo III/D/52/7917, 8135, 8156 and W. S. Churchill, Report on the Situation at Vilna, 10 Oct 1920. CAB 1/29/222–223. See also, FO Political Intelligence: Poland 008, 20 Mar 1920. CP 937. CAB 24/101/161–162. Wolf believed the boycott was the most difficult issue to resolve in any ultimate settlement of the Polish-Jewish problem. Morgenthau, after the enquiry the summer of 1919, found eight principal outbreaks against Jews in Poland. While whitewashing nothing, Morgenthau was 'anxious to hold the balance fairly evenly between Poles and Jews', while Homer-Johnson preferred to

dwell on Jewish 'defects' and exculpate the Poles. The Report ultimately cited 282 deaths. 'Strictly speaking there were no pogroms, but only military excesses within the zone of military operations.' PCD, 2, 5–7 Oct. Wolf, while putting these tragedies in a balanced light, hoped that ultimately the resolution of the Russian civil war and restoration of peace there would create an opportunity for eastward Jewish migration and reduce the Jewish presence and problem in the small succession states. PCD, 9–11, 6 Aug, 5, 8 Sept.

54 Wolf to Greenberg, 9 Dec 1919. BDBJ C 11/2/14. Wolf did not always deal in 'tranquillity'. He regularly added to Sir Basil Thompson's dossiers about subversive or potentially subversive individuals who always seemed to be Zionists or Jewish Nationalists. See, e.g., Wolf to Thompson, 15 Apr 1921. BDBJ C 11/2/16.

55 Wolf to Bigart, 26 May, 26 July 1925. AIU Angl IV/D/54/6910, 7031.

18

ASPECTS OF JEWISH SELF-GOVERNMENT IN ŁÓDŹ, 1914–1939

Robert Moses Shapiro

1. THE GENERAL PROBLEMS OF THE JEWISH *KEHILLA* IN ŁÓDŹ[1]

Introduction

Poland's second largest city and major industrial centre was home to nearly a quarter million Jews comprising a third of the city's population by 1939. Łódź was second only to Warsaw among the more than 800 *kehillot* in Poland.[2] Designated by government fiat in the 1820s to become a factory town, Łódź grew explosively as it attracted immigrants from near and far within the Tsarist empire. There are few works of rigorous scholarship on the history of the Jews in a city which was both a remarkable centre of proletarian movements in a predominantly agrarian country and at one and the same time a stronghold of Jewish tradition and secular Jewish socialism. There is also a dearth of studies of the local Jewish communities in interwar Poland, when their combined budgets amounted to 40 million złoty or more annually.[3]

There is in Poland, Israel and the USA a wealth of materials for the study of Łódź Jewry and its *kehilla*. Łódź was spared Warsaw's fate as a major battlefield, which deprived us of the records of the Ministry of Religions and Education's 'Mosaic Department', which had supervised the *kehillot* throughout the country, as well as the records of the Warsaw *kehilla*. In contrast, the archive of the Łódź *kehilla* was largely preserved, along with the records of local governmental agencies which had directly supervised and dealt with the *kehilla*. The extensive Yiddish and Polish press of both Łódź and Warsaw are an important resource, though partisan and inherently limited. The Łódź *kehilla* itself published and issued numerous reports, as well as a monograph on its first cemetery and the first periodical devoted to Jewish communal affairs in Poland. Unfortunately, few of the leaders of Łódź Jewry survived to publish memoirs or be interviewed by oral historians.[4]

Concepts and Consensus[5]

On the eve of Poland's rebirth there was a consensus among Polish Jewish groups that some form of self-governing communal organization was needed to unite and serve all Jews. The consensus extended to introduction of a democratic franchise, although the Orthodox opposed giving women the right to vote. All Jewish political parties favoured a federation of *kehillot* with a central council of Polish Jewry, with Yiddish as the principal Jewish communal language, although Zionists were champions of Hebrew and assimilationists were patriots of Polish. Most Jews held that the new *kehilla* should not only deal with religious affairs, but with social welfare and education, as well. Bundists would have restricted the *kehilla* to educational and cultural activities, while assimilationists opposed any ethnic separatism beyond the minimum needs of religion and philanthropy. Most Jews held that the *kehilla*, as the leading Jewish institution, should exercise supervision and guidance over all other Jewish public institutions. It was a given that the *kehilla* should have the power of taxation and should share in state funding for its activities.

Legal Status[6]

The legal status of the Jewish religious community in interwar Poland was rooted in legislation introduced by the German occupation administration in the Warsaw General-government in November 1916, which outlined a federal system of local and county bodies, with a 'Jewish Supreme Council' at the head. Entrusted to the Jewish community were administration of Jewish religious life, supervision of all Jewish religious and charitable organizations, as well as responsibility for both religious and secular education of young Jews and care of the Jewish poor. As a public-legal corporation embracing all Jews, the Jewish community was empowered to levy compulsory taxes on local Jews to supplement income from other sources. Literate male *kehilla* taxpayers over the age of 25 were eligible to vote in curial elections of *kehilla* councils,[7] with half of the councilmen to be chosen by a curia consisting of voters with secondary or higher education or rabbinic ordination. Several additional members of both major *kehilla* boards and the Jewish Supreme Council were to be nominated by the state, to which was reserved pervasive influence at all levels of Jewish communal organization. The German ordinance of 1916, which bore marked similarity to the Jewish communal legislation in the German states of Baden and Prussia, was never fully implemented, although elections were held in 218 communities, but not in Warsaw or Łódź. The new Poland's chief of state, Jozef Piłsudski, amended the German law of 1916, which he extended to include the whole of the former Congress Kingdom.

Piłsudski's amendments emphasised the religious nature of the *kehilla*, eliminated its responsibility for secular education, made social welfare merely an option and eliminated its power of supervision over private Jewish organizations. At the same time, the state's power over communal finances and rabbinic elections was enhanced. Only after years of delay and lobbying was the Piłsudski decree of 7 February 1919[8] eventually extended over the rest of Poland. The uniform text published in April 1928 remained the basic law governing Jewish communal affairs in Poland (except for autonomous Silesia).

Leadership[9]

Over the quarter century from 1914, the Łódź *kehilla* went through three Jewish regimes. For more than a decade, from October 1914 until April 1925, the Łódź *kehilla* was governed by a provisional board chosen by less than a score of men convened to fill the vacuum left by the absence from the city of the entire former board.[10] The provisional board was recognised by the Germans, who named additional members, retaining a majority of assimilationists and a minority of Hasidic and Orthodox Jews. Not permitted by the Ministry of Religions to resign until elections were held in 1924, the *kehilla* board was depleted by attrition. The second *kehilla* régime began in 1925, when the *kehilla* board elected as a result of the election of the previous year took office. No less than 14 lists contended for mandates on the 35–seat Łódź *kehilla* council, in an election with 34,596 eligible voters, of whom 48.4 per cent cast ballots. The results were indecisive, as the Orthodox *Agudas Israel* bloc won a plurality of 34.6 per cent of the vote but was unable to form a majority coalition.[11] The governing *kehilla* board elected by the council consisted of six *Agudas Israel*, four Zionists, three Non-party Religious, a Bundist and a Folkist.[12] A minority coalition of Zionists and Non-party Religious elected Zionist Sejm deputy and city councilman Dr. Jerzy Rosenblatt board president, while the *Aguda* had to settle for the vice-presidency. Endless bickering and the lack of a clear majority contributed to chronic, paralysing deadlocks for three years, as the board was divided by fundamental differences over such questions as voting participation of a rabbinate member on the board, the official language of the *kehilla*, support for secular and religious education and more. Moreover, the largest faction, the *Agudas Israel*, felt itself entitled to lobby the government to obtain reversal of majority decisions it opposed. The irregularly convened public sessions of the *kehilla* council were spectacles of squabbling and catcalls which only served to underscore the political division and immaturity of Łódź Jewry. By the end of 1927, all factions openly conceded the need for new elections to be called by the state.

This set the stage for the virtual 'coup d'état' in February 1928 which brought the *Agudas Israel* to power in the Łódź *kehilla*, where it would remain until 1939. With state support and collusion, the *Aguda* effectively seized power in the Łódź *kehilla* board as the Piłsudski regime supported a sympathetic and powerful faction on the Jewish street in an echo of the struggle for power in the *Sejm*. In effect, control of the Łódź *kehilla* may have been pre-payment for active support of the regime's BBWR list in the *Sejm* election of 4 March 1928. When legal challenges to the bizarre events of February-March 1928 eventually resulted in a court ruling invalidating the election of a new board, the government precluded the resumption of office by the former *kehilla* board president by the expedient of dissolving both the council and board and naming a provisional board with an *Aguda* majority led by Lejb Mincberg, who had come to power as *kehilla* board president in the 'coup' of 1928.[13]

Jacob Lejb Mincberg would remain president of the Łódź *kehilla* until 1939. A veteran member of the city council and a *Sejm* deputy for most of the interwar years, Mincberg was a manufacturer and a devoted follower of the Gerer Rebe. He was simultaneously very much the European businessman in a well-cut suit and hat and a *Hasid* who wore traditional garb on Sabbaths and holidays, including a *shtrayml* when on pilgrimages to Ger. Bundists attacked him as 'the diminutive Mussolini of the Łódź *Aguda*',[14] while the *kehilla* secretary admiringly characterised Mincberg's administrative style in 1938 as 'a sort of mosaic of dictatorship and liberalism, of strict piety and most modern technique'.[15] When a recalcitrant majority in the *kehilla* council in 1928 and 1929 attempted to obstruct adoption of Mincberg's budgets, the *Aguda* leader was able to prevail by means of illegal manoeuvres with the collusion of the county governor, the immediate supervisor of *kehilla* activities.[16]

The *kehilla* election of May 1931 enabled the *Aguda* to cement its hold on the Łódź *kehilla* by achieving an unprecedented absolute majority in both the *kehilla* council and board. This was accomplished with aid of the amended Jewish communal election regulation, issued in 1930[17] and bearing the stigmata of that year's corrupt parliamentary election which gave the Piłsudski regime an absolute majority. Its most notorious provision, 'paragraph 20', permitted disenfranchisement of 'persons who publicly come out against the Mosaic faith'. It was employed in Łódź against ten men, the leaders of the *Bund* and *Po'ale Tsion*, which, not surprisingly, provoked the socialists into boycotting the *kehilla* election. When the *Aguda* bloc won an absolute majority in an election in which the officially reported voter turnout was 57.4 per cent in remarkable contrast to Warsaw's mere 29.5 per cent, Zionists levelled blunt accusations of outright, blatant fraud.[18] But just as protests against abuses during the 1930 *Sejm* election were ignored by the régime, allegations regarding abuses committed by the *Aguda* were left uninvestigated. In 1936, in the wake of the Bundist plurality in the Warsaw *kehilla* election and the Łódź city council election in which the *Bund*-led bloc won nearly half the votes cast for Jewish lists, the Ministry of Religions ordered an indefinite postponement of the Łódź *kehilla* election which had been scheduled for 15 November 1936. Thus, the *Aguda* regime led by Mincberg remained in office until the outbreak of war.

Finances and Activities[19]

Between 1924 and 1936, annual spending of the Łódź *kehilla* grew from only 159,606 zł. to 1,758,177 zł.[20] The communal budgeting process in Łódź was complex and politically charged. Despite lip-service to the ideal of impartial supervision of the *kehilla*, the Polish state actively intervened in the financial administration of the Łódź *kehilla* both to further the interest of cooperative elements and to foil the aspirations of opposition groups. The various régimes of Poland pursued a policy of limited *kehilla* spending on religious needs and some aid for the poor. In reviewing proposed budgets submitted for confirmation, the state tended to compel reductions in the categories of social welfare, education and institutional subsidies. Such intervention into Jewish communal affairs and finances was analogous to similar policies in regard to incompetent or recalcitrant city council and municipal régimes.

For most of the interwar years, over 80 per cent of the Łódź *kehilla*'s revenues came from the direct *kehilla* tax and cemetery fees. Like some state taxes, the direct *kehilla* tax was assessed by committees of businessmen, artisans and workers which estimated the individual's ability to pay the tax, which ranged from 5 to 5,000 zł. in the 1930s, when a majority of Łódź Jewry was considered unable to pay even 5 zł. yearly.[21] Cemetery fees were a relatively progressive source of revenue, as most burials were provided free and only those willing and able to pay for choicer plots and tombstone permits were charged, although there was frequent bitter haggling. While cemetery fees produced over half of the Łódź *kehilla*'s revenue in the chaotic year of 1927, by the 1930s such fees declined to less than a fifth of total communal income. Less than 15 per cent of the communal revenue tended to come from a variety of minor sources, including voluntary contributions, endowments and bequests, synagogue and ritual bath fees, as well as fees for registration of births, deaths, marriages and divorces. Negligible amounts came from the city government toward the cost of *kehilla* care for orphans and the insane and for burials of the indigent. Unlike most Polish *kehillot*, Łódź did not depend for a significant part of its income on operation of kosher animal slaughter, which it only reluctantly took over at government urging at the end of 1933.[22]

Until the mid-1920s, religious items took a major part of the Łódź *kehilla*'s annual spending, which was typical of the minimal activities which a small community could undertake. As the *kehilla* budget grew, an increasing proportion went for social welfare. Thus, by 1930, over half of the *kehilla*'s spending went for social welfare, and religion took only a fourth. Yet Lejb Mincberg unwillingly presided over such growth in spending for what he, as a veteran city councilman, felt was properly a municipal responsibility. The Łódź *kehilla* board president declared that:

> Social aid has unwillingly become the broadest field of our interest. It is another story whether such unwilling activity as a result of bitter necessity is a normal thing.[23]

The regular activities of the Łódź *kehilla* for the benefit of the local Jewry fell into three principal areas: religion, education and social welfare. In none of these areas did the *kehilla* have a real monopoly; instead it worked alongside the numerous private Jewish organizations in each field. The *kehilla* was legally charged with responsibility for Jewish religious needs and only its rabbis were officially recognised, yet most Jews benefited from privately operated houses of worship, ritual baths, religious schools and the many privately supported rabbis (*'vinkl-rabonim'*). Polish law did not invest the *kehilla* and its rabbis with any coercive power to enforce Sabbath observance or *kashrut* beyond that of moral suasion and public opinion. The *kehilla* did have a monopoly on the operation of the Jewish cemetery, which could be used for coercion on occasion.

The Łódź *kehilla* provided small subsidies to dozens of religious schools and to some vocational educational programmes, as well as tuition grants for needy pupils. Not until 1931 did the *kehilla* open the first of two communal Talmud-Torahs providing both Judaic and secular education to several hundred boys from impoverished families. Most Jewish children attended the public elementary schools, which were under the overall supervision of a regional school council, to which the Łódź *kehilla* was regularly invited to name a representative. But the *kehilla* had no role in the legally mandated instruction in Judaism for the Jewish public school pupils. At times the *kehilla* did attempt to obtain improvements in the quality and quantity of such instruction.

For various reasons, including but not exclusively or predominantly because of anti-Jewish discrimination, many thousands of needy Jews were ineligible or unable to obtain municipal assistance in Łódź. The needy Jews turned to the network of private Jewish welfare organizations and institutions and to the *kehilla* for relief. By the latter 1930s, the *kehilla* annually allocated about 100,000 zł. in subsidies to scores of social welfare institutions chronically in financial crisis. Although the Łódź *kehilla* did not operate its own hospital, during the 1930s it regularly maintained 20 beds at the Poznanski Hospital and at the Marpe tuberculosis sanatorium in Otwock. The *kehilla* did operate an insane asylum with 59 beds, located in an inadequate building at the original Jewish cemetery on Wesoła Street. In a daring and ambitious move in 1938, Lejb Mincberg acquired the site of an unfinished mental hospital outside the city which he planned to complete at a cost of 1 million zł. as a 400–bed facility by 1941. The Łódź *kehilla* paid for the foster care of scores of Jewish foundlings and orphans annually and eventually funded two *kehilla* homes which housed over 70 children in 1937, while several hundred orphans were in Jewish orphanages subsidised by the *kehilla*. Direct aid to the needy by the *kehilla* took several forms, including Passover aid grants, free coal and emergency relief grants for the unemployed and homeless. Although it was not in a position to offer a regular relief dole, during 1930 the *kehilla* provided direct aid to 15,488 persons, who with their dependents amounted to over a third of Łódź Jewry.[24] Yet the number of Jews who benefited from municipal welfare programmes may have been larger than those receiving direct *kehilla* aid. Beyond emergency aid, the Łódź *kehilla* provided some 'productive aid' in the form of free loans and grants to buy business licenses or to renovate pushcarts and market stalls or for vocational retraining. There was also from 1928 a free legal consultation service at the *kehilla* chancellory.

Representation and Defence[25]

When Polish Jews felt in danger, they appealed to the government for protection through their elected representatives, as well as through influential businessmen. Frequently, those intercessors were also members of the *kehilla* leadership, like Jerzy Rosenblatt and Lejb Mincberg in Łódź. However, the *kehilla* was ill-equipped to act as a defence agency, although it might have been in a better position had the projected Religious Council of Jewish Communities ever been brought into being. Inability to achieve unity under any central, coordinated leadership was a principal weakness of Jewish political life in Poland. The significance of the *kehilla* grew in the increasingly hostile environment after Piłsudski's death, as Jewish representation in city councils and the *Sejm* declined. However, in spite of increasingly frequent anti-Jewish violence, including five bombings and several murders in 1936 alone, the Łódź *kehilla* does not appear to have taken any action to organize Jewish self-defence. Though Łódź had no university, the *kehilla* did adopt protest resolutions against the perennial violence on campuses and calls for anti-Jewish quotas. Yet, even as the ultimate crisis for Poland neared in 1939, the government did not involve the Łódź *kehilla* leadership in the plans for evacuation of the city's civilians in the event of war.[26]

In the struggle for a living, the *kehilla* sought to moderate the impact of the Sunday rest law by obtaining temporary exemptions to allow food stores and bakeries to operate additional hours on Saturday nights and

Sundays preceding major Jewish holidays, as was normally allowed before Christmas and Easter. However, the Łódź *kehilla* was rarely in the forefront of the struggle against discrimination faced by Jews in both public and private employment, including enterprises owned by Jews. Bundists railed incessantly against the hypocrisy of wealthy Hasidic *kehilla* councilmen and boardmen who piously threw themselves into the annual Passover relief campaign, but boycotted Jewish workers for the rest of the year. When Mincberg failed to employ any Jews during renovations on the Old Town Synagogue, the Orthodox worker representative in the *Aguda* faction castigated him the *kehilla* council:

> If the *kehilla* which ought to serve as a model employs no Jewish workers, how can one demand of Jewish industrialists that they should take on Jews for work.[27]

The law on 'humane slaughter' passed in 1936 was a direct assault on the religious, civil and economic rights of Poland's Jews, as well as a threat to the major source of revenue for most of the country's *kehillot*. Warsaw *kehilla* board president Elijah Mazur of *Agudas Israel* led an effort to mobilise other *kehillot* to use their connections to lobby for efforts to vote down or at least amend the proposed law, which *Sejm* deputy Lejb Mincberg characterised during debate as 'the local version of the Nuremberg laws'.[28] Once the law went into effect in 1937, the Łódź *kehilla* took the initiative in realising to the fullest the restricted opportunity left for kosher animal slaughter. Polish Jews had traditionally not consumed the hindquarters of animals, which ritually would require difficult and costly 'porging' or deveining (*nikur*); the portions had formerly been sold to non-Jewish customers, but that was no longer permitted. A large scale 'porging' facility and training programme were established by the Łódź *kehilla*, serving as model for Warsaw and other communities. By June 1938, the Łódź 'porging' institute had graduated 35 porgers and increased the quantity of kosher meat available, although many Jews continued to be reluctant to consume such porged meat in spite of repeated urging by the *kehilla* rabbinate. When the attempt to ban kosher slaughter entirely was renewed (unsuccessfully) in 1939, the Łódź *kehilla* joined in a nation-wide 16–day interdict of Jewish consumption of beef, proclaimed as an act of protest in March.

The Łódź *kehilla* spoke out on the treatment of Jews in Romania, the Soviet Union, Palestine and Germany. *Kehilla* resolutions were released to the press and sometimes sent to foreign governments or to the League of Nations. For example, six months before Hitler became chancellor, the Łódź *kehilla* board wrote in English to the League of Nations to protest against the anti-Jewish agitation in Germany and to appeal to the League to defend the Jewish people in Germany, for

> These unprecedented methods of destruction, recalling the dark medieval ages and forming a disgrace for the twentieth century, are awakening uneasiness among Jewish people as regards the fate of their brethren in Germany.[29]

Eventually, the *kehilla* became involved in the effort to aid Jewish refugees from Germany, both in 1933 and after the October 1938 expulsions of Polish Jewish nationals.

Although the Polish state permitted *kehillot* to budget funds for Zionist development in Palestine under the rubric of aid for poor emigrants, the *Aguda* faction in the Łódź *kehilla* generally blocked any grants for Zionist institutions or programmes until the latter 1930s, when a maximum of 6,000 zł. was allocated in 1938 for the various Palestine development funds. Yet the Łódź *kehilla* often spoke out on behalf of Jews in Palestine and the right of Jews to settle there. In response to the May 1939 British White Paper on Palestine, the Łódź *kehilla* board declared that

> This 'White Paper' signifies a [retreat from] the commitments of England to world Jewry and a liquidation of the Balfour Declaration. The Jewish people will not be deterred by the English machinations, being certain that the Land of Israel is appointed by Providence for the Jews.[30]

CONCLUSIONS

How autonomous was the *kehilla* in interwar Poland? It functioned under close state supervision and, at every stage of the elective process, the state reserved for itself and used various means to influence the composition of the Jewish communal leadership. State nominated commissioners often took over *kehillot* which were judged in danger of chaos. The trend toward such commissioner regimes in major *kehillot* grew from 1935, in tandem with the intensification of central governmental control over all local institutions. From 1928, the state consistently supported the *Agudas Israel* régime led by Lejb Mincberg, brought to power illegally with state collusion and kept in office with state cooperation.

Both before and during Mincberg's regime, the Łódź *kehilla* often and loudly proclaimed its patriotism and loyalty to the common Polish fatherland and its foreign policies. National holidays and the birthdays and name-days of the President of Poland and Piłsudski were marked with special services of thanksgiving in the *kehilla*'s Old Town Synagogue and with formal greetings sent by telegram. The annual Passover *sedorim* arranged by the *kehilla* for the hundreds of Jewish soldiers in the Łódź garrison were marked with patriotic addresses and singing of the Polish national anthem in the presence of invited government officials and military officers. When Poland sought to raise funds through national loans, the *kehilla* cooperated in the effort to mobilise Jewish subscriptions.

To what extent did the *kehilla* dominate Jewish communal life? Unlike its pre-modern predecessors, the Polish *kehilla* did not possess even a nominal monopoly over the most important facets of Jewish personal and public life, with the exception of official rabbinic functions and the operation of the cemetery.[31] Efforts to unite all Jewish institutions under the Łódź *kehilla*'s umbrella were considered but never realised. The *kehilla*'s ability to raise money through taxation could have been used to impose its leadership over the myriad Jewish social welfare, educational and religious institutions. However, both due to the poverty of a large part of Łódź Jewry and the limits placed on burdening of the well-to-do by both the state and the self-interest of communal leaders, the Łódź *kehilla* was unable to generate sufficient revenue to overshadow the wide array of privately organized and voluntarily funded organizations. Yet the *kehilla* leaders felt that they could and should speak out in the name of all Jews. *Kehilla* elections were public events involving a large part of the Jewish populace, validating claims to leadership. Indeed, the *kehilla* leadership was comprised of individuals who were members of the city's social, economic, political and religious élites, whose other positions in society reinforced their claims to communal leadership.

Organizationally, the Polish *kehilla* was a relatively primitive institution with a poorly developed structure. At the same time, the leaders of the Łódź *kehilla* were generally major merchants, industrialists and professionals who sought to introduce the kind of modern administrative methods which they employed in their own professional lives. The experience acquired by Mincberg and other members of the city council and of parliament in parliamentary methods and budgeting was certainly applied in the context of the *kehilla*. Similarly, the defects and weaknesses of Polish municipal and parliamentary life also hampered the operation of the Jewish community. Growth in the size and complexity of the Łódź *kehilla*'s activities during Mincberg's administration was reflected in the expansion of the communal payroll from 43 in 1928 to 130 a decade later.[32]

Although it was a local institution, the Łódź *kehilla* conducted what could be called a foreign policy. When prominent American or British Jews visited, they were received and informed about local conditions and needs, although with one eye on the reaction of Polish society to negative publicity. The American Joint or JDC was the single largest conduit of foreign aid for Polish Jewry, yet it tended to avoid dealing with the highly politicised and contentious *kehillot*, preferring instead to work through apolitical social welfare organizations and loan funds (*kasas*). Łódź *kehilla* leaders often spoke out on behalf of their brethren in Romania, the Soviet

Union, Palestine and Germany, sending protest telegrams to government and the League of Nations.

When in February 1939, Lejb Mincberg presented to the Łódź *kehilla* council what would be his final proposed budget, he expressed both his sense of the *kehilla*'s mission and his anxiety for the future:

> We have always striven that the Jewish *kehilla* should encompass ever more of our religious and national affairs and become the real representation of the separate groups and settlements in the country . . . The Jewish *kehilla* had to be and should have been the address of the entire Jewish people. [However], the Jewish *kehillot* – against our will – were changed into the sole address and who knows whether the course of events will not, heaven forbid, result in the basis of communal activity having to be still more expanded?[33]

Which leads to the controversial question, to what extent was the Nazi-German-imposed *Judenrat* an outgrowth or a continuation of the pre-war *kehilla*? Because of the role played by Mordecai Chaim Rumkowski, who had been a member of the Łódź *kehilla* board since 1932, some writers like Wolf Yasni[34] have argued that the Jewish ghetto administration was a malignant outgrowth of the former *kehilla* which had already pursued sycophantic policies toward the régime in power. Studies of the ghetto leadership by Isaiah Trunk and Lucjan Dobroszycki have underscored the progressive negative selection which took place with the passage of time.[35] Well before the introduction of the Łódź Ghetto in spring 1940, the *kehilla* had largely ceased to be a Jewish institution, although the Jews who worked within the ghetto administration generally honestly sought to assuage Jewish need while meeting German demands. The key factor in Rumkowski's power was not Jewish acceptance, but the threat of German retribution at the slightest resistance or obstruction. While both the medieval and modern *kehilla* were institutions sought and created by Jews to serve Jewish needs in the broadest sense, the Łódź *Aeltestenrat* was ordained by the Nazi Germans as an instrument of destruction of the Jewish community.

NOTES

1 This paper is based on my dissertation of the same title (Columbia University, 1987), which was written with the support of the YIVO Institute for Jewish Research, National Foundation for Jewish Culture, Memorial Foundation for Jewish Culture, Kościuszko Foundation, International Research and Exchanges Board (IREX) and the Institute of Contemporary Jewry at the Hebrew University in Jerusalem. *Kehilla* is the Hebrew Yiddish word commonly used by Jews to

designate their communal administration, also known by the Polish Yiddish word *gmine*. *Kehilla* and *Gmina* are the Polish equivalents, used here.

2 For lack of space, comparative material about other *kehillot* and municipal government has largely been excluded.

3 See the bibliography in my dissertation.

4 Ibid.

5 See ibid., ch. one, 'The Concepts of the Modern *kehilla* among Polish Jews'.

6 See my diss., ch. two, 'Legal Status of the Jewish Community'.

7 In most *kehillot*, the governing board was directly elected, while in the largest communities the board was to be chosen indirectly through the directly elected council. The minimum age for candidates was set at 30.

8 Piłsudski issued a series of decrees to establish the basic legal, administrative system of Poland pending legislation by the *Sejm*.

9 See ibid., ch. three, '*kehilla* Leadership and Elections'.

10 The initiative came from the Central Citizens Committee of Łódź to enable the Jewish Poznański Hospital, which was owed a large sum for treatment of indigent patients sent to it by the *kehilla*, to expand its operations.

11 The *Aguda* bloc received 34.6 per cent of the votes and 13 council seats; the Zionist bloc received 25.2 per cent and nine seats; the Nonparty Religious bloc 17.9 per cent and seven seats; *Bund* 9.2 per cent and three seats; *Po'ale Tsion* 6.6 per cent and two seats; Folkists 4.6 per cent and one seat; other 2 per cent and no seats.

12 The secularist Folkist won a seat on the board as a result of a deal with the *Orthodox Aguda* which also secured an additional seat for itself. Although the chief rabbi was *ex officio* also a member of the *kehile* board, the position remained vacant from 1920. The *Aguda* demand that a deputy rabbi be invited to fill the rabbinic seat on the board was rejected by the majority who understood that most of the rabbis would vote with the *Aguda*.

13 Mincberg's predecessor as *kehilla* board president was Benjamin Russ, leader of the Nonparty Religious and an Aleksanderer Hasid inclined positively toward Zionism and vehemently opposed to the *Agudas Israel*, which he saw as the instrument for the Gerer Hasidic drive to hegemony in the Jewish community. On Russ, see the manuscript biography by his son, Yitshak, in the Y. Grunbaum Archive (Central Zionist Archive, A127/352).

14 On Mincberg, see Hillel Seidman, *Ishim she-hikarti* (Jerusalem, 1970), pp. 327–34; *Polski Słownik Biograficzny*, vol.21 (Wrocław, 1976), pp. 281–2; and *Ilustrirter poylisher mantshester*, July 1929, p. 16. The Bundist quote is from the *Lodzher veker*, 8 June 1928, no. 25, p. 3.

15 *Yidishe Togblat*, 21 June 1938, no. 236. p. 5.

16 Provisions legalising such tactics were included in the Minister of Religions decree on Jewish communal finances of 9 Sept. 1931 (*Dziennik Ustaw Rzeczypospolitej Polski* [Hereafter *Dz. URP*], 1931, no. 89, poz.698.)

17 *Dz. URP*, 1930, no. 75, poz. 592.

18 Votes were cast by 15,571 voters out of 27,133 eligible. The *Aguda* bloc received 54.9 per cent of the votes and 15 out of 25 council seats; Zionists drew 23.3 per cent and five seats; Nonparty Religious 9.7 per cent and two seats; Folkists 8.1 per cent and two seats; and the assimilationist Economic Bloc 3.9 per cent and one seat.

19 See my diss., ch. four, 'Communal Funding and Functions'.

20 See my diss., Table 4.20.

21 For data on Łódź *kehilla* tax assessments, see ibid., Tables 4.10, 4.13–4.15 and 4.40.

22 See ibid., Appendix A: Łódź *kehilla* Budgets, 1915–1921, 1924–1934.

23 L. Mincberg, 'Der entviklungs-veg fun der lodzher yidisher kehile', *Ilustrirter poylisher mantshester*, April 1930, pp. 35–38; originally published as 'Yorn fun arbet

un aliye fun der lodzher kehile', *Khronik fun der yidisher kehile in lodzh*, no. 2–3, Oct.–Dec. 1929, pp. 7–16.
24 See my diss., Tables 4.36a-e.
25 See ibid., ch. five, 'Representative and Defender'.
26 See Isaac Lewin, 'Di gehayme evakuatsye-komisye', in *Lodzher yizkerbukh* (N.Y., 1943), pp. 77–80.
27 *Lodzer Tageblat*, 28 Dec. 1932, no. 301, p. 2.
28 Quoted after Emanuel Melzer, *Maavak medini be-malkodet: yehudei polin 1935–1939* (Tel-Aviv, 1982), p. 105.
29 Lodz *kehilla* Board to League of Nations, 27 July 1932 (League of Nations Archives, Geneva, Box R2166 [Minorities Section, Registry No.4/8772/8772, file of protests against the mistreatment of Jews in Germany, Poland, Austria, etc.]). I thank Mark Friedman for providing me with a copy of this letter.
30 *Yidishe Togblat*, 15 May 1939, no. 187, p. 5.
31 The legislation on Jewish communities did provide for the possibility of independent religious associations, which would have their own clergy and cemetery; but none was ever created.
32 See the draft budget for 1928 in the Łódź *kehilla* archive at the Łódzkie Wojewódzkie Archiwum Państwowe, record group 1057/436; and *Nayer Folksblat*, 15 Feb. 1938, pp. 4, 12.
33 *Nayer Folksblat*, 27 Feb. 1939, no. 50, pp. 7–8.
34 A. Volf Yasni, *Di geshikhte fun yidn in lodzh in di yorn fun der daytsher yidn-oysrotung*, 2 vols. (Tel Aviv, 1960–66).
35 I. Trunk, *Lodzher geto* (N.Y., 1962); id., *Judenrat: The Jewish Councils in Eastern Europe under Nazi Occupation* (N.Y., 1972); L. Dobroszycki, ed., *The Chronicle of the Łódź Ghetto 1941–1944* (New Haven, 1984).

2. COUP DE *KEHILLA*: THE *AGUDAS ISRAEL*'S SEIZURE OF POWER IN ŁÓDŹ*

Introduction

In 1928, control of Poland's second-largest Jewish community with its quarter-million Jews was seized by the conservative religious Jewish political party *Agudas Israel* with the active collusion of the Polish state authorities. The coup in the Łódź *kehilla*[1] was an echo of the struggle for power in the greater Polish political arena, as control of the Łódź Jewish community may have been pre-payment for active support of the Piłsudski regime in its struggle for control of parliament.

The Łódź *kehilla* election of 1924 had not produced decisive results. The *Aguda* bloc won a plurality of 13 seats, while the Zionist bloc drew only nine seats. However, the Zionists could look to the Non-party Religious (NR) as natural allies, for two of the seven NR councilmen-elect were known Zionist sympathisers and the rest were Aleksanderer *hasidim* vehemently opposed to the Gerers who were the bulk of the *Aguda*. However, the Zionists and NR held only 16 seats, two short of a majority.[2]

The July 1924 inaugural session of the new Łódź *kehilla* council adumbrated some unfortunate aspects of the future operation of the *kehilla*'s governing bodies.[3] When the outgoing board chairman Gerszon Neuman attempted to open the session, the Bundist and *Po'alei Tsion* councilmen met Neuman's Polish remarks with cries of 'Yiddish! Yiddish!' as they pounded on the table with sticks. Shmuel Edelman (PZ) took the floor to protest against the holding of the session behind closed doors, under police guard and in Polish; he called for the council to adjourn in protest. The Bundist Zelmanowicz then spoke at length against the circumstances of the council's first session and declared that the *Bund* would not permit speeches in Hebrew, as this would undermine the protest against the imposition of Polish. When the Zionist Senator Braude pointedly delivered his protest in ringing Hebrew, the socialists resumed their tablepounding with clubs and the disruption grew into loud yelling between the various factions. After a recess of several hours, Neuman attempted to resume the agenda despite the socialists' outcries and noise each time he spoke in Polish as required. The largest faction, the Agudists, walked out, followed by Edelman (PZ). The Bundists continued to demonstrate for Yiddish, although they abstained from the election of council officers, as Sholem Budzyner (NR) and Gerszon Praszkier (Z) were respectively chosen council president and vice-president.[4]

Concerted efforts at disruption and obstruction, the walkout by a major

* This paper is based on ch. 3 of my 1987 Columbia University doctoral dissertation, *Jewish Self-government in Poland: Łódź 1914–1939*.

faction, the decision of the rump factions to go ahead despite the absence of a large part of the council – all foreshadowed the ineffective squabbling and bickering which would dominate much of the *kehilla*'s time during the next four years. Moreover, the *Aguda* would succeed in getting the Łódź government commissioner to void the election of the council leadership in which the *Aguda* had not participated.[5]

After a three-month interval, with a heavy police guard at both the building entrance and before the door of the *kehilla* chancellory itself, only the 35 new councilmen and outgoing board chairman Neuman were admitted to the 23 October session. Sholem Budzyner (NR), a very wealthy industrialist and Aleksanderer Hasid known to have Zionist sympathies, again won election as council president with a plurality of 15 from the Zionists and NR; while Senator Asher Mendelson (A) received 14 votes and the Bundist Lichtenstein received three votes.[6]

A surprise development in the election of the 15–member *kehilla* board was an odd alliance of the Orthodox *Aguda* with the secularist, Yiddishist Folkists, which grew out of a last-minute breakdown in a Zionist-Folkist deal.[7] The election on 9 November 1924 produced a *kehilla* board in which the *Aguda* list held seven seats, the Zionists four, NR three and Bundists one.[8] Mincberg (A) and Rosenblatt (Z), the leaders of the two major factions, were both Sejm deputies. All nine of the *Aguda* and NR boardmen were merchants or manufacturers, while only one of the Zionists was. The other boardmen included two attorneys, a physician, a Bundist trade unionist and a Zionist artisan activist. Religiously, ten boardmen were strictly observant (Agudists, NR and Mizrachi Zionist Silberstein).[9]

Eventually, the NR joined with the Zionists to elect Dr Rosenblatt *kehilla* board president, while the Agudist Henekh Berger was chosen as vice-president. Interestingly, the Polish government never exercised its legal right to name three additional members to the board of the Łódź or any other *kehilla*.[10] The new Łódź *kehilla* board finally took office on 7 April 1925, during a session chaired by Berger in place of Rosenblatt, who was absent in order to attend the opening of the Hebrew University in Jerusalem.[11]

Endless bickering and the lack of a clear majority contributed to chronic deadlocks. Fundamental differences in ideological outlook divided the board over the role of the rabbinate, the language issue, support for secular and religious education and more. Moreover, the largest faction, the *Aguda*, was prepared to use its government connections to lobby for reversal of majority decisions. The other factions saw the *Aguda*'s demand that the various deputy rabbis fill the board seat reserved for the chief rabbi[12] as merely a ploy to increase *Aguda* strength as most of the rabbis could be expected to vote with the *Aguda*. Unable to break the board's quorum and failing to convince the majority to accept a rabbinate member, the *Aguda* faction obtained official directives requiring the *kehilla* board to invite a rabbinate representative or face having all its decisions declared invalid, including the all-important budget. The majority fruitlessly appealed to the provincial government, the Supreme Administrative Tribunal and the Ministry of Religions.

More than a month after the *kehilla* board took office, the *Lodzher Togblat* bitterly complained about the board's failure to get down to productive work. The Zionist daily declared that the *kehilla* board must demonstrate its political maturity, 'that it can free itself from the narrow four cubits of partisan ambitions and interests and satisfy the true needs of *all* circles and segments in the population.'[13]

Unfortunately, the first public session of the Łódź *kehilla* council provided a spectacle that only served to underscore the political division and immaturity of Łócź Jewry. The main room of the *kehilla* chancellory on the second floor of Plac Wolności 6 had been remodelled to provide boxes for the press and public to witness the deliberations on 25 May 1925. The public 'gallery' was separated from the council by a flimsy wooden barrier and allowed inadequate space for the hundreds of people who turned out for the first public session of the Jewish communal parliament. Most of the crowd were Hasidic Jews, including many children and youths. At least one woman in short sleeves and decolleté was compelled to leave the gallery by the pious crowd's objections to her immodest attire.[14] When council president Budzyner finally opened the session at 9 p.m. using Polish as required, he met a storm of protests and catcalls from the left. To limit the uproar, Budzyner had *kehilla* secretary Nadel read the agenda in Yiddish, since only the council president was bound by the order to use Polish.[15] Remarks by the Bundist Zelmanowicz provoked screams and whistles from the gallery. When the Nonparty Religious leader Benjamin Russ criticised at length both the *Bund* and the *Aguda* for obstruction which prevented aid for Jewish schools and the unemployed, his remarks were met with catcalls from the gallery, along with cries of 'Torah! Torah!' The disruption escalated, as the crowd sought to drown Russ out with yells of 'Get down! Crook! Uprooter of Israel! Shut your mouth! Apostate! Criminal!' Eventually, the crowd crashed over the wooden barrier and besieged the rostrum and the presidium table. When the meeting resumed, the squabbling continued unabated until the council adjourned at 2 a.m., without having adopted any decisions or considered any items on the agenda.

Writing in the *Lodhzer Togblat*, the Zionist educator Dr Natan Eck commented that the scenes acted out at the *kehilla* council's first public session were an embarrassment for the entire Jewish population.[16] Yet the wrangling, squabbling and violence which impeded the operation of the Łódź *kehilla* were not unique to Łódź Jewry. Such disruption of the legislative process was typical of general political institutions in Poland. The city council in Łódź was, if anything, worse than the *kehilla*.[17]

Frustration mounted as months passed and the *kehilla* board failed to achieve anything, and was unable even to adopt a budget. The *kehilla* council discussion of Rosenblatt's year-end report on 31 December 1925 was withering, with calls for dissolution of the *kehilla* board and a new council election to produce a stable majority. As the wrangling and mutual recriminations continued during the council session of 5 January 1926, Rosenblatt bitterly declared that 'The only rational act can be dissolution and setting of new elections.' Yet the board continued to limp along.

In February 1926, the *Lodhzer Togblat* characterised the first ten months of the Łódź *kehilla* board as 'a struggle of all against all' with no substantive achievements by any party. Council sessions had been marred by incessant infighting and mutual insults, to the amusement of the public gallery. Still, the Zionist daily believed that fruitful work was possible, given some good-will and responsibility, as well as mutual tolerance:

> If in the Polish government socialists can sit with Endeks at one table and govern, there is no reason to assume that in our Jewish local parliament a modus cannot be found for working in a similar manner of mutual concessions for the good of the Jewish populace, which the *kehilla* represents.[18]

During the last week of February 1926, the *Aguda* succeeded in forming a limited alliance with the Nonparty Religious, creating an Orthodox majority. However, the crisis in the Łódź *kehilla* dragged on for another year as the Orthodox majority was torn by internal differences and was unable to accomplish anything even in the religious field.[19] Despite a private conference between the Gerer *Rebbe* and the Aleksanderer *Rebbe*, the *Aguda*-NR alliance had collapsed by the beginning of March 1927.[20]

Shortly thereafter, Jerzy Rosenblatt announced his intention to resign as board president. Seeing that the Zionist, NR and Folkist factions had formed a majority coalition, the Agudists boycotted the election session of 16 March 1927 to block a quorum. Yet the Bundist Zelmanowicz provided the necessary quorum for the election of Benjamin Russ, a prominent Aleksanderer *hasid* and manufacturer, as the new *kehilla* board president.[21] Russ declared that he had set himself the 'goal of eliminating the chaos which reigns in the *kehilla* house [. . . by] conducting the work non-partisanly, entirely objectively, without any intentions for the benefit or harm of this or that side represented in the *kehilla*.'[22] Nevertheless, Russ proved to be no more successful than his predecessor in putting the Łódź *kehilla* on track.

By the *kehilla* council session of 4 December 1927, the need for new elections was generally accepted. The recent Łódź city council election had produced a socialist majority, and the *Bund* and *Po'alei Tsion* had won 37.3 per cent of the votes cast for Jewish lists. The *Aguda* and the Zionists had each declined to less than a fourth of the votes for Jewish lists. An *Aguda* motion of no confidence in the *kehilla* board and calling for it to resign was adopted by 14 to none, and another motion calling on the state to dissolve the council and board and hold new elections passed by 14 to one. The majorities apparently consisted exclusively of Agudists and the single Folkist, as the other factions abstained from voting for an *Aguda* motion although they conceded the need for new elections.[23]

Although the council decisions were non-binding, motions to accept them and call for the state to order new elections were adopted by seven to none at the board session of 21 December 1927, as the Zionists and NR abstained.[24] On 1 January 1928, Russ notified the council that the board had forwarded the council decisions to the state supervisory authority and that the board had essentially ceased to function.[25]

Council Vice-Pres. Mendelson (A) dropped a bombshell after he opened the *kehilla* council session of 8 February 1928 in the absence of Pres. Budzyner (NR). Mendelson read an official government notice dissolving the *kehilla* board and directing immediate election of a new board. The Zionists and NR protested that the matter had not been on the announced agenda. In point of fact, the government notice had been delivered to the *kehilla* chancellory only two hours before the council convened at 9 p.m. The socialists argued that dissolving only the board and not the council as well would 'not change the chaotic condition of the *kehilla*.' The Zionists and NR present declared that they would abstain from selection of the board election commission. Nevertheless, the *Aguda* had a majority of the 25 councilmen present and proceeded to elect a commission with Mendelson as chairman.

The *kehilla* election regulation provided that at least five days in advance of the election, the commission was to call on councilmen to submit lists of candidates signed by at least three councilmen.[26] The *Aguda*-dominated commission swiftly set the election of a new board for 14 February. In order to meet the technical requirement of five business days' notice, the Agudists astonishingly ordered that the *kehilla* chancellory be opened on Saturday, 11 February, from 9 a.m. to 3 p. m. For an avowedly Orthodox faction to open the *kehilla* offices on the Sabbath was scandalous.

Although the minutes of the 14 February 1928 council session are missing, it appears that the election took place in a tense atmosphere, with police present outside the meeting hall. As chairman of the election commission, Mendelson conducted the session with 33 councilmen present. Mendelson threatened to have the police remove board president Russ if he did not cease disturbing the proceedings by questioning the validity of an election held without official notification of the board. In the balloting, the *Aguda*-Folkist list received 16 votes, the Nonparty Religious only five and the Zionists only seven. The socialist bloc received five votes. Both the NR and Zionists each apparently suffered a defection to the *Aguda*. Moreover, the NR was deprived of the absent Budzyner's vote and the Zionist list was deprived of one vote due to a vacancy created by a resignation, as the Zionist alternate was not admitted. On the other hand, another Folkist alternate had been allowed to vote although his list had already exhausted its alternates.[27]

The ballots cast on 14 February 1928 were officially counted at a special *kehilla* board session convened the next day by Pres. Russ at express government order. The Zionists and NR each lost one mandate, while the *Aguda* and *Po'alei Tsion* each gained one and the Folkists and *Bund* each remained at a single seat. The *Aguda*-Folkist alliance had increased by only one seat, sufficient to give it an absolute majority, which would probably be reinforced by the rabbinic member of the board.[28]

Before the new *kehilla* board could take office, it had to elect its officers at a session chaired by the outgoing board president. Russ procrastinated in facilitating the accession of the new *Aguda*-controlled board. On Friday afternoon, 24 February 1928, after the *kehilla*'s regular office hours, *Aguda* leaders Berger and Mincberg had the *kehilla* messenger deliver to Russ's home an order from the government requiring him to call the session. Russ waited until the following Monday, 27 February, to contact the supervisory authority, which expressly ordered him to hold the election of the new board's officers that very day. Invitations to the meeting set for 9.30 p.m. were dispatched after noon that same Monday, even though the law required at least five days notice by registered letter. The Zionist and socialist boardmen objected to the improperly rushed meeting and to the various breaches of legal election procedure. Neuman (Z) objected that Mincberg (A) and his brother-in-law Makower (NR) could not legally serve simultaneously on the board. As the younger, Mincberg must withdraw and be replaced by an *Aguda* alternate. To this, Russ could only reply that he had been ordered to convene the new *kehilla* board according to the composition determined by the election commission on 14 February. The Zionists and Nonparty Religious could only abstain from the vote on new board officers by which Mincberg and Berger were respectively elected president and vice-president.

Even the final transfer of office from the old to the new *kehilla* board took place under a legal cloud, during a hastily called meeting on 5 March 1928. Mincberg had obtained a government directive to Russ, dated 2 March, ordering the outgoing president to convene the inaugural session on 5 March. Neuman, who had presided over the inauguration in 1925, objected to the inadequate notice for the session, as the board had not yet even been notified of the official state confirmation of the new officers. Mincberg simply replied that he had been directed by the government to take over from the former board president.

The *Aguda* coup in the Łódź *kehilla* was an echo of the struggle for power in the greater Polish political arena, as the government intensely supported a sympathetic and powerful faction on the Jewish street. Opponents of the *Aguda* pointed to the proximity of the 4 March 1928 Sejm election, in which the *Sanacja* regime sought to mobilise support for its BBWR list. *Kehilla* board president Russ had refused to adhere to the BBWR, while the *Aguda* allied itself with the government bloc. Control of the Łódź *kehilla* may have been pre-payment for active support of the Piłsudski regime. However, the BBWR won only a single Sejm seat in Łódź, while the Polish Socialists and Communists won a total of five seats and Zionist Jerzy Rosenblatt was elected on the National Minorities Bloc list. *Kehilla* council president Budzyner (NR) also won election to the Senate on the NMB list, while Mincberg failed to win re-election to the Sejm.[29]

However, Jacob Lejb Mincberg would remain president of the Łócź *kehilla* until the German invasion.[30] In his drive and aggressiveness as both a businessman and a political leader, Mincberg embodied the characteristic nervous energy, creative enterprise and ambitiousness of the stereotypical *Lodzher Mentsh* who had built Łódź into the textile centre of the vast Russian empire. A devoted follower of the Gerer *Rebbe*, Mincberg was at the same time very much the European businessman. Bundists denigrated the superficial up-to-dateness of the Agudists, who used modern terminology while retaining the old backward, reactionary positions of the 'black bourgeoisie'.[31] The Bundists referred to Mincberg as 'the diminutive Mussolini of the Łódź *Aguda*'.[32]

Benjamin Russ turned to the Polish civil courts to challenge the validity of the February 1928 Łódź *kehilla* board election. In November 1930, the Supreme Administrative Tribunal did indeed invalidate the 1928 election. Yet, although the state finally annulled the 1928 election in January 1931, Russ was not permitted to resume office. In February 1931 the Minister of Religions directed that new *kehilla* elections be held throughout the central provinces during May 1931. But unlike most communities, in which the outgoing boards remained in office until after the new elections, both the Łódź *kehilla* council and board were dissolved and replaced by a government-named provisional board. This was done in order to preserve *Aguda* control, as the 14 members named to the provisional board included 7 Agudists and a Folkist.[33]

The most striking result of the 1931 election was the absolute majority attained by the *Aguda* in Poland's second-largest *kehilla*.[34] That success could be attributed only partially to the effectiveness of *Aguda* campaigning. Zionists levelled blunt accusations of fraud, claiming that 'dead souls' had voted. There were also allegations of ballot-box stuffing, of persons voting in the name of others and of absentee voting, for which the law did not provide.[35] However, just as protests against official abuses during the 1930 parliamentary elections were ignored by the régime, the abuses which contributed to the success of elements considered sympathetic to the *Sanacja* on the Jewish street were left uninvestigated. *Aguda* control of the Łódź *kehilla* would be shielded and preserved again in 1936, when the government indefinitely postponed the Łódź *kehilla* election in the face of a likely socialist victory.[36]

NOTES

1 *Kehilla* is the Polish and *Kehile* is the Yiddish term for the more specific Polish expression *gmina wyznaniowa żydowska*.

2 *Lodzher Togblat* (*LT*), 8 July 1924, no. 159, p. 2; 11 July 1924, no. 162, p. 2; Edward Rosset, *Oblicze Polityczne* (Łódź, 1927), p. 110.

3 *LT*, 23 July 1924, no. 172, p. 4. It would not be until 1926 that the Minister of Religions finally authorised the *kehillot* to hold meetings in Polish, Hebrew and Yiddish, so long as all official protocols, records and correspondence with the state were in the 'state language': Ministry of Religions to Warsaw *kehilla*, 22 Jan. 1926, reprinted in Jakob Grynsztejn et al., eds., *Przepisy o organizacji gmin wyznaniowych żydowskich* (Warsaw, 1931), pp. 100–1.

4 *LT*, 20 July 1924, no. 178, p. 3.

5 *LT*, 1 Aug. 1924, no. 180, p. 7; 3 Aug. 1924, no. 181, p. 3.

6 *LT*, 24 Oct. 1924, no. 245, p. 6.

7 *LT*, 29 Oct. 1924, no. 249, p. 4; 6 Nov. 1924, no. 256, p. 3; 10 Nov. 1924, no. 259, p. 1; *Unzer Folk* (Łódź), 15 Apr. 1931, p. 15.

8 *LT*, 11 Nov. 1924, no. 260, p. 3; 12 Nov. 1924, no. 261, pp. 3–4.

9 See the previous note; Efroyim L. Zelmanowicz, *Epizodn fun mayn lebn*, (Mexico, 1956), pp. 208–9.

10 In June 1924, the Jewish parliamentary caucus adopted a resolution against any member party accepting such government-nominated mandates: *LT*, 19 June 1924, no. 143, p. 4.

11 Accounts of *kehilla* council and board sessions are primarily based on the respective protocol books in Record Group 1057 at the Archiwum Państwowe in Łódź. *LT*, 8 Apr. 1925, no. 83, p. 10.

12 The post of chief rabbi remained vacant from 1920.

13 *LT*, 17 May 1925, no. 112, p. 5.

14 *LT*, 19 May 1925, no. 114, p. 5; 28 May 1925, no. 122, p. 8.

15 Łódź *kehilla* council session protocol of 25 May 1925 and reports in the *LT* during the week immediately following.

16 *LT*, 28 May 1925, no. 122, p. 8.

17 In September 1923, the *Lodzher Togblat*'s *Sejm* correspondent attended a Łódź city council session and found the level of speeches to be embarrassingly low. Moreover, tea-drinking and smoking gave the hall the atmosphere of a *kawiarnia*, a coffee-house: *LT*, 7 Sept. 1923, no. 210, p .5.

18 *LT*, 22 Feb. 1926, no. 11, p. 3.

19 *LT*, 24 Feb. 1926, no. 13, p. 5; 26 Jan. 1927, no. 22, p. 5.

20 *LT*, 26 Jan. 1927, no. 22, p. 5; 2 March 1927, no. 52, p. 1.

21 *LT*, 14 March 1927, no. 62, p. 2; 17 March 1927, no. 65, p. 5; *Unzer Folk*, 15 Apr. 1931, p. 15.

22 *LT*, 17 March 1927, no. 65, p. 5.

23 The council did not have the power to dissolve itself under art. 21 of the *kehilla* statute.

24 The early departure of Silberstein (Z), Zelmanowicz (B) and Rabbi Friedel left the 6 *Aguda* and 1 Folkist in the majority anyway.

25 The board could not raise a quorum as the Agudists and Folkist stayed away.

26 Ministry of Religions (MWRiOP) decree of 25 Feb. 1921, arts. 53–62 (*Dziennik Urzędowy MWRiOP*, 1921, no. 4, poz.40); Decree of MWRiOP of 23 Dec. 1927, arts.64–71 (*Dz. Urz. MWRiOP*, 1928, no. 6, poz. 38).

27 Lists received as many alternates as seats won.

28 Łódź *kehilla* board seats in 1928 (and 1924): *Aguda* 7(6), Zionists 3(4), NR 2(3), Folkists 1(1), *Bund* 1(1), *PZ* 1(0).

29 *Lodzher Veker* (*LV*), 8 June 1928, no. 25, p. 3; Yitskhak Russ, 'R. Binyomin Russ Hy'd', (typescript biography of B. Russ by his son, in Central Zionist Archives, Jerusalem, A127/352); J. Hertz, *Di geshikhte fun bund in lodzh* (N.Y., 1958), pp. 331–3.

30 Hillel Seidman, *Ishim she-hikarti* (Jerusalem, 1970), pp. 327–34; *Polski Słownik Biograficzny*, vol. 21 (Wrocław, 1976), pp. 281–2; *Ilustrirter Poylisher Mantshester*, July 1929, p. 16.

31 H. Seidman, *Ishim she-hikarti*, p. 328.

32 *LV*, 8 June 1928, no. 25, p. 3.

33 MWRiOP directive of 3 February 1931, published in J. Dawidsohn, *Gminy Żydowskie* (Warsaw, 1931), pp. 96–7; *Lodzher gezelshaftlekhkeyt almanakh* (Łódź, 1938), p. 31; *LT*, 1 Dec. 1930, no. 275, p. 5; J. Hertz, *op. cit.*, p. 355.

34 Ibid.

35 Interpellation of 9 Oct. 1931 by Sejm Deputy Isaac Grünbaum et al., *Biuletyn Żydowskiego Instytutu Historycznego*, 1973, no. 1, p. 94.

36 R.M. Shapiro, *The Polish Kehile Elections of 1936: A Revolution Re-examined* (N.Y.: Yeshiva Univ., 1988).

19

THE IMAGE OF THE *SHTETL* IN POLISH LITERATURE

Eugenia Prokopówna

The word *shtetl* in Yiddish is a diminutive of the word *shtot* or 'town'; its exact meaning is, therefore, 'small town'. Not every small town, however, can be called a *shtetl*. The name refers not only to a physical entity, but to a particular cultural entity: a *shtetl* represents the *modus vivendi* of Jews in Eastern Europe. It was a bastion of traditional Jewish culture, and the word thus became a synonym for, and symbol, of that culture.

Though many Yiddish words were assimilated into the Polish language, *shtetl* was not one of them.[1] It was usually translated as *miasteczko*, 'small town'. This was the translation used for the title of Sholem Asch's famous novella *Shtetl*.[2] Alternatively it was printed in italics, as an unassimilated foreign word, in order to convey a specific milieu. This linguistic fact seems to indicate that the Jewish *shtetl* was not perceived as a socio-cultural phenomenon by the Poles.

There remains the question of Polish literature. Did it recognize the *shtetl* as an entity? Did it record the fact of its existence?

'The *shtetl* – a Polish phenomenon, a very Polish product . . . The *shtetl*. A flower which has grown out of our soil. But the Poles were little concerned with it . . . The *shtetl* was therefore not recorded by those writing in Polish.'[3] This judgement by Adolf Rudnicki is perhaps overly severe, for although it was understandably never as important a theme in Polish as in Jewish writing, the *shtetl*, as perceived in specific categories discussed below, did not go unremarked in Polish literature. The small Jewish, (or Polish-Jewish) towns scattered throughout the Polish province had already begun to appear in Polish fiction in the early eighteenth century and continue to do so to the present day: Andrzej Kuśniewicz's *Nawrócenie* (*The Return*); Waldemar Siemiński's *Kobieta z prowincji* (*A Woman from the Provinces*); Piotr Szewc's *Zagłada* (*Dissolution*) and Konwicki's *Bohiń*, are the most recent examples. In the eighteenth and nineteenth centuries, the theme of the *shtetl* was found predominantly in prose; in the twentieth century, and more specifically from the inter-war period, it also became a dominant theme in poetry.

How is one to explain Rudnicki's position? It is easily understood when one becomes familiar with his particular vision of the *shtetl* (*Krakowskie Przedmieście pełne deserów*, 1986 [*Krakowskie Przedmieście full of Desserts*]), which is presented in an idealized, romantic vein. This tone appeared in Jewish literature at the beginning of the century (the novel by Asch cited above is a prominent manifesto of this trend), and gained popularity after the Holocaust in a number of attempts undertaken at that time to present the phenomenon of the *shtetl*, whether in an anthropological way (E. Herzog, M. Zborowski, *Life is with People*, 1952) or in a more philosophical mode (A. J. Heschel, *The Earth is the Lord's*, 1950).

For Heschel – an outstanding philosophical 'norm-setter' in the idealization of East European Jewish culture and the forms created by it – the *shtetl* is neither a physical entity inhabited by Jews, nor a social organism, but the embodiment of a certain idea. His well-known essay *The Earth is the Lord's*, intended as a description of the everyday life of Jews in Eastern Europe – their rituals and traditions, values and aspirations – is in essence an attempt to capture its specific spirituality. The *shtetl*, where this way of life manifests itself, conceals a metaphysical purpose: *the place where the Scriptures are studied*, where in the synagogue and *beth hamidrash* the simple and learned, poor and rich discuss and deepen their knowledge of God's truth. Heschel informs us:

> Koretz, Karlin, Bratslav, Lubavich, Ger, Lublin – hundreds of little towns were like holy books. Each place was a pattern, an aspect, a way of Jewishness . . . The little Jewish communities in Eastern Europe were like sacred texts opened before the eyes of God, so close were their houses of worship to Mount Sinai. In the humble wooden synagogues, looking as if they were deliberately closing themselves off from the world, the Jews purified the souls that God had given them and perfected their likeness to God . . . Even plain men were like artists who knew how to fill weekday hours with mystic beauty.[4]

Like Heschel, Rudnicki does not acknowledge the description of Polish-Jewish towns that typically figures in Polish literature as part of the backcloth to the plot as being a true picture of the *shtetl*. In such descriptions, it should be added, the *shtetl* is almost always portrayed as rather ugly. Another reason might be the fact that the Polish image of the *shtetl* is usually of a Polish-Jewish, provincial 'miserable backwater' in which the Jewish world – shown in a fragmentary and episodic way – appears marginally in the background. This perspective is also common in contemporary historical works, for example in *Życie codzienne małego miasteczka w XVII i XVIII wieku* (*The Daily Life of a Small Town in the Seventeenth and Eighteenth*

Centuries) by Bohdan Baranowski (1975). In discussing various aspects of the everyday life of the Jewish inhabitants of these little towns, Baranowski says not a single world about the *shtetl* as a phenomenon.

But before the small town becomes part of a literary landscape, it is first of all part of the burning social question of towns and the middle class,[5] both in novels produced during the reign of Stanisław Augustus (the 'Stanisławowski novel') and then in the moralizing prose of enlightenment journalism in the first decade of the nineteenth century.

In Ignacy Krasicki's *Pan Podstoli* (*Mr Pantler*) (1778–98), or Michał Krajewski's *Podolanka w stanie natury wychowana* (*A Girl from Podole raised in a State of Nature*) (1784), 'the descriptions of the provincial towns are limited to ... a picture of destitution, neglect and decline, supposedly caused primarily ... by the Jewish population.'[6]

This socio-economic perspective, characteristic of an Enlightenment novel, is present, if variously stressed, in the image of the *shtetl* throughout the nineteenth century. It is particularly distinct in the novels of Stanisław Kostka Potocki, E.T. Massalski, and Jan Chodźko, who in the first half of the nineteenth century continue to debate the didactic problems of reform.[7] Linking the civic question[8] with the Jewish question meant, for Potocki or Massalski, that the most fundamental feature of an ideal town is its lack of Jews: 'We will not allow Jewish stallkeepers, for I am convinced that, without reform, any trade at all in their hands brings more harm than benefit to the country' – thus does Massalski's Podstolic express his reformatory *credo*.[9] Similar ideas reappear almost half a century later in the articles and prose of Klemens Junosza.

Independent of social tendencies or didactic aims, however, the use of the narrative device of a journey or peregrination that was employed so enthusiastically in the 'Stanisławowski' novel and early prose of the nineteenth century created a suitable and convenient opportunity to describe the provincial towns along the way. It was these frequently sketchy and stereotyped representations that gave rise to the cliché of the ugly scenery of the small town, the dirty 'miserable backwater', as Kraszewski was often to refer to it. 'Muddy, unpaved streets, covered with boards here and there, low houses, only a tenth part of them bricked, Jews and beggars everywhere', 'ill-built muddy towns, full of monasteries and Jews' – that is the view confronting the traveller's carriage journeying through Potocki's Ciemnogród.[10] This stereotype of the Jewish town must have been firmly entrenched in social consciousness, as in the 1840s a writer could introduce the scene of action in his novel as follows: 'I do not need to give a detailed description of Stanisławów for whoever has seen one Polish town has seen them all and knows that the Jewish element is predominant there'.[11]

Nor do we meet different portrayals in the work of Walery Przyborowski, *Hinda* (1869); Eliza Orzeszkowa, *Meir Ezofowicz* (1878); or Klemens

Junosza, *Czarnebłoto* (1895). Nor in Żeromski, whose hero Czaruś Baryka, in *Przedwiośnie* (*Before the Spring*) (1925)) is struck, on crossing the Polish-Russian border, by a sight which completely destroys his utopian vision of a Poland of glass houses:

> (spring) tried to shroud in its faint colours this *disgusting sight* [my italics, E.P.] which people had spread against its background, full of perpetually immortal beauty: a Polish-Jewish town. Cezary looked with gloomy eyes at the quagmire of muddy little streets, at the houses, all of various shapes, sizes colours and degree of filthiness, at the pigsties and puddles, at the farm buildings and burnt rubble. He returned to the market-place surrounded by Jewish shops, their doors and windows splashed with months-old mud, and unwashed beneath that for many quarters.[12]

Thus the small town of eighteenth-, nineteenth- and, very often, twentieth-century prose is a dark and ugly place. It is a very particular *locus obscurus*, a gloomy backcloth. Towns named or anonymous, real or fictional – Tenczyn, Berdyczów, Stanisławów, Brody, Radziwiłłów, Ostropol, Kazimierz, Szybów, Czarnebłoto, Kurzełapki, Cisy, Niemrawice – all are usually ruined, neglected, and wretchedly poor, greeting their visitors with the obligatory muddy puddle in the centre of the town square. Before the inter-war period the *shtetl* was not at all aesthetically ennobled. An attractive town was a striking exception, as was a clean town; so that when Julian Łętowski wants to give his pastoral tale of life in the *shtetl* ('Konkurencja' ['Competition'] 1890) an appropriate setting, he regards it as necessary to provide an appearance of verisimilitude: 'A small town, but clean and pretty. True, this first attribute is thanks to the river flowing through, its regular flooding and subsiding'.[13] Even in the twentieth century, the legend of Kazimierz on the Vistula, which Józef Czechowicz enthused about as a 'little town of paradise', was exposed as a harmful poetization of ugliness, wretchedness, and ruin. In Maria Kuncewiczowa's *Dwa księżyce* (*Two Moons*) (1933), Kazimierz, stripped of the idealizing veils in which the imagination of travellers, demanding the exotic and picturesque, had wrapped it, reveals the old, gloomy face of the *shtetl*.

Ugly and dilapidated it may have been, yet the provincial Polish-Jewish town was a typical element of the Polish landscape. Particularly in nineteenth-century prose – viewed from the noble's manor, from the windows of a traveller's carriage, through the eyes of a landowner going about his affairs via intermediaries from the town, or the eyes of a boy pausing on his way to school in the city – it can even constitute an important symbol of the familiar. In his novel *Latarnia czarnoksięska* (*The Magic Lantern*) (1844), Józef Ignacy Kraszewski asks: 'And do you know what makes every town Polish? The Jews. When there are no more Jews, we enter an alien country and feel, accustomed as we are to their good sense and services, as if something were not quite right.'[14] This sense of homeliness was still felt during the inter-war years when Ksawery Pruszyński, writing about two types of Polish town – the western Piast and eastern Jagiellonian, stresses that the towns on the Eastern borders were built by the nobleman and Jew.[15]

This last motif alluded to by Pruszyński seems to be fundamental. It appears that in the eyes of the *szlachta*, whose viewpoint was shared by Kraszewski and Pruszyński and is also the contemporary viewpoint of Kuśniewicz, the world of the *shtetl* is placed within the sphere of a specific understanding of familiarity, in which there is room for a paternalistic approach to 'our Jews in towns and villages'. I do not wish to suggest that for writers and story-tellers from the gentry the Jewish world was not an alien world. Indeed, it was exotic in its culture, but at the same time that exotic element perfectly harmonized with the Polish landscape, the landscape of 'our land', just as the Polish manor and Jewish town together harmoniously constructed a social landscape.

In as much as town scenes were common in eighteenth- and nineteenth-century prose, the *shtetl* as a cultural phenomenon was a rare theme. Polish literature usually portrayed individual Jewish types, characters removed from their native social context;[16] descriptions of the Jewish community and its specific organization and culture were rare. However, the proto-realistic prose[17] which arose during the period between the uprisings – travel reports such as J.I. Kraszewski's *Wspomnienia Wołynia, Polesia i Litwy* (*Recollections of Wołyń, Polesie and Lithuania*) (1840), and ethnographic works such as Ludwik Jucewicz's *Wspomnienia Żmudzi* (*Recollections of Żmudź*) (1842) – contained many generic images of life in Polish-Jewish towns. These were usually descriptions of market-fairs: short scenes recording what was then called 'Jewish trade', or characterisations of small-town merchants and tradeswomen. As a kind of documentary prose, these 'journeys' and 'memoirs' written between the uprisings give a certain outline of the history of the *shtetl*: in the towns of Kraszewski's Polesie and Wołyń, the memory of the massacre of Jewish communes, of the burning of towns at the mercy of the fire and sword of Chmielnicki's men during the Uprising is still alive.

The *shtetl* appears not to have been seen as a collective Jewish *modus vivendi* until the 1860s. It was then that Kraszewski, through his hero Jakub Hamon, the son of a tavern-keeper born in a village, who later comes to experience life in both small and greater towns, states his conviction that the experience of life in a Jewish community played an important role in recognizing, understanding and experiencing Jewish identity. Very characteristically, he regards the patriarchal elders of the *shtetl* as positive heroes, truly noble and ethical, embodying Jewish values and dedicated to a Jewish God, and contrasts them with semi-assimilated types, whom he regards as sceptics devoid of faith in anything.

The *shtetl* appears as a structure specific to Jewish life in the prose of the 1870s, in Eliza Orzeszkowa's *Meir Ezofowicz* (1878), described by the author as 'the short history of a small town';[18] and in subsequent decades in Wilhelm Feldman's *Żydziak* (*Jewboy*) (1889) and Klemens Junosza's *Czarnebłoto* (1895) and 'Słup' ('The Post') (1899). These were supplemented in the inter-war period by Kazimiera Alberti's novel *Ghetto potępione. Powieść o duszy żydowskiej* (*The Ghetto Condemned. A Novel of a Jewish Soul*) (1931). The title of Alberti's novel is extremely indicative. For writers adhering to Enlightenment-positivist ideals, the *shtetl* is identified with the ghetto, which they judge according to the standards prescribed by their own ideologies and obviously condemn. They see the *shtetl* as a community subjecting itself to the tyranny of completely inert laws which isolate it from the world. They consider it to be sunk in superstition, an anachronism and, indeed, a relic of barbarity in a Europe treading the road of progress. For them it represents the home of paupers and the Jewish question. The walls of the ghetto-town, they say, should be demolished, its inhabitants should be 'civilized', social and cultural reform should be carried out. They see no room for the approbation of traditional Jewish Eastern European culture, which they consider infinitely inferior to European culture even in its Polish version. For them, the *shtetl* was the subject of either serious arguments or satirical laughter. The latter attitude, less common, was an echo, interestingly enough, of the Jewish literature of the *Haskala*. The satirical portrayals of Czarnebłoto or Kurzełapki in Junosza – Mendele's translator – are clearly inspired by Mendele's incomparable Głupsk in *Przygody Beniamina Trzeciego* (*The Adventures of Benjamin the Third*).

The enlightenment-positivist criticism of the *shtetl*, outlined above in its standard variant, does acquire specific characteristics in the work of certain authors. These are undoubtedly most evident in the popular 'Jewish' novels of Klemens Junosza whose portrayals of small towns show the tangle of components constituting the author's outlook: Enlightenment ideals and a socio-economic perspective that sees the *shtetl* as an integral part of the Polish economic context, and finally, a satirical passion in which one hears the resounding note of the *szlachta*'s laughter.[19] Junosza also displays much interest in and understanding of the daily life of the *shtetl* and its structure, which demands that 'shopkeepers doze in their booths, Jewish women, settled on their thresholds, make stockings, and the learned rock over their tomes from morning till night.'[20]

The *shtetl* as it appears in the prose of the second half of the nineteenth century is in fact, as Orzeszkowa assures us, a place lying 'in one of the most secluded corners that can possibly exist in Europe today',[21] but these are corners which snippets of news and *Haskala* slogans can still penetrate, where emancipated, assimilated Jews still appear. Even in Szybów, far from the railway, arrivals from the provincial capital begin to settle – 'civilization's exiles', whose daughters amaze the local inhabitants with their boarding-school education and piano and French lessons; this, it is claimed, is a *shtetl* preparing for change, open to outside influences. In 'Słup', a story published by Junosza in 1899, the narrator, stylized as a naïve *shtetl* bard, allows the town's patriarchs to voice their complaints about the demise of the old ways: 'There *was* [my italics, E.P.] everything here: a quiet life, happiness, piety, wisdom, a little trade . . . Nothing was lacking. There was a school, a *mikva*, a *shokhet*, a rabbi'.[22] A sign of this decline is the slowly rotting post that marks the borders of 'the pious town of Kurzełapki', which finally falls over.

The *shtetl* motif undergoes a change in the inter-war years of the twentieth century with the appearance of a larger group of writers of Jewish descent who differ from their older brothers (e.g. Wilhelm Feldman) in their treatment of traditional Jewish culture. They no longer support the assimilationist ideology which demanded the rejection of traditional Jewish culture as the price for becoming European. On the contrary, for many Polish-Jewish writers (as they called themselves),[23] the heritage of the *shtetl* was something valuable which they did not wish to reject, which they were attached to and proud of, and which gave them roots in the world. They were the ones who made the *shtetl* a central theme in their writing. Thanks to Polish-Jewish poets, the *shtetl* also began to appear in poetry.

For Polish-Jewish writers, the *shtetl* was a physical entity, but above all an entity to which the first-person narrator is emotionally attached; therefore, although its physical appearance is still seen as ugly, it is evaluated in a different manner. It is a familiar and sympathetic entity, a happy and secure place, despite its aesthetic shortcomings. The *shtetl* now becomes, above all, the domain of childhood. It is not surprising, then, that it should be the affectionate abode of memory and imagination, an intimate entity. It is impossible to overlook or underestimate the importance of biographical experience in the construction of this image. This biographical element makes the *shtetl* a familiar and private domain, an area suffused with personal experiences and memories. Narratives of Polish-Jewish writers – Maurycy Szymel, Stefan Pomer, Czesława Rosenblattowa – about the *shtetl* are variations of the same story of having to leave the town in which they were born. Their creative writing is the memory reliving the places of childhood.

From these memories the *shtetl* emerges as a universal landscape, as it were, of Jewish biography. Its topography is characterized by its permanent features: the market-square, the synagogue, the inn, the spice shop, the crooked street, the Jewish cemetery. The synagogue, which is the true heart of the *shtetl*, is usually old and crumbling. Perceived with nostalgia,the whole landscape of the *shtetl* is the domain of the old and the ruined. The houses, synagogue, and cemetery are all dilapidated. The moss-covered walls crumble. Night can a throw a veil over this scene of decay, adding a layer of fantasy or other-worldliness to its dimensions.

This motif of decay, undoubtedly dominant in the description of the *shtetl* in Polish literature, was an undeniable reflection of the actual state of the Jewish provinces in the eighteenth, nineteenth and twentieth centuries. But while the *shtetl*'s dilapidation led writers who had rejected their links with the Jewish world to support demands for the reform of Jewish life, for Polish-Jewish writers the ruin of the *shtetl* was a symbol of the patriarchal world disappearing into the past. The native landscape infused with death became for them an elegiac theme. The first elegy on the Jewish town appears at the end of the 1920s, preceding Antoni Słonimski's *Elegia miasteczek żydowskich* (*Elegy on Jewish Towns*) by two decades. It was written by Stefan Pomer, whose volume *Elegie podolskie* (*Podolian Elegies*) (1931) was described in the inter-war years as 'a lyrical geography of Jewish settlements'.

It is a striking fact that in the work of writers from Jewish circles one looks in vain for the traditional Polish 'small town stories' that look at the Jewish world from the perspective of nineteenth-century Polish clichés (e.g. Kazimiera Alberti's *Ghetto potępione*). Seen from the inside, the *shtetl* does not appear as the compact social structure of old; the links once unifying its collectivity have weakened. The culture of the *shtetl* is no longer presented as a vital phenomenon worthy of ethnographic description (as Feldman saw it, for example). Usually, only fragments of this culture are mentioned, scenes of rituals fundamental to Judaism: the Sabbath, Yom Kippur, the Passover. Brief threads of folklore tradition, themes drawn from Jewish ballads, proverbs, and hasidic anecdotes appear in a stylized form. A whole gallery of small-town types are woven into the cast of characters: rabbis, beggars, tailors, salesmen, porters, and others. However, these, to use the title of one of the novels to emerge from the new Jewish circles are 'people who are still living' (C. Halicz [C. Rosenblattowa], 'Ludzie, którzy jeszcze żyją', 1934). This title effectively conveys the vision of the *shtetl* as a form which continued to exist, but which in essence already belonged to the past.

In any case, the literary hero and lyrical 'I' in the work of Polish-Jewish writers was also the inhabitant of the *shtetl*, 'the simple, believing Jew', as the authors claim. Though given a (Polish) voice, the town now clearly bears the mark of its times: one can meet a tragi-comic Charlie Chaplin in its streets, and, hovering above the *shtetl*, an aura of sadness, nostalgia, and melancholy, resounding in the music of the violin, the sentimental laughter that comes through tears.

Nor can one overlook the image of the *shtetl* in the work of two other writers of the inter-war period: Bruno Schulz and Adolf Rudnicki. In their work, too, the town becomes the intimate domain of childhood. For Schulz the town is a refuge for a hero worn out by the chaos of the world. The aura of the place emerges dimly from the sea of Schulzian metaphor, but in such a way that one cannot fail to see the market-square empty on the Sabbath like a biblical desert, houses fragrant with Sabbath smells while their inhabitants – Shlomo son of Tobias, Joseph son of Jacob – await the Messiah. In Rudnicki's *Szczury* (*Rats*) (1932), it is impossible not to identify in the depiction of the small town of Raj – the shops of Buch and Perlman, Groman's house – a particular leitmotif characterizing the hero's native milieu.

In post-war literature the *shtetl* inevitably becomes a historical theme, but it nevertheless persists as a theme. Who remembers it? Above all, Jewish writers born in a *shtetl* at the beginning of the century or in independent Poland, survivors, looking at the Jewish world from the other shore of the Holocaust, as it were. It is also remembered by their Polish contemporaries, those men and women from the provinces who, like Tadeusz Konwicki, grew up together with Jewish children in some

> provincial town, the quintessential small town on the outskirts of Wilno. This was a town among a vast archipelago of such towns, which produced the founder of Metro-Goldwin-Meyer and Józef Piłsudski, famous, miracle-working rabbis and the arch-traitor and tsarist spy Bałaszewicz, the leader of the Warsaw Ghetto Uprising, Wilner, and myself . . . All that was best in Europe and America came from there and pushed old Europe and young America forward . . .
>
> I remember Bujwidze better all the time. I dream of Bujwidze constantly. This microscopic town, this most typical of towns, in actual fact the name of the town alone without the town was something so characteristic and somehow formed types like myself, like Romain Gary, Soutine, David Halberstam and three-quarters of American directors, writers, actors and politicians.[24]

The Lithuanian Bujwidze, Galician Drohobycz (A. Chciuk, *Atlantyda. Opowieść o wielkim księstwie bałaku*, 1969) (*Atlantis. Tales of the Princedom of Lwów Argot*), or borderland towns are remembered by writers of the Galician or Lithuanian schools, to whom the Habsburg and Jagiellonian myths, offering a vision of open, multinational cultures, are dear. But the domain of childhood can equally be Kazimierz on the Vistula, disguised under the name of Laźmierz (W. Siemiński, *Kobieta z prowincji*, 1987). The vision of these provincial backwaters becomes so attractive that writers born in the 1940s, 1950s, and even the 1960s express a desire to inhabit them via their protagonists.

But the Holocaust stamps its seal on the memory and imagination of them all. A slaughtered town is, after all, something entirely different from a town gradually falling into decay. It is the term used by Kalman Segal in the title for his stories – *Tales from a Slaughtered Town* (*Opowiadania z zabitego miasteczka*, 1956). This death is also recorded by others – in an avant-garde style by Leopold Buczkowski (*Czarny potok* [*The Black Torrent*], 1954), realistically by Józef Wroniszewski (*Różdżka Jessego*, [*Jesse's Wand*] 1982). Szagalewo, the hero of Arnold Słucki's poetry, is indeed a surreal, Chagallian place with violins flying through the air, but it is also a place of suffering and death, bursting into ominous flames:

> There is a motionless world on the edge of the moving world,
> huts of clay and fire – strange towns.
> Orthodox chapels standing on the heads of burnt synagogues,
> drying like blind arks on their Ararats.[25]

The novels about inter-war Polish-Jewish towns by Artur Sandauer (*Zapiski z martwego miasta* [*Notes from a Dead Town*], 1963) and Andrzej Kuśniewicz (*Nawrócenie* [*The Return*], 1987) end on a chord of wartime fate; no turning back of memory, as Kuśniewicz would have it, can be a return to that world in a gesture of innocent ignorance.

Even Stryjkowski, concentrating on Jewish life with despair, clearly looks at that life as after a deluge; his gaze, made acute by the Holocaust, is sensitive to all portents of death. In his four-volume sequence begun in the 1940s (*Głosy w ciemności* [*Voices in Darkness*], 1946 [published 1956]; *Austeria* [*The Inn*], 1966; *Sen Azrila* [*Azril's Dream*], 1975; *Echo*, 1988), he gives us an account of the destruction of the internal structure of the town from the beginning of the century, a history of the breakdown of the codex of laws and hierarchy of values that united the Jewish community for a hundred years. The collective value of the *shtetl* cannot defend itself before the assimilationist, Zionist and socialist tendencies appearing among the Jews of Galicia. The patriarchal world perishes under the pressure of destructive contemporary forces. Stryjkowski does not depict the idyll of a *shtetl* dancing before the Lord. Instead, he tells the story of the family of a certain *melamed*, a teacher who is himself charmed by the 'wicked books' of the *Haskala*, but whose children betray their Jewishness: his daughter runs away with a *goy*, his older son joins the socialists, and the younger, who does not yet understand Polish well, finds himself in a Polish school. He tells the story of Tag and Azril, in whom desire for holiness and sinful desires do battle, and who, full of anxiety and guilt, cannot keep pace with the exigencies of loyalty to the ethical code of the community. True, for Stryjkowski the *shtetl* is marked by death, but it induced that death itself. The writer's heroes are unable to tread in the footsteps of their fathers (were their fathers really able to tread that path?); they betray their Jewishness or abandon it. The chain binding Jewish fathers and Jewish sons, a chain formed over a thousand years, breaks and falls apart; the chain of the covenant with the Lord suddenly snaps. The model given in traditional culture for forging the links of that chain proves impossible to repeat. Stryjkowski's hero, weak and easily fallible, is unable to fulfil his heavy ethical reponsibilities. The culture of the *shtetl* cannot survive as a particular form of existence, and this constitutes the nucleus of its death.

The inter-war *shtetl* that appears in prose from the 1950s on is always strongly invaded by waves of Polonization and secularization. In his *Zapiski z martwego miasta*, Artur Sandauer records its symbolic topography by causing his hero to wander between three spheres: the Jewish backwoods, the borderlands, and the centre of Polishness. He makes him a witness to a melodious dispute, conducted one Sabbath afternoon, by a family whose various members hum the Sabbath *zmirot*, Bialik's hymn 'Tehezakna', and the 'Red Flag' – a symbol of the dispute between traditional faith, Zionism, and socialism.

Similarly, in Kalman Segal's work, *The Town* (which remains anonymous, but is written with a capital) attempts to carry on its life according to the eternal rhythm in the valley of the San, but cannot isolate itself from the conflicts tearing inter-war reality apart. Though it clings to tradition, the latter is not the mainstay it once was. 'The old town was once a fortified castle with walls of granite and full of the wisdom of God and good customs like an ivory tower. This was a fortress and God was its foundations. What remains of the fortress? The shopkeepers and harlots shatter the Lord's holy temple. Fractious sons offend God and his prophets. Where is Isaiah, who will foretell their ruin?',[26] ask Segal's grey and bearded patriarchs.

The tone idealizing the *shtetl*, which in Segal's works rang out only in the voices of those literary heroes attached to traditional ways of life (Segal himself had a critical view, as expressed for example in the story 'Josełe' from *Opowiadania z zabitego miasteczka*), took on a different and more insistent character in the literature of the 1980s. The growing interest in the lost world of Polish Jews meant that the *shtetl* motif was now taken up by younger writers who had no memories of that world. Their towns, 'lying on the furthest reaches of the imagination',[27] can only (and this is no accusation) be visions constructed from inherited images. However, the choice made by Włodzimierz Paźniewski or Piotr Szewc, for example, from among the available clichés put forward by tradition, is extremely telling. Kuśniewicz's followers present the Polish-Jewish provinces of independent Poland in all their diversity, Kuśniewicz portrayed them as a gallery of types, amongst whom there were grey-beareded talmudists, lawyers' wives reading *Wiadomości Literackie* (what else), and communist tailors. But – and this is of great importance – Paźniewski and Szewc also write occasional prose elegies on the *shtetl*. Like Słonimski, a severe critic of traditional Jewish culture before the war,[28] who after the war lamented that never again would words of longing for Jerusalem be heard in Polish cherry-orchards, they too wish to see the picturesque and moving side of Jewishness, and also the exotic side: the warmth of spice shops, not to mention cinammon shops, and haberdasheries, the whirl of dancing *Hassidim*, the stillness of men poring over their sacred books.

This tone of nostalgic idealization, which can also be found in the writings of Holocaust survivors, is interpreted with psychological insight by Bogdan Wojdowski. His heroes in *Pascha*, living in contemporary Warsaw, watch the mystery-play of spirits in Perec's *Noc na starym rynku* (*Night in the Old Square*) at the Jewish theatre, resurrecting the *shtetl* in all its glory, but in all its conventionality also: 'The synagogue, the *heder* and the church stood on the market square together, and in the very middle, by the prompter's niche, was the well.'[29] Spiritually wounded and terribly sensitive, they long for a life among their own kind. As one character says:

> My whole youth. Among my own kind. And these walls? Let them collapse . . . I will exchange all I have, for such a small, the smallest of lives. So close to God. And God too in His place. And every sin and every good deed also in its place. The merchant behind his counter. The coachmen by their horses. Everything so small, so good and necessary.[30]

To him, the idyll of the *shtetl* means intimacy and imperturbable order in the world, certainty and security.

The idea of the spiritual beauty of the world of East European Jews and of Jewish traditional culture is proclaimed most fully in the voice of Rudnicki, who sensitively observes religious rituals and the spiritual truth still permeating them before the war (e.g. 'Lato', 1938):

> The *shtetl*. A complete triumph of the idea of a theocratic town, a theocratic state. The butcher, the writer, the rabbi – these are the ideological guardians of its life. Precise regulations speak of what is allowed and what is not allowed . . . A spiritual leader guides this life, is responsible for everything that happens. In the town one wakes with a prayer on one's lips, one falls asleep with a prayer. God is in every curve of the walls, everywhere. His shadow spreads over every meal, every word, over all work and rest. It might appear from the outside that the people were in the depths, that only a miracle could save them, but the miracle – in its own way – was their very life, their inner life.[31]

Clearly, Rudnicki does not attempt to paint an idyllic landscape of the town, but to show the depth and beauty of the Jewish tradition existing in the *shtetl*, a tradition which ordered the cosmos and everyday life. From ugly surroundings to a cultural terrain full of spiritual light, this statement could serve as a description of 'the Polish history' of the *shtetl*. A hidden light at first, but, as Heschel wrote, one whose brilliance would eventually penetrate all screens.

NOTES

1 See M. Brzezina, *Polszczyzna Żydów* (Warsaw, 1986), pp. 52–83.
2 S. Asch, *Miasteczko* (Warsaw, 1911).
3 A. Rudnicki, *Krakowskie Przedmieście pełne deserów* (Warsaw, 1986), pp. 39, 42, 43.
4 A. J. H. Heschel, *The Earth is the Lord's: The Inner World of the Jew in East Europe* (New York, 1950), pp. 89, 92, 93.
5 See Z. Leśniodorski, 'Miasta i mieszczanie w powieści stanisławowskiej', *Pamiętnik Literacki* 1–2 (1935); W. Wołk- Gumplowiczowa, 'Chłopi, mieszczaństwo i szlachta w powieści polskiej w pierwszej połowie XIX wieku', *Przegląd Socjologiczny* 1–2 (1939).
6 Z. Leśniodorski, 'Miasta i mieszczanie . . .', p. 188.
7 S.K. Potocki, *Podróż do Ciemnogrodu* (1820); J. Chodźko, *Jan ze Świłoczy, kramarz wędrujący* (1824), *Podróż do Pani Kasztelanowej* (1837); E. T. Massalski, *Pan Podstolic albo czem jesteśmy, czem być możemy. Romans administracyjny* (1831–3).
8 Similarly linked with the Jewish question was the so-called peasant question, which had a significant influence on the motif of the Jewish innkeeper and his inn in Polish literature. See M. Opalski, *The Jewish Tavern Keeper and His Tavern in Nineteenth-Century Polish Literature* (Jerusalem, 1986), pp. 21–2.
9 E. T. Massalski, *Pan Podstolic albo czem jesteśmy, czem być możemy. Romans administracyjny* (Petersburg, 1833), vol. ii, p. 55.
10 S. Potocki, *Podróż do Ciemnogrodu* (Warsaw, 1820), vol. 1, pp. 29, 146.
11 J. Brincken, *Józef Frank. Powieść historyczna z drugiej połowy XVIII wieku*. (Warsaw, 1845), vol. iii, p. 99.
12 S. Żeromski, *Przedwiośnie* (Warsaw, 1948), p. 109.
13 J. Łętowski, 'Konkurencja', in *Józefa Ungra Kalendarz Ilustrowany na rok 1890* (Warsaw, 1890), p. 18.
14 J. I. Kraszewski, *Latarnia czarnoksięska* (Kraków, 1977), series I, p. 271.
15 K. Pruszyński, *Podróż po Polsce* (Warsaw, 1937), p. 177.
16 See A. Hertz, *Żydzi w kulturze polskiej* (Paris, 1961), pp. 240, 241, 248, 254.
17 H. Markiewicz calls proto-realism an 'inter-uprising anti-romantic movement': see 'Próba periodyzacji nowożytnej literatury polskiej', in *Przekroje i zbliżenia. Rozprawy i szkice historycznoliterackie* (Warsaw, 1967).
18 E. Orzeszkowa, *Meir Ezofowicz* (Warsaw, 1988), p. 9.
19 See E. Prokopówna, 'Śmiech szlachecki w satyrycznych obrazach żydowskiego świata' (Studenckie Zeszyty Naukowe Uniwersytetu Jagiellońskiego), series VII, vol. 3; *Ironia. Parodia. Satyra* (Kraków, 1988).
20 K. Junosza, 'Froim', in *Łaciarz. Froim* (Warsaw, 1926), p. 34.
21 Orzeszkowa, op. cit., p. 9.
22 K. Junosza, 'Słup', in *Nowele i obrazki* (Warsaw, 1899), p. 12.
23 See E. Prokopówna, 'In Quest of Cultural Identity: Polish- Jewish Literature in the Interwar Period', *The Polish Review* 4 (1987).
24 T. Konwicki, *Wschody i zachody księżyca* (Warsaw, 1982), p. 86.
25 A. Słucki, 'Nieruchomy świat', in *Promienie czasu* (Warsaw, 1959), p. 51.
26 K. Segal, *Kochankowie w Sodomie* (Katowice, 1966), p.
27 K. Holzman, 'Truciciele publicznych studni', in *Krajobraz rodzinny i inne opowiadania* (Warsaw, 1981), p. 82.

28 See M. Opalski, 'Wiadomości Literackie 1924–1939: Polemics on the Jewish Question', typescript, p. 4. Paper given at the conference 'The Jews of Poland between the Two World Wars', Brandeis University, April 1986.
29 B. Wojdowski, 'Pascha', in *Krzywe drogi* (Warsaw, 1987), p. 19.
30 Ibid., pp. 29–30.
31 A. Rudnicki, *Krakowskie Przedmieście pełne deserów* (Warsaw, 1986), pp. 40–1.

20

THE POLISH JEWISH DAILY PRESS

Michael C. Steinlauf

In the period between the two world wars, the Polish-Jewish daily press was undoubtedly the most successful example of Jewish cultural creativity in the Polish language. Unfortunately, precious little has been written about this major cultural institution of modern Polish Jewish life. Over and beyond the obstacles to historical research created by the vast destruction of Polish archival institutions in World War II, difficulties which apply, though in different measure, to the reconstruction of both Polish and Polish Jewish history, particularly in the period just prior to the war, there is here a further barrier: the aversion albeit increasingly anachronistic of many Poles and Jews to phenomena whose locus is neither purely 'Polish' nor purely 'Jewish', as a result of which, the memory of the Polish-Jewish press has slipped into the void between two mutually exclusive national self-conceptions. Therefore this article. What follows is a sketch based on the skimpy existing literature[1] and a preliminary reading of the Warsaw daily *Nasz Przegląd*; my object is to assemble basic historical data, characterize general tendencies, and suggest areas for further detailed investigation – in short, to trace the rough dimensions of a marvellously complex yet neglected domain of recent Polish Jewish history.

FROM *IZRAELITA* TO *NASZ PRZEGLĄD*

The existence of the Warsaw daily *Nasz Przegląd* [*Our Review*][2] (1923–39), along with its sister publications in other large Polish cities, *Nowy Dziennik* [*New Daily*] (1918–39) in Kraków and *Chwila* [*Moment*] (1919–39) in Lwów,[3] represents a unique phenomenon in modern Jewish history: a daily press in a non-Jewish language.[4] Ever since the beginnings of the *Haskalah* (Jewish Enlightenment) at the end of the eighteenth century, there had been periodical publications published by and for Jews, at first primarily in the languages of the co-territorial nations, later, towards the end of the nineteenth century and particularly in Eastern Europe, increasingly in the Jewish languages – Hebrew and Yiddish – as well. Periodicals in the non-Jewish languages were published at intervals of a week, a month or more – they were never daily publications since it was assumed that once a Jew could read the language of the country in which he lived, he would avail himself of daily newspapers in that language for general news, and then turn to the Jewish press for subjects of Jewish interest. The first mass-circulation Jewish dailies arose to meet the needs of a large Jewish readership little conversant with non-Jewish languages, but who demanded the kind of window on the modern world which only a daily newspaper could furnish. Such dailies, inevitably in Yiddish,[5] were also intimately linked to the rise of Jewish national consciousness in Eastern Europe. Thus, the Warsaw Yiddish dailies *Haynt* (1908–39) and *Der moment* (1910–39), for example, both founded in the years just prior to World War I, furnished their readers with a complete account of world, local and Jewish community events, championed Jewish political struggles for civil and national minority rights, and were instrumental in publishing and supporting the newly-emerging Yiddish literary culture. With many adaptations based on the new conditions of life in an independent Polish state, the Yiddish daily press – which for most of the interwar period consisted of a least five dailies in Warsaw alone[6] – retained this fundamental profile as both news-purveyor and instrument of national renewal and resistance.[7]

The Polish-Jewish daily press, in contrast, did not come into its own until the end of World War I, and by virtue of a radical break with its past. For many decades, the Polish-language Jewish press, the oldest Jewish press in Poland – beginning with the short-lived *Dostrzegacz Nadwiślański* (1823–24)[8] and ending with the well-established and increasingly staid weekly *Izraelita* (1866–1913)[9] – upheld an assimilationist ideology which preached the transformation of Jews into 'Poles of the Mosaic faith' ['*Polacy wyznania mojżeszowego*'], and with the rise of Jewish national movements, opposed as 'separatism' any expression of national consciousness, be it Zionism or yiddishism. *Izraelita*'s social base was the Warsaw banking and commercial plutocracy which, tacitly supported by the orthodoxy, controlled the Warsaw *kehillah* (Jewish community council).[10] It was supported as well by certain groups of progressive Polish intellectuals, particularly the 'positivists', who welcomed assimilated Jews as partners in the development of Polish productive forces and political freedom. As both Jewish and Polish national movements – the latter frequently with an anti-Jewish orientation – began to gather force, however, *Izraelita* and what it represented began to be challenged, and several attempts were made in Warsaw to develop a different sort of press: *Izraelita* itself under the editorship of Nahum Sokolow (1896–1902);[11] the Zionist anthology *Safrus* (1905) edited by Jan Kirszrot;[12] the short-lived Zionist weekly *Głos Żydowski* (which was banned and then reappeared as *Życie Żydowskie*) edited in 1906–07 by Yitshak Grünbaum;[13] and from 1913–14, a daily newspaper – *Przegląd Codzienny*.

Przegląd Codzienny was founded at a prophetic moment in modern Polish-Jewish relations: when, amidst the furore resulting from the Duma elections of 1912 in which Jewish votes helped elect a candidate not supported by the nationalist Polish coalition, these groups declared a boycott against Jewish participation in Polish economic and cultural life.[14] The campaign, whose chief instrument was the new mass-circulation nationalist press, enlisted the support of many Poles previously well-disposed toward Jews, including the leading exponent of Polish positivism, Aleksander Świętochowski.[15] The editor of *Przegląd Codzienny* was Stanisław Mendelson, who had been an activist in the Polish Socialist Party, but had begun to move toward a Jewish national perspective (he was Nahum Sokolow's son-in-law). The paper, as Mendelson envisioned it, was intended for Jews (it covered in great detail the notorious blood libel trial of Mendl Beylis in Kiev),[16] but also for Poles; it was to provide for Polish society, he declared – in an expression identical to those that would be used in the interwar period by Polish-Jewish journalists to characterize their own activity – 'a mirror of Jewish life'.[17] Among the journalists it employed were Jakób Appenszlak and Natan Szwalbe, later founders of *Nasz Przegląd*, but also – unlike the interwar Polish-Jewish press – a number of Polish journalists as well.[18] Upon Mendelson's death and the start of World War I, *Przegląd Codzienny* folded.

With the collapse amidst a wave of anti-Jewish violence after World War I of the belief by significant numbers of either Poles or Jews that Jews could or should be assimilated into Polish society, and the passing, as a rule, of Jewish communal control out of the hands of assimilationist and religious oligarchies and to more democratic nationally-minded representatives, the Polish-language Jewish press emerged completely transformed. Although a small number of assimilationist Jewish publications continued to appear in the interwar period, their influence was minimal.[19] Rather, a new group of well-educated, largely middle-class journalists, whose notions of Jewish nationality had been shaped by the Yiddish and Hebrew press, who were primarily Zionist and frequently partisans of the Hebrew cultural revival[20] – began to found Polish-language Jewish publications. Thus in Warsaw, Appenszlak and Szwalbe, joined by Samuel Hirszhorn, Saul Wagman and Samuel Wołkowicz,[21] who had continued throughout the war and in the years immediately following to found short-lived Polish-Jewish newspapers, in 1923 established *Nasz Przegląd*. But why did this new generation of Polish-Jewish journalists found *daily* newspapers, a situation so unlike that in Western European countries? Why the need for a daily newspaper, a staple of modern life more commonplace than a telephone, to be 'Jewish', and what, if not language, did such an identification entail?

A JEWISH DAILY PRESS IN A NON-JEWISH LANGUAGE

Of greatest importance in the rise of the Polish-Jewish press was the rapid spread of the use of Polish among Jews. With the sudden availability of free primary education in the new Polish state, and despite the growth of Yiddish and Hebrew school systems, the majority of Jewish students in the interwar period nevertheless attended state schools in which the language of instruction was of course Polish.[22] Bi-lingualism (Yiddish and Polish) became increasingly prevalent among Polish Jews. Moreover, especially but by no means exclusively among educated youth and in sections of the middle and professional classes, Polish – particularly as a written language – began to make inroads over Yiddish.[23] In such circles, a preference for Polish over Yiddish and even an ignorance of Yiddish led to an estrangement from Jewish culture – yet rarely however to a renunciation of Jewish national identity. The irony is that precisely when the pre-World War I assimilators' dream of mass Polish-language education for Jews was finally fulfilled, linguistic assimilation was accompanied by relatively little of the national assimilation which had been their ultimate goal. Indeed, just the opposite was the case: Jews on the whole increasingly regarded themselves nationally as Jews, whether their language was Yiddish, Polish or both.[24] And it is precisely a population that was increasingly at home in Polish *yet* increasingly Jewish-identified that could constitute the mass base required for a Polish-Jewish daily press.

The strengthening of Jewish consciousness was, of course, at least in part a reaction to the growth of anti-Jewish feeling and violence in the interwar period. In an interesting defence of the Polish-Jewish press made, significantly, by a Yiddish journalist in a Yiddish daily, Sh. V. Stupnitski describes the origins of the Polish-Jewish daily press as follows: 'At a time when Jewish life developed, when Jews became involved in general political life – it then turned out that a Jew desiring to find out what is going on in the external world, as well as a non-Jew wanting to know what is happening among Jews, had simply no opportunity to do this, since nearly the entire Polish press is reactionary, Catholic, anti-semitic.'[25] Characteristic of the Polish press, Stupnitski points out, was that perhaps alone in all of Europe, it was '*judenrein* [free of Jews]', and even if occasionally there was a Jewish contributor, he was forced to change his name or sign his article with initials, and, certainly, could never write sympathetically of Jewish affairs. These then, concludes Stupnitski, were the 'objective reasons' for establishing a Jewish daily in Polish. 'It was simply a necessity for us, it was an act of national self-defense'.[26] This analysis is supported by the case of Jakób Appenszlak, the editor-in-chief of *Nasz Przegląd*. From an assimilated home, educated in Polish schools, Appenszlak began his journalistic career prior to World War I as theatre critic for the major Warsaw daily *Kurier Warszawski*. His decision to found a Polish-Jewish daily was partly a 'protest' against the pressure to change his name while he worked for the Polish paper.[27] Even more instructive is the origin of the Kraków daily *Nowy Dziennik*, founded during the last months of World War I as a direct result of Jewish outrage at the murder of a Jew by Polish hooligans, and the subsequent cover-up of the crime by the liberal Polish newspaper most widely read by Jews.[28] Moreover, the first Polish-Jewish daily, the short-lived *Przegląd Codzienny*, was, as we have seen, founded amidst the poisonous atmosphere of the first modern anti-Jewish press campaign in Polish history. Even when it was not overtly hostile to Jews and Jewish interests (for example, *Robotnik*, organ of the Polish Socialist Party), the Polish press was simply ignorant of and indifferent to Jewish matters.

To the 'objective reasons' for a Polish-Jewish daily press, Stupnitski then appends 'subjective reasons which justify [its] existence':

> Our development does not move along the path of Western Jews, among whom there rules a dualism, a double-entry bookkeeping in the relations between Jew and human being. The German Jew during the course of the entire week would read the *Frankfurter Zeitung*, a progressive, modern daily, and on Saturday would receive the weekly *Der Israelit* in order to square himself with Jewishness.[29] We read a newspaper as human beings and at the same time as Jews. We want therefore to find in it everything that can possibly interest the human being in the Jew and the Jew in the human being. As a result, there can exist among us a Polish-Jewish paper, whereas in France and England it is unneeded. . . .[30]

Stupnitski's words point to a significant difference between the sense of Jewish identity of Western and Eastern European Jews. In the West, the encounter with secularization generally meant the progressive diminution of the realms in which one could express one's 'Jewishness', its delimitation to family, synagogue, 'Sunday school', charitable institution or weekly newspaper. In interwar Poland, for a variety of reasons beyond the scope of this article, the transformation from traditional to secular world-view was, in this respect, not as disruptive, and was accompanied by the rise of an immense network of national institutions and ideologies within which one's day-to-day identity as a Jew could generally be taken for granted. Precisely *because* it was such a commonplace of everyday life, for many Polish Jews a daily newspaper, regardless of language, had to be Jewish as well.

CIRCULATION

Responding to these needs, the Polish-Jewish daily press rapidly attained a wide readership.[31] Establishing circulation figures, however, for these newspapers, and indeed for all of the Jewish press and even for the Polish press of the interwar period, is no easy matter. As a result of the massive destruction of Warsaw in the Second World War, most of the records of publishers and printers disappeared. For most of the years since the war, the only source of circulation statistics has been the catalogues, published during the interwar period by two Polish advertising firms,[32] to which the various newspapers themselves sent in figures. These are the data consistently utilized by Marian Fuks in his monograph on the Jewish press in Warsaw.[33] More recently however, Andrzej Paczkowski has turned elsewhere: to the records of the Polish Ministry of the Interior (that is, police) for the interwar period. These records are fragmentary: they do not exist at all for the 1920's, and for the 1930's only for certain years. Moreover, the manner in which they were obtained is unknown. However, Paczkowski makes a good case for the supposition that these figures, consisting of samplings often as frequent as every two weeks, and compiled exclusively for internal ministry use, are much more reliable than the single figure contributed to the advertising catalogues by newspaper publishers, and reproduced without any independent verification. Paczkowski first published the raw data in his article, '*Nakłady dzienników warszawskich w latach 1931–1938*',[34] and then published a monograph on the interwar Warsaw daily press, *Prasa codzienna Warszawy w latach 1918–1939*,[35] basing his conclusions as to circulation on an analysis of the data in his article. Since the figures for the Jewish press cited in his monograph are general

TABLE 1: AVERAGE CIRCULATION OF WARSAW JEWISH DAILIES, 1932–38

	Fuks	*Police Data*	*Nr. of samplings*
Nasz Przegląd	40–50,000	21,520	57
Piąta Rano[38]	40–50,000	14,745	57
Haynt	45,000	26,615	39
Der moment	30–40,000	23,315	42
Unzer ekspres	40–60,000	15,183	42
Folkstsaytung	18,000	16,494	42
Yudishe togblat	15–30,000	13,515	35
Hayntige nayes	75,000	19,843	41
Varshever radio	—	25,090	43

estimates, however, it seemed advisable to return to his sources. Therefore, in Table 1, I have presented average circulation figures for the nine major interwar Warsaw Jewish dailies in the 1930's (two Polish-Jewish morning papers, five Yiddish morning papers, and two Yiddish afternoon papers) according to Fuks, and according to my own analysis of Paczkowski's data in '*Nakłady dzienników warszawskich* . . .' (along with the number of samplings on which the latter figures are based).[36]

As is to be expected, the circulation figures based on the police data are, as a rule, significantly lower than those of Fuks. This is however in keeping with Paczkowski's overall analysis of Polish press circulation. Thus, for 1938, the only year for which comparable data are available, Paczkowski computes total circulation of the Polish daily press to have been 1,210,000 according to the advertising catalogues, and 770,290 according to the police data.[37] Moreover, the only case in which the figures are similar, that of the Bundist *Folkstsaytung*, supports the reliability of the police data, since Paczkowski independently notices a similar phenomenon for the Polish Socialist Party daily *Robotnik* (for which the police figures are actually higher than those in the catalogues), and attributes it to the possibility that the catalogue publishers reduced circulation figures for the socialist press.[39] The lower police figures receive further confirmation from Nakhman Mayzil, who in 1931 wrote that none of the five Warsaw Yiddish dailies attained a week-day circulation equal to that of the Moscow *Emes* – 31,000.[40] Furthermore, actual circulation figures were probably even lower than those given above, since Paczkowski calculates that about one-third of all Polish-language dailies were returned unsold;[41] if we assume that a similar proportion held for Yiddish papers (no statistics are available), then all the circulation figures in Table 1 must be reduced accordingly.

Using the police data, it is possible to compute total average circulation for the various types of daily newspapers in Warsaw in the 1930's. This has been done in Table 2. Based on these figures, the Polish-Jewish proportion of the total Warsaw Jewish daily press was 20.6 per cent, that is, for roughly every four Warsaw Jewish newspapers printed daily in Yiddish, one was printed in Polish. This proportion becomes more significant when viewed in the light of the fact that more of the Warsaw Yiddish than Polish-Jewish

TABLE 2: AVERAGE CIRCULATION OF WARSAW DAILY PRESS, 1932–38

Polish-Jewish[42]	42,014
Yiddish[43]	161,450
Jewish (Polish + Yiddish)[44]	203,463
Polish (non-Jewish)	632,058[45]
Total (Jewish + non-Jewish)	835,521

dailies were printed for readers outside Warsaw.[46] Furthermore, these figures may be compared to those for the period prior to World War I when, in 1906, for example, there were in Warsaw eight Yiddish and Hebrew dailies with a total circulation of 108,200, but no Polish-language Jewish dailies, and six Jewish weeklies with a combined circulation of 40,000, of which the two in Polish (*Izraelita* and *Głos Żydowski/Życie Żydowskie*) had a total circulation of 2,000.[47]

The police records also permit, to a limited extent, an analysis of the development of the daily press, at least in the 1930's. In Table 3 I have presented average circulation figures for two two-year periods: 1932–33 and 1937–38.[48]

TABLE 3: AVERAGE CIRCULATION OF WARSAW DAILY PRESS, 1932–33, 1937–38

	1932–33	*1937–38*
Polish-Jewish	48,057	35,970
Yiddish	170,249	152,650
Jewish (Polish + Yiddish)	218,306	188,620
Polish (non-Jewish)	546,499	717,617
Total (Jewish + non-Jewish)	764,805	906,237

The small decline of the Jewish press – 13.6 per cent – is made more significant by the simultaneous expansion of the non-Jewish Polish press – 31.3 per cent. Thus, in the course of a six-year period, the Jewish share of all the daily newspapers published in Warsaw declined from 28.5 per cent to 20.8 per cent.[49] Paczkowski suggests a number of possible reasons for this phenomenon: the relatively faster growth of the Polish population of Warsaw in the 1930's, the increase in the sale of Polish dailies outside Warsaw, but also, the increasing proportion of Jewish readers who turned to Polish papers.[50] He concludes: 'If the data on circulation on which I base my conclusions are true – and much indicates that they are – then it is possible to speak of an emerging crisis situation in the Warsaw Jewish press'.[51]

In order to specify the nature of the 'crisis' in the Jewish press, I have computed circulation figures for the major Warsaw Jewish dailies for the periods 1932–33 and 1937–38. These are presented in Table 4. The figures document a greater or lesser decline in the circulation of every major daily with the exception of *Nasz Przegląd*. Yet circulation of the other Polish-Jewish daily, the tabloid *Piąta Rano*, declined as well, so it would seem difficult to draw conclusions along linguistic lines. However, one of Paczkowski's major conclusions in his monograph is extremely helpful: 'If we

TABLE 4: AVERAGE CIRCULATION OF WARSAW JEWISH DAILIES, 1932–33, 1937–38

	1932–33	*1937–38*
Nasz Przegląd	20,391	22,649
Piąta Rano	16,167	13,322
Haynt	27,529	25,700
Der moment	25,130	21,500
Unzer ekspres	15,366	15,000
Folkstsaytung	18,737	14,250
Yudishe togblat	14,030	13,000
Hayntige nayes	21,951	17,734
Varshever radio	25,179	25,000

were to attempt to point to the most characteristic, the most important shift in the structure of the Warsaw press during the years of the Second Republic, then undoubtedly at the head, before all others, emerges the growing significance of the sensational press'.[52] The Jewish press was no stranger to this phenomenon: much was written about the 'pernicious' and apparently growing influence on Yiddish readers of the inexpensive afternoon tabloids such as *Hayntige nayes* and *Varshever radio*.[53] However, the above figures demonstrate, I would suggest, that if the Jewish reader was increasingly turning to tabloids in the late 1930's – as was his Polish counterpart – then it was not to Yiddish tabloids, nor even to a Polish-Jewish tabloid such as *Piąta Rano*, but to the non-Jewish sensational press in the Polish language.[54] On the other hand, among the readers of the more 'serious' (and more expensive) daily Jewish newspapers, Yiddish readers – as is to be expected by the spread of linguistic assimilation – declined, but Polish readers increased, an increase, however, which did not make up for the larger decrease in Yiddish readers.[55]

THE POLISH-JEWISH PRESS AND THE YIDDISH PRESS

In its overall democratic and Jewish national political orientation, in its function as guardian of Jewish civil and national rights in Poland and defender against anti-semitic attacks, in its consistent support for the development of Yiddish and Hebrew culture and struggle, as we shall see, against the 'danger of assimilation',[56] and in its ongoing concern for the building of a Jewish homeland in Palestine – the new Polish-Jewish press was very similar to the mass-circulation Zionist Yiddish press. Similar but not identical, however, the Yiddish press as a whole was more highly 'ideologized' than the Polish-Jewish. Thus during the interwar period, even *Haynt* and *Der moment*, which had been founded as politically independent newspapers, drew closer to and at various times formally affiliated with various Zionist factions.[57] *Nasz Przegląd*'s Zionism, in contrast, was 'non-party' and therefore independent, more of a 'tendency' than a firm 'ideology'. Only in *Nasz Przegląd*, for example, could one encounter – on the same page – articles by David Ben-Gurion and Vladimir Jabotinsky![58]

The philosophical similarity between the Polish-Jewish and the Zionist Yiddish press reflected many personal and organizational ties. Journalists and editors in one press often worked for the other as well; moreover, the same publisher was frequently responsible for publications in both Yiddish and Polish. Of the founders of *Nasz Przegląd*, for example, Natan Szwalbe, was diplomatic correspondent for *Haynt* in the 1920's, and both Samuel Hirszhorn and Samuel Wołkowicz were regular contributors to the Yiddish press as well as – most interestingly – founders of the Folkist Party, one of whose principles was the recognition of Yiddish as the national language of the Jewish people.[59] On the other hand, two of the figures whom Khaym Finkelshteyn, in his monograph on *Haynt*, calls 'the "big three" in the "*Haynt*-family"',[60] – Yehoshua [Osjasz] Thon and Nahum Sokolow – were closely involved with Polish-language publications[61] and were, indeed, skilled writers, editors and orators in Polish (as well as in Hebrew). This is also true of Yitshak Grünbaum, the charismatic Zionist politician who was probably the single most popular Jewish public figure of the 1920's. Grünbaum was instrumental in solidifying *Haynt*'s links to organized Zionism, and for a number of years was the paper's guiding spirit; he was simultaneously an editor and regular contributor to the Hebrew, Yiddish and Polish-Jewish press.[62] Moreover, the publishers of *Haynt* were directly involved in founding a number of Polish-language Jewish publications. Among them were the dailies *Kurier Nowy* (1919–20), *Nasz Przegląd*'s earliest post-World War I predecessor, whose editorial offices were the same as those of *Haynt*,[63] and *Nowe Słowo* (1931–32), and the weekly *Opinja* (1933–39).[64] The latter two, the most successful of these ventures, established partly in response to the supposed slackening of *Nasz Przegląd*'s oppositional politics, were edited by Mojżesz [Moyshe] Kleinbaum, a close associate of Yitshak Grünbaum.[65] '*Opinja*', states Finkelshteyn, 'said in Polish what *Haynt* propagated in the mother-tongue [*mame-loshn*, i.e., Yiddish]'.[66]

TWO KINDS OF 'BRIDGES'

And yet – despite this web of practical as well as ideological interconnection, the frequent identity of writers, publishers, political positions – language, in interwar Poland, was hardly an incidental matter, and a Jewish press in the non-Jewish language found itself before problems and opportunities which the Yiddish press did not face, and which, moreover, on occasion led it into conflict with it. First of all, employing the same language as the surrounding Polish nation meant that one was also speaking *to* it; a Polish-Jewish newspaper was therefore involved, as no Yiddish paper could or wanted to be, in the endeavour of 'reveal[ling] for Polish society, with whom we live on one land', as the first issue of *Opinja* puts it, 'a mirror in which it can see a faithful image of Jewish society',[67] or, in the words of Jakób Appenszlak in the founding issue of *Nasz Przegląd*: 'rendering accessible to Polish society an understanding of our national self, its laws and ideals'.[68] In relation to governing circles, the Polish-Jewish press attained the status of unofficial press organ of the Jewish community, in which reaction to policy could be gauged and political concerns noted. It also responded quickly and consistently to the Polish press, searching out rare expressions of goodwill, polemicizing with the proliferating anti-Jewish onslaughts, and thereby placing itself at the eye of the storm provoked by the 'Jewish question'. As a result of its 'visibility' in the Polish world, the tones of *Nasz Przegląd*'s political articles, for example, was generally less strident than that of its Yiddish counterparts. Moreover, *Nasz Przegląd* often stressed, more so than the Jewish-language press, Jewish patriotism to the Polish state.[69] The paper, in short, attempted to function as a bridge from 'darkest Nalewki'[70] to Polish society; but whether – aside from occasional Polish politicians and a multitude of journalists hungry for polemics – it reached any significant number of ordinary Polish readers is very doubtful.

In relation to its Jewish readers, *Nasz Przegląd*'s function as a bridge was more successful. First of all, it offered its Jewish readers a view of the Polish world they could not always find in the Jewish-language press: extensive national news, regular reviews of Polish theatre, accounts of behind-the-scenes parliamentary intrigues.[71] More important, however, was its role in returning 'Jewishness' to Jews. In the words of Appenszlak: 'For some may [the paper] be a gate of return, a stage in the approach to one's own nation [. . .] Among our own brothers we wish to intensify national feeling, expand the consciousness of the creative power and spiritual values of Jewry'.[72] In its founding issue, *Opinja* is even more explicit: 'our weekly undertook as a primary task to acquaint the Polish-reading Jewish intelligentsia with the breadth of Jewish knowledge, the history of the Jewish nation, the pearls of Hebrew and Yiddish literary creativity'.[73] Thus, the

Polish-Jewish press published articles by such eminent Jewish historians as Majer Bałaban, Ignacy Schiper and Mojżesz Schorr, who, although they also appeared in Yiddish and Hebrew publications, had chosen to write their major works in Polish, and were ultimately most at home writing for the readers of *Nasz Przegląd*.Even more important was the popularization of Yiddish and Hebrew culture. *Nasz Przegląd* published a great number of translations from Yiddish and Hebrew literature, both the 'classics' (Mendele Mokher Sforim, Sholem Aleichem, Y. L. Peretz, David Frishman) as well as contemporary authors (Sholem Asch, Z. Segalowicz, Y. Y. Trunk, Moyshe Nadir, Uri-Zvi Grinberg, A. Shlionski). New Yiddish and Hebrew books were extensively and seriously reviewed, as were Jewish music and theatre by writers thoroughly at home in several cultures.[74] One such writer, not untypical of this group, was the theatre and literary critic, feuilletonist and political commentator Mojżesz [Moyshe] Kanfer, who was based in *Nowy Dziennik* and published throughout the Polish-Jewish press. Kanfer, a childhood friend of the Hebrew writer Sh. Y. Agnon and a popular lecturer on Yiddish theatre and literature, was instrumental in founding the Kraków Yiddish Theatre, the first Yiddish theatre in Poland entirely financed by a Jewish community.[75] There were as well Yiddish and Hebrew writers, journalists and critics who wrote directly in Polish for the Polish-Jewish press.[76] As a result of these various efforts, in Warsaw for example, as Pola Appenszlak recalls: 'the fastidious crowd [of intelligentsia] which used to fill the Polish theatres and literary cabarets, began, thanks to [*Nasz Przegląd*], to attend the theatre of the Vilne Trupe, the Turkov-Kaminska theatre, Vaykhert's Yung Teater and the Azazel *kleynkunst* theatre',[77] and more generally: 'Yiddish culture, in *Nasz Przegląd*'s translation and under its patronage, acquired "civil rights"'[78] among Jews previously estranged from Jewish life. That is, through the mediation of *Nasz Przegląd* and its sister papers, Yiddish culture began to be associated with some of the prestige-value of high Polish culture.

UNIQUE FEATURES

Such dedication to Jewish literature and theatre was hardly unusual among Jewish newspapers. The Yiddish press had, after all, since its inception consistently written about Yiddish culture and published the work of Yiddish writers. Indeed, nearly all of the most prominent Yiddish prose writers first published their major works in the Yiddish dailies; the Yiddish press was their major source of readers and livelihood. What was unique in these endeavours of the Polish-Jewish press was entirely a function of language – the use of the Polish language to strengthen national consciousness and oppose 'assimilation' by transmitting an awareness of

Jewish culture to a group of readers who lacked the ability or inclination to find it in the Jewish-language press. The act of translation, moreover, permitted a symbolic reconciliation: Yiddish and Hebrew writers, frequently at odds ideologically, co-existed in the same newspapers, often on the same page, as nowhere else in the Jewish press. There were, however, in addition, several aspects of the Polish-Jewish press which were not a function of translation, which were not, that is, simply a Polish version of the Jewish-language press. These were features unique in themselves, and therefore also most relevant towards establishing a true picture of the extent and depth of a Polish-language Jewish culture in interwar Poland; here it is possible only to point toward areas which future research will fully document.

First of all, a pre-condition: the matter of style and aura. It was, after all, a very different thing to function amidst the middle-class world of Polish-speaking Jews and amidst the Jewish masses and their *mame-loshn*. Melekh Ravitsh, from a vantage point at the centre of interwar Warsaw Yiddish culture, recalls Jakób Appenszlak's 'Polish-aristocratic' manner,[79] and characterizes Paulina Appenszlak as the archetype of the young lady ['*panienke*'] whom young Yiddish poets dreamed of impressing: elegant, assimilated, and cosmopolitan.[80] And he marvels that a man such as Appenszlak, whose office was in the midst of Yiddish-speaking Warsaw, could remain so aloof in spirit and in practical knowledge of the Jewish masses around him.[81] The distance between these worlds was a matter of language, but also of class, a reproduction within the Jewish microcosm of the larger gulf between Polish and Jewish cultural circles.

The influence of class attitudes partly explains the commitment of the Polish-Jewish press to the popularization and support of Jewish fine arts. This is not to say that the Jewish-language press ignored Jewish painters and sculptors; yet, also doubtless because of remnants of the traditional Jewish preference for the written over the visual representation, Jewish visual artists, it seems, did not receive the same exposure in the Jewish-language press as their literary counterparts. In an article ironically entitled 'Is Jewish Art Needed?', a writer in *Nasz Przegląd*, for example, complains that 'publications such as *Haynt* and *Der moment* treat art with peculiar neglect'.[82] In the pages of *Nasz Przegląd*, on the other hand, a comparatively large amount of space was devoted to gallery reviews, criticism of past and contemporary Jewish art, Jewish art history, and, in the weekly illustrated supplement, reproductions of new works. Moreover, an organization founded by Jakób Appenszlak, the Society for the Propagation of Fine Arts [*Towarzystwo dla Krzewienia Sztuk Pięknych*], dedicated itself to raising money to enable young Jewish artists, to whom Polish galleries were frequently closed, to exhibit their works.[83] In an age when fine arts, even more than writing or music, constituted a link to a cosmopolitan

Western modernist culture, *Nasz Przegląd*'s efforts on behalf of Jewish art were encouragement for the 'europeanization' of Jewish culture.

Furthermore, the Polish-Jewish press also hosted the emergence of a new and as yet virtually undocumented literary phenomenon: a group of writers who chose to write fiction and poetry on Jewish themes in Polish. The most well-known of this group was Roman Brandstaetter, poet, translator and Zionist publicist;[84] the group included: Maurycy Szymel,[85] Anda Ekerówna, Horacy Safrin, H. A. Fenster, Daniel Ihr, Karol Dresdner, Stefan Pomer, Karol Rosenfeld, and Minka Silberman.[86] These were exceptions to the more well-known phenomenon of 'Polish writers of Jewish descent' such as Bolesław Leśmian, Julian Tuwim, Antoni Słonimski, Józef Wittlin and Mieczysław Jastrun – major Polish poets who, while widely attacked in the anti-semitic press for their supposed 'judaization' of the Polish language, in their interwar writings remained aloof from Jewish themes.[87] Yet there is also the case of Mieczysław Braun [Bronsztejn], whose modernist poetry rarely ventured into Jewish subject matter, but whose prose writings, frequently published in *Nasz Przegląd* and the Polish-Jewish weekly *Ster* (Warsaw, 1937–38), often did. And in an article entitled, 'Polish Writers or "Jewish Writers writing in Polish" or "Polish-Jewish [Writers]?"', Braun forcefully defends the first of these formulations and adds: 'The attachment of a Polish writer, a Jew, to the Jewish nation [. . .] is not incompatible with the natural tie which binds him to Polish culture and language in organic unity. There is no duality in this: belonging to the Jewish nation and to contemporary culture in its Polish form are reconcilable'.[88] Further research will doubtless reveal a broad and complex spectrum of approaches to the tangle of 'Polish-Jewish' literary identity.

In addition to its support of Jewish artists and Polish-language writers, *Nasz Przegląd* in particular also sponsored two special publications. One was *Mały Przegląd* [*Little Review*], which appeared as a regular supplement to *Nasz Przegląd* written exclusively by and for children. *Mały Przegląd*'s editor and guiding spirit was the legendary educator and writer of children's books Janusz Korczak, martyred, along with the children of his orphanage, at Treblinka in 1942.[89] The second of these publications was the weekly *Ewa* (1928–33), a journal for women edited by Paulina Appenszlak, the wife of the editor of *Nasz Przegląd*. *Ewa*, which announced in its founding issue that it would 'reflect the opinions, thoughts, problems and aspirations of the contemporary Jewish woman, struggling for complete liberation and active direct participation in the development of Jewish national life,'[90] was 'European' and broadly feminist in orientation;[91] it also, however, participated in another unique activity organized by *Nasz Przegląd*: the annual 'Miss Judaea' beauty contest.

'ASSIMILATION'

Despite the manifold ties between the Yiddish and the Polish-Jewish press, it was probably inevitable that the Yiddish press would come to regard a successful Polish-Jewish press with suspicion and often with outright hostility. First of all, since, as we have seen, a large proportion of Polish Jews in the interwar period were bi-lingual, Yiddish and Polish-Jewish papers were competing for many of the same readers. Thus, for example, in a bitter article in the Yiddish literary weekly *Literarishe Bleter* the young I. B. Singer accused the Lwów daily *Chwila* of manipulating the closing of its Yiddish rival *Lemberger togblat*, the last Yiddish daily in Galicia.[92] Moreover, the Yiddish press, indeed like all of Yiddish culture, consistently perceived itself as an embattled institution: one of the most commonly encountered words in the lexicon of contemporary Yiddish criticism was the word 'crisis', and one of the most commonly cited reasons for the 'crisis' was the increasing linguistic assimilation of Polish Jews, a perception which, of course, much in this article substantiates. Furthermore, there was in Polish Yiddish culture (as there was in Hebrew culture – and not only in Palestine) a tendency to perceive its mission as linguistically exclusive, that is, as the only 'authentic' Jewish culture. However much this tendency compromised with Hebrew culture (and when it did not, fanatical conflicts were the result), to the possibility of a Jewish culture in the Polish language it allowed no quarter. For all these reasons, it was also therefore inevitable, and this despite the commitment of the Polish-Jewish press to Jewish culture and national awareness, that the animosity directed toward it would take the form of accusations of 'assimilation' – that is, of seeking the disintegration of Jewish national consciousness in much the same way as its nineteenth century predecessor *Izraelita*. This was, after all, the occasion for Sh. Y. Stupnitski's previously cited 'justification' for the Polish-Jewish press.[93] And even in the pages of *Opinja*, a publication founded, as noted, by the publishers of *Haynt* and described as nothing else than its Polish version, space had to be devoted to refuting such charges. Replying to the reproach that the Polish-Jewish press was 'an instrument for the assimilation of Jewish society', and therefore had no right to participate in protests over the abrogation of the National Minorities Treaty,[94] an editorial in *Opinja* argues:

> If not malice, then amazing ignorance must have guided the author of this reproach. Isn't it known that every day the ranks increase of Jewish youth who emerge from Polish schools, denationalized and polonized, and therefore bereft of the opportunity of availing themselves of literature in Yiddish, and all the more so in Hebrew? Isn't is known that in assimilated Jewish circles hitherto

> completely estranged from the life of the Jewish masses – there has recently arisen a movement for a return to Jewishness [. . .] And shouldn't we, precisely for all these Jewish circles, create a bridge which would link them to Jewishness, and which only the Jewish press in the Polish language can constitute?[95]

To the evidence already brought undercutting such charges of 'assimilation', a final example: when, during the 1931 census, which failed to include a question on national affiliation, the Jewish press mounted a campaign to encourage Jews to use the question on 'mother-tongue' as a declaration of national identity,[96] that is, to answer Yiddish or Hebrew even if their primary language was Polish – the Polish-Jewish press participated as well. 'Entire Jewish families who speak neither Yiddish nor Hebrew', complains a writer in the assimilationist monthly *Zjednoczenie*, listed Yiddish as their mother-tongue 'because they were instructed to do so by the Jewish press *printed in the Polish language*'.[97] That is, for the sake of Jewish national interests, the Polish-Jewish press opposed documentation of the fact that many of its own readers existed!

CONCLUSION

Far from being a 'tool of assimilation', the Polish-Jewish daily press – as well as, I would suspect, the larger system of Polish-language Jewish culture which is yet to be explored – was an integral part of the complex, tri-lingual web, what Chone Shmeruk terms the 'polysystem',[98] of interwar Polish Jewish culture. The Polish-Jewish press, linked in a multitude of practical and ideological relationships to Jewish culture in Yiddish, and secondarily in Hebrew as well, shared with them the 'mission' of developing a modern Jewish national culture. Because Polish, however, was not an 'a priori' Jewish language, the Polish-Jewish press and the cultural system it represented lacked the ideological vitality, but also the frequent intolerance of Yiddish and Hebrew cultures. In contrast to the Yiddish and Hebrew cultural systems, each of which was associated with specific political ideologies (Bundist, Folkist, left Zionist, or non-assimilating Communist in the former case, Zionist in the latter), the Polish-Jewish cultural system as a whole 'had no well-defined overall political-ideological character'.[99] Thus, *Nasz Przegląd*'s readers, broadly Zionist or a-political, were generally less intensely 'politicized' than their Yiddish or Hebrew-reading counterparts. This apparent weakness of the Polish-Jewish press, in terms of the highly political standards of the age, was, however, in our own post-ideological hindsight perhaps, also its strength: a humility based on a consciousness of the limitations of its own possible claims to 'authenticity', which allowed it, first, to mirror the real breadth of Jewish cultural creation in Poland, and second, to continue to adhere to the flickering hope of fraternal relations with the non-Jewish world.

NOTES

1 Chone Shmeruk's article, 'Hebrew-Yiddish-Polish: a Tri-Lingual Jewish Culture' (to be published in Israel Gutman, Ezra Mendelsohn, Jehude Reinharz and Chone Shmeruk (eds) *The Jews of Poland between two World Wars*), is both from a theoretical perspective and on the basis of the observations and references with which it is filled, a fundamental starting point for the study of the Polish-Jewish press, and indeed for the study of interwar Polish Jewish culture in general. The authoritative bibliography of the Polish-language Jewish press is Paul Glikson's *Preliminary Inventory of the Jewish Daily and Periodical Press Published in the Polish Language, 1823–1982* (Jerusalem, 1983), with additions (soon to be published) by Alina Cała. For the interwar Yiddish press, the corresponding bibliography is Yechiel Szeintuch's *Preliminary Inventory of Yiddish Dailies and Periodical Publications Published in Poland Between the Two World Wars* (Jerusalem, 1986). Marian Fuks' pioneering monograph on the Jewish press in Warsaw, *Prasa żydowska w Warszawie, 1823–1939* (Warsaw, 1979), is an important but occasionally flawed source. Fuks is most reliable on the Polish-language press, but must, however, be used cautiously even here (see, for example, nn. 47 and 76 below). Andrzej Paczkowski's recent monograph on the interwar Polish daily press, *Prasa codzienna Warszawy w latach 1918–1939* (Warsaw, 1983), as well as an earlier statistical article, 'Nakłady dzienników warszawskich w latach 1931–1938' (in *Rocznik Historii Czasopiśmiennictwa Polskiego* [Wrocław-Warsaw-Kraków-Gdańsk], v. 15, 1976, pp. 68–97), examine the Jewish press as well, and bring new data to bear particularly on the question of circulation. (See pp. 214–7 below.) The anthology *Di yidishe prese vos iz geven* (Tel Aviv, 1975), edited by Dovid Flinker, Mordkhe Tsanin, and Sholem Rosenfeld, is a collection of reminiscences by Jewish journalists and editors; the following articles are relevant: Pola Appenszlak, '*Nasz Przegląd*', pp. 223–31; Moshe Sneh, '*Nowe Słowo* – a kemferishe tsaytung in der poylisher shprakh', pp. 232–35; Sholem Yededia, '*Pięta Rano*', pp. 235–36; Dovid Lazer, '*Nowy Dziennik* – 1918–1939', pp. 301–15. (Pola [Paulina] Appenszlak was a journalist and wife of the editor of *Nasz Przegląd*; Dovid Lazer worked for *Nowy Dziennik* from 1921 and was editor-in-chief during the latter 1930's; on Moshe Sneh see n. 65 below.) Melekh Ravitsh's quirky and illuminating *Mayn leksikon* (v. 1, Montreal, 1945; v. 2, 1947) includes profiles of several Polish-language Jewish journalists. Khaym Finkelshteyn's partly memoiristic monograph, *'Haynt' – a tsaytung bay yidn, 1908–1939* (Tel Aviv, 1978), contains incidental material on the Polish-language Jewish press as well. In addition: Pola Appenszlak, 'Ha-itonut be-polanit', *Enziklopedyah shel galuyot*, v. 1, Tel Aviv-Jerusalem, 1953, cols. 505–14; and Avraham Levinson, *Toledot yehudei Varshah*, Tel Aviv, 1953, pp. 305–06. For the sake of completeness, two pre-war Polish anti-semitic works: Paweł Czajkowski, 'Prasa żydowska w Polsce', *Przegląd Judaistyczny* (a pseudo-scholarly periodical devoted to the Jewish 'menace'), v. 1, 1922, pp. 197–212; and Zygmunt Jamiński, *Prasa żydowska w Polsce*, Lwów, 1936.

2 As if to emphasize the use of Polish for Jewish purposes, the word 'our' [*nasz*, *nasze*] was extraordinarily prevalent (over 12 per cent of Glikson's entries) in the titles of interwar Polish-Jewish publications.

3 For the purposes of this article there is little reason to distinguish among the papers published in these various cities. It should however be borne in mind that the

linguistic make-up of the Jewish populations of the Galician cities of Lwów and Kraków was very diffierent from that of Warsaw in Central ('Congress') Poland. The 1931 Polish census lists the following percentages of Jews declaring Yiddish as their mother tongue in these three cities: Warsaw, 88.9; Lwów, 67.8; Kraków, 41.3. (Cited according to Yankev Leshtshinski, 'Di shprakhn bay yidn in umophengikn Poyln', *Yivo bleter*, v. 22, 1943, pp. 147–62; these figures are somewhat inflated – see n. 24 below.) Thus, Kraków did not have a single Yiddish daily; Warsaw usually had at least five. Yet Jewish cultural and political life developed with a force of its own in Kraków, and primarily in the Polish language. And *Nowy Dziennik* in Kraków could become something that *Nasz Przegląd* never could in Warsaw: *the* Jewish newspaper.

4 As Shmeruk has pointed out ('Hebrew-Yiddish-Polish . . .'), the existence of a small number of obscure and widely scattered Jewish dailies in non-Jewish languages (see for example the listing of Jewish publications in *Jüdisches Lexikon*, v. 4, Berlin, 1930, pp. I–XXXV [insert to cols. 1104–05]) are exceptions which only underline the significance of the interwar Polish phenomenon.

5 Although Hebrew dailies existed in the interwar period (*Ha-zefirah*, with interruptions, to 1931, and *Ha-yom* from 1925–26, both in Warsaw), and in many circles great prestige was associated with the reading of a Hebrew newspaper, there were, however, never enough Hebrew readers in Poland to make a Hebrew daily a viable competitor of a Yiddish or even a Polish-Jewish daily, and a Hebrew paper could only exist because it was subsidized by Zionist organizations, for whom its existence was an important political statement. In the interwar years, moreover, as Shmeruk has pointed out, Poland increasingly lost ground to Palestine as the centre of modern Hebrew publishing. The circulation of the Hebrew dailies during the interwar period was a negligible proportion of the total circulation of the Jewish press.

6 In addition to *Haynt* and *Der moment*: *Unzer ekspres* (1927–39), an independent tabloid; *Folkstsaytung* (1921–39), organ of the Jewish socialist Bund; and *Yudishe togblat* (1929–39), organ of the orthodox Agudas Yisroel. *Haynt* and *Der moment* also published inexpensive afternoon tabloids: *Hayntige nayes* (1929–39) and *Varshever radio* (1924–39), respectively. In addition, almost all of the many Jewish political parties and 'tendencies' maintained their own, frequently irregular, periodical publications. Szeintuch lists a total of 1708 Yiddish periodical publications throughout Poland in the interwar period; a good number of these, of course, were short-lived.

7 If we interpret the notion of 'nationality' broadly enough, this may be said to characterize even the orthodox *Yudishe togblat*.

8 The weekly *Dostrzegacz Nadwiślański/Der Beobachter an der Weichsel*, printed in Polish and in Hebrew-character German, antedated by some forty years both the first Yiddish and Hebrew newspapers: *Varshoyer yudisher tsaytung* (1867–68) and *Ha-zefirah* (1862–1931), respectively. *Dostrzegacz* was a symbolically important but anomalous historical phenomenon: financially supported by the Russian government, it could not attract enough readers to justify its existence. *Dostrzegacz* has a comparatively large literature: Mordkhe Spektor, 'Di ershte tsaytung bay yudn', *Yudishe folks-tsaytung* (Warsaw), February 25, 1903; Majer Bałaban, 'Tsum 100-yorikn yubiley fun der yidisher prese in Poyln', *Bikher-velt* (Warsaw), v. 2, 1923, cols. 427–38, and 'Nasi poprzednicy i nauczyciele; prasa polsko-żydowska w XIX wieku', *Nasz Przegląd*, September 18, 1938; Azriel Frenk, 'Der "yontev" un zayn historisher hintergrunt', *Tsukunft*, March 1924; Nakhmen Mayzil, 'Di ershte yidishe tsaytung in Rusland mit hundert yor tsurik', *Tsukunft*, March 1924, and '125 yor zint der ershter yidisher tsaytung in Poyln', *Yidishe Kultur*, December 1948;

Yisroel Tsinberg, *Di geshikhte fun der literatur bay yidn*, v. 88, New York, 1943, pp. 220–21; Gershom Bader, 'Dray momenten in der antviklung fun der yidisher prese in Poyln', *Der polyisher yid, 11-ter yorbukh*, New York, 1944, pp. 60–61; Yankev Shatski, *Geshikhte fun yidn in Varshe*, v. 1, New York, 1947, pp. 290–92; Pola Appenszlak, 'Ha-itonut be-polanit'; S. Łastik, *Z dziejów oświecenia żydowskiego*, Warsaw, 1961, pp. 176–79; and Fuks, pp. 21–40. In terms of actual influence, the first Polish-language Jewish publication was the weekly *Jutrzenka* (1861–63). Significantly, although by the 1850's in Warsaw a potential readership for a Polish-Jewish periodical already existed, such a publication was only established under the impetus of the first Polish attacks on Jewish assimilation, the so-called 'Jewish War' of 1859. On *Jutrzenka*, see: B. Vaynrib, 'Tsu der geshikhte fun der poylish-yidisher prese', *Yivo bleter*, v. 2, 1931, pp. 73–79; Yankev Shatski, 'Der kamf arum geplante tsaytshriftn far yidn in Kongres-Poyln (1840–1860)', *Yivo bleter*, v. 6, 1934, pp. 61–83, 'A tsushtayer tsu der biografie fun Daniel Neufeld [editor of *Jutrzenka*] (1814–1874)', *Yivo bleter*, v. 7, 1934, pp. 110–16, and *Geshikhte fun yidn in Varshe*, v. 2, New York, 1948, pp. 245–47, 253–55, and v. 3, 1953, pp. 298–300, 318–19; Majer Bałaban, 'Nasi poprzednicy . . .'; Pola Appenszlak, 'Ha-itonut be-polanit'; and Fuks, pp. 41–61.

9 On *Izraelita*, see for example: Yankev Shatski, *Geshikhte fun yidn in Varshe*, v. 3, pp. 319–21; Fuks, pp. 85–102; and Alina Cała, *Kwestia asymilacji Żydów w Królestwie Polskim (1863–1897): Postawy, Konflikty, Stereotypy*, doctoral dissertation, Historical Institute, Polish Academy of Sciences (PAN), 1985.

10 See for example, Shatski, *Geshikhte fun yidn in Varshe*, v. 3, pp. 110–29.

11 The story was told that since by this time neither *Izraelita*'s subscribers nor its editorial board read the paper – they supported it as an institution, but in these circles actually reading a Jewish paper smacked of 'separatism' – it took years until someone noticed that this very 'separatism' had explicitly crept into the paper and Sokolow was fired. (See S. Hirszhorn, 'Początki żydowskiego ruchu narodowego w Polsce', *Nasz Przegląd*, September 18, 1938.) Nahum Sokolow (1859–1936), the most productive and influential of a number of tri-lingual nineteenth century Polish Jewish journalists, began working for *Izraelita* in the 1880's. For many years he also edited *Ha-zefirah*, founded numerous other Hebrew publications, and was closely involved in the birth of the earliest Warsaw Yiddish periodical, Y. L. Peretz's *Di yudishe biblyotek*. The Hebrew poet Haym Nahman Bialik said of Sokolow that if someone were to undertake the project of gathering all of his writings he would need three hundred camels to carry them. After World War I Sokolow served in the Zionist Executive, and in the 1930's as head of the World Zionist Organization. Although he lived in England for most of the interwar period (where he produced an English history of Zionism), Sokolow continued to publish in Poland in the tri-lingual Jewish press; among Polish Jews his authority as Zionist elder statesman was immense. For a bibliography of works about Sokolow and the Jewish press, see Robert Singerman, *Jewish Serials of the World: A Research Bibliography of Secondary Sources*, New York-Westport, Connecticut-London, 1986, pp. 109–112. On Sokolow and *Haynt*, see p. 218 below.

12 In the preface to *Safrus*, Kirszrot contrasts the old romantic promise of assimilation, 'a living idea, a creative and winged conception', with the contemporary result: 'a soul-less and mechanical process performed its work without a superfluous word, the work of disintegrating the nation, whose intelligentsia, tearing itself from the family trunk, in frenzied haste demolished all roads to the human soul'. ('Wstęp', p. 7.)

13 On *Głos Żydowski*, see the article by Hirszhorn in n. 11, and Fuks, pp. 153–55; on Grünbaum (1879–1970), see pp. 218–9 below. In the more democratic and

polonized situation in Galicia, Polish-language Zionist publications appeared with greater regularity: the fortnightly *Przyszłość* (Lwów, 1890–99?); and the weeklies *Wschód* (Lwów, 1900–12) and *Moriah* (Lwów, 1903–14); indeed, the Galician Zionist press as a whole was a Polish-language press.

14 The Duma was an elected representative body which met in St. Petersburg. Granted by the czar after the 1905 revolution, by 1912 the Duma's political importance was minimal. On the Duma elections of 1912 and the resulting anti-Jewish boycott, see for example *Żydzi w Polsce Odrodzonej*, Warsaw, [1932–33], pp. 482–85; the memoirs of the Polish-Jewish journalist Bernard Singer, *Moje Nalewki*, Warsaw, 1959, pp. 164–69; Finkelshleyn, p. 49–56; and Frank Bolizewski, *Polnishe-Jüdische Beziehungen 1881–1922* (Wiesbaden, 1981).

15 In 1913, in a major article entitled 'Jew-Poland' ['*Żydo-Polska*'], Świętochowski prophesied a 'war' between the Polish nation and the 'nation of Israel'. (*Tygodnik Illustrowany*, nr. 8.)

16 Fuks, p. 151.

17 Herman Czerwiński, 'Ze wspomnień dziennikarskich', *Nasz Przegląd*, September 18, 1938.

18 See Czerwiński.

19 In particular, the publications of the Union of Poles of the Mosaic Faith [*Zjednoczenie Polaków Wyznania Mojżeszowego*] such as: *Rozwaga* (1915–28) and *Zjednoczenie* (1931–33); for further sources, see Shmeruk.

20 The editors of the Kraków daily *Nowy Dziennik*, for example, were considered the most 'Hebraist' of any Jewish paper in Poland: most had received a Hebrew education and read and spoke Hebrew. On a visit to this Polish-language paper's offices, Haym Nahman Bialik is reported to have said: 'Here one can at least speak Hebrew!' (Lazer, p. 311.) The relationship between the small but prestigious Hebrew cultural circles and those Jewish circles among whom Polish was the language of choice was often particularly close. Polish-educated Jewish youth seeking a way back to 'Jewishness', for whom Yiddish was still – if sometimes only unconsciously – tainted with its lower-class origins and nineteenth century designation as 'jargon' (not to mention the new Zionist accusation that it was a product of Jewish exile [galut] and must be 'negated' along with it), often discovered in elitist Hebrew culture a bridge to a new Zionist identity. An example of this phenomenon is the case of the Polish Zionist youth group Hashomer Hatzair, whose members generally came from Polish secondary schools, had been influenced by Polish nationalism avoided Yiddish, and devoted their energy to cultivating a new and 'healthy' Jewish youth steeped in manual labour and Hebrew culture. (See Ezra Mendelsohn, *Zionism in Poland, the Formative Years, 1915–1926*, New Haven, Connecticut and London, 1981, pp. 81–87, 120–30, 290–96.) Another instructive example: in an article on the bitter Hebraist-yiddishist conflict, a writer in *Nasz Przegląd* (Jakób Zineman, 'O naszej kwestji językowej', September 6, 1928), while announcing an even-handed approach to the issue, in fact attributes most of the blame for the conflict to the 'barbarism' of the yiddishists, and accepts the correctness of most Hebraist arguments. For an enlightening discussion of the political aspect of this tie – the influence of Polish nationalism on Zionism, see Ezra Mendelsohn, 'A Note on Jewish Assimilation in the Polish Lands', in Bela Vago (ed.), *Jewish Assimilation in Modern Times*, Boulder, Colorado, 1981, pp. 141–49. The Hebrew-Polish nexus as a linguistic and literary phenomenon deserves further attention.

21 On the founders of *Nasz Przegląd*, see p. 15 below.

22 It should, however, be pointed out that many elementary school students attended public schools in the mornings, and religious or secular Jewish schools in the

afternoons. On the secondary level, more Jewish students attended private or community-supported Jewish schools than state schools, but in the majority of these schools Polish was the language of instruction. For an analysis of the trilingual Jewish educational system in Poland and for further sources see Shmeruk.

23 One example: in an article intended to reply to the widespread accusation that Yiddish culture was on the wane in Warsaw, Nakhmen Mayzil ('Vi halt es mit yidish in Varshe', *Literarishe bleter*, nrs. 18–19, May 3–10, 1935) nevertheless cites statistics that show that among the libraries of eight Warsaw Jewish secondary schools containing over twenty thousand volumes, there were only one hundred books in Yiddish! The phenomenon was most widespread but not limited to the middle classes. Thus, Zygmunt Turkov (*Di ibergerisene tkufe*, Buenos Aires, 1961, pp. 247–48) recounts how the organization Kultur-Lige, one of the bastions of Yiddish culture in the interwar period (among its activities was to manage one of the two Yiddish publishing houses in Poland), whose practice it had been to purchase blocks of seats to Yiddish theatre performances for its Warsaw working class membership, began in the late 1930's to patronize Polish theatre instead. Further research is required to establish whether such phenomena were more pronounced in Warsaw than elsewhere in Poland.

24 This is borne out by the results of two Polish censuses: in 1921, 74.2 per cent of those Jews declaring themselves Jewish by religion also identified themselves as Jews by nationality; in 1931, in the absence of a category for national affiliation, and in the face of a campaign mounted in the Jewish press to use the category of 'mother-tongue' (a particularly inappropriate notion in relation to the bi-and trilingual reality) as a political statement about national identity – 79.9 per cent of all Jews by religion declared Yiddish as their mother tongue and 7.8 per cent declared their mother tongue to be Hebrew. In Warsaw for example, there were more 'native' speakers of Hebrew (19,743) than of non-Jewish languages including Polish (19,305)! The percentage of 'native speakers of Jewish languages' in 1931 exceeded by 13.6 per cent the percentage of 'Jews by nationality' in 1921. Although these results are an unreliable source for Jewish linguistic affiliation, they are an excellent indicator of the growth of Jewish national consciousness – which appears to have been notably strengthened after ten years of independent Poland. (The figures are from Yankev Leshtshinski's analysis of the 1931 census cited in n. 3 above. On their actual significance, see Shmeruk, 'Hebrew-Yiddish-Polish . . .', as well as Leshtshinski.) It should be kept in mind, however, that there was a big difference between what a Zionist or Bundist, on the one hand, and an orthodox Jew, on the other, would have *meant* by Jewish nationality.

25 Cited from a Polish paraphrase of Stupnitski's article: (h), 'W młynie opinji. Czy potrzebne jest pismo polsko-żydowskie?', *Nasz Przegląd*, June 14, 1928. The original appeared in *Lubliner togblat* apparently as a reply to a 'great Jewish literary figure' who had stated in the *Sanacja* (government) newspaper *Głos Prawdy* that a Jewish daily in Polish was unnecessary. I have been unable to locate the original.

26 'W młynie opinji. Czy potrzebne jest pismo polsko-żydowskie?'.

27 Pola Appenszlak,'*Nasz Przegląd*', p. 227.

28 The victim, an orthodox Jew, was dragged from a trolley and beaten to death by a gang of Piłsudski's Legionnaires; on the following day the liberal *Nowa Reforma* carried a brief notice about the death, attributing it to a heart attack; at demonstrations surrounding the victim's funeral, the demand was raised for 'a daily Jewish national newspaper in the Polish language, which would serve as a combative tribune' against the wave of anti-semitism following the dissolution of the Hapsburg monarchy and the rise of an independent Polish state. (See Lazer, pp. 301–02, 304.)

29 Similarly, a Boston Jew today might read the daily ***Boston Globe*** and the weekly ***Jewish Advocate***.
30 'W młynie opinji. Czy potrzebne jest pismo polsko-żydowske?' These lines play on the well-known dictum of the nineteenth century Hebrew poet Yehudah Leyb Gordon: 'Be a Jew in the home, and a man on the street'.
31 During the 1930's there were between two and four Polish-Jewish dailies in Warsaw; for periodical publications throughout Poland in the interwar period, Glikson and Cała list some 700 titles, of which about 150 appeared only once.
32 The firms of Teofil Pietraszka and Franciszek Krajny, the latter later known as PAR (*Polska Agencja Reklamy* [Polish Advertising Agency]); the catalogues were published more or less every two years beginning in 1921.
33 See n. 1.
34 See n. 1.
35 See n. 1.
36 Because of an insufficient number of samplings, I omitted figures for 1931 and 1936; in addition, because of many apparent irregularities, I omitted figures for June 30, 1932. I then computed average circulation for each of the years 1932, 1933, 1937 and 1938, and took the average of these figures. Thus, for example, of the 57 samplings of the circulation of *Nasz Przegląd*, there were 19 for 1932, 24 for 1933, 7 for 1937, and 7 for 1938. Fuks' figures are on pp. 263, 275, 189, 197, 208, 215, 206, 189, respectively, of *Prasa żydowska* . . . .
37 'Nakłady dzienników . . .', p. 68.
38 *Piąta Rano*, a Polish-Jewish tabloid, was published from 1931–39; see further n. 54 below.
39 'Nakłady dzienników . . .', p. 69. Another possibility, suggested to me by Professor Joshua Rothenberg, is that they inflated circulation figures for the non-socialist press, but not for the socialist press which, in any case, was of small interest to the catalogue publishers since it carried very little advertising.
40 'Vu haltn mir mit unzer tog-prese in Poyln?', *Literarishe bleter*, nr. 22, May 29. This figure may not reflect the true circulation of *Der emes*; what is relevant here, however, is the figure itself and how it compares with Fuk's for the Warsaw press. Mayzil's statement that this is a week-day circulation figure suggests a further question, since it is well known that the circulation of the Yiddish dailies was much larger on Fridays – namely, was Friday circulation included in the police samplings in a statistically consistent manner? Checking the 45 cases of samplings for which specific dates are given permits an affirmative answer: 6 were on Fridays.
41 *Prasa codzienna* . . . , p. 260.
42 Based on the circulation of the following dailies: *Nasz Przegląd*, *Piąta Rano*, *Nowe Słowo* (Glikson nr. 308), *Pismo Codzienne* (nr. 348), and *Nasz Głos* [*Wieczorny*] (nr. 245) for the years 1932, 1933, 1937, 1938. For *Nasz Głos* in particular there is a degree of discrepancy between its dates of publication as given in Glikson and dates of samplings in the police data.
43 Based on the circulation of the following dailies: *Haynt*, *Der moment*, *Unzer ekspres*, *Folkstsaytung*, *Yudishe togblat*, *Hayntige nayes*, *Varshever radio*, *Tsvey baytog* (Szeintuch nr. 1523), *Dos vort* (nr. 685), *Dos naye vort* (nr. 1217), and *Yudisher kurier* (nr. 999) for the years 1932, 1933, 1937, 1938. For *Yudisher kurier* in particular there is a degree of discrepancy between its dates of publication as given in Szeintuch and dates of samplings in the police data. In addition, no distinction is made in the police records between *Dos vort* and *Dos naye vort*, and *Tsvey baytog* appears as '*Cwaj Bajtos*'.
44 From 1932–39 there were no Hebrew dailies in Warsaw.

45 Paczkowski's figures for the Polish-language daily press ('Nakłady dzienników . . .', p. 69) less my figures for the Polish-language Jewish daily press.

46 Paczkowski, *Prasa codzienna* . . ., pp. 242–43. *Nasz Przegląd*, for example, encountered more competition in other major cities from *Nowy Dziennik* and *Chwila* than did *Haynt* from local Yiddish dailies; *Nasz Przegląd* was therefore more of a 'Warsaw paper' than *Haynt*. Probably only Wilno, with its well-established Yiddish press, was an exception to the high level of penetration of Warsaw Yiddish dailies into other cities. On the other hand, more of the Warsaw Jewish daily press as a whole was printed for 'export' than was the case with its Polish counterpart (Paczkowski, *Prasa codzienna* . . ., pp. 259–60); in other words, the Jewish press in Poland was much more centralized in Warsaw than was the Polish press.

47 The statistics for 1906 from the offices of the Warsaw censor [*Warszawski Komitet Cenzury*], a rare and important find, are published in Fuks, p. 298. Fuks chooses to include the daily *Gazeta Nowa / Ludzkość* (with a circulation of 10,000) as a Jewish paper, but although its editor was Jewish, its politics were liberal and it was probably read primarily by Jews, it never explicitly addressed itself to a Jewish audience.

48 It should be noted that there are over three times as many samplings for the first period than for the second.

49 According to Paczkowski's calculations, the Jewish share of the Warsaw daily press declined from approximately 25 per cent for 1931–33 to 20 per cent for 1937–38; the first figure, however, is based on data which include the year 1931 which I omitted because samplings of Jewish press circulation for that year were extremely sparse. See *Prasa codzienna* . . ., p. 263 and the table on p. 257; there are other minor differences in Paczkowski's figures.

50 *Prasa codzienna* . . ., p. 263.

51 *Prasa codzienna* . . ., p. 263.

52 *Prasa codzienna* . . ., p. 275.

53 See for example, Nakhmen Mayzil's diatribe, 'Vu haltn mir mit unzer tog-prese in Poyln?', cited in n. 40.

54 Stanisław Świsłocki, the editor of *Piąta Rano*, expecting a large readership for a Polish-language Jewish tabloid, launched his paper in 1931 with a circulation of over 40,000, but was quickly forced to cut back to 'more realistic' numbers, and this at a time when the share of the sensational press as a whole in the Warsaw daily press went from 55 per cent in 1932–33 to 60–65 per cent in 1937–38. See Paczkowski, *Prasa codzienna* . . ., pp. 248–49 and 264–65.

55 Professor Joshua Rothenberg has brought to my attention a relevant and apparently undocumented phenomenon concerning readership of the Yiddish press in the 1930's. With the increasing pauperization of the Jewish population, coupled with the increasing sense of urgency about world news, the practice developed of paying 5 groszy (*Haynt* and *Moment* cost 25) to read a Yiddish paper on the premises of the local newspaper or book dealer, and then returning the paper to be sold or 'loaned' again. Yiddish papers inveighed against this practice, and even began to staple together the pages of their newspapers, but this didn't help: with the newspaper-seller's permission, the staples were removed and then replaced after the paper was read. Readers of *Nasz Przegląd*, generally of a wealthier class, did not need to 'share' their paper in the same way. Professor Rothenberg's observations stem from Radom and the shtetl Sandomierz. More research, including interviews with those who remember the period, is required in order to establish the prevalence of this phenomenon in Poland and its effect on the figures above.

56 Pola Appenszlak, '*Nasz Przegląd*', p. 226; see pp. 223–4 below.

57 *Haynt* affiliated with Yitshak Grübaum's *Al Hamishmar* faction of the General

Zionists, *Der moment* (after a link to the non-Zionist Folkist Party) first with the competing *Et Livnot* group, and in 1938 with Vladimir Jabotinsky's Revisionists. On the split in the Polish Zionist Federation, see Ezra Mendelsohn, *Zionism in Poland*..., pp. 245–52.

58 See for example *Nasz Przegląd*'s fifteenth anniversary issue, September 18, 1938. Ben-Gurion and Jabotinsky were leaders of two of the most antagonistic Zionist parties: Labour Zionists and Revisionists, respectively.

59 Hirszhorn (1876–1942), whose early years were spent in Polish-speaking circles, came to Yiddish as an adult. He was the author of a popular sketch of Polish Jewish history (*Historja Żydów w Polsce, od Sejmu Czteroletniego do wojny europejskiej [1788–1914]*, Warsaw, 1921) which he translated into Yiddish, and editor and for the most part translator of a Polish anthology of Yiddish literature (*Antologia Poezji Żydowskiej*, Warsaw, 1921). He liked to say that he wrote with two pens, Yiddish with the right hand and Polish with the left (Ravitsh, v. 2, p. 114). Wołkowicz (b. 1891), who was also a Yiddish-Polish translator, founded the series 'Biblioteka Pisarzy Żydowskich' which published Polish translations of Yiddish literature; in addition he was one of the founders of the Yiddish school system Tsisho. On Hirszhorn and Wołkowicz see *Leksikon fun der nayer yidisher literatur*, v. 3, New York, 1960, cols. 159–60 and 287–88, respectively; on Hirszhorn see also *Polski Słownik Biograficzny*, v. 9, Wrocław-Warsaw-Kraków, 1960–61, pp. 535–36. Appenszlak (b. 1891), on the other hand, read Yiddish fluently, but spoke with difficulty and with the 'accent of a *ger* [convert]'; see Ravitsh, v. 2, p. 98.

60 p. 146. The third was Moyshe Yustman [B. Yeushzon] (1889–1942), an extremely popular Yiddish columnist.

61 Thon (1870–1936), who served in the Polish *Sejm* [parliament], worked with *Nowy Dziennik* and also published in *Nasz Przegląd*; on his involvement in *Haynt* see Finkelsheyn, pp. 152–54. On Sokolow, see n. 11 above; on Sokolow and *Haynt*, see Finkelshteyn, pp. 154–57.

62 Finkelshteyn, pp. 132–45. On Grünbaum, see also p. 211 above. It would be worthwhile to compare the writings of a figure such as Grünbaum in Yiddish, Hebrew and Polish, in order to see how a political message may have changed depending on the linguistic audience.

63 Fuks, p. 258.

64 *Opinja*, an important and heretofore unexamined source for Polish-Jewish cultural history of the 1930's, was moved in 1935 from Warsaw to Lwów, where it appeared until 1939 as *Nowa Opinja* (according to Glikson, nr. 342) or *Nasza Opinja* (according to the catalogue of the Polish National Library). The publication may not have been able to continue in Warsaw because of political reasons: Cardinal Kakowski's displeasure over a Polish translation of Yosef Klausner's Hebrew study of the life of Jesus (Finkelshteyn, p. 302).

Other Polish-language Jewish publications published by *Haynt* were the dailies *Nowiny Codzienne* (1922) and *Nowy Czas* (1929), and the weekly *Nowa Palestyna* (1935) (Paczkowski, p. 248; Finkelshteyn, pp. 301, 302, 424, respectively). In 1939, after negotiations with the editors of *Nasz Przegląd*, the publishing cooperative 'Alt-Nay' (the publishers of *Haynt*) made plans for an illustrated Polish-language Jewish weekly which would begin to appear in September of that year (Finkelshteyn, pp. 300–03). The publishers of *Der moment* also founded Polish-language Jewish papers, among them the daily *Nowy Głos* (1937–38) (Paczkowski, p. 250).

In September 1929, Sh. Y. Yatskan, the flamboyant founding editor of *Haynt*, established an inexpensive a-political Polish tabloid with the purpose of weaning a mass Polish audience away from the popular anti-semitism fostered by the existing large-circulation Polish dailies, and thereby implicitly advancing Polish-Jewish harmony. The paper was launched by scores of newsboys distributing a special issue which proclaimed: 'Greatest sensation of the day! Revolution in press history! Daily of the newest type . . .!' *Ostatnie Wiadomości*, among the first successful attempts at yellow journalism in Poland, quickly attained a circulation of 100,000, making it the largest-selling Polish daily; throughout the 1930's, however, it gradually lost readers to other tabloids. Yatskan's involvement with the paper ended in 1934. (See Paczkowski, pp. 208–13, 264–65; Finkelshteyn, pp. 35–36.)

65 Kleinbaum (1909–1972), whose ties to Grünbaum inspired the nickname 'Kleingrünbaum', inherited Grünbaum's mantle when the latter emigrated to Palestine in 1933; under the name Moshe Sneh, he was the head of the Haganah (Jewish defense forces) in Palestine in the 1940's, and from 1951 the leader of the Israeli Communist Party (Maki). See Finkelshteyn, pp. 182–84, 301–02; and Sneh, pp. 232–34.

66 p. 301.

67 'Cele i zadania', nr. 1, February 5, 1933; as cited in Fuks, p. 279.

68 'Na posterunku', nr. 1, March 25, 1923; as cited in Jakób Appenszlak, 'Pietnastolecie "Naszego Przeglądu"', *Nasz Przegląd*, nr. 263, September 18, 1938.

69 Much was written, for example, about the Jewish part in Polish insurrections of the nineteenth century. This emphasis was generally balanced, however, by a realistic assessment of the actual state of Polish-Jewish relations, and demands for their improvement. Both these elements are implicit in the words with which Appenszlak continues the statement (written in the relatively hopeful early 1920's) cited above: 'As citizens of the Polish commonwealth, we desire a strong and enduring Poland, free and freedom-granting, drawing its power and prosperity from the concerted cooperation of all citizens without regard to creed, nationality, or point of view'. ('Na posterunku.')

70 A well-known street in the Warsaw Jewish quarter.

71 Bernard Singer (pseudonym 'Regnis', 1893–1966), *Nasz Przegląd*'s regular and extremely popular parliamentary correspondant, was on 'old-boy' terms with many Polish politicians. Characteristically, Singer wrote in Yiddish and Hebrew as well. See Finkelshteyn, pp. 197–99; and Ravitsh, v. 2, 121–23.

72 'Na posterunku.'

73 'Cele i zadania.'

74 The Polish-Jewish press was also highly receptive to Jewish writers in other non-Jewish languages. And therefore, for example, it was through the Polish-Jewish press that Franz Kafka was introduced to Polish readers. Of all the reviews, excerpts and mentions of Kafka's work in the Polish press in the interwar period, eighty per cent were in Jewish publications. See Eugenia Prokopówna, 'Kafka w Polsce Międzywojennej', *Pamiętnik Literacki*, v. 76, 1985, pp. 89–132, and especially the appended bibliography on pp. 131–32.

75 There is no entry for Kanfer in any of the Jewish or Polish encyclopedias or biographical dictionaries. The theatre he founded operated from 1926–28 with a permanent company of young amateur and professional, often Polish-trained actors; among the plays it produced were Yiddish versions of Stanisław Wyspiański's *Sędziowie* and *Daniel*, the latter staged for the first time in Poland, directed by the Polish director Antoni Piekarski. The theatre gained such artistic renown that, in a highly unusual gesture of recognition, the Kraków municipal council appropriated funds for its support. On this fascinating example of the complexities of interwar Polish Jewish culture, see: Sholem Fraynd, 'Dos ershte yidishe gezelshaftlekhe teater in Poyln (krokever yidish teater)', *Yidish teater*, v. 1, Warsaw-Vilna, 1927, pp. 214–30, and 'Krokever yidish teater', *Literarishe bleter*, May 27, 1927; Yonas Turkov, 'Ha-teatron ha-yehudi be-Krako', in *Sefer Krako, ir ve-*

em be-yisrael, Jerusalem, 1959, p. 352; and Rokhl Holtser, 'Yidish teater in Kroke', in *Yidisher teater in Eyrope tsvishn beyde velt-milkhomes, Poyln*, New York, 1968, pp. 276–85.

76 Among Yiddish writers: Leo Finkelshteyn and S. L. Schneiderman; among Hebrew writers, Yehudah Varshaviak, for example, published essays and reviews of Hebrew literature in *Nasz Przegląd*. Future research on the Polish-Jewish press will have to distinguish between writers who wrote directly in Polish and those whose works appeared in translation. Chone Shmeruk correctly criticizes the work of Marian Fuks for failing to make this important distinction. ('A Pioneering Study of the Warsaw Jewish Press', *Soviet Jewish Affairs*, v. 11, 1981, nr. 3, p. 38.)

77 '*Nasz Przegląd*', p. 228. These were the major Yiddish 'art' theatres in interwar Poland.

78 '*Nasz Przegląd*', pp. 228–29.

79 v. 2, p. 98; for many years Ravitsh was secretary of the Union of Jewish [i.e., Yiddish and Hebrew] Writers and Journalists, better known by its address, 'Tłomackie 13'.

80 pp. 100–01.

81 p. 101. For a comical comparison of the readers of five Warsaw dailies, including *Nasz Przegląd*, see: Der Tunkeler [Yoysef Tunkel], 'Der tsaytungs-farkoyfer', in *Dos amolike yidishe Varshe*, Montreal, 1966, pp. 318–22.

82 Norbert Rosse, 'Czy sztuk żydowska jest potrzebna?', May 19, 1925.

83 Pola Appenszlak, '*Nasz Przegląd*', p. 228.

84 After World War II Brandstaetter (b. 1906) converted to Catholicism, and is today a leading Polish Catholic writer and dramatist. He has published Polish translations of Psalms, Song of Songs, and Proverbs.

85 In the mid-1930's Szymel suddenly threw over a promising career as a Polish-language poet and, no longer as 'Maurycy' but as 'Moyshe', turned exclusively to Yiddish. See Ravitsh, v. 1, pp. 261–63.

86 Eugenia Prokopówna, a doctoral candidate at the Jagiellonian University in Kraków, is completing a dissertation on these writers. She has recently published an article on the depiction of the Jewish Sabbath in Polish literature which draws on some of this material: 'Sobota', *Fołks-sztyme* (Warsaw), nrs. 20–23, May 17–June 7, 1986; and see also her article in the forthcoming anthology *The Jews of Poland between Two World Wars* cited in note 1.

87 On such writers, see Artur Sandauer, *O sytuacji pisarza polskiego pochodzenia żydowskiego w XX wieku*, Warsaw, 1982.

88 'Pisarze polscy czy "pisarze żydowscy piszący po polsku" albo "polsko-żydowscy?"', *Ster*, 1937, nr. 16, as cited by Janusz Maciejewski in the introduction to his edition of Braun's *Wybór poezji*, Warsaw, 1979, p. 27. Braun (1902–42) is a relatively forgotten Polish poet; Maciejewski's small volume is the only edition of his poetry published since the war. Braun was also one of the rare Polish writers who attempted to direct the attention of Polish literary circles to Yiddish literature; see 'Literatura żydowska a polskie środowisko literackie', *Nowe życie*, v. 1, 1924.

89 Korczak wrote a book about Jewish children entitled *Mośki, Joski i Srule*, and a book about Polish children entitled *Józki, Jaśki i Franki* (See: c., 'Z piśmiennictwa', *Izraelita*, nr. 3, May 6, 1910). On *Mały Przegląd*, see: Janusz Korczak, *Ktavim pedagogiyim*, Tel-Aviv, 1954, pp. 135–58; Marian Fuks, '"Mały Przegląd" Janusza Korczaka', *Biuletyn Żydowskiego Instytutu Historycznego w Polsce* (Warsaw), nr. 105, 1978, pp. 3–28; and Leon Harari, '"Kleine Rundschau" – Korczaks Zeitung für die Kinder', in Werner Licharz (ed.), *Janusz Korczak in seiner und in unserer Zeit*, Frankfurt/Main, 1981, pp. 118–28.

90 'Od redakcji', February 19, 1928, as cited in Fuks, p. 282; on *Ewa*, see Fuks, pp. 282–85.

91 It should be noted that the orthodox Yiddish press often included a section in Polish for women, since many women in hasidic homes read Polish more fluently than Yiddish. Obviously, such women's publications were very different from *Ewa*.

92 B. Zinger, 'Der krizis fun der yidisher prese in provints', *Literarisher bleter*, nr. 129, October 22, 1926.

93 See pp. 212–3 above.

94 The treaty, guaranteeing Jewish political and cultural rights in independent Poland, was signed by Polish representatives as part of the Versailles Accords. Much Jewish political energy was expended during the interwar period attempting to realize its provisions.

95 'Pro domo sua', nr. 38, September 23, 1934, as cited in Fuks, p. 279. The article replies to an accusation made by 'one of our best journalists . . . at a certain Jewish journalists' conference'. Shmeruk ('Hebrew-Yiddish-Polish . . .') identifies the writer of the article as Moyshe Kleinbaum.

96 See n. 24 above.

97 'Statystyka a etyka', v. 1, 1932, pp. 10–12; as cited in Shmeruk, 'Hebrew-Yiddish-Polish . . .', emphasis in the original.

98 'Hebrew-Yiddish-Polish. . . .'

99 Shmeruk, 'Hebrew-Yiddish-Polish. . . .'

21

FROM 'NUMERUS CLAUSUS' TO 'NUMERUS NULLUS'

Szymon Rudnicki

Almost from the beginning of its activities the National Democratic movement used nationalist slogans in its propaganda campaigns, chiefly antisemitic ones. This propaganda eventually achieved the desired results. Clearly, though, the policy of the National Democrats was only one part of the so-called 'Jewish question', and the events described below were only a small part of the political programme of the National Democrats.

From the first days of the independent Polish state the National Democratic movement worked to curb the rights of the national minorities, particularly those of the Jews. Only a month after the assembly of the *Sejm Ustawodawczy* (Constituent Parliament) on 19 March 1919, the *Związek Ludowo-Narodowy* (Popular National Union) pointedly tabled a motion which resulted in a Commission for Jewish Affairs being set up. Its task was 'the comprehensive examination of the Jewish question, employing a questionnaire designed by those circles most familiar with the matter, and the presentation of conclusions so derived, with a view to resolving the problem'.[1] In the power struggle the *Endecja* (National Democrats) eagerly employed anti-semitic slogans, counting both on their universality and that they would be readily taken up by voters.[2] The slogans were matched by deeds. In the lands which had once belonged to Austria-Hungary, Jewish railway workers were dismissed. It began to be increasingly difficult for Jews to find work in state and municipal enterprises. As early as 1919, Itzhak Grünbaum complained about the introduction of a percentage quota system for students admitted to Poznań University.[3]

The universities became the testing ground for the National Democrats' propaganda and methods. The susceptibility and responsiveness of youth to patriotic appeals were exploited, and it proved simple to transform them into nationalist slogans. Advantage was taken too of the severe economic situation and poor employment prospects. Because of the lack of employment opportunities for intellectuals, it was easy to convince young people that posts occupied by others should belong to the host community – to the ethnic Poles. A fundamental rallying cry of nationalist youth, which it used to gain control at the universities, was the campaign against what it believed was the excessively high level of young Jews entering higher education. Although the Jews were the prime target for such attacks, in Lwów a campaign was also waged against the Ukrainians.

There were three stages in this campaign: (1) The 1920s and the efforts by young nationalists to gain power and influence in the universities. (2) The first half of the 1930s when the 'numerus clausus' slogan was replaced by the 'numerus nullus' one and the campaign over the 'ghetto bench' began. The campaign had also moved from the propaganda level to that of physical confrontation. (3) The second half of the 1930s, which was characterized by an intensification of campaign methods and notable successes for the young nationalists.

The young nationalists were initially concentrated in the *Narodowe Zjednoczenie Młodzieży Akademickiej* (*NZMA* – National Union of Student Youth) which they barely managed to control. They credited themselves with 'awakening resistance to Jewish influences'. And it is worth noting a sentence from the first issue of their journal *Głos Akademicki* of May 1920, that 'until recently our organization stood completely on its own in this struggle'. Since this reflected the contemporary situation, it was also an indication, as we shall see, of what an appropriate propaganda campaign, waged with persistence and ruthlessness, could lead to. Although a considerable number of students remained indifferent to this struggle at the universities and were concerned only with their studies, and the members of nationalist organizations were never in a majority, they nevertheless managed to gain control of the student organizations and impose their own views.

The battleground fought over by socialist and democratic organizations at the beginning of the 1920s was the *Bratnie Pomoce*, student self-help organizations. The first one to fall to the young nationalists was the *Bratnia Pomoc* of Poznań University. It was controlled by a Nationalist Bloc incorporating student associations and fraternities as well as the *NZMA*. After their success in elections held on 10 April 1921, they passed a resolution calling for Jews to be excluded from student organizations.[4] This pattern was to be repeated at other universities.

On the 25–26 March 1922, the first Congress of *Młodzież Wszechpolska* (All Polish Youth) took place. This was a nation-wide organization where adherents of the nationalist programme were concentrated. It immediately joined in the political campaigning before the 1922 parliamentary elections. From then onwards, the disparate activities at separate universities began to take on an organized shape.

From the beginning the nationalist students directed their activities towards limiting the number of Jews at universities to the same percentage they had in the nation as a whole; in other words, introducing the 'numerus clausus'. Why so many Jewish students should have been entering the universities is a question outside the scope of this paper. It should be pointed out, however, that they were chiefly concentrated in the Faculties of Medicine and Law – professions which could be pursued in private practice. In other faculties, and at other academic institutions, they were much less in evidence. For example, at Poznań University they never reached more than two per cent of the student total.

Młodzież Wszechpolska began a nationwide campaign aimed at forcing the government to introduce legislative measures for a Jewish quota. Their demands, however, did not end there. In a special issue of *Głos Akademicki*, of November 1922, devoted entirely to Polish-Jewish relations, they also called for a ban on the admission of Jews to student organizations and associations, and warned against maintaining social contact with Jews.

The 1922–3 academic year began with a series of rallies at different universities. As early as September a memorandum was addressed in Lwów to the senates of all universities demanding the introduction of a 'numerus clausus'.[5] At this time Jews were 42.5 per cent of the students at the Jan Kazimierz University, but at the Polytechnic they amounted to only 13.9 per cent, and only 13.7 per cent at the Academy of Veterinary Science. To back up their memorandum, a rally was called for 1 October, and the demand was renewed in February 1923. Among the resolutions passed at the rally was a call to restrict the number of Jewish students to 11 per cent of the total.[6] This was to be repeated at other universities with the exception of Poznań, where a limit of l per cent was demanded, the same percentage of Jews in the Wielkopolska region.[7] The fact was ignored that if this principle were applied to the other regions of Poland, then the percentage of Jews admitted would have come to considerably more than the stipulated 11 per cent.

In Kraków the Rector of the Jagiellonian University at first refused to agree to a rally of this kind. A number of student organizations also protested against attempts to hold one. After renewed requests, permission was granted and the rally took place on 23 October. Demands were made for a 'numerus clausus' for Jews in training colleges as well as in academic centres, and if necessary, in faculties of philosophy and law. These demands were renewed at a further rally on 19 March 1923, and on this occasion an appeal was also made for help in communicating these demands to the *Sejm*.[8]

The situation seemed much the same in Warsaw. A rally on 23 November 1923 passed a motion calling for the imposition of a 'numerus clausus'. This was handed to the Vice-Minister for Religious Affairs and Public Education. No Jews were admitted to this public meeting and no representative of the young socialists was allowed to address it. From then on this procedure became the norm. In addition, a students' association 'strong-arm squad' found its way into a meeting of the *Zjednoczenie -Organizacja Polskiej Młodzieży Akademickiej Pochodzenia Żydowskiego* (Organization of Young Students of Jewish Descent) – and broke down the doors of the hall where it was taking place.

These activities in Warsaw culminated in the all-student assembly called for 19 March in the Filharmonia. Here a resolution was passed, with a fourth point which stated that 'Jews should be excluded from membership of Polish ideological, training, scientific, self-help and other organizations, and [the assembly] expresses its approval and support for those organizations already observing these principles'.[9] The nationalists subsequently managed to introduce these principles into the *Bratnia Pomoc* organisations at the university and the polytechnic.

At the close of the assembly it was decided to hold a *Zjazd Ogolnoakademicki* (All-Student Rally) in Lwów at the end of May and the beginning of June. Delegates were chosen, in spite of the protests of young left-wingers, at local meetings on the majority vote system. Furthermore, at these meetings strong-arm squads, composed of members of *Młodzież Wszechpolska* and the student fraternities, admitted only their own followers and ejected those holding contrary views from the hall. In this way the desired composition of the national assembly was achieved. Young delegates of the Peasant parties, elected in Kraków, refused to participate. At first, the Catholic group *Odrodzenie* also wanted to withdraw from the convention. However, it eventually took part but abstained from voting on motions calling for a limitition on the number of Jews at Polish universities to the same proportion as in the overall population; and the waging of a struggle to support this measure using 'all necessary means to reach a successful outcome'. The assembly also approved the statute of the *Związek Narodowy Polskiej Młodzieży Akademickiej* (National Union of Polish Student Youth), which banned Jews from being members of the organization.[10] An unforeseen result of the assembly was a break in what had been, despite some violent differences of opinion, a solid, nation-wide student movement. After this convention, *Młodzież Wszechpolska* began to wield increasing influence at the universities.

Following resolutions passed at the assembly, a Main Committee and Local Academic Committees were set up to deal with the 'numerus clausus' issue. An action programme, extending far beyond the university sphere, was drawn up by the secretary of the Main Committee, Zbigniew Stypułkowski. He believed the ideal solution to the problem would be 'to employ those methods towards Jews, which would eradicate them and their influence from all Polish soil'. Because this was not possible for various reasons 'we must aim at a complete separation of Jews from Poles, and thus exclude them from all spheres of Polish life – government, national, economic, cultural, moral, family, social, etc. – leaving them complete freedom to organize their own ghetto.' As Dariusz Jarosz has shown, an identical demand was contained in the programme of *Młodzież Wszechpolska*, approved in 1925.[11]

The Parliamentary Club of the Popular National Union in the *Sejm* supported these demands. They did so after their defeat in the struggle for the presidency and at an unfavourable time for the National Democrats, following the assassination of Gabriel Narutowicz. On the one hand they wished to divert attention from recent events, while on the other the anti-Jewish campaign was treated as a part of a drive for support among young people. On 16 January 1923 a motion was proposed for changes in articles 85 and 86 of the Universities Act of 13 July 1920. These articles related to student admission procedures. In particular, attention was drawn to article 86, which gave faculty boards, with the approval of the Minister of Religious Affairs and Public Education, the right to limit the number of students accepted. The proposers of the motion wanted to add the following sentence to article 85, 'in Polish institutions of higher education, the number of students admitted to any given department who are of non-Polish nationality or of Jewish faith, must not exceed, as a percentage of the overall number of students of the same department, the percentage of the said national group, or Jewish faith within the overall population of the Polish State.'[12] As can be seen the motion was formally aimed at all minorities, in keeping with the doctrines of Polish nationalism. In practice, however it only applied to Jews, since only they exceeded the quota in the proposal.

The Education Committee of the *Sejm*, which considered this proposal, appointed as its spokesman the famous historian, Władysław Konopczyński. Besides being a professor at the Jagiellonian University, Konopczyński was also a deputy representing the *Związek Ludowo-Narodowy* and a member of the *Liga Narodowa* (National League). After he had spoken, Jewish and Socialist deputies rose to oppose the resolution. They demanded that the motion be sent to the Constitution Committee to test whether the proposed changes in the Constitution could be adopted legally.

The subject produced a bitter debate in the Constitution Committee. Ranged against the motion were Adam Pragier (PPS) and Ludwik Chomiński (*PSL-Wyzwolenie*) who argued that it was unconstitutional. I. Grünbaum asserted that it was the first step towards changing the Constitution. Władysław Kiernik (*PSL-Piast*) agreed that, as it stood, the proposal could not be reconciled with the Constitution. He redrafted it in consultation with *ZLN* members, linking the quota with the issue of a reduction in overall student numbers. Percentages were no longer mentioned, only a fair numerical relationship.[13]

The motion was returned to the Education Committee in its revised version and was then distributed to faculty boards with a query if its adoption would affect the running of higher education. Out of forty-two faculty boards, nine rejected the proposal, declaring themselves in favour of the *status quo*. Twenty-seven supported the proposal in its entirety. Seventy-five per cent of professors approved limiting student numbers and about half were in favour of a percentage quota.[14] In Kraków nine professors out of fifteen in the law faculty declared themselves in favour of limiting student numbers, and eight were in favour of percentage quotas. The medical faculty was unanimously in favour of such quotas. However, the professors in the philosophy faculty considered the proposal went against the dignity of the academic community. Thirty professors voted against the proposal, including the chairman of the Polish Academy of Learning, Kazimierz Morawski, and thirteen voted in favour of the quotas.[15] The Poznań members demanded a reduction of the quotas to one below the proportion of Jews in the population as a whole. The issue of percentage quotas also came up at the Conference of University Rectors (5–7 February 1923), but it did not generate any discussion.[16] In fact a number of faculties were already using percentage quotas, but the most extreme case, as mentioned above, was that of Poznań.

When the Education Commission received these figures and prepared to discuss the matter once more, the representative of *PSL-Piast* tabled a motion requesting its deferment until his party had formulated its own policy on the question. The motives behind this step are none too clear. Most probably, however, the move was connected with simultaneous discussion about the formation of a majority bloc in the *Sejm*, in which the *Piast* group would participate. As a result of these talks the so-called 'Polish majority' was set up in the *Sejm*, headed by the *ZLN* and *PSL-Piast*. One of the principles on which they cooperated was the tenet: 'Young Poles will be guaranteed the chance to be educated at secondary and tertiary level and at vocational institutes, according to the appropriate proportions of the national groups within the state.'[17] As can be seen the principle was also extended to secondary and vocational schools, and the issue was couched in terms which gave the impression that it was young Poles who needed defending, whereas in reality it was young Byelorussians and Ukrainians who were being the most unjustly treated.

The government of Wincenty Witos was formed on the basis of this agreement. Its Minister for Religious Affairs and Public Education was Stanisław Głąbiński, former chairman of the *ZLN*. At the same time, Kiernik's motion, in a slightly amended form, was returned to the Education Committee for further consideration and was approved on 19 June 1923 by sixteen votes to thirteen. Jewish representatives voiced their concern by tabling a counter motion, calling for the following passage to be added to article 86: 'the above restrictions [on admissions to universities] should not be applied on the grounds of nationality or faith.'[18]

With the resolution being passed by such a slender majority, the opposition demanded a third reading. The President of the *Sejm*, Maciej Rataj, sent the motion to the Legislative Committee. Here it came to a stop, since *PSL-Piast* considered it undesirable to introduce the 'numerus clausus' before reforming the Treasury. And this was the end of a first attempt to legislate for a percentage quota to be applied to students entering higher education. In the circumstances the only course open to Głąbiński was to transfer his authority to restrict the number of students admitted to the faculty boards. He did so by a letter circulated on 12 July 1923. The activities of the boards in this area were terminated by the May Coup in 1926.

The government formed after the Coup embarked on several initiatives aimed at reaching agreement with the national minorities. These moves culminated in the passage through the *Sejm* in January 1931 of a bill repealing emergency regulations relating to descent, nationality, language, race or religion. Jewish members had been pressing for such a bill since the first days of independence. If the Jewish minority were pleased with the bill, the mood of the Ukrainians following the pacification campaign of 1930 was one of hostility towards the government.

In the universities, this policy was expressed in the actions of the different ministers who assumed responsibility in turn for higher education. Before the start of the academic year, on 20 September 1926, Antoni Sujkowski cancelled the instructions circulated by Głąbiński. In July 1927 his successor, Gustaw Dobrucki, issued a reminder that the relevant law did not allow the introduction of limits based on nationality or religion. He received Jewish members of the *Sejm* at the beginning of the academic year and told them that 'the government of Marshal Piłsudski is absolutely opposed to the 'numerus clausus'.'[19] Continuing this policy, Sławomir Czerwiński advised university senates to be cautious in allowing assemblies which might result in anti-semitic brawls.[20]

These measures, however, were not matched by appropriate action in the universities. In fact, ceilings continued to be applied. The Rector of the Jagiellonian University, Leon Marchlewski, commented on this at a conference of university rectors, where consideration was given to which departments they should be introduced and in what form. Taking part in the discussion, the Minister, Dobrucki, declared that 'the recording of the actual number of Jews admitted by any one faculty is not desirable, since this cannot remain a secret.' In the end it was unanimously agreed that the Ministry should leave the 'numerus clausus' question untouched.[21] In fact it was not needed for, in practice, a Jewish percentage quota existed in places where the provision of laboratories had caused problems. The *Kurier Codzienny* of 2 October 1931, disclosed that this percentage was 12 per cent in medicine, 10 per cent in dentistry, and 8.5 per cent in pharmacy and veterinary science.

The medical faculties led the way during this early period of the campaign against the Jews. One pretext for the increasing number of confrontations which occurred each year was the so-called 'affair of the Jewish corpses'. On 26 June 1926 the director of the anatomy department of Warsaw University sent out a circular stating that because of a shortage of cadavers, Jewish students wishing to attend lectures and demonstrations would only be admitted if the Jewish community provided corpses.[22] It was claimed that the reason for this dispute was not political, but the result of the objection to Jews 'profaning consecrated corpses'.[23] The Jewish community could not provide the requisite number of corpses since Orthodox Judaism forbade dissection.

Młodzież Wszechpolska had no intention of abandoning its propaganda campaign. In May 1927, the Fifth Congress of Polish Student Youth (which it organized) advised its newly elected leaders to petition the academic authorities and the government to limit the number of Jews at university institutions.[24] Continuing efforts were being made, with some success, to exclude Jews from certain student organizations.

The economic crisis added a new dimension to the problem since it was a convenient starting point for unleashing chauvinism and anti-government activities. The governing council of the *Stronnictwo Narodowe* (Nationalist Party) organized a boycott of Jewish businesses. Similar activities were adopted among young people by the *Ruch Młodych Obozu Wielkiej Polski* (Youth Movement of the Camp for a Great Poland), which had been set up in April 1927. *Młodzież Wszechpolska* (*MW*) became an integral part of the latter organization as its student section. A special 'Jewish department' was created, attached to the central bureau of *MW*. Its activities were not confined to propaganda. In Lwów *MW* organized a blockade of Jewish shops, refusing to allow 'Christians' to enter them. The move was then repeated in other towns. During this period nationalist students began to sport green ribbons as a sign of their anti-semitism.

The nationalist camp was aware that the economic crisis facilitated the spread of anti-semitic propaganda. Appealing to feelings of social injustice, anti-semitism identified its source in a very primitive way, but one which was close to the popular imagination, in the figure of the Jew as competitor, the Jew as exploiter. In particular, the lower-middle-class who were suffering increasingly could see the elimination of Jewish competition as a way of solving all their problems. In the difficult economic situation, therefore, there was considerable support for the call for an economic boycott of Jews. It also attracted increasing support in the countryside. Similarly, the same argument was used in propaganda aimed at young people, namely that they were the victims of 'injustice' in their own country.

An advantage enjoyed by the anti-Jewish programme was its concrete nature and its convenient topicality. It provided a ready explanation for all the complex and negative phenomena of social, political and economic life. Hatred for a common enemy acts as an integrating force, welding together people from different social strata, classes and groupings and from different cultural levels. In Poland it was the Jew who was the obvious candidate for the position of public enemy. Not real Jews, although it was they who suffered from these policies, but mythical Jews – a mythologized, irrational group, the cause of all evil past and present. Consistent with this theory was the belief that the presence of Jews and Judaism meant disruption and disintegration for the Christian community, which was the ideal one by its very definition, and especially for the Polish Catholic community.

The nationalist camp's press organs stirred up the atmosphere to an even greater pitch of excitement.[25] At the beginning of December 1931, the official journal of *Obóz Wielkiej Polski* (*OWP*), *Szczerbiec*, reported: 'The ambition of the younger generation of Poles, who are now beginning to play an active part in social and political life, is to settle the Jewish question.' This policy statement was published at a time when a wave of anti-semitic disturbances, organised by *MW*, was sweeping across university campuses. The intention of the organizers was to influence young people beginning their studies. They aimed at provoking clashes with the police, which would then facilitate anti-government agitation and demonstrate the extent of its power to the youngsters.

Incidents started at the Jagiellonian University, beginning with the affair of the corpses: Jews were not admitted to anatomy lectures or practical experiments. Because of these incidents, lectures were suspended for a week, beginning again on 28 October. At Warsaw University trouble broke out in the faculty of law, which was a bastion of *MW* and where the greatest number of Jews in relative terms were studying. The result of these incidents, as *MW*, admitted, was to leave several dozen Jews severely beaten.[26] On 6 November lectures at the University were suspended, and similar action was taken at other institutions in the capital during the next few days. This step, which rectors frequently employed after such incidents, was inconvenient to the majority of students who had taken no part in the troubles, because it extended their term of study. Another 'inconvenience' was the announcement of fresh registration at the university.

Incidents also took place in other towns, including Wilno. Here, during an anti-Jewish demonstration after Jews had been turned away from the main university building, events culminated in tragedy. A Polish student of the law faculty, Stanisław Wacławski, was struck on the head by a stone during a brawl and died later in hospital. A wave of strikes and rallies organized by *MW* hit academic centres all over the country. Here motions demanding the introduction of a 'numerus clausus' were passed and, probably for the first time, the call for a 'numerus nullus' was heard, a slogan which replaced the other over the coming years.

The Senate of Warsaw University deplored these incidents. A number of individual professors protested against them, as they had done in 1923.[27]

Members of left-wing organizations consistently opposed them, risking threats and persecution. However, only the *Związek Polskiej Młodzieży Demokratycznej* (Union of Polish Democratic Youth) of the *Sanacja* organizations took an unequivocal stance, condemning the excesses and defending those attacked.

Just as in 1923, a resolution of the Nationalist Party of 18 December 1931, to regulate student numbers in academic institutions, came to be seen as an expression of support, which strengthened nationalist youth in its conviction that it was fighting for a just cause. The number of students was to be set annually by the Faculty Councils. 'Care should be taken in admitting students,' warned the movers of the resolution, 'that the number of Christian students in relation to the overall level outlined in Clause 1 should not be lower than the overall number of Christians in the national population as recorded in the last census.'[28] Unlike in 1923, it was rejected and was restricted to the Jewish population.

The resolution was sent to the Commission but never appeared before the *Sejm*. Its reading apparently led to stormy exchanges during sittings of the Educational Committee, but we have no records to indicate the positions adopted by individual Committee members. We know, however, the views of Professor Wacław Komarnicki, who moved the resolution. He justified it first on pedagogic grounds – to remove anything which might disturb academic work. Next he used arguments based on economic grounds. According to Komarnicki, young Jews were better off than their peers. As a direct result of too many of them entering universities, Jews were forcing Poles out of the professions. He insisted the state could not remain indifferent to the composition of the intelligentsia, all the more so as the influx of Jews into the arts and sciences was harmful. The introduction of a 'numerus clausus' was therefore a measure of national defence. To overcome the scruples of members of the Committee he cited the examples of restrictions on Jews introduced in Hungary and Rumania.[29] This statement was the broadest and most comprehensive expression of the motives behind the demands of the nationalists. By this time, however, these were not enough to satisfy *Młodzież Wszechpolska*. In May 1932, at a meeting of this Steering Committee, the previous demands on the Jewish question were extended considerably. Now all Jews were to be deprived of 'political rights with all that entails, and prevented by changes in the existing law from participating in the individual and collective life – both cultural and economic – of the Polish nation'.[30]

A further development of this resolution was the formulation of the 'Basic Principles underlying policy towards the Jewish, German and Slavic minorities' published in November 1932. The statement was published by the student section of the Warsaw *OWP*. Most space in the 'Principles' was devoted to the Jewish question. They assumed a complete separation of the two communities, with no chance of crossing the divide.

Mixed marriages, for example, would have been forbidden. All the restrictions would have appled to Jewish Christians as well. In the area we are discussing, they assumed the introduction of the 'numerus nullus' principle in all schools, starting from elementary level. Jews would have been forced to attend only their own lower and middle schools, which would not have enjoyed state rights. It was clearly a racist programme. Indeed, in the 'Principles' the concept of 'race' was used, although the nationalist press on the whole had avoided it.

From the outset the universities were an enclave of considerable independence. Both lecturers and students were critical of the regime. As a consequence, it might have been expected that the government would have tried to gain some say in the running of the universities, as well as acquiring a greater degree of control over faculty members and students. This would have been consistent with the general line taken by the authorities in the legislative sphere. After their victory at the 1930 elections and the achievement of a decisive majority in the *Sejm*, they began to introduce laws which increased their control over the nation. Consequently this was a period of considerable government activity in framing and carrying through legislation. On 1 March 1932 a bill was passed regarding assemblies and gatherings, on 27 October one regarding associations, and, following this, a bill relating to local autonomy. The high point of this anti-democratic course adopted by the government was the new constitution, which came into effect in 1935.

Government policies over schooling moved in a similar direction. On 12 January 1932 the government submitted the draft bill of a resolution for the reorganization of the school system. In the section dealing with the universities, it was proposed that the Minister for Religious Affairs and Public Education should have the power, after consultation with the faculty councils, to set compulsory, supplementary examinations at some universities and university faculties.[31] This proposal roused the anger of representatives of the national minorities. Milena Rudnicka, a Ukrainian representative in the *Sejm*, recognized that it gave legal sanction to a 'numerus clausus' which had existed in practice for several years over Ukrainian students. Emil Sommerstein, pointing to the decline in the number of Jews at the universities, condemned the proposal strongly, declaring that 'we have here the "numerus clausus", not in its brutal, naked form, as presented in the resolution of the Nationalist Group, but in a covert form, which has to rely entirely on those who are to carry it out.'[32]

A real storm erupted over the resolution relating to the universities. Even before it was submitted, on 21 January 1933 the Minister for Public Education spoke at a sitting of the *Sejm* Budget Committee. He pointed out that the academic authorities had not managed to use the relevant act to nip anti-semitic brawls in the bud, and this showed the need for a change in the law.[33] The draft bill, however, left no doubts as to the true intentions of its authors – the complete subordination of the universities to government control.

In principle the whole academic community opposed the scheme, although for widely differing reasons. The nationalists were concerned with defending the ground they had won; left-wingers considered it meant the destruction of the last vestiges of democracy. Scholars perceived a threat to academic values in the new proposals.[34] The opposition in the *Sejm* waged an unequal struggle against the bill. Representatives of the *Stronnictwo Narodowe* were also concerned at its far-reaching effects. The speeches of Professors Wacław Komarnicki and Bohdan Winiarski were calm and objective – pointing out the harm such measures would cause to academic life at the universities. But a very different voice sounded from the benches of the Nationalist faction. Tadeusz Bielecki declared that the new proposal would help Jews and was an attempt to 'disrupt the struggle of the younger generation against the Judaisation of the Polish community'.[35]

Immediately after the bill was passed the Minister for Public Education began to exploit the opportunities which it afforded him. Amongst other things the activities of student associations were only permitted on the site of specific universities. This resulted in the dissolution of all the nationwide student organizations which were controlled by the nationalist camp. Almost simultaneously the nationalists suffered an even more severe setback. The administration dissolved the *Obóz Wielkiej Polski* throughout the country. In practical terms this meant the end of a unified nationalist youth movement, since a split soon occurred, which led to the creation of the *Obóz Narodowo-Radykalny* (National-Radical Front).[36] All of these factions, however, adopted a uniform policy on the Jewish question.

The new law could not solve the very problem which had been one of the prime arguments for its introduction. Anti-semitic outbursts continued, increasing in force and brutality. On 24 October 1933 lectures were suspended at the University of Warsaw for one month because of clashes between a gang of toughs recruited by *MW* and members of the *Legion Młodych* (Youth Legion). A second reason was the introduction for the first time at Warsaw academic institutions of a 'ghetto bench'.

Anti-semitic activities grew in strength during 1935 after Piłsudski's death, when the National Democrats assumed for a while that they would gain power. 'The *Endecja* understood,' wrote Ludwik Krzywicki, 'that anti-semitic slogans were a useful means of controlling crowds and igniting passions. Indeed, students were to act in the vanguard in striking at the government with anti-Jewish slogans.'[37] The use of anti-semitic propaganda meant that the government could be attacked for its apparent philo-semitism, while the Left could also be attacked as an agent of 'international

Jewry'. This led to a series of street demonstrations throughout the country, symbolised by those at Przytyk, Mińsk Mazowiecki, and Myślenice. In 1936 a number of court cases occurred where members of the *Stronnictwo Narodowe* and the *Obóz Narodowo-Radykalny* were accused of placing bombs outside Jewish shops and similar activities.

Definite moves towards the introduction of a 'ghetto bench' began during the 1935–36 academic year, and gained in momentum during successive years. Disturbances began, as usual, at the beginning of the academic year, and because of this they were called 'autumn manoeuvres'. Often they were linked to events commemorating the anniversary of Wacławski's death.[38] They became wilder and more violent. Memoirs of students from the period are full of descriptions of those beaten and maimed, although the names of the organizers of these brawls are invariably missing. However, the attitudes of the latter are summed up in a leaflet, dated 26 January 1937:

> Progress, Learning, Democracy – they all sound wonderful. But what is hidden under this facade? The repulsive Jewish spirit. And this disgusting use of clubs which makes you recoil, is in fact a glorious struggle to free the nation from its Jewish fetters. Just think: you meet a Jew or a Communist in some dark place. And you set about him! You lay into him, driving the metal into his teeth! Just don't back away, you milksop![39]

Everyone came in for a beating, most of all Jews, but also those people who protested against the club-wielders – among them people who were not attached to any organization, but were motivated simply by common humanity.

Student organizations which protested against and actually opposed the activities of these gangs of thugs were the communist *Życie* (Life), *Związek Niezależnej Młodzieży Socjalistycznej* (Union of Independent Socialist Youth), *Legion Młodych-Fracja* (Youth Legion – Faction), the *Związek Polskiej Młodzieży Demokratycznej* (Union of Young Polish Democrats), and the academic grouping *Wici* (the youth movement of the Peasant Party). A number of these organizations formed the *Komitet Obrony Honoru Akademika* (Committee for the Defence of Students' Honour). They noticed that anti-semitism, besides its nationalist and racist face, was also an instrument which potentially threatened *all* liberal and democratic views.[40]

Individual professors frequently spoke out, dismayed by what was happening in the universities. Those who did so were not only people associated with the democratic camp. One of the most critical articles on the subject was written by Antoni Sobański, in the columns of the conservative periodical *Czas*.[41] Maria Dąbrowska also joined in the chorus of protest, throwing her personal popularity and moral authority on the scales. The voice of this author, sensitive to the human injustice being committed, and at the same time disturbed by the views of a section of the student body, was full of concern.[42] Her words, a reflection of the views and attitudes of the best section of the Polish intelligentsia, raised the spirits of the injured, but they did not affect the perpetrators of the violence, especially as many professors tolerated the thugs, or even supported them.

In February 1936 the Minister for Public Education, Wojciech Świętosławski, declared that he would not allow 'a handful of politically-motivated students to disrupt the normal work of the overwhelming majority'. A year later, in January 1937, he announced that he would not agree to the official introduction of student segregation: 'I regard the issuing of such an order as impossible.' Further statements along these lines were made.[43] They were composed in a tense atmosphere, when a number of the universities were closed because of attempts forcibly to introduce 'ghetto benches'. These attempts were being increasingly successful. Gradually more and more rectors were caving in.[44]

On 23 December 1936, a conference of university rectors approved a proclamation where the rectors attributed the nationalists' excesses to the influence of Hitlerism. They nevertheless acknowledged that the Jewish question was a difficult and serious one. While the proclamation denounced the violence, it was regarded, as Andrzej Pilch writes, as an encouragement to the troublemakers because in one section it admitted that students had the right to seek their own way of removing those ills that affected the life of the nation.[45]

Lack of decisive action encouraged the bully-boys. On 12 January 1937 the Rector of Wilno University, Władysław Jakowicki, having lost control of the situation, offered his resignation. However, support for the trouble-makers came from the former president of the *Sejm*, Julian Szymanowski. He accused the Jews of causing the disturbances by not accepting the Rector's proposal that Poles occupy separate seats. Attempts were made to impose segregated seating, amongst other places in the law faculty. All Jews were turned out of the university buildings and the library.[46] On their way out, ten Jews were set upon and beaten.

Although it was not a decisive factor, much depended on the attitudes of the faculty members. There was one case where a lecturer deliberately came late for class to allow time for Jews to be ejected from the lecture-theatre. Different attitudes can be seen clearly in the case of Wilno. Professor Tadeusz Czeżowski would not permit any disturbances at his lectures. When trouble threatened, Jews who did not want to occupy the seats intended for them and indicated by cards placed there were forced to remain standing during the lecture. Professor Pruffe recommended that the proctors remove the cards which divided the seating. The engineer Krasnopolski replaced his lecture with a talk on 'the systematics of culture'. Professor Panejko, however, requested all the Jews standing in the lecture-hall to leave before he would begin his lecture.[47] Professor Szymanowski's position has already been referred to. Similar events and similar attitudes could be encountered at other universities, among them Lwów, where the 'ghetto bench' had already been in force for a year.

In the circumstances the immediate action undertaken by the Minister proved ineffective. On 30 March 1937 he ordered the disbanding of the *Młodzież Wszechpolska* organization at Warsaw University, as well as the *Narodowy Związek Polskiej Młodzieży Radykalnej* (National Union of Radical Polish Youth) – the student wing of the *ONR*. It did not have a great deal of meaning or effect, since these organizations over a number of years had become used to acting on the edge of the law. This apart, the *Związek Młodej Polski* (Union of Young Poland) began to be active – a youth affiliate of the government *Obóz Zjednoczenia Narodowego* (Camp of National Unity). There was little to distinguish the *ZMP*'s views from *Młodzież Wszechpolska* or *ONR*, since the union was organized by members belonging to a wing of the latter body. This was all linked with the broader process by which the *Sanacja* began to appropriate for itself the slogans of the nationalist camp.

Partly because of this, the measures taken by the Minister could not put a brake on the action already set in motion. What is more, recourse to legal action was rendered impossible. In Lwów, during November and December 1936, eight students appeared in court accused of forcing Jews, by threats and by beatings, to occupy segregated seats. After a hearing at a Preliminary Court had found the defendants not guilty, the County Court confirmed this on appeal. *Wszechpolak* – the journal of *Młodzież Wszechpolska* – triumphantly informed its readers that, 'The ghetto cannot oppose the law.'

In July 1937 the Universities Act was amended. On the basis of this, at a rectors' conference of 24 September, the Minister made a further concession by allowing the rectors to issue public order instructions concerning segregated seating for Polish and Jewish youth in lecture theatres. This concession was received by the young nationalists as a great victory. A measure designed to calm the students had precisely the opposite effect. On 3 November 1937 *Młodzież Wszechpolska* proclaimed a 'day without Jews' at all institutions of higher education in Lwów. In following years a 'day without Jews and Ukrainians' was to appear. This initiative was seized on by other universities. The Executive Branch of *ONR* issued the following internal order: 'In bringing about the "numerus nullus", all *ONR* members are advised, when encountering a Jew at university, to beat him soundly and eject him from the campus. Should there appear to be too many Jews, or proctors who might come to the Jews' defence, then other colleagues should be called in to support you. The above order must be carried out ruthlessly. The "numerus nullus" must be forced through, as the "ghetto bench" was a year ago.'[48]

It was not only Jews who fell victim to the young 'nationalists'. On 18 July 1936, in the centre of Warsaw, distributors of the *ONR* journal *Falanga* repeatedly stabbed the young socialist leader, Stanisław Dubois. Cases of socialist and communist students being beaten up were not rare. In March 1939 members of strong-arm gangs broke into a talk organized by students affiliated to the Peasants' Party. The press reported that four victims of this attack lay in a critical condition in hospital.[49]

Various measures were employed against those faculty members who opposed the extravagant behaviour of the thugs. Explosive charges were laid at the doors of flats belonging to Konrad Górski in Wilno, and Kazimierz Bartel in Lwów. Mieczysław Wolffke was pelted with rotten eggs, and smoke canisters were thrown into the hall where he was to lecture. Cases of attacks on faculty members also occurred in 1933 during the dispute over the proposed Higher Education Bill. On this occasion a new device was introduced: lists of scholars, both Jewish and 'of Jewish descent', began to be published. On one of these was the name of Leopold Caro, vice-chairman of the Polish Primate's Social Affairs Council. This was linked to the demand, also being voiced at the time, for the imposition of a 'numerus nullus' for research staff as well. The so-called 'Aryan paragraph' – prohibiting Jews from belonging to certain organizations – was approved in 1937 by the Union of Non-Professorial Staff in Lwów Institutions of Higher Education. In the following year it was approved by the national Union of Associations of Non-Professorial Staff in State Institutions of Higher Education. Jews previously belonging to these organizations were immediately struck off the membership list.[50] This phenomenon extended far beyond university campuses. Similar resolutions were adopted by other associations and organizations, among other social and professional groupings composed of engineers, architects, doctors and so on. Exclusion from these organizations made continuing in one's profession difficult, if not impossible.

The issue spread to even more areas of public life. An attempt was made to divide city market-places into Polish and Jewish parts. Such a division was put into effect in Kalisz on 13 July 1937. The Association of Property Owners at Inowrocław passed a resolution calling for the eviction of Jews. But the most extreme step was taken by the local branch of the *Stronnictwo Narodowe* at Częstochowa, which proposed that Jews be banned from the town. A similar campaign was launched in Brześć nad Bugiem. The *Stronnictwo Narodowe* officially launched a campaign for residential ghettoes.[51] All this was done in accordance with the call to create a Catholic state of the Polish nation. Kazimierz Kowalski, chairman of the *SN* wrote that 'the one basic obstacle in achieving this goal is the Jews.'[52]

The number of street attacks on individuals, on Jewish shops and market-stalls, increased. When such incidents took place, the police generally arrived too late, or else ignored them. The economic crisis and the boycott action, often linked with the destruction of goods, caused a considerable decline in the part Jews played in trade and business.

The number of Jews at the universities fell rapidly. The Rector of Wilno University, Father Aleksander Wójcicki, wrote in his report for 1937 that, of those admitted to the first year of study, in the humanities eight out of eighty students were Jews, in law thirteen out of 150, in pharmacy four out of forty-five and in agriculture none. No Jews were admitted to Poznań University, to the medical faculty of the Jagiellonian University, nor to a number of other universities and faculties. Whereas, during the academic year 1928–9, 20.4 per cent of the overall student total were Jews, by 1936–7 this figure was 11.7 per cent and in 1937–8 only 7.5 per cent (1,183 out of 15,591 admitted); the figures in Warsaw were 4 per cent, in Lwów 7 per cent, in Kraków 10 per cent, in Wilno 7.3 per cent, and in Poznań none.[53] This reduction in the universities was achieved by means graphically described in *Wszechpolak* of 16 October 1939:

> Then the time arrived to apply for university places. The youth movement blocked the way of Jews so that it was difficult for them to complete all the formalities. There were cases at the medical faculty of UJK [the Jan Kazimierz University in Lwów] where a Jew, who had managed to get to the Dean's office and submit his application, had to be escorted out by ten proctors, and even then he could not leave by the main gate, but had to jump out of a window. Some could not manage to turn up for the entrance examination and even those who had already been admitted, turned up on registration day to find slogans scrawled up, saying 'Day without Jews', and then 'Second Day without Jews', and so on. Those who still wanted to make their way on to the university campus, faced being beaten up with knuckle-dusters and sticks decorated with razors.

This description of events at Lwów, which applied just as well to other towns and cities, preceded a confrontation with the Rector, Stanisław Kulczyński. He refused to allow a 'ghetto bench' to be introduced and, on 7 January 1937, offered his resignation. He defended his decision to resign in an open letter, where he maintained that he would not be a part in sullying the good name of the University. He would not give in to the terrorism of the young 'nationalists', who were trying to force the legal authorities to do the impossible. He asserted further that he was not against free choice over seating, but the introduction of a 'ghetto bench' took the issue of free choice 'on to the stage of emergency measures directed against a single national or religious group'. In this atmosphere academic life could not continue.[54]

Other rectors supported Kulczyński's views,[55] although the Rector of Poznań University did not. Although praiseworthy and honourable, Kulczyński's stand was of little avail. His successor, Rector Longchamps, issued an order on 12 January, the day that lectures were due to begin, that the segregated seating scheme should be imposed. The Pro-Rector Professor Ganszyniec refused to comply and wrote a letter of protest. He said, 'by submitting to the terror practised by *Młodzież Wszechpolska*, you have made the Rector's office both the expression and the executor of the absurd demands of these young people, and have sacrificed the victims of this campaign, without in return guaranteeing that peace or freedom to study, or the health and life of those condemned to the student ghetto, will be assured.' He commented, with regret, that he had failed to find in the Rector's order any words of condemnation of the organizers of the brawls.[56] Immediately afterwards, on the 6 February 1938, an article appeared in *Wszechpolak* claiming that Ganszyniec was in debt to the Jews, that he was an atheist and a socialist, and that his Jewish assistant was his lover. The late Rector, Kulczyński, on the other hand, was alleged to be a mason. In a similar way, twenty-six professors led by Bartel, protested against the introduction of an official ghetto at the Polytechnic, but the proposal was still approved by the senate.[57]

Voices were also raised in favour of the moves. After the above letter from the twenty-six professors had been made public, they were answered by Stanisław Głąbiński. He regarded it as improper to accuse the Rector of the Polytechnic, and other rectors, of acting contrary to the law by introducing segregation. They were only carrying out their duty. This argument was continually repeated. Głąbiński concluded his riposte with the demagogic assertion that in his student days seating had also been allocated.[58]

The Lwów professors were not the only ones to protest. Group petitions were drawn up and individuals spoke out, steps which demanded considerable moral courage in the circumstances. In December 1937 fifty-eight professors – the cream of Polish academic life – protested publicly against the introduction of restrictions based on creed, nationality or race. They came from various backgrounds and different political standpoints. They did so 'with a feeling of joint responsibility that the very thing which we have failed to prevent is now a dominant influence at the majority of universities'.[59] A number of them, in an expression of solidarity with Jewish students, delivered their lectures standing up. Henryk Lukerc wrote, '. . . although it may appear, judging from the words of some professors, that they criticize only the attack on academic freedom, forgetting other evils of totalitarianism outside the walls of the university, this movement is not exclusive, but is linked with the wider political movement of Polish democracy.'[60]

On 19 October 1937, Professor Mieczysław Michałowicz protested publicly in the auditorium of the Paediatrics Clinic of Warsaw University and explained his actions in this way, '. . . I want to follow my conscience, knowing I have remained faithful to Christian principles.'[61] This was not the first protest which appealed to religious principles. Immediately after Michałowicz's statement, however, two priests, Fathers Seweryn Popławski and Marceli Nowakowski, replied in an open letter, supporting the stand taken by the young nationalists.[62]

The propaganda of the nationalist movement followed closely on the heels of these representatives of the clergy. It did not take long for the effects of this activity to become apparent. On 16 January 1938, at an open meeting of the student Marian Sodality, it was agreed that individuals of Jewish origin could not become members.[63] A baptised Jew, Father Puder, was struck by an assailant in church. The Catholic press condemned this crime, but a few days after the incident, on 6 February 1938, Stanisław Mackiewicz wrote in *Słowo* that 'the one logical, clear criterion is, in fact, that adopted by Hitler. A Jew is a person who is of Jewish descent.' Ten days later he asserted that 'anti-semitism without racism is incomplete.' Voices were also raised demanding the enactment in Poland of anti-Jewish legislation along the lines of the Nuremberg Laws.[64]

Attitudes of this kind resulted in increasingly severe physical conflicts, involving ever wider sections of the community and inflicting new casualties. This is hardly surprising when one considers that, as a result of a search of three student hostels in Lwów in March 1939, the police found sixteen revolvers, two fowling-pieces, thirteen hand-grenades, thirty-four canisters filled with caustic gases and fluids, explosive materials, and so on.[65]

We do not know every incident that occurred. As Krzywicki writes, the censorship either did not allow articles on anti-Jewish excesses to appear, or else itself decided the guidelines on what should be written.[66] The searches described above took place following the murder in 1938 of three Jews, students of Lwów Polytechnic. A year later two university students were murdered, and in May that year, seven were severely beaten up, one a first-year student named Markus Landsberg, dying in hospital.[67]

Periodicals hostile to such deeds wrote of the incomprehensible tolerance, of the paralysis in acting against the wielders of clubs and cudgels, and they even wrote that there was silent admiration or support in some quarters. After the Landsberg killing, the Rector suspended lectures, and the senate condemned the crime. The Young Socialists' journal, *Młodzi Idą* commented bitterly on the steps taken by the university authorities: 'Here we go again. Events are following their usual course.' It called for resistance to such acts in deed as well as in word.[68]

The will to act was lacking. The administrative apparatus did not act, and when it did, it took inadequate steps and failed to achieve the desired results. This attitude should come as no surprise given the way the government bloc was evolving. Democratic, workers' and socialist organizations proved too weak to resist this wave of hate and barbarism. A regaining of collective sanity only occurred shortly before the outbreak of war, when the problems of national defence became the priority.

NOTES

1 Emergency motion of *ZLN* representatives concerning the establishment of a *Sejm* Commission on the Jewish Question. *Druki Sejmu Ustawodawczego RP*, no. 119.

2 One of the young socialist leaders wrote, 'Does anyone have any illusions that if it were possible to arouse the passions of the Polish people using some other platform than anti-semitism, that the *Endecja* would be prepared to discard immediately its anti-semitic propaganda . . .?' S. Dubois: 'Ohydna dywersja' in *Wyższe uczelnie pod blokadą reakcji* (Warsaw, 1937), p. 19.

3 Speaking during the discussion on Prime Minister Skulski's admission, 19 December 1919. *Sprawozdania Stenograficzne Sejmu Ustawodawczego*, p. 19.

4 D. Jarosz, *Młodzież Wszechpolska, 1922–1926* (Warsaw, 1983), p. 146.

5 'Memorial w sprawie zachowania polskości lwowskich akademickich uczelni', *Głos Akademicki*, November 1922.

6 'Środowisko lwowskie', *Akademik*, 20 March 1923.

7 'Wiec akademicki młodzieży poznańskiej', ibid., 25 January 1923.

8 'Młodzież akademicka w Krakowie w sprawie numerus clausus', *Goniec Krakowski*, 21 May 1923. Also D. Jarosz, op. cit., pp. 122–3.

9 'W sprawie numerus clausus', *Gazeta Warszawska*, 20 March 1923. Also Jarosz, op. cit., pp. 106–8.

10 'III-ci Ogólny Zjazd Polskiej Młodzieży Akademickiej we Lwowie', *Akademik*, 30 June 1923. See also *Prąd*, June–July 1923, and Jarosz, op. cit., pp. 48–51.

11 Z. Stypułkowski, 'My i Oni', *Wiadomości Akademickie*, 10 December 1924; also Jarosz, op. cit., p. 72.

12 *Druki sejmowe*, Okres I, Druk nr 94; for an account of the struggle to have this resolution accepted, see 'Walka o numerus clausus', *Przegląd Wszechpolski*, November–December 1923, pp. 848–72.

13 The text of the motion is in W. Komarnicki, *Numerus clausus w szkołach akademickich* (Warsaw, 1932), p. 28. The speech was delivered before a sitting of the Education Committee of the *Sejm*, on 3 March 1932.

14 Ibid.

15 The latter declared that 'the universities are being flooded with Jews', the introduction of the numerus clausus will calm the ferment at the universities, and is not incompatible with the moral and constitutional equality of rights. 'Declaration of a minority of professors of the Philosophy Faculty of the Jagiellonian University concerning the "numerus clausus", decided at a sitting of the Faculty Council on 9 March 1923', *APAN Kraków*, *Teki Zielińskiego*, file no. 7837.

16 *Konferencje rektorów szkół akademickich w Polsce w latach 1919–1931* (Warsaw,1932), p. 55.

17 'Zasady współpracy stronnictw polskiej większości parlamentarnej w Sejmie w r. 1923', *Materiały źródłowe do historii polskiego ruchu ludowego*, vol. 3 (Warsaw, 1967), p. 81.

18 K. Czerwiński, *Szkoły wyższe w Polsce. Ustrój, organizacja studiów* (Warsaw, 2nd ed. 1930), p. 26.

19 'Numerus clausus', *Akademik Polski*, 18 October 1927.
20 A. Pilch, *Studencki ruch polityczny w Polsce w latach 1932–1939* (Kraków, 1972), p. 129.
21 'Twelfth Conference, 23–24 April 1927', *Konferencje rektorów* . . ., p. 118–20.
22 'Okólnik', *Akademik Polski*, 20 January 1927.
23 J. Zański, 'U progu nowego roku akademickiego na medycynie', ibid., October 1930.
24 'Uchwały Piątego Zjazdu Ogólnoakademickiego w Poznaniu', ibid., 20 June 1927.
25 The conservative *Dzień Polski* of 15 November 1931 commented on these attempts as follows, '*Gazeta Warszawska* writes in a language which incites its readership not only to spread violence and confusion, but at times even to pogroms. The National Democrats do not pause to consider what effects these Hitlerite policies may have when transferred to Polish territory.'
26 'Zajścia antyżydowskie', *Akademik Polski*, December 1931.
27 R. Ganszyniec, *Sprawa numerus clausus i zasadnicze jej znaczenie. Antysemityzm akademicki jako objaw antysemityzmu społecznego* (Warsaw, 1925), p. 23. Also T. Kotarbiński, 'Po burzy 22 XI 1931', *Racjonalista*, December 1931, pp. 177–84.
28 *Druki Sejmowe*, Okres III, Druk nr 434.
29 W. Komarnicki, op. cit., pp. 31–40.
30 'Zjazd Rady Naczelny M. W. (15–17 V)', *Akademik Polski*, 7 June 1932.
31 *Druki sejmowe*, Okres III, Druk nr 451.
32 Stenographer's report of the 61st session of the *Sejm* on 22 February 1932, pp. 38 and 51.
33 One of the supporters of the bill, Professor Wałek-Czarnecki wrote: 'In Poland the government of Marshal Piłsudski represents a solid tower of strength against which all the efforts of Hitler's imitators will fail. This government will not look on with indifference while the "nationalist" club-wielders and their protectors among the older generation indulge in their antics.' T. Wałek-Czarnecki, *Sprawa szkół akademickich* (Warsaw, 1933), p. 47.
34 These problems have been discussed in an article by S. Rudnicki, 'Ustawa o szkolach akademickich z dn. 15 III 1933', *Więź*, 1985 no. 4–6, pp. 166–80.
35 Stenographer's report from the 91st session of the *Sejm*, on 20 February 1933, p. 111.
36 A book devoted to these issues is that by S. Rudnicki, *Obóz Narodowy-Radykalny. Geneza i działalność* (Warsaw, 1985). See p. 392.
37 L. Krzywicki, 'Burdy studenckie', *Wspomienia*, vol. 3 (Warsaw, 1959), p. 292.
38 'On the anniversary of Wacławski's death, Jewish blood must flow. On that day Jewish homes and businesses, acquired by wrongs done to Poles, and even by their deaths, must burn.' *ONR.AAN*, *Druki ulotne*, vol. 154.
39 B. Chrzanowski, *Wspomnienia. Rozdział o miłości i dobroci*, BN III 6480/2 (typescript). The following is an extract from an *ONR* leaflet quoted by *Czas* on 2 November 1936: 'You will shudder at the idea of so many setting on one person. The sight of blood will disturb you . . .. Don't be put off by the blood – keep hitting, beating everywhere, strike with whatever comes to hand, use whatever suits you best.'
40 The *OMTUR* journal wrote: 'Anti-Jewish demagogy is just a screen for these unruly knights. Behind it are hidden the reactionary, fascist endeavours of Dmowski-ism.' 'Nauka i kastet', *Młodzi Idą*, 15 November 1936. A representative of *Wici* wrote in a similar fashion: 'The *Endeks* are advocating a biological, animal kind of anti-semitism. "Beat the Jew" – just because he is a Jew. They are attempting to use this racial hatred to drown all the aspirations of the peasant masss towards real and necessary changes of attitude.' T. Rek, 'Endecki antysemityzm', *Młoda Myśl Ludowa*, June–July 1936.

41 A. Sobański, 'W odpowiedzi panu Dembińskiemu' *Czas*, 8 November 1936.
42 M. Dąbrowska, 'Doroczny wstyd' *Dziennik Popularny*, 24 November 1936.
43 Speech by the Minister for Religious Affairs and Public Education at a session of the *Sejm*, 21 February 1936, *Oświata i Wychowanie*, ii, 1936, p. 103. 'You must not assume that the behaviour of any of you will be tolerated, where that behaviour is incompatible with the law, and with a sense of honour and dignity.' J. Ujejski (Vice-Minister of Religious Affairs and Public Education), 'O lepsze warunki życia młodzieży akademickiej', Address delivered over the radio, 5 October 1936, ibid., p. 640.
44 'A number of rectors were unhappy about the disturbances and unhappy about the anti-semitic excesses and the creation of ghettoes within the precincts of the universities. But their desire for peace and quiet was even greater. Peace at any price.' L. Krzywicki, op. cit., p. 348.
45 A. Pilch, op. cit., p. 160.
46 'He was working in the university library on one of the upper floors. *ONR* supporters broke into it, dragging him out by his hands and feet and hurling him down onto the marble floor of the lobby.' H. Obiezierska, *Pamiętnik* (in private hands).
47 'Żydzi są sami winni zamknięcia uniwersytetu w Wilnie', Copy of an article by Professor J. Szymanowski, *Wszechpolak*, 21 January 1937. 'Zajście żydowskie na USB', ibid., 11 February 1937. 'Zajście żydowskie na Uniwersytecie Wileńskim', ibid., 18 February 1937. 'Prowokacje zydowskie na uniwersytecie wilenskim', ibid., 25 February 1937.
48 S. Rudnicki, op. cit., p. 306.
49 J. Swirski, 'Protestujemy', *Młoda Mysl Ludowa*, February, 1939.' Hitlerowska napaść', *Epoka*, 15 March 1939.
50 'Paragraf aryjski w Związku Asystentów', *Wszechpolak*, 4 February 1937. S. Ossowski, 'Nowa grupa etniczna w szkołach akademickich', *Epoka*, 25 February 1939.
51 'O ghetto terytorialne', *Wszechpolak*, 17 October 1937. 'Ghetto akademickie', ibid., 10 November 1937. 'Ghetto w Inowrocławiu', ibid., December 1937.
52 From the foreword to J. Giertych, *O wyjściu z kryzysu* (Warsaw, 1938), p. 8.
53 'Odżydzenie USB', *Wszechpolak*, 17 October 1937. 'Z materiałów liczbowych WRiOP', *Oswiata i Wychowanie*, vol. 6 (1938) pp. 556–7. A. Pilch, op. cit., pp. 157–8.
54 S. Kulczyński, 'Nie chciałem złożyć podpisu. List otwarty', *Dokumenty chwili* (Kraków, 1938), pp. 17–19.
55 Letter to Rector Kulczyński, ibid., p. 14.
56 R. Ganszyniec, 'Zarządzenie sprzeczne z etyką i elementarną sprawiedliwością', ibid., p. 15.
57 'Open letter by Lwów professors', *Epoka*, 5 February 1938.
58 'Professor Głąbiński's reply', *Wszechpolak*, 6 February 1938.
59 'Lux in tenebris lucet', *Epoka*, 5 January 1938. The list of signatories is also in S. Rudnicki, op. cit., pp. 373–4.
60 H.L., 'Spisek przeciwko szermierzom światła', *Epoka*, 5 February 1938.
61 'Statement by Professor Michałowicz'. In *Dokumenty chwili* . . ., p. 10.
62 They wrote: 'Because those comments may cause some mental anguish among the young, we the undersigned, experienced teachers of young people, wish to assert that the positive attempts of the faithful in choosing to separate themselves from Jews, does not conflict with the aims, the teaching and the dictates of the Church.' Quoted from *Czas*, 24 October 1937.
63 Concerning the aryan paragraph in the *ASM*, *Wszechpolak*, 30 January 1938. The moderating priest of *ASM* annulled the resolution.

64 S. Rudnicki, op. cit., p. 375.
65 A. Pilch, op. cit., p. 156.
66 L. Krzywicki, op. cit., p. 377.
67 *Kurier Warszawski*, 28 May 1939; *Epoka*, 15 March 1939, 5 June 1939.
68 'Na innych szpaltach', *Młodzi Ida*, VI, 1939.

PART IV

The Second World War

22

JEWS AND POLES UNDER SOVIET OCCUPATION (1939–1941): CONFLICTING INTERESTS

Paweł Korzec and Jean-Charles Szurek

INTRODUCTION

The attitude of a considerable number of Jews to Soviet power between 17 September 1939 and 21 June 1941 in the Polish territories annexed by the USSR has still not been adequately studied and the issue causes mutual resentment. One of the most commonly accepted points of view charges the 'Jews' with betraying the Polish state and 'collaborating' with the enemy, on the basis of the favourable welcome they gave the Soviet troops, for example, or the prominent position they held in the new administration.[1]

What is important, in the framework of the Jewish perception of twentieth-century Polish national history, is to establish whether available sources confirm the 'collaboration' of Polish Jews with the Soviet invader as an actual fact and, if so, how to characterize it, and to understand what place it occupies in Polish history.

Curiously enough the accusation of collaboration is rare in Polish historical works published in the West.[2] It appeared for the first time at the outbreak of war in reports on the situation in occupied Poland drawn up by the delegates of the government in London. These reports are a sort of synthesis in which underground observers mix on-the-spot information with their own political analyses. They note Jewish collaboration with the 'reds' but rarely supply precise facts, probably because of the difficulties in collecting them, presenting them, and conveying information from inside the area of Soviet occupation to the outside world. These observers were by no means independent investigators and they were also expressing the varying sympathies of the Polish government.

One of the earliest reports was written by Jan Karski, key witness in Claude Lanzmann's film *Shoah*. Karski's evidence is interesting on more than one count. First, he was the first courier to go to the Soviet zone at the end of 1939 and, as early as February 1940, to be able personally to inform the Polish government in exile, still at Angers, of the facts of the German and Soviet occupations. Secondly, although his report on the Soviet occupation is relatively vague compared with information which got through later, it expresses, in our view, the real complexity of the situation: a complexity based on the 'dialectic' of the two occupations. Karski was neither a typical witness nor hostile to the Jews, as his unique evidence on the Warsaw ghetto shows. His testimony reveals much of the spirit of the times. Thirdly, the fate which befell this text is also a reflection of the times, since two versions exist which have only been discovered recently. There were two versions because the author, at the request of the Polish government, modified passages which emphasized the growth amongst the population of an anti-semitism encouraged by the Nazi occupation. Government leaders, frightened by the negative image which emerged from it, asked Karski to soften and even reverse the import of this statement. But though it was harsh on the Jews, they did not ask him to change his description of their co-operation with the Bolshevik power.

The following are some of the significant points from the initial version of this report:[3]

The Situation of the Jews in the Territories Annexed by the Third Reich

The situation of the Jews in these territories is clear, uncomplicated, easy to understand.

They are outside of the law . . . Officially they are intended, through the use of force, law, and propaganda, for destruction or removal.

Jews are being thrown out of these territories, their goods are being confiscated, the 'guilty' are being imprisoned – the intent is toward the complete cleansing of this area of the Jewish element.

Jews are deprived there of practically all possibilities of living – if they live, they do so surreptitiously, in fear, with no rights . . .

All wear stars or patches (the same as in the Generalgouvernement), which indicate that they are Jews. Those who shun this obligation are threatened with severe repression . . .

In several cases (also in the Generalgouvernement) the restrictions, ordinances and moral atmosphere surrounding the Jews pertain also to the Polish people. This, of course, occasions a quiet satisfaction among the Jews and all the more rancour, disappointment, and consciousness of humiliation among the Polish people.

Relations in the Generalgouvernement[4]

The tendency is towards a resettlement of all Jews from the annexed territories to the Generalgouvernement. The assumption of the Germans is that these territories, 'essentially German but disgracefully Judaized by the Poles,' should be returned re-Germanized without Jews.

In the Generalgouvernement, the Jews who are resettled from the annexed territories are housed in the preponderant number of cases in Lublin and its environs. This creates the impression that the Germans would like to create there something along the lines of a ***Jewish reservation*** . . .

In the territory of the Generalgouvernement the situation of the Jews is similar (as above), but it is mitigated by all of the consequences stemming from the facts that: 1) there are more Jews here; 2) Jews cannot be sent farther away from there; 3) the German population on these territories is quite small – and the Polish population does not yet at any rate reveal a disposition toward relations with the Jews along the lines of the methods and atmosphere being established by the Germans.

No less, however, do the Jews here have stars or patches, and the same injunctions as in the annexed territories apply to them here . . .[5]

The Jews – the Invaders – the Poles

(a) Under German Annexation (Occupation)

Usually one gets the sense that it would be advisable were there to prevail in the attitude of the Poles toward them the understanding that, in essence, both peoples are being unjustly persecuted by the same enemy. Such an understanding does not exist among the broad mass of the Polish populace.

Their attitude toward the Jews is overwhelmingly severe, often without pity. A large percentage of them are benefiting from the rights that the new situation gives them. They frequently exploit those rights and often abuse them.

This brings them, to a certain extent, nearer to the Germans . . .[6]

(b) Under Bolshevik Annexation (Occupation)

The situation of the Jews in these territories is fundamentally different. After all 'there are no distinctions made here among nationalities or religious groups.' 'Everyone finds conditions for work, and the protection of the law.'

The Jews are at home here, not only because they do not experience humiliation or persecutions, but [also because] they possess, thanks to their quick-wittedness and ability to adapt to every new situation, a certain power of both a political and an economic nature.

They are entering the political cells; in many of them they have taken over the most critical political-administrative positions. They play quite a large rôle in the factory unions, in higher education, and most of all in commerce; but, above and beyond even all this, they are involved in loansharking and profiteering, in illegal trade, contraband, foreign currency exchange, liquor, immoral interests, pimping, and procurement.

In these territories, in the vast majority of cases, their situation is better both economically and politically than it was before the war.

This applies first of all to the classes of petty merchants, artisans, proletarians, and the half-educated. The wealthiest and more educated circles [owners of homes, larger plants, factories, stores, as well as lawyers, doctors, engineers, etc.] are subject in principle to the same restrictions and pressures, and also to liquidation as a social group, as are other nationalities within the Soviet system.[7]

The attitude of the Jews towards the Bolsheviks is regarded among the Polish populace as quite positive. It is generally believed that the Jews betrayed Poland and the Poles, that they are basically communists, that they crossed over to the Bolsheviks with flags unfurled.

In fact, in most cities the Jews greeted the Bolsheviks with baskets of red roses, with submissive declarations and speeches, etc., etc.

However, one needs to insert here certain reservations.

Certainly it is true that Jewish communists regardless of the social class from which they came adopted an enthusiastic stance towards the Bolsheviks. The Jewish proletariat, small merchants, artisans, and all those whose position has at present been improved *structurally*, and who had formerly been exposed primarily to oppression, indignities, excesses, etc., from the Polish element – all of these responded positively, if not enthusiastically, to the new régime.

Their attitude seems to me quite understandable.

However, there are worse cases, where they [the Jews] denounce the Poles, Polish nationalist students, and Polish political figures, when they direct the work of the Bolshevik police force from behind their desks or are members of the police force, when they falsely defame the relations [between Poles and Jews] in former Poland. Unfortunately it is necessary to state that such incidents are quite common, more common than incidents which reveal loyalty towards Poles or sentiment toward Poland.

In contrast, I have the impression that the intelligentsia, the wealthiest Jews and those of the highest level of culture [with, of course, certain exceptions, and not counting the pretenders], rather think of Poland often with a certain fondness and would happily greet a change in the present situation [leading to] the independence of Poland . . .

I am familiar, for example, with an authentic incident in which a Jew, the well-known attorney from Lwów, Mr. 48, warns Poles about the danger from the GPU, about threats of legal action against them, and about communist lawyers . . .[8]

The Jewish Problem as an Element of Internal German Policy in the Polish Territories

The attitude of the Jews toward the Poles and vice versa under German occupation is an extremely important and extremely complicated problem, much more important and much more consequential than their attitude under the Bolshevik conquest . . .[9]

'The solution of the Jewish Question' by the Germans – I must state this

with a full sense of responsibility for what I am saying – is a serious and quite dangerous tool in the hands of the Germans, leading toward the 'moral pacification' of broad sections of Polish society.
It would certainly be erroneous to suppose that this issue alone will be effective in gaining for them the acceptance of the populace.
However, although the nation loathes them mortally, this question is creating something akin to a narrow bridge upon which the Germans and a large portion of Polish society are finding agreement.'[10]

Hundreds of other reports followed Karski's and interpreted the Jews' role under the Soviet occupation in accordance with the information conveyed and the sympathies of their authors.

Jan Karski's text is, in our view, interesting in that, from the start, he emphasizes the specific features of each occupation. Thus he shows that, from the beginning, with the Polish army barely defeated, the German occupation was already imposing unparalleled war and living conditions on the Jews. The process of extermination was not yet in train, but segregation, the concentration of the mass of Jews – Karski visited the camp at Bełżec in December 1939 and said 'that he never saw anything so horrible'[11] – and arbitrary rule, had brutally erupted. This arbitrariness was calculated, and was specifically intended to draw the Polish population into the destruction of moral norms. The special *anomie* which set the Jewish population apart and which appealed to the Poles, constituted for Karski the most serious moral danger. During the first weeks of the war, a wave of 300,000 to 400,000 refugees flowed eastwards, fleeing the German threat,[12] and gave the Soviet troops a euphoric welcome because their presence meant that their lives were saved. Almost all these refugees were Jews.[13] In addition, the evidence indicates that they were mainly young and from politically conscious families.[14] Thus 15 to 20 per cent of all Jews from the German-occupied zone left. It is clear that the German danger and the Soviet presence did not weigh on Jews and Poles to the same degree.

Equally clearly the two populations could not view the Soviet occupation in the same light. Moreover, in order to live, this mass of refugees had to seek work, and found it notably in administration, that same administration which until a few months before had been closed to them by the Polish state. The effect of 'collaboration' would thenceforth be visible, physical, and would naturally feed witnesses' reports and memoirs. There was also active ideological collaboration – we will return to this. Here, we want to emphasize two aspects of this complex situation which Karski reveals: first, despite the inter-ethnic clashes, there was not *one* Jewish community with homogeneous attitudes, but social and political groups with interests which diverged and converged at different times. Under the German occupation, the Jewish community formed an objective entity, while on the other side of the Bug (the river which separated the two zones) national differences were subordinated to Sovietization and therefore *in principle* there was equality before the law. When discrimination reached the Poles, it was not in the name of hostile ethnicity *per se* but in the name of a social and political programme. Secondly, it follows from this that, because of the different nature of the two occupations, certain words have differing meanings. Thus ideas of collaboration, or betrayal – even if they are expressed in this vocabulary – have different connotations. Karski, patriot that he was, clearly stated right from the start that there was no possible parallel between the two zones, between the Jews' 'betrayal' and the demoralization to which the Germans subjected the Poles.

Better to understand what was involved here, we must now approach the specific character of eastern Poland (the *kresy* or borderlands) and the nature of the Soviet occupation.

THE SPECIFIC CHARACTER OF EASTERN POLAND

On the morrow of World War I, the frontiers of the Second Polish Republic, especially its eastern frontiers, were discussed at length. What territorial shape should Poland take after 123 years of eclipse as a state? Should it return to its boundaries of 1772, which included a considerable number of nationalities, or to a more limited but ethnically more homogeneous territory? France, in favour of a Poland strong enough to resist the Bolsheviks, supported the first option, Britain the second. The principal Polish political leaders (Dmowski, Piłsudski), certainly followed by the majority of public opinion, fiercely defended the idea of a state extended eastwards, even if they had different policies on ethnic minorities.[15] Military conflicts, which finally settled the matter, were favourable to Poland (the Polish-Soviet war of 1920, and the struggles with the Ukrainians and Lithuanians). Poland thus found itself ruling over a large area where national minorities represented about 35 per cent of the population and where Poles were not in the majority in more than half of it.

This situation was most marked in eastern Poland, that is to say in the territories situated east of the Curzon line – which the USSR invaded on 17 September 1939. Polish identity, traditionally preserved by a minor nobility and a not very large peasantry, had weakened in the nineteenth century, whereas nationalism had increased amongst the Ukrainians, Lithuanians and Byelorussians.[16] Frequently surrounded by hostile ethnic groups, the Poles were only in the majority – and at times only slightly so – in a few regions: Białystok, Wilno, Nowogródek, Lwów. If Poland had consisted solely of the eastern territories, it would only have been represented by a third of its nationals.[17] And it is clear that the majority of Byelorussians, Ukrainians, Lithuanians and Germans found themselves, involuntarily, in a state they rejected.

Relations between the Second Republic and the Jews were equally difficult, and characterized by mutual mistrust. Here too a certain sociological and political heterogeneity must be noted within the Jewish minority. There was a world of difference between assimilated Jews, such as those who had fought for Polish independence in Piłsudski's legions, and the 'Litvaks' from the Wilno or Polesie regions, who spoke Russian or Yiddish better than Polish. Generally, if the Jews on the eastern borders of the Polish state spoke Yiddish amongst themselves, they used their respective languages with the ethnic majorities. The language of the Jewish intelligentsia was Russian in Lithuania, and Polish and German in eastern Galicia. This linguistic imbroglio best symbolizes the tangle of national, religious and social identities which the new state inherited. In towns such as Białystok or Wilno, the Jews bordered on 50 per cent of the population.[18] At the political level, a common characteristic of all the main units was opposition to the nation-state which Dmowski stood for. Whether they were Zionists, Bundists, socialists or communists – all, in their own way, saw a solution to Jewish identity elsewhere than in the increasingly hostile framework of the Second Republic. From this point of view the Jews were scarcely distinguishable from the other national minorities. But they never displayed irredentist and independent tendencies – unlike the other minorities, especially the Ukrainians, who did not hesitate, despite everything, to ally themselves with Germany. On the contrary, by and large they advocated a policy of status quo, peace, integrity and the security of the Polish state. The Jewish demand, as politically and publicly expressed, complied with a legal requirement, namely that the Jewish *national* minority be integrated into the Polish state. The 'national' claim therefore necessarily covered a variety of forms.

The problem of nationalities undermined this state from its birth. The power holding élites as well as most of the social body adhered to the nationalistic ideology of the National Democrats which looked forward to the Polonization of the Ukrainians and Byelorussians and the emigration of the Jews. This policy was applied in regions where Ukrainians predominated; for example, the government introduced Polish as the main language in the administration and education, arousing a wave of manifest discontent amongst the Ukrainians.[19] This discontent lasted throughout the inter-war period.

The policy was also applied to the Jews. As early as 1935, 'Jewish questions' were handled by an emigration department of the Ministry for Foreign Affairs. According to this department, there was 'an essential contradiction between the interests of Poland and the Jewish interest', and 'a state of war existed, without war being formally declared', between the two populations. 'The Jews waged the war both defensively and offensively.'[20] The Polish government of the day put forward a policy of emigration, even making contact with Zionist organizations, notably that led by Jabotinsky, envisaging the transfer of the Jewish population to Palestine, Uganda or Madagascar. The expulsion of the Jews was also sought through economic methods: the government supported the boycott of Jewish enterprises, especially businesses, carried out by militant nationalists in 1938–9. This was, indeed, one of their main goals. 'The economic struggle, certainly,' exclaimed Prime Minister Sławoj-Składkowski in open parliament, in a phrase which has remained famous. General Skwarczyński, the principal leader of the government group, for his part, stated that 'the assimilation of the Jews cannot be the aim of a policy on nationalities,' pointing his finger beyond the frontiers of Poland.[21] A draft law at that time even foresaw stripping all Jews of their citizenship, another only the Jews in the east, and it is a well-known fact that numerous Polish leaders followed the measures adopted in Germany attentively.[22] The place the 'Jewish question' occupied on the eve of war is best symbolized by the Camp Zbąszyn affair, which took its name from the Polish-German frontier post where thousands of Polish Jews crowded for several months during the winter of 1938–9. They had been expelled by Germany, and the Polish government refused to allow them to set foot on the national soil. It is therefore no exaggeration to say that a sort of obsession surrounded the 'Jewish problem', and this was shared by an increasing number of organizations, and fed by the economic difficulties of the country and an outbreak of violence.

The difficulty of resolving social and national conflicts *at the same time* was particularly clear-cut where they were intermingled: east of the Bug. The weakness of the Polish presence in the eastern territories even led the State authorities to develop a colonization programme in the twenties and a programme to re-polonize the minor nobility in the thirties. The colonization programme exacerbated social and national tensions in a quite exceptional manner. We will pause for a moment to study this question because it makes it easier to understand Soviet policy in 1939.

Colonization was at first military; then, from 1923, civil. In the east, colonists could obtain free land formerly belonging to Russian landowners. Often it was also the land of former Polish nobles which had been confiscated (because of participation in uprisings) and entrusted to Russian dignitaries. The colonists could enjoy preferential loans, and free buildings and means of production. The local populations – Byelorussian peasants, for example (predominant in the north-east of the country) – were opposed to this, all the more so as the agrarian structure there was polarized. Vast landed properties in the hands of the Polish landowners, who were often nobles, side by side with a mass of small Byelorussian farmsteads, made for a deep-seated hunger for land. The colonization had a strategic character: the colonists had weapons and constituted military associations, a sort of reserve army which also watched over the frontiers for smugglers. They were the object of particular hatred, noted an observer from the government camp.[23] The land taken over for colonization exceeded the land assigned for agrarian reform in the Polesie and Nowogródek regions, and, according to one of the best-known Polish historians, 'most of the colonists left the land derelict'.[24] Part of this land was sometimes even sold to merchants, or rented out.

Some Polish historians today do not hesitate to describe the policy pursued towards eastern Poland as colonial.[25] Colonization was not only ethno-military, it also took the form of the export of raw materials (particularly wood), the absence of investment and consumption which represented only a quarter of the national total, whereas population was almost equally divided between Poland A (west) and Poland B (east), according to a Polish administrative formula of the day.

> In every administrative region, every town hall, commune, not to mention the police, even the post office, even in the streets of towns and villages of the eastern region, the atmosphere, the social order, was different from that in the rest of the country. Likewise the laws, which apparently had nothing to do with the nationalities policy, became instruments to oppress the local population.[26]

Repression struck equally at the Orthodox population forced by the authorities to embrace Catholicism,[27] and at Catholic Byelorussians who had not wished to abandon their nationality.[28] As for the programme to re-polonize the *'szlachta zagrodowa'*, (peasant-nobles) a product of the minor nobility of the pauperized and largely peasant-dominated borders, it aimed in a very concrete fashion to recall Poland's historic roots in these territories. The authorities organized ceremonies for this minor nobility, manifestations of national cohesion. Genealogies were researched. They sought to convince the peasants that they were former nobles and to make them join associations. The peasants frequently declined this offer so as not to become estranged from their Byelorussian or Ukrainian neighbours. These peasants also enjoyed different privileges, especially in the area of education. It was primarily the military authorities who encouraged this quest for identity in the borders, but this *szlachta zagrodowa* movement – a final attempt to give substance to a historic right denied in practice – remained of slight extent.[29]

In short, it would seem that the borders and the territories to which, sometimes ephemerally, they gave access elude established 'attempts at classification',[30] to use the formula of Czesław Miłosz, who was born there. Criss-crossed by ethnic groups and nationalisms, the borders symbolized a frame of reference, a foundation myth for the Ukrainians and the Poles, the Byelorussians and the Lithuanians. Similarly, the Jews who were driven by poverty or anti-semitic oppression to leave them for America, Palestine or Western Europe, retained an equally idyllic image of the 'old country'. A town like Wilno, so important for Polish culture or history, was also a cultural capital for the Jewish world. This was something the Polish élite knew nothing about. Miłosz described, long after the war, with candour as nostalgic as it was profound, in a work which is more evocative than any scholarly treatise of that 'Commonwealth' that the *Kresy* were:

> The Jewish religious literature, born in this part of Europe and translated into many languages, has become famous throughout the world: you merely have to open an anthology of religious thought to alight on Hasidic parables and learn to revere those sages who were natives of the lost villages, the Baal Shem Tov, Rabbi Nachman of Braclaw, Rabbi Itsik of Lublin, Rabbi Pinkas of Korzec, men who on all evidence reached the heights of evangelical love. Here too were born secular Yiddish prose and poetry, full of both tragedy and incomparable humour. On the spot in Wilno where these books were printed for the international market, we knew absolutely nothing about it. I was able to learn about a few elements of it much later, when I bought books in New York: in other words one had to learn English to reach what one had on one's doorstep.[31]

Partial heir to the breakup of empires, Poland also inherited ethnic conflicts for which the Polish nation-state, represented by the Second Republic, was certainly not prepared. The question of its 'betrayal', especially in the east, when the Polish presence there was in the minority, and enforced, cannot convey the entanglement of conflicting interests. Which is far from meaning that Poland had no legitimate rights there. On the contrary, the *Kresy*, a geographical, historical and literary area, constituted one of the symbolic landmarks in Polish culture, a legendary territory from where the greatest Polish writers came. But these were precisely those writers for whom the spirit of liberty opposed the ethnic cult: writers such as Mickiewicz or Miłosz. Again it is Miłosz who best expresses the spirit of an area which, because of its multicultural composition, abolished frontiers – until the policy of the Second Republic forced all the protagonists to erect new ones:

> I myself must confess that it is precisely the strangeness of the region from which I come and the impossibility of communicating anything of its past to strangers which has been my obsession since the beginning of my life as an émigré. Because when I am asked about my country of origin, I cannot reply 'Poland', even if that is what is expected of someone who writes in the Polish language. I have to add

> that my years at school and university were spent in a town which changed hands thirteen times in the course of this century, thirteen, I have counted them. Having said that, I have worked assiduously and with a persistence which is a proverbial Lithuanian virtue to bring my native region to life in all my writings.[32]

If the rise of Polish nationalism had the effect of broadening the irredentism of national minorities other than the Jews, it also provoked 'centrifugal' tendencies amongst the Jews. The Zionist organizations accelerated plans for departure; the *Bund*, in its struggle against the authorities' anti-Jewish intrigues, found it increasingly difficult to propose 'cultural autonomy' and drew closer to the communists. As for the Jewish communists, they campaigned actively within the Communist Party (KPP), in which they formed an energetic and conspicuous minority, particularly in the eastern territories,[33]. The relationship between the Jews and communism cannot be summarized here in a few words, any more than the orientations of all the Jewish parties, especially the predominant religious parties. It is certain, none the less, that communist messianism attracted the Jews, particularly the Jewish youth, all the more so because the Polish nation state denied them assimilation and a place as citizens. The communist ideal suited the Jews even more because it reduced the 'national question' to a perspective in which all ethnic programmes could be absorbed. Even if communism was supported only by a minority of Jews in Poland, it none the less played a notable part in the left/right cleavage. Communism radically opposed the fascism which was in its turn based on the Catholic national tradition. It authorized the Jews to abandon their traditional social links (religion, family, community) and embrace the ideals of Progress, Reason and Modernity inherited from the Enlightenment. Was there no place, one might ask, to maintain these ideals within the nation-state? Perhaps, but in inter-war Poland, where the Jewish minority saw its areas of identification reduced, the Jews' national hope, when it existed, could most easily adopt either Zionism or, by 'disguised inversion', communism. The latter, by its abstract internationalism and its social teleology, also constituted a method – or rather, a hope – for assimilation into the nation-state. From this point of view, the Soviet Union, perceived as stripped of national impediments, and as the 'homeland of the workers', also constituted a homeland for the Jews. It was not a nation-state like the others, nor an empire like those before 1914. The Jews who wanted to stay in Poland, and claimed the status of a national minority, did not have territorial claims. They did not identify territories with 'homelands', above all in eastern Poland where all the minorities fought for power and where the Jews themselves, particularly those who spoke the Russian language, saw their destiny closer to revolutionary Russia than to the Poland 'of the colonels'.

REFLECTIONS ON THE NATURE OF THE SOVIET OCCUPATION

The Sources

Although no overall work exists on Polish-Jewish relations under the Soviet occupation, there are a considerable number of archives, memoirs and testimonies dispersed in different collections (the Hoover Institution at Stanford, the Sikorski Institute at London, the Institute of Jewish History in Warsaw, the Yad Vashem archives, etc.), as well as numerous literary sources, which make it possible to approach this question. Much of what follows will be based on the testimonies published by the sociologist Jan T. Gross. They come primarily from Polish sources and illuminate some essential aspects of this period.[34] However, what is lacking, as far as we know, are syntheses built on Soviet, Byelorussian, Ukrainian, Lithuanian and Jewish sources. It goes without saying that we cannot here – it would need a book – do more than sketch out the arguments necessary to our thesis.

The Sovietization of the Western Ukraine and Western White Byelorussia

The Soviet seizure of eastern Poland was carried out under this heading. In fact, since the twenties the Soviet Union maintained that Byelorussia and the Ukraine should be reunified.[35] In attacking the 'Polish landlords', Soviet propaganda justified the Red Army's invasion by a double liberation, social and national.

The testimonies of the first days of the occupation emphasize the form that the Soviets intended it to take and that it took – or did not take. A short analysis of these first days also makes it possible to highlight the interests at stake.

Right from the start, the Soviets tried to raise the Ukrainians, the Byelorussians and the Jews against the representatives of the Polish state, even trying to convince the Polish soldiers to turn their arms against their officers.[36] It is certain that all the nationalities, except the Poles of course, welcomed the Soviets' arrival, often with open demonstrations of joy. It was primarily the end of Polish rule that was fêted, noted Jan T. Gross, rather than adherence to the new régime.[37] Of course, the Ukrainians hoped to see the question of their national independence resolved, the Byelorussians – particularly the peasants – their social and national struggle, while the Jewish proletariat hoped for equal rights.

Accumulated hatred provoked the settling of local accounts, and blood flowed 'without Bolshevik participation'.[38] During those first days,

> the principal victims were the Poles: the military colonists, the minor nobility of the borders, the landowners, the police, the forest guards, as well as small groups of soldiers and officers from units of the Polish

army broken up by the German offensive. In the course of a few days in September, the Ukrainians, the White Russians and the 'locals' had made those who had been the instruments of the Polonization of the provinces of the south-east for the past twenty years pay for it. What aggravated the confrontation was that the Soviet occupation excluded certain categories of the population from rights, people in the service of the Polish state as well as 'class enemies' – that is to say landowners and rich peasants – and that it simultaneously subjected them to 'official' terror. Nevertheless, there too the local population (rapidly regrouped into sections of the militia, including not only the Ruthenian national minorities but also numerous Jews) committed acts of direct violence.[39]

Sovietization did not aim at the destruction of the Polish nation but at the subjection of purported interests in the local populations – social and national – to the Kremlin's aims. That is why the Soviet authorities essentially attacked the representatives of the state and the 'propertied classes': police, army, colonists, forest guards, landowners, rich peasants. In short, they attacked all the bureaucratic-economic caste abhorred by the Byelorussian and Ukrainian peasantry, who thus saw their social and national hopes become a reality. The Polish witnesses often believed that they were the object of repression on account of their national origin, whereas it was actually their social role which was the target. The terror of the first days, particularly that practised by the peasants, was tolerated by the Soviets as 'rightful anger of the masses'. Then the political organs (including the NKVD and the army) organized the occupation.

In the militias and revolutionary committees which were spontaneously created or initiated by the Soviet authorities, the Jews certainly played a role, which was important although not exclusive, since they also contained the newly 'dominant' nationalities as well as common-law prisoners freed by the Soviets in the name of the class-struggle. But there too, the Jews did not form a homogeneous entity: it was primarily the Jewish youth and the poverty-stricken masses who were a real mainstay of the new power.[40] This qualified aspect of the Soviet occupation is confirmed by Jewish evidence: 'The Russians relied primarily on the Jewish element when allocating positions, naturally distinguishing between the bourgeoisie and the proletariat.'[41]

The 'class struggle' remained the basic motive of pro-Soviet Jews, and they applied it with revolutionary intransigence in respect of the whole bourgeoisie, including the Jewish bourgeoisie, as noted by Max Wolfshaut-Dinkes:

> . . . I must confess that I found the conduct of the Jewish communists during the Soviet occupation terribly repugnant: they had a far too

> brutal attitude towards their employers. The Polish and Ukrainian employees did not denounce their employers as exploiters so that their undertaking would be nationalized and they themselves sent to Siberia; unfortunately, the Jewish communists had no hesitation in doing this.[42]

The social/national conflict thus recurs: the Jewish communists, supported by a radicalized youth, reckoned that an essential revolution, with themselves as the heroes, was coming about thanks to their support. The Ukrainians and Byelorussians, during the first weeks at least, believed that the Soviet presence would settle the question of their national independence. Note that, according to the testimonies in Gross's book, the bloodshed which the Polish populations complained of during the beginning of the occupation came much more from inter-ethnic conflicts than from the 'class struggle'. Revolutionary intransigence proved less sanguinary than the quest for national frontiers. This detail is frequently forgotten when 'Jewish collaboration' is discussed, as if the 'betrayal' of the Byelorussians and Ukrainians must naturally be self-evident and naturally cause blood to flow.

The social programme which Sovietization embodied brought the Jews equal rights with *others*. That is what the Jewish testimonies indicate, as reported by Gross: 'The changes which began to occur in the village after the Russians' arrival were a total surprise . . . To the Jews, they could only consider it a dream, as if the Messiah had come. The Russians raised their status, they gave them something – a status that they had never had in their lives'.[43] Gross mentions the case of a rich millowner who, although he did not like the Bolsheviks 'because they valued a thief or a murderer more highly than us and he had more chance of living than us', nevertheless added, 'There was no racial or national persecution and, for the first time, the Jew was not a second-class citizen'.[44]

If Sovietization meant the destruction of Jewish community structures (liquidation of political parties, prohibition of the teaching of Hebrew, closure of religious schools), it did, on the other hand, permit Jews to occupy the symbolic places of employment which were inaccessible to them previously: administration, university, a variety of jobs.

The 'Judaeo-Bolshevik' alliance and the equality of nationalities, apparently in effect, were actually subject to the logic of Sovietization. In the politico-administrative hierarchy which was set up, it was the *vostochniks*, that is to say, the people from the east (officials, factory managers, trusted Soviet agents intended to make the occupation secure) who occupied the key positions. They included Russians and Ukrainians, Byelorussians and Jews from the east. Then came the local Ukrainians and Byelorussians whose 'homelands' were to be joined to the Soviet Union by a semblance of elections. Then the Jews, whom the Soviets called on for help and who, for the reasons indicated, would not fail them. The Jewish presence was all the more conspicuous because the Byelorussian and Ukrainian populations, uneducated and consisting to a vast extent of peasants, could not occupy the administrative machinery which was created under the Soviet umbrella.[45] Henceforth, every Pole who lost his job applied to an official, a teacher, an examining magistrate – many of whom were Jews. And yet there too the attitude of the 'Jews' cannot be reduced solely to acceptance of Sovietization.

JEWISH ATTITUDES UNDER THE SOVIET OCCUPATION

For many, the arrival of the Red Army meant relief in comparison to the advance of the Germans, whose crimes against the Jews were already known: at Przemyśl, for example, the Germans shot 640 communal notables as soon as they entered the town.[46] 'With the Soviet entry into the town,' Max Wolfshaut-Dinkes recounts, 'the people calmed down a little. They were no longer afraid of massacres'.[47]

During the first fifteen days of September, between the German advance and the disbanding of the Polish army – and before the Russian army intervened – the Jews were most afraid of pillage and seizures. 'With the arrival of the Germans [Lwów region], pillage and persecution of the Jews began, not only at the hands of the Germans; the Ukrainian-Polish underworld also utilized this period against the Jews'.[48]

It was therefore *spontaneously*, in the absence of any authorities, that urban militias formed, composed of numerous Jews and with a primarily *civil* role. In the town of Dubno, for example:

> Because of the progress of the German army, the local Polish authorities decided to leave the town . . . The police also left the town and a militia . . . was created in its place. Note . . . that numerous young Jews were to be found in this militia, they were armed and guarded the bridges and military stores, abandoned by the Polish army. The town was disturbed and the Jews were afraid of the Polish and Ukrainian anti-semites.[49]

The joy with which the Jews, including the bourgeoisie – who were to lose their fortunes and often their liberty from contact with the Bolshevik 'revolution' – welcomed the Russian troops was born of the guarantee of *order* they assured. This joy already expressed the anguish of a minority race who, in the years of the war, would suffer the German hordes, the Ukrainian peasants, the Polish 'indifference'. Note that Poles and even Ukrainians were fleeing westwards,[50] though to a much smaller degree than the Jewish exodus eastwards. It is in the light of this 'exchange of ethnic groups', to use Max Wolfshaut-Dinkes's phrase, that the upheaval in the borders under the double Soviet-German impact can be understood: the choices open to the Jews and the collaboration by some of them.

Consequently, the Jews' pro-Soviet attitude cannot solely be explained, even superficially, by their adherence to communism. Moreover, this attitude was qualified: the assimilated bourgeoisie of Lwów, for example, although it was protected by the Soviet presence, was offended by this 'fourth partition of Poland'. It is also well known that a section of the Jewish communists were troubled by the pact and by the transport of Soviet merchandise to Germany. And the numerous refugees from western Poland expressed particularly ambivalent attitudes towards the USSR.

As time went on, this mass of refugees posed problems for the Soviet authorities, not only because it was difficult to house them and to find them work, but particularly because their critical and sometimes slightly mistrustful attitude to the new power made Sovietization more difficult. The authority decided to deport them to the interior of the USSR, as it had already done with 'enemy' categories (there were four large deportations: in February 1940, peasants and colonists were deported; in April 1940, their families; in June 1940, the refugees from central Poland, therefore primarily Jews; in June 1941, a mixture of these categories – in all, over a million people).

The deportation of June 1940 is of especial interest here. In fact, there is a certain degree of coherence about Soviet policy even if all the testimonies concur in indicating that arrest and deportation could fall indiscriminately on anyone. The aim of the first deportation was in principle the eradication of all the categories which symbolized the Polish state (colonists, police forces, minor nobility, reputedly rich peasants, forest guards). How could the deportation of a mass of reputedly friendly Polish Jews logically be included here?

Once the attachment of western Byelorussia and the western Ukraine to the Soviet Union had been proclaimed, the authorities instituted a compulsory census of refugees. The questions asked were simple: (1) Do you wish to adopt Soviet citizenship? (2) Do you wish to return to your country of origin [therefore, as it might happen, to Germany]? There was considerable disarray amongst the refugees who did not know the rules of the Soviet game in weighing up what was at stake. They were given no explanation and communal institutions had been closed since the beginning of the occupation. The census was conducted by 'committees of aid for the refugees', in actuality auxiliary organs of the NKVD. A majority registered for return: fear of Soviet citizenship and of simultaneously losing Polish citizenship partly accounted for this decision.[51] Some people considered this measure unrealistic and did not imagine that the Soviets could surrender them into German hands, particularly not such a massive number of individuals. Others thought that they could escape the problem under the German occupation.

The aim of the census was revealed when people who had declared themselves Polish were arrested and deported in June 1940. Note that – a cruel and paradoxical irony of history-deportation saved the lives of several hundred thousand Jews, while the minority who became Russian and who remained in this territory were exterminated during the German occupation.

Another aspect of Sovietization and 'collaboration' was the search for jobs. The destruction of trade, crafts and the liberal professions – predominantly Jewish sectors – meant that the Jews had to look for a place in the new structure:

> People tried to find work in the administration because their origin was unfortunate ... Some of the craftsmen joined the *artels*, others thought that the time was ripe for possible social advancement ... some even went into the militia ... Most of the people reckoned that collaboration with the Soviets was an obligation, but deep down inside they opposed it ... Everyone thought that the Jews served the Soviet power with enthusiasm and joy because it was in their interest for the Bolsheviks to remain. The Jews were afraid of explosions from other minorities, victimized by the Soviets.[52]

This account, written by an inhabitant of Volhynia and not by a refugee, shows the reasoning which governed the conduct of numerous Jews: more than 'collaboration', it was participation, even passive participation, which the régime wanted of them. They had no other solution, either because of economic uprooting or as a result of inter-racial conflicts. This was the same reasoning which led all citizens, including the Poles – except those at the bottom of the social scale – to participate in the semblance of elections intended to legitimize the annexation. There was never any question, as Jan T. Gross says, of convincing the local populations, but of making them accomplices,[53] through successive losses of personal autonomy. Fear, brainwashing, the search for well-being in a wretched environment remained determinant elements of Sovietization for all.[54]

The word 'Jews' therefore covers a varied spectrum. What was the common factor between the Jewish communists who participated actively in Sovietization and those who, although communist, rejected it; between the refugees who, although grateful to the Red Army for having saved them, refused Soviet citizenship, and those who, pauperized, accepted administrative jobs willy-nilly; between those who accepted the Soviet order with relief so as not to be engulfed in the ethnic-social conflicts, and those who saw an unprecedented equality of rights being achieved?

Is it really possible to talk of 'collaboration' in all these cases, and particularly in the case of Jews, who were not assimilated and not identified with the Polish state and who welcomed the change of régime? The word has too many echoes of the 'other' collaboration and does not seem to convey a complex reality, a reality which was in no way comparable with the German occupation, even for the Poles.

The Soviet occupation of 1939–41 embraced a heterogenous Jewish population, in the grip of a historic involvement with other peoples, where the resentments of the inter-war period, the exodus, adherence to Bolshevism and many other factors interacted. Finally, it is not irrelevant to recall that the 'Jewish' price in deportations to the Soviet camps was not negligible: 30 per cent of the deportees were Jews, 52 per cent Poles, 18 per cent Ukrainians and White Russians.

CONCLUSION

There are at least two ways of talking about betrayal. One is positivist: it is steeped in the aims of nation states, of their dominant forces, and to some extent espouses them, defending their frontiers with greater or lesser conviction, and acknowledging that different or conflicting national schemes can lead to betrayal. Thus the positivist approach can express any national scheme: for example, the Ukrainians would set out the reasons for their betrayal and their rapprochement with Poland's enemies; the Jews would suggest that it was the Polish state which betrayed them and not vice versa.

The positivist categories do not, in our opinion, take Polish-Jewish relations under the 1939–41 Soviet occupation sufficiently into account, whether methodologically or epistemologically. The imbroglio of ethnic groups and nationalisms, the Second Republic's policy on nationalities, the Soviet-German impact on the borders, the presence of communism amongst the Jews – all these factors require a multi-dimensional reading of the objectives discussed, capable of surmounting any frontier. 'Betrayal', if this term is appropriate to the ethnic clashes and still means anything, then takes on a completely relative sense. This second, somewhat analytical approach, in our view, makes it possible to assess the conflicting arguments.

If, as we hope we have shown, ideas of 'betrayal' and 'collaboration' are inapplicable to the situation described here, how has their use in this context become so widespread? It was primarily spread in the clandestine press during the occupation and in reports by correspondents of the Home Army (*AK*). Moreover, close reading of these reports shows that the information they contain is much less exact than the sources used here, which were often, of course, drawn up after the 1939–41 period, or hedged about with caveats.[55] Let us advance the hypothesis – which is after all quite commonplace – that the use of 'betrayal' was conveniently integrated into the political strategies of the different underground parties, extending, in radicalized terminology, to the 'Jewish question' debated before the outbreak of war: did not some Polish leaders for example, make every effort to propose a transfer of Jews to the Odessa region during the winter of 1940?[56] The charge of betrayal also made it possible to justify and put in relative terms the unbridled anti-semitism of the population which Karski talks about. This anti-semitism was therefore widely developed well before the fusion of the two zones of occupation under German control, which made it possible to become familiar with the 'behaviour' of the Jews in the east.

And what should we think of the use of these words today? Do they make it possible to combat the negative stereotypes which overcome the Poles as soon as the Jewish question is broached? Is it rather a question of showing that it was communism, and therefore the Judaeo-Bolshevik alliance, which fundamentally increased an anti-semitism which was scarcely more excessive – and perhaps even less – than before? This hardly makes sense. Destiny ordained that the murder of the Jews of Poland, the largest Jewish community of Europe, took place on Polish soil, in the greatest of isolation. The mechanisms are often still incomprehensible, but it does not seem to us sensible to explain them by arguments which seem to be of a political nature.

'Betrayal' belongs to the classical anti-semitic vocabulary, as much moreover as it does to the vocabulary of a Jewish literature which loves to dwell on fantasy.[57] Its use seems to us best treated with reserve.

NOTES

1 This question has been raised recently in several works, particularly in Aleksander Smolar, 'Les Juifs dans la mémoire polonaise', *Esprit*, 127 (June 1987), pp. 2–8; Krystyna Kersten, *Narodziny systemu władzy 1943–1948* (Paris, 1986), 172.

2 The taboo which surrounded Polish-Jewish relations, particularly in a Soviet dimension, not to mention the Soviet occupation, made publication inconceivable in Poland. However, the vast amount of underground published material is beginning to broach both aspects equally.

3 The English translation is taken from David Engel, 'An Early Account of Polish Jewry under Nazi and Soviet Occupation Presented to the Polish Government-in-Exile, February 1940', *Jewish Social Studies* 45:1 (1983), 2–16.

4 The western part of the Polish territories had been annexed to the German Reich; another part, situated in the south-east, with Kraków as its centre, had been transformed by the occupying forces into a sort of protectorate called the 'General-Government'.

5 Engel, 'Early Account', 1–2.

6 Ibid.

7 Ibid.

8 Ibid.

9 Ibid.
10 Ibid.
11 In fact Karski was to revisit Bełżec, which later became a death camp.
12 The estimate generally put forward. Cf. Franz Beranek, 'Das Judentum in Polen', in Werner Markert (ed.), *Osteuropa Handbuch Polen*, (1959), 124.
13 Cf. the memoirs of Gina Mehr, Yad Vashem, 3042/170–N, or those of Reiss Walter, an inhabitant of Lwów, who writes: 'In September, 1939, the Russian army came to Lwów, and the Germans, who were already in the suburbs, withdrew behind the San. This fact was welcomed very joyfully by the Jews of Lwów, although nothing very good was expected from Soviet power,' Yad Vashem, 03–2241.
14 Personal memory of Paweł Korzec, who was one of the refugees in 1939.
15 Dmowski's nationalist camp put forward a theory, known as incorporationist, which aimed at incorporating the non-Polish ethnic groups into the nation state; Piłsudski's was a federalist solution: both collapsed quite quickly.
16 Cf. Andrzej Chojnowski, 'Problem narodowościowy na ziemiach polskich w początkach XX w. oraz w II Rzeczypospolitej', in *Z dziejów Drugiej Rzeczypospolitej*, a collective work edited by A. Garlicki (Warsaw, 1986), 177–94. See particularly p. 177, where the author writes that 'on the other side of the Bug, the phenomenon of obliteration of national identity brought about the regrouping of Polish peasants and minor nobility'; and 'If the assimilationist effect of Polish culture on the native population there was limited, this was the result of the Russifying action of the Tsarist government and the national activation of the Lithuanians, Ukrainians and Byelorussians.'
17 In the Polesia region (*województwo*), they only formed 14.5 per cent of the population; in Volhynia, not much more than 16 per cent.
18 Chojnowski 'Problem narodowościowy', 180.
19 Whereas the number of Polish schools was unchanged, the number of Ukrainian schools in eastern Galicia decreased in five years (1924–8) from 2,151 to 716. In their place and during the same period, the number of schools described as bilingual had increased from 9 to 1,793. The bilingualism, which introduced Polish as the first language, was only a screen for Polonization.
20 Quoted by A. Chojnowski, *Koncepcje polityki narodowościowej rządów polskich w latach 1921–1939* (Kraków, 1979), 222.
21 Quoted by Chojnowski, ibid, 226.
22 At the time of the discussions between Ribbentrop and Lipski (Polish ambassador to Berlin) on 24 October 1938, a real *Gesamtlösung* was envisaged in respect of Jewish emigration, cf. Artur Eisenbach, *Hitlerowska polityka zagłady Żydow* (Warsaw, 1961), 123.
23 K. Srokowski, *Sprawa narodowościowa na kresach wschodnich* (Kraków, 1924), 19.
24 W. Pobog-Malinowski, *Najnowsza historia polityczna Polski* vol. 2 (London, 1956), 441.
25 Aleksandra Bergman, *Sprawy białoruskie w II Rzeczpospolitej* (Warsaw, 1984), 101.
26 Ibid.
27 Cf. Chojnowski, *Koncepcje*, 193.
28 Cf. Bergman, *Sprawy białoruskie*, 102.
29 Cf. Chojnowski, *Koncepcje* A contemporary military report indicated that the 'nobility factor . . . has remained . . . as the sole link between this group of the population and Polishness.' Quoted by Chojnowski, p. 228.
30 Daniel Beauvois (ed.), *Les confins de l'ancienne Pologne, Ukraine, Lituanie, Bielorussie*, Preface by C. Miłosz (Lille, 1988), 11.
31 Czeslaw Milosz, *Une autre Europe* (Paris, 1964), 100.
32 Beauvois, *Les confins*, 9.
33 There is a copious literature on the relationship between the Jews and communism.

Localized descriptions are thinner on the ground: 'In our town, May 1 was described as a Jewish holiday. In fact, Jewish youth occupied a leading place in the processions with flags and posters bringing together all shades of the Left.' Miłosz, *Une autre Europe*, 97. 'In our town I never knew a non-Jewish communist,' says Max Wolfshaut-Dinkes, a native of Przemyśl; cf. Max Wolfshaut-Dinkes, *Echec et mat. Recit d'un survivant de Przemyśl en Galicie*, published by Association des fils et filles des deportés juifs de France, (Paris, 1983), 21.

34 Jan Tomasz Gross and Irena Grudzińska-Gross, 'W czterdziestym nas matko na Sybir zeslali' in '*Polska a Rosja 1939–42*' (London, 1983). This book, with a preface by Jan Gross, brings together a sample of testimonies from adults who left the USSR with the Anders army, and from children evacuated by the Polish authorities. These documents, which describe their perception and experience of the Soviet occupation, were drawn up at the request of the Polish government. They can be found at the Hoover Institution, Stanford. Cf. also Jan T. Gross, 'Wybory', *Aneks*, 45 (1984), 129–60, 46/47 (1988), 171–210. These articles are the theme of his book, *Revolution from Abroad: Sovietization of Western Ukraine and Western Bielorussia, 1939–1941* (Princeton, 1988).

35 The existence in Poland of distinct communist parties (Communist Party of Western Byelorussia, Communist Party of Western Ukraine), although subordinate to the Polish Communist Party, constitute one of the symptoms of this.

36 Cf. Jan T. Gross, 'W czterdziestym' 16.

37 Ibid., 20.

38 Ibid., 17.

39 Ibid., 18.

40 Ibid., 28.

41 Ibid., testimony 033/666 at Yad Vashem.

42 Wolfshaut-Dinkes, *Echec et mat*, 22. Or again: 'The Jews lived in fear, haunted by the prospect of expropriation and deportation to Siberia. They mistrusted one another and, above all, they feared the Jewish communists. These latter were fanatical supporters of the régime, zealous servants of the authorities. Faithful to their "duty", they fought unscrupulously against the "terrible" class enemy, composed of shopkeepers and craftsmen,' Ibid., 36.

43 Gross, 'W czterdziestym', 30, quoting Testimony 03/2821 at Yad Vashem.

44 Ibid., quoting Testimony 03/3381 at Yad Vashem.

45 Testimony of Fela Schnek, drawn up on 10 December 1947 at Yad Vashem (E/664, p. 1), indicates that in the Lwów region, 'From the start the Jews occupied most of the positions in the Soviet administration, although the key posts were always in the hands of Soviet officials.'

46 Cf. Wolfshaut-Dinkes, *Echec et mat*, 30.

47 Ibid., 31.

48 Account by Gina Mehr, Yad Vashem 03/3381, pp. 2–3. She adds (p. 3) that it was fortunate that she was separated from her husband because a great danger would then have threatened him: 'With the help of the local Ukrainian intellectuals, headed by Dr. Birecki, a list of 70 people to be eliminated had been drawn up and my husband and his brother figured on it. Fortunately this sentence was not carried out because the Germans, as a result of the agreement with the Soviets, were to withdraw behind the San, and after an agonizing 14 days, we were freed by the Soviets.'

49 Moshe Kahan, 'Two years of Soviet rule in Dubno', in the *Yizkor-buch* of Dubno, ed. Yaazov Arimi, (Tel Aviv, 1966).

50 'Many Polish and Ukrainian families left the side of the village occupied by the Soviets and went into the German-occupied region. This was, as it were, an exchange of ethnic groups.' Wolfshaut-Dinkes, *Echec et mat*, 31.

51 Cf. Kahan, 'Two years'; personal memory of Pawel Korzec, who opted for Soviet citizenship.

52 Pat Yacov (general editor), *Fun noentn over*, 3 vols., published by Congress for Jewish Culture (New York, 1957), testimony of Beti Ajzensztajn-Kesher, 'The Jews in Volhynia, 1939–41', pp. 3–30. The author adds that 'it was the Jewish communists who abolished the teaching of Hebrew and the Hebrew schools, in two months. The non-Jewish *politruks* (political commissars) did not even know that Hebrew was taught.'

53 Gross, 'Wybory' (see above, n. 34), p. 204.

54 Soviet 'discipline' even reached the Polish partisans, who were the most zealous supporters of the Soviet régime: thus Wanda Wasilewska, the communist writer who gave great support to the Kremlin's policy, was present in Lwów in 1940 at the assassination by unknown persons of her husband, a worker who did not refrain from criticizing the system. Cf. Ola Watowa, *Wszystko co najwazniejsze* (London, 1983) 30–1.

55 We have a certain number of these 'situation' reports in our possession, but their analysis goes beyond the scope of this article.

56 This suggestion was made by Roman Knoll, former ambassador to Berlin and leading government personality, in a report sent from Warsaw in March 1940 to the authorities in exile in Angers. The suggestion was taken up by the Minister of the Interior, Stanisław Kot. Knoll added that the Polish people would not tolerate a return to the pre-1939 situation and that only the territorial solution that the Zionists envisaged would prevent the use of violent methods. The choice, he wrote, was between 'Zionism and extermination' (for him a Zionist solution might well have been carried out on the coast of the Black Sea). Cf. David Engel, *In the shadow of Auschwitz: The Polish Government-in-Exile and the Jews, 1939–1942* (Chapel Hill, North Carolina, 1987) p. 65.

57 In his book, *Bruno Schulz* (1989), Henri Lewi brings up the idea of betrayal as essential to salvation present in Schulz's work, and derived from a mystical tradition which goes back to the seventeenth century.

23

THE WESTERN ALLIES AND THE HOLOCAUST

David Engel

> Our entire people will be destroyed. A few may be saved, perhaps, but three million Polish Jews are doomed. This cannot be prevented by any force in Poland, neither the Polish nor the Jewish Underground. Place this responsibility on the shoulders of the Allies. Let not a single leader of the United Nations be able to say that they did not know that we were being murdered in Poland and could not be helped except from the outside.

This, reported the emissary from underground Poland, Jan Karski, was the 'solemn message' entrusted him by a central figure of the Jewish *Bund* in Warsaw in October 1942 for delivery to 'the great leaders of the Allies'.[1] On the same occasion, according to Karski, the *Bund* spokesman, together with a Zionist representative, presented specific demands for a response on the part of the Western Allies to the relentless, methodical murder of their people which has since, for better or worse, come to be called the Holocaust. Some of these demands – their appeal to the Western powers to 'begin public executions of Germans, any they can get hold of', for example, or their call to 'threaten the entire German nation with a similar fate [to that then being meted out to the Jews] both during and after the war' – were, it seems, primarily the product of desperation, and those who advanced them did not seriously anticipate a favourable Allied response.[2] But others – exchanging Jews for German prisoners or ransoming them for money, or dropping leaflets from the air upon German cities informing the German people of the fate of Europe's Jews – were actually quite modest suggestions which Karski's informants appear to have anticipated would be given due consideration by the leaders of the free world. Clearly they expected the two great Western Allies to hear their cry and come to their aid. 'The democracies', they insisted, 'cannot calmly put up with the assertion that the Jewish people in Europe cannot be saved.'[3]

Yet, as nearly two decades of careful and extensive research has revealed, the democracies could, and in fact did, do precisely that. Beginning with Arthur Morse's much publicized 'chronicle of American apathy' in 1968,[4] and followed in short order by the more sophisticated works of David Wyman,[5] Henry Feingold,[6] and Saul Friedman,[7] the response of the United States to the successive stripping of the dignity, freedom and – ultimately – the lives of six million European Jews has been revealed as one of at best indifference, and perhaps even of complicity, in what the Nazis termed the 'Final Solution' of the Jewish question.[8] Though Joshua Sherman, in a 1973 study, showed the British Government's attitude toward assisting Jewish refugees from Nazi rule between 1933 and 1939 to be 'comparatively compassionate, even generous' when contrasted with that of the United States and other countries,[9] Bernard Wasserstein found 'an ocean of bureaucratic indifference and lack of concern' in his examination of British policy during the war years published six years later.[10] More recently Monty Penkower, endeavouring to provide the 'broad perspective' which he found lacking in these previous works, has detailed, among other things, the manner in which both major Western Allies' thinking on the Jewish question actually served to reinforce each other's unwillingness to respond positively to European Jewry's cries for help,[11] while Wyman has extended the scope of his indictment of American policy through 1945.[12] Canada's response to the Jewish crisis has also come under scrutiny, with Irving Abella and Harold Troper maintaining that that country's record of assistance to Germany's victims is 'arguably the worst' of that of any in the free world.[13] And still, with more books on the way, the final word remains to be said.[14]

The unanimity in the tenor of the brief against the Allies is striking, as is the fact that in nearly twenty years there has been no serious scholarly attempt to defend the free world's record during the war years.[15] In the American case, the recurrent combing of by now familiar terrain – the Evian Conference; the Schacht-Wohltat-Rublee negotiations; the Congressional debates over immigration policy and practices; the administration's handling of visa matters, resettlement schemes, and relief programmes; the response to specific proposals for the rescue of Balkan and Hungarian Jewry; the meeting at Bermuda; the establishment of the War Refugee Board; and the reception of the suggestion to bomb Auschwitz – in increasing detail, and on the basis of an ever-expanding reservoir of documents and oral testimonies, has rendered the verdict of willful refusal to come to the aid of European Jewry when reasonable opportunities to do so presented themselves, most difficult to contest. The British case, to be sure, has not yet been subjected to such repeated scrutiny, but a number of scholars, who in the course of work on other aspects of Holocaust history or British-Jewish relations, have had occasion to deal with certain specific issues in the problem under discussion have tended on the whole to underscore Wasserstein's assessment.[16] Whether further investigation of the Canadian Government's record will result in a similar strengthening of Abella and Troper's evaluation remains to be seen; but whatever the case, the notion that many Jews' lives might have been saved, had the two chief Western Allies been especially interested in seeing this happen, appears at this juncture firmly established by historical investigation.

Yet if serious objection to this fundamental point has yet to be heard, there are nonetheless other basic issues which divide the various authors in their approaches to the subject at hand. Perhaps the most obvious concerns the purpose which they assign to their research. Morse's goal was avowedly hortative: 'If genocide is to be prevented in the future, we must understand how it happened in the past – not only in terms of the killers and the killed but of the bystanders.'[17] His stridently moralistic tone, however, drew immediate fire from Feingold, who maintained in the Introduction to his own book that the time had come to 'move beyond the moral aspect to examine the political context in which America's response was conceived'.[18] Their exchange limned the poles of a dilemma which all who have approached the subject have had perforce to confront. Most have insisted upon their commitment to objectivity: as Wasserstein explained, 'the motto which I have adopted as the ideal toward which to strive is the motto of that French writer who said, "Je ne propose rien, je n'impose rien, j'expose."'[19] Yet at the same time he acknowledged the difficulty of maintaining detachment toward a subject so emotionally resonant; and, indeed, it seems that no one has been altogether successful in masking his personal abhorrence of his subject's behaviour. Some, in fact, have made no visible attempt to do so. Penkower, for one, echoes Morse in this sense; his explicit theme is the West's 'decay of conscience' and 'abdication of moral responsibility',[20] and in his narration, analysis and explanation are often overshadowed by a recurrent sermon in which the Allies are held to bear equal guilt with the Germans for the gas chambers and crematoria.[21] Friedman also seems to hold the moral purpose in high regard; in a review of Wasserstein's book he looked askance at the latter's 'effort to render a balanced account and avoid being chastised for Jewish partisanship', and castigated him for failing to 'remind all of the Biblical injunction contained in Genesis IV:10 – "The voice of your brother's blood cries out to me from the ground."'[22] Friedman's own work does indeed exude considerably greater passion than those of Wasserstein, Feingold, or Wyman, and his moral ardour is evident throughout; but unlike Penkower, his major thrust remains always analytical. So too does that of Abella and Troper, whose feelings about their subject are never disguised, yet at the same time always subtly and unobtrusively presented.

For the majority of writers, then, the essential task in investigating Allied responses to the Holocaust is less one merely of exposing and condemning Western callousness toward the fate of European Jewry than of uncovering the reasons for it. And it is upon this issue that the primary historical debate is centred. Here the literature reveals three principal points of conflict. The first concerns the role of anti-semitism as a cause of the general reluctance to assist Jews. Feingold places particular emphasis upon this factor, maintaining that anti-Jewish prejudice strongly coloured the attitudes and actions of those State Department bureaucrats most directly responsible for the administration of refugee matters. At the top of the list he places Assistant Secretary of State Breckenridge Long, head of the Department's Special War Problems Division and supervisor, *inter alia*, of its Visa Section, whose anti-semitism, though 'not as crude as that of the Nazis, . . . held many of their assumptions'.[23] Until 1944, when pressure by Treasury Secretary Henry Morgenthau finally led to the creation of the War Refugee Board outside the State Department's sphere of influence, Feingold reports, Long 'usually had his way', and he used the position which he had assumed in January 1940 'to halt, as soon as possible, the trickle of refugees to the United States'.[24] Ostensibly he did so in the interest of national security, in order to prevent the infiltration of German agents in refugee guise; but Feingold views this as motivated in large measure by a personal 'distaste for Jews'.[25] The 'security gambit' was, moreover, most difficult for refugee advocates to counter, as, too, for the American President, who, according to Feingold, did sincerely hope to see at least some action to aid Hitler's victims. In this situation, and constrained as well by both a restrictive immigration law and the 'Jew Deal' epithet which some of his opponents had attached to his administration, master politician Roosevelt sought, Feingold suggests, to strike 'a balance between the opponents and advocates of a more active rescue policy'.[26] The result, as Feingold sees it, was an 'uncertain mandate' which 'zig-zagged between those who favored and those who opposed a more active rescue policy', and in which 'the prize often went to those who had better access' to the Oval Office.[27] Long, himself a consummate politician with 'a keen knowledge of the inner workings of government and a wide circle of friends' in high places, was able successfully to 'control . . . the flow of information to the White House' and thus 'to curtail the humanitarian activity of the Roosevelt Administration'.[28]

Wyman and Friedman both dispute this claim. Wyman sees Long less as an anti-semite than as an 'atavistic nationalist', an exponent of '"100 percent Americanism" . . . concern[ed] to preserve American resources for American citizens and fear[ful] of the alien as a threat to American culture. . . '.[29] He also makes no attempt to link Long's fear of incoming refugees serving as a camouflage for the infiltration of Nazi agents with anti-Jewish or anti-alien feelings. Yet on the other hand, he places considerably more emphasis than Feingold upon popular anti-semitism, reportedly on the rise in the United States between 1937 and 1944, as 'a major element in public resistance to immigration of refugees'.[30] 'Viewed within the context of its times,' he concludes, 'United States refugee policy from 1938 to the end of 1941 was essentially what the American people wanted;'[31] his second book suggests that the same statement could be made with regard to the years of America's actual involvement in World War II. Friedman, in contrast, while agreeing that 'ultimately . . . the blame for inaction lies with the faceless mass of American citizens', not only exonerates Long from all suspicion of Jew-hatred ('in fact,' he notes, 'Long apparently was genuinely concerned about the fate of European Jewry'), but assigns to neither official nor popular anti-semitism a significant role in explaining the American response to the Holocaust.[32] There were, he acknowledges, some anti-semites in the consular service and in the lower echelons of the State Department, but for the most part the actions of the bureaucrats can be regarded as simply a 'rigid adherence to the letter of the law'.[33] If the State Department initially suppressed reports of mass murders of Jews in Eastern Europe which reached it during the Summer and Fall of 1942, including Gerhart Riegner's famous cable describing a Nazi plan systematically to annihilate all of European Jewry 'at one blow', this, argues Friedman, is better explained by the legacy of scepticism toward 'atrocity stories' and disillusionment with humanitarian causes in general left by the experience of World War I, as well as by a certain inurement to suffering experienced by those who could recall the cruel and heart-wrenching deaths of thousands or even millions of innocent victims of the Armenian massacres, the civil wars in Russia and Spain, Stalin's campaign against the kulaks, or the Japanese occupation of China, than by anti-semitism on the part of government functionaries.[34] Even the failure of the Bermuda Conference in April 1943, he maintains, was not the result of 'malice', but rather of 'the belief that special efforts on behalf of the Jews would signal vicious reprisals against them in Europe'.[35] Nor does Friedman hold anti-semitism primarily responsible for public apathy toward the Jewish plight. Though many Americans may indeed still have clung to 'the medieval view that persecution of Jews was a fit retribution for the Jewish sin of deicide', of greater importance, he holds, was the fact that 'Americans were too preoccupied with jobs in 1938, with the Japanese menace in 1942, and with their own biases against [Mexican-American] Zoot Suiters and Negroes in 1943 and 1944 to care about Jews'. Even those who professed outrage over Nazi brutality were more interested, he suggests, in 'punishing the guilty than in succoring his victim'.[36]

The British case admits of similar controversy. Although Wasserstein reports that 'anti-semitism was in the air in Britain during the war', and that 'there was a definite Government tendency . . . to bend with the wind of hostility to refugees, rather than give a lead or build upon the more generous elements in public opinion', he insists that 'conscious anti-semitism should not be regarded as an adequate explanation of official behaviour'.[37] But shortly thereafter he remarks that 'when set in the context of total war and of British policy towards Allied nations in general, the Jews received peculiarly ungenerous treatment'. As examples he cites 'the welcome accorded to tens of thousands of Yugoslav and Greek refugees from Nazism in the Middle East after 1941 and the more chilly reception accorded to Jews'; 'the wholesale operation by which the Allies supplied the entire food needs of the population of Axis-occupied Greece between 1942 and the end of the war', as opposed to 'the niggardly quantities of food relief which the Ministry of Economic Warfare permitted to be sent to Jews under Nazi occupation'; 'the contrast between the official preparations ... for the reception of up to 300,000 Dutch and Belgian refugees in Britain, and the consistent refusal of the Home Secretary to consider the admission ... of more than one or two thousand Jewish refugees'; and 'the disparity between the extraordinary efforts devoted by the Western powers to the provision of assistance to the Warsaw rising ... and the unanswered cries of the Jewish rebels in the Warsaw Ghetto' a year earlier.[38] His explanation for this discrimination is centred upon the exigencies of the ongoing British retreat from the Balfour Declaration and the government's determination to prevent Jews from gaining state sovereignty in Palestine. This policy, he holds, required that the Jews not be recognized as an Allied nation; and without such recognition, the 'limited horizons of bureaucratic thinking' could allow the Jews no special claim for help.[39] Yet the paramount relevance of such thinking is readily apparent only in the first-cited of his examples; it would seem to require a good bit more explication to show why this purported application of different standards to Jews than to non-Jews – which many might reasonably regard as a primary symptom of anti-semitism[40] – ought not to be regarded as as much anti-semitically as politically motivated. Thus Colin Holmes (himself a sophisticated student of British public attitudes toward Jews) has contended, for one, that although 'Wasserstein is correct in his refusal to regard antisemitism alone as the force behind British policy', he 'runs the risk of underplaying its significance'.[41]

In the Canadian situation, as presented by Abella and Troper, in contrast, there appears little room for dispute that popular and bureaucratic antipathy toward Jews consistently reinforced one another to the point where governmental refugee policy came to be guided by an unabashed anti-semitism. Abella and Troper have first of all uncovered a Canadian counterpart to the American Long – Frederick Charles Blair, Director of the Immigration Branch of the Department of Mines and Resources. A wealth of quotations from the private correspondence of this veteran civil servant who, the two scholars report, almost single-handedly 'made [Canadian immigration] policy and implemented it' reveal him – with a definitiveness absent from Feingold's characterizations of Long – as a 'tough-minded bureaucrat ... [whose] contempt for the Jews was boundless'. By the same token, though, Abella and Troper point out, Blair's actions in the final analysis 'reflected the wishes and values of his superiors'.[42] They hold that Prime Minister Mackenzie King, despite what they take to be his genuine 'humanitarian and religious instincts', also did not want 'foreign strains of blood' entering Canada, and he was in their view strongly influenced by an 'unofficial, unholy triumvirate', consisting of the Immigration Branch, the Cabinet, and the Department of External Affairs, which was determined to keep refugees – especially Jewish ones – out of the country.[43] Virtually all of the politicians and officials of these arms of government, they hold, were heirs to a tradition of ethnic prejudice which could, in theory, tolerate non-white or non-Christian immigrants 'as long as they were out of sight' in the mines, lumber camps, or farms of the distant north and west, but which at the same time regarded Jews as incapable of remaining 'on the farm or in the bush' where they belonged.[44] In this, Abella and Troper note, they were in step with a general increase in public expressions of anti-semitism, which especially in Quebec had recently begun to take on political overtones. In such conditions, even those who might personally sympathize with the Jewish plight understood perforce that support for liberalized immigration rules was a severe political liability.[45]

Abella and Troper's strong emphasis on anti-semitism notwithstanding, however, the major trend since the late 1970s has been to seek the principal motivation for Allied inaction and callousness in other directions. For some, the key problem is more cognitive than affective – the ostensible existence of a gap between information and knowledge which prevented news of the Holocaust from being believed and internalized even after it had been reliably reported and confirmed. Among the first to call serious attention to this notion was Yehuda Bauer. He raised it, however, more in the context of an observation that the Jews of the free world seemed at the time unable to comprehend that the Nazis were bent on a programme of total biological annihilation of the Jewish people, even though from June 1942 on they 'had all the information . . . that was needed to establish the facts'.[46] A year later Wasserstein raised the possibility that the British Government, too, may have suffered from 'an imaginative failure to grasp the full meaning of the consequences of decisions'.[47] Interestingly, he invoked this consideration not in his discussion of British responses to the first news of the Holocaust (where disbelief was presented as more wilful than psychologically unavoidable), but as a tentative explanation of why those whom he regarded as at bottom good and decent people, 'who would probably have played the . . . Good Samaritan if their neighbour had fallen among thieves . . . "came and looked, and passed by on the other side"' when it came to thc murder of European Jewry. He suggested that since 'the average British official lived in a different mental world from that of the Jewish refugee', he could not grasp that 'the agony of European

Jewry was enacted in a separate moral arena, a grim twilight world where [his] conventional ethical code did not apply'.[48]

Perhaps such speculations are what prompted Walter Laqueur[49] and Martin Gilbert[50] to probe the limited problem of Allied reactions to the news of the Holocaust more deeply. Laqueur, who never intended a broad analysis of what the Allies did or did not do for the Jews and why, judiciously avoided the temptation to posit disbelief of the horrible reports coming out of Europe in 1942 as the primary explanation of Allied indifference to the Jewish plight: 'Even if the realities of the "final solution" had been accepted in London and Washington,' he argued, 'the issue [of aid for Jews] would still have figured very low on the scale of Allied priorities.'[51] Gilbert, in contrast, exceeded these cautious limits and suggested that the perceptual failure was the prime cause of Allied inaction on the Jews behalf. He attempted to show that the most crucial piece of information about the Holocaust, the existence of a mass murder camp at Auschwitz-Birkenau and its role as the destination of most transports of Jews from outside of Poland, was not known in the West until the third week in June 1944. For him, the test of the Allied reaction to the agony of European Jewry came only after this date, and in consequence he devoted the final quarter of the book to detailing the British and American responses to the various proposals to bomb the camp and the rail lines leading to it. Unfortunately, in his all too brief discussion of the Allies' underlying motivations in rejecting these requests, he neglected to consider seriously anything but the problem of information. Thus he left the strange and rather self-contradictory impression that, whether the Allies knew about Auschwitz or not, their 'failures . . . were those of imagination, of response, of Intelligence, of piecing together and evaluating what was known, of co-ordination, of initiative, and even at times of sympathy'.[52] His own evidence, though, as critics have noted,[53] strongly suggested that much more was involved, and his failure to examine other factors – not even the 'political considerations and . . . prejudice' that he noted in passing in his Introduction[54] – prevented him from proving the primacy of faulty perception as an explanation of Allied behaviour toward Jews during the Holocaust.

Still, the perceptual explanation continues to exert influence. Penkower, for one, insofar as he analyses motivation at all, considers virtually exclusively the problem of information and belief. In this vein he goes even further than Gilbert. Not only, he maintains, did British and American officials continue to disbelieve reports of the mass murder of Jews until the war's end, but 'Allied callousness toward the Jewish people reflected a different elementary failure of perception' as well. 'Having at first misjudged the dimensions of the Holocaust', he argues, 'London and Washington continued to deny Jewry' the status of an Allied nation. This was because, Penkower claims, they did not grasp that Jews were being persecuted not as Poles or Czechs or Belgians, but solely as Jews, and thus could not sensibly be regarded on the basis of their citizenship alone.[55] Here Penkower is in explicit disagreement with Wasserstein, who views this aspect of the Allied attitude toward the Jews as essentially politically motivated.

Wyman, too, in his more recent book, considers the problem of disbelief, but from a different angle; and he does not accord it near the explanatory significance of Gilbert or Penkower. In keeping with his interest in popular attitudes, he notes, on the basis of a survey of 19 American metropolitan dailies, the failure of news about the Holocaust to make any significant impact upon the American mass media or public as a whole. Americans, he claims, were thus not aroused to demand Government action on the threatened Jews' behalf, so that there was no available political counterweight to the State Department's obstinate refusal to become involved in such activity. But, he adds, two forces which might have been able to arouse the public and mobilize it to put pressure on the Government – the churches and the organized Jewish community – failed to do so.

In raising the issue of American Jewry's behaviour in the face of the Holocaust, Wyman boldly enters the third area of dispute among those who consider the reasons underlying the Western Allies' inaction. Indeed, the question of the response of the Jews of the free world to the slaughter of their brethren in occupied Europe has recently emerged in its own right as no less significant a focus for scholarly attention than that of the response of the democracies. In many respects the academic debate over this issue echoes an extended and often heated public argument within Jewish circles over the charge – first voiced even during the war itself – that the leaders of free-world Jewry failed to speak out with suitable vigour and daring against the unwillingness of the Allied governments to come to the aid of their threatened European brethren. The public controversy, which appears of late to have become increasingly heated, displays many overtones of internal Jewish political strife, and these are not absent from the scholarly debate as well.[56] Thus most aspects of this contest exceed the scope of the topic under consideration here. Nevertheless, it is of relevance, since, as Wyman's work, among others, shows, a scholar's attitudes toward it stand also to influence his explanation of the reasons for the Allied responses to the Holocaust.

It must be noted, though, that, in contrast to the virtually unchallenged negative scholarly assessment of Allied behaviour, the accusation of Jewish passivity is by no means universally accepted. Feingold strongly denies it with respect to American Jewry, Abella and Troper in the Canadian case, and Wasserstein with regard to the Jews of the free world as a whole.[57] For these scholars, obviously, Jewish behaviour could not form a significant part of an explanation of Allied inaction in the face of the Holocaust. But even among those who – often in palpable anguish – believe they have found documentary confirmation of the charge, there is still dispute over the purported fact's practical consequences. Friedman, who was the first to criticize the American Jewish leadership within the framework of a scholarly study, concludes that the Jews who 'deified' Roosevelt bore 'some responsibility' for the lack of American rescue efforts, but nevertheless refrains from assigning them the major blame. In balancing the picture he points out, much as do those who reject his indictment, that the mass marches and civil disobedience called for by critics of the Jewish establishment 'would have been regarded by Americans in 1942–1943 as seditious behavior designed to immobilize the government and thereby jeopardize American fighting men abroad'. In the end, he states, 'the fault lay . . .' most of all 'in a society which had created an atmosphere in which a leader of a minority did not feel free to speak the terrible news he had learned of persecution abroad for fear of generating that same persecution at home.'[58] Wyman seems to assign Jewish passivity a somewhat greater weight: he writes that the 'effectiveness [of Jewish action] was importantly diminished by [the] inability to mount a sustained or unified drive for government action, by diversion of energies into fighting among the several organizations, and by failure to assign top priority to the rescue issue,' thereby implying that had these self-imposed obstacles been overcome, American Jews might have been able to make a significant impact upon the Roosevelt administration's policy.[59] Two researchers who have yet to publish their findings in book form, on the other hand, evidently regard Jewish actions and inactions as a decisive determinant of the American Government's behaviour. David Kranzler, who is studying the Rescue Committee (*Va'ad ha-Hatsalah*) sponsored by the Union of Orthodox Rabbis of the United States and Canada, holds that 'had American Jews been less ideological and more pragmatic . . ., most certainly many more Jews would have been spared from the Holocaust'. He also maintains that the march of 400 Orthodox rabbis on Washington on 6 October 1943 was directly responsible for the establishment three months later of the War Refugee Board.[60] Eliahu Matz, a former doctoral student at the City University of New York who was reportedly preparing a dissertation on American Jewish responses to the Holocaust, posits similar effectiveness for the Emergency Committee to Save the Jewish People of Europe, the group led by the emissary of the Palestinian *Irgun Tsva'i Le'umi*, Hillel Kook (alias Peter Bergson), which challenged established Jewish organizations to adopt more aggressive tactics toward the American Government and which attracted widespread public attention.[61]

For all of the fervour which this debate has generated, though, there seems to be little disagreement between the two sides over the basic facts of the case. Instead, the controversy exists almost entirely on the interpretive level. The same can be said for the other two areas of dispute outlined here as well. An indication of this is the failure of the large quantities of hitherto untapped primary source material exploited by Penkower and Wyman to yield compelling evidence in support of any of the various conflicting theses. Indeed, it seems unlikely that the continued mining of archives and interviewing of participants in the events in question will by itself lead to a significant clarification of the issues.[62] Thus it appears that in the future investigators will need to expand their interpretive framework in order to prevent the discussion of the subject from degenerating into a vapid retelling of well-known tales. Fortunately, there is much room to develop in this regard. The controversy over the role of anti-semitism in the formulation of Allied policy, for instance, would be well served, among other things, by a more careful consideration of the similarities and differences between governmental attitudes toward relief and rescue for Jews and for other civilian populations in occupied Europe. Much has been made in this regard of British willingness to suspend the blockade of shipments to occupied territory in order to relieve famine in Greece as contrasted with the unwillingness to do the same for Jews in the Polish ghettos; yet recent research on British-Greek relations suggests that there were sound political and strategic reasons for feeding the starving Greek population which were absent in the Jewish case.[63] The Polish Government-in-Exile made repeated requests of the British and American Governments that German cities be bombed in retaliation for atrocities committed against Polish citizens, yet these, like those from Jewish sources, were refused.[64] The Allied armies made no visible attempt to interfere with the 'death marches' of concentration camp prisoners in the Winter of 1945, despite their ability to do so with little difficulty, even though the majority of those involved were non-Jews.[65] And the attitude of the American Government, as, for that matter, of Christian Americans as a whole, toward the plight of non-Jewish refugees from Nazi Germany has recently been described – by a Jewish historian – as one of 'apathy'.[66] The thinking which underlay Allied behaviour in these cases deserves not only to be systematically explored, but also to be taken into account in analysing the motivations of Allied actions toward the Jews.

Similarly, in the context of the discussion of faulty perception as an explanation of the failure to rescue, it seems helpful to ask whether and how Allied attitudes toward the Jewish situation changed immediately following the war, when the shock of the face-to-face encounter with the concentration camps was fresh in the public mind. Of all who have explored the issue at hand thus far, only Abella and Troper have carried their narrative forward to 1948. They find that the indisputable evidence of the Final Solution revealed to the Canadian authorities following the liberation of the camps had virtually no impact upon the Government's immigration policy.[67] The conclusions of Leonard Dinnerstein's study of America's behaviour toward the displaced persons are not quite so apodictic, but they also indicate that clear knowledge about the

Holocaust did not cause a revolution in American thinking.[68] Proponents of the perceptual explanation have yet to come to grips with these considerations.

Regarding the role of free-world Jewry in Allied policy formulation, it seems to me necessary to consider this within the broader context of the influence of public opinion in general, and of special interest groups in particular, upon the calculations of the Allied Governments during wartime. In the British case, which has been most thoroughly studied, it seems that public opinion was actually quite sympathetic to the Jewish cause, and church leaders stood resolutely beside Jewish demands for relief and rescue; yet this moved the British Government but little.[69] The situation could well have been different in the United States, of course, where the normal adversary relationship between the political parties continued in force, for the most part, throughout the war. But this proposition deserves more thorough consideration. To what extent, for example, was administration war policy designed with an eye to domestic political considerations? Was the Jewish vote regarded by political leaders as an important factor in the Congressional elections of November 1942, or in the Presidential election two years later, and how might this have affected policy? To what extent was the United States Government prepared to take action on any matter involving the war zone in opposition to the wishes of its British ally? What efforts were made by other immigrant groups to elicit government action on behalf of their brethren in Nazi-occupied Europe, and how successful were these? Examination of questions such as these ought to place the controversy over the ability of American Jewry to move the American Government from its policy of inaction in a perspective more conducive to informed analysis.

Greater attention ought also to be given to a fact mentioned in passing by some of the scholars under consideration but never sufficiently developed by them. At the close of World War I, world Jewry had been widely regarded in Western diplomatic circles as a force to be reckoned with. Britain had issued the Balfour Declaration, the Versailles Conference had imposed the Minorities Treaty upon the newly created states of East Central Europe, and the League of Nations had mandated Britain the task of establishing a Jewish National Home in Palestine. Yet by the time Hitler came to power in 1933, this same ostensible world power found itself almost entirely without leverage in its endeavour to enlist international assistance in protecting its charges under Nazi rule. The actual 'abandonment of the Jews', to borrow Wyman's title, took place not during World War II, but well before. This precipitous decline in the ability of Jews to utilize the international political arena as a forum for defending their rights and interests was a necessary preparatory step toward the formation of the callous attitude with which the Allied Governments were to respond to their pleas for help during the Holocaust. Its tracing and analysis ought thus, it would seem, to form an important part of the discussion of the subject at hand.

Perhaps, when all of these aspects of the problem have been thoroughly treated, attention will come to be directed to an observation offered unobtrusively by Feingold, which for 15 years has remained, sadly, on the periphery of the discussion. In the Introduction to his book Feingold spoke, almost as an aside, of 'the great difficulty of assigning to a modern nation-state a humanitarian mission to rescue a foreign minority for which it had no legal responsibility'. During the Holocaust, the Allies were essentially being asked – as Karski's informants pointed out in Warsaw in October 1942 – to 'adjust [the strategy of war] to include the rescue of a fraction of the unhappy Jewish people'.[70] Yet because during the previous two decades the Jews had lost whatever ability they once had had to appeal to the Western powers with political arguments, the only basis upon which such a demand could be put forth was a moral one. For the Allies, on the other hand – whatever their propaganda might have reported on the home front – the war was being fought to preserve and advance vital national interests. When all is said and done, the Allied Governments did little to extricate the Jews of Hitler's Europe from their mortal peril because they could see no compelling political, strategic, or legal reason to do so. Thus, as Feingold pointedly observed, 'the villain of the piece, in the last analysis, may not be the State Department or even certain officials but the nature of the nation-state itself'.[71]

NOTES

1 Jan Karski, *Story of a Secret State* (Boston, 1944), p. 323.
2 Ibid., pp. 325–6.
3 Ibid., p. 327.
4 Arthur D. Morse, *While Six Million Died: A Chronicle of American Apathy* (New York, 1968).
5 David S. Wyman, *Paper Walls: America and the Refugee Crisis 1938–1941* (Massachusetts, 1968).
6 Henry L. Feingold, *The Politics of Rescue: The Roosevelt Administration and the Holocaust, 1938–1945* (New Jersey, 1970).
7 Saul S. Friedman, *No Haven for the Oppressed: United States Policy Toward Jewish Refugees, 1938–1945* (Detroit, 1973).
8 The word 'complicity' is employed explicitly by Friedman, p. 7. Feingold, generally less caustic, though no less emphatic in his condemnation of American policy toward the Jews of Europe, speaks of 'seeming compliance with the goals of the Final Solution', p. x.
9 A. J. Sherman, *Island Refuge: Britain and Refugees from the Third Reich 1933–1939* (London, 1973), p. 267.
10 Bernard Wasserstein, *Britain and the Jews of Europe 1939–1945* (Oxford, 1979), p. 345.
11 Monty Noam Penkower, *The Jews were Expendable: Free World Diplomacy and the*

Holocaust (Illinois, 1983). Penkower considers Britain and the United States to be 'accomplices to history's most monstrous crime', p. vii.

12 David S. Wyman, *The Abandonment of the Jews: America and the Holocaust, 1941–1945* (New York, 1984).

13 Irving Abella and Harold Troper, *None is Too Many: Canada and the Jews of Europe, 1933–1948* (Toronto, 1982), p. x.

14 Cf. Richard Breitman, 'The Allied war effort and the Jews, 1942–1943', *Journal of Contemporary History*, vol. 20 (1985), pp. 135–56. Breitman and Alan M. Kraut are reportedly working on a 'study of American refugee policy and European Jewry, 1933–45'.

15 The nearest approximation to a defence is offered by John P. Fox in two reviews of Wasserstein's work. Fox maintains that 'within the context of Allied military operations during 1943, Germany's own effective "sealing of all escape routes", and above all the intensity and haste of the extermination process, it really is a *non sequitur* to talk of "significant relief" not being offered to the Jews and the non-efficacy of "Allied rescue efforts"'. But his principal objection seems to be to the implication that 'the Allied nations . . . must also be held responsible for the Final Solution or Holocaust, notwithstanding the fact that the first and final responsibility for that crime rests with Nazi Germany'. He makes no effort to dispute the general charge of British indifference to the fate of Jews subject to a policy of deliberate and systematic murder and acknowledges that 'a great deal' in Wasserstein's book 'makes for disturbing reading'. *International Affairs*, (January 1980), pp. 143–4; see also *European Studies Review*, (January 1980).

16 Wasserstein's book was the subject of a symposium held at Tel Aviv University in 1982, whose proceedings were subsequently published: Anita Shapira, ed., *Diyun al Britaniah ve-Yehudei Eiropa 1939–1945* (Sugiyot be-Toledot ha-Tsiyonut ve-ha-Yishuv, no. 3, Tel Aviv, 1983). In addition, there are a number of articles which deal with specific issues with regard to the British response to the Holocaust, most notably with the prospects for rescuing Hungarian Jewry in 1944; among them are Yehuda Bauer, 'The Mission of Joel Brand', in *The Holocaust in Historical Perspective* (Seattle, 1978), pp. 94–155, 164–71; J. S. Conway, 'Between apprehension and indifference: Allied attitudes to the destruction of Hungarian Jewry', *Wiener Library Bulletin*, nos. 30/31 (1973–4), pp. 37–48; Bela Vago, 'The Horthy offer: A missed opportunity for rescuing Jews in 1944', in Randolph L. Braham, ed., *Contemporary Views on the Holocaust* (Boston, 1983), pp. 23–45. See also the contributions by Bauer, Vago, and Nathaniel Katzburg in *Rescue Attempts during the Holocaust: Proceedings of the Second Yad Vashem International Historical Conference* (Jerusalem, 1976). In addition, the works by Walter Laqueur and Martin Gilbert, cited below, strongly support Wasserstein's view of the character of British attitudes.

17 Morse, Introduction (unnumbered page).

18 Feingold, p. ix.

19 Wasserstein's remarks in Shapira, p. 24.

20 Penkower, pp. vii–viii.

21 These tendencies are most in evidence on pp. 146–9, 179–82, 222, 286–8, 301–2.

22 *American Jewish History*, vol. 69, (1980) no. 4, pp. 529–32.

23 Feingold, p. 135.

24 Ibid., pp. 297, 136.

25 Ibid., p. 159.

26 Ibid., p. 298.

27 Ibid., 2nd edn. (New York, n. d. [1980]), pp. xiv–xv.

28 Ibid., pp. 136, 297.

29 Wyman, *Paper Walls*, pp. 10, 146. He quotes from Long's diary to show that the

Assistant Secretary held a negative opinion not only of 'the Russian and Polish Jew . . . but . . . of all that Slav population of Eastern Europe and Western Asia'.

30 Ibid., p. 23.
31 Ibid., p. 213.
32 Friedman, pp. 230, 116–7.
33 Ibid., pp. 117–9.
34 Ibid., pp. 137–8.
35 Ibid., p. 180.
36 Ibid., pp. 230–1. The final citation is quoted by Friedman from a 1938 editorial in the *New Republic*.
37 Wasserstein, pp. 351–2.
38 Ibid., pp. 352–4.
39 Ibid., pp. 132, 353.
40 Cf. the comments by Dina Porat in Shapira, p. 45.
41 Colin Holmes, 'Britain and the Jews of Europe: Review article', *Jewish Journal of Sociology*, vol. 22 (1980), pp. 59–72. Holmes continues, '. . . there is clear evidence that . . . a cultural antipathy towards Jews . . . was at work in the circumstances we have been describing' (p. 68).
42 Abella and Troper, pp. 7–9.
43 Ibid., pp. 17, 50.
44 Ibid., p. 5.
45 Ibid., pp. 17–18, 50–1.
46 Yehuda Bauer, 'The Holocaust and American Jewry', in loc cit., pp. 19–28. Feingold and Friedman had also noted both Jewish and Allied disbelief of atrocity reports, but they did not incorporate this fact in any significant way in their explanations of Allied inaction.
47 Wasserstein, p. 356.
48 Ibid., pp. 356–7. For another perspective on this problem, see the review of Wasserstein by David Vital in *Commentary*, vol. 69 (1980) no. 2, pp. 80–3.
49 Walter Laqueur, *The Terrible Secret: Suppression of the Truth about Hitler's 'Final Solution'* (Boston, 1980).
50 Martin Gilbert, *Auschwitz and the Allies* (New York, 1981).
51 Laqueur, pp. 7, 10, 203–4. In fact, he actually turned the perceptual failure argument on its head, claiming that it was precisely the low priority given to the Jewish situation in Allied government circles that permitted State Department and Foreign Office bureaucrats to pass lightly over reports of mass murder without seriously considering their implications.
52 Gilbert, pp. 339–41.
53 Cf. Deborah E. Lipstadt, 'Witness to the persecution: The Allies and the Holocaust: A review essay', *Modern Judaism*, vol. 3 (1983) no. 3, p. 329.
54 Gilbert, p. viii.
55 Penkower, pp. 295–8, passim.
56 Such overtones are quite noticeable in, *inter alia*, Lucy S. Dawidowicz, 'Indicting American Jews', *Commentary*, vol. 75 (1983) no. 6, pp. 36–44, and the many Letters to the Editor in response, ibid., vol. 76 (1983) no. 3. It is indicative of the nature of the debate that some scholars have chosen to express their views primarily in Jewish public-affairs reviews such as *Commentary* or *Midstream* rather than in purely academic forums.
57 Feingold, paperback edition, pp. 321–9; Abella and Troper, pp. 283–4; Bernard Wasserstein, 'The Myth of "Jewish Silence"', *Midstream*, vol. 26 (1980) no. 7, pp. 10–16.
58 Friedman, pp. 152–4, 230.
59 Wyman, *Abandonment*, p. ix.

60 David Kranzler, 'Letter to the Editor', *Midstream*, vol. 27 (1981) no. 3, p. 58. The letter was a response to Wasserstein, 'Myth' (above, note 57).

61 Eliahu Matz, 'Political actions vs. personal relations', *Midstream*, vol. 27 (1981) no. 4, pp. 41–7. Matz's comments on this subject (sometimes offered under the name Eliyohu Matzovsky) have appeared frequently in articles, book reviews, and letters to the editor published in *Midstream*. It should be pointed out that Feingold and Friedman do not view pressure from the sources indicated by either Matz or Kranzler as instrumental in the creation of the War Refugee Board, while Penkower and Wyman assign the Emergency Committee a certain – if not the decisive – weight. There is also a detailed (though as yet unpublished in book form) study of Anglo-Jewry's influence on the British response to the Holocaust, which concludes that while greater organizational unity and vigour would not likely have affected British policy, dramatic, extraordinary protest offered by prominent British Jews outside of the Jewish organizational establishment might have: Meir Sompolinsky, Ha-Hanhagah Ha-Anglo-Yehudit, Memshelet Britaniah ve-ha-Sho'ah (unpublished PhD dissertation, Bar-Ilan University, 1977), pp. 229–30.

62 This is not to suggest, of course, that nothing is to be gained from the exploration of new sources. Penkower, for example, has provided many new details which provide a better-rounded picture of the events he describes. Among other things, he has identified one Eduard Schulte as the anonymous German industrialist whose information concerning a German plan biologically to annihilate all of European Jewry formed the basis of the Riegner telegram of 8 August 1942 [the same identification was made independently by Breitman and Kraut; cf. Richard Breitman and Alan M. Kraut, 'Who Was the "Mysterious Messenger"?' *Commentary*, vol. 76 (1983) no. 4, pp. 44–7]. The point here is simply that such details, however interesting, aid understanding of the larger issues involved but little, and that the chances of discovering what Yehuda Bauer has called a 'documentary Rosetta Stone' which will do substantially more than fill out details are small.

63 Cf. Procopis Papastratis, *British Policy towards Greece during the Second World War, 1941–1944* (Cambridge, 1984), pp. 114–18; see also the comments by Bauer in Shapira, pp. 64–5.

64 Ironically, the Poles believed that world Jewry could help influence the British and American Governments in their favour; cf. inter alia, Reprezentacja Żydostwa Polskiego, *Sprawozdanie z działalności w latach 1940–1945* (n.p., n.d.), pp. 54–5.

65 Yehuda Bauer, 'Tse'adot ha-mavet, Yanuar-Mai 1945', *Yahadut Zemanenu*, I (1983), pp. 199–221.

66 Haim Genizi, *American Apathy: The Plight of Christian Refugees from Nazism* (Ramat-Gan, 1983).

67 Abella and Troper, pp. 190–279.

68 Leonard Dinnerstein, *America and the Survivors of the Holocaust* (New York, 1982).

69 Sompolinsky, p. 228. The limited impact of public opinion in Britain during the 1933–1939 period is analysed by Haim Shamir, *Be-Terem Sho'ah: Redifat Yehudei Germaniah ve-da'at ha-kahal be-ma'arav Eiropa 1933–1939* (Tel Aviv, 1974).

70 Karski, p. 327.

71 Feingold, p. xiii. Helen Fein also noted 'the organizational incapacity and unreadiness among nation-states to protect members of other nation-states,' but she, too, failed to place this idea at the centre of her summary of Allied and neutral responses to the Holocaust. Helen Fein, *Accounting for Genocide: National Responses and Jewish Victimization during the Holocaust* (New York, 1979), p. 166.

24

THE CONDITIONS OF ADMITTANCE AND THE SOCIAL BACKGROUND OF JEWISH CHILDREN SAVED BY WOMEN'S RELIGIOUS ORDERS IN POLAND 1939–1945

Ewa Kurek-Lesik

The world's religious orders for women constitute a rather picturesque landscape, and, there is little point in denying it, quite a confused one for the historian. Apparently not even in Rome do they know exactly how many orders there are and what they do. The picture is no clearer in Poland. Both before the Second World War and throughout its course no one, it seems, was possessed of comprehensive information as to their number, location or of the nature of activities carried out by the nuns. Each group, if I may use such a term, followed its own path. It had its own authorities – whether in Poland, Rome or elsewhere – its own goals, its own kind of spirituality and its own habit – or lack of one. There was no overall authority that could coordinate the female religious orders on a national scale, set out a concrete programme of action or formulate any kind of position. Furthermore, every group had different capabilities and suffered a different fate during the occupation. All this had a fundamental effect on the question of admitting Jewish children into the convents.

The hiding of Jewish children in Polish convents during the Second World War presents the historian with very difficult problems. The fundamental difficulty is the lack of sources. Rescuing Jews and their children in Poland was carried out in the strictest conspiratorial conditions and obviously the nuns during the war did not record these activities. After the war, political conditions and the pressure of day-to-day work, as well as the sisters' own attitudes, were not conducive to the task of completing or supplementing the archives with notes or statements concerning their wartime activities, As for the children themselves, they were collected by their parents or relatives after the war or by Jewish organisations, and left the convents for all corners of the world, or were scattered throughout Poland and are rarely able, or willing to visit the places where they spent their wartime childhood. Therefore, in my travels in Poland, Israel and America collecting information, I had to create my own sources.

Naturally, forty years after the war and given the above obstacles, it is difficult to claim a comprehensive grasp of the subject. That is why what I have managed to reconstruct, which I will summarise here, can constitute only a part of the whole picture.

Directly before the outbreak of the Second World War there were 84 communities of nuns in Poland, comprising over 20,000 sisters, whose opportunities to take action were limited during the Occupation by German policies towards the Church, which differed significantly in different parts of Poland. Those sisters who were situated in parts of the country incorporated into the *Reich* in October 1939 were not able to do anything. They filled the prisons and labour camps, were relocated or had to go into hiding. Those sisters, who were in areas occupied by the Soviet Union until June 1941, were forced to take up paid work and to put aside their habits, some were sent to Siberia and their houses and goods were ransacked by the Soviet authorities, all of which – together with the Ukrainian massacres in Wolynia and Galicia – also made any work impossible after June 1941. As far as conditions during the war are concerned, in as much as one can speak of normal conditions, these applied only to convents in the *General Gouvernement* and for this reason my information relates to this geographical area.

Among the many activities and responsibilities which the war created for the sisters, they saw the most important as being the rescue and care of children who were made most helpless by war and who suffered most harm because of it. This is why it was mainly children, among all the others requiring help, who passed through convents. The children were of various nationalities: apart from Poles, there were Ukrainians, Jews and Gypsies and, towards the end of the war, the children of the enemy also – German children.

The rescue of Jewish children was a special task for Polish nuns, for from October 1941 every Pole rescuing a Jewish adult or child paid for it with his life if discovered by the Germans. In Poland, during the last war, neither the cassock, habit or Bishop's mitre provided protection from death. For this reason, two sisters of the Order of the Immaculate Conception and eight Sisters of Charity paid the highest price. They were shot by the Germans for helping Jews and their children.

Female religious orders had 2,289 houses in Poland just before the war; 15–20 per cent of these ran orphanages or boarding-schools. It was here above all that Jewish children found refuge. To date I have located 189 convents hiding Jewish children during the war, of which 173 were in the *General Gouvernement*. The most active were the sisters in Warsaw and its environs – in the capital alone 23 houses hid Jewish children and 41 houses on the outskirts of Warsaw performed the same function. These figures are not definitive, of course. My original information on convents concealing Jewish children was derived from convent sources. Today I can only complement them, together with information given by those who were saved.

The sisters of 37 communities were engaged in this work, or rather this is the number I have been able to ascertain. In six of these communities, the sisters involved are no longer alive, nor have I been able to locate the children themselves – the memory of the activity survives only in the oral tradition of the communities concerned. Furthermore, six of the communities helped only adult Jews. In all, two-thirds of the 74 female religious communities in Poland took part in helping Jewish children and adults.

There is today no way of ascertaining the number of children saved. The chief reason for this is the fragmentary nature of the sources and, more specifically, forty years after the war, the death of the majority of the Mothers Superior of the Convents concerned who alone knew the exact number of refugees housed in their establishments. Nevertheless, it seems that the number of children saved was not less than 1,500 – how many more there may have been will probably always remain a mystery.

The convents which hid Jewish children fell into different groups.

The first category consisted of those among whom admittance of Jewish children was a response to directions from above, from the order's general or provincial authorities. 'The rescue action conducted by the sisters of the Family of Mary,' writes Sr Teresa Frącek, 'was arranged from above, and directed by the Mr General – Ludwika Lisówna, and the provincial Mother Superior Matylda Getter. The order's houses were situated in Lwów and Warsaw. The directives of the order's authorities were realized due to the self-sacrifice of the sisters. Following the example and with the approbation of their superiors, the sisters in almost all the convents helped the Jews.'[1] A similar situation existed among the Grey Ursulines. Mother Andrzeja Górska says: 'The order's house, known as "the Grey House" during the occupation, on Wiślana Street in Warsaw played an important part in this action. It already functioned as the order's general house and was the seat of the Mother General, Mother Pia Leśniewska, the question of aid for the Jews also rested in her hands.'[2]

The admittance of Jewish children into the houses of the Grey Ursulines or Franciscans of the Family of Mary depended on the attitude of their superiors and, although I do not believe that participation in such actions was encouraged by the superiors in the form of recommendations, the sisters of particular convents automatically adopted a stance resembling that of their superiors towards the question of these children. This situation proved to be the most beneficial both for the sisters and the children themselves as it freed the superiors of particular convents and individual sisters from the need to take the final decision and it contributed to their self-confidence and daring in carrying out such a difficult task for those times. For Jewish children it meant that the convent gates were open to them at all hours of the day or night.

If both the conditions of occupation and the order's democratic traditions allowed, decisions on accepting Jewish children were taken by all the sisters. 'I will never forget the conference called by Sr Wanda Garczyńska,' writes Sr Maria Ena.

> It was 1942–43. The school on Kazimierzowska had been closed. The SS was based in a huge block opposite our house, where the RGO kitchen was open and functioning almost without a break. The people, too, came in a constant stream – children, young people, adults with canisters for soup. Only for soup? For everything. Kazimierzowska pulsated with life – from the nursery to the university. Amongst this hive of activity there were also Jewesses. Real ones. With red, curly hair, freckled, with prominent ears and unusual eyes. Thoroughbreds. There could be no mistake. It was well-known that concealing a Jew meant the death sentence.
>
> The sister knew that other orders had already been warned and searched. So she hid nothing, withheld nothing. She called us together. She began the conference by reading a fragment of the Gospel of St John 15 vs 13–17. She explained that she did not wish to jeopardise the house, the sisters, the community. She knew what could be awaiting us. There was no thought of self. She knew: you should love one another as I have loved you. How? So that He gave His life.
>
> I lowered my head. I did not dare look at the other sisters. We had to decide. If we said one word, openly, honestly admitted to fear for our own skins, our own lives, the lives of so many sisters, the community. . . . Was it prudent to risk it for a few Jewesses? It was our decision whether or not they would have to leave.
>
> Silence.
>
> No one stirred. Not a single breath. We were ready. We would not give up the Jewish children. We would rather die, all of us. The silence was overwhelming. – we did not look at each other. The sister was sitting with closed eyes, her hands folded over the Gospel. She was no doubt praying.
>
> We got up. We did not even pray together as we normally do . We went to Chapel. We felt light and joyful, though very grave. We were ready.[3]

The general authorities were able to take a central decision in only very few communities. The frontiers, geographical considerations and the conditions imposed by war made contact with the central authorities difficult if not impossible. The particulars of operations in which timing often meant the difference between life and death meant that as far as action was concerned – not only that of saving Jewish children – individual houses were autonomous even though in peacetime the principle of central authority was applicable to all women's communities. Furthermore, in my opinion, in many communities the admittance of Jewish children was deliberately left as an open question because of the death penalty it incurred – the vow of religious obedience did not extend that far. Sr Aleksa, a Josephite, says: 'Dr Fryderyk S. granted permission for me to take his 6-year-old daughter to Lwów where she was to stay with a certain Polish family. I consulted my superior as I did not know what to do. The Mother Superior said she could neither issue an order nor forbid me to do it as it was a question of risking one's life.'[4]

Saving Jewish children, taking them in was thus to a great degree the result of decisions taken by the superiors of individual religious houses. From the accounts of the sisters this certainly appears to be the case in most situations. Sr Ludwika (order of St. Elizabeth), says: '. . . here the decision rested entirely with the Superior of the house, Sr Gertrude Marciniak and I simply carried out her recommendations – though she was always careful to point out that, because of the danger involved, the decision was mine.'[5] Similarly Sr Jolanta, a Franciscan Missionary of Mary: '. . . whoever came, any child in need of help, the Mother Superior, Katarzyna Clawrey, ordered that they should be taken in. The admittance of children was her decision.'[6]

But there were also cases where individual sisters, bold, intelligent and of uncommonly strong personality, individually took part in actions rescuing Jewish children and who influenced their superiors by their conduct or at least gained their warm approbation and assistance. That was probably the case with Sr Syksta, a Pleszew nun (*Służebniczka Pleszewska*), and Sr Ludwika Małkiewicz (order of St. Elizabeth) among many others. When Rachel stood at the door of the Convent of Trzesówka, the Mother Superior happened to be away and to wait for her return would have meant death for the child. It fell to the kitchen sister to make the decision to take her in.

Jewish children behind convent walls were not a novelty of the occupation for all women's religious communities in Poland. A certain number of children already lived in orphanages run by Polish sisters from before the war. It is difficult to determine on a general scale why Jewish children happened to find themselves in those particular orphanages before the war as the circumstances surrounding their admittance have been ascertained in only three cases. 'Krzyś was admitted to the orphanage officially as a Jew with papers stating that he was an illegitimate child of Jewish extraction with the surname Eisenberg. He was brought there as a small child.'[7]

'Janek B. came to us before the war. His parents had left for Germany where they died, the Germans returned the child. A sister travelled to the border to collect him. He was not yet walking when he came to us. When the war broke out Janek was eleven years old.'[8] 'Lotka, who had not yet been weaned when the war broke out, was sent by the hospital in Gdańsk to the orphanage of *Służebniczek Pleszewskich* sisters in Gdynia-Oksywie.'[9] These were most probably children whose parents did not want them and there were also other orphans who had no one to care for them.

The outbreak of war, the confusion, the first repressions and resettlements meant that, among others, Jewish children also began to arrive at convent gates. Sporadically at first, as, for example, at the Grey Ursulines in Zakopane, where in December 1939 the Germans liquidated the Bishop of Kraków's Committee's sanatorium for children with tuberculosis. The Grey Ursulines took in the children who had been left at the roadside. 'We took 15 children, 2 Jewish ones among them: Rysio Krupka – 10–12 years and Anita Goldman aged 10. In 1942 as a result of a search hunting out Jews, the President of the Jewish Council in Nowy Targ issued an order forbidding Jewish children to be sent there and then ordered that they should be brought to the Warsaw Ghetto. Sr Bieryłło who was accompanying the children outwitted their "guardian" along the way and took them instead to the sisters at Tamka Street in Warsaw. Anita survived the war but Rysiek went back to the ghetto on the wishes of his parents and died there on 15 August 1942.'[10]

At the turn of 1940–1, the Germans issued a decree in accordance with which the sisters would have to send their Jewish charges to the ghettos which had been set up. The nuns responded to this decree of the occupier as they did to so many of the others and sought ways to keep the children in the orphanages. The above-mentioned child by the name of Eisenberg 'the superior was sorry for and asked the directress of social welfare not to let him go. But the child had papers which clearly indicated that he was Jewish. After long and insistent behest on the part of the Mother Superior the directress decided to destroy his papers and from then on he was known as Krzysztof X.' At the Michalitki 'one of the children was to be taken and put in the ghetto. The sisters bribed the social services, received a receipt that the child had been handed over and hid the little girl.'[11]

The sisters did not manage to keep all the Jewish children who came to their orphanages before the war or in its initial years. Sometimes they were unsuccessful in fighting for a child to stay in their establishment, sometimes the sisters fought perhaps too insistently, especially as the Jewish Councils themselves were demanding that they be sent to the ghetto. But no one knew at the time the ghettos were established that their inhabitants were destined to die.[12]

It is characteristic that the enclosure of Jews in the ghetto and the issuing of German decrees concerning the removal of Jewish children from institutions run by nuns, coincided with the time of the first wave of arrivals in the religious houses. In the words of Sr Amabilis: 'Jewish children began to come to us from the moment the ghettos were closed off. In the beginning they usually came for a short period and then disappeared. We did not even regard them as permanent pupils. The periods for which they came to us as boarders were equally as short as those they spent at the day school.'[13] These shortlived visits during the ghetto's closing-off period could indicate that convents, particularly those running schools with boarders, served as a form of 'repository' for children for the time that it took their parents to organize themselves on the 'aryan side' or while they decided whether or not to live in the ghetto. Some of the children who arrived during that first period remained within the convent walls until the end of the occupation. At that time the sisters who provided shelter for Jewish children were still not risking a great deal. It was not until 15 October 1941 that Hans Frank ordered that 'Jews who leave their designated area without permission are liable to incur the death sentence. The same sentence applies to those who knowingly harbour Jews.'

In the spring and summer of 1942, the Germans in Poland began to realize 'the final solution' in respect of the Jews, that is they began the process of liquidating the ghettos and the murder of their inhabitants. To quote Sr Amabilis again: 'The influx of Jewish girls began in the years 1942–43'. The period she quotes is typical of almost all the female religious orders sheltering Jewish children. The time link between the beginning of the German mass murder of Jews on the one hand and the growing influx of Jewish children to convents on the other is clear.

In what way did these Jewish children, deprived of their right to life, come to find themselves behind convent walls during this most tragic period for Jews in Poland? The first group consisted of those who were taken in at the request of Poles who knew them, priests or simply ordinary people – Poles and Jews. In Kielce the orphanage's patron, Fr Jan Jaroszewicz, 'was approached by Jewish mothers who begged him to take in their children, confident that no harm would come to them there.'[14] '. . . a young Jewish doctor came to the Resurrectionists in Lwów in tears and gave her children into their care. She offered a small sum of money as she had no more. She could not take her children with her, she could not bear to leave them on the street.'[15]

It sometimes happened that in seeking to save their children, parents unexpectedly also found help for themselves.

> Early in the spring of 1943 a woman appeared in the institution with a request that her two children who had been christened the year before – a boy in the third class and a girl in the fifth – should be

> taken in. She looked very semitic. After conversing with her I decided that I would try to help her. The director of IHP was Dr. Kazimierz Dąbrowski, a psychiatrist living in Zagórze. I had to confer with him. The doctor agreed to admit the children who arrived at our institution shortly afterwards. A few days later their mother came to help in the sewing room, half furtively and half in the open. She continued to live in Radość – I did not know the address – and sometimes spent the night with us. She was very discreet in view of our children who were unable to keep any secret. She said her husband had been arrested.[16]

Jewish parents often had the chance to save only themselves, or they ceased to care about their own safety at all, wishing at all costs to save the lives of their children. A number of them came to the conclusion that they would be safest within convent walls. Having no contacts they simply arrived at the door, as at the Turkowice establishment where 'M. was brought by his own father who said to the Mother Superior:

– Sister, I am a Jew, a dentist. There is nowhere for me to hide for I am well-known here. I will live for as long as I am useful to the Germans, but I will surely not survive. I have brought you my son. If you can, I would ask you to take him in.'[17]

The admittance of Jewish children sometimes constituted an almost tragic scenario. 'I remember Antoś T.' says one sister. 'That is what the sisters called him as no one knew his real name. When the ghetto in Ostrowiec was being liquidated an old bearded Jew ran up to one of the sister's windows and threw the baby up to her crying "Hide him! He's yours now!"'[18]

But in most cases, Jewish parents wishing to place their children in establishments run by sisters went via Poles they knew who played the role of patron and intermediary. For example at the Sisters of the Name of Jesus in Klimontów Sandomierski where 'two little girls, Iwonka and Lusia, were brought by the Opatów *starosta*, and a third, two year old Marysia, was brought by the lady of the manor, Mrs Ropelewska,'[19] and the Magdalen Sisters were brought 'Krystyna G., by her nanny, a Catholic who saved the child from the ghetto'.[20] Quite often the roles of middleman and of those who rescued children from the ghetto were played by priests. Children were brought out of the Warsaw Ghetto by Fr Prelate Marceli Godlewski of All Saints Church, and from the Częstochowa ghetto by '. . . the late Fr Prelate Antoni Godziszewski, who had contacts within the ghetto from where he smuggled children out into the appropriate establishments. In our institute (Oblate Sisters) there were only girls. They were admitted by the Mother Superior who was also director of the establishment.'[21] Priests, by means known only to themselves, sought out Jewish children and brought them to the sisters. At the Grey Sisters' Boduen house 'Fr Piotr Tomaszewski, the chaplain of the house, excelled in this activity. He brought 3-year-old Monika W. to the sisters at their recreation.'[22]

Because of the fragmentary nature of these accounts, which is also a result of simple lack of information on the part of those who related them, it really is difficult to distinguish those Poles who were involved in placing children in orphanages from those who carried out their own small rescue actions in an individual capacity. Sr Szczęsna tells how: 'Jewish children were brought to the house in Częstochowa from various places. Some were brought by people we knew, others – by complete strangers. The teacher Kitówna, I don't remember her first name, brought several such children. Dr. Franke from Częstochowa brought us an older girl with a christening certificate. Some nun from an order that did not wear a habit also brought a few Jewish children to us.'[23] From the accounts of the sisters of this house it appears that the teacher Kitówna paid for the help she gave these children with her life.

> . . . A certain lady came to the Albertines in Kraków with a question – how could she save a child from the ghetto. She received the reply: it's quite simple, bring it here. This she did. The child's father came out via the sewers and handed her the one-year old boy and she brought it to the sisters' creche.[24] We took Ruth N., the daughter of Max and Rose N., to the Order of St. Elizabeth house in Otwock in November, 1942 at the request of her parents, who were in hiding after the liquidation of the ghetto. With the agreement of the convent's superior, I drew up false Catholic papers using the name Teresa Wysocka. We enacted the abandonment of the child. One evening Ruth's mother stealthily and apparently unnoticed by anyone, left the little one in a corridor. The barely three year old child began to cry and the religious and lay members of the establishment rushed out to see what was going on. Little Ruth had a little bag around her neck containing the false certificate and a letter asking that they care for the child for a short time. The mother wrote that her husband had been taken to work in Germany and she herself was engaged in bartering and trading and had nowhere to leave little Teresa and in her difficult situation she was counting on the compassion of the sisters – the mother signed herself Wysocka of course. The child was with us for about two years. Ruth's parents survived in hiding in Warsaw at Peplinska Street in the district of Praga.[25]

The accounts quoted above reveal a further method of getting Jewish children into Polish convents, an enacted abandonment. The sisters, especially in orphanages, were required to produce records concerning the children they had taken in, their identity papers and registration cards, which had to be presented every time there was a German control check. It was simplest, therefore, to avoid the whole procedure of formally taking in the child and to enact its abandonment. However, most Jewish children did arrive in convents, not necessarily orphanages, as authentic foundlings. In Warsaw at the Fr Boduen house '. . . Jewish children were found on the steps, at the gates, in church porches and lobbies, often by the Boduenska gate. The greatest influx of children began early in 1943, just after the ghetto was finally liquidated. In the space of three months, 57 girls and 66 boys arrived in this fashion.'[26] The same order of Grey Sisters was forced to set up a creche adjoining the hospital in Kielce in 1942 '. . . because so many foundlings were being left near the hospital. I, myself, returning from town one day, found such a child on a path near the hospital. It could not have been more than ten days old. They were in all probability Jewish children, ten of them. In 1945 a few of the children were hunted out and taken back by their parents who had somehow managed to avoid death. Others were handed over to orphanages. One happy mother came all the way from Canada to reclaim her child in 1946.'[27]

According to Sr Hermana from the Albertines' Kraków house: 'During the anti-Jewish actions the number of children left at the creche increased. They could be recognised as the boys were usually circumcised or had semitic features.'[28]

Individual Jewish children were left with sisters belonging to a variety of orders. In Samborz 'a little child of two was left, one of the sisters cared for him with great devotion for over a year. When the child began to walk it was handed over to the town's Bazylianki sisters as our order ran an old people's home.'[29]

> During the war we ran a nursery school at Lotnicza Street in Kraków. Jewish women would bring their children to our gates, of course we fed them for as long as we could. One Jewess asked if her daughter could stay at school a little longer. One day she did not come for the child. The sisters kept her at the convent for a while, later Sr Agnieszka Szymczyk hid her with a lady she knew and continued to look after her. After the war her uncle came from Palestine and took her away. She wrote beautiful letters to Sr Agnieszka.[30]

As I have already mentioned, from Autumn 1941 Poland became the only occupied country in Europe where hiding or helping Jews was punishable by death. The Poles soon learnt that this was no empty threat on the part of the Germans. From 1942 in particular, that is from the moment the total extermination of the Jews began, this terrible penalty was meticulously executed. This was also a period when individual Jews – including children – managed to escape from the murderous ghettos. Children wandered the streets. Some of them, the figures are not known, failed to find shelter and sooner or later fell into the hands of the Germans. Some were hidden by Poles. Sometimes, however, on finding their paths crossed by a Jewish child, the Poles did not dare to give it shelter. However, conscience forbade them to condemn such children to death and so they directed them to the nearest convents. The fact that the sisters rescued Jewish children was apparently an open secret. 'In the order's Lublin house,' Sr Michael relates, 'there were a few Jewish girls hiding from the Germans. One of them, 10 or 11 years old, whose parents had been shot and whose house had been burnt down, tried to run away and hid first of all with some Polish farmers. But they were afraid to hide a Jewish child and sent her to us.'[31]

Sr Mistera remembers Frania Aronson:

> She was walking along the road from Warsaw and crying. Hungry, homeless, scantily dressed, she attracted the attention of a passing woman who pointed out the house with the church spire and advised her to go there. The sisters there would help her. This was in Ignacow. And indeed that is what happened. After the war she left for Palestine. She writes letters, expressing her gratitude. In the archives of our Central House there is a letter testifying to this.[32]

'I was ten years old,' writes Maria Klein from Israel.

> I was taken from the labour camp in Przemyśl when the ghetto was being liquidated. People were burnt alive, murdered, robbed and, as it was a shame to waste ammunition on children, they were caught by the legs and their heads smashed against a wall. I can see their shattered brains to this day. The Poles were generally very hostile and very willingly handed Jews over to the Gestapo. I write this because I was brought out of, or rather I ran away from, the camp to Mrs. Romankiewiczowa's who lived nearby and she took me, along with milk for the orphanage, to the Sisters of the Sacred Heart. We met our former charwoman along the way. I had the impression that she recognized me and was terrified that she would give everything away to the Germans. But thanks to the prayers of the sisters nothing happened. The sisters took me in with great love and understanding, there were already children from the ghetto there. The sisters arranged things so that we could talk in the lavatories in order not to arouse the suspicions of the other children. We were formally introduced to all the children, meanwhile we would lead each other into the ways of convent life and could be alone and talk without being heard.[33]

It is quite possible that Icek arrived at the Samaritan Sisters convent in Henryków in a similar fashion. Zdzisław Umiński describes the boy's arrival: 'It happened during the Holocaust years, when human life was worth very little. But sometimes it seemed particularly valuable as it did to this nun. One day a small Jewish boy of about ten years old rang at the door and one of the sisters, the portress, opened the door.

– Will I get something to eat? – he asked, trembling with cold.

– Come in – said the nun. I was nearby as I had just brought some wood back from the forest and the snow was still melting in the seams of my jacket. It was snowing lightly and I had omitted to brush myself off. The horse and cart were standing in front of the gate, I had to go in through the main door in order to open the iron gates which screeched horribly.

– Look Zdzich – the nun said to me, pointing at the little one's clothes. Long rows of fleas were marching all over him. In the sudden warmth they had crawled out and it was only now that one could see how infested the boy was. I took him to the laundry and prepared some water for him, I burnt his rags in the steamer they used to boil beetroot for the swine. He got new clothes, and, when he had eaten, the Sr portress said they would hide him in the attic where he would somehow pass the winter. – There's a little room there – she explained – the chimney goes up right beside it so he won't be too cold. When it gets darker, then one of the sisters will take him for a walk, so that the girls don't see (the girls were prostitutes working without black books, the [pre-war] police brought them to the institution for so-called rehabilitation), and he will get food enough to ease his hunger.

– But Lola is hungry – he protested. He got up and said he had to go to Lola.

– Who is Lola? – asked the sister.

– She's my sister, we ran away together when the men in black on the wall shot mama. Mama called: Icek take Lola and run – because I am Icek Wilf and my papa was Mosze Wilf and had a soapworks and now they have made soap out of him. Because when they took papa to Oświęcim they made soap out of him there and you get it on ration cards – that's what mama said. They gave us Jews little green bars of soap but we didn't want to soap ourselves though, how could we soap ourselves? It was human soap wasn't it, not real soap?

– Where is Lola? – I interrupted.

– She's by the Płudy because I said I'd be coming.

– Has she been waiting long?

– Might not seem long to you, miss, or to me because we've eaten and aren't hungry, but for her in this frost it's a long time. I'd like to go there now.

– You will have to wait a little while – said the sister. She had already spoken to the superior and the boy had been assured of a place. But now there was this Lola of his.

– I will go to Mother and explain about the girl. The Sister portress was an energetic woman but had to consult with the superior on every decision. She returned a few minutes later saying that, as dusk was falling, Icek and I should go soon to fetch Lola.

We rode off. The hoarfrost clung to the horse's mane as we followed the road to the Płudy. We stopped at a sandy hillock whose peak was covered by convulsingly twisted little firs.

– She's waiting there – said Icek and called softly: Lola, come on over here, there's bread and sausage as well and it's warm in the house. White walls and these ladies in funny clothes.

However, Lola did not want to come out so we had to go to her.

– Aj vaj – moaned Icek – something's happened. It's like she's lying under a quilt, but it's not, it's the snow.

– I think she's dead – I said leaning over the girl. I began to tug at her, wiping her little mouse-like face, but to no avail. Hunger and the cold had killed her.

– Lola, what have you done! Now I'll probably die, because I've been left all alone.

He did not die. We buried Lola marking her grave with a stone. The stone is there to this day, pushed into the sand. It is not far from the housing estate which has grown up there over the last few years.

It was then, at the beginning of 1943 that the sister took in not only the boy, but also a doctor and his wife and child, a few other people, strangers to me, and of course I, too, was sheltered by the sisters.'[34]

Younger children were brought, some carried, to the sisters. In Kraków at the Ursulines '. . . one day another four year old tenant arrived. A tram conductor brought him saying that the child had been riding around the tram all day, chewing on a piece of bread. We called him Antoś.'[35] At the Albertines in Tarnopol '. . . one afternoon, during the period that the greatest campaign against the Jews was being waged, a policeman arrived carrying a little basket with a baby inside, a little boy who can't have weighed more than four kg. The policeman said he'd found him in an empty house.' And in Kraków 'On evening at 9 o'clock two people, a woman and a ferryman brought a one year old child dressed in a white astrakhan coat and claimed that while crossing the Vistula in a boat they heard some splashing, then they saw a white object in the water and rowing in its direction they fished the child out of the Vistula. The boy was completely soaked through, blue in the face and unconscious. Sr Fidelisa spent four hours by his side before she was able to bring him round but the little boy caught pneumonia. Fortunately, however, he survived it and grew healthily.'[36]

Finally, the sisters themselves were engaged in actually gathering Jewish children.

> During the Warsaw uprising a five year old boy was found wandering near the Children's Institute in Wołomin. He was wretched, in rags, hungry and flea-ridden. The boys from the Institute chased him away a few times and even threw stones at him. When one of the sisters noticed this she called him to her, washed him, fed him, and changed his clothes and he stayed in the Institute. He was unable to say anything about himself. Since he had a dark complexion the other children called him the 'gypsy'. At first he was frightened and timid but he changed after a few days and the boys came to like him very much. He stayed until September 1946. Then the sister who had taken him in was transferred to the convent at Siedlce where a certain Jewess was going around the local Institutions looking for her child. She showed his photograph and the sister recognized the 'gypsy' from Wołomin. The happy mother collected her son and in gratitude offered the sisters leather for shoes.[37]

Krystyna O. born in 1939, arrived from Warsaw on 20 October 1943. The child climbed out from the sewer canal on Nowolipki Street in Warsaw. Sr Julia Sosnowska, a Grey Sister, came across her by chance as she was passing. Knowing Ignaców, she took her to the Institute there. Krysia had a card with her bearing her name and date of birth and she was registered accordingly at the Institute. She stayed in Ignaców until 26 October 1945. She was then transferred by the education authorities to the Institute at 75 Nowogrodzka Street. Apparently she completed secondary school and settled in Silesia.[38]

The most beautiful page written into the history of the rescue of children during the Second World War, or, to put it another way, the most open of them all, steeped in limitless compassion and the will to help, was demonstrated by the Franciscan Missionaries of Mary. The sisters were few in number, their community was poor. There were two houses: in Zamość and in Łabunie. Sr Jolanta says:

> In June 1941 the Germans moved us and the children to Radecznica, about 50 km from Łabunie. It was very good there, although food was a problem. The Germans alloted a ration to the children, but what did that amount to – a little cereal and fermented marmalade. The Franciscan Fathers fed us. They gave us a plot of land to grow vegetables, somewhere to keep cows and horses, they turned over a building in the courtyard to us for the girls and the dining-room for the boys. Now children began to pour in, day and night. Boys began to arrive and girls too, before then it had been only girls. Before we had about fifty children, now they began to arrive quickly and soon there were 150. The *RGO* did not send any children to us. I remember Zygmuś, a little Jewish boy of about six or seven.

> Generally, whenever someone arrived, a child perhaps needing help, the Mother Superior, Katarzyna Crowley, ordered that they should be admitted.[39]

Sister Zofia, of the same community, who worked in Zamość during the war says:

> The Rotter family was also hidden by our order. The whole family were hidden at Zamość, but I don't know the exact details. There was also one sandy-haired Jewish boy, Lis, I think that's what he was called. But no one really bothered about whether a child was a German or Jewish or what. Only: you are a child and we take in children. We did not even know how many there were of each different background.
>
> Our Mother Superior was an Irish woman, Catherine Crowley. She doted completely on the children. We took them all in. And as far as the children were concerned, the Mother Superior knew about all of them, we knew the identity of some of them. Sometimes we had no idea that a child was Jewish.
>
> During the war we were inundated with children. Everyone: policemen, neighbours, if anyone met a child along the road they would all bring them to us. We had a house at Zdanów Street in Zamość. At one point there was no more room even in the corridors. In the old building we had quite a big chapel and eventually we turned that into a dormitory for the children. We made the chapel so small that there was room only for a small altar and the priest – we would hear Mass standing in the corridors. But it was all too small and finally we took over the school in Łukasińska Street. As we could not accommodate all the children even there, we farmed them out, when possible, to Polish families. I worked at Łukasińska Street. Those were very difficult times. I cared for the babies and ran the Infirmary. There were three groups of children. We worked 24 hours a day. No one received extra subsidies for the children. We had collections to get money. Our whole fortune lay in them, our children.[40]

The Franciscan Missionaries of Mary acknowledged that the condition for the admittance of a child under their roof was a straightforward, childish need. A place had to be found. And there was a particularly large number of needy children in the Zamość region.[41] The sisters made no enquiries about a child's nationality, despite the sentence threatening them with regard to Jewish children. The account below testifies, among others, to the fact that they did not lack a place in the houses of the Missionaries: 'Some man from Komarów, who had been resettled from the Poznań region, gathered up Jewish children and sent them to Radecznica. Apparently he had some mandate to do so on behalf of the Jews. The children he discovered all found themselves there and were brought up by the nuns.' It was not possible to study the background to this action in any more detail.[42]

Poles, driven by an initial impulse of human solidarity or mercy, or for reasons of material benefit, often decided to hide Jewish children. But with the passing of time and the intensification of the extermination programme, as news began to filter through from all sides about the murder and the burning of whole Polish families for hiding Jews, those people still hiding children were gripped by fear. Some of them, unable to overcome it, sent the children to the nuns. '. . . a farmer from a village brought a three year old girl to the Albertines in Siedlice as he was too frightened to hide her any longer. The girl was in deadly fear of the Germans, she did not even want to look out of the window in case someone should see her.'[43] Wanda was left at the house of the Franciscan Missionaries of Mary in Zamość. 'She was very nicely dressed, two or three years old, a little card hung around her neck: "Wanda has been christened"' Sr. Zofia remembers. 'During the war I was housemistress at Zamość and after the war I ran a house for small children in Łabunie. Towards the end of the sixties I had a telephone call asking if an abandoned child named Wanda had ever been entered in the house's register. Some time later I got a letter from Israel: 'I am that Wanda, my name now is Tamara. I was adopted by Jewish parents but I would like to learn about my own history and would like to ask your help. I was not at all happy with my new parents. I only learnt that I was not their child when I married and had children. Then they finally told me. Where did I come from, who were my parents and where were they from?'

It was very fortunate then that Sr Azaria was still alive and when she heard about it she said: – Do you know, sister, I once met a woman at the bus stop who peeled potatoes for us during the war and who was interested in Wandzia. We talked for a while and then she said she was going to Skierbisze.

And that was all. I wrote to the parish priest at Skierbisze asking him to announce that I was searching for a woman who at more or less such and such a time had left Wanda with the sisters at Zamość.

And sure enough some time later I received news from the priest that such and such a woman had come to see him. I wrote to her and she came to see me and told me Wandzia's story:

– I am not her mother. I met Wanda's mother at the market in Zamość. She was selling something, I was selling something, we got friendly and she started to tell me about her life. She came from Bydgoszcz. They had killed her husband there and she and her little son escaped to the east. Wandzia was then still 'on the way', she was carrying her. She gave birth to Wanda on the train – it was 1939. She came to Zamość and tried to earn a living by trading. I don't remember her surname now.

Once the Germans rounded up her children in the market place to send them to the children's camp. Somehow she managed to get them back but then became afraid because it had emerged that she was Jewish, that these were Jewish children. So she asked me to take care of Wandzia in the hope that perhaps she would survive. She herself decided to stay with her son. Some time later they were taken to Izbica and shot.

I stayed in Zamość with Wanda and took care of her. One day some Germans came to my house asking who the child was. I answered that she was my niece and when questioned Wandzia confirmed that I was her aunt. But from then on I feared for both myself and the child. I came to the conclusion that I could do nothing but leave her with the sisters. I opened the gate of the convent courtyard and pushed the child in, in this way it was impossible to tell – who? what? . . . an abandoned child. Wishing to know what had happened to her, I reported to the sisters to peel potatoes.'[44]

'First I was sent to some people near Dębice,' relates Rachel, a Jewish girl, saved by the Josephites. 'My parents and younger sister were hiding under assumed names near Tarnobrzeg. Then it began to get really bad, there were already a few informers revealing the fact that they were Jews. When I was with those people at Dębice my father paid me visits over a short period of time. We were put in the attic – there was no question of showing oneself anywhere – and this was all at night, in secret. I remember my father picking off the fleas which I had, of course. And then one day my father didn't come. I learnt eventually via someone else that my father had run away somewhere and that something had to be done with my mother.

I do not know to this day where he went and what happened to him. The people I was staying with were extremely worried by this situation. They were terribly afraid. Then there were some attacks on Jews – I don't remember it all so well now but I do remember Jewish children running by, looking for somewhere to hide, yes, like animals baited by dogs. No one wanted to take these children in, they ran over the fields with the Germans shooting at them. And I could not admit to anything – I was not allowed to say anything. And so I lived, in a kind of stupor.

Then one day my landlord decided something had to be done with me. They must have been very much afraid. They had robbed my parents – but that was another story – now they fell into a panic. They came to the conclusion that I should be sent to a convent.

Something has to be done with the mother and the little one and this one will have to be taken somewhere – such were the snatches of conversation that reached me. From what I was able to hear between my mother and the landlord it appeared that she later committed suicide.

– I tried to do it once but when I got into the water the little one said mummy the water's so cold . . . and I couldn't do it . . .

And then . . . .it was tragic. It must have been 1942, just before Holy Week. First they took me to Tarnobrzeg where my mother and sister were hiding. My father was no longer there. My mother decided to commit suicide with the help of my landlord. It was to be suicide by drowning. Together with the little child. The child, my sister, was then three years old.

I was left further along the river – I was to wait there. I was completely stupefied. It wasn't normal. First I saw my mother. She said goodbye so sincerely somehow. And then I saw the little one. I didn't know what was going on.

It took some time. At last the man returned and said: It's all over. Let's go.

He took me in my stupefied state to Trzesówka. The convent could be seen from a distance as the village was built of wood and the only stone building with more than one storey was the convent. The landlord left me in a field nearby and said:

– Go over there and they'll take you in for sure.

It was Palm Sunday. I trudged dully towards the convent. Sr Roberta wasn't there then. It was Sr Adolfina who ran the whole household. She was a large and . . . well . . . severe sort of nun. But she welcomed me so cordially and then, just as in the film *Polskie drogi* she asked me to say my prayers. Of course I knew my prayers. I rattled them off and heard her say:

– Very well, you shall stay here.

She was a wise nun. She realized at once what was behind it all and the next day she christened me with water. She knew immediately what was going on.'[45]

Led by instinct or because the convent was the one nearby centre they were familiar with, in moments of danger Jewish children themselves came to ask for help. 'There was a little Jewish boy living with us,' says Sr Czesława who supervised the dining room in Lublin during the war. 'He was fourteen or fifteen years old. He had run away from the Germans. The boy knew of us because our school was well-known before the war as was the institute we ran. When the Germans were in the process of liquidating the ghetto, the boy ran to us and begged us to hide him. Trembling, he repeated:

– Please hide me! Please hide me!

Naturally we hid him.'[46]

Sister Maria tells the following story: 'Behind our convent in Samborz there was a Jewish cemetery. One day, on Sunday, I heard shooting at about 11 o'clock in the morning. Half an hour or so later a girl appeared. Pale, and bearing little resemblance to a child, she seemed to be mere skin and bones. I had never seen anything like it. She was 11 years old. She threw her arms around Mother Superior's neck and said:

– The Germans have just killed my papa and mama. Sister, you'll be my mother now!'[47]

The first organized attempts to rescue Jewish children were made by the workers of Warsaw Council's Welfare Department, the Main Welfare Council and some underground organizations. The task of the children's welfare department, operating within the framework of Warsaw's Social Welfare department, was directing and sending homeless Polish children to the appropriate establishments. However, this area of work was secretly extended to include Jewish children also. Jan Dobraczyński, the head of the Children's Welfare department at that time, writes:

> Very early on – right after the ghetto was closed – the question of Jewish children was raised in the department. A number of Jewish families had remained outside the ghetto. The parents usually hid separately from the children. Then when rumours began to spread among the Jews inside the ghetto that the Jewish population was to be murdered, many families began to try to get their children out of the ghetto and to find a place with Poles for them. We were faced with the problem of what to do with the dozens of Jewish children, their numbers growing by the hundred.
>
> Officially, we could not concern ourselves with them. A Pole who helped Jews could be sure if the 'crime' was discovered, he would be killed . . . Individual welfare workers got around this regulation by drawing up false papers. . . .
>
> But the problem continued to grow. The number of Jewish children needing help grew daily. The sporadic actions of individual workers could lead to a catastrophe of unforeseeable consequences and extent should the Germans ever discover that records had been forged.
>
> One day my ladies, that is to say the group of social workers in the department came to me concerning this affair. The whole group – to name only Irena Sendlerowa, Jaga Piotrowska, Nonna Jastrzębska, Halina Kozłowska, Janina Barczakowa, Halina Szablakówna – had for some time been carrying out actions on their own initiative aimed at rescuing Jewish children from the ghetto and placing them in a tutelary institute with false papers, after first agreeing the matter with the director of the establishment in question. But their own capabilities were becoming exhausted.
>
> As the son of a former Director of Welfare whose name was still very familiar in all the institutes, especially religious ones, I was very popular with their various directors. When I became their superior – as director of the department – the directors came to me in all sincerity to consult with me on their most difficult problems. I decided to call on their help. I selected those institutes – all religious

> ones – whose heads I could trust completely and laid my case before them quite openly. I said that we would be sending a certain quantum of children to them and they had to know that these were Jewish children who would be coming to them with false records. They would recognize them by the fact that the letter directing them to a particular institute would be signed by myself personally.[48]

Jadwiga Piotrowska has the following to add to the above account:

> . . . in order to place a child in an institute it was necessary to provide false papers, to obtain a forged birth certificate. Letters recommending children to tutelary establishments were issued on the basis of these papers. Records were written up by trusted welfare workers. Many Catholic parishes were willing to provide false certificates, and the letters directing children to various establishments were signed by the director of the department, Jan Dobraczyński. This method proved to be exceptionally successful. Of the several hundred children placed in this way, only two boys were killed. The rest of the children survived the occupation.
>
> The institutes, run mainly by convents, took in every Jewish child without exception, in complete awareness of the danger that threatened them. After all, it could mean a death sentence for the whole convent.[49]

The department also took into its care those children whom it was itself able to rescue from the ghetto, as well as those who managed to get over to the Aryan side themselves. Similar actions were carried out by the Main Welfare Council whose children's department was headed by Aleksandra Dargielowa.

If it were not for the positive attitude of the sisters, if it were not for their completely conscious and responsible consent to take in Jewish children, then the efforts of the welfare workers and the *RGO* would have had no result. Furthermore, the sisters not only accepted the children but also helped actively; if the situation demanded it, they fought for every one of them. 'Alfred B.', says Sr Ludwika,

> was born in Baden-Baden. His mother, née Roder, was German, his father was a Jew. After the murder of his father in the Warsaw Ghetto, Alfred and his mother escaped to the Polish side with no means of living. The mother begged for bread for herself and her child from German soldiers without reporting to the German authorities fearing that they would take her child away to the ghetto. It was thus that an Austrian woman, Marta Harf, met her in the street. Seeing her ill and tearstained, she decided to help her. The

> mother was taken to hospital and Marta Harf took the child in herself. The child's mother died in hospital and before her death she asked Marta Harf to send little Alfred to Baden-Baden. The German authorities refused to agree to this and the boy was to be returned to the ghetto. Marta Harf, an honest and noble woman, did everything she could to save the life of the child.
>
> Finally, I was sent by the Mother Superior to see Marta Harf and there, having acquainted myself with the case, I was to decide whether to bring the boy back with me or not. There was some concern, expressed by director Chaciński from the welfare department, that it might be some ruse on the part of the Germans for Harf had insisted at the department that the child was of pure German blood which prompted one to ask what, then, was he doing in a Polish orphanage?
>
> If I had not taken the boy he would have been forced to return to the ghetto. So I took little seven year old Albert with me to our house in Swirga. It was 1941. The boy stayed with us until the end of the war and then he moved to Grabia near Toruń with a group of other children. He was very clever and went to the Lycée in Aleksandrów and then to engineering school in Radom.[50]

In the summer of 1942, when the fate of Jews in Poland gradually ceased to be a mystery to either the Jews themselves or the Poles, a plan took shape in the Information and Propaganda Bureau of the Home Army High Command to create a special, secret institution which would concern itself with help for the Jews and which would be subsidized by the authorities of the Polish Underground. Prior even to this and as far as their humble means would allow, a small organization called the Polish Renaissance Front (*FOP*), headed by Zofia Kossak, tried to help those escaping from the ghetto. *FOP* got funds to help Jews from contributions given by landowners and the intelligentsia, where Zofia Kossak's personal contacts from pre-war religious and military circles enabled her to acquire papers 'on the side' for those in her care and to find places for women and children behind convent walls. Among other efforts, but mainly thanks to those of Zofia Kossak, on 27 September 1942, a committee was established initially called The Social Committee for Aid to the Jewish People, and for conspiratorial reasons – the Konrad Żegota Committee.

On 4 December the temporary Jewish Aid Committee was transformed into the Council for Jewish Aid. Earlier still, for it was in November 1942, a meeting took place between the representatives of 'Żegota' and Irena Sendlerowa who represented the body of workers from the Welfare Department of the City of Warsaw and Aleksandra Dargielowa who ran the children's section in the *RGO*.

The Council of Help for the Jews recognized from the beginning of its existence that the problem of Jewish children was a major priority demanding special attention. As actual aid for the children was already being organized by both the *RGO* and the Social Welfare department, the *RPŻ*, who supervised the actions of the two organizations above, concentrated its efforts on making contact with the ghetto easier for them and also provided as much financial help as they could.

The activities conducted with the aim of helping the Jews including Jewish children were, for obvious reasons, carried out in conditions of secrecy and conspiracy in Poland. Placing the children in institutions run by sisters depended on the personal contacts of *RGO*, Welfare or *RPŻ* workers with the convents.

A consequence of the principle of conspiracy was the lack of documentation of actions carried out, and a present lack of interest in the problems of forty years ago means that the collaboration of the sisters with the Welfare Department, *RGO* and *RPŻ* in saving Jewish children can only be roughly reconstructed as far as Warsaw and its environs are concerned, or in the case of convents situated further away, only if contacts with Warsaw are obvious as, for example, with Łomża or Turkowice. It is possible, however, that the admittance of Jewish children into convents in other towns operated according to similar principles. For example, the Sisters of the Sacred Heart and the Felician sisters remember the welfare provisions in Przemyśl:

> There was a Magdalena S. who had been sent by the Welfare. She was nine years old and did not participate at all in religious instruction along with the other children. Children were prepared for their first Communion there. And then the girl admitted that she was a Jewess and her name was Greta Sirberg. Her parents in Lwów, seeing the danger, managed to get papers for her and put her on a train to Przemyśl; they themselves perished. In Przemyśl she found the Welfare and they directed her to the sisters.[51]

Sr Ligoria Grenda (Order of the Sacred Heart), says: 'I too witnessed an incident where a fourteen year old girl reported to the *RGO* saying she was lost and asking for help – she was directed to the orphanage. Later it turned out that she was Jewish.'[52]

It is impossible to say whether or not the *RGO* and Welfare workers in Przemyśl were aware that these were Jewish children. And even if they were, we do not know if their actions were the result of individual decisions or the realization of some common outlined programme of help for Jewish children. Both Sr Eliza, a Sister of Nazareth, and Sr Emilia, an Oblate Sister maintain that it was the Welfare who sent children to their institutes in Częstochowa. At the Seraphile Sisters' in Drohobycz '... Jewish children were not officially taken in, they were abandoned or brought by someone from the Welfare committee anonymously and without registration cards.'[53]

From the sources I have consulted so far, it appears that Jewish children directed by the *RGO*, *RPŻ* and Welfare departments were taken in by at least the following orders: the Albertines, Sisters of the Order of St. Elizabeth, The Oblates, the Felicians, the Franciscans of the Family of Mary, the Samaritan Sisters, the Seraphites, the *Służebniczki Starowiejskie*, the Grey Sisters, the Grey Ursulines, the Ursulines of the Union of Rome, the Resurrectionist Sisters, the Sisters of Nazareth.

Nuns in Poland who actively took part in the opposition movement helping partisans and underground organizations, occasionally mention Jewish children who came to them as a result of conspiratorial connections. Here, for example, is the account given by Maria Rumińska:

> During the years of the Nazi occupation, as a member of the underground organization *ŻWŻ-AK*, I tried, as far as I was able given the material resources available to me, to help the forsaken and unfortunate people whom the occupier had deprived of their families and means of survival, in particular children and the aged. During the period I made contacts with the Warsaw ghetto. I helped those wretched people, supplying them with food and medicine, but I cared especially for the children. I was helped in this work by the convents with great sacrifice and self-abnegation. And particularly by those nearest Warsaw, the Służebniczki Sisters from the Convent of the Immaculate Conception of the Blessed Virgin Mary in Czersk on the Vistula, who ran an orphanage where children from the Warsaw Ghetto found shelter and loving care. Sr Syksta acted as the link between myself and the convent. I kept the children rescued from the ghetto in my flat at 17 Poznańska Street until Sr Syksta came to collect them and take them to the orphanage.[54]

It is difficult to ascertain looking at this account or that given by Sr Syksta, whether Maria Rumińska rescued Jewish children because those were the instructions of the parent cell of the *AK*, or perhaps unaware of that, she was, for example, another link in the newly-established *RPŻ*. But this last is contradicted by the fact that Rumińska handed over her last Jewish child to the sisters in 1943. This would indicate that the work undertaken by her ceased as a result of loss of contact with the now completely isolated Warsaw Ghetto.

Now, no one will ever find out how many similar actions were undertaken independently by *AK* cells or other organizations. No one will ever determine the circumstances surrounding the admittance by convents of Jewish children sent there via this route.

When taking in these children, were the sisters always aware of their background? No. There are doubtless many whose genealogy is not known to this day. A Resurrectionist sister talks, among others, of 'the mother of Janka Kowalska who, when visiting her, made the sign of the cross on her forehead – she also entreated her to do everything just as her Catholic girl friends did. Janka went to mass with the rest of them and took Holy Communion – she had not been christened. It was not until after her mother had been killed and according to the wishes she had earlier expressed that Janka told her housemistress about herself.'[55] And according to Sr Roberta: 'If a child was not particularly striking in any way, if it was not circumcised, then we did not even know it was a Jewish child. I had a little blond boy in my group. No one, not even I, knew that he was Jewish. After the war a Jew appeared to collect the child with a complete set of clothes for him (they were the right size!) and said it was his son. To prove it, he described the scar the boy had on his body. The child left with his father.'[56] In some orders, the Franciscan Missionaries of Mary, for example, the sisters were quite uninterested in the children's racial background.

Psychologically, the situation was easier for the sisters if they did not know that their wards were Jewish. They could sleep peacefully, they could, if need be, deny the children's Jewish descent with complete conviction. But for the children themselves it was perhaps the most difficult of situations. They were thrown completely onto their own resources. The sisters, unaware of their true background, were not in a position to guarantee them the kind of asylum that their situation might demand. For children whose true descent was revealed at the time of arrival, the sisters usually became confidantes and provided much consolation. Even if the children were still forced to dissemble before the rest of their 'guardians', then the sister at least was someone, the one person before whom they did not need to watch their words, they could be themselves. Those children who were advised to keep their secret, from the sisters too, were denied all this.

T. Berenstein and A. Rutkowski write that 'In some convents Jewish children thus found themselves bearing a double burden of conspiracy: before the occupier and before their guardians.'[57]

The suggestion that the children were forced into this position by the attitude of the sisters has no grounds in the source material. The boy whose father claimed him from Sr Roberta would have been cared for by the Samaritan Sisters even if they had known about his descent. And he was not the only one. Similarly Janka Kowalska – the moment she revealed her secret to the sister it had no meaning. In my opinion, the children were forced into this double conspiracy by the mistrust of their parents. The war and the cruelty they had experienced had shaken their faith in people to the point where they felt it was safe to trust no one. Even the sisters. Apart from that, in the case of religious Jews, their unwillingness to christen their children played a not trivial role.

Jewish children were taken in primarily by those convents whose sisters ran educational or fostering establishments: orphanages, nurseries, boarding schools. Children were also left at convents where the sisters did not care specifically for children and they were usually sent on to the nearest convent-run children's institution or, if conditions allowed, they were kept and hidden in the convents they had originally come to. At the Carmelites of the Child of Jesus in Sosnowiec, little Tela, a Jewish girl, began the 'Babies House'. The sisters farmed out the children, especially the very little ones, to Polish families as the sisters did not have the facilities to care for them properly.

Payment to cover the children's stay at convents was equally dependent upon the type of activity the sisters of a given convent were normally engaged in, as upon the nature of the circumstances surrounding the child's arrival. Boarding schools, and a few orphanages, demanded the normal fee, although in the case of Jewish children who very often had no one to pay for them, the sisters often made an exception. Maria Szymańska whose niece was cared for by the Resurrectionist Sisters at the school they ran writes that none of the parents of Polish girls '. . . despite the constant threat of danger which hung over the convent, took their child away. Some paid enough to cover two children to pay for those who were being sheltered there. From time to time, very irregularly, insignificant amounts of money would arrive for Jasia, I don't know from what source. The sisters occasionally received discreet gifts from people of good will.'[58]

At the Resurrectionists in Lwów, a doctor, a Jewess, leaving her two sons in the care of the sisters '. . . left some very small sum as it was all she had'. In intermittent cases and only when the parents personally placed their children in convents, would the sisters receive money for the child's keep. This occurred more often at the time the child was reclaimed, after the war. The parents, overjoyed at finding that their son or daughter was alive, offered the sisters what they could, whatever they were able to afford. Leather and lengths of cloth – unusually valuable at that time as the sisters recall – were received by the Albertines and in Klimontów Sandomierski '. . . a child's father rewarded the institute with a sum of money, placing it in the hands of Sr Maria Herman, the director of the orphanage.'[59]

Rewards were not always accepted. Sr Ludwika Małkiewicz writes: 'Ruth's parents survived by hiding in Warsaw's Praga district. After the war they wanted to give us the rest of the money they had left in return for saving the child's life. The Mother Superior would accept nothing, so then they wanted to give the money to me – of course, I did not take it either.'[60]

But a decided majority of Jewish children were taken in with no provision for their keep, which the sisters attempted to raise with the help of donations from charitable institutes or gifts received from collections.

'The parents of Anita and Rysio were Orthodox Jews, believers, and well educated. One of our older wards who worked in a factory in the ghetto which produced woollen articles, maintained contact with Hanka's family. As far as our remaining wards are concerned. I know nothing as the Welfare department gave me no information beyond the fact that they were orphans' says Sr Augustyna.[61] A similar situation was encountered in almost all the houses. The sisters did not always know the details of their wards' social backgrounds. In principle, it is easiest to ascertain the social background of children who found shelter in boarding schools run by nuns. These schools, one should add, were of a very high standard. Mother Andrzeja Górska says: 'The children staying at Milanówek came mainly from intellectual families. Perhaps because it was a private establishment of a high standard and, like the summer colonies, it charged fees.'[62] Of the children hidden by the Order of the Immaculate Conception one sister says – 'The children staying with us came to us via conspiratorial cells and were from intellectual circles: the children of manufacturers, industrialists, scholars.'[63] Similarly Sister Amabilis regarding the girls at the Nazareth Sisters' Warsaw school: 'They came most often from intellectual, mixed families.'

As regards the rest of the children, those from orphanages, nurseries, hidden in the convents individually or in small groups, it seems sensible to employ a criterion of age, that is, to distinguish those children who could talk from those who had not yet begun to do so.

> In the town of Luboml there lived three sisters who worked wherever they could during the war in order to earn a living. The wife of the local miller, a Jewess, was hiding from the Germans. It was about 1942. In the autumn she had to leave the town to avoid being caught. She could not easily run away together with her child – a two-year-old girl – without risking both her own life and that of the child. So she hid the child in some bushes. The housekeeper of the local parish priest happened to hear the child crying. She took the girl and brought her back to the priest's house. In the evening the priest came to the sisters with the plea that they should take the child in and care for her. The sisters willingly did so. After considering the consequences that threatened them for hiding a Jewish child, they tried to find a way around the difficulties of the situation. One of the sisters began to teach the child Polish and the simplest knowledge about God. As the child was developed beyond her years and already spoke quite a lot of Yiddish, the sisters were worried that she would betray herself in the presence of strangers.
>
> The girl quickly learnt many Polish words and a short prayer. On the advice of the village soltys, a pious man who practised his faith, the sisters reported the child to the police, taking advantage of the parish pilgrimage when parents often lost their children.

> The sisters dressed the child and took her to the appropriate offices. In the office a German soldier sat at a desk with a portrait of Hitler hanging on the wall behind him. During the sisters' conversations with the soldier, the child, pointing at the portrait, said: 'Oh, it's God!' The soldier heard this and exclaimed that she could not possibly be a Jewish child as she had mentioned God in Polish. He advised the sister to announce the fact that the child had been found in the newspaper, and if no one claimed her to put her up for adoption.'[64]

The account above is the only one which mentions a child who could not speak Polish at the time of coming to the convent. The girl came from a typically Jewish background where Yiddish was spoken at home. In some accounts, though they are extremely rare, one can find statements suggesting that not all Jewish children knew Polish particularly well, or that their knowledge was not sufficient to allow them to use Polish freely beyond the convent. The Franciscans of the Family of Mary in Lwów '. . . at Kurkowa Street, hid a little girl of typically semitic features under a barrel during a search. If discovered, she was to pretend to be dumb.'[65] This was often the only way, for adult Jews too, to conceal their slightly incorrect Polish.

Of the Jewish children hidden by Polish sisters during the last war who could talk at the moment of arriving at the convent, almost one hundred per cent spoke perfectly correct Polish; they came therefore, from homes where the Polish language was generally used. From families – if a good knowledge of the Polish language can be accepted as a criterion of assimilation – who were also assimilated.

From reports from orphanages to which the majority of children came via the Social Welfare, the *RGO* or *RPŻ*, the prevalent opinion was that these were children coming from families of the intelligentsia. In Chomotów '. . . children of Jewish descent, making up about 10% of the total, came for the most part from assimilated families of the intelligentsia. They differed markedly from the rest of the children, who came from a completely different milieu, generally from the margins of society.'[66] Similarly at the orphanage in Częstochowa where 'Jewish children spoke Polish. Those who came to us came from educated families. They were of school age and were aware of their critical situation.'[67]

Among the children who came to the sisters themselves or who were directed to them by Poles, one can find the children of tradesmen or craftsmen. 'During the war a little Jewish girl came to us, her mother supplied our household management school in Lublin with fruit'[68] and Maria Klein who was at the Sacred Heart convent in Przemyśl writes: 'I came from a non-religious Jewish family, my father had been a member of the *PPS* for many years and was a tailor by trade.'[69] But even in this group the majority of children generally came from educated families. Very often doctors, vets, lawyers and dentists are mentioned.

It might appear that due to the religious character of the orphanages run by the sisters, the greatest percentage of children in hiding came from Catholic families of Jewish descent. The sources do not bear this out. Problems with papers and legalization of the Jewish children's residence indicate that a definite majority of the children used false birth certificates, or the sisters had to find certificates for them. They were not christened either. The children's behaviour or their confidences often indicated that they had been brought up in Jewish, religious families.

In the second group of children, those who could not yet talk, the chances of survival were even better. It is also more difficult, even roughly speaking, to ascertain their social background. The children themselves were unable to reveal anything about their families and moreover in this group the majority were children who had been abandoned, found by the sisters or brought to them by random Poles. Finally, it is even difficult to calculate how many of the children abandoned and left with the sisters during the last war were Jewish, as only in the case of boys who had been circumcised could there be any certainty.

Generally, Jewish children taken in by convents came mainly from assimilated, educated families who sometimes did not practise the Jewish religion. This situation arose as a result of the realities of the holocaust and the circumstances surrounding the rescue of Jews in Poland. I think at least a few elements were important in saving Jewish children coming from these circles. A basic and essential element was the knowledge of the Polish language and contact with Poles; these conditions were fulfilled almost exclusively by polonized Jews, almost always from the intelligentsia. As parents, they had the greatest chance of finding help for their children. A second, and not trivial aspect of the issue, was the psychological possibilities of polonized Jews. It is well known that opinions prevailing in the ghettos regarding the attitude of Poles to Jews were generally negative, regardless of whether there were actual grounds for them or not. Izabela Czajka-Stachowicz who was saved by a blacksmith writes '. . . there in the ghetto they said: here there is death and there also is death – you will not escape death on the "Aryan" side, the Poles will hand you over to the Germans first.'[70] Polonized Jews were more resistant to this kind of neurosis for the simple reason that they knew Poles. Parents who decided themselves to leave their children in the care of Polish nuns must surely have had their own opinions as to the latter – positive to the extent that they trusted them. I think that the process of Polonization must also have included something in the form of 'infection' with the Polish distrust of the Germans. A distrust which caused Jewish families to search for ways of escape early enough to mean that escape for their children was still a possibility.

The admission of Jewish children into the houses of women's religious communities in Poland from 1939–1945 was presided over, throughout its course, by the sign of chance, so to speak. The interested parties – the Jews as well as the religious communities – did not set up any organization or institution which would co-ordinate, work out or agree the principles and conditions of admitting Jewish children.

The sisters themselves functioned in an unorganized fashion in Poland, that is to say, they did not have a central authority which could have maintained contact between communities on a national level. Furthermore, the political realities of occupied Poland excluded the possibility of a public declaration on the part of any community concerning the rescue of Jewish children, as this would have been tantamount to incurring the death sentence of the sisters as well as of the children they had taken in.

Ringelblum writes of the reasons why the Jews left the question of placing their children in Polish convents to chance:

> It is worth remembering, for historical reasons, a project to organize the placing of several hundred Jewish children in convents according to the following conditions: children of ten years and above would be accepted, the fee for a year would be 8,000 zloties, paid in advance, and the children were to have papers and evidence of their residence in the country so that they could be claimed after the war. This project was discussed in Jewish circles and met with the opposition of both Orthodox and certain nationalist circles. Objections were put forward that the children would be christened and would be lost for ever to the Jewish nation. It was argued that future generations would accuse them of not keeping up to the mark and of not teaching our children *kiddush hashem* (martyrdom of faith), in the name of which our forefathers died in the flames of the Spanish Inquisition. The advice of social activists on this issue did not lead to a unanimous conclusion, no resolution was adopted, which left the Jewish parents with a free hand.[71]

The condition governing the admission of a Jewish child into the house of a female religious community in Poland during 1939–45 was its fortuitous arrival at the convent gates. This is the picture presented by the sources which I have listed. Perhaps I will come across others in the future which will allow me to extend its limits, bringing in new important elements – or which will change it completely. In this sense, the question remains an open one.

NOTES

1 T. Frącek, 'Zgromadzenie sióstr Franciszkanek Rodziny Maryi w latach 1939–1945', from: *Kościół Katolicki na ziemiach Polski w czasie II wojny światowej*, vol. 11, p. 288.
2 Related by Mother Andrzej Górska, Grey Ursulines, private records.
3 Related by Sister Maria Ena, of the Order of the Immaculate Conception, private records.
4 Related by Sister Aleksa Żółtek, Order of St Joseph, private records.
5 Related by Sister Ludwika Małkiewicz, Order of St Elizabeth, private records.
6 Related by Sister Jolanta Zienkiewicz, Franciscan Missionaries of Mary, private records.
7 Sister Magdalena Kaczmarzyk, 'Pomoc udzielana Żydom przez Zgromadzenie Sióstr Albertynek w czasie II wojny światowej' (Kraków, 1961), typescript, from: AGZ, Albertine Sisters.
8 Related by Sister Apolonia Nienałltowska, Passionist, private records.
9 Related by Sister Gregoria Klaczyńska, *Służebniczki Pleszewskie*, private records.
10 Sister Joanna Chrostek, 'Przeżycia wojenne domu zakopiańskiego', manuscript 1946, p. 13, from: AGZ, Grey Ursulines.
11 E. Japol 'Zgromadzenie sióstr św. Michała Archaniola' a dissertation at KUL, p. 278.
12 Sisters and children from orphanages which found themselves incorporated into the *Reich* were in a particularly difficult situation. From Autumn 1939, the Germans began liquidating or resettling those orphanages and the children were subjected to a detailed 'racial examination' with the aim of picking out the 'nordics' from among them who were then ear-marked for germanization. The Sisters did not manage to get all the Polish children through these selections successfully. Only occasionally during resettlements was it possible to smuggle out and save Jewish children. Usually, however, the sisters were helpless as, for example, in the case of the Passionist sisters when, during the liquidation in February 1941 of an orphanage for small children in Płock '. . . the Germans took a Jewish boy of around seven years to the hospital because he had some skin complaint. Apparently they shot him.' Related by Mother Stanisława Żebrowska, Passionist Sisters, private.
13 Related by Sister Amabilis Filipowicz, Sisters of Nazareth, private records.
14 Related by Sister Alina Wilczyńska, from: AGZ, Daughters of Mary Immaculate.
15 L. Mistecka, 'Życie i działalność sióstr Zmartychwstanek w okupowanej Polsce', doctoral dissertation, KUL, p. 259.
16 Related by Sister Barbara Bojanowska, Grey Ursulines, private records.
17 Related by Fr Michał Kot, private records.
18 Related by Sister Maria Sawicka, Franciscans of the Family of Mary, private records.
19 Related by Sister Cecylia Solecka, p. 59, from: AGZ, Sisters of the Name of Jesus.
20 O. Abramczuk, 'Zgromadzenie Matki Bożej Miłosierdzia w latach 1939–1945', from: *Kościół Katolicki na ziemiach Polski w czasie II wojny światowej*, vol. 10 (Warsaw, 1981), p. 186.
21 Related by Sister Emilia Stopka, Oblate Sisters, private records.
22 'Pomoc udzielana dzieciom i osobom dorosłym pochodzenia semickiego przez siostry św. Wincentego à Paulo', typescript, from: APZ, Grey Sisters.
23 Related by Sister Szczęsna, Sisters of Nazareth, private records.
24 Sister Magdalena Kaczmarzyk, op. cit.
25 Related by Sister Ludwika Małkiewicz, Order of St Elizabeth, private records.

26 A. Słomczyński, *Dom ks. Boduena, 1939–1945* (Warsaw, 1975), p. 117.
27 'Pomoc udzielana dzieciom i osobom dorosłym pochodzenia semickiego przez siostry św. Wincentego à Paulo', typescript, from: APZ, Grey Sisters.
28 Sister Magdalena Kaczmarzyk, op. cit.
29 Ibid.
30 Related by Sister Benedykty Biedroń, from: AGZ, Sisters of the Holy Spirit.
31 Related by Sister Michaeli Bieńkowska, Pasterki, private records.
32 'Pomoc udzielana dzieciom i osobom dorosłym pochodzenia semickiego przez siostry św. Wincentego à Paulo', typescript, from: APZ, Grey Sisters.
33 Related by Maria Klein from Israel, private records.
34 A. Umiński, 'Album z rewolwerem' (Warsaw, 1984), p. 18.
35 Related by Sister Maria Stella Trzecieska in: *Ten jest z ojczyzny mojej* (Kraków, 1969), p. 242.
36 Sister Magdalena Kaczmarzyk, op. cit.
37 Ibid.
38 'Pomoc udzielana dzieciom i osobom dorosłym pochodzenia semickiego przez siostry św. Wincentego à Paulo', typescript, from: APZ, Grey Sisters.
39 Related by Sister Jolanta Zienkiewicz, Franciscan Missionaries of Mary, private records.
40 Related by Sister Zofia Makowska, Franciscan Missionaries of Mary, private records.
41 The leaders of the Third German *Reich* foresaw, in their plans, the germanization of the occupied stretches of Eastern Europe, which also included a plan to create a so-called German settlement around Zamość. According to Himmler's recommendations, from 6–25 November 1941 the Polish population from seven villages near Zamość was resettled, and on 27 November 1942 a programme of mass resettlement was begun of Poles from the Zamość, Hrubieszów and Tomaszów regions. The Poles thus evacuated and concentrated in a camp in Zamość were divided into four groups by the Germans. The first two, recognized to be of 'racial value' (of German descent or with some German blood), were to be germanized. The Poles from the third group were sent to work in Germany, and the fourth group was destined to die in Oświęcim. Children from the third and fourth groups who were less than fourteen years of age were taken from their parents by the Germans – their fate was a tragic one.
42 'Zamojszczyzna w okresie okupacji hitlerowskiej' (Warsaw, 1968), p. 47.
43 Sister Magdalena Kaczmarzyk, op. cit.
44 Related by Sister Zofia Makowska, Franciscan Missionaries of Mary, private records.
45 Related by Rachel, saved by the Josephite Sisters, private records.
46 Related by Sister Czesława Kulpińska, The Servants of Jesus, private records.
47 Related by Sister Maria Sawicka, Franciscan Missionaries of Mary, private records.
48 J. Dobraczyński, *Tylko w jednym życiu* (Warsaw, 1978), pp. 241–247.
49 *Słowo Powszechne*, 19 April 1968.
50 Related by Sister Ludwika Małkiewicz, Order of St Elizabeth, private records.
51 'Zgromadzenie Sióstr św. Feliksa z Kantalicjo w latach 1939–1947', from: *Żeńskie Zgromadzenia Zakonne w Polsce 1939–1947*, vol. 1 (Lublin, 1982), p. 51.
52 Related by Sister Ligoria Grenda, Order of the Sacred Heart, private records.
53 Related by Sister Janina Watychowicz, Order of the Seraphile Sisters, private records.
54 Statement by Maria Rumińska, from: AGZ, *Służebniczki Pleszewskie*.
55 L. Mistecka, op. cit.
56 Related by Sister Roberta Fiedorczuk, Samaritan Sisters, private records.

57 T. Berenstein, A. Rutkowski, 'O ratowaniu Żydów przez Polaków' from: *Biuletyn ŻIH* Nr 35, 1960, p. 33.
58 M. Szymańska, *Byłam tylko lekarzem* (Warsaw, 1979), p. 145–156.
59 Related by Sister Cecylia Solecka, from: AGZ, Sisters of the Name of Jesus.
60 Related by Sister Ludwika Małkiewicz, Order of St Elizabeth, private records.
61 Related by Sister Augustyna Szczepańska, Grey Ursulines, private records.
62 Related by Mother Andrzej Górska, Grey Ursulines, private records.
63 Related by Sister Maria Ena, Order of the Immaculate Conception, private records.
64 Related by Sister Teresa Przystupa, Sisters of St Teresa, private records.
65 T. Frącek, *op. cit.*, p. 291.
66 Related by Helena Kozłowska, in: *Ten jest z ojczyzny mojej* (Kraków, 1969), p. 805.
67 Related by Sister Emilia Stopka, Oblate Sisters, private records.
68 Related by Sister Czesława Kulpińska, Servants of Jesus, private records.
69 Related by Maria Klein from Israel, private records.
70 Izabela Czajka-Stachowicz, *Ocalił mnie kowal* (Warsaw, 1956), p. 23.
71 E. Ringelblum, 'Stosunki polsko-żydowskie', *Biuletyn ŻIH*, no. 29 (1959), p. 39.

PART V

After 1945

25

THE CONTEXTS OF THE SO-CALLED JEWISH QUESTION IN POLAND AFTER WORLD WAR II

Krystyna Kersten and Paweł Szapiro

Any historian seeking a better insight into the nature and dynamics of Polish-Jewish relations after World War II, must force his way through areas which have been distorted for many years by two types of falsehood: lies of silence and lies of word and deed. Both have their causes – great fear and petty cowardice, deep defeatism and everyday opportunism, occasionally feelings of shame, but, all too frequently, purely tactical considerations. When the lie of silence persists too long and its failure to hide the truth becomes evident, the authorities try to prevent their further discrediting in world and national opinion, while the nation, even more sensitive to world opinion, strives also to drown out the voice of its conscience. At this point the silence is shattered. As this change does not usually stem from a love of the truth, but is rather an unwilling concession to avoid opprobium and condemnation, the areas passed over in silence are then deliberately filled with bogus models which project a mystified reality in order to mask the genuine situation. These facades are in fact half-truths based on conveniently selected facts, some unauthenticated and some genuine, manipulated to convey false messages. So that these constructs can perform their camouflaging function effectively, they are set within carefully chosen contexts which permit the clearly pejorative character of even universally condemned views and actions to be concealed, thus making them appear as elements of a higher order.

This mechanism, likely to be a universal one, has been widely applied in the game of appearances played in Poland over the last 40 years, and has allowed the masking of anti-semitism to gain dangerous popularity. Given the thorough discrediting of anti-semitism, negative attitudes towards Jews were forced to seek out contexts that could legitimize and even ennoble existing prejudices, antipathy, hostility, and discrimination. Consequently, cunning collages known to influence public opinion were created; in order to cloak the shameful nakedness of anti-semitism, they had to present themselves as apparently cleansed of racial criteria. Thus, both among the rulers and the ruled, the depiction of Jews exclusively as 'emanations of Jewishness' became, as it were, a taboo subject. Instead, depending on the needs of the moment and on specific opinion-moulding groups, the image of the Jew was linked with other factors conveying something alien or hostile – with communism or anti-communism, with the régime in power or its opponents, with cosmopolitanism, freemasonry or Zionist nationalism. In one way or another, the myth of the Jew – never sufficiently Polish – remained in force.

Another method of diverting attention from the significant presence of anti-semitism has been the institutionalization of official rites designed to furnish proof that sympathy for the memory of the Holocaust victims is still alive. These ceremonies were clearly mere façades, however, for their contents were quite obviously biased, and demonstrated disregard for historical truth. These alibi-creating manoeuvres were orchestrated to convey the message that Polish society's attitudes towards Jews were, on the whole, positive, and that helping Jews and heroic attempts to save them during the Nazi occupation were typical responses. In fact, the propagation of this touched-up image led world opinion to swing to the opposite extreme. Both of these half-truths employed a hackneyed technique: *pars pro toto*, for they focused on the actions of a decided minority, while consigning to oblivion the dominant attitudes of society, in all their complexity.

On the part of the régime, manipulation, both through the use of such contexts and the construction of façades, was, for the most part, a conscious operation, reflecting current political trends. For society, however, these were exercises in self-deception – defensive reactions aroused by a strong feeling that the nation's existence was threatened, consequently promoting an even stronger need for national self-affirmation. The label 'Polish anti-semites' was incompatible with the cliché 'Poland – inspiration of the world'.

We touch here on one of the most important factors in the vicious circle of Polish-Jewish relations. For historical reasons, a feeling of threat has been so thoroughly encoded in each of these peoples that the sensation of being threatened remains even when real danger begins to vanish. This, in turn, arouses psychologically understandable defensive reactions, the evolution and consequences of which could prove to be even more sinister than their initial sources: there is less and less room for any rational appraisal of the situation, and more and more for irrational thinking, dominated by aggressive tendencies, which perceive evil or hostility in all that hinders the fulfilment of the psychological needs of the individual, group or nation. History shows that in unfavourable circumstances, populations sharing the same homeland – especially populations so battered by fate as the Jewish and Polish – almost inevitably fall into insidious traps which direct defensive reactions against one another rather than against the threat itself. The intensity and near fatalism of these reactions, so often aggressive, are clearly displayed in the interaction of old and new aspects of the Jewish question in Poland over the last four decades. These arose through the overlapping and mutual reinforcement of several causes of conflict: first the burden of archetypes in how Poles and Jews looked at each other, still functioning in the realms of both the sacred and the profane; second, the direct and indirect consequences of the German occupation; and finally Poland's situation after the Second World War.

Let us review the expectations of Poles and Jews at the end of the war in the face of the tragic and antagonistic roles allotted them by history. Poland emerged from the war subjugated, with a régime imposed on her, and one which the majority of society considered to be alien and threatening to the nation's spiritual existence. What is more, even with their glorious record of resistance against the Germans, the nation's sons now found themselves persecuted by a new régime. Fratricidal struggle was the hallmark of the era, claiming new victims. Thus victory over the Germans did not bring Polish misery to an end; liberation from the nightmare of Nazi occupation did not lead to the anticipated sovereignty. The programme of rebuilding the country after the ravages of war did not eliminate an almost universal frustration which was deepened by a feeling of isolation, already familiar to the participants in the Warsaw Uprising, accompanied by disillusionment with the Western allies, a feeling growing since Yalta. Finally, there was anxiety, even fear, in the face of everything that came from the East, because of a series of painful experiences stretching back to 1939. It is not surprising, then, that the imperative of biological and spiritual survival and of the defence of national identity were instilled into the behaviour of Poles, and that the call for resistance, variously conceived, remained alive, and was directed against everything seen as subjugation and, consequently, against those perceived as its perpetrators.

The expectations of Polish Jews, who owed their salvation largely to the Soviet Union where they had spent the war, or who had survived in Poland – hidden by Poles or with the help of so-called Aryan papers – to be later liberated by the Soviet army, could not possibly have been the same. Nor were different expectations held only by those who decided relatively early to emigrate. Of those Jews wishing to remain in Poland, many maintained the belief, dating from before the war or from during it, that a system proclaiming social justice would finally end racial and ethnic discrimination.

Others, at first far from being communists – and there were many – maintained the belief that the introduction of a communist régime in Poland would eradicate anti-semitism and bring real, not merely formal, equality, and they therefore pushed ideological and political reservations about the new order aside. The memory of bitter and inhuman past experiences and, above all, the shocking discovery that anti-semitism had survived the Holocaust, inclined many of those unwilling or unable to emigrate towards acceptance of the new reality. Some of the slogans propounded by the new régime were welcomed: the cliché of 'reaction' was already functioning, linking all opposition to the authorities with the right, nationalism and anti-semitism. This mystification, which was achieved by including many who approved neither of the new order nor of anti-semitism within the category of so-called 'reaction', proved effective, though not as effective as the stereotype of the 'communist Jew'. Ultimately, these were two, almost contradictory, distortions reflecting the functioning of the same process - namely constructing in the mind a concocted, synthetic image of the enemy. Mystical thinking came into play here, seeking to rationalise the negative feelings produced - of hostility, enmity, aggression - and born of a sense of helplessness in the face of threats towards established values and even towards the security of individuals and society as a whole. The road to making minds captive to the logic of higher reasons lay wide open, reasons meant to justify hostile archetypes and contemporary prejudices and, furthermore, to absolve them of their ominous consequences. Neither the adherents, nor the opponents of the new system managed to avoid this road. Mutual Polish-Jewish relations also failed to avoid it, and, paradoxically, became even more sensitive than hitherto. This worried those Jews who at that time were not susceptible to any propaganda, and who had decided to rebuild their lives in Poland despite the painful conviction that their feelings towards the country were not reciprocated. All they could hope was that the mutual resentments sustaining anti-semitism and feelings of alienation would gradually fade.

Thus the expectations of the majority of Polish Jews did indeed differ from those of the majority of Poles, even given the heterogeneity of the group classed as Jewish. After all, these were people of diverse beliefs, whose ethnic, religious, and cultural links with the Jewish world were at times strong, at times weak, and often extremely tenuous; at times they were awakened only as a manifestation of normal human dignity, or as a community spirit among victims of discrimination. When reference is made to Jews in this essay, we have in mind all Jews: from those Poles of Jewish descent so closely fused with Polishness that the word assimilation understates the strength of this tie, to Jews who tried to preserve a separate ethnic, religious, or cultural identity in Poland, their homeland.

What, then, were the hopes of the Jews who had survived? They believed, desired to believe, and, indeed, had to believe, that after the inhuman experiences of Nazism, endured by Poles and Jews together, they would live normally, as Poles or as Polish Jews, without the imposed, or at times adopted, handicap of Jewishness, without ostracism, of whatever kind. The death-knell of anti-semitism - this was to be the posthumous triumph of Polish Jewry. Too often the opposite was the case:

despite these natural human expectations, the few who escaped annihilation met less with rejoicing and welcome from their surroundings than with indifference, antipathy and even hostility. This hostility was on occasion vented in atrocities, not only in the infamous Kielce pogrom. Of course, it would be simplest to attribute such acts of violence exclusively to the barbarity bequeathed by the war, to the kindling of provocation or to civil war. But it must not be forgotten that at this time it was not rare for Jews to be killed by Poles just because they were Jews.

This atmosphere, in which Poles and Jews harboured different hopes, produced the scenario for the future drama. The régime, perceived by Poles as a hostile one, seemed to Jews to safeguard their lives and to offer the chance for equal rights. Past and present meshed to produce a situation boding ill for Polish-Jewish relations. Logically, this would seem absurd. The virtual total annihilation of Polish Jews removed from the Polish scene a numerically significant community which had expressed its distinctiveness through its separate religion, speech, dress and behaviour. Generally speaking, then, the previous bases for antagonism and antipathy – even the economic ones – that existed before 1939, had disappeared. While it is true that Nazi methods evoked condemnation, these persecutors of Poles and Jews alike had practically fulfilled the programme or dreams of Polish anti-semites – Poland was well-nigh free of Jews. Attempts to revive the Jewish community in 1945–48 failed. Most of the survivors left Poland during the first five years after the war.

But, as the old saying goes: when reason sleeps, ghosts walk. Millions of Polish Jews had perished, yet the Jewish question in Poland persisted. New post-war antagonisms, reinforced by different experiences during the war, overlapped with everlasting irrational prejudices and phobias. The common martyrdom of Jews and Poles proved to be less significant than the difference in fates assigned to them in the occupier's policies. These had shown a different intention, scale, and timetable in persecuting Poles and Jews. The argument over which side had suffered the most victims and martyrs was a new, tragic component in the Polish-Jewish entanglements, clouding mutual perceptions and affecting mutual relations. Furthermore, the stereotype imposed by the Nazi racist selection criteria was absorbed into the consciousness of all living through the day-to-day realities of occupation. Even with full awareness of the criminality of these criteria and with their complete rejecting in theory, it was difficult to ignore them, since they defined the fate of individuals: they divided society into those who were condemned to immediate execution and those for whom this sentence was suspended, allowing them to live for a while. Their different fates left deep, traumatic scars in the consciousness of both Poles and Jews. Jewish survivors not only remembered that some Poles had maintained contact with them, helped them and rescued them, at a risk to their own lives, while others had blackmailed them or betrayed them to the

Germans. They also remembered their fear, not only of the Germans but also of their 'Aryan' fellow citizens. But what persisted above all was the consciousness of the indifference during the war of most of those around them, sometimes coloured with sympathy, but often with antipathy. The position of the Jews was too dreadful for them to afford the luxury of objective reasoning which would enable them to see that these embittering attitudes and disillusioning behaviour did not stem entirely from anti-semitism, but also from the intensification of terror, which was far greater in Poland than in the occupied western countries. Feelings of abandonment and isolation dominated everything, together with the perception that the dying Jewish population was separated from the Polish population by a wall built of more than just bricks.

The memory of this isolation was to persist for years, decreasing and increasing its impact, depending on circumstances. These feelings were a reminder that in conditions of terror, both the awareness of fellow victims and solidarity with them can awaken and grow, but that they can also fail to be awakened and may even die out. The consciousness will also grow, that in those inhuman times, moral norms and codes of behaviour were affected not only by reprehensible motives - prejudices and hostility, indifference or callousness - but simply because fate forced a person to choose between alternatives all of which involved a decision or action which was both human and inhuman and did not fit into the natural realms of human imagination. Keeping faith with these norms and codes, a readiness to provide concrete aid to save a life, sometimes had to be limited - in the face of cruel reality - to the symbolic sphere, to showing feelings of brotherhood and solidarity. Such a position cannot, of course, replace attempts to save lives, but it can protect the condemned from feelings of isolation and apathy, and those to whom they look so desperately for help, from the accusation of indifference, callousness and passivity. Moreover, it may create an atmosphere mobilising both the victims and the potential rescuers to overcome the fatalistic approach of which the practical consequences cannot be underestimated. But even this position was far from universal. And so the 'sin of abstention' became one of the stigmas of that time, although - later on - this designation happened to be unjustly extended to all acts of abstention, some of them unavoidable. The truths of these times are thus complicated and multidimensional: they explain much, allow much to be understood, but they do not absolve everything. They indicate that human lack of imagination does not make it easier to understand the dilemmas of the human fate of others, that it does not enable one to overcome mutual misunderstanding. Once again it appears that one's own hell and that of others, like one's own truth and that of others, are weighed on different scales.

The memory of Poles after the war was dominated by the consciousness of their own martyrdom and of the dramatic history of the resistance movement. Reminders of the awkward role played by mostly passive witnesses to the Holocaust were an unwelcome disturbance to this image. This troubling awareness was not uncommonly relieved by evoking a myth portraying Jews as the bearers of evil, a myth rooted in the Christian tradition, which was later adopted by the ideology of extreme nationalism. Even during the war this myth fed on every convenient argument, whether valid or deceptive; for example, reports on the pro-Soviet behaviour of national minorities, including Jews, to the east of the Bug in 1939–41. After the war, this myth was nurtured by the highly visible presence of Jews in the ruling apparatus, especially in the security services, and even by those supporting or acceding to the new order proclaimed by the communists.

The image of Jews as internal enemies was thus strengthened in society, this time by attributing to them the role of communist oppressors of the Polish nation – all the more for being concealed in Polish national costume. With the passage of time, the authorities cynically accepted this argument in their attempt to direct the authentic aspirations of society into the course of anti-semitic resentment to suit one of the subsequent tactical twists of the régime. It was used against persons of Jewish origin, first to settle scores within the establishment, and later, for many years, in the struggle with the opposition. Knowing that the fundamental contexts for the Jewish question and its dynamics since 1945 have been determined by the inimical relationship between the régime and society puts the problem of anti-semitism into concrete historic perspective and reminds us that the so-called Jewish question in Poland, is after all, also a Polish question. It is this political context that caused the widening vicious circle of mutual Polish-Jewish resentments, a rationalisation of mutual prejudices which many Poles and Polish Jews were unable to free themselves from completely.

Let us survey the complicated dynamics of these contexts over the past four decades.

In the first decade after the war, the régime, following its doctrinal premises, declared war against anti-semitism and employed accusations of anti-semitism to discredit its ideological and political opponents. As a matter of fact, this policy unintentionally served to strengthen in public opinion the linking of Jews and the authorities as a threat against Polishness. Things got even worse as a consequence of the authorities' attempts to camouflage the background of people of Jewish descent who occupied responsible positions at various levels of the administration.

The world of façades constructed with great care in this first decade according to doctrinal and political demands, and meant to mask reality, collapsed with the system's first crisis in 1956. Tendencies surfaced which expressed differences in views among both the ruling élite and in society. These were to become a permanent element in Polish life for some time to come. The Jewish question did not escape this process. Part of society was aware of frequent anti-semitic occurrences in Poland, but always saw this as a reprehensible phenomenon; others, also condemning anti-semitism, denied its existence as a social phenomenon, especially as in many strata of society and among some generations it was not at all noticeable. Another, quite notable, sector of society still displayed vital, though repressed, resentment and prejudices. The more they had previously been suppressed, the more actively they erupted at a moment of crisis for the régime. This was helped by the fact that many Jews held important political positions, which *eo ipso* made them jointly responsible for the actions which society demanded should be called to account. Simultaneously, among the ruling élite, which was divided over how to react to threats to its authority, there emerged a group propagating nationalistic and populistic slogans. At first timidly, and then more and more blatantly, this group gave these slogans anti-semitic overtones. Proposals to eliminate Jews from government were advanced to prove the authorities' national character and divert attention from fundamental problems, and to saddle Jews with the blame for all past evils, thereby freeing the communist party from responsibility.

In 1956 such tendencies were not allowed to be voiced openly, but they were observed by society, in which a new movement to defend sovereignty, truth, and freedom began to take shape. This was composed partly of workers, but at its heart was an important section of the political, intellectual, and cultural élite, which included many Jews, who had diverse reactions to the deep ideological and political crisis. For various reasons, some Jews acknowledged this crisis as a sign of the bankruptcy of the idea that Poland could have a future for them, and they emigrated; around 40,000 people left Poland at that time. Others continued to identify in a general sense with the order introduced in Poland in 1945, or saw in the Polish October either a reflection of the proper direction of change, or a necessary, but palliative cosmetic operation. Still others, aligning themselves with the aspirations of society, opted to merge even more with it; and even if some of them had until then maintained close ties with the régime, they sooner or later broke them and gradually moved to definite opposition. As a result, a new cliché appeared in the 60s: Jews as enemies of the Polish People's Republic, opponents of socialism, sowers of discord. Alongside this cliché a renovated stereotype was propagated of Jews as national nihilists, alien to Polishness and the mainstays of Stalinism.

In 1968 these new and revived make-believe constructs which had served to mask xenophobic and basically racist attitudes, employing descent criteria instead of self-identification, and which were propagated with some success by one of the factions in power in the mid-1960s, revealed their spiritual kinship to the Nuremberg laws. The authorities, disturbed by processes under way in society undermining their authority, welcomed an option to appeal to anti-Jewish resentment. This time the strategy was immediately successful: Jews were attacked and the framework of society was disturbed. Society was disoriented, intimidated and divided, and remained unaware – with the exception of a few groups – that one of the most important aims of this action was to disarm the nation both morally, and, as later became clear, intellectually. The instigators of this operation anticipated that the attack on Jews would be met in part with passivity, and in part with society's approval, thus helping to divert attention from the real causes of increasing dissatisfaction. And in fact, the resurgence of anti-semitic slogans, coupled with populistic and anti-intellectual appeals, did not disappoint these expectations. This campaign, which did not hesitate to adopt old *ONR* models, reactivated old stereotypes: Jews as Jew-Communists, the Jewish mafia, Jewish freemasons. In addition, a new phantom appeared: the Jew as Zionist. In creating this, the evident and, not only Jewish, welcoming of Israel's success in the Six Day War, had to be suppressed by raising an artificial furore about a supposed fifth column, which had allegedly revealed itself, and was meant to show that Polish Jews considered Israel to be their true homeland.

This hate campaign revived among Jews the seemingly extinct fear felt during the war or even before it. The subsequent purge not only deprived people of their positions or even of the possibility to practise their professions: it also attempted to strip them of their dignity. This led to an exodus of almost 20,000 Jews from Poland who were ultimately reproached merely with being Jewish – the racist key behind this purge could not be hidden, despite attempts at ideological camouflage. The authorities did not hesitate to link the pretence of voluntary emigration with the supposed repudiation of the Polish homeland, although it was clear that many of the departing Jews would continue to live culturally as Poles, even as *émigrés*. It is difficult to describe the deep grief, outrage and shame of those Poles who fully realised that this was, in fact, expulsion provoked by the authorities; but also that this banishment could never have attained the scale it did, had quite a few social groups not allowed fear, indifference or silent consent to overshadow condemnation of the methods employed.

The emigration following the events of March 1968 virtually completed the removal of Jews from Polish land. In a perverse historical paradox, the Jewish question did not die out, but instead began in subsequent years to acquire a new dimension. March 1968 proved to be a deep-seated, traumatic experience. It was deeply imprinted on the consciousness and subconsciousness of the victims of this ignoble witch-hunt; it affected the consciences of the thousands and the thoughts of the millions who had witnessed it. What is more, in the long run, it took its toll among the hunters and their aides themselves, who later experienced more than one disappointment. It also affected those who were linked with them in various power-relationships and who opportunistically did not oppose but sometimes even helped them in March, not sensing that the odium from their shameful silent cooperation would cling to them for good. The policy of anti-semitism was taught an unequivocal lesson: the Jews departed, but the plagues remained.

The March inheritance accelerated the polarisation of already differentiated positions, expressing not only the mutual antagonism between the authorities and society, but also the divisions within these structures. For these positions to crystallize, a new, historically significant factor had to find its voice: the attempt by society to organize itself, an attempt which emerged increasingly openly for the first time in many years. This process – combined with the need to consider critical world opinion – forced the authorities to shatter the lie of silence, although not immediately.

New contexts for the Jewish question began to function against this background. The façades meant to hide the existence of anti-semitism were constructed with greater and greater calculation, but authentic tendencies of renewal also began to appear more strongly in society, which had had its fill of both the lie of silence and the lie of speech or 'Newspeak'. As far as the régime in general is concerned, the hunters and their aides maintained and continue to maintain the sinister equation created in the 1960s of Jews as eternal enemies of socialist Poland. But at the same time, within the establishment itself, among people who were perhaps genuinely ashamed, but who knew that to maintain their cowardly silence confirmed their joint responsibility for the régime's shameful and unforgettable actions in 1968, aspirations emerged to remove the stigma with which the régime was stamped. This tactical approach won out among the authorities shortly after the crushing of Solidarity, but the measures undertaken were far from truly cathartic. As was true for the authorities' general strategy towards society, actions towards the 'Jewish question' were, and still are, incomplete, inconsistent, and timid. Still fearing open and unequivocal condemnation of the actions of 1968, and still permitting the undisturbed continuation of March discriminatory practices in certain areas, the authorities balance between truth and falsehood.

This policy was expressed in the sudden, almost ostentatious interest shown in the topic of Jews. It is now essential for Poland's rulers that there be much discussion of Jews. They are adopting this policy (not so much *glasnost* as *głośność* [vociferousness]) on an unprecedented scale and a scope that probably astonishes even them. In the new domestic and international situation, the authorities felt forced to present society with truthful and valuable information long denied to it. Thus in the media, in publishing houses and in theatres, products of Jewish culture, both old and contemporary, began to appear more frequently; the viewer, listener, and reader were given the opportunity to get to know the literature, art, and religious and secular customs of a community that for centuries had been a part of the multi-national Republic.

Alongside these actions, delayed for an entire generation, the old deceptive stereotypes continue to exist. The sudden zealous observance and publicizing of anniversaries to honour Holocaust victims are the most evident façades. Activities designed to show only one side – the praiseworthy and heroic one – of Poles' relations to Jews during the war – also jar, with their half-truths. The illusion is thus created that it is the authorities who represent moral values which were in fact upheld by the opposition movement developing in the last ten years as an expression of the independence regained by society. This is not the first appropriation committed by the authorities.

It is undeniable that emancipation movements before Solidarity – in particular the most powerful of these, the Committee for Social Self-Defence, KOR, together with the sectors of society coperating with it – not only unequivocally condemned anti-semitism, but also exposed the façades which concealed it. Among the ideals of this movement was the need for authentic – and not illusory and alibi-creating – absolution for the sin of indifference towards anti-Jewish actions and for their silent concealment especially when they were undertaken by Poles. This was thus an expression of the need for a genuine catharsis with respect to such actions, those of the distant past, and those more recent, both those resulting from the régime's policies – that is from the adversaries – and those from society itself. It was painfully clear that, although the Jewish community had almost vanished from the Polish scene, the ghost of the Jew still wandered through Poland, and, unfortunately, for a large part of society, it still has symbolic meaning: that of the outsider, someone not to be trusted, someone to be guarded against, to be blamed for every failure, even for the disasters of fate.

The supernatural strength of this symbol was felt during Solidarity's sixteen-month existence. This was surely an indirect consequence of society revelling in pluralism, or more concretely, of its willingness to listen to all viewpoints provided they claimed the legitimacy of opposition to the authorities. Now, however, these basically anti-semitic tendencies, whether directed against the authorities or against persons or groups within the opposition, found determined resistance. A significant majority had no doubt that this was an inadmissible contamination of the emancipatory, democratic, and humanistic ideals on which Solidarity was based. This majority included people of different generations and outlooks, with different past histories: those involved in the resistance movement during the war and who had been harassed or imprisoned after it, but who had never tolerated witch-hunts or the search for scape-goats; and those fascinated in their youth by the imported New Faith, who, finally grasping the connection between the capture of consciousness by the logic of higher goals and the dehumanization of the human condition and that of the nation, recognized they had to demystify reality, a reality which courageously challenged the authorities but was not always popular with society; and those among believing Catholics who found in Christianity an *imprimatur* for their support of the harsh régime's opponents who were not always admirers of religion; and those believers and non-believers for whom the Church had become a buttress and an ally in the difficult struggle to save the internal sovereignty of the nation; and finally, those who in the brutal lesson of 1968 discovered the link between the anti-semitism peering out from behind ideological masks and the shattering of society through its moral and, at times, intellectual disarmament.

This link not only laid bare the cynicism with which these false stereotypes of Jews as Zionists, cosmopolitans, national nihilists, and trouble-makers were created, but also demonstrated that opposing anti-semitism - everywhere, in all its forms and masks - is an inseparable part, but only one part, of the struggle to heal social life threatened by deprivation. It also showed that this goal cannot be attained exclusively by attacking the authorities; it is necessary in addition, to find the strength and courage to identify and demonstrate the negative phenomena rooted in society itself. And the nation - or indeed any nation - does not like this at all.

Condemnation of anti-semitism was therefore part and parcel of this moral renewal of society from the start. It was important, especially in Poland, a country of such deep-rooted Catholic traditions, that the Church hierarchy after Vatican II joined in secular efforts to break down ancient unfavourable stereotypes of the Jews. In the religious sphere these measures removed the centuries-old anathema on Jews and Jewry, and, moreover, created a propitious climate for Christianity and Judaism to meet on the basis of philosophical discourse and mutual respect for existing differences.

The suppression of Solidarity - the movement which confronted the lie of silence and persistently exposed spoken lies for the first time on such a scale - did not deter the nation's real determination to end the shameful failure to recognize the history of the Jewish community on Polish lands, and the practice - by no means limited to Poles - of distorting the picture of Polish-Jewish relations. True, one still meets attitudes that almost automatically continue the traditional embellishment of the Polish nation's past, thus avoiding unpalatable truths about Polish-Jewish issues among others. But a new spirit is in the air, leading to greater hope because it is developing especially among the younger generation. It is still embryonic and takes many forms. It includes believers and non-believers, Poles and Jews alike. Its central aim - in this case not directed at the construction of façades - is to find out about the history of Polish Jews, to restore the Jewish culture of these lands to its place in the treasury of Polish culture, so impoverished and distorted by the long practice of the cult of the single-nation state, and, what is most difficult but also most important, to reveal the whole truth, even in its most unpalatable form, about Polish-Jewish relations. In spite of psychological inhibitions, fears of misunderstanding, semantic difficulties, a gradual, courageous and genuinely purifying removal of masks and exposure of pathologies and prejudices has begun; not in order to accuse others or to accuse oneself, not to admit one's sins and beg for forgiveness, not in the name of philosemitism, but to satisfy the real need to comprehend the dramatic entanglements of human relations. For the truth about Poles and Jews, living side by side and subjected in the last half-century to various forms of totalitarianism, is a part of the universal truth about man's fate.

Though human fate obviously and naturally varies according to the histories of particular individuals, groups, nations, in different times and places, it is none the less similar in general. This should be remembered in any discussion of the causes, nature and consequences of Polish antisemitism, as well as of the contexts in which it is manifested. Although there is no doubt as to its specific character, it is at the same time an illustration of a much more widespread phenomenon, namely the origin and maintenance of stereotypes which perceive with animosity those who are different, labelling them as alien or hostile. These stereotypes tend always to become generalisations, within which feelings of hostility are transferred from the individual to the group and from the group to the nation.

This phenomenon arises from unsatisfied needs, from disappointments, from dissatisfaction with oneself or one's life, or in the face of opinions – one's own, those of one's surroundings or of the world – about oneself, one's group, one's nation. It emerges from the desire to compensate for feelings of inferiority, from the unsatisfied need to affirm one's worth. It is born under the pressure of experience and emotions arising most often from fear, out of the feeling that the individual, a group, or a national, religious, or ideological community is under threat, whether real or imagined. This process is characterised by exaggerated defensive reactions directed against real or imagined rivals or adversaries; as a rule it evolves toward views which, often helped by irrational thinking, serve to rationalise and justify negative emotions and aggressive defensive reactions. These can – but do not have to – lead to the sort of vicious and even criminal attitudes and acts often seen in the past; and they are all the more threatening because they claim the legitimacy of high aims: *ad maiorem Dei aut nationis gloriam*.

In this century, in which both crimes have been perpetrated, and scientific progress achieved, on an unprecedented scale, all beliefs, doctrines, systems, and revolutions – whether political, social, religious, scientific or technological – have proved helpless in the face of this pathology which appears as various anti-isms all over the world. History knows no successful prescription for the ailment. Experience none the less shows that a major role in the development of such phenomena is played by conflict between the truth, that is reality, perceived variously in the recent past or present, and the hierarchy of values recognised by the individual, group, nation or any specific community, often dominated by immoderate egocentrism or individual or collective egoism. The historian's duty is thus to tell the truth so that the often vulnerable individual and collective psyche can learn to accept often unpalatable conclusions. The proliferation of facts will not suffice to achieve this. What might help would be to reveal the role of mechanisms – both those imposed from without and those which facilitate self-deception and sustain professed notions, even in defiance of the facts. Becoming aware that our truths are only partial truths, and that even praiseworthy notions reach disproportionate dimensions under the influence of egocentric and egoistic attitudes, often distancing us, step by step, from the claims of humanism, helps us to endure less painfully the cruel test of time. The ancient historian understands this: the great distance of time assists him. For the modern historian, it is different: he must assist time, he must stir up truth so that it does not become barren; he must stir up, agitate, the hierarchy of values so that it does not become inhuman.

26

IS THERE A JEWISH SCHOOL OF POLISH LITERATURE?

Jan Błoński

Between the wars, the small but picturesque town of Kazimierz-on-the-Vistula was a favourite holiday resort of artists and writers. It was also extremely popular among Jews, who predominated among the local population. Adolf Rudnicki dedicated to Kazimierz his charming essay, 'Summer' written in 1938.[1] He pointed out two seemingly contradictory phenomena in connection with the town. In the first place, 'the ghetto was triumphant'. Why? Because 'prodigal sons' were returning to it, seeking shelter from increasing anti-semitism. They wished to feel at home and to find a firm base among their own people, in the faith and customs of their fathers that survived only among the simple and uneducated. Yet upon their return they found that change had come to their stable backwater, for now 'the Jewish masses usually speak Polish, their everyday life is conducted in this language' (even though this Polish was often poor and rather limited). Paradoxically, the growth of nationalism among the Jews was accompanied by the gradual abandoning of their distinctive language.

Rudnicki noticed similar contradictions among the élite. The assimilated intellectuals 'as they returned to the faith which, they had hoped, they had abandoned once and for all . . . found that their thinking, until then sharp and clear, rational and materialistic, became touched with . . . that despondency that kills all belief in the feasibility of progress.' And what of artists and writers? Those who expressed themselves in Yiddish (or avoided all association with Poles) 'displayed their own complexes towards Poles. Generally speaking these amounted to nothing more than the complex of the poor.' It was not surprising that 'the works of the assimilated justify the specific role of Jewry in the world, while the purists only add to their specific fields some works which are usually untranslatable.'[2] In other words, the generation born about 1910 found propitious conditions for the creation of a 'Jewish school' in literature. Life – including their most inner life – was lived through the Polish language. Yet this life was marked by unexpectedly strong Jewish features.

Jews had certainly made themselves felt in Polish literature much earlier. Already at the turn of the century, writers of Jewish descent played an important role in the intellectual élite. Their role was to increase considerably in independent Poland. However, those who desired assimilation had to abide by the tacit understanding that they were not to explore their Jewish experience, at least not in their literature. Thus the first intellectuals to surface as identifiably Jewish in their work were critics and historians, starting with Klaczko. Then came poets, among them figures as eminent as Leśmian and Tuwim. Yet prose writers were significantly absent. Was it a coincidence? It seems unlikely. Novelists base the substance of their work on their life experience, particularly the experience of youth. The Polonized Jews preferred to leave their past in the dark. Perhaps they feared that their autobiographical experiences, even if transformed into fiction, would seem provincial and uninteresting, perhaps even degrading. Certainly their collective past must often have seemed too painful and too difficult to express. Their Polishness caused – at least then – an emotional block in their memory and imagination which made novel-writing difficult. Or so it seems to me.

It is possible to assert that these writers were not really Jews. Certainly they did not identify themselves as Jewish writers. Their break with the past did not, for a long time at least, find literary expression. The rules of assimilation assumed that even if the newcomer did not conceal his past, he would not hearken back to it either. This rule was apparently applied everywhere in Europe, and not exclusively to Jews. It was, perhaps, a somewhat different story on the other side of the ocean.

The first signs of change in literature appeared initially in poetry, and then only in the form of careful allusions, as masks. According to Sandauer, 'the result of assimilation to a society which demonized Jews was, in Tuwim's case, his self-demonization:'[3] he viewed himself as a changeling, a devil marked with a mysterious stigma. Was it the stigma of art or the stigma of his descent? The answer depended on the reader. Only in 1943, influenced by the news of the Holocaust, did Tuwim declare that he spoke in the name of 'those Shloyms, Sruls, Moskis, hooknoses, sheenies, shonks',[4] and thus as an abused and contemptible Jew. Yet he neither could, nor would, repeat this confession in his poetry: his 'Song about Beating' remained unpublished. Similarly, in the poetry of Słonimski or Jastruń, clear allusions to their origins can only be found after 1945. Yet already in the 1930s a few young poets appeared who made the main theme of their work their perplexity at being torn between two nations and two cultures. Writing about his love for 'the wide, grey land of Mazowsze', Słobodnik says that his 'brothers' will regard it as treason, while 'the children of this land' will regard it as an expression 'of foreign blood, old and unhealthy'. Thus he will always walk 'between two . . . brands of hatred'.[5] Brandstaetter puts it even more clearly. He begs 'the

Hebrew language' to forgive him, for he will not 'carry his ripe crops to your barns'; yet he lays at its feet 'all [his] most secret pains' in a poem woven of 'Polish sweet-smelling rue and fresh herbs of thyme',[6] that is, of the flowers closely associated with Mickiewicz. At that time, Brandstaetter also wrote a singular poem about 'the Jerusalem of light and darkness'. He praises 'the holy homeland' being restored in Israel by 'pioneers'; he constantly 'prays for its greatness' and fears for its future; yet he also curses it if it does not drive away 'pimps' and 'usurers', if, inspired by 'national virtue', it kindles hatred and brings about bloodshed.[7] It is in fact a Zionist poem, written in Polish, and modelled on the poetry of the Romantic poets who were accustomed to describe their own enslaved country in similar words.

Yet these various voices do not constitute a literary trend. It would be difficult to include Bruno Schulz in a so-called 'Jewish school': he is too unique, too individual, and also too great to fit into the synthesized picture I plan to propose.[8] For I believe that if it were not for the extermination of the Jews, such a school might have taken root in Poland. This is indeed corroborated by a most cruel paradox: Jews became much more conspicuous in Polish literature after the Holocaust.

The major theme of this literary school, or group, was the condition of the Jewish intellectual. It was, after all, the Jewish intellectual who most keenly faced the problem of national identity. It meant for him both self-determination and self-understanding; it penetrated all levels of his life, from the religious to the erotic. Polish literature could only absorb the Jewish intellectual; the world of the tradesman, the artisan, and the poor had been abandoned to Yiddish literature. Orzeszkowa, Prus and Żeromski cast their heroes as doctors, scholars and students, while other authors (called contemptuously 'jargon writers') preferred to follow the fortunes of craftsmen, pedlars or labourers.

This paper will review some of this literature in order to draw a portrait of the Polish intellectual of Jewish descent, or perhaps the Polish-speaking Jewish intellectual.

An intellectual (and this is even more true of an artist) is often born when, as a child, he is struck by 'difference'. The child did not feel different in its own familiar circle; it had its own place in the natural order of a community, both within the family and among neighbours. But suddenly someone appears who excludes him from the community by referring to him as different. Perceived as a changeling, he can (although he does not have to) begin to fathom his 'difference'. In this way he constructs his individuality; he not only adjusts himself to his environment by accepting its standards and concepts, but he also creates new ones, trying to see the world differently, if only on a limited scale, trying to remodel the world in line with his thoughts and imagination. This sense of 'difference' may also include some perception of differences between Jews and the Gentiles.

It was Brandys who in his *Little Book* showed clearly the moment of being struck by 'difference'. His hero as a child plays with his playmates in the park. They are ordered about by the thin, dark- skinned Pola (Pola!) in whom – as the writer recalls – 'everything' was disturbing, 'everything' meaning, sex, which the boy had not noticed before. He invites her to his home, showers gifts on her, until the moment when the girl (he does not know why) excludes him from the group:

> 'Go away,' she mumbled, 'you. . . .' And she repeated the word. And I suddenly realized, understood, remembered! Yes, it was the same . . . word with which the beggar woman had cursed my father . . . I was petrified. Then I began to retreat slowly towards the bushes, with a desperate, backward movement of a donkey.[9]

The fatal word, which is not difficult to guess, is never mentioned in Brandys's book, which gives it a special flavour. The same scene, suitably transformed, recurs elsewhere, for instance in *Samson*, where a colleague brings it to the hero's notice that the Jews once left their land:

> Jakub was surprised again for it had never entered his mind that he had left his country. This country was enough for him, and he did not long for any other.[10]

The literary characters of Brandys are excluded from the primary community owing to the powerful word 'Jew'. In contrast, in Stryjkowski's works the gesture of repudiation is performed by Jews. The six or seven-year-old Aronek is called 'an enemy of Israel', a defiled Jew about whom 'the rabbi knows nothing', 'a *szajgec*, who should not touch the holy book.' So he looks forward to entering the Polish school with curiosity and relief. Aronek suffers repudiation as a result of the behaviour of his father, a pious Jew, whose views do not fit the practical religious routine of a little Galician town:

> 'Rabbi Tojwie does not experience ethical unity in himself anymore', a learned Viennese comments. 'On the one hand rabbinical formalism, on the other an inner need for true holiness . . . un-Jewish naivety. I have put it wrong – the word is biblical.'[11]

Is it indeed biblical? Formalism functioned well as long as the Jews were a closed community. It began to crack when the gates of the ghetto were thrown open. Tojwie became entangled between his longing for knowledge and his observance of the rules. He let his daughter become a teacher for he could not foresee she was going to fall in love with a gentile. Subjectively speaking, he is innocent, but it is men of lesser moral worth who are opposed to him among the Jews. Thus Tojwie introduces a new kind of moral criteria: the purity of the heart, yet at the price of despair and revolt. So the father's 'biblical' piety resulted in the polonization of his children!

It may happen that the hero is brought up as one who has already been repudiated, or at least is in the process of transition from one community to the other. This process is usually spread over a couple of generations. This is the case in Sandauer's *Notes from a Dead House*. As he says himself,

> I had no door to prise open as they were wide open already . . . it was my father who had made the effort to break out of the Jewish Middle Ages for me . . . I was born in a home already Polish, Socialist and atheist.

So why does the 'liberated' son continue searching for his roots? Born in 'middle-of-the-way' Targowica, he belongs in spirit to the Polish market-place whose 'balustrades and cupids' teach him 'a sense of beauty', which will lead him to classical studies. He retains, however, dispassionate self-criticism. He ridicules himself in the character of the grotesque Maurycy Rosenzweig, admirer of everything Polish. Yet it is only during the Nazi occupation that he returns to his family nest, to the area called Blich, where his great-grandfather Aron is dying, 'having shut himself out by strict rules from the loathsomeness and confusion . . . in which we, the people on the edge of society are accustomed to live'. Blich is near to hell, bisected by the modern Cocytus, a city sewer, where the fugitives from the ghetto are soon to perish. And what stretches beyond Blich? Dniester meadows, seductive because of their wild Ukrainian and erotic glamour. Even during the war the hero manages to perform a unique trick, both practical and symbolic. He spends his days in the ghetto, and his nights in the fields, which makes it possible for him to survive, but it also gives him a sense of the absurd resulting from his split social identity.

Such mythical topographies can sometimes be found in memoirs and novels. They emphasize the significance of the place which, by shutting him in or liberating him, determines an individual who is intrinsically incapable of social integration. For as Sandauer says, 'self-determination was always to present me with unsurmountable difficulties'. In his family, Orthodox piety, international Socialism and Zionism existed side by side: towards all of them he experienced 'that feeling of futility usually felt towards things already overcome'.[12] Overcome? Perhaps simply un-assimilated and non-internalized?

The feeling of being excluded was encouraged in two ways. First of all, by the ever-present anti-semitism, which was rarely cruel or consistent, yet dogged and nasty. And who was more susceptible to humiliation than an intellectual, who had come over to the camp of those who insult and who speaks their language? Traditional Jewish communities were indeed less sensitive to anti-semitism than more 'enlightened' ones. The former interpreted their Jewish otherness – and Jewish affliction – in a religious way. Their religious faith acted as a bulwark, at the cost of obscurantism, thus resembling the Polish Church in the most difficult period of the partitions.

An avalanche of anti-semitic nonsense was now released. 'Everybody's mind was so confused,' Sandauer remembers about the spring of 1939, 'that no one was surprised if. . . an anti-Nazi meeting ended in beating up Jews.'[13] Thus the beginning of the war, as perceived by Stryjkowski, becomes a paroxysm of nonsense. A Jew will always be suspect, whatever he does. If he does not roll with laughter when an actor mocks Hitler, he can feel the censorious eyes of the audience on him and hear meaningful murmurs. If he laments over the inadequate anti-aircraft defence, he is accused of defeatism. If he repeats the terrifying (but true) rumours, it is suggested that he sides with the Germans. Are not all Jews Communists? Has not Ribbentrop just signed a pact with Moscow? Peasants say that the Germans have dropped two Jewish spies by parachute. And what do old pious Jews do? They profiteer, as they shut their shops on a Saturday![14] One could quote examples by the hundred. Such accusations and inventions were particularly numerous in the university and the army, the two institutions that an assimilated Jew was particularly keen to enter. These institutions, by the way, were probably much less anti-semitic than others, but the pain was felt sharpest in the place that should have been the safest.

The sufferings of the intellectuals also had other sources, less evident but also more vicious. They had been brought up conscious of crisis and decadence. 'The older a nation, the richer its past . . .' Rudnicki wrote. 'The older a nation, the older each man seems to be born.'[15] Yet there is more bitterness than dignity in this old age, turned back towards the past, incapable of action, doomed to suffering. Thus the Jews see themselves, thus they feel. The chosen people are at the same time the cursed people. 'Anyone can enter our house, can kill, can defile!' cries old Tag in *Austeria*. 'What a price we pay for having been chosen by God!'[16] Abandoning Jewry means ceasing to be exceptional. To be as others are, as all are! A place for everybody – also for the Jews, relieved from the stigma of their otherness – will be found in the Europe of freedom, equality and brotherhood. The rabbi will be replaced by the physician, Jerusalem by Paris, and the jealous Jehovah by progress with a capital P.

The leadership of Jewish opinion in the inter-war period already belonged not to the religious authorities, but to the lay, liberal, rationalist and sometimes free-thinking élite. The lawyer Kirsche was

> a humanitarian, individualist, aesthete, liberal, democrat, in short – a true nineteenth-century man. He was everything a well-mannered

> lawyer ought to be: a Socialist (although he understood national democracy), an assimilationist (although he recognized the achievements of Zionism), and an anti-fascist as well (although he held German efficiency in high esteem).

However, the war comes, and with it the German occupation, the Jews are marked with the yellow star and enclosed behind the barbed wire. Where does Mr Kirsche end up with his rational views and socially valuable virtues? In naive and cowardly submission, without even a streak of humility. Kirsche becomes the chairman of the Judenrat in Stryj, or Sambor. As Kirsche boasts, the SS-man Gabriel 'said recently: You are the only man in the whole town I can talk to'.[17] What does Gabriel like to talk about? About Goethe and Nietzsche. At the same time he decimates the Jews, pretending to their chairman that he is trying to protect the ghetto from the total annihilation that Berlin demands.

No one has ever castigated the enlightened Jewish élite more cruelly than Sandauer. Yet *The Death of a Liberal* seems to be too programmatic and systematic. Sandauer ridiculed, one by one, all the liberal and rational values cherished by the enlightened middle class: conscientiousness which now, in 1942, contributed only to the slow extermination of those who worked; respect for the law, when the law aimed only at the debasement and subjugation of fellow men; rationality as a principle of human behaviour, when both death and survival depended on chance alone; the dignity of the individual, an empty and meaningless concept in the world where man had become, literally, a merely quantifiable object.

The same line of argument was often followed by Rudnicki, whom Sandauer ironically could not bear (the feeling was mutual). In *A Merchant of Łódź* he presented the appalling story of Chaim Mordechai Rumkowski who 'with German blessing ruled over the Jews shut in the Łódź ghetto'. There were more than two hundred thousand Jews there; 'in the area of a few streets' they formed a state, 'isolated from men and the world', governed with an iron fist by the Emperor, as Rumkowski was sometimes called. He was not educated, he was a businessman. Tough, pig-headed, vigorous, hard-working, obviously a good organizer, he belonged – in a sense – to the social élite. Before the war he used to collect money from the Jewish community for an orphanage and for the Palestine Land Purchase Fund.

Rumkowski was a sensible man. 'His own inner reality . . . was . . . cheap, respectable, decent, business-like.' Rumkowski quickly realized that a Jewish policeman would always be preferable to a German one, that 'people must eat, children must learn . . . and the sick need medical care', and particularly, that the Jews could not oppose the Germans effectively. They could only sell their own labour – for survival, for a bowl of turnip soup. 'What partner would not accept such terms? What normal man needed the corpses of hundreds of thousands of men? . . . He knew only that he himself would never kill a man, that he would agree to such terms.' So he got angry when 'his subordinates did not share his belief'.[18] His anger was formidable and grew progressively. He ruthlessly controlled and allocated everything and everybody: the synagogue and money (he had enough of his own), the rich and the poor, music and horse transport. Work and order were the Emperor's watchwords. Thus this tiny totalitarian state of beggars and starvelings was created in the anus of the totalitarian Reich. And Rumkowski firmly believed that it was not going to be excreted via the chimney.

Common sense makes one think first of all about the living, protection of life is a primary duty. But in fact not all can be rescued. Then reason counsels the rescue of some at least. Even under the most difficult circumstances one should try to reach an agreement with one's enemy as some norms and liabilities then follow. If you want to gain something, you must give something in turn, for human actions are governed by self-interest. That is why it is important to understand the situation. You should not lose your head, panic, change your behaviour in the face of sudden danger. Experience suggests that one must accept the inevitable. Rumkowski possessed all these features of character and skills. They were certainly positive features. Modern societies value them as they help people to adjust to new circumstances. They make it possible to adjust one's own life to the requirements of individual and social good. As in a nightmare, these features got out of hand in the Łódź ghetto and became destructive, converting Rumkowski into a man mad both with fear and with a lust for power.

The confusion of principles, as well as the confusion and interchange of the roles of the executioner and the victim, had already been described in 1946 by Borowski in his Auschwitz stories. Totalitarianism is not appeased until it destroys its victim, not only physically but also morally. It must make him accept this new, sordid world. The executioner does not want the victim to accept his values, for he neither has any nor understands any. The victim must rather recognize the absence of any values, since this clearly proves the necessity of submitting to sheer power. Heaven must become empty and the very idea of moral law unimaginable. What remains is power. This will – sooner or later – lead to the realization that 'nothing can be done'. Such a surrender, according to Borowski, Sandauer and Rudnicki, is the inevitable result of liberal and enlightened middle-class culture.

It is the passivity and the divisions of the Jewish community that present the most painful problems to the intellectual. Abandoning his religion, he had found shelter in a kind of a humanistic – or humanitarian – Vulgate, inherited from the Enlightenment and tinted either with liberalism or with Socialism. The bankruptcy of this Vulgate, based upon the happiness and welfare of the individual, became obvious once the ghetto was established. The Jewish élite could neither understand the process leading to the Holocaust, nor oppose it in any way except passively. 'I realized then why my position was so ridiculous,' says Sandauer's hero, 'it was the lack of any principles. I fought only for my own life . . . People wondered that we went to our death – by the thousand, meek as sheep. But what were we to revolt for? . . . To die in order to avoid death, does not make any sense, you will agree . . . What did I die for? For the faith I did not share? For the nation I did not feel I belonged to?'[19] Hence his chaotic, discordant behaviour, ending in suicide. Brandys puts similar thoughts into the mouth of his Samson: 'I am afraid to die just for the reason that I have a certain type of face . . . This face has been tormenting me all my life . . . People find in it everything they hate the Jews for.'[20] Samson does not see himself as a Jew; he has become a Jew because of others. Taking up arms, Samson accepts responsibility for his own fate, the fate of a Jew, and – as we can guess – of a Communist, potentially at least. Yet he is killed too soon for his gesture to become anything more than a mere symbol.

So where is our intellectual to find shelter? From where is he to acquire certainty? He feels alienated from the community he has been brought up in, repudiated by the community he wanted to join. He is disillusioned with, indeed, appalled by the failure of the enlightened ideas which promised him an all-European homeland. He can resort only to the most extreme and radical ideas, either abandoning the world for the Jewish people and interpreting its religious tradition in a political and secular manner, or ignoring completely his own nationality, identifying himself with the triumphant progress of the world proletariat. For the intellectuals threatened with anti-semitism, Zionism and Communism were different answers to the same challenge. 'With a considerable part of the Jewish intelligentsia, the Zionist idea was replaced by Communism', maintains Stryjkowski who himself travelled along this path. 'Communism was believed to offer the only panacea to the Jewish problem. For example: the Soviet Union. We sincerely believed that . . . But . . . only a tiny part of the Jewish intelligentsia went Communist at all seriously.'[21] True enough. Yet they have left abundant literary evidence of the specifically Jewish path to Communism.

We can perceive here a singular paradox. Choosing Communism meant as a rule a radical rejection of all nationalism, including Polish nationalism. However, in literature it clearly favoured the Polish language and Polishness generally. The story of Henryk in *A Black Rose* is clearly autobiographical, although Henryk is not a Jew, which is exceptional with Stryjkowski. It seems as if the writer parted symbolically with his own past. The other choice, of Zionism, assumed indeed the abandonment of Polish as a literary language (as well as that of Yiddish).

'Going Communist' was often fed by a fear of loneliness, by a desire to feel a sense of community with others. 'I learned the need for that friendship and its essential sense,'[22] writes Hertz, 'among crowds in big meeting halls . . . I contrived to go everywhere in order to quench my thirst for reality.' Rudnicki writes about 'the perennial dream of the loners': 'to be with someone, be together, be rooted in life, resist exclusion, find one's group, be inside, be involved'.[23] Such dreams are quite common among intellectuals, but were experienced by Jewish intellectuals like a paroxysm. It was Flaszen who once wrote about Brandys:

> He cannot produce a sound unless he becomes lost and annihilated in some 'we'. . . . A complex of otherness? Probably; hidden deeply and diffidently under the changing masks. We intellectuals, we Communists, we citizens, we Poles. . . . The writer puts on only those masks which are conventionally accepted and socially sanctioned. And that is his undoing.[24]

In his *Little Book* Brandys revealed the source of his obsessive themes, thus reinforcing his position in literature.

The need to belong to a community is an inner necessity in all these three cases. In Sandauer's self-analysis it is presented as the result of the need to act. He perceives the ghetto, shut in by the Germans, as 'a community . . . in a state of decomposition'. Lack of hope goes along with the demoralization of the people 'fascinated by the Nazi terror and concerned only with salvaging their own lives'. Thus they are 'dazzled' when they hear about the existence of the conspiracy, the party, the underground army. It is resistance that gives a chance of survival; and a certain minimum of solidarity is required for it to develop. Yet with Sandauer active self-preservation is stronger than community spirit. As he says, it is 'a construction aiming at something but devoid of any goals: an ideologist without ideology, a prophet without faith'. He writes in order 'to go beyond himself, to experiment within his own psyche'.[25] In this way, most probably from a thirst for novelty and from national uprooting, Sandauer was transformed into a critic. Yet one can ask whether such activism does not quite closely resemble the enemy it was to combat, nihilism?

Not all Jewish intellectuals felt the need to soothe their loneliness with activity or their lack of roots with blind faith. To those intellectuals who were close to the simple Jewish people the Communist doctrine appeared an eschatology of brotherhood. The belief in revolution was born out of the fusion of religious tradition and social despair. Little Sztajer – I quote Rudnicki –

> in the spell between two summers became sad, his face heavy, listless, blank, as if too mature, and he did not know life yet . . . Looking at him I knew what was going to happen to him . . . deprived of a living

> source, he became cynical, nothing seemed noteworthy to him ... His father at least had been expecting the Messiah ... I learned to my relief that he remained faithful to his father and his nation; he believed now in Madrid, in China, he, a son of the ancient nation which had long earned the right to receive alms from mankind.[26]

The author's 'to my relief' indicated that Rudnicki identifies the revolutionary beliefs of little Sztajer with the preservation of human dignity in the man whose inner self is laid bare by the hopelessness of destitution.

To the question concerning the source of his youthful Zionism, Stryjkowski gives the following answer: 'It meant turning away from the way of life of petty shopkeepers, pedlars, craftsmen ... which lay as a burden on us young people, longing for beauty, freedom, vitality, an ideal homeland. ... We were concerned with good, justice, beauty – nothing less than that. ...'[27] Yet exactly the same can be said about the evolution towards Communism! The example of Henryk in *A Black Rose* corroborates this. His judgement of the comrades he meets with is predominantly moral: 'Henryk began to respect Tyszyk; he was a noble and splendid type of revolutionary. He was a tough man ... he was supposed to be a Ukrainian, which confirmed his idealism.'[28] Henryk meticulously follows the party code and later the prisoners' code; with childlike conscientiousness he learns the rudiments of Marxism and repeats worn-out slogans with the zeal of a convert. He perceives, although he does not understand – he does not want to understand – the suspicion, ruthlessness, and sectarianism spreading within the party. Released from prison, he makes his way to the Soviet Union: without preparation, without any warning, with the confidence of a crusader knocking at the gates of paradise.

The motives behind 'going Communist' are thus rarely based on the economic situation or the product of an examination of society. What predominates is the moral imperative and the anticipation of great change. When there are neither masters nor slaves, neither exploiters nor exploited, then there will be neither goys nor Jews. The party is the place where that word which once so struck the hero of *A Little Book* is never mentioned. This, at least, is what is believed by Henryk, who, although a Gentile, seems to have a similar biography to Artur in *The Great Fear*. Some time also elapses before Artur hears – or rather overhears – this word. However, the solution of the 'Jewish problem' will only be the least important benefit conferred by the radically new world after the revolution. After many years and much disillusionment, Rudnicki describes the following dream which is perhaps an illumination or a revelation:

> Without knowing I knew, without seeing I saw. Drunk with the white sun, dazed with the scent, I waited. I waited, being absolutely certain that it was going to happen, that soon the sea would part and the

> Man would emerge out of the deep. That this Man would say the Word, and History would start its progress once again . . . this time without those terrible sufferings known to everybody.[29]

Is this not a perfect example of the projection of religious hope onto history? Who is going to emerge from the deep, a Messiah or Marx? Yet Rudnicki already knows that all historical Messianism is an echo, derived from the 'first creation of the world'.

Although it became common to abandon both Messianic and political dreams, only Stryjkowski presented a detailed account of disillusionment with Communism. Yet, as if admitting failure, he concedes that 'not much of it has remained as literature'. He has produced an interesting document, courageously and conscientiously recording events in Lwów between 1939 and 1941. By carefully distancing himself from the hero, he has presented his 'unintended thoughtlessness'.[30] Yet *The Great Fear* seems to be somewhat colourless, at least when compared with Stryjkowski's other novels. His hero's adventures among the Communists do not stir the deep store of his imagination. Is it because, by abandoning his infatuation and 'thoughtlessness', the hero adopts common sense, which does not always stimulate literary creativity? Or is it that not all taboos have been broken in this report on a political love-affair?

The spiritual pilgrimage that I have briefly recalled ends either in failure or in bankruptcy. The Jewish people have perished. Israel has been repudiated. The revolutionary dream is no more. What is left to our hero? What strategy will he adopt, if he is not to seal his lips, if he wants to speak about those things which were once dear to him, which are still dear to him?

He finds his place in the apocalyptic vision of the world. It corresponds perfectly with the repudiated hope for general happiness. The end of the world has come. Yet somehow there is no end to this end; the world continues sinking deeper and deeper into death. In his *Our Fiddles on the Willows* Stryjkowski describes a meeting with a Jewish community in America, reconstructed by the rescued friends of his childhood. There is nothing they lack there in California! There is a rabbi (married to a Hawaiian woman converted to Judaism), there is kosher food, and a Zionist association. Yet all this is not really authentic. It is the Californian carnival of the 1960s. The Jews seem to appear in the same show as the shaved followers of Krishna or long-haired flower children. They dream a dream that allows them to escape from the world of luxury cars and computers. 'Never and nowhere had the Jews had it so good as in America.' Yes, it is true, that as long as they are Jews, they must return to the past. However, this past is more and more faint, less and less understood. A Sephardic rabbi has never heard about the Marranos; instead of history, 'I teach boys not to be afraid of anybody', he says. Nobody seems to understand Hasidic songs. 'I clapped my hands. Others joined me in clapping. Yet without enthusiasm. The young did not know the psalm, had no idea what it had sounded like in their fathers' and grandfathers' time.'[31] In short, the reconstructed Jewish community seems thoroughly unauthentic to the stranger from Poland. Yet he himself has no other. So he becomes attracted to the substitute, but then feels compelled to escape from it. To fill his cup of bitterness, the Jews accuse him of faint-heartedness and treason. Has he not abandoned his Zionist youth for a career as a Communist 'official', a career which ended, of course, in failure? If he at least settled in California! But no, he does not want to. He returns to the Polish cemetery, dreaming vague and alluring dreams about a crazy student, Louise Madrid de Arietti. He imagines she is of Marrano descent. Thus – simply – a new novel is looming in his mind.

No solution – apart from an imagined one – is any longer possible. The intellectual becomes limited to the role of a writer. He should, however, justify his work. Rudnicki sees himself as a privileged eyewitness. He has survived the Holocaust which he considers as a final and uncommunicable experience. He has survived in order to bear witness to the limits of things human. His duty is only to report. But what to report? Great events? No, because it is not feasible either to report heroism or martyrdom. One can, however, preserve the atmosphere, mood, and tone rescued from the Holocaust. One can recall those human values which were revealed in the days of annihilation – or afterwards, demonstrate that there are no limits to man's abilities. There is nothing he will not attempt in the process of his self-determination. The economy of Jewish life balances human fate in a quite unforeseeable way. Various values – beauty, language skills, perceptiveness, competence in shoemaking, philosophical education or ability to cook – converge and cancel each other in this incomprehensible equation of the fate of man, pressed hard by events, fate which transgresses everything that an individual or a community have ever experienced.

There is the danger of dandyism in Rudnicki's attitude. Is not the writer walking in the cemetery searching for trinkets? And the danger of narcissism: for he who has become skilled in the extraordinary, tends to see himself as extraordinary as well. However, with passing years Rudnicki has learned caution, and perhaps also modesty. His search has become opalescent with religious meaning.

> I know the truth [we read in his *Actor*] although I do not need it, I am not looking for it. What is more – I do not want it. Each time I am the truth and its very opposite . . . If it were only me, a poor shammer, no one would ever mind, but my poverty is only pretended, for in fact I am powerful, and my house is amongst the oldest, it came into being in the first moment of creation, just then when the words were spoken: Let there be light . . . So there was light, yet it did not

> disperse darkness. Since then, with the annihilation of unity, my career has begun. I am a proof against the unity which we have been trying to achieve. . . .[32]

In other words, I bear witness to otherness; I prove everything that is unforeseeable and unique in man. To be sure, he will prove it in a distorted way, 'what I do, these are crude things'; an actor (impersonator), by means of an echo (word), evokes 'the thing' (creation). Yet there is no other solution: even an 'echo' differentiates darkness by destroying the primeval unity, the unity older than creation, older than the spirit's intervention; or the unity which will follow the end, when the spirit leaves the world and abandons it to perpetual agony.

There is, however, something particularly optimistic in this chronicler of Jewish suffering. Even if everything has perished, a tear is left, a kind word, wisdom, a joke, which may come in useful some time. In contrast, the best books of Stryjkowski, who himself did not witness the extermination of Polish Jewry and has not written a single line about it, seem to be marked with finality and clearly aim at tragic apotheosis. It is fear that predominates, not a physical and common fear, but a holy, godly fear: in the memory of the heroes the father rises and thus also the prophets, and the patriarchs and He whose name must not be mentioned and makes them conscious of sin. Tojwie, and Azriel, and Tag, all of them have sinned. A godless act, even if not committed consciously, follows man and demands redress: 'Vengeance is mine, saith the Lord.' Thus affliction (which in Stryjkowski's works is a foreboding and augury of the Holocaust) must be accepted as something one deserves. Has not the whole nation left the path of righteousness? For the sin of an individual is – as in antiquity – the sin of a community; it falls as a burden on the whole nation. It returns in a dream that tells you to leave the house and make a pilgrimage to your father's grave, in the voices in the dark, in the thought of a sacrilege the memory of which makes the hair stand on end. From the broken law emanates a tragic aura. Oh, for the religion of the heart, the confidence of a child dancing joyfully before the throne of the Everlasting! Hasidism is the comfort and temptation of Stryjkowski's heroes. Yet they remember that to be a Jew means above everything else to keep the Law. Awe-inspiring responsibility. An impossible task. For human thoughts and efforts contradict and cancel each other; outcome belies purpose, which in the end appears only illusory. Both Rabbi Tojwie, who spent his days poring over the Torah, and Henryk, a revolutionary who never thought about God, were overcome by emotions they did not understand, and by circumstances that they mistook for their own decisions. Henryk at least was given the illusion of hope which makes one blind to the results of his actions.

Yet the suffering of Tojwie, the agony of Azriel, and particularly the wisdom of old Tag in *Austeria*, penetrate deeper, discover more. The ordered world – the world of Jewish tradition and European order – really collapsed in 1914. The Russian offensive, which marks its progress through the Carpathian Mountains with pogroms, seems to predict the Apocalypse. But it cannot be avoided: the fugitives reach only the edge of the wood, Tag's inn (*austeria*). While the town is ablaze, townspeople discuss the war in a very sensible, enlightened way, in the firm hope that they are going to salvage from it both their heads and their furniture. A group of *Hasidim*, together with their rebbe, is not even aware of disaster; they sing and dance, praise God and celebrate the joy of being a Jew. A stray bullet kills the beautiful Asia. Her fiancé, dumb with pain, is arrested for the alleged murder of a Cossack, and hanged. That is how the young – beauty and the future – die while Jewish bribes see to it that the town centre is not destroyed.

This time ransom has postponed annihilation. Yet injustice remains, and no one wants even to mention it. Tag takes upon himself a final duty: affliction has struck his house, so he must accept it himself. He must at least tell the Russian commander that he has committed the crime, in the same way as Antigone, who when burying her brother announced that the world order had been destroyed. Tag finds someone to accompany him, a priest, a teacher of religion, a friend of the Jews, who had secretly baptized Tag as a child in order to save him from the flames of hell. Pathetic and absurd, they both walk slowly to meet their death. They go to atone for the crime which they did not want, but which was born out of the *difference* they themselves embody. Only the word remains to redeem them.

> The word is a great thing. Emanation of man's spirit . . . Literature is eternal. It is the only truth. Prose, poetry. Eternal, as the word is eternal, as man is eternal. For there is certainly eternity . . . If so, there may be a God. Perhaps he is eternity?[33]

These are the words of faith burdened with doubt, the only ones that befit a literature which, in expiring, seems to seek an audience in eternity.

NOTES

1 A. Rudnicki, *Lato*, (Warsaw, 1946), pp. 132, 129, 135, 129, 133–4.

2 See A. Hertz, *Żydzi w kulturze polskiej*, (Paris, 1961).

3 A. Sandauer, *O sytuacji pisarza polskiego pochodzenia żydowskiego w XX wieku*, (Warsaw, 1982), p. 28.

4 J. Tuwim, *My Żydzi polscy*. Reprinted in the anthology: *Piesn ujdzie cało*, (Warsaw, 1947).

5 W. Słobodnik, Szeroka, szara . . .', in *Wiersze*, (Warsaw, 1936), p. 48.
6 R. Brandstaetter, 'Elegia na mowę hebrajską' in *Węzły i miecze*, (Warsaw, 1933), p. 20.
7 R. Brandstaetter, *Jerozolima światła i mroku*, (Warsaw, 193–), pp. 7, 11.
8 The only one who wrote about the Jewish roots of Schulz's prose was A. Sandauer in 'Rzeczywistość zdegradowana' in *Zebrane pisma krytyczne*, (Warsaw, 1981), pp. 557–81.
9 K. Brandys, *Mała księga*, (Warsaw, 1975), p. 42.
10 K. Brandys, *Samson. Antygona*, (Warsaw, 1949), p. 19.
11 J. Stryjkowski, *Głosy w ciemności*, (Warsaw, 1971), pp. 417, 454, 456, 461.
12 A. Sandauer, 'Zapiski z martwego miasta', in *Proza*, (Cracow, 1972), pp. 111, 171, 184, 117.
13 Ibid. p. 131.
14 J. Stryjkowski, *Wielki strach*, (Warsaw, 1980), pp. 22–55.
15 A. Rudnicki, *Lato*, p. 121.
16 J. Stryjkowski, *Austeria*, (Warsaw, 1966), p. 227.
17 A. Sandauer,'Śmierć liberała', in *Proza*, pp. 7–8, 9.
18 A. Rudnicki,'Kupiec łódzki' in *50 opowiadań*, (Warsaw, 1963), pp. 81, 106, 91, 106.
19 A. Sandauer, op. cit., pp. 55–56.
20 K. Brandys, *Samson* . . ., p. 177.
21 J. Stryjkowski, *Odejście*; T. Krzemień, Interview with J. Stryjkowski, *Kultura* 1961, no. 30.
22 P. Hertz, *Sedan*, (Warsaw, 1966), p. 151.
23 A. Rudnicki, *Noc będzie chłodna, niebo w purpurze*, (Cracow 1977), p. 90.
24 L. Flaszen, 'Brandysowskie remanenty', *Przegląd kulturalny*, 1952, nos. 51–2.
25 A. Sandauer, 'Zapiski z martwego miasta', in *Proza*, pp. 187, 182, 117.
26 A. Rudnicki, *Lato*, p. 125.
27 J. Stryjkowski, *Odejście*.
28 J. Stryjkowski, *Czarna róża*, (Warsaw, 1962), p. 330.
29 A. Rudnicki, *50 opowiadań*, p. 555.
30 J. Stryjkowski, *Odejście*.
31 J. Stryjkowski, *Na wierzbach . . . nasze skrzypce*, (Warsaw, 1974), pp. 189, 231, 177.
32 A. Rudnicki, *50 opowiadań*, pp. 444–445.
33 J. Stryjkowski, *Odejście*.

27

A VOICE FROM THE DIASPORA: JULIAN STRYJKOWSKI

Laura Quercioli Mincer

Pesach Stark, who was later to adopt the pseudonym Julian Stryjkowski, was born on 27 April 1905 in Galicia, that legendary land of Jews, Poles, Ukrainians and many other peoples, that country in which, according to Paul Celan 'men and books lived':

> There was a great deal of tolerance in Austria. It was possible for a Jew and a priest to meet and become friends; at school, Jews, Poles and Ukrainians sat on the same bench. The exasperation that followed did not yet exist. I do not mean that there was no anti-semitism; there has always been anti-semitism, but it did not reveal itself so bitterly. There were friendships between Poles and Jews. Even more often, there were friendships between Poles and Jewish women. And this was the last and only time of well-being in that country. Under the wing of Emperor Franz Joseph.[1]

Stryjkowski was born near Lwów (as it was called by the Poles, Lemberg by the Jews and Germans and Lviv by the Ukrainians) in a small town called Stryj from which he was to take his name. Austria-Hungary and Galicia in particular form the countryside and the 'raison d'être' of most of his works, which are marked with a nostalgia for that lost land, that far off and unrepeatable Atlantis, which clearly has the universal and unchangeable contours of epic countrysides. Stryjkowski became the bearer of the great myth of Middle Europe and of that lament which is for Lwów, Prague and Trieste.

> Noch einmal, noch einmal, Father
> my old Jew, recite
> a passage from Genesis, from Deuteronomy
> and also if you can, from the marvellous world
> which disappears with you.

> Trieste, Südhahnhof, Sunday morning,
> the Vienna express via Ljubljana.
> Give me your little hand – you said
> and you repeated it in German.
> And I fervently followed you.[2]

As the 'Vienna express via Ljubljana' was to Fölkel, who came from Trieste, so the road to Duliby or the Hetmańskie Valleys at Lwów had for Stryjkowski all the obviousness of symbols and did not require explanation. 'In *Austeria* Stryjkowski often evokes the road to Duliby, a village of thieves, just as if all his readers in every latitude knew perfectly well where the village of Duliby was and what it represented. It was like saying Jordan, Lethe, Troy, or the Capitoline Wolf; as if Duliby were part of a universal geography and part of a common cultural heritage. The country of one's childhood has no need of explanations.'[3]

In conjunction with this epic transfiguration there is a marked indifference to the actual natural countryside, whose presence is almost only always hinted at. In this Stryjkowski seems to hark back to *ostjüdisch* visual tradition, by which I mean that of people unaccustomed to contact with nature, nature being a long way from the town centres where most Jews lived, and then tragically absent from the Nazi ghettos where they were destroyed.

> Too often we forget that they were citizens of the desert, that they still look after this desert within themselves as their own internal space and they perpetuate it in history, greatly surprised at those human trees which are 'other mortals'. Perhaps one should add that they made the desert not only into their own internal space but that they continued it *physically* in the ghetto. Anyone who has visited a ghetto cannot help but noticing that it has no vegetation, no flowers, and everything is dry and desolate: it is a strange little island, a small rootless universe, which was well suited to its inhabitants, who were as far from life on earth as angels or ghosts.[4]

The 'desert' of which Cioran speaks was a painful but privileged prospect for the author. It was what lay behind that Jewish 'exoticism' that is often considered in Poland to be one of the salient characteristics of Stryjkowski's work: an exoticism which does not come from distance in geographical terms, but from distance in time and in internal space. Stryjkowski's father was a religious *hasid*, an elementary school teacher, a *melamed*; he refers to his mother as 'a simple Jewess'. The family was very poor but the author did not like to talk about it. It is only rarely that he mentions the 'horrible poverty' which he experienced as a child.

> The world is the homeland of the writer. In this world there is a little street on which the writer grew up.[5]

The 'little street' of *Hasidic* orthodoxy along which his parents travelled soon became too narrow for Stryjkowski, who was never to forget the severe and uncomplicated moral upbringing of his childhood.

> Recently the French journal *Libération* asked me to take part in an enquiry by answering the question 'Why do I write?' I understood suddenly that in all my travels this was the question I had never asked myself. And my road had been longer than that of others. At home we spoke only Yiddish and when my father took me to school when I was six, he told me that when the teacher asked me my name I must answer: present. It was the only word with which I went to the Polish school, my only provision for the road. And when the school mistress asked me what such and such made, I replied: present ! And I gave the same answer to all the questions. After every 'present' of mine, my young colleagues burst out laughing, and I didn't know why. I didn't know whether it was a good or a bad thing for the Jews. But I didn't know either that the word 'present' which my father entrusted me with, was the most important in my life.[6]

At twelve years old Stryjkowski ran away from home and became a Zionist:

> I wanted to burn my bridges, sociologically, with the entire class of 'people with ringlets', that is, the class of Orthodox *Hasidic* Jews. I detested them from the start, even when I was six.[7]

The artistic apprenticeship of the young author was long and difficult. He published some writings in Hebrew which are now unobtainable and some literary criticisms and translations, Amongst these was a translation of *Mort à crédit* by Celine ('He taught me the most important thing: how to take an uncompassionate look at myself.') He ended his studies at the University of Lwów under the famous Professor Kleiner, by writing an unusual thesis entitled, 'Women Criminals in Romantic Literature'. Romanticism is the only literary debt that Stryjkowski acknowledged (since he was always intent on emphasising his own isolation and his uniqueness on the Polish scene): 'Słowacki is the only one who is close to me; indeed it is to him that I owe my formation from Polish romanticism.'

The writer was no longer so very young when he passed from Zionism to Communism:

> I was threatened with unemployment and there was no unemployment in the Soviet Union. I was threatened with anti-semitism and there was no anti-semitism in the Soviet Union. Our belief in this was unshakeable.[8]

Nonetheless he continued to feel that his writing was intended to be different from mere political writing:

> I always considered myself to be a writer who did not write. This was my illness. I suffered much from it – I was a martyr to artistic impotence.[9]

It was during these years that he ultimately came to regard Zionism as a Utopian movement. In 1934 he became a member of the illegal Communist Party of the Western Ukraine and remained one until its dissolution by Stalin in 1938. From the end of the war until 1966 he was a member of the Polish United Workers' Party (as it was called after 1948). In 1966 he handed in his Party card in protest at the expulsion of Professor Leszek Kołakowski. His membership of the Communist Party also cost him a year in prison from 1935 to 1936.

When the Nazis entered Lwów in 1941, Stryjkowski succeeded in escaping to the Soviet Union, where he was to remain for the duration of the war: 'The happiest years of my life.'[10] It was in Moscow in 1943, on hearing the news of the destruction of the Warsaw Ghetto, that he wrote his first novel in Polish, *Głosy w ciemności*, (Voices in the Dark) choosing what was to be the language of his future writing:

> I felt then that I was touched by the hand of God . . . and understood that I had to start writing, that I had to erect a tombstone to the memory of my people who had died . . . the real rôle of literature is to immortalize something which is dead. Literature as the epitaph of the world.[11]

The world whose epitaph we find in this novel is that of the *shtetlach* of the Jews, and of the infancy and youth of the author:

> For me it is like retrieving Atlantis from under the sea. Buried memories. It did not seem possible even to me to be able to remember unexpectedly things that I thought now were lost. But by working with one's memory it is perhaps possible to recover things which have already been pushed beyond the boundaries of consciousness.[12]

This is the often quoted 'dream writing' (*pisanie snem*) of the romantic Słowacki: a state of semi-trance, to which the author abandons himself at the moment in which he 'is touched by the hand of God'. It is a divine touch which is partly equivalent to the 'spirit of narration' of Thomas Mann, or the need to bear witness to and be part of the 'flotsam and jetsam' of Jewish life that remained in Poland. Stryjkowski places himself at an intersection between the tradition of romantic writing dictated by inspiration, the automatism of modern writers and the humility of a writer simply affirming: I have something to say, something to show. Tolstoy was among his masters and is one of the few writers he admires. It was Tolstoy who made Natasha exclaim, 'You know, I have the impression that . . . when we abandon ourselves to recalling, recalling, recalling, we end up, by dint of continually recalling, remembering things which happened even before we came into the world.'

The composition of *Głosy w ciemności* represents the fragmentary and sometimes obscure flowering of his memory. It is a piece of writing that seems to trace the disconnected and distorted geography of the citizenship of Eastern Galicia in which it is set and the frantic and uncertain pace of life of the *Luftmenschen* who inhabit it. Jan Błonski has disparagingly defined its structures as being put together 'grain by grain', underlining the fragmentariness, the crossing of various stories and the multitude of *dramatis personae*. But really this kind of composition which has also been defined as 'circular' seems more suited than any other, to give the sense and the atmosphere of what is being described, with its apparent confusion and also its appearance of being immovable and closed in upon itself: the exuberance of Jewish society and often its underestimated heterogeneity, its insecurity and its bitter presentiment of its end.

The action takes place in Galicia in the year 1912. The main characters are the young Aronek, the *alter ego* of the writer, and his father, reb Tojwie, 'the village Acosta', 'policeman of God', a character of biblical grandeur, destined for biblical suffering. In the background is a society divided between the most completely closed dogmatisms and the libertarian ambitions of the young people, between the wisdom that is thousands of years old and the consciousness of being alive, of which the respective spokesmen are the rabbi and his learned daughter seen against a background of the emergence of new forces like Zionism and triumphant Capitalism. It is a world whose rhythms and language are still often archaic and different; a world which speaks Yiddish, Ukrainian and Polish, which writes in German and which prays in Hebrew. The surrounding Polish society is drawn as if in another dimension: although it is near and concrete, it is always foreign, indifferent, hostile.

This linguistic and cultural complex in which Jews in that part of Europe lived, as well as the ancient *substratum* of their world, have not always been translated into cultural richness; sometimes they have become a limitation and an impediment. According to Kafka, the middle European Jewish writer must face three impossibilities: it is impossible for him not to write, impossible to write in German and impossible to write in any other language. 'One could almost add a fourth impossibility: it is impossible to write.'[13]

This is perhaps an internal schism that the writer in Yiddish does not suffer from, since he uses the language of his own childhood and of his own social and religious community. It is rather the assimilated Jewish writer who suffers from it, having chosen as his own the language of the country in which he lives, but in so doing has denied himself any real means of dialogue either with his own community of origin or with the surrounding non-Jewish environment, which is usually hostile and has little interest in writing.

If one reads Stryjkowski's works, what emerges from them very clearly is a search for a Jewish identity in the diaspora, in Poland. A Jewish identity which for him was to come in the end to coincide with his origins, in his two last romantic, biblical novels on Moses and King David.

Stryjkowski came to write through the catastrophe of his own people. After the *Shoah*, the destruction, writing became a duty, the fulfilment of an act of piety towards the world that had been lost. According to a famous statement of Adorno, after Auschwitz poetry could no longer exist; but after Auschwitz, epic is possible.

> I knew that the hour would come for me also. Unfortunately that hour was the tragic hour of extermination. In Moscow, where I was working on *Wolna Polska*, weak echoes reached us of what was happening in Poland under the Nazi occupation. It was late, I do not know why, when I heard about the insurrection in the Warsaw Ghetto. I learnt that from one day to the next a Jewish people had ceased to exist and that that people after the extermination was again mine. A Communist Jew is no longer a Jew. But I felt myself to be a Jew again.[14]

The fact of having escaped alone from the *Shoah* necessarily later on weighed him down with the bitterest sense of guilt. Stryjkowski shouldered his guilt and accused himself of it in every novel; the problem could always be traced to that of the responsibility towards his community.

At a distance of about ten years from each other, two more novels set in Galicia appeared: *Austeria* (1966) and *Sen Azrila* (The Dream of Azril, 1975) – 'Variations on the world after the catastrophe and in the face of the catastrophe'.[15] The themes of the Galician novels and to a certain extent their narrative technique make Stryjkowski comparable with the other great contemporary writer of the Yiddish world, Isaac Bashevis Singer. Neither Stryjkowski nor Singer ever explicitly mentions the *Shoah* or the period of the Nazi occupation. The world of their novels is thereby made all the more dramatic, in that the tragedy which annihilated it is always implied and never described. This kind of bitter consciousness makes the work of these two writers very different from the writings of other writers or portraitists of the Yiddish world before the war, in that the *shtetlach* for Singer as for Stryjkowski 'are not a community but a society in disorder.'[16]

Their language also makes the two writers similar. The language of Singer is Yiddish, which he often translates into English, reflecting in the translation the syntactic construction and typical intonation of the original. Singer, of course, is not the only Yiddish writer to have transplanted his linguistic style into English. The critic Leslie Fielder, has said of the best of these writers, that when reading their English texts one could see the writing going from right to left. The linguistic operation of Stryjkowski is similar. He admits when talking about *Głosy in ciemności*:

> Certainly the book is written in Polish, I would even say in classical Polish, but the rhythm of the book and its internal melody is translated word to word from Yiddish.[17]

More than one doubt has been raised as to the validity of the Yiddish-Polish prose of Stryjkowski, which in Poland sometimes seems to reawaken the ghosts of sleeping dogs that people would rather let lie, and which is also not easy to understand, at least for young readers. This is not the case for Singer in America, where all practical reference to this style is lacking, and in Poland the writings of Stryjkowski are, as the title of a novel by Kuśniewicz proclaims, 'lessons in a dead language'.

In writing this prose, Stryjkowski is not attempting to charm the Polish reader (an accusation that has often been brought against him) but is showing that he belongs, in a thoroughly personal way, to the triple linguistic, cultural and literary heritage of the Polish Jews. Before the Second World War, Polish Jewish culture was expressed substantially in three languages: Yiddish, the most conspicuous on the literary scene, Hebrew, the language chosen by Zionists (and the young Stryjkowski), and lastly Polish. After the war Hebrew literature disappeared in Poland, whilst until 1957 various authors continued to express themselves in Yiddish, which is now limited to publications of the Jewish Historical Institute (*Żydowski Instytut Historyczny*). Even in Yiddish literature, linguistic paradoxes, though rare, are not lacking. For instance how can one describe in Yiddish events which took place in Poland? Israel Joshua Singer in *Altshot* resolves the problem by frequently putting into the mouth of his hero, a Jewish antiquarian who lives in the Old Town of Warsaw, long sentences in Polish, sometimes actually in rhyme. In contrast with the language of the dialogue, that of the narrator is 'classical Yiddish', as foreign as possible from Polish idiom and rich in typically Yiddish expressions.[18]

In the writings of Stryjkowski, the Jewish characters often use an extremely colourful and even extravagant Polish ('More than one green worm comes out of you!'[19]) which are faithful translations of typical slang, whereas the language of the narrator is harmonious and literary. In the stories of Singer, the use of Polish on the part of the hero indicates and underlines his complete lack of links with the Jewish community; the ghosts of the lost world of Stryjkowski give voice in their exotic 'Yiddishing' Polish to an absolute distance.

In Poland the myth of *Żydokomuna*, 'Jewish communism', is still very much alive. This myth, which was fomented by Stalin but had much earlier origins, was that all communists were Jews and that all Jews were at least potential communists. Stryjkowski tells us how at school the teacher used to draw a star with five points on the blackboard and to say turning to the class. 'This is the star of David, isn't it?'.[20] Even today the Poles have not forgiven the writer the years between 1946 (when he returned to Poland) and 1956 (the Polish thaw) during which he was considered to be one of the strongest exponents of the régime. Three of these ten years Stryjkowski spent in Rome as the Polish Press Agency's foreign correspondent. During that time he wrote what was to be his most successful publication, which was to be translated into all the languages of the countries behind the Iron Curtain, *Bieg do Fragala* (The Race to Fragala), a novel about the struggles of the peasants of Calabria, illustrated by Guttuso, which resulted in Stryjkowski being expelled from Italy and his being given the first state prize in Poland (whereas Guttuso only obtained second prize).

In 1956, after a wait of ten years, *Głosy w ciemności* was published. Some literary critics have praised this novel and its author. They say that *Głosy w ciemności* is the best Polish novel since the war and compare Stryjkowski to Thomas Mann.[21] Other critics, on the other hand, feel that the author has shown a 'want of tact' in addressing a subject so extravagant as that of the *shtetlach* of the Jews, on which it would have been better to keep quiet.

Głosy w ciemności, like the subsequent novels, is founded 'on the problem of the defeat of a strong individuality, which has done a great deal of wrong in life to itself and to others, dogmatically convinced of its own (non-existent) rightness'. These words taken from an interview with the author in 1962, seem to invite political interpretation. In fact, without ever having given himself up to mortifying self-criticism or denying his own past, Stryjkowski for some time had distanced himself from Party orthodoxy. The moment of his public self-detachment from the Party can be placed in 1962, when *Czarna Róża* was published, a largely autobiographical novel about communist society in Lwów before the war. Although it stays within the limits of realistic prose, this book is really a manual on what is not a definition of a young communist, and on what should not be one's reasons for joining the class struggle, and on how not to behave when one is a political detainee, and so on. *Czarna Róża* provoked impassioned and violent discussions (we recall one at the Jewish Cultural and Social

Organisation in Warsaw, in the course of which the author ran a serious risk of being physically attacked) and resulted in the author almost completely ceasing to publish.

> I don't need to write . . . But there was one thing I couldn't do: cease to consider myself a writer . . . I don't need to write at all. And I feel alright. But that's only for a certain time. I never know for how long I'll be able to remain 'silent'. Until something happens that I have to 'reveal'. Unfortunately this is becoming more and more difficult.[23]

In 1966, the second of Stryjkowski's Galician novels appeared, *Austeria* (The Inn), which takes a markedly more pessimistic position than its predecessor. In *Głosy w ciemości* we find ourselves face to face with a society, which, although seeing the abyss into which it is about to fall ('We were afraid like insects before the storm. How long shall we be able to pretend to be alive?' p. 373), continues nevertheless to consider itself a society. In it, interpersonal relationships, although they are strained and disturbed, are respected and the earthly order, a reflection of the transcendental law, is still valid and stable. In *Austeria* premonitions of the impending destruction of the world of farthest Eastern Europe are much stronger.

The 'concentric' action of *Głosy w ciemności* is of a one-year duration whilst that of *Austeria* is of a few hours, from the afternoon to the dawn of the following day. This is the first day of the Great War and the action takes place in a Jewish inn 'on the road to Duliby near Skole, in an almost deserted place, a very long way from school and synagogue'. During the course of the action, which rigorously respects the three unities of Greek drama, the society of the Jewish *shtetl* separates before our eyes. In the inn kept by the elderly Tag, there is no longer any law, or any human contact, but only a busy commotion in an attempt to flee from the catastrophe, what Stefan Zweig has called the collapse of 'the world of yesterday' and of the 'age of gold and safety'.

Austeria is the most Austrian work of Stryjkowski and is well adapted to the framework of the Habsburg legend, although from its own point of view it is rigorously Jewish (and one can recall in passing that the Jews were certainly the people who suffered most from the fall of Austria-Hungary): in fact 'no people and no language venerates the Emperor like the Jews' (p. 48); and the lament for 'the Emperor with a Jewish heart' (p. 35) is always vivid, as is the lament for those times in which 'it was possible to live to be seventy without knowing how a pitchfork is made'. The historical perspective of the novel, a 'Galician ecumenism', that is, the ecumenism of those who, with obstinate nostalgia, see in the region a symbol of the peaceful meeting of different peoples, cultures, languages and religions. The elderly Tag, the central character in *Austeria*, is the only person in the Yiddish world of Stryjkowski to be a friend not only of a *goy*, a gentile, but even of a priest, entirely without being tempted to become a Christian, as indeed none of Stryjkowski's characters is (with the single exception in *Przybysz z Narbony*):

> What do you want, Father?' – rejoined Tag to the priest, who was an untiring missionary – 'You know very well that I am Jewish and I will remain Jewish until my death. A Jew is always a Jew. Even if he is baptised.' – 'You are different.' – 'All Jews are alike. As no other people is. I am not different from other Jews.'(p. 171)

Although he keeps to the faith and customs of his fathers, the inn-keeper Tag has a Christian mistress. The theme of the love of the old inn-keeper for the Ukrainian girl, Jewdocha, a 'cow-girl', rather than being one of the signs of the scarce and spurious Jewish conscience of the writer, harks back to a well-known model of Jewish folklore. The theme of the male or female Jewish inn-keeper in love with a Christian (often a pork merchant), which was already present in the legends circulating around the figure of Baal Shem Tov, the founder of Hasidism, is also to be found in Israel Joshua Singer's story *Blut* (Blood) in which the son of a guilty union becomes a violent anti-semite and dies while trying to kill his own family.[24]

At the beginning of the 1960s Stryjkowski went to Los Angeles. Three short stories resulted from his encounter with the American reality, which are contained in a book entitled *Na wierzbach . . . nasze skrzypce* (On the Willows . . . our Violins).

> The waves grow smaller, the sea is silent. I shall come down to earth like Columbus. I am young and strong. The sea calms me down, the dead wave passes, the land invites me. A great happiness awaits me, a discovered treasure. I put out to sea on the narrow canoe, on the red sky, I am four years old again, the horse snorts and stamps with its hooves on the stone street.
> – Let us go down there, down there. – My mother points
> to the red sky.
> The sky is violet.
> The country evening is coming down,
> without lamps.
> The smell of wormwood,
> of cows,
> of smoke.
> – Ssh, there is a country, there, there is our house.[25]

Amongst those who have escaped from the concentration camps and the ghettos, among the friends and acquaintances from the past, who are now perfectly settled in the American reality, the narrator does not manage to find even an unimportant person (a deputy *melamed*) from his own home and from the world that has disappeared in Europe. The rabbi has his head covered with a very small *yarmulka*, 'a ritual relic . . . as shameful as a fig leaf' (p. 101). In Nysen's villa the little valley of the cypresses ends in 'a hedge in the form of the star of David' (p. 132). The narrator, a Polish writer, 'a dignitary' in his own home country, has nothing to communicate on the other side of the Atlantic:

> 'What can I say? – I reflected, as if I really wanted to make a declaration that from the first moment they had been expecting from me . . . The seconds passed in silence. I dried the sweat on my forehead with my handkerchief.
> – My dear friends – I began – I have nothing to say to you.
> The guests looked at each other and returned to their dinner. (p. 117)

Even Jakub, the author-narrator's former close friend, finds his desire to return to Poland strange and incomprehensible, 'irrational' or dictated merely by motives of self-interest.

After this brief American interlude, Stryjkowski returned to Poland, the country he had never considered abandoning.

> A whole people has perished. How can you walk on that earth? Under every stone is a brother who has been killed . . . – But I belong to the cemetery. (p. 109)

In 1975 the third Galician novel of Stryjkowski was published, *Sen Azrila* (The Dream of Azril), one of his most hermetic texts. It is set at the beginning of the century and tells of the return of Azril, a rich widower, to his native land. The whole of the action takes place during the course of a single night, illuminated by a moon which is 'as thin as a cut fingernail', (p. 31) and can be interpreted as the description of a dream or nightmare, during which the hero returns to his own country, but after the *Shoah*, hoping to find again some trace of the places and peoples once known to him. He cannot, however, even find the tomb of his father.

> The chain is broken . . . I have forgotten the words. What do they say? . . . I have not been here for twenty years, and the memory of the living is the balm of the dead. Reb Pinches the scribe. The voice was sucked out of the void. Your son AZRIEL . . . There is no father, there is no son. The chain is broken.[26]

The novel ends with the death of Azril: his return has been in vain, in his birthplace he has not found either the tomb of his parents or any reason to live in a world which now is no longer his. And he cannot do otherwise than die.

In *Sen Azrila* Stryjkowski continues his search for a *lingua franca*, immediately comprehensible not only to the few Jewish or 'Jewishing' readers, but also, even if not primarily, for Polish readers; the linguistic atmosphere comes from the music and the internal rhythm of the sentences. In this, which is perhaps the most Jewish of Stryjkowski's books, although the language used by the characters is exclusively Yiddish, the rendering into Polish of almost all foreign expressions is very striking, and this includes both Yiddish or Hebrew expressions, and even those which would not present difficulties for the Polish reader to understand (as for example Sholem Aleykhem).

With the death of Azril, it seems that Stryjkowski's Galician cycle has ended. In order to speak of Jewish matters, the writer turns now to more remote settings; biblical Israel, or Spain under the Inquisition. In particular, the novel with the Spanish setting, although a long way away from the Austro-Hungarian Empire and from the days of the Emperor, seems rather to be a continuation of the Galician novels than one of their far off antecedents. At least, this is the indication contained in the dedication, 'to the insurgents of the Warsaw Ghetto'. 'The Galician theme – Stryjkowski has said – is the theme of my life to which I must always return.' During recent years, the author now in his eighties, has returned 'like a madman' to his first novel, *Głosy w ciemności*, which he is starting to write the sequel to, perhaps to take the characters through the horrors of the war.

In 1980 and during the Solidarity period, Stryjkowski was to join the then current cultural self-justification of those years of renewal and hope, by publishing with the independent publisher *Nowa* (and simultaneously in London with *Zapis*) a novel which was violently anti-Soviet, *Wielki Strach* (The Great Fear) which deals with the occupation of Eastern Poland by the Red Army. But by taking this line he does not seem to have brought himself any closer or made himself any more credible to his Polish readers. Possibly his last two novels have contributed more to that result: *Odpowiedź* (The Answer) and *Król Dawid żyje* (King David is alive), where the biblical theme and the emphasis on the religious foundations common to Jews and Poles, seem to be convincing and more is gained from them than just a repudiation or a critique of communism. The only public meetings which the author participates in now are those organised by the Church and both *Odpowiedź* and *Król Dawid żyje* have been published by Dominican publishers:

> You ask me whether my friendship with the clergy causes me any problems. What do you want me to answer? It is merely a question of aesthetics. They are always very kind and very well educated. I have

never heard a word that could displease me. The Church to-day is the only place in which one can talk, where one can feel a little freedom. 'Church' does not mean only believers but atheists as well.[27]

In 1986, when this article was written, Poland under General Jaruzelski had succeeded in relegating all culture not pertaining to the regime into the narrow confines of the Church and cloisters and this enforced polarisation (Church – Party) had certainly not offered openings for quiet reflection and dialogue. Nevertheless, the 'normalisation' was not interrupt, but rather, paradoxically, favoured, two phenomena which give room for hope in the future of Polish society. A part of the clergy and the Catholic intelligentsia seemed willing to approach Judaism and to consider critically, perhaps for the first time for decades, one of the most painful chapters of their own recent history, that of the relationship between Jews and Poles. In other parts of society as well, particularly in families where there is a communist or socialist tradition, with the result that they are Polonized and 'assimilated' even if they are of Jewish origin, the next generation was growing closer to Judaism and its values, which to them represented cosmopolitanism and a defence of tradition, and national and religious identity; and this was a rediscovery of Judaism, which in the particular situation of Poland, necessarily and most of all entails a search for that spirit of tolerance which for many decades seemed to have abandoned that country.

This is the background against which the figure of Julian Stryjkowski was continually acquiring greater significance, for he was one of the very few writers who had never forgotten his Jewish origins, even during his period of militant communism (even if 'a Jewish communist is no longer Jewish'.)

Literature owes its significance to the fact that it is about the struggle of good against evil . . . Faustism is one of the more famous variations on this problem and even appears in the Bible, in the Book of Job. . . . One aim of literature can be to help man, showing him that he is not alone in his struggle, that he has a hinterland.[28]

Warsaw has been destroyed, and Polish Judaism has been wiped out. The Poles have reconstructed their city; on one of the buildings in the centre, on the corner of Aleje Jerozolimskie and Nowy Świat, the words 'The whole people is rebuilding its capital' are engraved. It is in the ghostly and upsetting city that Styjkowski now lives.

His windows look out over the large Łazienki Park. In his house, next to several reproductions of Michelangelo, there is a portrait of the Emperor Franz Joseph, which the author shows to his guests saying, 'There is the portrait of a good man. The last one.'

A great silence reigned. The sky had become clear, as after a storm. The stars had become animated and twinkled. I looked for Sirius, the most trembling, the most unquiet and the most loved amongst the stars. But I could not find it. It was not there. And when I saw the Great Bear, with its rod broken, I shivered . . . I understood what it means to be a stranger everywhere. . . . Everywhere suspended between the beginning and the end of the road. 'Not the goal' – the Jewish actress sang – 'But the approach to it, not the bank, but the road that leads to it, because it is in dreams that I am well, I am well in illusions . . . in dreams the sky is more blue than blue' . . . These soap bubbles set the Jewish singers free . . . Where are you, poets of the air? . . . Free yourselves on the miserable ant hill of the towns, on the peacock wings of the poetry of Itzik Manger. Scattered jewels of guttural words. Let us sit down in front of the Great Theatre, in the Hetmanskie Valleys, under the monument of King John on horseback. I am Polish: you are Jews. I, because I disliked your raucous speech, took refuge in the 'sacred songs of the lamp, the sacred songs of *viburno*' . . . But today allow me to sit down beside you. How are you? Have you a grosz for dinner? How beautiful your language is. Like a full saucepan. Listen, I have translated the ballad of 'The Golden Peacock'. It tells how the peacock flies to the rabbi with a letter from the woman who loves him: on the letter 'there are three tears'. Oh, would you like something on your, on our, common death? . . . 'The night is cloudy and the Polish sky is above us, and above the old town. The town is the urn containing the ashes of our lives.' The actress like a crow sat down on the back of the chair; soon Leah will come out onto the stage in her white wedding dress; her thick hair winds round the shaken body of Dybuk. The Market Place is crowded; in the disfigured town the noisy, authentic and real life on Polish earth unravels itself and nothing remains, nothing. I have fled alone, but I have shouted, 'Save yourselves if you can!'. Everyone has died as in times past on the pyres of faith. Only I remain, I alone.[29]

NOTES

1 J. Stryjkowski, *Na wierzbach . . . nasze skrzypce*, (Warsaw, 1974), p. 5.
2 F. Folkel, *Monade. 33 poesie del giudeo*, (Milan, 1978), p. 36.
3 W. Chołodowski, *Stryjkowski*, (Warsaw, 1982), p. 8.
4 E. Cioran, *La tentation d'exister*, (Paris, 1974).
5 Interview with Z. Taranienko in *Literatura* (Warsaw), vol. II,(1972), no. 15.
6 Interview with the author, March 1984 (to appear in *La rassegna mensile di Israel*).
7 Ibid.
8 G. Origlia, Introduction to the Italian edition of 'Przybysz z Narbony' ('L'uomo venuto da Narbona', Rome, 1985), pp. 7–8.

9 Interview with the author, March 1984.
10 Interview with T. Krzemień, *Kultura* (Warsaw), vol. XIX, (1981), no. 22.
11 Interview with J. Nieczkowski, *Współczesność*, vol. XVI, (1971), no. 22, pp. 1–3.
12 Interview with the author, March 1984.
13 F. Kafka, *Briefe*, (Frankfurt-am-Main, 1966), pp. 337–8.
14 Interview with the author, March 1984.
15 L. Ligęza, 'Umiejętność milczenia', *Więź*, (1962), no. 1, p. 147.
16 I. Knopp Zadowsky, *The Trial of Judaism in Contemporary Writing*, (New York, 1975).
17 Interview with W. P. Szymański in *Tygodnik Powszechny*, vol. 18, (1964), no. 21.
18 Ch. Shmeruk, 'Jews and Poles in Yiddish Literature in Poland Between the two World Wars', Polin no. 1 (Oxford, 1986).
19 *Głosy w ciemności*, (Warsaw, 1956), p. 36.
20 Krzemień, *Kultura*, (1981).
21 Z. Bieńkowski in *Kultura* (Warsaw), vol. II, (1964), no. 7.
22 Szymański, *Tygodnik Powszechny*.
23 J. Stryjkowski, 'Dlaczego piszę', *Nowa Kultura*, vol. X, (1959), no. 17.
24 Cf. Shmeruk.
25 *Na wierzbach . . . nasze skrzypce*, p. 42.
26 *Sen Azrila*, (Warsaw, 1975), p. 160.
27 Interview with the author, 23 January 1986.
28 Taranienko, *Literatura*.
29 *Na wierzbach . . . nasze skrzypce*, pp. 80–2.

28

POLES AND POLAND IN I. B. SINGER'S FICTION[1]

Monika Adamczyk-Garbowska

When Isaac Bashevis Singer was awarded the Nobel Prize in 1978, most Polish people heard his name for the first time. Singer's absence from the Polish literary scene had been caused to a great extent by the general silence surrounding Jewish topics after 1968; the campaign against Jerzy Kosinski's *The Painted Bird* did not help to introduce another writer with similar roots, either. Paradoxically enough, while commenting upon the award, some Polish journalists tried to present Singer as a Polish writer, attempting in this way to gain a Polish Nobel Laureate; let us remember that this was before Miłosz and Wałęsa and some Poles had a complex about not being sufficiently appreciated on the international forum.

Although Singer is not a Polish writer, but a Yiddish one, his work is deeply rooted in the Polish Jewish past. And yet he cannot be described as a mere chronicler of the vanished Jewish world. As Eli Katz observes, 'his towns of Goray and Bilgoray, Frampol and Zamość, all of which can be located historically and geographically, are more products of the imagination than the invented Tuneyadevke and Glupsk of Mendele, or Sholom Aleichem's Kasrilevke and Kozodeyevke'.[2] This sentence rightly points at one of the most important aspects of Singer's fiction. His imagination has a transformatory power, changing historical reality into his own fictitious one. The fact that he himself is a post-Holocaust chronicler of the pre-Holocaust world makes his vision substantially different from those of classic Yiddish writers whose reality could have been threatened by pogroms and legal decrees, but was nevertheless perceived as relatively stable and static.

What makes his work attractive to the Polish reader is not only the depiction of the Jewish community, exotic to the modern Polish audience, but also his image of Poles and Poland, his views on Polish customs, history, politics, and so on. Reading *The Manor* or *The Estate*, the Polish reader is fascinated and puzzled to find a different interpretation of certain historical events or social phenomena from the one he knows from classical Polish literature.

In Poland, Singer has received mainly favorable criticism, but this seems partly due to the fact that only some of his novels[3] and stories were translated into Polish and also because he is not directly concerned in his fiction with the Holocaust, which appears to be the most controversial issue for Polish critics. It is possible, however, that if *The Slave* or *The King of the Fields* were translated into Polish, the unfavourable image of Poles as a collective could evoke some negative response as in the case of William Styron's *Sophie's Choice*.[4]

Singer is well-known for his literary technique that involves stereotyping, typification, and tendencies of focusing on and exploring the negative aspects of human nature. For this he has been fiercely attacked by critics of different orientations, who sometimes overlook the fact that they are a part of his artistic technique rather than a willingness to deprecate one particular group.[5]

I should like to examine his Polish characters and depiction of Polish reality to see how his tendency toward stereotyping is displayed in this respect, to what extent his perception of Poland resembles that of other Yiddish authors, and what is the significance of Polish topics in his work as a whole.[6]

Polish topics constitute only a part of his writing. In some novels and stories Poles do not appear at all, in others they appear as more or less marginal characters, and in several stories and one novel, *The King of the Fields*, they come to the fore, constituting a majority. Poles are practically the only Gentiles appearing in Singer's fiction. In his novels or stories taking place in America the characters are exclusively American or European Jews. Clive Sinclair rightly observes that 'America never dominated the imagination of the Singer brothers, as it had the generation of immigrants that preceded them'.[7]

Nevertheless, in comparison to Jewish characters, Poles usually constitute a minority and therefore the scale of characters must be more limited. One can distinguish two distinctive stereotypes, that of a Polish nobleman and a Polish peasant woman.

The first stereotype has its rich source in Yiddish literary tradition in which the Polish *porets* is usually a negative or at least highly ambivalent figure; often pictured as arrogant, violent, thoughtless, indulging in food and alcohol.[8] It would be worth briefly comparing how the nobleman is presented in Polish literature. Generally speaking, one can say that violence and arrogance are presented as bravery and pride, thoughtlessness as idealism, and if drunkenness or gluttony are mentioned they usually receive a comic touch. However, in some Polish literature with leftist tendencies the *pan* (nobleman) bears some features resembling the Yiddish stereotype.[9]

Singer stressed a number of times that his characters are based on people whom he knew very well and that he avoids writing about people of whom he does not possess enough knowledge.[10] It is obvious, however, that he does not base his descriptions of nobles on personal experience – the more so since noblemen appear mainly in his historical novels – but takes them from various literary sources, Yiddish rather than Polish. Considering the image the *porets* has in the Yiddish tradition and the writer's demonic imagination, as well as his interest in sexuality in its most unusual forms, it is no wonder that all the vices of the Polish *pan* are further intensified in Singer's writing. The Polish nobleman becomes a real demon, sexually promiscuous and perverse; unable to accumulate wealth, he can only waste what he inherited or what he acquired exploiting peasants and – to some extent – Jews.

Proceeding in the historical order encountered in Singer's works, we find a prototype of the Polish *pan* in *The King of the Fields* in the figure of Król Rudy, who at the beginning seems quite civilized compared with his savage subjects but soon loses control over them and indulges in excessive drinking, bloodshed and rape to the same extent as his *wojaks*. Finally he loses his mind and behaves as a wild animal rather than a human being. His early efforts at creating a well-organized Polish state fail owing to his own weaknesses and the corruption of his people. While working on *The King of the Fields* Singer consulted a Polish classic *Stara baśń* (An Ancient Tale) written in 1876 by Józef Ignacy Kraszewski and covering approximately the same period, i.e. the beginnings of the Polish state.[11] Kraszewski's version of the early Polish history, however, is highly idealized presenting the mythical founder of the Polish state, Piast (Kraszewski's *kniеź* Piastun) as a very well-balanced, wise and noble man; contrary to Król Rudy, he succeeds in consolidating the pagan Slavic tribes who have to defend themselves from German aggressors.

Another embodiment of the Polish nobleman is Count Adam Pilitzki from *The Slave*, an emotionally unstable and totally depraved character. 'It was said that his daughter had drowned herself after having been possessed by him. His son had gone mad and had died of jaundice'.[12] Although he is directly responsible for the collapse of his family and indirectly for the decline of Poland, he always tries to put blame on others.

> At every opportunity Adam Pilitzki warned that Poland would have no peace until Protestants, Cossacks and Jews were killed – particularly the Jews who had secretly bribed the traitor Radziszewski and conspired with the Swedes.[13]

He mistreats everybody, especially peasants and Jews, and at some stage of his life becomes a fanatical Catholic, which, however, does not lead him to follow Christian principles in his life but rather intensifies his contempt and hatred for those who think differently.

His wife is even more demonic – 'The rumour was that [she] was his procuress and had taken the coachman as her lover. Another that she copulated with a stallion'.[14] As Gladsky notices, she is the only Polish female in Singer's fiction perceived in such an unfavourable light.[15]

The nineteenth-century equivalents of Król Rudy and Count Pilitzki are the Jampolski father and son who appear in *The Manor*. Their pathological behaviour is partly explained by the traumatic experiences they undergo, such as participation in the January uprising of 1863, expulsion to Siberia and loss of faith in the sense of fighting for Polish independence.

These are, however, only superficial reasons; more pertinently their downfall seems to be encoded in their genes. Apart from serving as representatives of their disappearing class, they also stand for some modern positivist ideas of the period, of which they are faulty followers. Their main role is to counteract the Jewish characters since they are to some extent the modus leading to the rise and fall of the Calman Jacoby family. As the Jacoby's rise to riches is devoid of dignity – he prostrates himself in front of the Russian duke – and his marriage to Clara based on lust and vanity, he is also doomed to the final fall. As a consequence of becoming the lords of the manor, Calman and his family depart from their community and forsake their heritage to a lesser or greater degree.

Lucian Jampolski is the most demoniac of all Singer's characters, a figure resembling some Dostoevsky protagonists. Apart from representing his depraved self and the moral degradation of Polish émigrés, he personally contributes to the fall of the Jacoby family by seducing Calman's daughter Miriam Lieba.

In Polish literature the image of a January insurgent would receive completely different treatment. The old count after returning from Siberia would lead a decent and austere life in the aura of heroism and martyrdom, loved and admired by his neighbours, and his son would probably choose a positivist road, comprising, among other things, a friendly attitude towards Jews.

Janek Zazhitsky from *The Family Moskat* belongs to the same infamous gallery. Although not really an aristocrat he comes from the pauperized nobility and gradually becomes a member of the ruling class. His ascent up the social ladder corresponds with his gradual moral degradation. A former teetotaller, he becomes a drunkard; a former philo-semite, he turns to anti-semitism. He repeats Pilitzky's prejudices in a modernized version, believing that Jews involved in some international plot are responsible for the coming downfall of Poland. His marriage to Masha causes her pain and disaster.

The motif of the seduction of a Jewish girl by a Gentile *pan* appears in earlier Yiddish literature and it always leads to tragedy.[16] It also constitutes the topic of one of Singer's stories, 'One Day of Happiness', where a bizarre figure of a Polish 'general-poet', handsome and apparently *charmant* like Lucian at the beginning of his relationship with Miriam Lieba, turns into a beast raping the Jewish girl. The stereotypic Polish chivalry is handled with irony when he sends the girl, driven to commit suicide, an impressive bouquet of roses, 'red as blood'.[17]

In his depiction of noblemen Singer continues the Jewish tradition in which in descriptions of the *shtetl*, the *porets* was a necessary element, most often appearing in the background. The figure of a violent and vicious *pan* really suits Singer's imagination and his role is either to show the basic evil of human nature or create a certain counterbalance to sicknesses tormenting the Jewish community.

The figure of the Polish peasant woman stands at another extreme. Gentle, kind-hearted, obedient and quiet, she is the opposite of the carnivorous Polish male whom she usually despises. She is also sensitive and/or passionate enough to be a mate for the Jewish protagonist. Her stereotype comprises features often used by foreign writers to depict Polish heroines (for example we encounter more refined versions of the Singer Polish woman in Leon Uris's *Mila 18* or Styron's *Sophie's Choice*).[18]

In the *King of the Fields* Laska and Yagoda, although not strictly representatives of Poles, but Lesniks - a highlanders' tribe conquered by Poles and speaking nearly the same language - are again historical prototypes of the Slavic woman, submissive and utterly devoted even if mistreated and betrayed. Yagoda becomes a wife of Cybula who, although non-Jewish, resembles in many respects such Jewish protagonists as Yasha Mazur, Asa Heshel Bannet and Herman Broder in his sensitivity (compared with other pagans), pessimism and sexual promiscuity. In this particular novel, Kosoka, the woman in love with the Jewish protagonist, Ben Dosa, is a Tartar girl, but the pattern of their relationships is a historical prototype of Polish female-Jewish male relationships in *The Slave* or *Enemies*.

In *The Slave,* Wanda, the most fully developed among Singer's Slavic heroines, greatly differs from her savage kinsmen. She seems city-bred, wears nice and clean clothes, can express herself clearly, quite unlike other peasants who 'could scarcely speak Polish, grunted like animals, made signs with their hands and laughed madly.'[19] In her village she bears the nickname of 'The Lady' since apart from the above-mentioned characteristics she is good-looking:

> [She] was twenty-five and taller than most of the other women. She had blonde hair, blue eyes, a fair skin, and well-modelled features. She braided her hair and twisted it around her head like a wreath of wheat. When she smiled, her cheeks dimpled and her teeth were so strong she could crush the toughest of pits. Her nose was straight and

she had a narrow chin. She was a skilful seamstress and could knit, cook and tell stories which made one's hair stand on end.[20]

She combines a certain refinement and class with the peasant's strength and endurance. Because of her love for Jacob the Jew, Wanda abandons her heritage and converts to Judaism, taking the name of Sarah. It is interesting to mention in this context that in the Polish literary and folk tradition the name Wanda stands for a woman who prefers to commit suicide rather than depart from her Polishness.

The relationship of Jacob and Wanda is presented as ideal for in spite of the final tragedy, they never betray each other. Their misfortunes are caused by external factors or God's will rather then their own behaviour. In other cases the Polish females are often mistreated by the Jewish protagonists for reasons embedded in the latter's personalities. And thus Magda in *The Magician of Lublin* is driven to commit suicide and Yadwiga from *Enemies* ends up abandoned, having been previously betrayed several times.

The stereotype of the Polish female also applies to her physical appearance, generally that of a healthy, blonde and rosy wench. Yadwiga, for example, has rosy cheeks, pug nose, light-coloured eyes, flaxen hair and high cheekbones. She smells of camomile and beetroots.[21] Tekla, a maidservant from *Shosha*, has 'muscular legs and firm breasts' and 'her cheeks [are] the colour of ripe apples. She gave forth a vigour erupted in the earth, in the sun, in the whole universe [. . .] She wanted to give, not to take. If the Polish people had produced even one Tekla, they had surely accomplished their mission'.[22]

Magda differs from the other women both in her background and physical appearance. She comes from pauperized petty gentry and she is 'barely skin-and-bones'[23] and has pimply skin. But still she has grayish-green eyes, snub nose and high cheekbones. Her looks must be different from those of other heroines to fit the tasks she has to perform as a magician's companion.

The relationships of the Jewish male and Polish female are also doomed to disaster like the ones of the Polish male and Jewish female, though they are devoid of the violence characteristic of the latter. The mixed relationships are usually childless, and if a child is born it either causes enormous pain as in the case of Jacob and Wanda or it is unwanted and abandoned by the father as in the case of Yadwiga and Herman.

In Singer's fictionalized memoirs, we encounter a passage symbolizing the mutual attraction and peculiar entanglement of Polish and Jewish fates. The narrator, fantasising about a sexual relationship with a maidservant Marila, another strong kind-hearted blue-eyed girl with 'a high bosom and round hips'[24] says:

> I know full well that this will complicate our accounts even more, bring new reincarnations and maybe prolong the Diaspora, but even though free choice was bestowed upon us, everything is predestined. The divine ledger is manifold. Marila is the eleventh generation of a coachman who seduced the wife of a peasant, and I the thirteenth generation of a milkmaid raped by a squire. It's all noted in our genes.

He foresees, however, that 'a year hence, Marila will marry her fiancé, the soldier Stach, son of Jan, and for me there also awaits somewhere an ovary and a womb that will give birth to my son or daughter. God is the sum total not only of all deeds but also of all the possibilities'.[25] It seems then that according to Singer, in spite of the mutual attraction and affinity it is the safest for each party to follow his or her traditional way. Singer's characters, however, try to select some of the rare 'possibilities' and this leads them to their downfall.

In sum the Polish female is the embodiment of everything feminists would object to, and a representative of one of the types distinguished by Evelyn Torton Beck, that of the 'passive, willing victim',[26] although Beck in her article does not mention any Polish characters.

It is worth noticing that similar types appear also in Polish literature, for example in Zofia Nałkowska's *Granica* (Boundary Line, 1935), where Justyna, the seduced and abandoned peasant girl resembles in her fate Singer's Jewish heroines mistreated by their Polish lovers and in her appearance and submissiveness Singer's Polish females.

In spite of possible literary sources, it seems that in the case of Polish women Singer draws to some extent from first-hand experience. He certainly must have had more contact with Polish peasant women than with members of the ruling class, whether in his grandfather's *shtetl* or in Warsaw. Most probably the main contact he had with the Gentile world was through similar women. In contacts between hostile or estranged communities women are often a kind of link and do not undergo negative stereotyping to the extent males do. A Jewish counterpart of Singer's Polish heroines in Polish literature may be, for example, the figure of Esterka, who is idealized both in Yiddish and Polish literatures.[27] Esterka's devotion to King Casimir is parallel to Singer's heroines' devotion to their Jewish lovers.

But again, owing to Singer's originality as a writer, he offers his own interpretation of the stereotype, enriching it with the features that suit his literary vision. Since for Singer the world basically consists in a struggle between the opposites: good and evil, faith and betrayal, ignorance and knowledge – it is not surprising that obedient, devoted, self-sacrificing, simple-minded and patient females often serve as counterparts to rebellious, unfaithful, selfish, intellectual and restless males. This pattern works in both types of relationships, regardless of whether the male is Jewish of Polish. The main difference is that Jewish women attracted to Polish men usually come from well-off families and are rather well-educated; their acquaintance with Polish romantic literature makes them even more prone to seduction.

Apart from these individual stereotypes we encounter a collective stereotype in Singer's fiction: that of Poles as a group or community. In *The King of the Fields* they are *wojaks*, in *Satan in Goray* or *The Slave* peasants, and in *The Family Moskat*, *Shosha* and the writer's memoirs, the anonymous mob encountered usually on the train.

In the tenth century Król Rudy's men kill, rape, set fire to homes and crops, constantly quarrel, drink vodka and mead, and in their rare moments of sobriety shout patriotic slogans. The simple folk live in ignorance and filth and serve obscure gods.

In *Satan in Goray* where peasants stand far in the background, they are presented as very backward and easily manipulated against Jews. Although this is the seventh century of Christianity in Poland they still perform pagan rituals and worship idols: 'In the village of Maidan the peasants lured a witch into the woods, chained her to a tree, and built a fire about her, after stripping her of her clothes'.[28] In *The Slave*

> the village abounded in cripples, boys and girls with goitres, distended heads and disfiguring birth-marks; there were also mutes, epileptics, freaks who had been born with six fingers on their hands or six toes on their feet. In summer, the parents of these deformed children kept them on the mountains with the cattle, and they ran wild. There, men and women copulated in public; the women became pregnant, but climbing as they did all day on the rocks, bearing heavy packs, they often miscarried. The district had no midwife and mothers in labor were forced to cut the umbilical cord themselves. If the child died, they buried it in a ditch without Christian rites or else threw it into the mountain stream.[29]

Sometimes the priest is also an element of the collective being presented in a very unfavourable light like Dziobak, in *The Slave*, who is always drunk.

The peasants coexist daily with all sorts of savage and mischievous spirits and perform all kinds of sorcery, believing in similar powers as the pagans in *The King of the Fields*. Singer admitted that while working on *The Slave* he carefully studied Polish demonology. In this savage milieu Jacob undergoes similar experiences to those of Kosinski's Boy in *The Painted Bird*. Any connection in this case is highly improbable, but it is possible that both writers drew some of their material from similar sources.

The collective stereotype combines violence and drunkenness characteristic of aristocrats with passivity, simple-mindedness and enslavement typical of Slavic women. The collective is unclean, stinking of sweat and vodka and threatening to the Jews.

The stereotype of peasants also comes partly from the Yiddish tradition. Even in the Yiddish literature written between the wars, excluding leftist novels where peasants are treated with pity, Polish *poyerim* are often characterized as stupid and simple in contrast with the educated Jews,[30] as the peasants in *The Slave* are contrasted with the learned Jacob. This stereotype is not unique but typical of the perception of 'the stranger' by a folk community. In the Polish folklore Jews as a collective are also perceived as a dark and mysterious community, performing strange rituals, unclean and stinking of onion and garlic.[31] Even the element of violence is present only in a more camouflaged form with the belief in Jews kidnapping Christian children for Passover *matzot*, which has its milder Jewish counterpart in the belief in forced conversion of Jews to Christianity. Olga Goldberg stresses that the negative stereotype of a Jew in Polish folklore is 'invariably a male figure'[32] which can be to great extent applied to the Yiddish tradition in general and Singer's fiction in particular. Besides, there is always the magic element present, making the stranger both 'destructive and positive'.[33] In the case of Polish peasants as perceived by Singer the destructive element is drunkenness and ignorance, the positive strength and endurance.

Each rule, however, has its exceptions and as in classical Yiddish literature good *goyim* also appear , so they do in Singer's fiction. Such good *goyim* are, among others, Duke Wiśniowiecki, a protector of Jews, appearing in *Satan in Goray* as 'the Polish nobleman Wisniewski the friend of the Jews, who had impaled *haidamaks* on wooden poles',[34] or 'domesticated' Gentiles, coexisting peacefully with *shtetl* Jews and constituting a part of the *shtetl* landscape. As Sholom Aleichem put it:

> If Fyodor, the gentile who extinguished the lights in Kasrilevke on Friday nights; pockmarked Hapke, the woman who whitewashed the houses and milked everyone's goats; and other such non-Jews could be labelled the 'other people' . . . the Jews could have remained in their village until the advent of the Messiah, for since time immemorial they had fared well with these 'other people' so well, in fact, that one might even have thought it couldn't be any better.[35]

However these 'other people' are en masse hostile and the singled out exceptions only confirm the rule.

In Singer's writing, such domesticated Gentiles usually appear in works where he employs first person narration or narrative monologue.[36] The narrator is either the author himself – as in his autobiographical fiction – or an anonymous or named inhabitant of the *shtetl* (e.g. Aunt Yentl). These narrators present the domesticated Gentiles with sentiment and affection and as Fyodor or Hapke they are described as a bit *meshuge*. For example,

Yash from 'The Chimney Sweep'[37] simple-minded and modest, liked by all Jewish housewives in the shtetl, turns out to be a clairvoyant.

A *porets* can be domesticated as well, like Jan Chwalski from 'Strong as Death'[38] an eccentric with a heart of gold: sending Purim gifts to his court Jew, dancing Cossack dances with Jews, sending for a doctor if any of his peasants gets sick and madly in love with a wife of another nobleman, very stereotypic for a change. Since a characteristic feature of stereotypes is that once broken they go to the other extreme, while all other noblemen never get sober, Jan Chwalski is portrayed as a teetotaller.

In 'The Litigants'[39] two quarrelling and finally reconciled noblemen are also treated with a dose of sympathy and humour but they are by no means perceived as normal.

In one of the stories from *A Day of Pleasure*, the alien and threatening Polish collective represented by Gentiles occasionally passing the young narrator, laughing at him and speaking 'incomprehensible language'[40] is counterbalanced in another story with a rather neutral figure of the janitor coming for his 'Friday money'. He waits politely at the door with his hat taken off.[41] The story focuses on the character of a Polish washerwoman bearing 'certain pride and love of labour with which many Gentiles have been blessed'.[42] The washerwoman stands for a symbolic coexistence of the two communities, since she washes Jewish holy garments while Singer's mother is praying for her when she senses that something bad must have befallen the old woman. On the other hand by a humorous example Singer shows the disparity of the two worlds:

> She was especially fond of me and used to say I looked like Jesus. She repeated this every time she came, and Mother would frown and whisper to herself, her lips barely moving, 'May her words be scattered in the wilderness'.[43]

What is considered the greatest compliment by the Gentile washerwoman is considered a blasphemy by Singer's mother. The story ends with the most beautiful invocation, similar to that from 'Strong as Death':

> And now at last her body, which had long been no more than a shard supported only by the force of honesty and duty, had fallen. Her soul passed into those spheres where all holy souls meet, regardless of the roles they played on this earth, in whatever tongue, of whatever creed. I cannot even conceive of a world where there is no recompense for such effort.[44]

Here the paradise is perceived in ecumenical terms, while in 'Strong as Death' it is a separate paradise for Gentiles. The difference is justified by the different narrator, Singer himself in the first case, and a simple woman in the other. In this context one cannot resist an analogy with the concept of the 'righteous gentiles' which Madeline G. Levine finds rather offensive.[45]

There are also some characters who do not fall into the above-mentioned categories but who constitute certain stereotypes, closer however to the Polish literary tradition than the Yiddish. Such characters are, for example, Doctor Marian Zawacki and his wife Felicia. Being related to the Jampolski family (Felicia is Jampolski's sister) they serve as their counterparts, decent and unthreatening. It is difficult to say to what extent Singer knows Polish literature and draws from it (he mentions Mickiewicz, Słowacki, Wyspiański both in his novels where his Jewish characters read them, as well as in his autobiographical works and interviews) but there is a striking resemblance between Doctor Zawacki and Doctor Judym from Stefan Żeromski's *Ludzie bezdomni* (Homeless People) and between Felicia and a number of heroines from positivist literature, pauperized Polish noblewomen mourning the national tragedy after the January uprising, pious, modest and devoted, altruistic and concerned mainly with serving others. If not directly from Polish literature, Singer could have drawn inspiration for the character of Doctor Zawacki from one of Peretz's stories.[46]

Both the noble doctor and the demonic noblemen express very critical views on Polish history and try to explain the reasons for the collapse of the Polish state. Doctor Zawacki seems to be the most reliable voice owing to his sanity and lack of direct responsibility for the decline of Poland, since he himself comes from a simple family and has gained his education and prestige by his patience, endurance and self-sacrifice.

Although Singer is a mystic, he does not mystify the reality of Polish-Jewish relations. He never demonizes Polish anti-semitism, presenting it together with other 'isms' which according to Singer are so dangerous and inseparable from human nature, and interpreting it as a constant struggle to power which is 'the essence of human history. Today the Poles tormented the Jews; yesterday the Russians and Germans had tormented the Poles . . . Even the allegedly good people are evil. Yesterday's martyrs often become today's bullies.'[47] One is tempted, however, to try to answer the question asked by Chone Shmeruk, whether Singer offers us 'a reconstruction of a certain state of affairs in the past or a version of affairs today.'[48]

In my opinion in Singer's fiction we encounter constant intermingling of the past with the present. Often the same ideas are presented in completely different epochs and expressed in various forms but they remain basically alike. The best illustration of this statement is ***The King of the Fields*** whose savage characters express surprisingly modern ideas, including homosexuality, vegetarianism and feminism, and the only Jewish character, Ben Dosa, forced to leave the community freshly implanted with Christianity, foreshadows the disappearance of the East European Yiddishland as much as *Satan in Goray*, 'The Last Demon' or *The Family Moskat*.

Contrasting with the critical image of Polish history and Poles as a collective is the great affection with which Singer presents the Polish landscape, either through his own voice or that of his characters. The two places that have found particularly thorough description in Singer's writings are Bilgoray and Warsaw.

Bilgoray is presented as a kind of mythical place, a paradise on earth (worth noting is the semantic coincidence since paradise in Polish is *raj*). Described by means of impressions and images rather than exact topographic descriptions, Bilgoray bears a strong resemblance to the Holy Land:

> In the fading light, everything became more beautiful, blossoms seemed more distinct, everything was green, juice-filled, radiant with the light of the setting sun, and aromatic. . . . It seemed to me that these fields, pastures, and marshes must resemble the land of Israel. The sons of Jacob were herding sheep nearby. Before Joseph's stacks of grain, other stacks bowed down. The Ishmaelites would arrive soon, riding camels, their asses and mules loaded with almonds, cloves, figs and dates . . . The world seemed like an open Pentateuch. The moon and the eleven stars came out, bowing before Joseph, the future ruler of Egypt . . . The fields were all shapes and colors, squares and rectangles, dark green and yellow . . . I wished I could stay here forever.[49]

Poland thus seems to be a paradise for the Jewish people. However, such idyllic descriptions of the *shtetl* are usually devoid of Poles since they might threaten the idealized vision.

Warsaw on the other hand is described in more realistic terms. Just as on the basis of Bolesław Prus's *Lalka* (The Doll), so on the basis of Singer's novels and stories one can recreate the map of pre-war Warsaw, especially of the Jewish quarter, though not exclusively. Warsaw is presented both in its beauty and ugliness, but the ugliness makes it even more real and human. 'Spring in Warsaw could make one crazy with longing' and the sky over the city makes one think of the sky in the Holy Land, 'clear and perfectly cloudless', reflecting 'the deep night-blue of those climates where the sun doesn't set during the summer months'.[50] And Singer himself seems to express his own feelings through Hadassah's words when she writes in her diary:

> Warsaw, dear city of mine, how sad I am! Already, before I have left you, I long for you. I look at your crooked roofs, your factory

> chimneys, your thickly clouded skies, and I realize how deeply rooted you are in my heart. I know it will be good to live in a strange country, but when my time comes to die I want to lie in the cemetery on Gensha, near my beloved grandmother.[51]

In a recently published novel *Umschlagplatz*[52] Jarosław Marek Rymkiewicz patterns one of his characters on Singer. A writer Icyk Mandelbaum who miraculously escaped the Holocaust continues his life in Manhattan, eventually becoming a recipient of the Nobel Prize. In the mid-eighties he comes to Warsaw trying to find some of his nearly non-existent past.

This is obviously only Rymkiewicz's poetic licence; Singer himself has never wished to visit Poland after the war since apart from eliciting in him feelings similar to those of other survivors in whom such a visit must evoke traumatic reflections, it could undermine his artistic integrity. He lives in the Warsaw of his youth which serves him as an inexhausible source of literary inspiration. As he stated in one of his interviews when asked about his attitude towards Poland:

> The truth is that I am still living there. I lived there my first thirty years; and you know that your experiences in childhood are the most important for a writer. So for me the Poland of my youth still exists.[53]

The vanished Poland of his youth which constitutes his lost Yiddishland makes him, as he himself half-jokingly observed, a Yiddish Homer.[54] As the mythical Homer drew from the earlier oral tradition so Singer draws from his own, both oral and written, transforming it into a work of high literary merit. And since in Singer's Troy apart from the Jewish world there existed a Gentile one, however indifferent, separate or even threatening, Polish characters and Polish landscape are necessary elements to record and recreate the destroyed reality in all its richness.

NOTES

1 This is a revised version of a paper presented at an international conference on the image of Poles in English and American Literature held in Sosnowiec in June 1989.

2 Eli Katz, 'Isaac Bashevis Singer and the Classical Tradition' in *The Achievement of Isaac Bashevis Singer*, ed. Marcia Allentuck (Carbondale, 1969), p. 21.

3 *The Manor*, *The Estate*, and *The Magician of Lublin*.

4 A critical review of *The King of the Fields* by a Polish critic appeared in English. See Ewa Kuryluk, 'Nightmares of the Poles and the Lesniks' *The New York Times Book Review*, October 16, 1988, pp. 12–13. The reviewer criticises among other things, Singer's depiction of Poles and Poland.

5 Singer was criticized by a number of Yiddish critics for abandoning the Yiddish

tradition and presenting the false image of Jews. See e.g. Jacob Glatstein, 'The Fame of Bashevis Singer', *Congress bi-Weekly*, no. 17, 1965, pp. 17–19; Sol Liptzin, *The Maturing of Yiddish Literature* (New York, 1970). From the feminist point of view he was criticized for his portrayal of women. See e.g. Evelyn Torton Beck, 'The Many Faces of Eve: Women, Yiddish and I.B. Singer', in *Studies in American Jewish Literature. Isaac Bashevis Singer. A Reconsideration*, pp. 118–22.

6 Selected aspects of the 'Polish side' of Singer's fiction were discussed before by Thomas S. Gladsky, 'The Polish Side of Singer's Fiction', in *Studies in American Jewish Literature. The Varieties of Jewish Experience*, no. 5 (Albany, 1985), pp. 5–14, Chone Shmeruk, 'Polish-Jewish Relations in the Historical Fiction of Isaac Bashevis Singer', *The Polish Review*, no. 4, 1987, pp. 401–13.

7 Clive Sinclair, *The Brothers Singer* (London, 1983), p. 86.

8 See e.g. Israel Bartal, 'The *Porets* and the *Arendar*: The Depiction of Poles in Jewish Literature', *The Polish Review*, no. 4, 1987, pp. 357–69; Chone Shmeruk, 'Jews and Poles in Yiddish Literature in Poland between the Two World Wars', *Polin*, vol. 1, 1986, pp. 176–95.

9 See e.g. Leon Kruczkowski, *Kordian i Cham*. First published 1932.

10 See e.g. *Isaac Bashevis Singer on Literature and Life*, ed. Paul Rosenblatt and Gene Koppel (Tucson, 1979), p. 31.

11 This fact is mentioned by Chone Shmeruk in 'Polish-Jewish Relations in the Historical Fiction of Isaac Bashevis Singer'.

12 Isaac Bashevis Singer, *The Slave*, transl. by the author and Cecil Hemley (New York, 1962), p. 149.

13 Ibid. p. 150.

14 Ibid.

15 See Gladsky, p. 7.

16 See the articles mentioned in footnote 8.

17 Isaac Bashevis Singer, 'One Day of Happiness', in *The Image and Other Stories* (New York, 1985), p. 31.

18 E.g. Uris's Gabriela Rak who is in love with Andrei Androfski, a character based to some extent on Mordechai Anielewicz, is a 'classic Polish beauty' with honey hair and blue eyes, and Styron's Sophie, submissive and utterly devoted to Nathan, has straw-coloured hair and Slavic cheekbones. Both of them reject their Polishness guided by their love for Jewish protagonists.

19 *The Slave*, p. 9.

20 Ibid., p. 10.

21 Isaac Bashevis Singer, *Enemies. A Love Story* (New York, 1972), p. 4.

22 Isaac Bashevis Singer, *Shosha*, transl. by Aliza Shevrin, Elizabeth Gottlieb and Joseph Singer (New York, 1960), p. 29.

23 Isaac Bashevis Singer, *The Magician of Lublin*, transl. by Elaine Gottlieb and Joseph Singer (New York, 1960), p. 23.

24 Isaac Bashevis Singer, *Love and Exile* (New York, 1984) p. 106.

25 Ibid., p. 155.

26 Beck, p. 120.

27 See Chone Shmeruk, *The Esterke Story in Yiddish and Polish Literature. Case Study in the Mutual Relations of Two Cultural Traditions* (Jerusalem: The Zalman Shazar Center for the Furtherance of the Study of Jewish History, 1985).

28 Isaac Bashevis Singer, *Satan in Goray*, transl. by Jacob Sloan (New York, 1958), p. 171.

29 *The Slave*, pp. 9–10.

30 See Shmeruk, 'Jews and Poles in Yiddish Literature in Poland between the Two World Wars'.

31 See e.g. Olga Goldberg-Mulkiewicz, 'Polish Folk Culture and the Jews'; Władysław T. Bartoszewski, 'Polish Folk Culture and the Jews', both in *Proceedings of the Conference on Poles and Jews: Myth and Reality in the Historical Context held at Columbia University, March 6–10, 1983*, eds. John Micgiel, Robert Scott, Harold B. Segal (Institute on East Central Europe, Columbia University, New York, 1986), pp. 479–90 and 591–506.
32 Goldberg-Mulkiewicz, p. 486.
33 Ibid., p. 488.
34 *Satan in Goray*, p. 131.
35 Sholem Aleichem, 'The Great Panic of the Little People, in *Old Country Tales*, selected and transl. by Curt Leviant (New York, 1966), p. 102.
36 For discussion of Singer's narrative monologue see Chone Shmeruk 'The Use of Monologue as a Narrative Technique in the Stories of Isaac Bashevis Singer', in I. Bashevis-Singer, *Der shpigl und andere dertseylungen* (Tel Aviv, 1975), pp. v–xxxv.
37 Issac Bashevis Singer, 'The Chimney Sweep', in *A Friend of Kafka and Other Stories* (New York, 1970).
38 In *The Image and Other Stories*.
39 Ibid.
40 See Isaac Bashevis Singer, 'Reb Asher the Dairyman', in *A Day of Pleasure. Stories of a Boy Growing Up in Warsaw* (New York, 1969), p. 54.
41 See 'The Washwoman', ibid., p. 77.
42 Ibid., p. 78.
43 Ibid., pp. 78–9.
44 Ibid. pp. 83–4.
45 See Madeline G. Levine, 'The Ambiguity of Moral Outrage in Jerzy Andrzejewski's "Wielki Tydzień"', *The Polish Review*, no. 4, 1987, p. 385, footnote 1.
46 Israel Bartal notices that the character of a Polish pharmacist in Peretz's 'In postvogn' is influenced by Polish positivist writers, Bartal, p. 367.
47 *Love and Exile*, p. 46.
48 Chone Shmeruk, 'Polish-Jewish Relations in the Historical Fiction of Isaac Bashevis Singer', p. 413.
49 'Bilgoray', in *A Day of Pleasure*, p. 194.
50 *Love and Exile*, p. 146.
51 Isaac Bashevis Singer, *The Family Moskat*, transl. by A. H. Gross (New York, 1950), p. 162.
52 See Jarosław Marek Rymkiewicz, *Umschlagplatz* (Paris, 1988).
53 Marshall Breger and Bob Barnhar, 'A Conversation with Isaac Bashevis Singer', in *Critical Views of Isaac Bashevis Singer*, ed. Irving Malin (New York, 1969).
54 See Isaac Bashevis Singer and Richard Burgin, *Conversation with Isaac Bashevis Singer* (New York, 1985), p. 73.

Notes on Contributors

MONIKA ADAMCZYK-GARBOWSKA is a lecturer in the Department of English at Marie Curie-Skłodowska University, Lublin. She specializes in translation theory and comparative literature and is the author of *Polskie tlumaczenia angielskiej literatury dziecięcej. Problemy krytyki przekładu* (Polish Translations of English Children's Literature: Problems in the Criticism of Translation) (1988). She has published several articles on Isaac Bashevis Singer in Polish and English and is currently writing a book about the Polish aspects of Singer's fiction.

ISRAEL BARTAL is Professor of Modern Jewish History at the Hebrew University of Jerusalem and Director of the Center for the History and Culture of Polish Jews. He is the author of several articles on eastern European Jewish history and on the history of the pre-Zionist Jewish community in Palestine. His monograph, *Non-Jews and Gentile Society in East European Hebrew and Yiddish Literature 1856–1914* will soon be published by Hebrew Union College. He edited the minute book of the Council of the Four Lands, and is co-author, with Magdalena Opalski, of *Poles and Jews: A Failed Brotherhood* (1993).

DAVID BIALE is Koret Professor of Jewish History and Director of the Center for Judaic Studies at the Graduate Theological Union at the University of California, Berkeley, and Adjunct Associate Professor in the Department of Near Eastern Languages, also at Berkeley. He is the author of *Gershom Scholem: Kabbalah and Counter-History* (1979), *Power and Powerlessness in Jewish History* (1986), and *Eros and the Jews* (1992).

EUGENE C. BLACK is Ottilie Springer Professor of History at Brandeis University. He is author of *The Association: British Extra-parliamentary Organization, 1769–1793* (1963), and editor of *European Political History 1815–70* (1967) and *Victorian Culture and Society* (1973). At present he is working on a study of the political activity of Lucien Wolf.

JAN BŁOŃSKI is Professor of the History of Polish Literature at the Jagiellonian University in Kraków. His many publications include *Poeci i inni* (Poets and the Others) (1956), *Zmiana warty* (The Changing of the Guard) (1961), and *Odmarsz* (Departure) (1978).

NORMAN DAVIES is Professor of Polish History at the School of Slavonic and East European Studies, University of London, and has been Visiting Professor at McGill, Hokkaido, and Stanford universities. He is an MA (Oxon), Ph.D. (Kraków), and Fellow of the Royal Historical Society. His books include *White Eagle, Red Star, the Polish–Soviet War 1919–20* (1972); *Poland Past and Present: A Bibliography of Works in English on Polish History* (1976); *God's Playground: A History of Poland* (2 vols., 1981), and *Heart of Europe: A Short History of Poland* (1984). He is at present writing a history of Europe.

DAVID ENGEL is Professor of Jewish History at New York University and co-editor of the journal *Gal-Ed: Studies on the History of Polish Jewry*. Among his many publications are: *In the Shadow of Auschwitz: The Polish Government-in-Exile and the Jews, 1939–1942* (1987) and *Facing a Holocaust: The Polish Government-in-Exile and the Jews 1943–45* (1993).

JACOB GOLDBERG was Lecturer in History at the University of Łódź until 1967 and has since been Research Fellow, and subsequently Senior Lecturer and Professor of History, at the Hebrew University of Jerusalem. He has published over forty books and articles on the social and economic history of the Jews in the Polish–Lithuanian Commonwealth. Among his books are *Stosunki agrarne w miastach ziemi wieluńskiej w drugiej połowie XVIII wieku* (Agrarian Relationships in the Towns of the Wielun District in the Second Half of the Seventeenth and Eighteenth Centuries) (1960) and *Jewish Privileges in the Polish Commonwealth: Charters of Rights Granted to Jewish Communities in Poland–Lithuania in the Sixteenth to Eighteenth Centuries: Critical Edition of Original Latin and Polish Documents with English Introduction and Notes* (1985).

GERSHON DAVID HUNDERT is Professor of History and chairs the Department of Jewish Studies at McGill University. He is the author of *The Jews in a Polish Private Town: The Case of Opatów in the Eighteenth Century* (1992) and co-author of *The Jews in Poland and Russia*. His major research interest has been the history of the Jews in early modern Poland.

KRYSTYNA KERSTEN is Professor at the Institute of History of the Polish Academy of Sciences, Warsaw. Her main interest lies in contemporary Polish history and her works are devoted to the social and political history of Poland after 1944 and to the movements of the population during and after the war. She is the author of *Repatriacja ludności polskiej po II wojnie światowej* (The Repatriation of the Polish Population after the Second World War) (1974), *Polska 1943–1948: Narodziny systemu władzy* (Poland 1943–1948: Origins of the System of Government) (1986), and *Polacy, Żydzi, Komunizm: Anatomia półprawd, 1939–1947* (Poles, Jews, Communism: The Anatomy of Half-Truths, 1939–1947) (1993).

STEFAN KIENIEWICZ was Emeritus Professor at the University of Warsaw until his death in 1992. He wrote extensively on Polish history in the nineteenth century, and his books include *Społeczeństwo polskie w powstaniu poznańskim 1848* (Polish Society in the Poznań Uprising, 1848), *Historia Polski 1795–1918* (The History of Poland 1795–1918), and *Powstanie styczniowe* (The January Uprising).

PAWEŁ KORZEC was Professor at Łódź University until 1968 and is now a researcher at the Centre National de la Recherche Scientifique in Paris. His most important book is *Juifs en Pologne* (1980).

EWA KUREK-LESIK wrote her doctorate at the Catholic University of Lublin on the concealment of Jewish children in nunneries in Poland in the years 1932–1945. She has undertaken research in Poland, the USA, and Israel and has recorded the memories of many nuns and rescued children on videotape. Her thesis has been published under the title *Gdy klasztor znaczył życie* (When the Cloister Meant Life) (1992).

MAGDALENA OPALSKI teaches at Carleton and York University in Ontario, Canada. She is the author of *The Jewish Tavern-Keeper and his Tavern* (1986), and co-author, with I. Bartal, of *Poles and Jews: A Failed Brotherhood* (1993) on the legend of 'Polish–Jewish brotherhood' in 1863 in Polish and Jewish literature. She has also edited a special issue of *The Polish Review* devoted to Polish–Jewish cultural relations (1987).

MARIA AND KAZIMIERZ PIECHOTKA are architects and architectural historians. They have practised as architects in post-war Poland and together have written over 130 books and articles on the history of architecture, housing developments, and the mechanization of construction. Among their works are *Bóżnice drewniane* (Wooden Synagogues) (1955, English translation 1959) and *Założenia techniczne zintegrowanego przemysłu budowlanego* (The Technical Bases of an Integrated Building Industry) (1978).

EUGENIA PROKOPÓWNA teaches modern Polish literature at the Jagiellonian University of Kraków. Her major essay 'Kafka w Polsce międzywojennej' (Kafka in Inter-war Poland), originally published in Polish in *Pamiętnik Literacki*, will soon appear as a monograph in the series *Studies on Polish Jewry* in Jerusalem.

LAURA QUERCIOLI-MINCER is an Italian scholar and works in Rome with Jewish organizations. She has held research scholarships in Poland and at the Oxford Institute for Polish–Jewish Studies and has published several articles about Polish Jewish literature in post-war Poland.

MOSHE ROSMAN is Senior Lecturer in Jewish History at Bar-Ilan University. Educated at the Jewish Theological Seminary of America and Columbia University, for the past ten years he has resided in Israel. He is the author of *The Lord's Jews: Magnates and Jews in the Eighteenth Century Polish–Lithuanian Commonwealth* (1990).

SZYMON RUDNICKI is Professor of History at Warsaw University and pro-Dean of the Historical Faculty. He is a member of the Israeli–Polish Historical Commission and of the Scholarly Council of the Jewish Historical Institute in Warsaw. He is, above all, interested in the politics of the right and fascism, Polish–Jewish relations, and large landowners. Among his books are *Działalność polityczna polskich konserwarystów 1918–1926* (The Political Activity of Polish Conservatives 1918–1926) (1981) and *Obóz Narodowo-Radykalny: Geneza i dzialalność* (The National Radical Camp: Its Evolution and Development) (1985).

PAWEŁ SAMUŚ is Professor of History at the University of Łódź. His main interest is in the social and political history of Poland at the end of the nineteenth and the beginning of the twentieth centuries. His many publications include *Dzieje SDKPiL w Łodzi 1893–1918* (The History of the SDKPiL in Łódź 1893–1918 (1984).

ROBERT MOSES SHAPIRO, a former fellow of the Max Weinreich Center at YIVO, teaches history at Yeshiva University, New York. His 1987 Columbia University doctoral thesis on Jewish self-government in Poland focused on Łódź Jewry between the world wars. During 1989/90, he was a Yad Hanadiv/Barecha Foundation Visiting Research Fellow in Jerusalem. He is preparing a comprehensive history of the Jews of Łódź.

CHONE SHMERUK is Professor of Yiddish Literature and Chairman of the Academic Board of the Center for Research on the History and Culture of Polish Jews at the Hebrew University of Jerusalem. He is a member of the Israel Academy of Sciences and Humanities. His most recent publications include *Sifrut Yidish: Perakim letoldoteha* (Yiddish Literature: Aspects of its History) (1978), *Sifrut Yidish befolin* (Yiddish Literature in Poland) (1981), and *The Esterka Story in Yiddish and Polish Literature* (1985). He is editor, with Irving Howe and Ruth R. Wisse, of *The Penguin Book of Modern Yiddish Verse* (1987).

SHAUL STAMPFER is a lecturer in the Department of Jewish History at the Hebrew University of Jerusalem. He is the author of *Shalosh yeshivot litaiyot* (Three Lithuanian Yeshivas) (1982) and has written widely on demographic topics.

MICHAEL C. STEINLAUF is Assistant Professor of East European

Jewish History at Gratz College. In 1983/4 he spent a year in Poland as a Fulbright Fellow. He devotes himself to Polish Jewish cultural history and Polish–Jewish relations in the nineteenth and twentieth centuries. He is currently studying the development of Yiddish theatre in Poland, and translating works by Y. L. Peretz into English.

PAWEŁ SZAPIRO is a research worker at the Jewish Historical Institute in Warsaw.

JEAN-CHARLES SZUREK is a researcher in the Centre National de la Recherche Scientifique in Paris. He has written *Aux origines paysannes de la crise polonaise* (1982) and a number of articles on Jewish–Polish relations.

JANUSZ TAZBIR is Professor at the Historical Institute of the Polish Academy of Sciences, Warsaw. He is the editor of the annual *Odrodzenie i Reformacja w Polsce* (Renaissance and Reformation in Poland). He works on the history of Polish culture in the sixteenth and seventeenth centuries and of religious movements in this period. Among his publications are: *A State Without Stakes: Polish Religious Tolerance in the Sixteenth and Seventeenth Centuries* (1973), *Geschichte der polnischen Toleranz* (1977), *La République nobiliare et le monde: Études sur l'histoire de la culture polonaise à l'époque du baroque* (1986). He is a contributor to *History of Poland* (edited by S. Kieniewicz, 1968).

JERZY TOMASZEWSKI is Professor at the Institute of Political Science and Head of the Mordekhai Anieliewicz Research Center on the History of Jews in Poland at Warsaw University. He is a member of the Council and Board of the Jewish Historical Institute in Poland. Among his publications are *Rzeczpospolita wielu narodów* (A Republic of Many Nations) (1985), *Z dziejów Polesia 1921–1939: Zarys stosunków społeczno-ekonomicznych* (On the History of Polesia 1921–1939: An Outline of Social and Economic Conditions) (1963), and *Ojczyzna nie tylko Polaków: Mniejszości narodowe w Polsce w latach 1918–1939* (A Fatherland not only for Poles: National Minorities in Poland in the Years 1918–1939) (1985).

PAUL WEXLER is Professor of Linguistics at Tel Aviv University. He is the author of numerous articles in the fields of Jewish linguistics (especially Yiddish, Judaeo-Ibero-Romance, Judaeo-Arabic) and Slavic linguistics. His recent books include *A Historical Phonology of the Belorussian Language* (1977) and *Explorations in Judeo-Slavic Linguistics* (1986).

ANNA ŻUK is a lecturer in the Institute of Philosophy and Sociology at the Marie Curie-Skłodowska University in Lublin. Her main interest is in the interpretative reconstruction of the philosophical context of Judaism, on which she has published a number of articles.

Chronological Table

POLISH HISTORY	GENERAL HISTORY
4th–6th cent. Slavonic migrations west of the Odra and south of the Carpathians	**4th–7th cent.** The great migrations of people
beginning of 7th cent. Formation of political organizations of the Slavs south of the Baltic	**5th–7th cent.** The Merovingian State
middle of 9th cent. Foundation of small regional Slavonic states in the Odra and Vistula basin	**800** Charlemagne's Imperial coronation
	*c.*830 Foundation of the Great Moravian State
	843 Treaty of Verdun
2nd half of 9th cent. Expansion of the Great Moravian State into the area of southern Poland; foundation of the State of the Polanie (the Piast dynasty) in Great Poland	**9th cent.** Foundation of the Bohemian State
	end of 9th cent. Foundation of the State of Kiev
1st half of 10th cent. Conquest of Mazovia by the Piasts	**906** Fall of the Great Moravian State
before 963 to 992 Reign of Mieszko I	**950** Bohemia recognizes the suzerainty of the Empire
	962 Otto I crowned Emperor
966 The Polish court adopts Christianity	
972 Conquest of western Pomerania by Mieszko I	
	987 Beginnings of the Capet dynasty in France
	988–9 Duke Vladimir of Ruthenia adopts Christianity

POLISH HISTORY		GENERAL HISTORY	
992–1025	Reign of Bolesław the Brave		
1000	Emperor Otto III recognizes Poland's independence; foundation of the archbishopric in Gniezno		
1004–18	Bolesław the Brave's war against the Germans		
1018	Peace of Bautzen (Budišyn); Bolesław the Brave's expedition against Kiev and the incorporation of the Czerwień Castles into Poland	**1024**	Beginning of the Salic dynasty of the Franks in Germany
1025	Bolesław I the Brave crowned King of Poland		
1025–34	Reign of Mieszko II		
1033	Mieszko II renounces the royal crown		
1034–58	Reign of Kazimierz I the Restorer		
1037	Kazimierz I the Restorer expelled from Poland; anti-feudal and anti-Christian rising of the people		
1038 or **1039**	The Bohemian Duke Břetislav invades Poland		
1039	Kazimierz I the Restorer returns to Poland; reconstruction of the state begins		

1058–79	Reign of Bolesław II the Bold	**1054**	Beginning of the eastern schism
1076	Bolesław II the Bold crowned King of Poland	**1066**	The Norman conquest of England
1079	Revolt of the nobles and expulsion of Bolesław II the Bold	**1077**	Henry IV in Canossa
1079–1102	Reign of Władysław Herman		
1102–38	Reign of Bolesław III the Wrymouth	**1096–9**	First Crusade
1109	Invasion of Poland by Emperor Henry V		
1121–2	Western Pomerania reincorporated into Poland	**1122**	Concordat of Worms
1124–8	Christianization of western Pomerania		
1138	Death of Bolesław III the Wrymouth; beginning of Poland's territorial division with a Grand Duke as senior among the provincial rulers		
1138–46	Reign of Władysław II as Grand Duke of Poland		
1146–73	Reign of Bolesław IV the Curly as Grand Duke	**1147–9**	Second Crusade
		1152–90	Reign of Emperor Frederick I Barbarossa
		1154	Beginning of the Plantagenets' rule in England (Henry II)
		1171	Conquest of Egypt by the Seljuks

POLISH HISTORY

1173–7 Reign of Mieszko III the Old as Grand Duke

1177–94 Rule of Kazimierz II the Just as Grand Duke

1180 Congress of Łęczyca, concessions by Kazimierz II the Just in favour of the clergy

1181 Western Pomerania made dependent on the Empire

1202–27 Reign of Leszek the White as Grand Duke

1226 Conrad of Mazovia brings the Teutonic Knights into Poland

1227 Death of Leszek the White; decline of the institution of Senior Duke

1232–4 Conquest of Little Poland and a part of Great Poland by the Silesian Duke Henry the Bearded

GENERAL HISTORY

c. **1200** Foundation of the University of Paris

1202 Establishment of the Order of Knights of the Sword in Livonia

1204 The Crusaders capture Byzantium

1206 Establishment of the Mongolian State and beginnings of Mongolian expansion

1215 *Magna Charta Libertatum* in England

1228–9 Sixth Crusade

1240 Tartars capture Kiev and conquer Ruthenia

1241	First Mongol invasion of Poland; battle of Legnica, death of Henry the Pious
1249–52	Conquest of the Lubusz Land by the Margraves of Brandenburg
1291–2	Conquest of Little Poland by King Wacław II of Bohemia
1295	Coronation of Przemysł II as King of Poland
1296	Death of Przemysł II
1300–5	Reign of Wacław II as King of Poland
1306	Władysław I the Short conquers Little Poland
1308–9	The Teutonic Knights capture Gdańsk and eastern Pomerania
1314	Władysław I the Short conquers Great Poland
1320–33	Reign of Władysław the Short as King of Poland; end of territorial division
1325	Polish–Lithuanian alliance against the Teutonic Knights
1331	Battle of Płowce, victory of Władysław the Short over the Teutonic Knights
1333–70	Reign of Kazimierz III the Great, the last king of the Piast dynasty

*c.***1241**	Establishment of the Hansa
middle of 13th cent.	Foundation of parliaments in France and England
1254–73	The Long Interregnum in Germany
1302	The States-General constituted in France
1309–77	The 'Avignon captivity' of the Popes
1316–41	Reign of Giedymin and unification of the Lithuanian State
1328	Ivan Kalita gains the title of Grand Duke of Muscovy

POLISH HISTORY		GENERAL HISTORY	
1335	Congress of Vyšehrad: John of Luxemburg renounces his claims to the Polish throne and Kazimierz III the Great his rights to Silesia	**1337**	Outbreak of the Hundred Years War
1340–9	Poland occupies the greater part of Vladimir and Halicz Ruthenia	**1342–82**	Reign of Louis d'Anjou as King of Hungary
		1346	Battle of Crécy
middle of 14th cent.	The Statutes of Great Poland and Little Poland—first codification of the common law	**1348**	Foundation of the University of Prague
1355	Privileges for the gentry granted by Louis d'Anjou in Buda in return for the recognition of his succession in Poland		
1364	Foundation of the University of Kraków		
1370–82	Reign of Louis d'Anjou	**1371**	Beginning of the reign of the Stuarts in Scotland
		1377–1417	Western schism
1384	Jadwiga, daughter of Louis d'Anjou, becomes Queen of Poland	**1380**	Battle of Kulikovo Pole, victory of Demetrius Donskoi over the Tartars
1385	Polish–Lithuanian Union at Krewo		

1386	Baptism of the Lithuanian Grand Duke Jagiełło and his marriage to Jadwiga		
1386–1434	Reign of Władysław Jagiełło; beginning of the Jagiellonian dynasty	**1397**	Union of Denmark, Norway, and Sweden at Kalmar
1399	The Lithuanian Grand Duke Witold in the battle with Tartars on the Vorskla river		
1400	Restoration of Kraków University	**1409**	Theses of Ian Hus
1410	Battle of Grünwald	**1414–18**	Council of Constance
1420	Władysław Jagiełło rejects the Bohemian crown offered to him by the Hussites	**1419–34**	Hussite wars
1422–33	The gentry obtain the charter *Neminem captivabimus nisi iure victum*	**1429**	Joan of Arc in Orléans
1434–44	Reign of Wladyslaw III		
1440	Władysław III ascends to the Hungarian throne; Kazimierz IV to the Lithuanian throne; the Prussian Union formed		
1444	Battle of Varna and death of Władysław III		
1447–92	Reign of Kazimierz IV in Poland	*c.***1450**	Discovery of print by Johannes Gutenberg
		1453	Constantinople captured by the Turks; end of the Hundred Years War
1454	Incorporation of Prussia into Poland		

POLISH HISTORY

1454–66	Thirteen Years War with the Teutonic Knights
1466	Peace of Toruń with Teutonic Knights
1473	First printing shop in Kraków
1492–1501	Reign of John Albert
1492–1506	Reign of Alexander in the Grand Duchy of Lithuania
1496	Statutes of Piotrków: the rights of peasants and burghers abridged
1497	John Albert's defeat in Moldavia
1501–6	Reign of Alexander
1505	*Nihil Novi* Constitution
1506–48	Reign of Zygmunt I the Old
1514	Muscovite troops take Smoleńsk; Polish–Lithuanian victory at Orsza
1515	Meeting in Vienna of Zygmunt I the Old, Władysław Jagiełło (son of Kazimierz IV),

GENERAL HISTORY

1455–85	War of the Roses in England
1462–1505	Reign of Ivan III and liberation of Russia from Tartar dependence
1481	Inquisition established in Spain
1492	Discovery of America; conquest of Granada—the end of Spain's *reconquista*
1497–8	Discovery of the sea-route to India (Vasco da Gama)
1503–13	Pope Julius II

	and Emperor Maximilian Habsburg: the Habsburgs receive the guarantee to succeed to the Bohemian and Hungarian thrones in the case of the extinction of the Jagiellonian dynasty
1518	Arrival in Poland of Bona Sforza, wife of Zygmunt I the Old
1520	First royal edicts against dissenters
1525	Secularization of the Teutonic Order in Prussia; the Prussian Prince Albrecht pays homage to Zygmunt I the Old
1526	Extinction of the Mazovian line of Piasts; incorporation of Mazovia into the Crown
1529	Zygmunt II Augustus ascends to the throne of Lithuania

1517	Theses of Martin Luther
1519	Charles V becomes Emperor
1519–21	Conquest of Mexico by Hernán Cortés
1519–22	Ferdinand Magellan's expedition round the world
1521	The Edict of Worms outlaws Martin Luther as a heretic
1524–5	Peasant war in Germany
1526	The succession of the Habsburgs in Bohemia and Hungary; 'Sacco di Roma'
1531–6	Conquest of Peru by Francisco Pizarro
1534	Establishment of the Jesuit Order; separation of the English church from Rome

POLISH HISTORY	
1543	Nicolaus Copernicus' *De revolutionibus orbium coelestium*
1548–72	Reign of Zygmunt II Augustus
1561	Secularization of the Livonian Order; incorporation of Livonia and establishment of the Duchy of Courland
1563–70	The Seven Years Northern War
1564	Jesuits brought into Poland
1569	The Union of Lublin
1570	Compact of Sandomierz—agreement of the Protestant denominations for the defence of religious freedom
1573	The principle of the free election of kings adopted; religious peace guaranteed
1573–4	Reign of Henri de Valois
1576–86	Reign of Stephen Batory
1577	War with Danzig
1577–82	War with the Grand Duchy of Muscovy for Livonia
1578	Foundation of the Wilno Academy

GENERAL HISTORY	
1545–63	Council of Trent
1547–84	Reign of Ivan the Terrible in Russia
1556–98	Reign of Philip II as King of Spain
1558–1603	Reign of Queen Elizabeth in England
1572	St Bartholomew's Night in France
1574–89	Reign of Henry III de Valois as King of France
1576	Outbreak of revolt in the Netherlands
1579	Establishment of the Republic of United Provinces in the Netherlands

1580	First meeting of the Council of the Four Lands		
1587–1632	Reign of Zygmunt III Vasa	**1588**	Victory of the English navy over Spain's Great Armada
1594–6	Cossack uprising under Severin Nalevaiko	**1589–1610**	Reign of King Henry IV in France
1595	Foundation of the Zamość Academy		
1595–6	Union of Brześć		
1600	Outbreak of the war with Sweden	**1600**	Establishment of the East India Company in England
		1603	Death of Elizabeth Tudor, beginning of the Stuart dynasty in England
1604–6	Polish participation in the action of the False Demetrius		
1605	Victory over the Swedes at Kirchholm		
1606–7	Rebellion of Mikołaj Zebrzydowski		
1609–19	War with Russia		
1610	Stanisław Żółkiewski's victory over the Russian army at Kłuszyn	**1611–32**	Reign of Gustavus Adolphus in Sweden
		1613	Beginning of the rule of the Romanovs in Russia
		1618	Beginning of the Thirty Years War
1620	Defeat of the Polish army in the battle with the Turks at Cecora	**1620**	Defeat of the Bohemians at Bílá Hora

POLISH HISTORY		GENERAL HISTORY	
1621	Defence of Chocim and peace with Turkey		
1627	Battle of the Polish and Swedish navies at Oliwa		
1629	Victory over the Swedes at Trzciana; truce with Sweden		
1632–4	War with Russia	**1632**	Battle of Lützen and death of Gustavus Adolphus
1632–48	Reign of Władysław IV Vasa	**1642**	Beginning of Revolution in England; the Long Parliament
1648	Outbreak of the rising under Bohdan Chmielnicki (Khmelnytsky) in the Ukraine	**1648**	Peace of Westphalia
1648–68	Reign of John Kazimierz	**1649**	Execution of Charles I Stuart
1651	Victory over Bohdan Chmielnicki's army at Beresteczko		
1652	Sejm broken up by the first *liberum veto*	**1653–8**	Protectorate of Oliver Cromwell
1654–67	Polish–Russian war	**1654**	Compact of Perejasław between Ukraine and Russia
1655–60	Polish–Swedish war		
1657	Treaties of Wehlau and Bydgoszcz; Poland renounces the Prussian fief		
1658	Arians (Antitrinitarians) expelled from Poland; compact of Hadziacz		

1660	Peace with Sweden at Oliwa	**1661–1715**	Reign of Louis XIV
1665–6	Rebellion of Jerzy Lubomirski		
1667	Truce of Andruszów		
1669–73	Reign of Michael Korybut-Wiśniowiecki		
1672	Turkish invasion of Poland		
1673	Victory over the Turks at Chocim		
1674–96	Reign of John III Sobieski		
1683	Siege of Vienna by the Turks and the Polish relief	**1682–1725**	Reign of Peter the Great in Russia
		1684	Creation of the first anti-Turkish League
1686	Peace with Russia (the Grzymułtowski treaty)		
1697–1733	Reign of Augustus II the Strong		
1699	Peace with Turkey at Karlowitz	**1699**	The Habsburgs complete the conquest of Hungary
		1700–21	The Northern War
		1701	Proclamation of the Kingdom of Prussia
		1701–14	The Spanish war of succession
1702	Swedish invasion of Poland		
1704	The opponents of Augustus II proclaim an interregnum; election of Stanisław Leszczyński		
1709	Augustus II again recognized as King		

POLISH HISTORY		GENERAL HISTORY	
		1714	George I ascends to throne in Great Britain; beginning of the Hanover dynasty
1715–16	The Confederation of Tarnogród		
1717	The 'Dumb Sejm'	**1716–20**	The affair of John Law in France
1733	Double election of Augustus III and Stanisław Leszczyński		
1733–5	The struggle of Stanisław Leszczyński against Augustus III for the Polish throne		
1734–63	Reign of Augustus III		
1740	The Collegium Nobilium established by Stanisław Konarski	**1740–8**	The Austrian war of succession and the Silesian Wars
		1740–86	Reign of Frederick II in Prussia and of Maria Theresa in Austria
		1742	Frederick II occupies Silesia
		1756–63	The Seven Years War
		1762–96	Reign of Catherine II in Russia
1764–95	Reign of Stanisław Augustus Poniatowski		
1764–6	Constitutional reforms carried out by the 'Convocation Confederation'		
1766–8	Russian intervention on the side of reactionary opposition		

1767	The Confederation of the Dissenters and the Confederation of Radom	**1767**	James Watt's steam engine
1768–72	The Confederation of Bar		
1772	First partition of Poland		
1773	Establishment of the Commission for National Education	**1773**	The Jesuit Order dissolved
1775	Establishment of the Permanent Council		
		1776	First workers' union organized in England
		1776–82	The American War of Independence
		1787	Proclamation of the Constitution of the United States of America
1788–92	The Four Year Sejm		
1789	'The Black Procession' of burghers in Warsaw	**1789**	Outbreak of the Great Revolution
1790	'Warnings for Poland' by Stanisław Staszic		
1791	Constitution of 3 May		
1792	The Confederation of Targowica and war with Russia	**1792**	Overthrow of the monarchy in France
1793	Second partition of Poland		
1794	The Kościuszko Insurrection		
1795	Third partition of Poland	**1795–9**	The *Directory* in France
1797–1803	Polish Legions at the side of the French army	**1799**	The revolt of 18 Brumaire
1800	The Society of Friends of Sciences established in Warsaw; reorganization of the University in Wilno		

POLISH HISTORY		GENERAL HISTORY	
		1804	Napoleon Bonaparte Emperor of the French
1806	Napoleon's Prussian campaign; rising in Great Poland; Warsaw occupied by the French	**1806**	End of the Roman Empire of the German Nation
1807	Establishment of the Duchy of Warsaw; its Constitution	**1807**	Peace of Tilsit
1808	Introduction of the Code of Napoleon		
1809	Polish–Austrian war; the territory of the Duchy of Warsaw extended	**1809**	French–Austrian war
1811–23	Enfranchisement of peasants in Polish provinces under Prussian rule		
1812	The army of the Duchy of Warsaw participates in Napoleon's Russian campaign	**1812**	Napoleon's campaign in Russia
		1814	Napoleon abdicates; George Stephenson's first locomotive
		1814–15	Congress of Vienna
1815	Foundation of the Kingdom of Poland and of the Free State of Kraków	**1815**	The 'Holy Alliance' formed
1816	Foundation of the University of Warsaw		
1817–23	Activities of the Philarets and Philomaths in Wilno		
1819–25	Activities of the National Freemasonry and of the Patriotic Society		

		1820–3	Liberation of the Latin American countries; revolutionary movements in Spain and Italy; liberation of Greece
1823–5	Contacts of the Patriotic Society with the Decembrists in Russia		
1828	Establishment of the Bank Polski	**1825**	The Decembrist rising in St Petersburg
1830–1	The November Insurrection	**1830**	The July Revolution in France
1831	Beginning of the Great Emigration	**1830–2**	Revolution in Belgium
1832	The autonomy of the Kingdom of Poland abridged; the Polish Democratic Society formed in France	**1832**	Electoral reform in Great Britain
1833	Józef Zaliwski's expedition	**1833**	Abolition of slavery in the British colonies
1834–6	Activities of the secret independence organization 'Young Poland'	**1834**	Giuseppe Mazzini forms the 'Young Europe'
1834–40	Construction of the 'Huta Bankowa' ironworks		
1835	The association 'Lud Polski' (Polish People) formed (The Grudziąż Commune)		
1835–8	Szymon Konarski's activities in Podolia, Ukraine and Lithuania	**1837–1901**	Reign of Queen Victoria in Great Britain
1840–4	Father Piotr Ściegienny's activities in the Kielce region	**1839–42**	Opium War in China
1842–5	Activities of the 'Plebeian Union' in Poznań		
1846	Kraków revolution; peasant rising in Galicia; the Free State of Kraków abolished		

POLISH HISTORY

1848	Uprising in Great Poland; revolutionary ferment in Galicia and Silesia; Warsaw–Vienna railway inaugurated; enfranchisement of peasants in Galicia
1848–9	Polish participation in the revolutionary events in Europe
1851	Customs union of the Kingdom of Poland and the Russian Empire
1853	Ignacy Łukasiewicz discovers the kerosene lamp
1860–2	Patriotic demonstrations in the Kingdom of Poland
1862	Central Committee of the Reds established in Warsaw; Aleksander Wielopolski becomes chief of the civilian government in the Kingdom of Poland; inauguration of the Main School (University) in Warsaw
1863–4	The January Insurrection
1863	Manifesto on the enfranchisement of peasants issued by the leadership of the insurrection

GENERAL HISTORY

1847	The Workers' Union formed in London
1848–9	Revolution in France, Austria, Germany, Italy, Hungary; the *Communist Manifesto* of Karl Marx and Friedrich Engels
1850–64	Taiping rebellion in China
1852–71	The Second Empire in France
1853–6	The Crimean War
1857	Uprising in India
1859–60	Struggle for the unification of Italy
1861	Enfranchisement of peasants in Russia; Abraham Lincoln inaugurated as US President: American Civil War (1861–5)

Poland		World	
		1864	The First International formed
1866–85	Gradual elimination of the Polish language from the schools in the Kingdom of Poland	**1866**	Prussian–Austrian war; battle of Sadova
1867	Autonomy of Galicia	**1867**	The Austrian State transformed into a dual monarchy
		1869	Opening of the Suez Canal; establishment of the Workers' Social Democratic Party in Germany
		1870–1	Franco-Prussian War
		1871	Proclamation of the German Reich; the Paris Commune
		1871–86	The *Kulturkampf*
1873	The Academy of Sciences and Letters established in Kraków		
1876	Abolition of separate judicature in the Kingdom of Poland and introduction of the Russian language into courts		
1878	First socialist organizations formed in Poland	**1878**	The Congress of Berlin
1880	Trial of Ludwik Waryński and his associates in Kraków		
1882	The 'Proletariat' formed	**1882**	The Triple Alliance formed
1885–6	Trial of the 'Proletariat' leaders		
1886	The Colonization Commission in Great Poland established by the Prussian authorities; foundation of the Polish League		

POLISH HISTORY		GENERAL HISTORY	
1889	Polish Workers' Union formed	**1889**	The Second International formed
1890	The first Workers' May Day in Poland	**1890**	The first workers' May Day celebrations in London
1892	Foundation of the Polish Socialist Party		
1893	Foundation of the Social Democratic Party of the Kingdom of Poland (since 1900: Social Democratic Party of the Kingdom of Poland and Lithuania) and of the Polish Social Democratic Party of Galicia and Silesia; foundation of the National League		
1894	The 'Hakata' formed in the Prussian-annexed part of Poland	**1894**	The Russo-French Alliance
1895	Foundation of the Peasant Party in Galicia (from 1893: Polish Peasant Party)		
1897	Foundation of the National Democratic Party		
1898	Anti-Polish emergency laws in the Prussian-annexed part of Poland	**1898**	Discovery of radium by Pierre Curie and Marie Curie-Skłodowska
		1900	Establishment of the Labour Party
1901	Strike of schoolchildren in Września against the Germanization of schools		
		1903	The Nobel Prize awarded to Antoine Henri Becquerel, Pierre Curie, and Marie Curie-Skłodowska
1905–7	Revolution in the Kingdom of Poland	**1905–7**	Revolution in Russia

1906	The Polish Socialist Party (PPS) split into the PPS Left and the PPS Revolutionary Wing		
1906–7	School strike in the Prussian-annexed part of Poland	**1907**	The Triple Entente formed
		1911–12	Revolution in China and proclamation of the Republic
		1912–13	The Balkan Wars
1914	Supreme National Committee in Galicia; formation of the Polish Legions at the side of the Austrian army	**1914**	Outbreak of First World War
1915	The Kingdom of Poland occupied by the German and Austrian armies		
1916	Act of the German and Austrian governments on the Polish question (5 Nov.)	**1916**	Battle of Verdun
1917	The Legions dissolved; establishment of the Polish National Committee in Lausanne (it later functioned in Paris); establishment of the Regency Council	**1917**	February Revolution in Russia, Tsardom overthrown; USA enters war; victory of the Great Socialist October Revolution in Petrograd; the Petrograd Workers' Soviet recognizes Poland's right to independence
1918	Ignacy Daszyński forms the Cabinet in Lublin; Józef Piłsudski becomes chief of the independent Polish State on 11 November; establishment of the Polish Communist Workers' Party (since 1925: Communist Party of Poland (KPP))	**1918**	Woodrow Wilson's 14 Points of Peace; declaration of the Soviet government on the annulment of treaties on the partitions of Poland; outbreak of revolution in Germany; surrender of Austria and Germany

POLISH HISTORY		GENERAL HISTORY	
1918–19	Uprising in Greater Poland; Councils of Workers' Delegates in Poland		
1919–20	Polish–Soviet war	**1919**	Peace treaty signed in Versailles; establishment of the League of Nations; the Third International formed
1919–21	Silesian uprisings		
1920	Plebiscites in Warmia, Mazuria, and Powiśle		
1921	The Constitution of March voted; peace treaty of Riga; plebiscite in Silesia		
1922	Assassination of President Gabriel Narutowicz; Stanisław Wojciechowski elected president	**1922**	Benito Mussolini's *coup d'état*
1923	Second Congress of the KPP; workers' uprising in Kraków		
1924	Financial reforms of Władysław Grabski; establishment of the Bank Polski; construction of the port of Gdynia launched	**1925**	Treaties of Locarno
1926	Józef Piłsudski's May *coup d'état*		
1929	The 'Centrolew' (Centre-Left) formed	**1929–33**	The great depression
1931	The trial of Brześć		
1932	Non-aggression pact with the USSR	**1933**	Hitler assumes power; the Reichstag fire trial
1934	Non-aggression pact with Germany		
1935	The Constitution of April passed	**1935**	Remilitarization of Germany; Italian aggression in Abyssinia

1936	Strikes in Kraków and Lwów; peasant strikes in Little Poland
1937	National Unity Camp formed
1938	The Communist Party of Poland dissolved by the Communist International; annexation of the Zaolzie region (part of Cieszyn Silesia) by Poland
1939	Nazi Germany attacks Poland (1 Sept.); the September campaign (1 Sept.–5 Oct.); the Soviet army enters West Ukraine and West Byelorussia (17 Sept.); Gen. Wladyslaw Sikorski forms the Polish government-in-exile in France; establishment of the General-gouvernement by the Nazi occupying power

1936	The Berlin–Rome Axis formed
1936–9	Fascist *coup* and civil war in Spain
1937	Japanese aggression in China; Italy joins the German–Japanese pact
1938	Annexation of Austria by Germany; Germany occupies the Sudetenland; the Munich agreements
1939	Annexation of Czechoslovakia by Germany; Soviet–German non-aggression pact; outbreak of Second World War

HISTORY OF POLAND AFTER THE OUTBREAK OF THE SECOND WORLD WAR

1939–45	Second World War
1939	September Campaign: Poland partitioned by Germany and USSR (28 Sept.)
1941	German invasion of USSR: Polish–Soviet Treaty. Implementation of Nazi 'Final Solution' begins
1943	USSR severs diplomatic relations with Polish government-in-exile. Warsaw Ghetto Rising (Apr.)
1944–5	Liberation: complete occupation of Polish lands by Soviet army
1944–7	Civil War: liquidation of all resistance to Soviet supremacy
1944	Lublin Committee formed by Soviet patronage (22 July)
	Warsaw Rising (1 Aug.–2 Oct.)
1945	Transfer of international recognition from Polish government-in-exile in London to Provisional Government of National Unity in Warsaw (28 June); Potsdam Conference (July)
	Formation of Provisional Government of National Unity
1946	Referendum (30 June)
1947	First elections to Sejm (19 Jan.): Allied protest

1948–56	Period of Stalinism
1948	Formation of Polish United Workers Party: One-Party State launched
1952	Constitution of Polish People's Republic (22 July)
1955	Formation of Warsaw Pact by USSR
1956	Eighth plenum of party independently elects W. Gomułka as First Secretary
since 1956	Poland governed by national Communist regime
1958	Reconstitution of COMECON (23 May)
1966	Celebration of the Polish Millennium
1968	March events: student riots followed by anti-Jewish purge
1970	Baltic riots; fall of Gomułka; E. Gierek First Secretary
1976	Constitutional amendments; June events: rise of political opposition
1978	Cardinal Karol Wojtyła elected Pope John Paul II (16 Oct.)
1980	Emergence of Solidarity
1981	(Dec.) Introduction of martial law
1989	Establishment of first non-Communist government

Maps

1. *The Kingdom of Bolesław the Brave in 1025*

Source: A. Zamoyski, *The Polish Way*; copyright © 1987 John Murray (Publishers) Ltd. Reproduced by permission.

2. *Poland under Kazimierz the Great, 1370*

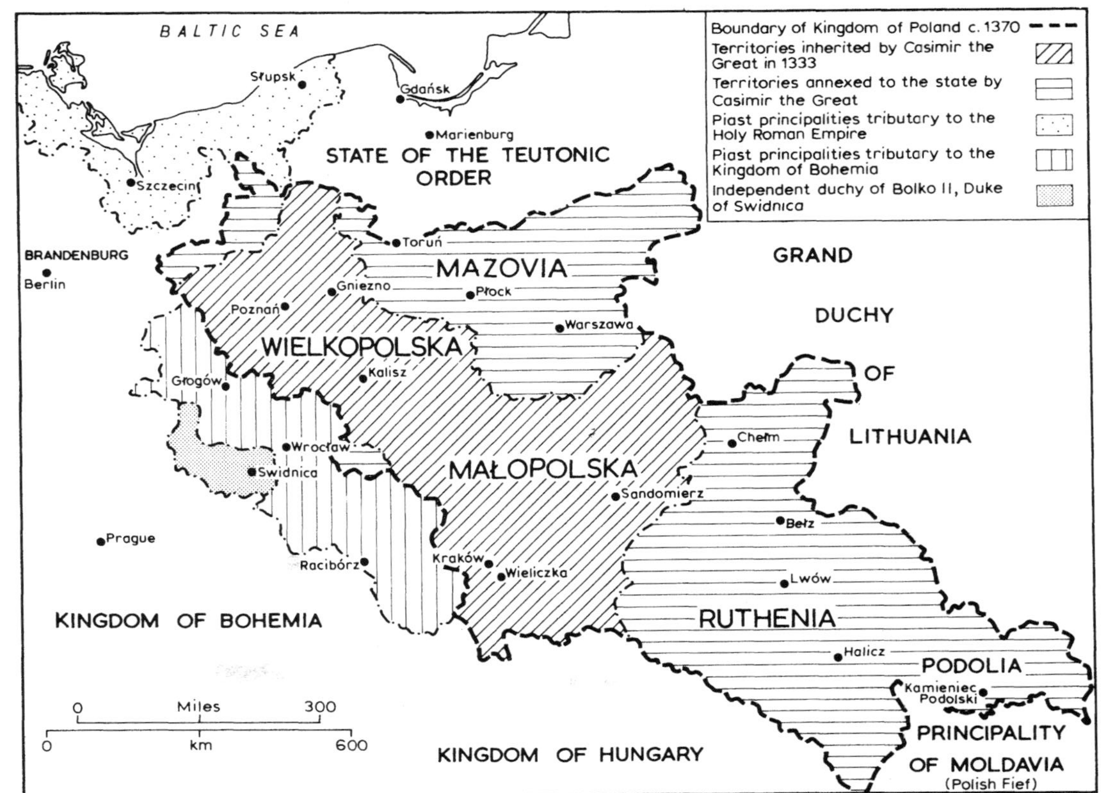

Source: A. Zamoyski, *The Polish Way*; copyright © 1987 John Murray (Publishers) Ltd. Reproduced by permission.

3. *Poland in 1771*

Source: H. Kaplan, *The First Partition of Poland*; copyright © 1962 Columbia University Press. Reproduced by permission.

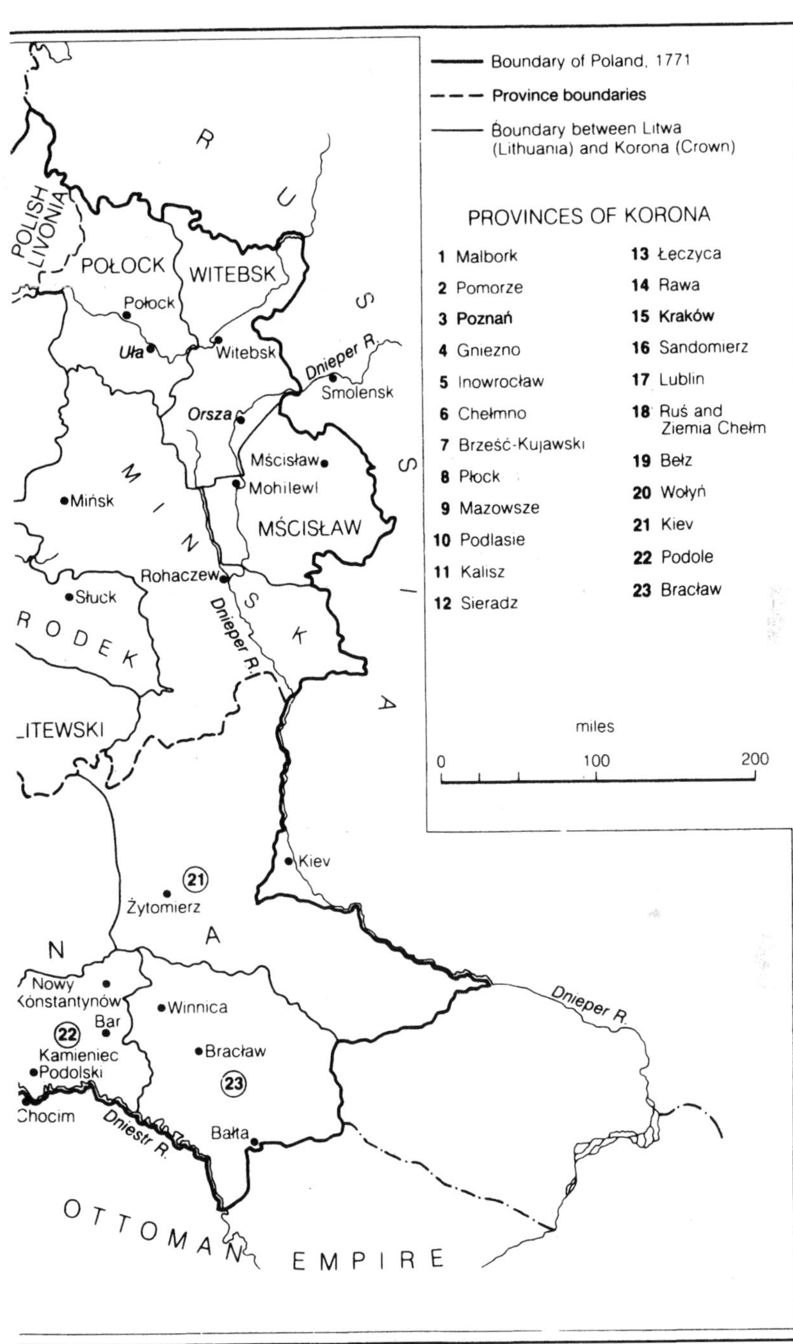

Boundary of Poland, 1771
Province boundaries
Boundary between Litwa (Lithuania) and Korona (Crown)
PROVINCES OF KORONA
1 Malbork
2 Pomorze
3 Poznań
4 Gniezno
5 Inowrocław
6 Chełmno
7 Brześć-Kujawski
8 Płock
9 Mazowsze
10 Podlasie
11 Kalisz
12 Sieradz
13 Łęczyca
14 Rawa
15 Kraków
16 Sandomierz
17 Lublin
18 Ruś and Ziemia Chełm
19 Bełz
20 Wołyń
21 Kiev
22 Podole
23 Bracław
miles
0
100
200
POLISH LIVONIA
POŁOCK
Połock
WITEBSK
Witebsk
Uła
Orsza
Dnieper R.
Smolensk
Mścisław
Mohilew
MŚCISŁAW
Mińsk
Rohaczew
Słuck
LITEWSKI
Kiev
Żytomierz
Nowy Konstantynów
Bar
Kamieniec Podolski
Winnica
Bracław
Bałta
Chocim
Dniestr R.
OTTOMAN EMPIRE

4. *The Partitions of Poland*

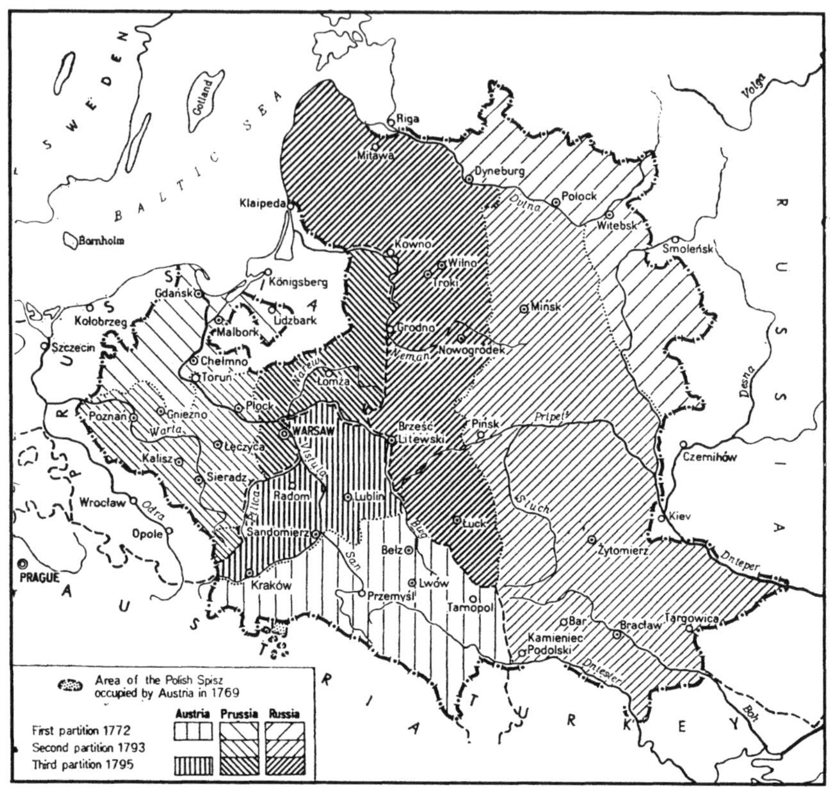

Source: S. Kieniewicz (ed.), *History of Poland*; copyright © 1986 PWN—Polish Scientific Publishers.

5. *Poland in Napoleonic Europe*

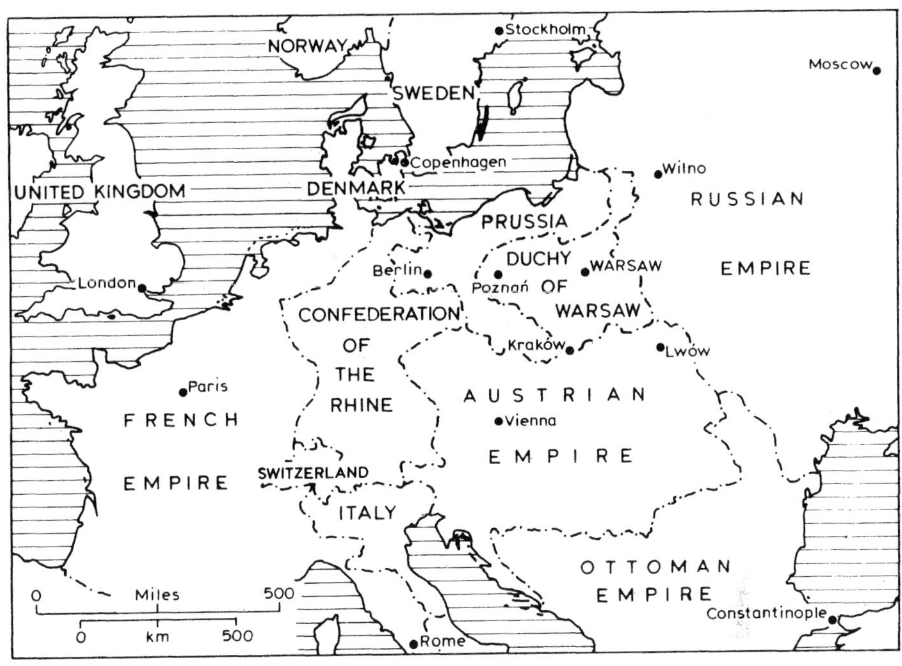

Source: A. Zamoyski, *The Polish Way*; copyright © 1987 John Murray (Publishers) Ltd. Reproduced by permission.

6. *The Territorial Settlement of 1815 in Eastern Europe*

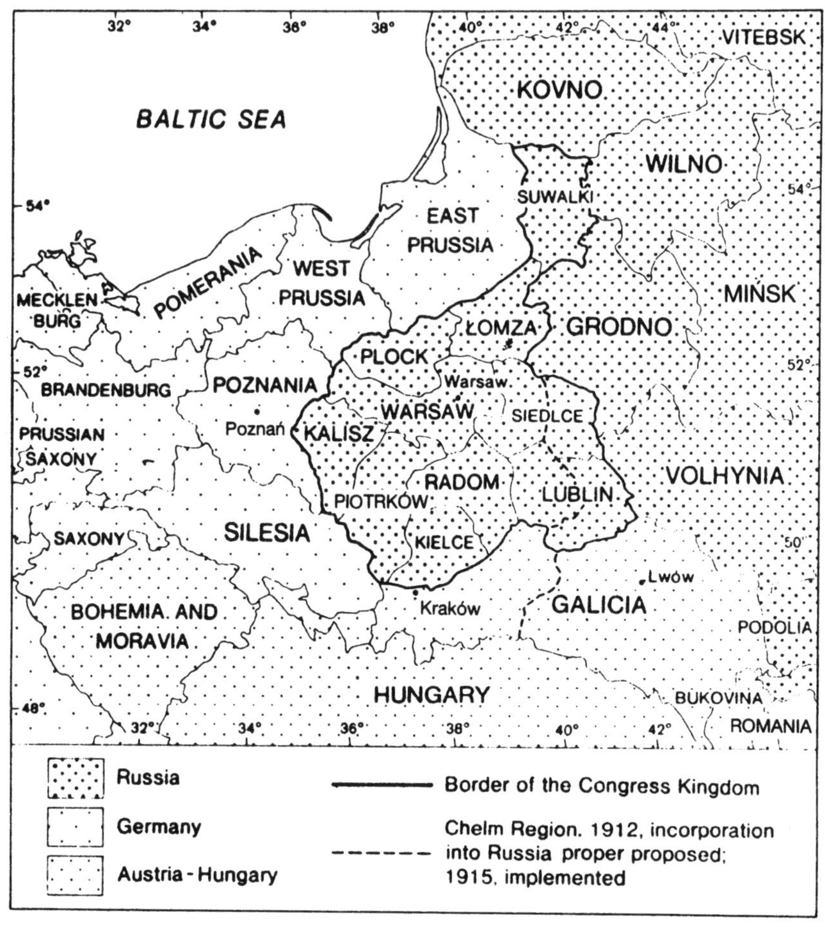

Source: R. A. Prete and A. Hamish Ion (eds.), *Armies of Occupation*; copyright © 1984 Wilifrid Laurier University Press. Reproduced by permission.

7. *The Congress Kingdom of Poland*

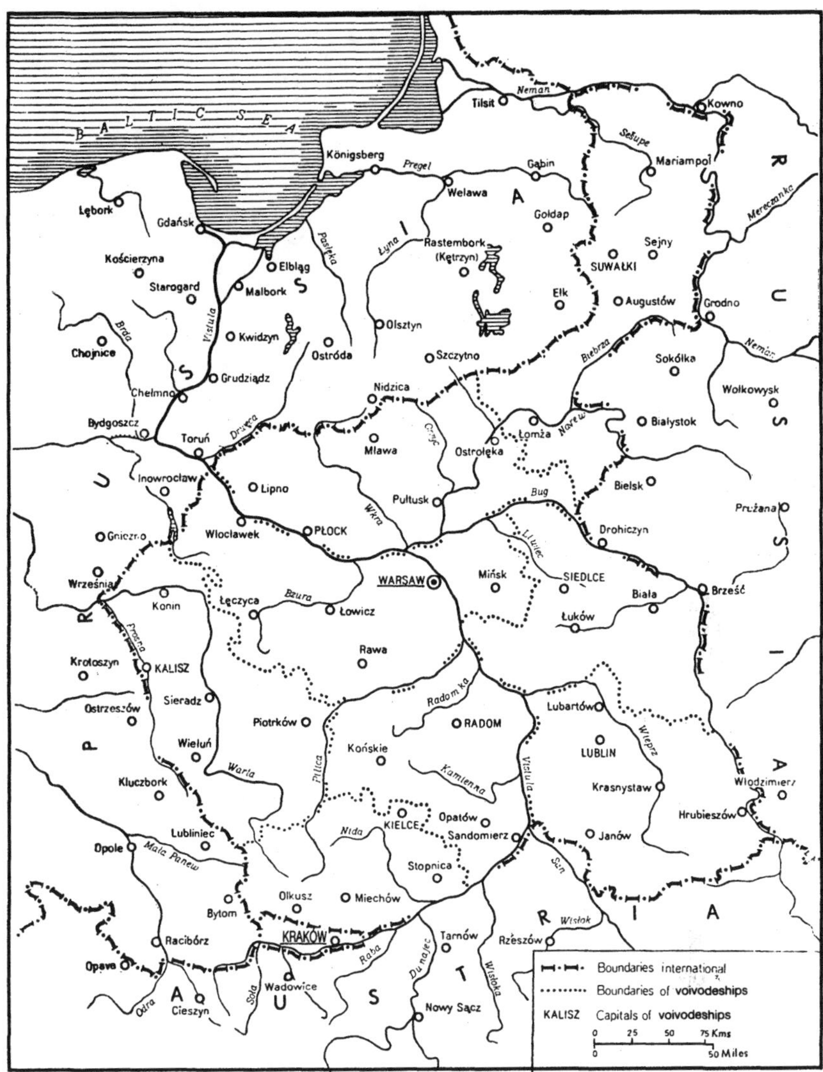

Source: S. Kieniewicz (ed.), *History of Poland*; copyright © 1986 PWN—Polish Scientific Publishers.

8. *The Territories making up the Polish State in 1921*

Source: Abramsky *et al.*, *The Jews in Poland*; copyright © 1986 Basil Blackwell Publishers. Reproduced by permission.

9. *The German Occupation, 1939–1945*

Source: N. Davies, *God's Playground*, vol. ii; copyright © 1981 Oxford University Press. Reproduced by permission.

10. *Post-war Poland*

Source: N. Davies, *God's Playground*, vol. ii; copyright © 1981 Oxford University Press. Reproduced by permission.

Glossary

Akhdushnikes A name used both by its supporters and its opponents in Łódź to refer to adherents of the **Bund**.

arenda A lease of monopoly rights, usually of an estate.

arendarz The holder of an arenda.

beit hamidrash (Hebrew: lit. 'a house of study'). A building attached to a synagogue where Jewish men assemble to study the Torah.

biletowy The tax Jews had to pay until 1862 to stay overnight in Warsaw.

bimah Raised area in the centre of a synagogue where the cantor stands when leading the service and where the public reading of the Torah takes place.

Bund General Jewish Workers' Alliance. A Jewish Socialist Party, founded in 1897. It joined the Russian Social-Democratic Labour Party, but seceded from it when its programme of national autonomy was not accepted. In independent Poland it adopted a leftist, anti-Communist posture, and from the 1930s co-operated increasingly closely with the Polish Socialist Party (PPS).

Chamber of Deputies (Polish: *izba poselska*) The lower house in the **Sejm** containing representatives from each **voivodeship** (*województwo*) in Poland (the **Crown**) and the Grand Duchy of Lithuania. It was elected by the ***szlachta*** of each voivodeship, meeting in the local **dietine**. (Polish: *sejmik*). It started to meet regularly after 1493 and, in accordance with the privilege *Nihil novi* of 1505, the king promised that no new legislation would be introduced without the joint consent of the Chamber of Deputies and the **Senate**.

Commonwealth (Polish: *Rzeczpospolita*) The term *Rzeczpospolita* is derived from the Latin *res publica*. It is sometimes translated as 'commonwealth' and sometimes as 'republic', often in the form 'Nobleman's Republic' (*Rzeczpospolita szlachecka*). After the union of Lublin in 1569 it was used officially in the form *Rzeczpospolita Obojga Narodów* (Commonwealth of the Two Nations) to designate the new form of state which had arisen. In historical literature, this term is often rendered as 'The Polish–Lithuanian Commonwealth'.

Confederation (Polish: *Konfederacja*) A union of nobles called together to defend the country or obtain certain defined political objectives. After 1652, but mainly in the eighteenth century, the indiscriminate use of the ***liberum veto*** regularly paralysed the **Sejm**: confederations, which were not subject to the veto, were the only means available for achieving political objectives in an emergency.

This glossary is partly based on that in Artur Eisenbach, *The Emancipation of the Jews in Poland*, ed. A. Polonsky (Oxford, 1991).

Congress Kingdom (also 'Kingdom of Poland') A constitutional kingdom created at the Congress of Vienna (1814–15), with the Tsar of Russia as hereditary monarch. After 1831 it declined to an administrative unit of the Russian empire in all but name. After 1864 it lost the remaining vestiges of the autonomy it had been granted at Vienna and was officially referred to as 'Privislansky kray' (Vistula territory).

corvée Compulsory labour service due from peasants to their landlord. It remained in effect after the formal abolition of serfdom in the Grand Duchy of Warsaw in 1808 but was abolished by Alexander Wielopolski in 1863.

Crown (Polish: *Korona*) The Polish part of the *Rzeczpospolita* (Republic, or **Commonwealth**), as distinct from the Grand Duchy of Lithuania, with which it was dynastically linked from the fifteenth century and constitutionally united in 1569 by the Union of Lublin. In addition to its ethnically Polish core territories, it included Royal Prussia and the Ukraine, which after 1569 was transferred from the Grand Duchy to the Crown.

Diet *see* Sejm (Seym in eighteenth-century Polish spelling)

dietine (Polish: *sejmik*) A local assembly of the ***szlachta*** operating in each **voivodeship** of the **Commonwealth**. It elected deputies to the **Sejm** and provided them with instructions governing their conduct there. Dietines met much more frequently than the Sejm and by the end of the seventeenth century had much more importance in the regions. They were the basic forum for the political activities of the *szlachta* and by the eighteenth century had become subject to influence and manipulation by the magnates, who used them as a tool for their own political purposes.

Duchy of Warsaw State created in 1807 on the basis of the Treaty of Tilsit and enlarged after the French defeat of the Austrians in 1809. Its structure was laid down by the Constitution of 1807 and its Duke was Frederick August I, King of Saxony. It was abolished by the peacemakers at Vienna.

Endecja Popular name for the Polish National Democratic Party, a right-wing party which had its origins in the 1890s. Its principal ideologue was Roman Dmowski, who advocated a Polish version of the integral nationalism which became popular in Europe at the turn of the nineteenth century. The Endecja advanced the slogan 'Poland for the Poles' and called for the exclusion of the Jews from Polish political and economic life. *see also* Obóz Wielkiej Polskiej

Four Year Sejm (Diet) This **Sejm**, which was transformed into a **Confederation** in order to avoid being bound by the ***liberum veto*** met in Warsaw from 6 October 1788 to 29 May 1792 under the leadership of the Marshal of the Sejm, Stanisław Małachowski. Making use of the favourable international situation (the involvement of Austria and Russia in a war with Turkey), the 'Patriotic' Party introduced a number of reforms in the social and political system of the **Commonwealth** which aimed to free it from the hegemony of the Tsarist empire and re-establish its independence. These included the abolition of the *liberum veto*, the strengthening of the power of the central administration, and an increase in the size of the army. These reforms were embodied in the Constitution of 3 May. The changes introduced by the Four Year Sejm were overturned by the reactionary Confederation of Targowica acting with the assistance of the Russians, and the new order was given 'legal' sanction by the Sejm of Grodno in 1793.

Frankists Followers of Jacob Frank (1726–91). Frank was the head of a mystical antinomian sect among Polish Jews whose followers hailed him as the Messiah. His conflict with rabbinic Jewish leaders led him to adopt Christianity in 1759 along with over 500 of his followers. They were patronized by an important section of the Polish nobility, including King Augustus III, who acted as Frank's godfather. In 1760 he was imprisoned by the Polish authorities on the grounds that his conversion was not 'sincere'. He was released in 1772 and moved to Moravia, where he continued to head his sect along with his daughter Eva. After his death his followers, who may have included the great Polish poet Adam Mickiewicz, continued to believe that their cult was destined to usher in the messianic age.

General-gouvernement An administrative unit created in Poland during the Nazi occupation from some of the territory seized by Germany after the Polish defeat. Established on 26 October 1939 the General-gouvernement comprised four districts: Kraków, Lublin, Warsaw, and Radom. Its capital was Kraków and its administration was headed by Hans Frank. After the Nazi invasion of the Soviet Union another province, Galicia, made up of parts of the pre-war Polish provinces of Łwów, Stanisławów, and Tarnopol, was added. The Germans pursued a policy of mass murder of the Jewish population in the area and reduced the Christian Poles to slaves who were to provide a reservoir of labour for the Third Reich.

goyim (Hebrew: lit. 'people') A term used by Jews for non-Jews, sometimes with pejorative overtones.

Great Emigration (Polish: *Wielka Emigracja*) After the failure of the Polish Insurrection of 1830–1 between 8,000 and 9,000 of those who had participated emigrated. Because of its political and cultural significance this group became known as the 'Great Emigration'. It was made up of those who were not included in the amnesty proclaimed by Tsar Nicholas I on 1 November 1831 and those who were unwilling to acquiesce in the new political order in Russian Poland. They were mostly officers and civil servants who had worked for the insurrectionary government and they were predominantly noble in social origin. The majority settled in France, mostly in the provinces because of restrictions imposed by the French government. They were deeply divided politically between the more conservative followers of Prince Adam Jerzy Czartoryski (the Hotel Lambert group) and the more radical supporters of the Polish Democratic Society. Among leading Polish writers and artists who were associated with the Great Emigration were Frederic Chopin, Zygmunt Krasiński, Adam Mickiewicz, Cyprian Kamil Norwid, and Juliusz Słowacki.

HaBaD An acronym derived from the Hebrew words *hokhmah, binah, da'at* (wisdom, understanding, knowledge). It was applied to a sect of **Hasidism** which developed in the Grand Duchy of Lithuania and whose leading advocate was Rabbi Shneur Zalman of Liozna (or Liady). He preached a more rationalistic and ordered faith than the Hasidism of central and southern Poland. The Lubavich dynasty of rabbis, also called *HaBaD* Hasidim, is descended from Rabbi Shneur Zalman.

Hajdamaki The name used to describe armed groups which were active in the Polish Ukraine in the eighteenth century. The Hajdamaki included both ordinary bandits and peasant insurrectionaries.

halakhah (Hebrew: lit. 'the way') A word used to describe the legal part of Jewish tradition and norms of religious observance, especially in the sense of 'way of acting', 'habit', 'usage', 'custom', and 'guidance'.

Hasidism A Jewish mystical movement which grew up in the eighteenth-century Polish–Lithuanian Commonwealth. The Hasidim (from *hasid* (Hebrew) 'a righteous man') sought direct communion with God by various means including singing, dancing, and communion with nature. Originally opposed by the bulk of the Orthodox establishment in Poland, who described themselves as *misnagdim* (lit. 'opposers', i.e. of Hasidism), the movement soon became particularly strong in central Poland (the Congress Kingdom), southern Poland (Malopolska or Galicia), and the Ukraine.

Haskalah (Hebrew: lit. 'wisdom' or 'understanding', but used in the sense of 'Enlightenment') A rationalistic movement which emerged in the Jewish world under the impact of the European Enlightenment in the second half of the eighteenth century. It first became important in Germany under the influence of Moses Mendelssohn and soon spread to the rest of European Jewry, first in the west and then, more slowly, in the east. The *maskilim* (followers of the Haskalah), while retaining the Jewish religion, sought to reduce Jewish separateness from the nations among whom they lived and to increase their knowledge of the secular world. The movement also fostered the study of biblical rather than talmudic Hebrew and emphasized the poetic, critical, and scientific elements in Hebrew literature, aiming to substitute the study of modern subjects for traditional ones. In eastern Europe it opposed Hasidism and what it regarded as the relics of Jewish fanaticism and superstition. It also sought Jewish emancipation and the adoption by Jews of agriculture and handicrafts.

heder (Hebrew: lit. 'room') Colloquial name for a traditional Jewish elementary school.

hevra (pl. ***hevrot***) A mutual benefit society made up of people in the same occupation or who are devoted to performing some social or religious task (charity, burial, early morning prayer, etc.).

jurydyki Areas within towns not subject to the legal control of the municipal administration, but owned by noble or ecclesiastical dignitaries.

kahal, kehilla (Hebrew: lit. 'congregation') The lowest level of the Jewish autonomous institutions in the Polish–Lithuanian Commonwealth. Above the local *kehillot* were regional bodies, and above these a central body, the *Va'ad arba aratsos* (Council of the Four Lands) for the **Crown** and the *Va'ad lita* (Council of Lithuania). The *Va'ad arba aratsos* was abolished by the Polish authorities in 1764, but local autonomous institutions continued to operate until 1844 in those parts of the Polish–Lithuanian Commonwealth directly annexed by the Tsarist empire, and longer in the **Congress Kingdom** and the remaining parts of Poland.

Kresy The eastern provinces of Poland between the two world wars. Today they form parts of Lithuania, Belarus, and Ukraine.

liberum veto The right of every deputy in the **Sejm** to overturn legislation of which he did not approve or for which his **dietine** had not provided him with instructions. The legal basis of this privilege seems to originate in the Statutes of Nieszawa (1454) which promised that no royal legislation would be introduced into a province without the consent of its local dietine. When dietine deputies began meeting regularly in the Sejm this was taken to mean that unanimity was required for all new legislation. In the sixteenth century, and even into the seventeenth century, decisions were still taken by majority vote, but in 1652 Władysław Siciński exercised his veto as an individual to 'explode' the Sejm; thenceforth there was continuous and irresponsible use of the veto, rendering normal parliamentary activity impossible. According to the practice, once a veto was used the Sejm was suspended and all legislation hitherto introduced in the session was declared invalid.

Magistrat The name for the municipal administration in pre-partition Poland.

Malopolska (Polish: lit. 'lesser Poland') Southern Poland, the area around Kraków. Also referred to under the Habsburgs as Galicia.

maskilim *see* Haskalah

melamed (Hebrew: teacher) A teacher in a ***heder***. A distinction is made between a *melamed dardeki* who taught children of both sexes to read and write Hebrew and also a chapter or two of the weekly lesson from the Pentateuch, and a *melamed gemara* who taught Bible and Talmud to boys and also, when they were older, the *Shulchan arukh*.

mitnaged (***misnagid***) (pl. ***mitnagdim***) (Hebrew: lit. 'opposer') The rabbinic opponents of Hasidism.

November Insurrection The unsuccessful Polish insurrection against Tsar Nicholas which began in November 1830 and which was followed by the **Great Emigration**.

Obóz Wielkiej Polskiej (Polish: the Camp for a Greater Poland) Extreme right-wing and pro-fascist organization founded in December 1926 by

Roman Dmowski because of his dissatisfaction at the weak reaction of the National Democratic Party (*see* Endecja) to the coup of May 1926 which brought Józef Piłsudski back to power.

pan (Polish: 'lord', 'master', or 'noble') Also used today as the polite form of the second person singular.

Patriotic Society A revolutionary organization founded in December 1830, after the outbreak of the **November Insurrection**. It represented the more radical wing of the insurrectionaries and aimed to ensure the effective pursuit of the goals of armed struggle for independence and social reform.

pogłówne (Polish: poll tax) A tax imposed in the Polish–Lithuanian Commonwealth (*see* Commonwealth) on Jews, Gypsies, and Tatars, ostensibly in return for the protection they received from the Republic, since they did not perform military service. Between 1580 and 1764, the responsibility for levying this tax on Jews fell to the Council of the Four Lands (see also *kahal*).

Polish Commonwealth *see* Commonwealth

porets Yiddish: nobleman. see also *pan, szlachta*

poyerim Yiddish: peasants.

rebbetzin Yiddish: rabbi's wife.

Revir A section of a town in which Jews were required to live.

royal (free) town A town directly dependent on the king, and subsequently on the government of the Grand Duchy of Warsaw and the **Congress Kingdom** of Poland. Burghers in royal or 'government' towns had greater rights than those in towns controlled by the nobility.

Rzeczpospolita Polish: Republic or Commonwealth. *see* Commonwealth

Sanacja From the Latin *sanatio*, meaning healing, restoration. The popular name taken by the regime established by Józef Piłsudski after the coup of May 1926. It referred to Piłsudski's aim of restoring health to the political, social, and moral life of Poland.

Sejm The central parliamentary institution of the **Commonwealth**, composed of a **Senate** and a **Chamber of Deputies**; after 1501 both of these had a voice in the introduction of new legislation. It met regularly for six weeks every two years, but could be called for sessions of two weeks in an emergency. When it was not in session, an appointed commission of sixteen senators, in rotation four at a time, resided with the king both to advise and to keep watch over his activities. Until the middle of the seventeenth century, the Sejm functioned reasonably well; after that, the use of the ***liberum veto*** began to paralyse its effectiveness.

Senate The upper house of the **Sejm**. Its origin was the medieval Royal Council. It was composed of all the great officials of the government, the **voivodes**, hetmans, marshals, and treasurers, headed by the archbishop of Gniezno, who also served as *interrex* on the death of the king. The members of the Senate were overwhelmingly drawn from the class of magnates (see *szlachta*) which came to dominate Polish society in the seventeenth and eighteenth centuries.

shadkhan Yiddish: marriage broker.

shiddukh Yiddish: a marriage, as arranged by a ***shadkhan***.

shtetl (Yiddish: small town) The characteristic small town of central and eastern Poland, often with a Jewish majority.

shtibel A small Hasidic meeting-place for prayer.

soltys (German: *Schultheiss*; Latin: *scultetus*) During the period of extensive German colonization and immigration during the middle ages, the *soltys* was the agent who organized the establishment of new villages; as a reward, he was given one-sixth of the village's land, together with other privileges. This made these agents an extremely wealthy and influential group, posing a challenge to the ***szlachta*** itself. By the Statute of Warta (1423), the nobility were given the right to buy out the lands of the local *soltys*. This group thereafter disappeared as a social force, but the office of *soltys* remained in the form of a local administrator acting for the landlord of a village.

starosta A royal administrator, holder of the office of *starostwo*. From the fourteenth century, there were three distinct offices covered by this term: the *starosta generalny* (general starosta), in **Wielkopolska**, Rus, and Podolia (Ukraine), represented the crown in a particular region; the *starosta grodowy* (castle starosta) had administrative and judicial authority over a castle or fortified settlement and its surrounding region; and the *starosta niegrodowy* (non-castle starosta) or *tenutariusz* (leaseholder) administered royal lands leased to him.

szlachta The Polish nobility. A very broad social stratum making up nearly 8 per cent of the population in the eighteenth century. Its members ranged from the great magnates, like the Czartoryskis, Potockis, and Radziwiłłs, who dominated political and social life in the last century of the Polish–Lithuanian Commonwealth, to small landowners (the *szlachta zagrodowa*) and even to landless retainers of the great houses. What distinguished members of this group from the remainder of the population was their noble status and their right to participate in political life, the **dietines**, the **Sejm**, and the election of the king.

tekhinot, ***tekhines*** Prayers published in Yiddish for those people who could not read Hebrew (generally women).

tsaddik (Hebrew: lit. 'the just one' or 'a pious man') A leader of a Hasidic sect (or community). Hasidim often credited their *tsaddikim* or *rebbes* with miraculous powers and saw them as mediators between God and man.

Tse'ena urena A seventeenth-century Yiddish paraphrase of the Pentateuch written primarily for women. It has gone through innumerable editions, including one recently issued in Israel and New York.

voivode (Polish: *wojewoda*) Initially this official acted in place of the ruler, especially in judicial and military matters. From the thirteenth century the office gradually evolved into a provincial dignity; between the sixteenth and eighteenth centuries, the voivode conducted the local **dietine**, led the *pospolite ruszenie*, the *levée-en-masse* of the ***szlachta*** in times of danger to the **Commonwealth**, and occasionally governed cities and collected certain dues. By virtue of his office, he sat in the **Senate**.

voivodeship (Polish: *województwo*) A province, governed by a **voivode**.

Wielkopolska (Polish: lit. Greater Poland) Western Poland, the area around Poznań.

wójt (German: *Vogt*) During the medieval establishment of towns, he was the official who organized the new town and occupied the leading place in its local administration as the head of the town's courts. The office was hereditary and was provided with one-fifth of the dues and one-quarter of penal fines collected by the town. After the rise of town councils, the office was bought out by the larger and richer towns. By the eighteenth century the *wójt* was generally the chief administrator of a group of villages.

yeshivah A rabbinical college, the highest institution in the traditional Jewish system of education.

zogerkes Women who had the responsibility of helping less able women attending synagogue to follow the liturgy and find where they were in the service.

żydek (pl. ***żydkli***) (Polish: lit. 'little Jew') A mildly derogatory word used by Poles of Jews.

Printed and bound by CPI Group (UK) Ltd, Croydon, CR0 4YY

10/06/2025

14686708-0001

Index

Note: Polish–Lithuanian Commonwealth is abbreviated throughout to PLC.

Index compiled by Lilian Rubin